ROUTLEDGE HANDBOOK OF THE DIGITAL ENVIRONMENTAL HUMANITIES

The *Routledge Handbook of the Digital Environmental Humanities* explores the digital methods and tools scholars use to observe, interpret, and manage nature in several different academic fields.

Employing historical, philosophical, linguistic, literary, and cultural lenses, this handbook explores how the digital environmental humanities (DEH), as an emerging field, recognises its convergence with the environmental humanities. As such, it is empirically, critically, and ethically engaged in exploring digitally mediated, visualised, and parsed framings of past, present, and future environments, landscapes, and cultures. Currently, humanities, geographical, cartographical, informatic, and computing disciplines are finding a common space in the DEH and are bringing the use of digital applications, coding, and software into league with literary and cultural studies and the visual, film, and performing arts. In doing so, the DEH facilitates transdisciplinary encounters between fields as diverse as human cognition, gaming, bioinformatics and linguistics, social media, literature and history, music, painting, philology, philosophy, and the earth and environmental sciences.

This handbook will be essential reading for those interested in the use of digital tools in the study of the environment from a wide range of disciplines and for those working in the environmental humanities more generally.

Charles Travis is Associate Professor of Geography and GIS in the Department of History at the University of Texas, Arlington, USA, and Associate Research Fellow at the Trinity Centre for the Environmental Humanities, Trinity College Dublin, Ireland.

Deborah P. Dixon is Professor of Geography at the School of Geography and Earth Sciences at the University of Glasgow, Scotland.

Luke Bergmann is Associate Professor of Geography and Canada Research Chair in GIS, Geospatial Big Data and Digital Geohumanities with the Department of Geography at the University of British Columbia, Vancouver, Canada.

Robert Legg is Professor of Geography with the Department of Earth, Environmental, and Geographical Sciences at Northern Michigan University, Marquette, Michigan, USA.

Arlene Crampsie is Assistant Professor of Historical Geography at the School of Geography at University College Dublin, Ireland.

ROUTLEDGE HANDBOOK OF THE DIGITAL ENVIRONMENTAL HUMANITIES

Edited by Charles Travis, Deborah P. Dixon, Luke Bergmann, Robert Legg, and Arlene Crampsie

Routledge
Taylor & Francis Group
LONDON AND NEW YORK

Cover image: THEPALMER@iStock

First published 2023
by Routledge
4 Park Square, Milton Park, Abingdon, Oxon OX14 4RN

and by Routledge
605 Third Avenue, New York, NY 10158

Routledge is an imprint of the Taylor & Francis Group, an informa business

British Library Cataloguing-in-Publication Data
A catalogue record for this book is available from the British Library

Library of Congress Cataloging-in-Publication Data
A catalog record has been requested for this book

ISBN: 978-0-367-53663-3 (hbk)
ISBN: 978-0-367-53669-5 (pbk)
ISBN: 978-1-003-08279-8 (ebk)

DOI: 10.4324/9781003082798

Typeset in Bembo
by Apex CoVantage, LLC

CONTENTS

ILLUSTRATIONS

Figures

Tables

CONTRIBUTORS

Jayakrishnan Ajayakumar, Researcher, Department of Population and Quantitative Health Sciences Case Western Reserve University School of Medicine, USA.

Claudia Berger, Researcher, School of Information, Pratt Institute, New York, USA.

Ursula Biemann, artist, writer, and video essayist, Zurich, Switzerland.

Wendy Burk, independent poet and translator, Las Cruces, New Mexico, USA.

Chiara Cavalieri, Professor of Urbanism and Territorial Management, LAB SST UCLouvain-Université catholique de Louvain, Belgium.

Aude K. Chesnais, Senior Researcher, Native Lands Advocacy Project, and Visiting Fellow, School of Global Environmental Sustainability Colorado State University, USA.

Nigel Clark, Professor, Lancaster Environment Centre, Lancaster University, United Kingdom.

Andrew Curtis, Co-Director of the GIS Health & Hazards Lab, Department of Population and Quantitative Health Sciences Case Western Reserve University School of Medicine, USA.

Mickey Dennis, Researcher, School of Information, Pratt Institute, New York, USA.

Deborah P. Dixon, Professor of Geography, School of Geographical and Earth Sciences, University of Glasgow, Scotland.

Gwenyth H. Dobie, Associate Professor, Acting Area Coordinator, School of the Arts, Media, Performance, and Design, York University, Toronto, Canada.

Lauren Drakopulos, Postdoctoral Fellow, Department of Global Development, Cornell University, USA.

Marcus Foth, Professor, QUT Creative Industries Faculty, Brisbane, Australia.

L Frank, Tongva-Acjachemen Artist, Santa Rosa, California, USA.

Ian Garrett, Associate Professor of Ecological Design for Performance, Department of Theatre, School of the Arts, Media, Performance & Design, York University, Canada.

Paolo Giardullo, Researcher, Department of Philosophy, Sociology, Education & Applied Psychology, University of Padua, Italy.

Matthew N. Hannah, Assistant Professor, Social Sciences, and Education Library, Purdue University, USA.

William Hansard, PhD Digital Collections Specialist, Theodore Roosevelt Center, Dickinson State University, North Dakota, USA.

Desirae Harp, Vocal Contributions (Wappo), California Native Collaborator, Groundworks, Toasterlab, Canada.

Steven Hartman, Visiting Professor, Faculty of History and Philosophy, University of Iceland, Iceland.

Roberta Hawkins, Associate Professor, Department of Geography, Environment, and Geomatics, University of Guelph, Canada.

Kelli Hayes, Researcher, School of Information, Pratt Institute, New York, USA.

Poul Holm, Professor of Environmental History and Director Trinity Center for Environmental Humanities, Trinity College, the University of Dublin, Ireland.

Ryan Horne, Sinai Manuscripts Digital Library Data/Metadata Coordinator, Charles E. Young Research Library, University of California, Los Angeles, USA.

Viðar Hreinsson, independent literary scholar and environmental activist, Icelandic Museum of Natural History, Reykjavík, Iceland.

Guðrún Ingólfsdóttir, Research Fellow, Árni Magnússon Institute for Icelandic Studies, Reykjavík, Iceland.

Finn Arne Jørgensen, Professor of Environmental History at Department of Cultural Studies and Languages at University of Stavanger, Norway.

Dick Kasperowski, Professor, Linguistics, Logic, and Theory of Science Unit, University of Gothenburg, Sweden.

Ras K'Dee, Music Production (Makamo Mahilikawna, Kashaya, Ha Bida-Afro/Pomo), California Native Collaborator, Groundworks, Toasterlab, Canada.

John Kendall, PhD Candidate, College of Liberal Arts, University of Minnesota, USA.

Sokvisal Kimsroy, Researcher, Department of Geography, Kent State University, USA.

Tatiana Konrad, postdoctoral researcher, Department of English and American Studies, University of Vienna, Austria.

Conor Kostick, Researcher, Trinity Center for Environmental Humanities, Trinity College, University of Dublin, Ireland.

Parker Krieg, Instructor in Exploratory Studies and English, Department of English, University of Nebraska at Omaha, USA.

Elena Cogato Lanza, Senior Scientist, LAB-U ENAC, EPFL (École polytechnique fédérale de Lausanne), Switzerland.

Jiyoung Lee, Researcher, School of Information, Pratt Institute, New York, USA.

Francis Ludlow, Associate Professor of Medieval Environmental History, Trinity Center for Environmental Humanities, Trinity College, University of Dublin, Ireland.

Kok-Chhay Ly, Researcher, Department of Geography, Kent State University, USA.

William J. Mackwood, Associate Professor, Graduate Programme Director in Dance, School of the Arts, Media, Performance, and Design, York University, Toronto, Canada.

Eric Magrane, Assistant Professor of Geography, Department of Geography, New Mexico State University, USA.

Pablo Mansilla-Quiñones, Director of "Territorios Alternativos Lab," Director of Project ANID FONDECYT n° 11181086 "Deshabitar los Extremos: nuevos modos de habitar lo Rural en Magallanes," Instituto de Geografía, Pontificia Universidad Católica de Valparaíso, Chile.

Rhonda McGovern, Researcher, Trinity Center for Environmental Humanities, Trinity College, University of Dublin, Ireland.

Peta Mitchell, Professor of Digital Media, School of Communication, QUT, Brisbane, Australia.

Andrés Moreira-Muñoz, Director of "BioGeoArt project, SOC 180040," Instituto de Geografía, Pontificia Universidad Católica de Valparaíso, Chile.

Kevin Moskowitz, PhD Candidate, Department of History, University of Texas, Arlington, USA.

Ruth Mostern, Associate Professor, Department of History, World History Center, University of Pittsburgh, USA.

Dumisani Z. Moyo, Researcher, School of Geographical and Earth Sciences, University of Glasgow, Scotland.

Gizem Naz Gezgin Direksiz, PhD Candidate, Social Psychology, Dokuz Eylül University, Turkey.

John Nicholls, Data Manager, Trinity Center for Environmental Humanities, Trinity College, University of Dublin, Ireland.

Eric Nost, Assistant Professor, Department of Geography, Environment and Geomatics, University of Guelph, Canada.

J. Albert Nungaray, PhD Candidate, Department of History, University of Texas, Arlington, USA.

Astrid E.J. Ogilvie, Senior Research Associate, Stefansson Arctic Institute, Akureyri, Iceland, and Institute of Arctic and Alpine Research, University of Colorado, Boulder, USA.

Selin Süar Oral, Assistant Professor, Department of Digital Game Design, Faculty of Fine Arts, Istanbul Aydin University, Turkey.

Hasan Volkan Oral, PhD Researcher, Department of Civil Engineering, Faculty of Engineering, Istanbul Aydin University, Turkey.

Tiśina Parker, Production Manager/Costume Design (Ahwahnee Miwok, Kucadikadi Paiute), California Native Collaborator, Groundworks, Toasterlab, Canada.

Francesco De Pascale, Teaching Assistant, Department of Culture and Society, University of Palermo, Italy.

Ana Peraica, Visiting Professor, Danube University Krems, Austria.

Jesse Peterson, Postdoctoral Researcher, Department of Ecology, Swedish University of Agricultural Sciences, Sweden.

Juan Carlos Jeldes Pontio, Director of MADLAB & AconcaguaFabLab, Escuela de Arquitectura y Diseño, Pontificia Universidad Católica de Valparaíso, Chile.

Laura Lo Presti, Researcher, University of Padua, Italy.

Shanmugapriya T. Priya, AHRC Postdoctoral Research Associate, Department of History, Lancaster University, United Kingdom.

Lucy Sabin, PhD Candidate, Department of Geography, University College London, United Kingdom.

Kanyon Sayers-Roods, Vocalist/ Musical Contributions (Mutsun-Ohlone & Chumash Native from Indian Canyon Nation), California Native Collaborator, Groundworks, Toasterlab, Canada.

Hasan Saygin, Researcher, Application and Research Center for Advanced Studies, Istanbul Aydin University, Turkey.

Darius Scott, Assistant Professor of Geography, Department of Geography, Dartmouth University, USA.

Hira Sheikh, PhD Candidate, Design Lab, QUT Creative Industries Faculty, Brisbane, Australia.

Ragnhildur Sigurðardóttir, Ecologist, Svartarkot Culture-Nature, Iceland.

Jennifer J. Silver, Associate Professor, Department of Geography, Environment and Geomatics, University of Guelph, Canada.

Bernadette Smith, Dancer/Singer/Concept for Spirits Within (Coastal Pomo), Dancing Earth, Groundworks, Toasterlab, Canada.

Chris Alen Sula, Associate Professor, School of Information, Pratt Institute, New York, USA.

Deborah Sutton, Senior Lecturer in Modern South Asian History, Department of History, Lancaster University, United Kingdom.

Bronislaw Szerszynski, Professor, Department of Sociology, Lancaster University, United Kingdom.

Blair Talbot, Researcher, School of Information, Pratt Institute, New York, USA.

Rulan Tangen, Choreographer/Artistic Director, Dancing Earth, Groundworks, Toasterlab, Canada.

Charles Travis, Associate Professor, Geography & GIS, Department of History, University of Texas, Arlington, USA and Associate Research Fellow at the Trinity Centre for the Environmental Humanities, Trinity College Dublin, Ireland.

James Tyner, Professor of Geography, Department of Geography, Kent State University, USA.

René van der Wal, Professor of Environmental Citizen Science, Department of Ecology, Swedish University of Agricultural Sciences, Sweden.

Serhat Yilmaz, Researcher, Disaster Training Application and Training Center, Istanbul Aydin University, Turkey.

Josephine Zimba, Researcher, School of Geographical and Earth Sciences, University of Glasgow, Scotland.

INTRODUCTION

Routledge Handbook of the Digital Environmental Humanities

Charles Travis, Deborah P. Dixon, Luke Bergmann, Robert Legg, and Arlene Crampsie

Introduction

The harnessing of fire by *Homo sapiens* approximately one million years ago, described after the invention of inscription and chronicling of language in the geo-myth of Prometheus – bringer of the sacred flame to mortals – set into motion the geophysical process of combustion, which "facilitated the transformation of much of the terrestrial surface . . . and in the process pushed the parameters of the earth system into a new geological epoch" (Dalby 2018, 721). While not as yet formally acknowledged as a time period distinct from the Holocene by the International Commission on Stratigraphy (ICS) – despite the recommendation of the Anthropocene Working Group of the Sub-commission on Quaternary Stratigraphy (SQS) – the name "Anthropocene" nevertheless emphasises the cumulative anthropogenic forcing of the earth's physical processes. Combustion has continued to play a crucial role in this physical transformation as the elemental technology fueling a carbon-based Industrial Revolution but also as a trigger for nuclear weapons testing.

Indeed, it is the globe-encircling material signal of nuclear weapons testing that has been proposed by the Anthropocene Working Group as the "marker" denoting the arrival of the Anthropocene in the stratigraphic record of the Earth. It was first embedded in Gaia's planetary memory on 16 June 1945 by the detonation of the Trinity plutonium device (the second "Promethean event" in human history) over a New Mexican desert plain named *el Jornada del Muerto* (*the Journey of Death*) by 17th-century Spanish conquistadores seeking an illusory city of gold. Yet the emergence of the Anthropocene in geologic debates and the ensuing emphasis on material markers within a stratigraphic record overshadow a series of histories and geographies that speak to power and violence and the making, breaking, and remaking of knowledge about the planet, its inhabitants, and the relations between and betwixt these. The renaming and reframing of cultural and physical landscapes and phenomena during early modern imperial processes and hemispheric exploitations of environmental resources, peoples, and places served as precedents for the socio-material discourses of 21st-century anthropogenic global warming. Before the New Mexican desert plain became a testing ground, it was settled by Indigenous communities named by the colonising Spanish the "Pueblo." Furthermore, the site was repurposed and utilised as a "Petri dish" to test calculations that created a towering, polychromatic mushroom cloud and an invisible wave of lethal radiation to crest over the dry desert floor. Indeed the Manhattan

DOI: 10.4324/9781003082798-1

Project can be "directly tied to the start and rise of the digital age. The prominent nuclear signal in the novel strata appears also as a material effect of computational power" (Rosol et al. 2018).

Digital Origins

The etymology of the word *digital* in Western civilisation is traced back to the Latin *digitus*, denoting a "finger" or "toe." Its use is illustrated in the ancient Roman statesman Marcus Tullius Cicero's *Epistulae ad Atticum* (68–44 BCE), in which he complains to his friend Atticus about a case of usury – which Cicero says can be plainly ascertained *si tuos digitos novi* ("if your fingers know") how to calculate interest rates. By the medieval period, "digital" denoted a number less than ten (after counting fingers on both hands). Its use waned until the 1930s when analogue computing devices devised a new system of *digits*, which evolved into the binary *digital* computer language of 0s and 1s. And now, in the 21st century, we are again employing our digits on computer keyboards and touch screens to communicate, invent, calculate, imagine, compose, and visualise.

However, our human digits also facilitated interplays between inscription, tabulation, and visualisation systems, creating ancient computational methods that shaped the development of Egyptian, African, Babylonian, Chinese, Indus Valley, Mississippian, Aztec, Mayan, Incan, and other Indigenous and Agricultural Revolution civilisations: "from cuneiform tablets in Mesopotamia, papyrus in the Roman Empire and medieval codices to modern typesetting, telegraph signals in submarine cables or the time critical data infrastructure created in the wake of automated finance, information media offer ever more discrete ways of signaling and mobilizing ever greater societal and material systems" (Rosol et al. 2018). The astronomer Edward Charles Krupp (1997, 17) defines "cosmovision" or a "world view" as "the link between the architecture of the universe, the pattern of nature, the fabric of society, and the personal environment." Indeed, coding and mapping the multifaceted phenomena of perceived and experienced universes have been practised over many millennia. From the songline practices of the ancestors and current generation of the Warlpiri people in central Australia to "the smallest society of nomadic hunter-gatherers, such as the San people of the Kalahari, to the large-scale societies of Egypt, China, the Greeks, and the Romans" (Krupp 1997; Wynter 2003; Norris and Harney 2014).

In turn, inscription, tabulation, and visualisation systems can be traced back to the pre-Columbian Mesoamerican Olmec tablet, Aztecan and Mayan codices, and South American Incan *khipu*. The *Cascajal Block*, a stone writing slab etched with hieroglyphs discovered in Mexico, is dated to 900 bce and represents one of the earliest writing systems discovered in the Americas. The Mayan *Popol Vuh* and the Aztec *Yoalli Ehēcatl* are examples of sophisticated codices. The latter depicts the *Tlalocs* – the four corners of the universe – watering maize fields with different types of rains. Codices were integrated with astronomical, surveying, and timekeeping systems that by the "sixth century A.D. the Maya solar calendar was more accurate than the Gregorian calendar now in use in the western world" (Fuson 1969, 498; Smith 1984; Sherman 2015). Codex systems employed non-linear, visual languages to convey simultaneous levels of meaning and information through the applications of various dyes, pigments, and deer and other animal skins. In turn, Armida de la Garza (2016, 57) observes that although the Incas "had no written or visual language like the indigenous peoples of Central America," they were able to consolidate "a vast empire, *Tawantinsuyu* or 'The Empire of Four Directions' between 1438 and 1533" by employing recording and tabulation systems known as khipus. Spun from a rhizomatic network of different-coloured cords and knot "codes," khipus were used to administrate and tally censuses, maintain food and agricultural inventories, map villages and other population centres, keep calendars, and record and archive genealogies. As analogue corollaries to current digital, statistical, accounting, and narrative information platforms, khipus were originally considered to function as mnemonic aids for data storage and narration. However, studies of the arrangements and patterns of cords and knots in surviving khipus reveal the existence of complex mathematical semantical systems. It is posited that the Incan Andean civilisation "encoded language in a similar way to the binary code employed by today's computer" (Urton 2003; Garza 2016, 57). Khipu weavers "could choose between a number of yes/no conditions to be met, such as using cotton or wool, a spin or a ply direction" to create data strings by weaving 24 colours and using distinct knotting styles. By employing such methods, 1,536 data permutations could be "coded" by "knowledge weavers" on a khipu (Urton 2003; Garza 2016, 58).

Paper and transferrable type first emerged in ancient China, but the mechanisation of printing originates with Johannes Guttenberg's press. The device modelled on medieval and Mediterranean wine and olive oil presses published the first print edition of the Bible in 1455 (Barbier 2017). Indeed, similarities between systems to process organic materials into substances for human use and consumption and early computing systems are commensurate with the advent of modernity. Dorothy Kim (2021, 145) notes that in the early days of the Industrial Revolution, the Jacquard silk-weaving loom, first exhibited in 18th-century Lyon, France, was like modern-day computers as design utilised "a binary code for processing infinitely complex information," to produce intricately patterned cloths (Sikarskie 2016, 1). In 1822, Charles Babbage built a computing device in Britain called the *difference engine*, for which, in 1843, Ada Lovelace, niece of poet Lord Byron, scripted a Bernoulli algorithm. Babbage's second computing device, the *analytical engine*, was described as a machine that wove "algebraical patterns just as the Jacquard loom weaves flowers and leaves" (Menabrea and Lovelace 1842). The demonstration of Samuel Morse's coded electrical pulses in 1838, George Boole's *The Laws of Thought* (1854) and Herman Hollerith's electronic tabulator, a punch card machine that tallied the results of the 11th US Census of 1890, preceded the development in the 1940s of the US Army's ENIAC programmable electronic computer and Alan Turing's Enigma cypher-breaking calculating machine – itself a precursor for 21st-century artificial intelligence (AI) applications (Turing 2004; Chandra 2013).

An undersea cable strung between Ireland and North America in 1858 was a precursor to contemporary global digital infrastructures. The insulated copper wire bundle carried its first transatlantic message, a Morse-coded conversation between Queen Victoria and President James Buchanan, which took 16 hours to pulse across the 3,200-kilometre line. In addition to expanding communication and travel networks in the 19th century, time zones were established America to standardise arrival and departure times for the country's transcontinental railroad. In 1958, the launch of the Russian satellite Sputnik signalled the incorporation of extraterrestrial space in computational efforts. In transforming human cultures, the industrial artefacts functioned as the result of extractive industries that supplied coal, steel, iron, copper, and wood all assembled in cases by exploited labour. In the 20th and 21st centuries, nuclear, space, and digital technologies have formed a symbiosis. As human artefacts, they have entered the biosphere feedback loops connected to the litho-, hydro-, and atmosphere of the Earth's planetary system.

Digital Divides and Reconciliations

John Durham Peters (2015, 2) muses in *The Marvelous Clouds* that it was "impossible to say whether the nitrogen cycle or the internet is more crucial to the planet's maintenance." It has been argued that our level of knowledge concerning the digital-computational transformation impacts of the last eight decades is currently at the stage where Earth systems research was 30 years ago. The increasing integration between the planet's litho-, hydro-, bio-, and atmosphere and a "'technosphere' densely populated with digital devices" requires "new forms of joint human-Earth system research that focuses on the co-evolution and internal dynamics of the interactions between both domains" (Rosol et al. 2018). In 2005, John Udell predicted that "in the very near future, billions of people will be roaming the planet with GPS (Global Positioning System) devices. Clouds of network connectivity are forming over our major cities and will inevitably coalesce. The geoaware Web isn't a product we buy; it's an environment we colonize" (2005, 28). Sylvia Wynter (2003, 261) contends that this spread of digital imperialism reinforces a neocolonial Western *Homo economicus* "dynamic of overconsumption on the part of the rich techno-industrial North paralleled by that overpopulation on the part of the dispossessed poor, still partly agrarian worlds of the South [composing the] . . . differing facets of the central ethno-class Man vs. Human struggle."

Both the digital revolution and the wicked problem of global warming are phenomena originating in the human condition of Western civilisation, and their threats are disproportionally affecting the Global South (South and Mesoamerica, Asia, Africa, and places like Tuvalu in Oceania, slowly sinking under the waters of the Pacific with sea-level rise) and Indigenous, subsistence-based communities existing on the peripheries of the industrial world. In this regard, the words of Sukarno, leader of Indonesia's revolution against the Dutch colonial system, echo prophetically from the past to describe the ambivalence of the Global South towards Western-centric solutions. In an address titled *Tahun Vivere Pericoloso* (*A Year of Living Dangerously*), delivered on 17 August 1964, Sukarno stated,

> I am not saying that we do not need technology. . . . More than those skills, we need the spirit of a nation, the spirit of freedom, the spirit of revolution. . . . What is the use of taking over the technology of the Western world if the result of that adoption is merely a state and a society à la West . . . a copy state?
>
> *(Mortimer 2006, 82–83)*

The cultural tools of cartography, computation, composition, and commerce have been historically employed in the establishment of colonial settlements that acted as foundations for the creation of empires in the Americas, Africa, and South and East Asia. The applications of these tools often reshaped or destroyed the landscapes of Indigenous civilisations. To recover and restore such places, Jordan Clapper (2021, 433) notes that *indigenisation* is "a strategy of queering the landscape of narrative and interactive storytelling." The United Nations Declaration on the Rights of Indigenous Peoples (UNDRIP) has attempted to address the problems of recovering such landscapes. However, Tahu Kukutai and John Taylor (2016, xxi) find that it "is ironic that even with the emergence of the global 'data revolution' these problems persist in many countries where indigenous peoples live." They assert that "the twin problems of lack of reliable data and information on Indigenous peoples and the biopiracy and misuse of their traditional knowledge and cultural heritage are issues that have been grappled with in the process of drafting and negotiating" the declaration (Kukutai and Taylor 2016, xxi). Recently, video games shaped by Indigenous perspectives and knowledge systems have emerged to resurrect ancient Olmec, Mayan and Aztec visual narrative tropes, as well as traditional storytelling methods employed by First Nations peoples of North America. Elizabeth LaPensée (2014, 20–21), a digital media artist who "writes" such games, notes that

> the Internet and three-dimensional representations have always existed for Indigenous people. We have always perceived the connectivity between all and life in many dimensions. . . . While many commercial games still rely on flattened space that is

> mapped and claimed by players in ways that reinforce colonial values, I hope to offer experiences rooted in the gifts of sky, land, water, plants, animals, insects, our people, stars and manidoo . . . – games that shift perspectives and reinforce ours.

As Amanda Coole and Samatha Frost (2010, 6–5) observe, both the digital revolution and the existential threat of global warming are forcing our collective species to "reorient . . . profoundly in relation to the world, to one another, and to ourselves." During the last quarter century, accelerating rates of CO_2 emissions and global temperature rise have converged and, in some cases, impacted "global capital and population flows" and the "biotechnological engineering of genetically modified organisms." The proliferation of mobile computing technologies and devices has led to "the saturation of our intimate and physical lives by digital, wireless, and virtual technologies." Coole and Frost (2010, 5) note that "we are finding our environment materially and conceptually reconstituted in ways that pose profound and unprecedented normative questions" and thus need to "think in new ways about the nature of matter and the matter of nature; about the elements of life, the resilience of the planet and the distinctiveness of the human." In the 1990s, as personal computers were becoming mainstream devices it was observed that

> for the most part, our computing takes place sitting in front of, and staring at, a single glowing screen. . . . From the isolation of our work station we try to interact with our surrounding environment, but the two worlds have little in common. How can we escape from the computer screen and bring these two worlds together?
>
> *(Wellner, Mackay, and Gold 1993, 26)*

However, in the first decades of the 21st century, with advances in fibre optic, chip, software, and hardware technologies, in addition to mass proliferation of online and social media platforms, computers seem to be "an extension of one's thoughts rather than an external device on which one types. The embodiment then takes the form of extended cognition, in which human agency and thought are enmeshed within larger networks that extend beyond the desktop computer into the environment" (Hayles 2012, 2–3). Deborah P. Dixon and Mark Whitehead (2008, 606) contend that "the meat, bones, nerves, synapses not only of individual human bodies, but all manner of corporealities," manifest in a nexus that fuses geography and technology. In turn, Mike Crang (2015, 354) opines that the "percolation of new media into everyday life suggests that separations of real and virtual, material and cyberspace are misconceived" and ruefully observes that we cannot "opt out of new technologies, not even by using a retro notebook. We are all now digital scholars – even if it is 'digital lite' in terms of using various forms of digital mediation in various aspects of our work."

Towards the Digital Environmental Humanities

In 1978, William Rueckert coined the term ecocriticism in *Literature and Ecology: Experiment in Ecocriticism*. Drawing on biophysicist James Lovelock and microbiologist Lynn Margulis' *Gaian* tropes, Rueckert conceptualised reciting poetry as part of "a larger system of energy exchanges where poems act like green plants, revitalizing the ecosystem and the reader" (Posthumus and Sinclair 2014, 257). *Gaia* (a geo-biological symbiosis which regulates planetary homeostasis) is reacting due to the impact of human agencies and their "slow violence" against the earth's systems. Donna Haraway (2016) states that *Gaia* as an "intrusive force" is in turn slowly eroding the "tales and refrains of modern history" and contends,

> This intrusion threatens not life on Earth itself – microbes will adapt, to put it mildly – but threatens the livability of Earth for vast kinds, species, assemblages, and individuals . . . *Gaia* does not and could not care about human or other biological beings' intentions or desires or needs, . . . *Gaia* is not about a list of questions waiting for rational policies.

As digital environmental humanities (DEH) projects and initiatives manifest in collective and independent scholarship, research, and activism, they do so by engaging technology, media, and tools "to challenge geographical borders as well as reconsider transnational contexts" of the multiple and cross-catalysing global climate and environmental cultural crises (Weidner, Braidotti, and Klumbyte 2019, 17). Consequently, arts, humanities, and scientific scholars are working across disciplinary boundaries and media platforms. Kirill O. Thompson (2021, 11), a comparative philosopher interested in agricultural and food ethics and concerned about the environment and climate change, posits that "social science and humanities scholars offer *perspectives* on the on the human and natural forces in play in the Anthropocene while the scientists register and analyze the basic data, to compile *account books* of the cumulative human geo-impact." The DEH provides a common, dialectical space to create an ascending methodological helix to synthesise both approaches in order to interpret, question, catalogue, address, formulate, and provide avenues and networks for practical solutions to the wicked problem of global warming beyond the limited imagination of the Western *Homo economicus*. In addition, as Peters notes, digital platforms, devices, and techniques are providing "new life to age-old practices such as navigating, cultivating, stargazing, weather forecasting, documenting, and fishing" (2015, 8), which warrant DEH perspectives and research, and engagement in spheres located within and beyond the Cartesian pales of the academy. Echoing the etymology of the word *ecocriticism* (derived from the Greek, *oikos* and *kritis*, to coin the term "house judge" – Noel Castree (2021, 434–36) applies an interesting metaphor when he states that the environmental humanities have

> placed a roof over a large but half-built house, in the process allowing stairways and corridors to be constructed and, increasingly, some extensions too [creating] a powerful feeling of, if not family, then certainly community and solidarity. As the house is upgraded and enlarged more people choose to become long-term residents [often disagreeing productively among themselves].

Within this metaphorical space, the DEH would aptly supply the wiring, the smartphones and sensors, tablets, laptops – the internet – and the altar nooks where we can summon the digital goddess *Alexa*. However, as the band R.E.M. "murmured" back in the 1980s, is the DEH applied in conjunction with this metaphor being "*martyred, misconstrued*"? (Berry et al. 1983). Indeed, the DEH is a sum greater than just a discursive confluence between the digital and environmental humanities. A better analogy perhaps for the DEH would conjure its metamorphosis from various disciplines in the arts, humanities, and sciences as a caterpillar hatching from an egg followed by its cocooning into *chrysalis* (or *pupa*) from which the *imago* will emerge utterly transformed. Each stage which creates a butterfly is related, but each phase represents a distinct organism with specific levels of consciousness, purpose, and scale of agency. The aim of the DEH to appropriate and paraphrase an idea conceived by John Corrigan (2010) is to chase and understand the morphology of a butterfly and its migrations, interactions, and environments rather than just pinning its gossamer wings to the leaf page of an antiquated sheet of parchment.

Part I. *Overviews*

This opening part, edited by Charles Travis, provides an entrée to emerging works, as well as their precedents in the field of the DEH, to illustrate how arts, humanities, and science scholars are working in collaboration across disciplinary boundaries by employing hybrid methodologies and mediums to broaden the scale and scope of environmental perception, representation, study, inquiry, and pedagogy. In the chapter "Cowboys, Cod, Climate, and Conflict: Navigations in the Digital Environmental Humanities," Charles Travis et al. showcase how various DEH theory, and methods are applied in three internationally funded research projects: Larry McMurtry's Literary Geography, NorFish (Environmental History of the North Atlantic Fisheries, 1500–1800), and the Climates of Conflict in Babylonia.

Finn Arne Jorgensen's chapter "The Armchair Guide to the Digital Environmental Humanities" provides a reprint of a seminal DEH paper which discusses Wolfgang Schivelbusch's thesis of machine mediated landscape perceptions for our digital age as means to examine the spatiality of digital media and the natural world. In the chapter "Deep Weather," Ursula Bieman discusses a video essay juxtaposing Alberta Oil Sand carbon geologies with the hydrogeographies of the near-permanently flood threatened Ganges Delta of Bangladesh to underscore how the rapid transformation of our physical environment urges us to find modes of re-perceiving and re-representing the multifaceted dimensions of global warming.

Andrew Curtis et al.'s chapter, "Adding Spatial Context to the 17 April 1975 Evacuation of Phnom Penh: How Spatial Video Geonarratives Can Geographically Enrich Genocide Testimony," utilises thick mapping and inductive visualisation techniques to geographically reconstruct the environment of the forced evacuation of Phnom Penh through first-hand accounts taken while retracing the route. In "Normalised Alterity: Visualising Black Spatial Humanities," Darius Scott discusses how animations created from audio clips chronicling African American oral histories collected in rural communities in the US South counter historical erasures of Black voices without reinforcing a dominant hegemony of Eurocentric cartographic perceptions and representations. Lastly, Charles Travis' chapter "New Machines in the Garden: The Digital Environmental Humanities" dissects the premises Western humanism and environmental consciousness as they intersect with analogue/digital technologies by seeking insights from the poetry of Walt Whitman and Emily Dickinson, the science fiction of Octavia E. Butler and Philip K. Dick, and irreverent social commentary of Michel Houellebecq and Umberto Eco.

Part II. *Voicing Indigeneity*

In this part edited by Arlene Crampsie, scholars and activists, independently and collectively, highlight the potential for the DEH to actively participate in the decolonisation of environmental knowledge. In offering exciting new possibilities for recentring Indigenous lifeways, knowledge, and systems of knowing, the DEH facilitates the sharing of beliefs, practices, and values among and between Indigenous communities locally and globally. In addition, it can foster encounters with wider society, enhancing understanding and awareness of the challenges faced by and facing these communities. Ironically, it is in the reclaiming and repurposing of the core tools of imperialism and colonialism – cartography, computation, data collection and technological innovation – that Indigenous communities are decolonising and resurrecting their environmental knowledge and experiences. These tools are also used to facilitate active resistance, highlighting and challenging the accepted sociocultural norms and continued systemic inequalities inherited from the de-territorialisation of Indigenous communities. As the chapters in this section illustrate, digital technologies such as countermapping, data collection and data (knowledge) recovery and preservation, (re-)storying data, virtual reality, digital audio, audiovisual media, network analysis and social media can all be utilised effectively to capture, interpret and exhibit the valuable insights of Indigenous knowledge, practices, values, and resistances.

J. Albert Nungaray chapter, "From Localised Resistance to the Social Distance Powwow: Movements in the World of Indigenous Americans," discusses how Indigenous resistance and community building movements have appropriated entertainment, broadcast, and digital mediums and technologies from *Buffalo Bill's Wild West* show in the late 19th century, to the Lakota Sioux Dakota Pipeline protests in the 21st century. Chris Alen Sula et al.'s chapter, "Countermapping Plants and Indigenous Lifeways in North America: A Case Study of Tending to Turtle Island," explores geographic information system (GIS) mapping and countermapping techniques, particularly in relation to histories and impacts of colonialism on *Lenapehoking* and other Indigenous spaces, cultures, and lifeways on *Turtle Island* (North America) in order to link bodies, plant life, and stories to place. In the chapter "The Double Data Movement towards the Ecological Pluriverse: The Case of the Native Land Information System," Aude K. Chesnais focuses on issues of data colonialism, land, and food systems statuses to discuss the validation of culturally appropriate knowledge data systems, to assert native sovereignty and the need for a sustainable pluriverse.

Ian Garrett et al.'s chapter, "Groundworks: Re-storying Northern California with Emplaced Indigenous Media," discusses a decolonising theatre project connecting artists, communities, and key issues of land use, water rights, food security, and data infrastructure to places of Indigenous significance by the use of geolocated immersive media. In the chapter "Datafication, Digitisation, and the Narration of Agriculture in Malawi: From Productivity Measures to Curated Folklore," Dumisani Z. Moyo and Deborah P. Dixon discuss a data-rich national agriculture monitoring and evaluation system in the sub-Saharan country of Malawi in concert with an emerging digital archives programme to collect stories from a farming-centred culture, which offers an avenue for agro-decolonisation efforts. And lastly, in another chapter focusing on Malawi, "Spatial Video Geonarratives: Digitising Indigenous Folklores in Urban Flooding Lived Experiences," Josephine Zimba describes ethical and practical dimensions of employing spatial video geonarrative techniques to digitise folklores about the increasingly urban flooding of informal settlements of Mzuzu City.

Part III. *Geopoetics and Performance*

Deborah P. Dixon, the editor of this part, asks, "What kind of work do we want a prefix to do – and what does it indeed perform?" The term *geopoetics* might well be seen as another in a proliferating list of *geo*-inflected words: to be sure, it joins with geography, geology, geoscience, geopolitics, geohumanities, and geoethics, to name most but not all of the *geo*-prefixed words. For some concerned with etymologies, such a prefixing offers a way of foregrounding the ways in which particular kinds of doings – to inscribe, to conduct science on, to study, to play politics with, and to care for – draw on the materialities of the Greek-derived *geo* ("earth," "ground," or "land") for their animation and shape that same *geo* into spaces and places, landscapes and habitats, ecologies and systems. The *geo* here is a double-sided object, at once a resource and a product. To prefix poetics with such a *geo* is to feel for a language – embodied in song, verse, recitation, storytelling, composition, art, and so on – that expresses not so much our being in the world but rather the groundedness in our being of the Earth. In the midst of a planetary-wide Anthropocene that lays out with ever-more stark detail entanglements of colonialism and deep history, global capitalism, and Earth systems, and the violence, precarity, and vulnerabilities that have and will ensue from these, it is perhaps unsurprising to find a *geo*-inflected poetics. Poetics is a means of expressing our cares and anxieties, our preoccupations and concerns, but it is also an effective call to solidarity and action. Digital geopoetics is additive – it adds to our modes of expression while also offering new forms of effects and new audiences. The data-heavy spectacle of Anthropocene itself becomes a new creative resource. Yet in its performance, the prefix of *geo* is doing more than indicate an object, the Earth. It is also a feeling for the borders of our agency, our understanding, and our means of expression: a feeling for a poetics of an Earth without us.

Pablo Mansilla-Quiñones et al.'s chapter, "Exploring Sensible Virtual Immersive Spaces through Digital Georamas," investigates 19th-century panoramas, dioramas, and georamas, to illustrate how digital projects similarly enable dialogues of knowledge on ways of seeing the Earth but in contrast opening avenues to pluriverse representations. In "The Digital Poetics of Lost Waterscapes in Coimbatore, South India," Shanmugapriya T. Priya and Deborah Sutton discuss a digital literary visualisation project on water stress in Southern India that works with local activists and communities in compiling open-access data concerning lost and precarious landscapes of water in manners challenging presumptions of imperial pasts and state-sponsored science. Eric Magrane and Wendy Burk's chapter, "Relationality in the Online Literary Journal *Spiral Orb*," considers experiences of editing and the resulting digital ecology of authorship, screen, text, and online reading. The chapter suggests that hyperlinked journal design lends vibrancy and performativity – one not centred on individual works but on juxtapositions and interrelations enacted and de- and re-composed, presented in the online text environment.

In "Chemo Creatures in a Digital Ocean! The Making of a Speculative Ecosystem," Lucy Sabin describes the video exhibit *In Search of Chemozoa*, designed by digital artists and scientists to poetically grapple with the restless balancing acts between cells, their milieux, communities, and resources. William J. Mackwood and Gwenyth H. Dobie's chapter "Innovative and Creative Geographies: The Shifting Boundaries of Inside, Outside, Real, and Imagined Spaces" chronicles the experiences and productions of theatre artists who work at the critical intersection of nature and art and ponder what it means to have a digital lab and performance studio in the verdant forest of the Canadian Northwest. Lastly, Tatiana Konrad's chapter, "The Sound of Environmental Crisis: Silence as/and (Eco)Horror in *A Quiet Place*," explores the role of soundscapes in transmitting performances of environmental degradation to cinema audience by arguing that silence in the film directed by John Krasinski illustrates humanity's neglect of responsibility in regards to global warming.

Part IV. *Species, Systems, Sustainability*

Chapters in this part, edited by Robert Legg, highlight how the DEH can inform deeper understandings of digital turns in environmental education, conservation, governance, and interactivity. Authors deconstruct and assess current state-of-the-art projects and address how digital systems record, communicate, and shape narratives about the Earth's species. Discussing how the proliferation of digital techniques and platforms encourages environmental citizenship and crowdsource science contributions and awareness, the authors focus on how the emergence of new framings, perceptions, and interactions with planetary species facilitate embodied and emplaced DEH applications, practices, and pedagogies.

Ana Peraica's chapter, "Genotype, Phenotype, Phototype: Digital Photography, Biological Variety, and Excessive Overpopulation of Types," introduces the concept of phototype, along with genotype and phenotype, and defines the field of photogenetics to approach new lifelike forms. Jesse Peterson et al.'s chapter, "(Inter)National Connections: Linking Nordic Animals to International Data Banks," explores how non-human organisms become registered data points for international biodiversity observation networks and raises issues related to intimacy, dataveillance, and competition. Lauren Drakopulos et al.'s chapter, "A Shark in Your Pocket, a Bird in Your Hand(Held): The Spectacular and Charismatic Visualisation of Nature in Conservation Apps," parses conservation surveillance techniques employing Twitter, interactive platforms, and crowdsourcing apps to discuss how tracking technologies reshape nature-society relations by creating distinct visualities.

In "Images of Nature through Platforms: Practices and Relationships as a Research Field and an Epistemic Vantage Point of DEH," Paolo Giardullo draws on science and technology studies to illustrate how digital photography and citizen science projects offer opportunities to study cultural practices, people's interactions with nature and how research is shaped and enacted on web platforms. Lastly, Selin Süar Oral et al.'s chapter, "A Novel Method Suggestion for the Achievement of Environmental Citizenship Behaviour in the Digitising World," outlines a new five-stage model for creating an educational programme that uses interactive games to encourage environmental awareness and practice.

Part V. *Digital Chronicles of Environment, Literature, Cartography, and Time*

In *The Neanderthal's Necklace: In Search of the First Thinkers* (2003), palaeontologist Juan Luis Arsuaga posits that humans evolved as a storytelling species. In the 21st century, when digital and Anthropocene discourses are increasingly preoccupying our human condition, Charles Travis, editor of this part, states that the DEH is posed to explore different kinds and types of storytelling and asks what digital practices are being undertaken by what kinds of actors, with what human-technical agencies, and for what audiences, users, and communities of interest and practice? Travis notes that Hanna Arendt (2006, 258) states that "the political function of the storyteller-historian or novelist is to teach acceptance of things as they are. Out of this acceptance, which can also be called truthfulness, arises the faculty of judgment." In such a manner, digital storytelling practices can reflect the dynamic fluidity of human-environmental relations intimated by the heuristic of the Anthropocene.

Steven Hartman et al.'s chapter, "Online Transcription of Regional Icelandic Manuscripts Initiative," discusses the design, curation and launch of a citizen science online platform that enables collaborative research on transcriptions of Icelandic literary documents created between 1550 and 1950. In "'Thick Mapping' for Environmental Justice: EJScreen, ArcGIS, and Contemporary Literature," Parker Krieg and Matt N. Hannah layer literary spaces with the United States Environmental Protection Agency data. Intersecting spatial theory with critical environmental justice frameworks, the chapter illustrates how geo-hermeneutic GIS techniques enrich our understanding of "lived" and "narrated" worlds.

Laura Lo Presti's chapter, "One Map Closer to the End of the World (As We Know It): Thinking Digital Cartographic Humanities with the Anthropocene," highlights visuality, materiality and movement to contextualise anthropocentric and post-human digital and analogue cartographies into configurations that reveal the wide spectrum of rhythms imbued in mapping practices at "the end of the world as we know it." In "The Deafening Roar of the Digital Environmental Humanities: Case Studies in New Scholarship," William Hansard and Kevin Moskowitz employ the *fin de siècle* American circus and mid-20th-century US auto industry as case studies to investigate the role of the "digital turn" in the environmental humanities to expose or create "silences" in the historical writing process and "corpus" (historiography) due to the conversion of quantitative archival data into narrative-friendly formats. Lastly, Francesco De Pascale and Charles Travis' chapter, "The COVID-19 Testimonies Map: Representing Italian 'Pandemic Space' perceptions with Neogeography Technologies," provides a qualitative geospatial technology survey of citizen testimonies framed by "sense of place" conceptualisations discussed in the works of humanistic/human geographers Armand Frémont, Torsten Hägerstrand, Anne Buttimer, and Yi-Fu Tuan.

Part VI. *Algorithmic Landscaping*

As will have been apparent, states Luke Bergmann, editor of this part of the handbook, there are many threads which weave together these chapters and the DEH. But with this section, "Algorithmic Landscaping," we highlight the land as digital, and even in some senses, the digital as a form of "land." The digital has often been dominated by anthropocentric projects of representation and ordering. But if the digital is more than a human project – if it is of the land and for the various processes and beings that constitute and inhabit it – then these chapters help us to listen to the many others who participate in our digital worlds. In some cases, this is a matter of changing databases or database practices. Sometimes, it is a matter of moving to other forms of digital representation, such as the semantic web, where knowledge claims can be more self-consciously interpretative and more easily seen as contested. It can be a matter of understanding the digital as always-already expressive of the informatic processes of the Earth and its life. The chapters of this section thus offer both interpretative practices and creative engagements, among the human, the non-human, and the entanglements of the land.

In the chapter "Digital Oil and the Planetary Oilfield," John Kendall invites us to think of oil as a digital object as we interrogate its material and symbolic relations by employing recent insights from the philosopher Yuk Hui and emergent research on the "planetarisation" of extraction. Chiara Cavalieri and Elena Cogato Lanza's chapter, "Between Digital and Territorial Turns: A Forking Path," offers a rich exploration of territorial and digital turns that have renovated the planning of cities and their hinterlands by discussing the histories of *transformational cartographies* enacted by urbanists and architects to envision regional bodies out of heretofore separate entities. Ryan Horne and Ruth Mostern's chapter "Landscapes in Motion: Cartographies of Connectivity and the Place of Physical Geography in the Environmental and Spatial Humanities," cognisant that many spatial history projects assume static physical landscapes and atemporal weather and climates discusses the environmental data required for long-term and large-scale spatial environmental history projects, by featuring the Tracks of Yu Digital Atlas, Pleiades, and the World Historical Gazetteer projects.

In "(Re)Imagining the Ibis: Multispecies Future(s), Smart Urban Governance, and the Digital Environmental Humanities," Hira Sheik et al. state that environmental sensing and monitoring technologies now gather an unprecedented amount of data about the Earth, including its biodiverse species. The chapter encourages us participate more meaningfully in digital knowledge practices on non-human lives using different sorts of databases and theoretical negotiations. Lastly, Bronislaw Szerszynski and Nigel Clark's chapter, "Elemental Computation: From Non-human Media to More-than-Digital Information Systems," invites us to consider what it means for the Earth to compute. Whereas it may be more common to use computation as a metaphor to understand the world (akin to how organic or mechanical metaphors are used), Szerszynski and Clark invert the direction of inquiry to understand computation and digital information as "elaborations" upon the Earth and its life.

Sources

Arendt, H. 2006. *Between Past and Future*. London: Penguin.
Arsuaga, Juan Luis. 2009. *The Neanderthal's necklace: in search of the first thinkers*. Chichester: John Wiley.

Barbier, F. 2017. *Gutenberg's Europe: The Book and the Invention of Western Modernity*. Translated by Jean Birrell. Malden: Polity Press.

Berry, B., P. Buck, M. Mills, and M. Stipe. 1983. "Laughing." *Murmur*, I.R.S. Records, April 12, 1983.

Castree, Noel. 2021. "Making the Environmental Humanities Consequential in 'The Age of Consequences' the Potential of Global Environmental Assessments." *Environmental Humanities* 13 (2): 433–58.

Chandra, V. 2013. *Geek Sublime: Writing Fiction, Coding Software*. London: Faber & Faber.

Clapper, Jordan. 2021. "Ancestors in the Machine: Indigenous Futurity and Indigenizing Games." In *Alternative Historiographies of the Digital Humanities*, edited by Dorothy Kim and Adeline Koh, 427–72. Santa Barbara: Punctum Books.

Coole, Diana, and Samantha Frost. 2010. "Introducing the New Materialisms." In *New Materialisms: Ontology, Agency, and Politics*, edited by Diana Coole and Samantha Frost, 1–43. Chapel Hill: Duke University Press.

Corrigan, J. 2010. "Qualitative GIS and Emergent Semantics." In *The Spatial Humanities: GIS and the Future of Humanities Scholarship*, edited by David Bodenhamer, John D. Corrigan, and Trevor Harris, 76–88. Bloomington: Indiana University Press.

Crang, Mike. 2015. "The Promises and Perils of a Digital Geohumanities." *Cultural Geographies* 22 (2): 351–60.

Dalby, S. 2018. "Firepower: Geopolitical Cultures in the Anthropocene." *Geopolitics* 23 (3): 718–42, Ref. 721. doi:10.1080/14650045.2017.1344835.

Dixon, D. P., and M. Whitehead. 2008. "Technological Trajectories: Old and New Dialogues in Geography and Technology Studies." *Social & Cultural Geography* 9: 601–11.

Fuson, R. H. 1969. "The Orientation of Mayan Ceremonial Centers." *Annals of the Association of American Geographers* 59 (3): 494–512. doi:10.1111/j.1467-8306.1969.tb00687.x.

Garza, Armida, de la. 2016. "Aboriginal Digitalities: Indigenous Peoples and New Media." In *The Digital Arts and Humanities*, edited by Charles Travis and Alexander von Lunen, 49–62. Cham: Springer Press.

Haraway, D. 2016. "Tentacular Thinking: Anthropocene, Capitalocene, Chthulucene." *e-Flux, Journal* (September): 75. www.e-flux.com/journal/75/67125/tentacular-thinking-anthropocene-capitalocene-chthulucene/.

Hayles, N. K. 2012. *How We Think: Digital Media and Contemporary Technogenesis*. Chicago: University of Chicago Press.

Kim, Dorothy. 2021. "Embodying the Database: Race, Gender, and Social Justice." In *Alternative Historiographies of the Digital Humanities*, edited by Dorothy Kim and Adeline Koh, 145–202. Santa Barbara: Punctum Books.

Krupp, E. C. 1997. *Skywatchers, Shamans and Kings: Astronomy and the Archaeology of Power*. New York: Wiley & Son.

Kukutai, Tahu, and John Taylor. 2016. *Indigenous Data Sovereignty: Toward an Agenda*. Canberra: ANU Press, xxi.

LaPensée, Elizabeth. 2014. "Indigenously-Determined Games of the Future." *Kimiwan Zine Issue 8: "Indigenous Futurisms"*: 20–21.

Lovelock, J., and B. Appleyard. 2019. *Novacene: The Coming Age of Hyperintelligence*. London: Allen Lane.

Menabrea, Luigi Federico, and Ada Lovelace. 1842. "Sketch of the Analytical Engine Invented by Charles Babbage." Translation of Menabrea, L. F. 1842. "Notions sur la machine analytique de M. Charles Babbage." *Bibliothèque universelle de Genève*. Nouvelle série 41: 352–76.

Mortimer, Rex. 2006. *Indonesian Communism under Sukarno: Ideology and Politics, 1959–1965*. Singapore: Equinox Publishing, 82–83.

Norris, R. P., and B. Y. Harney. 2014. "Songlines and Navigation in Wardaman and Other Australian Aboriginal Cultures." *Journal of Astronomical History and Heritage* 17 (2): 141–48.

Peters, J. D. 2015. *The Marvelous Clouds: Toward a Philosophy of Elemental Media*. Chicago: University of Chicago Press, 2.

Posthumus, Stephanie, and Stéfan Sinclair. 2014. "Reading Environment (S): Digital Humanities Meets Ecocriticism." *Green Letters* 18 (3): 254–73.

Rosol, Christoph, Benjamin Steininger, Jürgen Renn, and Robert Schlögl. 2018. "On the Age of Computation in the Epoch of Humankind." *Nature Outlook* 563 (7733): 1–5.

Rueckert, William. 1978. "Literature and Ecology: Experiment in Ecocriticism." *The Iowa Review* 9 (1) (Winter): 71–86.

Sherman, J., ed. 2015. *Storytelling: An Encyclopedia of Mythology and Folklore*. London: Routledge.

Sikarskie, Amanda, Grace. 2016. *Textile Collections: Preservation, Access, Curation, and Interpretation in the Digital Age*. New York: Rowan and Littlefield.

Smith, Michael E. 1984. "The Aztlan Migrations of the Nahuatl Chronicles: Myth or History?" *Ethnohistory* 31 (3): 153–86.

Thompson, K. O. 2021. "Preface." In *Narratives in the Anthropocene Era*, edited by Charles Travis and Vittorio Valentino, 9–32. Lago: Il Sileno Edizione.

Turing, A. M. 2004. *The Essential Turing*. Oxford: Oxford University Press.

Udell, John. 2005. "Annotating the Planet with Google Maps: Open, XML-Based Design Makes It a Service Factory for the Geospatial Web." *Infoworld* 4.

Urton, Gary. 2003. *Signs of the Inka Khipu: Binary Coding in the Andean Knotted-String Records*. Austin: University of Texas Press.

Weidner, C., R. Braidotti, and G. Klumbyte. 2019. "The Emergent Environmental Humanities: Engineering the Social Imaginary." *Connotations: A Journal for Critical Debate* 28: 1–25.

Wellner, P., W. Mackay, and R. Gold. 1993. "Back to the Real World." *Communications of the ACM* 36 (7): 24–26.

Wynter, S. 2003. "Unsettling the Coloniality of Being/Power/Truth/Freedom: Towards the Human, After Man, Its Overrepresentation—An Argument." *CR: The New Centennial Review* 3 (3): 257–337.

PART I

Overviews

1

COWBOYS, COD, CLIMATE, AND CONFLICT

Navigations in the Digital Environmental Humanities

Charles Travis, Poul Holm, Francis Ludlow, Conor Kostick, Rhonda McGovern, and John Nicholls

Introduction

The digital engages five broad research strands emerging in the humanities: firstly, the creation of web-based collections, archives, and text-encoding initiatives; secondly, the reading and analysis of electronic hypertexts; thirdly, the application of geospatial and discursive mapping and coding technologies; fourthly, approaches deploying gaming and 3D immersive visualisations; and fifthly, the explosive growth of big data, social computing, crowdsourcing, and networking opportunities (Holm, Jarrick, and Scott 2015). Digitally enabled syntheses between old (books, archives, maps, paintings, film, etc.) and new types of media (qualitative analysis software, geographic information systems [GIS], social media, gaming and virtual reality platforms, etc.) are becoming increasingly salient to the study of human-environmental relations. In turn, research and teaching initiatives coalescing under the umbrella of the DEH are beginning to address three interrelated phenomena characteristic of the 21st century: the digital revolution, global warming, and sociopolitical agency related to environmental change (Travis 2018). In this milieu, the "new human condition," to crib a phrase from the political philosopher Hannah Arendt (1961, 59), finds that "the world we have come to live in . . . is much more determined by [humans] acting into nature, creating natural processes and directing them into the human artifice and the realm of human affairs."

Concerns of the DEH include, firstly, how we come to *know* – with masses of information becoming increasingly available in diverse forms and platform – and secondly, how we *work* – in collaborative, "glocally" scaled endeavours that integrate physical and virtual environments which are changing techniques, workflows, and the ontology of research and teaching practices – and thirdly, how we *understand* – as cybernetic tools and methodologies provide radically new insights into and integrations of "old analogue," "new digital," and "natural archival" types of data. These concerns inform the three DEH case studies featured in this chapter. The first offers a geo-literary *eco-digital* geo-hermeneutic on 19th-century US expansion and environmental degradation in the American West; the second offers a "data canon" *precis* on the North Atlantic

DOI: 10.4324/9781003082798-3

"Fish Revolution" between 1500 and 1800; and the third features computer-automated readings of ancient astronomical diaries to analyse ancient relations between climate and conflict in the Fertile Crescent kingdoms of Babylon and Assyria.

Larry McMurtry's Literary Geography: Eco-Digital Geo-hermeneutics (Charles Travis)

This project engages a panoramic literary geography of the 19th-century American West depicted in a tetralogy of novels by the Texas author Larry McMurtry (1936–2021) collected under the title of the *Lonesome Dove Chronicles* (2010). Humanities geographical information systems (HumGIS) applications were deployed to explore McMurtry's literary perceptions and representations of the American Southwest and Rocky Mountain West during the expansion of the United States in the 19th century. The *Larry McMurtry's Literary Geography* (*LMLG*) project funded by the University of North Texas Libraries at McMurtry's *alma mater* draws on the *Portal to Texas History* digital data collection to perform an *eco-digital* geo-hermeneutics on his collective works.[1]

McMurtry's saga on the closing of the American West, McMurtry borrowed character tropes from Miguel de Cervantes' (1547–1616) *Don Quixote* (1605–1615) to depict the lives of Augustus "Gus" McRae, a raconteur from Tennessee, and his stolid partner, Woodrow Call, and recount their days as filibusters, Texas Rangers, and cowmen. McMurtry observes that the "crazy old knight and the peasant pragmatist" comprised "an essential pair" and were "the ultimate source of Gus and Call" (McMurtry 2008, 10). The duo's rambles through the American Southwest and Rocky Mountain West regions during the expansion of the United States in the 19th century were inspired in part by Charles Goodnight (1836–1929) and Oliver Loving's (1812–1867) pioneering cattle drive from Texas to Montana in 1866. The *Chronicles* spans five decades of western historical and cultural geography, despite chronological slippages between the four novels that comprise it. It commences in the 1840s with *Dead Man's Walk* (1995), then spans the 1850s–1860s in *Comanche Moon* (1997). Its titular novel, *Lonesome Dove* (1985), ranges from the late 1870s, and *The Streets of Laredo* (1993), the *Chronicles*' concluding work, is set in the 1890s.

By navigating the online 3D Google Earth tours of the four novels on the *LMLG* project page, one can journey with Gus and Call as Santa Fe filibusters, and Texas Rangers and join their cattle drive from Texas to Montana (Figure 1.1). Reading the *Chronicles* while navigating the Goggle Earth tours illuminates an observation Annie Proulx (2008, 8) made in *Dangerous Ground: Landscape in American Fiction* on the experience of a "viewer/writer/reader" of a text who

> stands metaphorically in both the unwritten and the written landscapes, enters the territory on the page the same time it is created in the mind – a profound involvement with place through real three dimensional landscapes and the described and imagined landscape.

By zooming in and out on the Google Earth tours, a reader can hop from Mexico City to the Rio Grande in south Texas and jump to the west of the Pecos River and the Great Plains in the Oklahoma and Kansas Territories. One can traverse the Palo Duro Canyon, the arid *Llano Estacado* (Staked Plains) of west Texas, cross the Powder River basin of Wyoming and ford the Missouri River to the lush pastures of the Milk River Valley in northwestern Montana. The historian John Lewis Gaddis (2011, 48) notes that the most distinctive characteristics of Russian novelist Leo Tolstoy's (1869) epic *War and Peace* (*Война и миръ*) are "the great shifts of scale that

Figure 1.1 Homepage of the *Lonesome Dove* Google Earth tour.

Source: The Portal to Texas History and Charles Travis.

take place within it." Tolstoy, Gaddis writes, "zooms out . . . to show us great armies sweeping across Europe, and the back in to focus on . . . the ordinary soldier's point of view," concluding "Google Earth, for all its own zooming in and zooming out, has nothing on Tolstoy." The *Chronicles* encompasses similar shifts in scale, and though accepting Gaddis' point, reading McMurtry's work in concert with the Google Earth tours, one can undertake an *eco-digital* geo-hermeneutic journey across the Great Plains and Rocky Mountains.

Proulx (2008, 7) defines a "deep landscape novel" as a work "in which the story that unfolds can only happen . . . *where* it happens." The *Chronicles* adheres to Proulx's classification and "deep mapping" concepts juxtaposing textual, virtual, and actual landscapes that provide heuristics to integrate literary, cultural, and historical geography with HumGIS methods and literary and textual studies and conduct this chapter's *eco-digital* geo-hermeneutics on McMurtry's works. By incorporating a "reflexivity that acknowledges how engaged human agents build spatially framed identities and aspirations out of imagination and memory," deep mapping techniques deployed in the creation of the Google Earth tours (Figure 1.2) illuminate "how the multiple perspectives constitute a spatial narrative that complements the prose narrative traditionally employed by humanists" (Bodenhamer, Harris, and Corrigan 2015, 20; Travis 2020a, 2020b).

By navigating across the tours' remotely sensed landscapes, readers can hermeneutically transpose the *Chronicles*' apocalyptic sunsets, raging rivers, majestic cloud-filled horizons, dew-laden mornings, alkaline badlands, buffalo skull pyramid racks, and grasshopper swarms on the digitised environments produced by a Landsat/Copernicus satellite lens. In addition, one can locate in the tours where deadly biblical scale dust, hail, and lighting storms kill one cowhand and a poisonous nest of moccasin vipers kills another – boys just on the cusp of manhood, never to partake of the ritual pleasures of life in the saloons and bordellos of Ogallala, Nebraska, a place Gus describes as the "Sodom of the Plains" (McMurtry 2010, 1313). In this regard, McMurtry's

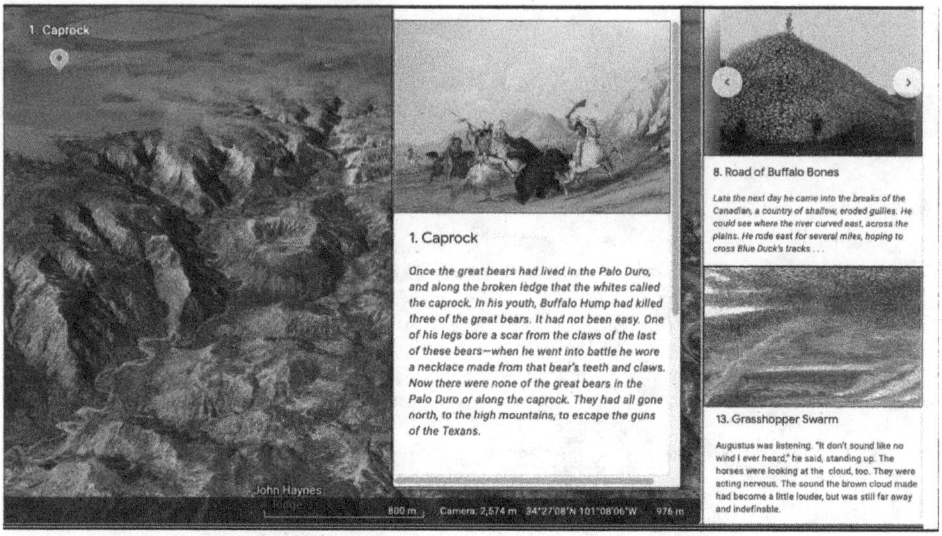

Figure 1.2 3D Google Earth tours of a Comanche bear hunt on the edge of the Llano Estacado, Road of Buffalo Bones in the Canadian River basin, and Great Plains grasshopper swarm, featured on *The Larry McMurtry's Literary Geography* project page.

Source: Larry McMurtry and Charles Travis.

Chronicles, like Cervantes' *Don Quixote*, "does not disentangle the story from the history, but points its telescope at the ill-defined frontier itself" (Wardropper 1965, 5). Contemplating the settlement of the United States west of the Mississippi River, McMurtry (1990) observes,

> To understand the westward expansion, one needs not merely the explorer and the scientist, but the artist as well. From the beginning artists were part of the enterprise – and a vital part of it, for it was the artists, rather more even than the explorers or the scientists, who ended up selling the West to the East. To a great extent that there was a West of the imagination – and this was the West that most Americans knew – it was the artists, not the pioneers, who created it.

McMurtry's writing weaves together Gaelic and Indigenous "folklore and American frontier history" and storytelling to depict transgressions of "physical, psychic, and geographical borders" symbolised in the "Western" as "a simple adobe wall, an otherworldly dimension, or a mountain chain" (Quintelli-Neary 2004, 44). It is not a stretch of the imagination to hear echoes of the seventh-century Irish epic *Táin Bó Cúailnge* (*The Cattle Raid of Cooley*) in McMurtry's storylines. In the *Chronicles*, the Mexican-American War (1846–1848) and American Civil War (1861–1865) manifest as distant thunder over the narrative horizon of its four novels. The US Army and Plains Indian Wars (1865–1890) and General George Armstrong Custer's denouement at Little Big-Horn (1876) are also depicted peripherally.

In contrast, McMurtry's fictive renderings of the freebooting 1841–1842 Texan–Santa Fe and Mier Expeditions (*Dead Man's Walk*), the Texas Ranger–Comanche Wars with the *Penateka* war chief Buffalo Hump between 1850–1870 (*Comanche Moon*), Goodnight and Loving's 1866 pioneering cattle drive (*Lonesome Dove*), and the rise of the Railroad Barons in the 1880s–1890s (*Streets of Laredo*) provide period detail, if not pedantic history. In the *Chronicles*, McMurtry

(2010, 1203) depicts one of Gus' rueful reflections on the "closing" of the Western "frontier" as a panoramic coda:

> In the north, the Army had finally taken the fight against the Comanches away from the Rangers and had nearly finished it. . . . After the [American civil] war, the cattle market came into existence and the big landowners in south Texas began to make up herds and trail them north to the Kansas railheads. Once the cattle became the game . . . he and Call quit rangering. It was no trouble for them to cross the river and bring back a few hundred head to sell . . . they had roved too long, Augustus concluded. . . . They were people of the horse, not of the town; in that they were more like the Comanches than Call would ever have admitted.

In his epic poem *Cycle of the West* (1919–1941), Nebraska poet laureate John G. Neihardt (1881–1973) portrayed the industrial re-territorialisation of the Great Plains from an Indigenous perspective:

> In all this wild beginning; saw with fear
> Ancestral pastures gutted by the plow,
> The bison harried ceaselessly, and how
> They dwindled moon by moon . . . (2018, 315)

Neihardt's poem cycle imparts "the last great fight for the bison pastures of the Plains between the westering white men and the prairie tribes" as "the struggle for the right of way between the Missouri River and the Pacific ocean" (Miller 1928, 125). Though Indigenous subsistence hunts did contribute to winnowing the massive herds, in particular the culls of American buffalo hunters, in search of hides and the incidental "sport" of easterners who shot the animals for amusement from passing trains, dwarfed the bison harvests of the Great Plains tribes. Ironically, the explorer Charles Frémont stated that bison trails should direct the US transcontinental railway in the Rocky Mountain West, arguing "that the buffalo was the best engineer, because he found that the great herds when going North for the winter crossed the upper passes, following the line of least resistance" (Rogers 1905, 272). McMurtry's *Chronicles* intertextually echoes the biogeographical destruction of the North American species lamented in Neihardt's verses. During a cattle drive, Gus is stopped in his tracks by the desolation in the Canadian River basin wrought by hunters and the industrial east's market for "buffalo coats":

> [He] was amazed to see an enormous pyramid of buffalo bones perhaps fifty yards from the water. The bones were piled so high. . . . Down the river a quarter of a mile there was another pyramid, just as large. . . . He saw five pyramids of bones between the crossing and Aus Frank's camp, each containing several tons of bones.
>
> *(McMurtry 2010, 1567)*

Another example of McMurtry's biogeographical eye is his depiction of a massive grasshopper swarm on the Great Plains. The extinct Rocky Mountain locust (*Melanoplus spretus*) once covered the West in leviathan swarms until the end of the 19th century. One famous Nebraska sighting in 1874 was estimated to range 198,000 square miles in size, weigh 27.5 million tons and speculated to comprise 12.5 trillion insects (Garcia 2000). In McMurtry's cattle-drive novel *Lonesome Dove*, the Hat Creek crew find themselves on the Great Plains in high summer when they spy a towering dark cloud looming on the horizon. The grasshopper swarm, vivid and tactile in McMurtry's depiction, revives memories of 19th-century extinctions like the passenger pigeon:

> The sound the brown cloud made had become a little louder, but was still far away and indefinable. Suddenly Augustus realized what it was. "Good lord," he said. "It's grass-hoppers, Lorie." . . . The cloud covered the plain in front of them from the ground far up in the air. It was blotting out the ground as if a cover were being pulled over it. . . . The hum they made as they spread over the prairie grass was so loud Lorena had to grit her teeth. . . . The cowboys who saw the cloud while on horseback were mostly terrified. . . . The sunshine glinted strangely off the millions of insects.
>
> *(McMurtry 2010, 1657)*

The historical geography described in the *Chronicles* maps out the expanding borders of the United States from the 1840s to the 1890s. During this period, the statistical cartography of the US Census Bureau (Figure 1.3) enumerated the lower 48 states, and the Indigenous and colonial *conquistador* trails of the West were transformed into an industrial webbing of railway lines, telegraph wires, and steamboat routes which contributed to populating and re-territorialising the natural and cultural landscapes of the once North American frontier.

Socially, McMurtry compares *Lonesome Dove* to George Eliot's (1819–1880) provincial British Midlands novel *Middlemarch* (1871–1872), set in 1831 during agricultural and parliamentary reforms dominated by the "technological and empiricist practices of an expanding capitalism" and ensuing industrial re-territorialisation. *Middlemarch*, historically contextualised by emerging English railways, the accession of King William IV and the passage of the Whig-sponsored 1832 Great Reform Act by the British Parliament, is also in a period that finds railway surveyors mapping rural landscapes meeting violent resistance from local farmers (Breen 1993, 48; Walton 1994).

In turn, the *Chronicles* counter the east-to-west geographical teleology under pinning the spatial historiographies of American expansion. The historian Patricia Limerick (1992, 1022) called for a revision of "east-to-west process" geo-historiographical model of US exploration and settlement by recognising the prior presence of Indigenous communities and the northward,

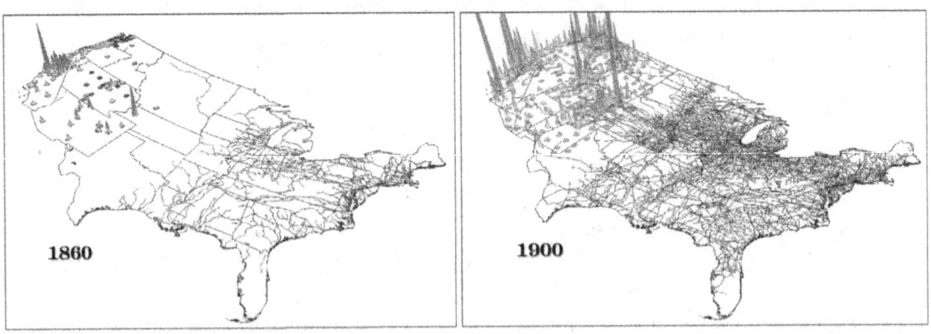

Figure 1.3 Railway and urban population expansion in the American West, 1860–1900.

Source: United States Census Bureau Data 1860 and 1900, sourced from Steven Manson, Jonathan Schroeder, David Van Riper, and Steven Ruggles. *IPUMS National Historical Geographic Information System:* Version 14.0 (Database). Minneapolis, MN: IPUMS. 2019; Railroad Networks 1870–1890. *Jeremy Atack, "Historical Geographic Information Systems (GIS) database of U.S. Railroads and Steamboat Routes for 1860, 1900."* Maps: Charles Travis.

southward, and eastward migrations of peoples from Mexico, Canada, and Asia. The Google Earth tour mappings of McMurtry's tetralogy illustrate (Figure 1.4 a and b) that the geographical arcs of the *Chronicles* run on a south-to-north axis from inside Mexico to the Canadian border rather than along the traditional east-to-west axis portrayed in John Gast's (1842–1896) 1872 painting *American Progress* or by historian Frederick Jackson Turner (1861–1932), who asked the audience of his 1893 address *The Significance of the Frontier in American History* to

> [s]tand at Cumberland Gap and watch the procession of civilization, marching single file – the buffalo following the trail to the salt springs, the Indian, the fur-trader and hunter, the cattle-raiser, the pioneer farmer – and the frontier has passed by. Stand at South Pass in the Rockies a century later and see the same procession.
>
> (Turner 1893)

However, Herbert Bolton (1870–1953), Turner's student, viewed US history from a hemispheric perspective in *The Epic of Greater America* (1933). Arguing that traditional historiography obscured subjects that "seemed secondary," Bolton contends that through a "borderland" heuristic lens, such narratives become "outstanding and primary" and vital to understanding the cultures that created the United States (1933, 473–74). In regards to American *tabula rasas* concerning the West and frontier, Limerick states, "The notion of a pristine wilderness is deservedly in tatters; the discoverers now appear as late arrivals in an already fully occupied and much affected landscape" (1992, 1022). She recommends "to think of the West as a place – as many complicated environments occupied by natives who considered their homelands to be the center, not the edge" (1987, 26), in addition to a physical landscape that is "actual, material, and substantial – something in the soil, a set of actual places . . . holding layer upon layer of memory" (2000, 28).

Furthermore, Walter M. Kollmorgen (1969, 216–17) notes that the "early range cattle industry of the West" depicted in *Lonesome Dove* "had its antecedents in the pastoral activities of Spanish America and, more remotely, in the *meseta* of Spain," the high Castilian plateau of La Mancha, where Cervantes set his novel *Don Quixote*. Gus and Call, as American reincarnations of the Errant Knight and Sancho Panza, illustrate Bolton's remapping of the West as a "meeting place and fusing place of two streams of European civilization, one coming from the south, and the other from the north" (Hämäläinen and Truett 2011, 341).

The geonarrative trajectory (Figure 1.4) of the *Chronicles* ranging from Mexico City in the south to Montana's Milk River Valley in the north parallels Bolton and Limerick's perspectives, as well as Pekka Hämäläinen's observation that "the rise of Plains Indian horse cultures along an orientation of grasslands, which meant that the northward spreading frontier crossed several climatic belts" (2003, 835) and its temporal setting intersects with the period during which the Industrial Revolution in England was catastrophically unsettling the agrarian and labour market economies of the British Isles. Prime examples include the Scottish Highland Clearances in the 18th and 19th centuries in the shadow of the 1746 Jacobite loss at the Battle of Culloden and the 1848 Irish Famine. Marguerite Quintelli-Neary (2004, 22) observes that such events caused the "despised races of the Celtic fringe" from "Wales, Ireland and Scotland" to migrate to America. Many headed West, beyond the boundaries of the Anglo-centric East Coast of the United States. Woodrow Call, who claims fierce allegiance to his American identity, is a member of this Celtic/Welsh/Gaelic "fringe" diaspora and is reminded by Gus, "You was born in Scotland . . . I know they brought you over when you were still draggin' on the tit, but that don't make you no less a Scot" (McMurtry 2010, 1144). McMurtry, a scion of a modest cattle-ranching family based in Archer City, northeast Texas, drew inspiration for the *Chronicles* from his first-hand experience with cattle, family memories, and genealogical lore, recalling:

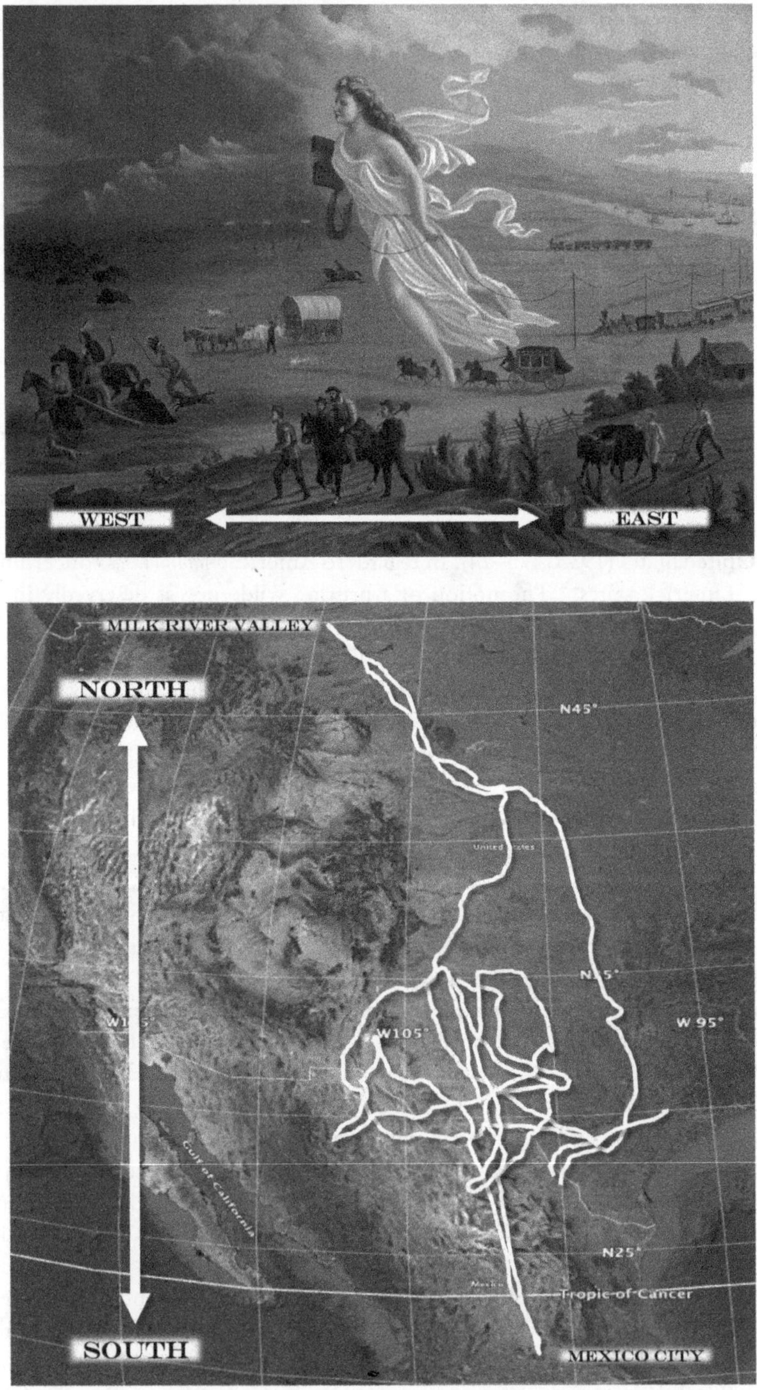

Figure 1.4 (a) *American Progress*, 1872, by John Gast, east–west axis geonarrative teleology. (b) Composite of *Lonesome Dove Chronicles* north–south axis geonarrative teleologies: *Dead Man's Walk*, *Comanche Moon*, *Lonesome Dove*, and *Streets of Laredo*.

Sources: Wikimedia Commons and Charles Travis.

> Before I was out of high school I realized I was witnessing the dying of a way of life – the rural, pastoral way of life. In the Southwest the best energies were no longer found in the homeplace, or in the small towns; the cities required these energies and the cities bought them. . . . The cattle range had become the oil patch; the dozer cap replaced the Stetson almost overnight. The myth of the cowboy grew purer every year because there were so few actual cowboys left to contradict it.
>
> *(McMurtry 2006, 11)*

Like Cervantes' depiction of the Plains of La Mancha, McMurtry parses the cultural and physical geographies of the American West, Southwest, and Rocky Mountain regions through the cracked lenses of myth, fiction, and history.

The NorFish Project (Poul Holm and John Nicholls)

The lack of quantitative assessment of the early modern fisheries has caused fishery scientists and historians to seriously underestimate the impact of pre-modern fishing efforts and total landings of two main commercial fish species: North Atlantic cod and Northeast Atlantic herring. This was the hypothesis of the NorFish project (Environmental History of the North Atlantic Fisheries, 1500–1800) (Holm et al. 2019), which employed big data analytics, deep chart mapping, and historical ocean productivity, modelling on the basis of multinational, multi-archival research (Travis and Holm 2016; Travis et al. 2020; Rankin and Holm 2019). In the end, NorFish published data concerning 25 fisheries containing more than 6,000 landing records (of

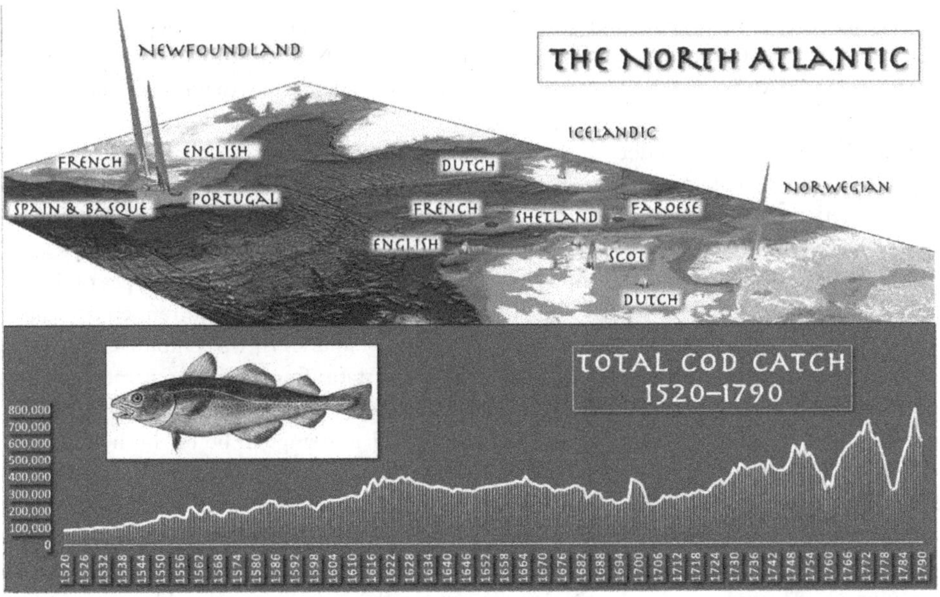

Figure 1.5 North Atlantic cod harvest, 1520–1790. Spikes in 3D visualisation symbolise the number of cod harvested by country per location during the period.

Source: P. Holm et al. 2021. *Extractions of North Atlantic cod and herring, 1520–1790*; cod image, *Wikimedia Commons*. Graph and 3D visualisation: Charles Travis.

typically ten or more variable attributes) in addition to a historical cartography and qualitative document database on the site Figshare (Holm et al. 2021). The project adopted a multidisciplinary, humanities-led approach to establish a robust quantitative framework of maritime extractions, supplies, and prices while also chronicling and parsing the subjective preferences and political motivations of actors who took part in the early modern Fish Revolution across the North Atlantic.

Employing DEH methods, NorFish discovered that marine extractions during the early modern period, c. 1520–1790, vastly exceeded previous assumptions. The project found that North Atlantic fisheries for cod and herring were of an order of magnitude comparable to levels measured during the Industrial Revolution, challenging notions of relatively unimpacted pre-industrial-age marine ecosystems. We identified two periods of Accelerated Marine Extractions (AME) respective episodes between 1540–1620 and 1750–1790, when growth rates of fish landings were higher than human demographic growth. These periods of AME point to the contribution and impacts of fish supplies on the expansion of early-modern societies (Holm et al. 2021). Quantifying data extracted from historical sources, such as archival records, documents, and cartography, in addition to scholarly publications, is a multifaceted task. The NorFish team was composed of multilingual historians (Scandinavian, German, Flemish, French, Spanish, Portuguese, and English), as well as archaeologists, biologists, geographers, and a mathematician. All NorFish researchers produced data requiring curation by a full-time data manager. In a landmark development, data on French and English, Northwest Atlantic cod fishing and catches were rigorously analysed and processed. In turn, data derived from combinations of archival materials, existing scholarly articles and academic datasets revealed large gaps created by missing and/or unknown data points. To obtain viable estimates of actual catches, a novel capacity trend method (CTM) was created. The application of CTM filled gaps in port records by extracting a simple progression extrapolation (variable trend) from aggregated annual effort values of primary ports to fill missing data on secondary ports and determine complete annual capacity trends with transparent levels of detail and accuracy (Nicholls, Allaire, and Holm 2021). Subsequently, CTM may be used to analyse other historical data series that have patchy coverage across time and space.

While historians focus on deriving meaning, insights, and facts from qualitative and quantitative information, a data manager seeks to impart a scientific taxonomy upon extracted data by applying meticulous planning, verification, and formatting to transform raw data into thematic datasets. Data are only as good as the quality of the research that led to their discovery and are meaningless unless accurately cited and sourced. The project identified various types of data outputs that had to be constructed into viable thematic datasets and series and rendered compliant with the NorFish data management framework. At the basic level, the Dublin Core (DubC) standard was employed to formulate data strings into a static foundation of named fields that were clearly defined and rooted in data management conventions. The NorFish cartography data was handled in such a manner, enabling complex data strings to be established in simple, well-defined terms (e.g. Travis et al. 2020; Rankin and Holm 2019). Similarly, the documented outputs of the project, including large online databases, were formatted into DubC standard structures to ensure transparency and simplicity.[2]

In addition, NorFish generated a large number of multidimensional datasets with spatio-temporal and taxonomic elements. Interspersed with and contextualised by relevant quantitative and qualitative datum fragments, these sets contributed information for the project's various peer-reviewed publications. The DubC standard was applied to these sets to enable data to reach its full and relevant research potential. The addition of specific species data in taxonomic fields meant that the refined and robust Darwin Core (DwC) standard could be superimposed on these datasets. DwC incorporates a rigorously validated taxonomic perspective into DubC, enabling clear metadata to be established and underlying data to be formatted to optimal effect. A positive by-product of applying such criteria was that it conforms to de facto standards for representing marine species data, attracting inclusion in the United Nations Educational, Scientific and Cultural Organization's Ocean Biodiversity Information Systems (UNESCO OBIS) big data platform. As the largest public domain resource of marine animal species biodiversity in the world, the UNESCO OBIS includes 80 million individual records from over 4,250 datasets, including well over 150 million measurements and facts.[3] Furthermore, this criterion complements and supplements the Oceans Past Initiative (OPI) legacy History of Marine Animal Populations (HMAP) data store, making OPI a major provider of historical datasets.

A rigorous process of formatting, testing and verification was required to produce each DwC-ready dataset. The NorFish data was placed in correct pre-defined fields, several of which were exclusively created and required to ensure interaction with the larger DwC environment. For NorFish, named data fields were matched exactly to data gathered from meticulous research. Lists of data then had to be verified manually and computationally. Visual checks were carried out to account for any obvious errors or omissions. This was followed by having the data run through established DwC "R" programmed sequences to test various elements, such as the correct use of taxonomic naming conventions, viable coordinate locations, and temporal reliability. Following any corrections and revisions that may have been necessary, the NorFish DwC data were entered into an Integrated Publishing Toolkit (IPT) established by the Global Biodiversity Information Facility (GBIF). The data then followed yet another series of verifications and checks before being harvested into the OBIS database.

While this level of detailed scrutiny provided clean data, it was also necessary to generate supporting documentation so that the datasets could be accurately contextualised within their historical settings. These documents provide anyone who accesses NorFish datasets with a full description of the data fields but also provide datum sources and brief historical backgrounds for clarity. Published academic articles and outputs from the NorFish data canon routinely reference these datasets, which are integral to understanding the conclusions reached by the NorFish project (Nicholls, Allaire, and Holm 2021).

The comprehensive documentation of historical North Atlantic fisheries enables future researchers to ask questions previously considered unanswerable. An example of the enduring value of NorFish's data is a newfound clarity on changes in fish consumption preferences from the late medieval to the early modern period. The most important human benefit of elevated marine exploitation during this period was increased food security. The annual consumption of herring and cod almost doubled during the 16th-century Fish Revolution, reaching from 2.9 to 5.7 kilograms per capita by 1790. Indeed, total seafood consumption in West Europe averaged 10 kilograms by 1790, but with significant regional differences. This amount stands in comparison with the global average fish consumption of close to 10 kilograms in 1960. Access to the cheap, dried protein offered by herring and cod was critical to food security in pre-industrial societies. Dried or salted fish kept well and was generally less expensive than beef during spring months when grain and meat stocks ran low. Consequently, its increased availability likely played a significant role in the demographic rise of modern Western Europe.

The NorFish project's mixed-methods approach highlighted geographical shifts in fishing from east to west, finding that herring was increasingly sourced from the North Sea rather than the Baltic, while cod was harvested more predominantly from the Northwestern Atlantic rather than its Northeastern waters. Geopolitically significant, this reorientation was also discovered, occurring at regional levels, with fluctuations found in the Irish and Celtic Seas, the Danish North Sea fisheries, the Baltic and the North Atlantic islands. As fish shifted from being an expensive and limited resource in the late Middle Ages to a relatively cheap and abundant commodity by early modern times, environmental and societal changes ensued.

The Fish Revolution of the 1500s impacted demographics, politics, and market-driven economies, with the strategic importance of the trade becoming evident to all major Western European powers. Inverse effects of war and peacetime were reflected in fish stock increases during periods of conflict as fishing slowed or halted. NorFish concludes that the "Great Fishing Experiments" of the First and Second World Wars saw similar respites that increased Newfoundland cod stocks during the Napoleonic Wars. Warfare largely mirrored downturns in fishing and upturns in stocks. From the 1630s until the Treaties of Utrecht (1713–1714) – a period of protracted wars – fish stocks rose as fishing fleets were pillaged or destroyed, leading to lower catch landings. Fishing crews were often taken captive, with their vessels appropriated for naval refitting and warfare. Volatility was the norm, with piracy and conflict in full sway. Fish markets outside of European theatres of conflict fared slightly better, such as the Newfoundland, Caribbean, and Iberian trade triangle, but cargo interceptions and attacks on fishing grounds were commonplace. Despite these dangers, rising prices sometimes encouraged fishing crews to risk going to sea. Peace brought a steady rise in fishing efforts as relative periods during the 16th and 18th centuries witnessed elevated marine extractions and ensuing prosperity.

Impacts of climate change, as documented by fall in temperatures and increases in storms late in the 17th century, more than likely had a negative impact on fishing efforts as fish stocks fell due to the reduced abundance of zooplankton in the oceanic food chain. Additionally, predator-prey phenomena and volcanic eruptions may have contributed to the geopolitical contexts of fisheries. The phenomenon of oscillating production levels between Northwestern and Northeastern waters may potentially be explained by biophysical changes across the North Atlantic. These questions will now be addressed on the basis of solid evidence by the funded for a six-year period through 2027 by the European Research Council.[4] In this sense, NorFish is proof of concept that assembling a global environmental history of humans and marine resources with contributions from various DEH methods can indeed be undertaken.

The CLICAB Project (Francis Ludlow, Conor Kostick, Rhonda McGovern)

The Climates of Conflict in Babylonia (CLICAB) project is an interdisciplinary venture that considers evidence from natural and human archives using quantitative and qualitative methods to pursue two central hypotheses. Firstly, climatic changes, including periods of extreme weather, influenced patterns of violence and conflict in the ancient Near East, thereby playing a key role in this formative region and era of world history. Secondly, the nature of any linkage between climate change, violence, and conflict varies through time and space according to evolving socio-economic, political, cultural, and broader environmental contexts. To test these hypotheses, the CLICAB project has focused upon the kingdoms of Assyria and Babylonia (centred in present-day Iraq and Syria) during the first millennium BCE, with four aims.

First Aim: Reconstructing Assyrian and Babylonian Hydroclimates

Written sources available for these Fertile Crescent kingdoms are rich with relevant observations, so producing new climatic reconstructions from such documents has been the project's first aim. Limited access to important environmental data due to regional conflicts and hydropolitics over water access (associated with dam building) have obstructed record-keeping and promoted secrecy. As a result, records from ancient Babylon may provide longer and higher-quality time series of variables, such as monthly Euphrates River levels, than do modern era data sources (Yilmaz 1995; Vörösmarty, Fekete, and Tucker 1996; Slotsky 1997; Lein 1998; Kirschner and Tiroch 2012; Huijs, Pirngruber, and van Leeuwen 2015). Ancient measurements were preserved in "astronomical diaries" created by Babylonian court astronomers who systematically recorded daily celestial and meteorological phenomena between the eighth and first centuries (Haubold, Steele, and Stevens 2019). With few exceptions, the meteorological content of these diaries has not been assessed for environmental reconstructions (Huijs, Pirngruber, and van Leeuwen 2015; Sigl et al. 2015; Ludlow, Kostick, and Morris 2022). Categorisation and extraction of this data for the first four centuries BCE, the period in which surviving diaries are most heavily concentrated, forms the foundation of CLICAB's climatic reconstructions.

More disparate sources, including annals and chronicles (e.g., Luckenbill 1924; Grayson 2000 [1975]; Glassner 2004; Budge 2009 [1902]), inscriptions (e.g., Piepkorn 1933; Nissen 2003), administrative records, personal and official correspondence (e.g., Parpola 1987; Lanfranchi and Parpola 1990; Moran 1992; Hunger and Cole 1996; Parpola 2014), astrological reports (e.g., Hunger 1992), and even some literary texts, such as epics and the Sumerian city laments (e.g., Vanstiphout 1980), yield important data on the incidence and perceptions of meteorological and related environmental phenomena, in addition to incidences and responses to societal stressors, such as epidemic disease, subsistence crises, migration, and conflict (e.g., Kleber 2012; Radner 2015). While such sources cannot offer systematic observations as found in the diaries, collectively they offer greater chronological and geographical span and scope, allowing the creation of a "master chronology of extreme weather, conflict and societal stress" for the first millennium. CLICAB has to date surveyed 18 (of 21 presently available) online volumes of the *State Archives of Assyria*, a landmark series that has published many such sources.[5] Overcoming challenges in using such materials requires methods from the field of historical climatology, which sits at the intersection of climatology and environmental history (Pfister 2007). The field's methodological advances have involved identifying, categorising, and assessing the historical reliability of written descriptions of relevant phenomena and quantifying such information for the purpose of reconstructing past climates. Even if not explicitly using the term DEH, STEAM research by Ludlow and Travis (2019) and the "consilient" approaches of Izdebski et al. (2022), and others adopt such methods.

Although computerised content analysis applied to an ever-growing body of digitised historical sources can empower all work in the humanities, automated close and distant reading methods can also promote detachment from the source material and its historical-geographical context, potentially undermining credible interpretations.[6] However, this is not limited to the digital age; for example, Thomas Short's *A General Chronology of the Air, Weather, Seasons, Meteors, Etc.* (1749), an infamous early modern work in historical climatology, was critiqued for paying too little attention to the reliability and independence (or "witness status") of its sources. Indeed analogue or digital reconstruction biases are often compounded by inclusions of misdated, duplicated, exaggerated, misidentified, fabricated, or otherwise dubious reports (Bell and Ogilvie 1978; Ogilvie and Farmer 1997).

While historical climatologists now widely stress the need for the assessment of source reliability using methods from critical philology and literary textual and source analyses, a persistent lack of practical guidance and case studies to meet this need exists. In addition, positivist stances of many historical climatologists on determining source reliability rarely acknowledge indeterminate cases, in addition to the subjectivity and potential for error on the part of the assessor. In creating a chronology of extreme weather reports from the medieval *Irish Annals*, Ludlow (2010) established a simple scale of *apparent reliability* (AP) reflecting this reality. Allowing readers to see all potentially relevant reports annotated by the AP scale rather than silently excluding those reports deemed unreliable opens avenues for further analysis if a report proves to be genuine or receives independent corroboration, in addition to providing insight into how chroniclers perceived and interpreted natural phenomena.

Informed by this work, CLICAB has designed a schema for coding and extracting the content of the astronomical diaries and more disparate sources. Enhanced by DEH-relevant textual analysis and encoding tools, the schema provides the means to reconstruct precipitation, cloudiness, atmospheric opacity, and wind direction (Figure 1.6) alongside ancient Euphrates River levels and other regional hydroclimatic variables. It was also recognised that climactic records could be considered "politically sensitive" as celestial and terrestrial phenomena such as comets, eclipses, earthquakes, storms, floods, and droughts were considered potential omens in the Ancient Near East that might portend fortune or misfortune for rulers and their societies.

It was thus posited that such phenomena might influence what court astronomers recorded in the diaries, potentially impacting the completeness and type of content recorded. For example, after the Neo-Babylonian Empire fell to the Persians in 539 BCE, rulers such as Darius III and Xerxes were known to have decommissioned temples and removed priests and scribes in a deliberate snub to the Babylonian way of life and a shift away from "cuneiform culture" (Robson 2019).

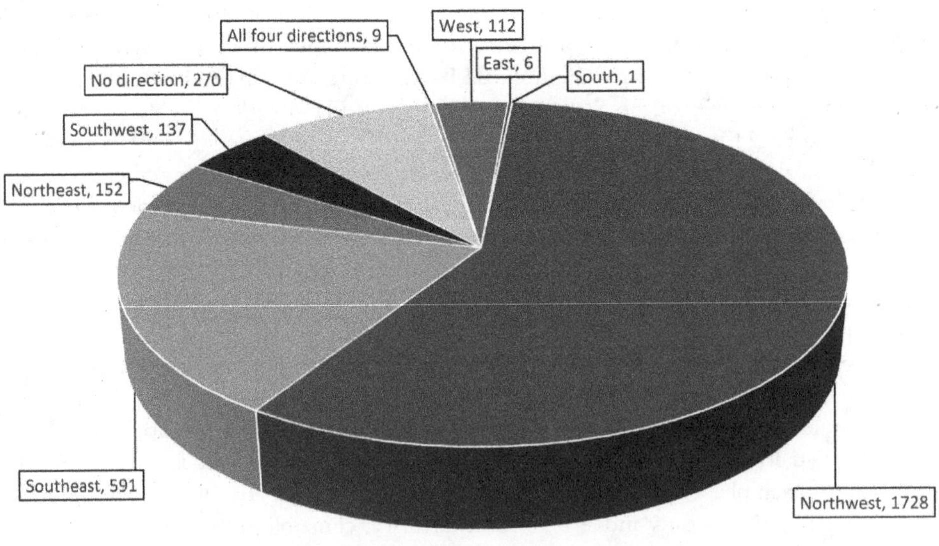

Figure 1.6 *Wind Direction Observations, Astronomical Diaries 652–61* BCE. exemplifies the meteorological data abundantly reported in the surviving diaries, with this figure following the categories offered by the astronomical diaries themselves.

Source: Rhonda McGovern (provisional data).

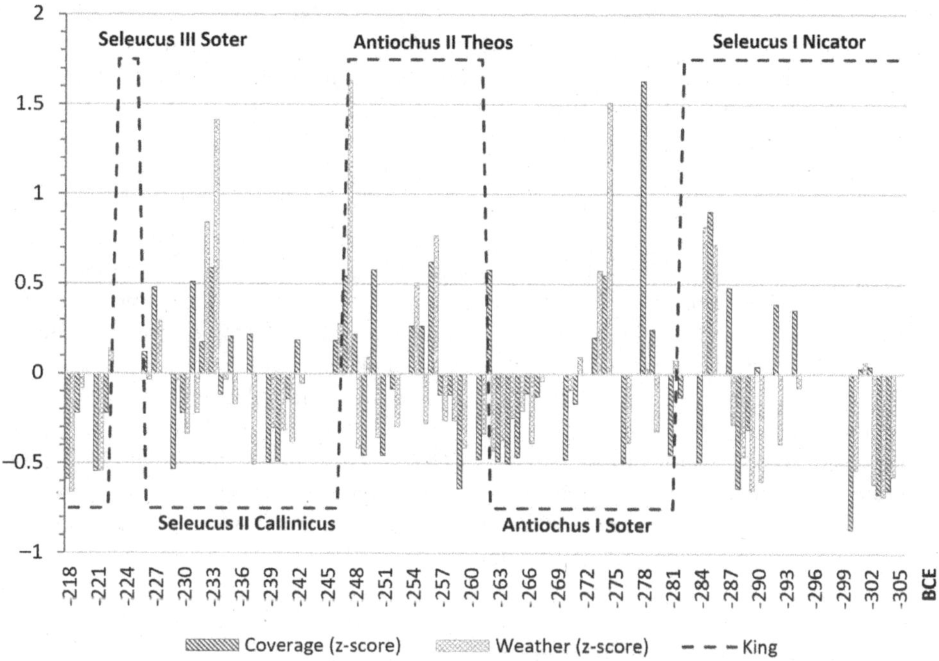

Figure 1.7 Standardised frequency plot (in z-scores on the vertical axis) for weather and total coverage (i.e., including non-weather reports) provided per year (305–218 BCE) from surviving astronomical diaries, alongside transitions between Fertile Crescent kings. Higher positive values signify greater coverage, and vice versa.

Plot: Francis Ludlow and Rhonda McGovern.

Thus, attention has been paid to the historical context in which the diaries were recorded, nuances in meaning, the likely intent of the diarists and their patrons, their intended audiences, and their general worldview. This is key to assessing the reliability of any report or observation and speaks to the issue of "representivity" in climatic reconstruction, which concerns how well any observed trends, such as in reports of heavy rainfall (or precipitation indices based upon combined reports of rainfall, flooding, drought, etc.), describe actual occurrences through time (Ludlow 2010, 2012). The possibility exists that derived trends will be distorted by multiple such factors, as well as the more obvious existence or lack of diaries surviving from certain periods. Such distortions can be potentially controlled statistically, and CLICAB has paid considerable attention to the coding of missing data, whether arising from lost diaries, damage to existing diaries, or silent changes in the type and volume of content even when diaries are available and apparently undamaged (Figure 1.7).

Second Aim: Assessing Associations between Climate, Conflict and Violence

Establishing whether extreme weather and abrupt climatic changes are statistically associated with violence and conflict in the first millennium BCE kingdoms of Babylonia and Assyria is the project's second aim. CLICAB's team holds considerable experience in categorising and quantifying violence documented in medieval Ireland and ancient Egypt (e.g. Ludlow and Manning 2016; Manning et al. 2017; Ludlow and Travis 2019), as well as societal stresses (e.g. famine, epidemic disease, political transitions, mass migrations) potentially generative or resulting from violence and conflict as documented in medieval European, Near Eastern, and Chinese annals and chronicles (Ludlow et al. 2013; Kostick and Ludlow 2015; Sigl et al. 2015; Gao et al. 2016; Kostick and Ludlow 2019). A source-critical approach is again needed here to avoid either treating the material without due caution or erroneously dismissing it as unreliable.

In categorising and quantifying violence and conflict, the project also aims to capture valuable nuance from the sources concerning the scope and scale of war, civil war, and forced mass population transportations. The Neo-Assyrian kings (and those of other regional polities) undertook military campaigns on an annual basis to gather tribute, restore order, or expand their territories. To achieve a more meaningful insight into the scope, intensity, and impact of these campaigns, CLICAB is developing a simple schema to denote whether a given campaign was minor – the ruler marching armies to unreliable cities to collect revenue – or represented a massive upheaval such as when the major regional powers of Elam and Assyria attempted to decisively eliminate each other by mobilising significant resources. Our working schema is presently a simple ordinal scale of 1 to 3, following straightforward criteria that return similar decisions by different assessors. While it is possible to adopt a finer scale to capture more detailed variations of the campaigns (e.g. a scale of 1 to 10), when this was trialled, assessors made increasingly subjective judgements – with greater disagreement even when apparently adhering to the same criteria. The advantage of such quantification methods when complemented by qualitative practice is that they provide a bird's eye view of change across times and places, enabling statistical comparisons with inherently quantitative climatic data sourced from natural archives.

CLICAB is also examining the use of sudden climatic "shocks" as "tests" of human response to reveal prevailing vulnerabilities and resilience. Dispersed through time, such shocks can let us examine whether and how responses evolve according to changing economic, political, and cultural contexts. An analysis based upon repurposing the superposed epoch analysis (SEA) method (used on continuous time-series studies of natural phenomena like tree-ring growth values) has already been undertaken by CLICAB. Discrete human events such as the incidence of revolts or the collapse of kingdoms/dynasties occurring across a range of years after a climatic shock have, for example, already been examined in this manner (Manning et al. 2017; Gao et al. 2021). The project employs this approach to assess whether associations exist between the timing of four climate-altering explosive volcanic eruptions dated 750, 723, 703, and 676 BCE: (Cole-Dai et al. 2021) and counts of documented violence, conflict, and other societal stresses between 750 and 650 BCE. Initial results illustrate a clear increase in the average of these counts in the first decade following these eruptions (Figure 1.8). While this increase may have occurred simply by chance, the advantage of a quantitative approach is the ability to calculate the likelihood that the observed counts occurred randomly or not. Statistical analysis suggested that there was less than a 10% chance that elevated counts in the years immediately following the eruptions were random. Forthcoming ice core volcanic reconstructions will provide more event dates to examine. These, combined with an examination of violence, conflict and stressors by individual type, as well as the application of the previously described scale of intensity, will provide a more nuanced analysis. This will help determine whether the manner of sociopolitical conflict responses observed in Figure 1.8 are maintained, say, for all 50-year sub-periods across a broader time range or are notably absent or reduced for particular periods and/or types of violence. This will, in turn, provide clues as to potential changes in underlying socio-economic and political contexts that might promote greater environmental resilience and offer new questions to be pursued by scrutinising documentary and archaeological evidence.

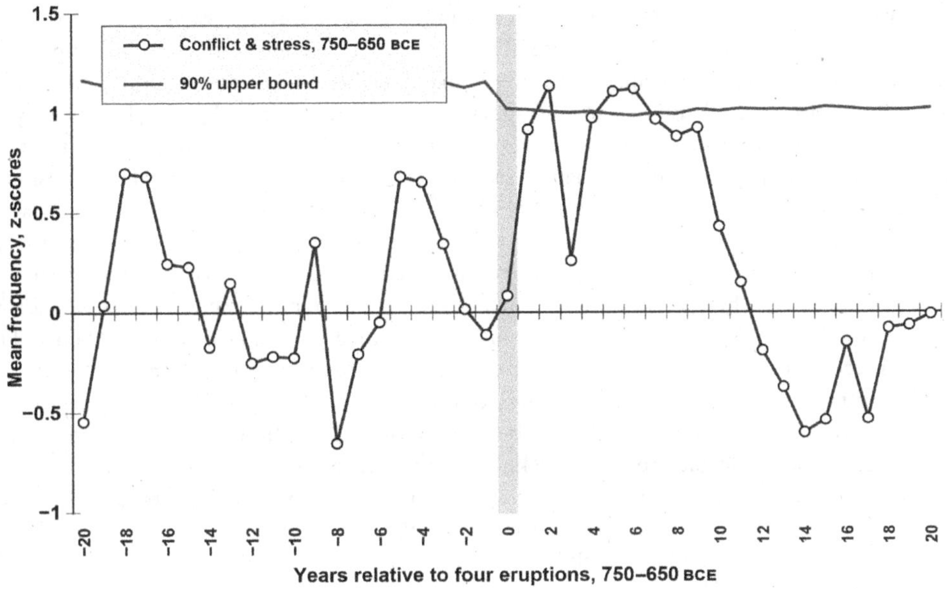

Figure 1.8 Superposed epoch analysis, showing the mean frequency of documented conflict and societal stress counts for each of the 20 years before four major volcanic eruptions seen in polar (Antarctic) ice cores (i.e. years −20 to −1 on the horizontal axis), the years of these eruptions (i.e. year 0, horizontal axis), and each of the 20 years following (i.e. years 1 to 20, horizontal axis). The average frequencies are notably elevated in the first decade following these eruptions, with the probability of observing such high values at random being less than 10%. Figure redrawn after Ludlow, Kostick, and Morris (2022).

Third and Fourth Aims: Pathways from Climate to Conflict and Importance of Historical Context

CLICAB's third and fourth aims are to delineate pathways by which climatic changes may have catalysed violence and conflict and assess if and how ancient Near Eastern societies developed mitigation strategies depending on their changing historical contexts. The project's contribution to *The Cambridge World History of Genocide* (Ludlow, Kostick, and Morris 2022) illustrates the latter's importance in mediating and or amplifying climatic influences by providing new insights into the fall of the Kingdom of Israel in 722 BCE. In that year, a revolution occurred in Assyria, possibly leading to the death of King Shalmaneser V and a likely opportunistic attempt by Israel to escape Assyrian domination (put simply). But a quick internal consolidation of power by the new Assyrian king Sargon II crushed the rebellion, and the population of Israel was dispersed by mass transportation (Frahm 2019; Hasegawa 2019). Until now, discussions of the pathways by which such violence and conflict erupted have largely excluded climate. Indeed, historian Bob Becking (2019, 23) states that

> climate in the Iron Age II–III period remained stable in ancient Israel. We can therefore assume that no specific impulses from a (sudden) change in climate would have influenced the course of events leading to the end of the kingdom.

However, recent ice core data from Antarctica identifies a massive, possibly tropical volcanic eruption in approximately 723 BCE (Cole-Dai et al. 2021).[7] The severe drop in temperature and disruption of seasonal precipitation patterns that likely followed, alongside the introduction of new, onerous taxes, plausibly acted as catalysts for internal revolt in Assyria. This, it may be posited, raised existential questions for the ruling elite of the Kingdom of Israel – was the time right to take advantage of the Assyrian crisis and risk challenging their subordinate position? Ultimately, their decision to do so can therefore be hypothesized as an indirect and partial outcome of the eruption but also a fatal misjudgment leading to the destruction of Israel. This case study is only one example of previously unobserved coincidences between major historical events in the ancient Fertile Crescent region and the incidence of extreme weather and abrupt climate changes documented in natural archives such as ice cores and cave speleothems. The detailed reconstruction of the historical Near Eastern climate (which now stands to be considerably advanced by the DEH-informed study of the astronomical diaries) is likely to reveal further such coincidences, as well as prove to be relevant for present climate change concerns. For example, explosive volcanic eruptions are known to impact river flow in many regions, but the size and number of eruptions in the modern period are limited by historical standards (Iles and Hegeral 2015). Examining responses to eruptions in the ancient Near East may thus prove salient to water supply issues following the next large contemporary eruption in an already acutely hydro-sensitive region. We hope that the CLICAB project showcases how a self-reflective and self-critical "digital" environmental humanities can co-produce new insights with colleagues (and methods and sources) from the natural sciences into societal vulnerabilities and resiliencies to environmental change.

Conclusion

As a liminal field, the DEH is an adaption to 21st-century cybernetic, climactic, and sociopolitical transformations. Featuring innovative approaches, research, and pedagogical questions, the DEH promotes the study of past and present human-environmental relations in order to cultivate better understanding of future potential and sustainable paths. The case studies featured in this chapter showcase how theory, techniques, and scholarship in literary geography, open-source geospatial hermeneutics, maritime environmental history, data taxonomies, historical climatology, automated digital reading, and statistical analysis find confluence and coherence in this emerging field. Collectively, the projects provide evidence that by no means are the arts and humanities in "intellectual crisis" but rather are becoming increasingly relevant to understanding how to address social, environmental, and digital threats and opportunities of our "new human condition" (Holm and Travis 2017). Our generation has been gifted with enormous computing power, including the means to inform and misinform itself about the state of the world, not least on the causes and mitigatory practices concerning human-induced climate change. The DEH may – and should – face up to the challenges that humanity faces as we discover the true positive potential of our environmental-social-political agency.

Acknowledgements

Charles Travis acknowledges funding from the University of North Texas Library, the Portal to Texas History Research Fellowship and the University of Texas, Arlington, COLA Faculty Research Endowment. Poul Holm (principal investigator) and John Nicholls acknowledge support from a European Research Council Synergy Grant (4-OCEANS project, grant agreement ID 951649).

Francis Ludlow (principal investigator), Conor Kostick, and Rhonda McGovern acknowledge support from an Irish Research Council Laureate Award (CLICAB, Award IRCLA/2017/303), and thank Joe Manning, Bert van der Spek, and Reinhard Pinrgruber for useful discussion.

Notes

1 *Larry McMurtry's Literary Geography* (https://blog.uta.edu/travisc/research/larry-mcmurtrys-literary-geography) project features 3D Google Earth tours of the four novels that comprise the *Lonesome Dove Chronicles* and *Portal to Texas History* (https://texashistory.unt.edu).
2 *NorFish Platform: Databases & Cartography Hub* (http://cehresearch.org/norfishplatform).
3 *UNESCO OBIS* (https://ioc.unesco.org/our-work/ocean-biodiversity-information-system).
4 *4-OCEANS project* (www.tcd.ie/tceh/4-oceans).
5 *State Archives of Assyria Online* (http://oracc.museum.upenn.edu/saao).
6 In addition to exploiting text search and encoding software like MaxQDA and open-source alternatives, CLICAB focuses on the complete "close reading" of texts to appreciate the context in which project-relevant references to drought or other phenomena are recorded.
7 Personal communication: Michael Sigl, University of Bern, 2020. Eruption location is important in determining climatic impacts.

Sources

Arendt, H. 1961. *Between Past and Future: Eight Exercises in Political Thought*. New York: Penguin.

Becking, B. 2019. "How to Encounter an Historical Problem? – '722–720' as a Case Study." In *The Last Days of the Kingdom of Israel*, edited by S. Hasegawa, et al., 17–34. Berlin: De Gruyter.

Bodenhamer, D., T. Harris, and J. Corrigan. 2015. *Deep Mapping and Spatial Narratives*. Bloomington and Indianapolis: Indiana University Press.

Bolton, H. E. 1933. "The Epic of Greater America." *The American Historical Review* 38 (3): 473–74.

Bell, W. T. and A. E. G. Ogilvie. 1978. "Weather Compilations as a Source of Data for the Reconstruction of European Climate During the Medieval Period." *Climatic Change* 1: 331–48.

Breen, R. 1993. "Place and Displacement in the Works of Brian Friel and Seamus Heaney." Unpublished PhD Dissertation, University of Warwick.

Budge, E. A. Wallis, ed. 2009 /1902. "The Annals of Ashur-nasir-pal." In *Annals of the King of Assyria: The Cuneiform Texts with Translations and Transliterations from the Original Documents*. London: British Museum.

Buell, Lawrence. 1995. *The Environmental imagination: Thoreau, Nature Writing, and the Formation of American Culture*. Cambridge, MA: Belknap Press of Harvard University Press.

Campbell, B. M. S., and F. Ludlow. 2020. "Climate, Disease and Society in Late-Medieval Ireland." *Proceedings of the Royal Irish Academy* 120C: 159–252.

Cole-Dai, J., et al. 2021. "Comprehensive Record of Volcanic Eruptions in the Holocene (11,000 years) from the WAIS Divide, Antarctica Ice Core." *Journal of Geophysical Research: Atmospheres* 126: e2020JD032855.

Frahm, E. 2019. "Samaria, Hamath, and Assyria's Conquests in the Levant in the Late 720s: The Testimony of Sargon II's Inscriptions." In *The Last Days of the Kingdom of Israel*, edited by S. Hasegawa, et al., 55–86. Berlin: De Gruyter.

Gaddis, J. L. 2011. "War, Peace, and Everything: Thoughts on Tolstoy." *Cliodynamics* 2 (1).

Gao, C., F. Ludlow, O. Amir, and C. Kostick. 2016. "Reconciling Multiple Ice-Core Volcanic Histories: The Potential of Tree-Ring and Documentary Evidence, 670–730 CE." *Quaternary International* 394: 180–93.

Gao, C., F. Ludlow, A. Matthews, A. R. Stine, A. Robock, Y. Pan, R. Breen, and M. Sigl. 2021. "Volcanic Climate Impacts Can Act as Ultimate and Proximate Causes of Chinese Dynastic Collapse." *Communications Earth & Environment* 2: Article Number: 234.

Garcia, M. 2000. "Melanoplus spretus (On-line)." *Animal Diversity Web*. Accessed January 1, 2020. https://animaldiversity.org/accounts/Melanoplus_spretus/.

Glassner, Jean-Jacques. 2004. *Mesopotamian Chronicles*. Atlanta: Society of Biblical Literature.

Grayson, A. K. (ed.) 2000 [1975]. *Assyrian and Babylonian Chronicles*. Winona Lake: Eisenbrauns.

Hämäläinen, P. 2003. "The Rise and Fall of Plains Indian Horse Cultures." *The Journal of American History* 90 (3): 833–62.

Hämäläinen, P., and S. Truett. 2011. "On Borderlands." *The Journal of American History* 98 (2): 338–61.

Hasegawa, S. 2019. "The Last Days of the Northern Kingdom of Israel." In *The Last Days of the Kingdom of Israel*, edited by S. Hasegawa, et al., 1–16. Berlin: De Gruyter.

Haubold, J., J. Steele, and K. Stevens, eds. 2019. *Keeping Watch in Babylon: The Astronomical Diaries in context*. Leiden: Brill.

Holm, P., A. Jarrick, and D. Scott. 2015. *Humanities World Report 2015*. Cham: Springer Nature.

Holm, P., F. Ludlow, C. Scherer, C. Travis, B. Allaire, C. Brito, P. W. Hayes, A. Matthews, K. J. Rankin, R. J. Breen, R. Legg, K. Lougheed, and J. Nicholls. 2019. "The North Atlantic Fish Revolution, c. AD 1500. Hypotheses, Methodologies, and Ways Forward." *Quaternary Research* 1–15. doi:10.1017/qua.2018.153.

Holm, P., J. Nicholls, B. Allaire, P. Hayes, and J. Ivinson. 2021. "Accelerated Extraction of North Atlantic Cod and Herring, 1520–1790." *Fish and Fisheries*. doi:10.1111/faf.12598.

Holm, P., and C. Travis. 2017. "The New Human Condition and Climate Change: Humanities and Social Science Perceptions of Threat." *Global and Planetary Change* 156: 112–14.

Huijs, J., R. Pirngruber, and B. van Leeuwen. 2015. "Climate, War and Economic Development: The Case of Second-Century BC Babylon." In *A History of Market Performance: From Ancient Babylonia to the Modern World*, edited by R. J. van der Spek, B. van Leeuwen, and J. L. van Zanden, 128–48. London: Routledge.

Hunger, H., ed. 1992. *Astrological Reports to the Assyrian Kings*. Helsinki: Helsinki University Press.

Hunger, H., and S. W. Cole. 1996. *Nippur IV – The Early Neo-Babylonian Governor's Archive from Nippur*. Oriental Institute Publications, 114. Chicago: University of Chicago.

Iles, C. E., and G. C. Hegerl. 2015. "Systematic Change in Global Patterns of Streamflow following Volcanic Eruptions." *Nature Geoscience* 8: 838–42.

Izdebski, A., K. Bloomfield, W. J. Eastwood, R. Fernandes, D. Fleitmann, P. Guzowski, J. Haldon, F. Ludlow, J. Luterbacher, J. G. Manning, A. Masi, L. Mordechai, T. Newfield, A. R. Stine, C. Senkul, and E. Xoplaki. 2022. "The Emergence of Interdisciplinary Environmental History: Bridging the Gap between the Humanistic and Scientific Approaches to the Late Holocene." *Annales*.

Kirschner, A. J., and K. Tiroch. 2012. "The Waters of the Euphrates and Tigris: An International Law Perspective." *Max Planck Yearbook of United Nations Law Online* 16: 329–94.

Kleber, K. 2012. "Famine in Babylonia: A Microhistorical Approach to an Agricultural Crisis in 528–526 BC." *Zeitschrift für Assyriologie und Vorderasiatische Archäologie* 102: 219–44.

Kollmorgen, W. M. 1969. "The Woodsman's Assaults on the Domain of the Cattleman." *Annals of the Association of American Geographers* 59 (2): 215–38.

Kostick, C., and F. Ludlow. 2015. "The Dating of Volcanic Events and their Impacts upon European Climate and Society, 400–800 CE." *European Journal of Post-Classical Archaeologies* 5: 7–30.

———. 2019. "Medieval History, Explosive Volcanism and the Geoengineering Debate." In *Making the Medieval Relevant: How Medieval Studies Contribute to Improving Our Understanding of the Present*, 45–97. Berlin: De Gruyter.

Lanfranchi, G. B., and S. Parpola. 1990. *The Correspondence of Sargon II, Part II*. Helsinki: Helsinki University Press.

Lein, R. A. 1998. "Still Thirsting: Prospects for a Multilateral Treaty on the Euphrates and Tigris Rivers Following the Adoption of the United Nations Convention on International Watercourses." *Boston University International Law Journal* 16: 273–93.

Limerick, P. N. 1987. *Legacy of Conquest: The Unbroken Past of the American West*. New York: W. W. Norton.

———. 1992. "Disorientation and Reorientation: The American Landscape Discovered from the West." *The Journal of American History* 79 (3), Discovering America: A Special Issue (December): 1021–49.

———. 2000. *Something in the Soil: Legacies and Reckonings in the New West*. New York: W. W. Norton, 28.

Luckenbill, D. D., ed. & trans. 1924. *The Annals of Sennacherib*. Chicago: University of Chicago.

Ludlow, F. 2010. "The Utility of the Irish Annals as a Source for the Reconstruction of Climate." Unpublished PhD Dissertation. University of Dublin, Trinity College.

———. 2012. "Assessing Non-Climatic Influences on the Record of Extreme Weather Events in the Irish Annals." In *At the Anvil: Essays in Honour of William J. Smyth*, edited by P. J. Duffy and W. Nolan, 93–133. Dublin: Geography Publications.

Ludlow, F., C. Kostick, and C. Morris. 2022. "Climate, Violence and Ethnic Conflict in the Ancient World." In *The Cambridge World History of Genocide*, edited by Ben Kiernan, Tracy Maria Lemos, and Tristan Taylor, Vol. 1. Cambridge: Cambridge University Press.

Ludlow, F., and J. G. Manning. 2016. "Revolts under the Ptolemies: A Paleoclimatic Perspective." In *Revolt and Resistance in the Ancient Classical World and the Near East: The Crucible of Empire*, edited by J. J. Collins and J. G. Manning, 154–71. Leiden: Brill.

Ludlow, F., A. R. Stine, P. Leahy, E. Murphy, P. Mayewski, D. Taylor, J. Killen, M. Baillie, M. Hennessy, and G. Kiely. 2013. "Medieval Irish Chronicles Reveal Persistent Volcanic Forcing of Severe Winter Cold Events, 431–1649 CE." *Environmental Research Letters* 8 (2): L024035.

Ludlow, F., and C. Travis. 2019. "STEAM Approaches to Climate Change, Extreme Weather and Social-Political Conflict." In *The STEAM Revolution: Transdisciplinary Approaches to Science, Technology, Engineering, Arts, Humanities and Mathematics*, edited by A. de la Garza and C. Travis, 33–65. New York: Springer.

Manning, J. G. 2018. *The Open Sea: The Economic Life of the Ancient Mediterranean World from the Iron Age to the Rise of Rome*. Princeton: Princeton University Press.

Manning, J. G., F. Ludlow, A. R. Stine, W. Boos, M. Sigl, and J. Marlon. 2017. "Volcanic Suppression of Nile Summer Flooding Triggers Revolt and Constrains Interstate Conflict in Ancient Egypt." *Nature Communications* 8: Article 900. doi:10.1038/s41467-017-00957-y.

McMurtry, L. 1985. *Lonesome Dove*. New York: Simon & Schuster.

———. 1990. "How the West Was Won or Lost." *New Republic* 203 (17): 32–38.

———. 1993. *The Streets of Laredo*. New York: Simon & Schuster.

———. 1995. *Dead Man's Walk*. New York: Simon & Schuster.

———. 1997. *Comanche Moon*. New York: Simon & Schuster.

———. 2006 *In a Narrow Grave: Essays on Texas*. New York. Simon & Schuster.

———. 2008. *Books: A Memoir*. Vol. 1. New York: Simon and Schuster.

———. 2010. *The Lonesome Dove Chronicles*. New York: Simon & Schuster.

Miller, Mary. 1928. "Recent Poetry on the Prairie." M.A. Thesis, University of Kansas.

Moran, W. L. 1992. *The Amarna Letters*. Baltimore: Johns Hopkins University Press.

Neihardt, J. G. 2018. *A Cycle of the West: The Song of Three Friends, the Song of Hugh Glass, the Song of Jed Smith, the Song of Indian Wars, the Song of the Messiah, Annotated by Joe Green*. Introduction by Alan Birkelbach. Lincoln: University of Nebraska Press.

Nicholls, J., B. Allaire, and P. Holm. 2021a. "The Capacity Trend Method. A New Approach for Enumerating the Newfoundland Cod Fisheries (1675–1790)." *Historical Methods* 2021: 1–14. https://doi.org/10.1080/01615440.2020.1853643.

Nissen, Martti. 2003. *Prophets and Prophecy in the Ancient Near East*. Atlanta: Society for Biblical Literature. (Prisms A & B).

Ogilvie, A. E., and G. Farmer. 1997. "Documenting the Medieval Climate." In *Climates of the British Isles: Past, Present and Future*, edited by M. Hulme and E. Barrow, 112–34. London and New York: Routledge.

Parpola, S., ed. 1987. *The Correspondence of Sargon II, Part 1*. Helsinki: Helsinki University Press.

———. 2014. *Letters from Assyrian and Babylonian Scholars*, State Archives of Assyria X. Indiana: Eisenbrauns.

Pfister, Christian. 2007. "Climatic Extremes, Recurrent Crises and Witch Hunts: Strategies of European Societies in Coping with Exogenous Shocks in the Late Sixteenth and Early Seventeenth Centuries." *The Medieval History Journal* 10: 33–73.

Piepkorn, A. C., ed. & trans. 1933. *Historical Prism Inscriptions of Ashurbanipal* (Prism D, E, & K). Chicago, IL: University of Chicago Press.

Proulx, A. 2008. "Dangerous Ground: Landscape in American Fiction." In *Regionalism and the Humanities*, edited by R. Mahoney Timothy and J. Katz Wendy J, 6–25. Lincoln and London: University of Nebraska Press. www.jstor.org/stable/j.ctt1dgn4v0.6.

Quintelli-Neary, M. 2004. "Establishing Boundaries in the Irish American West." *Études Irlandaises* 29 (2): 44.

Radner, K. 2015. "Royal Pen Pals: The Kings of Assyria in Correspondence with Officials, Clients, and Total Strangers (8th and 7th Centuries BC)." In *Official Epistolography and the Language(s) of Power*, edited by S. Prochazka, et al., 61–72. Wien: Österreichische Akademie der Wissenschaften.

Rankin, K., and P. Holm. 2019. "Cartographical Perspectives on the Evolution of Fisheries in Newfoundland's Grand Banks Area and Adjacent North Atlantic Waters in the Sixteenth and Seventeenth Centuries." *Terrae Incognitae* 51 (3): 190–218. https://doi.org/10.1080/00822884.2019.1679487.

Robson, E. 2019. *Ancient Knowledge Networks. A Social Geography of Cuneiform Scholarship in First-Millennium Assyria and Babylonia*. London: UCL Press.

Rogers, J. M. 1905. *Thomas H. Benton*. Philadelphia, PA: G.W. Jacobs.

Short, T. 1749. *A General Chronological History of The Air, Weather, Seasons, Meteors, etc*. 2 Vols. London.

Sigl, M., M. Winstrup, J. R. McConnell, K. C. Welten, G. Plunkett, F. Ludlow, U. Büntgen, M. Caffee, N. Chellman, D. Dahl-Jensen, H. Fischer, S. Kipstuhl, C. Kostick, O. J. Maselli, F. Mekhaldi, R. Mulvaney, R. Muscheler, D. R. Pasteris, J. R. Pilcher, M. Salzer, S. Schüpbach, J. P. Steffensen, B. M. Vinther, and T. E. Woodruff. 2015. "Timing and Climate Forcing of Volcanic Eruptions for the Past 2,500 Years." *Nature* 523: 543–49.

Slotsky, A. L. 1997. *The Bourse of Babylon: Market Quotations in Astronomical Diaries of Babylonia*. Bethesda: CDL Press.

Tolstoy, L. 1869. *War and Peace* (*Война и миръ*). Moscow: The Russian Messenger.

Travis, C. 2018. "The Digital Anthropocene, Deep Mapping, and Environmental Humanities' Big Data." *Resilience: A Journal of the Environmental Humanities* 5 (2): 172–88.

———. 2020a. "Historical and Imagined GIS *Borderlandscapes* of the American West: Larry McMurtry's Lonesome Dove Tetralogy and L.A. *Noirscapes*, Special Issue University Consortium of Geographic Information Science." *International Journal of Humanities and Arts Computing*. https://doi.org/10.3366/ijhac.2020.0249.

———. 2020b. "Digital GeoHumanities." In *International Encyclopedia of Human Geography*, edited by A. Kobayashi, Vol. 3. 2nd ed., 341–46. Elsevier. https://dx.doi.org/10.1016/B978-0-08-102295-5.10538-4.

Travis, C., and P. Holm. 2016. "The Digital Environmental Humanities – What Is it and Why Do We Need It? The NorFish Project and SmartCity Lifeworlds. In *The Digital Arts and Humanities: Neogeography, Social Media and Big Data Integrations and Applications*, edited by C. Travis and A. V. Lünen. Cham: Springer.

Travis, C., F. Ludlow, J. Matthews, K. Lougheed, K. Rankin, B. Allaire, R. Legg, P. Hayes, R. Breen, J. Nicholls, L. Towns, and P. Holm. 2020. "Inventing the Grand Banks: A Deep Chart. Humanities GIS, Cartesian, and Literary Perceptions of the North-West Atlantic Fishery ca 1500–1800." *GEO: Geography and Environment*. https://doi.org/10.1002/geo2.85.

Turner, F. J. 1893. "The Significance of the Frontier in American History." *American Historical Association*. Accessed July 4, 2021. https://www.historians.org/about-aha-and-membership/aha-history-and-archives/historical-archives/the-significance-of-the-frontier-in-american-history-(1893).

Vanstiphout, H. L. J. 1980. "The Death of an Era: The Great Mortality in the Sumerian City Laments." In *Death in Mesopotamia*, edited by B. Alster, 83–89. Copenhagen: Akademisk Forlag.

Walton, R. J. 1994. *Larry McMurtry and the Victorian Novel*. College Station: TAMU Press.

Wardropper, B. W. 1965. "'Don Quixote': Story or History?" *Modern Philology* 63 (1): 1–11.

Yilmaz, S. 1995. "Bridge Over Troubled Waters: Hydropolitics of the Tigris and Euphrates." Unpublished M.A. Dissertation, Princeton University.

Data Sources

Atack, Jeremy. 2015. *Historical Geographic Information Systems (GIS) database of U.S. Railroads and Steamboat Routes for 1860 and 1900*. Nashville: Vanderbilt.

Brito, Cristina, Nina Vieira, John Nicholls, and Richard Breen. 2020. "SeaCite Database." http://cehresearch.org/SeaCite/seacite.php.

Holm, Poul, Richard Breen, Zhen Yang, and John Nicholls. 2018. *DANdoc Database. 2018*. Trinity College Dublin. http://cehresearch.org/DanDoc/DanDoc.php.

Holm, Poul, John Nicholls, Patrick Hayes, Josh Ivinson, and Bernard Allaire. 2021. *Extractions of North Atlantic cod and herring, 1520–1790. Figshare*. Dataset. https://doi.org/10.6084/m9.figshare.13614452.v14.

Holterman, Bart, and John Nicholls. 2018. *HANSdoc Database*. Deutsche: Schifffahrtsmuseum. https://hansdoc.dsm.museum/.

Nicholls, John, Poul Holm, Patrick Hayes, Josh Ivinson, and Bernard Allaire. 2021. *Norfish Data Collection*. figshare. Collection. https://doi.org/10.6084/m9.figshare.c.5514351.v1.

The Portal to Texas History (2004–2021). University of North Texas Libraries. https://texashistory.unt.edu/.

Rankin, Kieran. 2018. *Cartographical Perspectives on the Evolution of Newfoundland's Grand Banks Fisheries in the Sixteenth, Seventeenth, and Eighteenth Centuries*. Trinity College Dublin. http://cehresearch.org/norfishplatform/collections/show/1.

Travis, C. 2021. *Larry McMurtry's Literary Geography Project Page*. Arlington: University of Texas. https://blog.uta.edu/travisc/research/larry-mcmurtrys-literary-geography/.

United States Census Bureau Data 1860 and 1900, sourced from Steven Manson, Jonathan Schroeder, David Van Riper, and Steven Ruggles. 2019. *IPUMS National Historical Geographic Information System: Version 14.0* [Database]. Minneapolis, MN: IPUMS.

Vörösmarty, C. J., B. Fekete, and B. A. Tucker. 1996. *River Discharge Database, Version 1.0 (RivDIS v1.0), Volumes 0 through 6. A contribution to IHP-V Theme 1.* Technical Documents in Hydrology Series. Paris: UNESCO.

Wang, P., K. H. Lin, Y. C. Liao, et al. 2018. "Construction of the REACHES Climate Database Based on Historical Documents of China." *Scientific Data* 5: 180288. https://doi.org/10.1038/sdata.2018.288.

2

THE ARMCHAIR TRAVELLER'S GUIDE TO DIGITAL ENVIRONMENTAL HUMANITIES[1]

Finn Arne Jørgensen

> The empirical reality that made the landscape seen from the train window appear to be "another world" was the railroad itself, with its excavations, tunnels, etc. Yet the railroad was merely an expression of the rail's technological requirements, and the rail itself was a constituent part of the machine ensemble that was the system. It was, in other words, that machine ensemble that interjected itself between the traveler and the landscape. The traveler perceived the landscape as it was filtered through the machine ensemble.
>
> – *Wolfgang Schivelbusch*[2]

Introduction

The armchair traveller explores the world from the comforts of home. Through the printed word, still photographs, moving pictures, and sound, scenic locations and remote landscapes come alive, conveying some form of filtered and mediated experience of the world. You are armchair travelling when you read a Lonely Planet book about someplace you may or may not be planning to actually visit, when you watch the Travel Channel on cable TV, or when you watch penguins in Antarctica on Google Street View. Armchair travel is a way of seeing the world with age-old traditions. The genre has tight connections to nature writing, seeking to build an understanding of, knowledge about, and attachment to natural and cultural places. At the same time, armchair travel is about estrangement, as Bernd Stiegler argues: to not just learn about new places but also to see familiar places in a new light.[3] As such, armchair travel is a deeply humanistic practice, weaving a web of meaning, narratives, and connections across the world, but always centred in the physical location of the armchair traveller. The media of armchair travelling, however, is in constant change. In recent years, geolocative technologies and networked screens have seemingly extended the range and immersive depth of what we now think of as virtual travel experiences. Using examples from Norwegian travel mediations, this article asks what happens when new media forms and networked digital technologies become part of the armchair travel experience. What are the affordances of media technologies and the modes of storytelling and experience in the digital representation of travel?

 DOI: 10.4324/9781003082798-4

The technological mediations of near and distant cultures and environments have long fascinated scholars and the public alike, and it seems like this interest peaks around times of large-scale technological transition, when new modes of transportation and mediation become available. Few scholars have analysed this relationship between technology, media, and the perception of landscape as convincingly as Wolfgang Schivelbusch, who famously argued that the landscape perceived by railway travellers was filtered through the machine ensemble of the railroad system, creating a new panoramic view of the landscape that was not possible before the railroad. *The Railway Journey* – which was published in German in 1977 and translated into English two years later – has had a considerable influence on the way historians of technology understand the relationship between technology and the experience of travel and place.

For Schivelbusch, *The Railway Journey* is a story of new transportation technologies, of "annihilation of space and time" by speed. His big argument is that the railway destroyed the traditional relationship, the close contact, between travellers and their environment and replaced it with a panoramic experience of time and space. For him, the railway was the first truly *modern* mode of transportation, where mobility replaced the physical act of movement, and his main goal with the book was to capture this subjective experience of railroad travel at the very moment it was new.[4] Schivelbusch's original argument can very well apply to each successive generation of transportation technologies, where faster modes of transportation – be it cars, boats, aeroplanes, or others – continue to shrink space over time.

A corresponding argument would be that reverting to older forms of transport technology slows down the passage of time and expands the sense of place. As travel slows down, a new consciousness emerges, more deliberate and more attuned to the landscape being travelled through. In the spirit of Schivelbusch, we should consider this slowness an often-romanticised narrative invoked in depictions of railroad travel. The actual travel time between two locations can, in some circumstances, be less by the slow and steady movement of a train than through the increasingly stressful and antagonistic experience of modern aeroplane travel. Slow travel is a carefully cultivated state of mind more than anything else and one that needs to be historicised and contextualised in order to be fully understood.

Building on Schivelbusch's thesis, this article explores new media types of storytelling – in other words, armchair travel – that have emerged around this form of slow travel, arguing that new media technologies function as a medium that enables particular relationships between people and the world. With the coming of the railroad, the viewpoint for observing landscape was no longer a static one. The focal point changes – nearby is a blur, further away is clear – but slowly moving. Railway travel frames the experience, literally and metaphorically. The landscape of train travel is not experienced directly on the body but through a window. In some ways, this particular framing of nature can be seen as a predecessor to screen-based media.

Following Schivelbusch's emphasis on the sensory and experiential quality of the human-landscape relation, I will focus on the roles media forms can play in shaping relationships between people and landscapes. From such a perspective, Schivelbusch's insights in *The Railway Journey* give us an opportunity to think about the relationship between the digital and the material and about the technological affordances of mediation in ways that are critical for the environmental humanities. We seldom experience nature fully directly and unfiltered, but instead mediated through, even enabled by different technologies.[5] The rapid movement of bodies through landscapes in trains on railroad tracks is one example. Technology provides a connecting bridge between the different timescales of human and environmental change. However, technology is not a neutral mediator. The newness or oldness of a particular technology at any given point in time shapes our understanding of both the mediated phenomenon and ourselves.[6] For most technology, newer means faster, more powerful, and more sophisticated, simultaneously making older technologies seem less so, despite how advanced they had seemed when they were new (as most smartphone owners discover upon the release of a new and much more advanced model). When thinking about change over time, however, it is imperative that we recognise how old technologies were all once new, as Carolyn Marvin argues.[7] Technologies we today consider stable, unchanging, and devoid of transformative power, when compared to the new, were once disruptive, changing social relationships and the built environment alike.

Slow Travel and Sustainable Tourism

The world is a much smaller place than it used to be. Commercial airlines fly to almost every corner of the planet, which means that there are very few places in the world that are actually hard to visit. Travellers complain about the indignities of security checkpoints and being crammed into ever-narrower plane seats, but the fact remains that we live in a time with unprecedented amounts of travel opportunities across larger distances and at a much higher speed than before. We are bombarded with images and narratives of exotic and enticing travel locations across the world in advertising, entertainment, and culture, and more and more people actually have the opportunity to seek out these places for themselves.

Vacation travel has become a marker of affluence and personal satisfaction and is today a consumer and leisure experience on a large scale.[8] Particularly faraway and exotic travel destinations can function as a sort of conspicuous consumption, as Thorstein Veblen defines it, but also the more everyday chartered flights to mass tourism sites like Gran Canaria matter.[9] As a result of this dramatically increased travel activity, many have questioned and criticised the sustainability of extensive travel and tourism.[10] Climate change discussions frequently reference the high and growing emissions from air travel, and in more local contexts, noise pollution from transport infrastructure has also become a concern. Furthermore, the sheer numbers of tourists represent significant wear and tear on natural and cultural landscapes.

Slow travel is one of the responses to these environmental challenges in the emerging literature on sustainable tourism.[11] For instance, Dickinson et al. define slow travel as "an emerging conceptual framework which offers an alternative to air and car travel, where people travel to destinations more slowly overland, stay longer and travel less."[12] Yet there seems to be a lack of consensus over the appropriate modes of transportation. Instead, slow travel should be seen as a group of associated ideas, a mindset rather than a tangible product.[13] Other literature on slow travel explores the connection between speed and positive values in modernity, such as freedom and progress, whereas slowness and stillness are seen as undesired. Molz examines how pace becomes socially encoded in media, demonstrating that slow travel opens the door to a more nuanced story of modernity.[14] It is precisely this story this article investigates, with slow travel as a way of making sense of a changing world.

This emphasis on speed and slowness, paired with an underlying narrative of modernity and environmental degradation, resonates with Schivelbusch's story of the railway ensemble. When travellers today place railroad travel in the slow travel category, we see clearly what a relative phenomenon speed is. The "slow" is attributed by us, accustomed to higher speeds. Contemporary sources to Schivelbusch, on the other hand, emphasise the speed of train travel, the feeling of almost flying when travelling on a train.[15] What was once new and modern seems to have become slow, deliberate, and authentic. What do these alternating senses of speed and modernity mean for the relationship between travel, experience, and landscape?

Landscapes of Textually Mediated Travel

Narratives of travel to distant locations have been a foundational element of literature. Romance, politics, war, and other interpersonal relationships are all distributed in time and space, which means that travel and mobility have been essential components of storytelling for as long as humans have shared tales around a fireplace. In written literature, Marco Polo is perhaps one of the most well-known travel narratives, having inspired armchair travellers for centuries, but the genre is much older. Pausanias' ten-volume *Description of Greece* dates to the second century, for instance, and the *Odyssey* is even older.

Travel literature as a genre became extremely widespread in the 18th century, particularly through British writers reporting on the far places in the British Empire and elsewhere.[16] These British travellers also visited Norway at the end of the 18th century, joining a small but prolific group of Norwegian explorers.[17] Scientists, folklorists, authors, journalists, painters, and more or less professional explorers can be found among the travellers. The books, articles, and artworks that these travellers published represent a simultaneous mapping of the countryside and of modernisation, as modern transportation infrastructures followed in the footsteps of the pioneering travellers. Railroad travel came to feature frequently in contemporary travel reports. These narratives of railroad travel mainly took place in textual media in Norway, in travel books, and in short articles in the popular volumes of the Norwegian Trekking Association, published annually since 1868.

Schivelbusch attempted to capture the experience of a large-scale technological transition and contrasted railway travel with walking. Travel was slow before the railroad. We would think it was painfully slow, but as Schivelbusch writes about the nostalgia for pre-railroad travelling, it had more "soul." There is an inherent assumption in his writing that travel by foot was contemplative, rich, and full of details. Furthermore, referring to Georg Simmel's writings on urban perception and John Ruskin's writings on travel, Schivelbusch reflects on the quality of sensory input at different speeds. The less input, the more time we have to dwell on it. In this sense, change is bad. Ruskin writes, "[T]o any person who has all his senses about him, a quiet walk along not more than ten or twelve miles of road a day, is the most amusing of all travelling; and all travelling becomes dull in exact proportion to its rapidity."[18]

We find similar sentiments in the writings of the early explorers of the Norwegian countryside. A posthumous tribute to three trekkers, Mayor P. Birch-Reichenwald, Professor Axel Gudbrand Blytt, and Dr Marius Sophus Lie, portrayed them all as old-fashioned tourists, spending the summers on foot, getting to know Norwegian nature. They were all active and influential people in science and politics but gained the energy for this work while trekking in the mountains.[19] The pioneering explorers were hardy men, revelling in the challenges of the road. The so-called old tourists, however, were a breed of men that were fast disappearing at the turn of the 19th century. These old tourists claimed to enjoy (most) of the hardships of the road by foot and shared their experiences in the form of travel reports, many published in the annual reports of the Norwegian Trekking Association since 1868. Written travel narratives of this kind can be found in abundance, and they started appearing around the late 1700s. In the 1800s, it seemed like the Scandinavian countryside, in particular, was full of rather well-to-do travellers who all ended up writing about their experiences.[20] These travellers, in practice, mapped and catalogued Scandinavian landscapes, identified scenic locations, explained the best routes and modes of transportation to get there, and attempted to convince other urbanites that getting there was worth the trouble.[21] These narratives attached considerable romance to the old form of trekking, before modern transport infrastructure civilised the countryside, in ways that can be construed as anti-modern. Yet we can also read these narratives as expressions of complex negotiations over the changing relationship between technology, nature, and national identity.

The narratives in these books changed as the railroads between the major cities started opening up. Travellers such as the history and geography professor Yngvar Nielsen – the most prolific Norwegian travel writer of the period – described the new way of travelling in ways that are very much in line with Schivelbusch.[22] But to him, the railroad was just one of a whole flood of technologies that heralded the coming of modernity. In his memoirs, Nielsen describes personally being present at pretty much the first arrival of every single piece of new technology. Trains, electricity, telegraphs, telephones – he had seen it all. It is not a coincidence that the appreciation for nature experiences as a leisure activity increased so dramatically during this period of rapid technological change.[23] While clearly appreciative of these new technologies, Nielsen's writings were also tinged with nostalgia over a disappearing mode of experiencing Norwegian nature.

The railroad was not the only rapidly expanding transport infrastructure at that time, but it was one of the most immediately visible on the landscape. W. Matthieu Williams, a British scientist, wrote a book comparing the travel experience of 1853 and 1876 and pointed out how the new railroads that were built had taken over much of the tourist traffic in 1876. He wrote that the railway between Oslo and Trondheim was "emphatically a tourist's railway; the portion I have traversed presents the most splendid panorama of scenery I have ever seen from any railway." Despite this strong promotion of the panoramic qualities of the railroad, he considered the railroad less authentic and less proper than walking by foot. The railroad would "take all the luxurious and hurried traffic – [A]mericans and others who are 'doin" Europe, &c, and whill [*sic*] leave the old carriole roads to the full and healthful enjoyment of those who desire and are able to leisurely travel through Norway with a knapsack."[24] As with Schivelbusch, there's an implied interpretation that older ways of travelling had been freer. The new went on a track, predetermined. The machine ensemble of the railroad thus annihilated more than just time and space; it also endangered the healthy relationship to nature that many sought.

Yet railroads and travel books went together in an almost symbiotic fashion. Together, they opened up a way of intimately knowing the landscapes of the young country, both in a material and a meaningful sense. Written travelogues became a widely read genre at the same time as travel became more broadly available for ever-larger groups of people. As such, they both reflected the growing interest in travel and served to reinforce this interest. The books were as much guides for directions as they were guides for emotion – what you were supposed to feel when travelling, the sense of discovery and the sublimity of nature combined with a certain appreciation of physical and cultural hardship. However, as both David E. Nye and David Blackbourn suggest in their explorations of the technological and natural sublime in respectively the United States and Germany around the same period, nostalgia was not the only possible response to the technological face of modernity.[25]

Travel in New Media

When travel narratives met moving images, time began to matter in a different way. A book lives outside of time in many ways. While authors pace their narratives at different speeds and draw the attention of readers to particular elements of the story, people read at different speeds, and a book can be put down and taken up again at the reader's leisure. A film, on the other hand, has a duration. The camera takes in a whole scene, demanding the viewer's attention at any given time. "The camera's fundamental relationship to the world around us and its recording of other cultures has always dogged documentary," writes Andrew Utterson.[26] As travelogue first moved into film media and later into the digital age, the relationships between viewers, landscape imagery, and the increasingly networked world shifted.

In Erkki Huhtamo's recent history of moving panoramas, he demonstrates how the 360-degree moving panoramas were a media spectacle without equal at that time and became a big fad in the decades preceding the railroad. This passed when the railroads opened, and the panoramas were completely swept away when movie theatres began opening across Europe and the United States. But for this brief window of time, panoramas offered viewers immersive landscape paintings of close and distant places. The panoramas could take their audience to exotic and scenic locations, often far away, without the inconvenience, hardship, and expense of travelling.[27]

Trains arrived with the film medium, in a sense. The first film at the very first public showing of moving film, arranged by the Lumière brothers in Paris in 1895, was *L'Arrivée d'un train en gare de La Ciotat*. For viewers in the 21st century, the film is nothing spectacular, really. We have become so accustomed to moving pictures that we no longer see what the big deal is. A train arrives at a station, and the passengers get off. It's all over in 48 seconds. A frequently told story is that the first audience ran away in panic when the train came towards them, but this is likely only a myth.[28] But newspaper articles and commentaries from the time indicate that the audience found the milling about of the passengers on the platform as fascinating as the movement of the train through the landscape.[29] The movement of the train and its passengers became entangled in the newness of moving pictures as a medium.

Railroads have continued to capture the imagination of travellers and armchair travellers worldwide. In 2009, the Norwegian Broadcasting Corporation aired a seven-hour-long programme following Bergensbanen, the railroad between Bergen and Oslo in real time, minute by minute. In this pre-recorded programme, aired on the 100th anniversary of the railroad's opening, the TV audience could see the view from a front-mounted camera, leaving the train itself invisible. The viewpoint is thus not that of the driver but perhaps of the train itself. In front of the train, we see the track winding its way through the landscape, as illustrated in Figure 2.1.

Figure 2.1 The Bergensbanen railroad penetrating a snowy landscape at Finse. Norwegian Broadcasting Corporation, *Bergensbanen: Minutt for minutt*, 2009.

Source: Reproduced by kind permission from Duke University Press and Finn Arne Jørgensen.

More than a million Norwegians watched the show, "almost paralyzed" by the real-time and mostly unedited slow journey through the Norwegian countryside.[30]

This Norwegian show was not the first of its kind. The Deutsche Bahn operated a TV channel called Bahn TV from 2001 to 2010. One of the programmes, *Bahn TV in Fahrt*, showed the view from the cab of a moving train, following the regular train lines between cities in Germany, Austria, and France. Initially started as an internal staff television channel, it expanded into a niche channel that some cable subscribers could get from 2005 to 2006. After 2008, the channel shifted to a pure webcast. The NRK *Bergensbanen* programme was similar in scope in that it did not significantly augment this plain video feed with digital content. An audio signal and superimposed text notified viewers of train station and tunnel names, but beyond that, the slowly changing landscape penetrated by the railroad tracks took centre stage. This was to change in a later iteration of the slow railroad travel TV idea, which thoroughly embedded born-digital perspectives on place and mobility in the show.

The *Nordlandsbanen: Minutt for minutt* programme first aired in late December 2012, following the train from Trondheim to Bodø, over almost ten hours, through 729 kilometres, 42 stations, 156 tunnels, and 361 bridges. The new element added here was that NRK recorded the journey four times, one for each season. The four video feeds were then synchronised using GPS data recorded during the journey. The website gave viewers the option to watch the seasons individually or all at once, as we see in Figure 2.2. The NRK editors pointed out that this was an incredibly time-consuming and intricate process. Microphones mounted on the train recorded sound both inside and outside of the train, adding to the mediated experience of the journey. Viewers got a bit more feeling of speed as a result of the forward-facing camera, but the overall impression is still one of slowness, of painstakingly making your way through a landscape.

Watching and exploring this train ride becomes strangely hypnotic, with the clickety-clack sound of the train on the tracks (I keep it on in my office when writing sometimes, as a kind of white noise). But the experience we get is not the compression of time and space that

Figure 2.2 Four seasons in sync. Norwegian Broadcasting Corporation, *Nordlandsbanen: Minutt for minutt*, 2012.

Source: Reproduced by kind permission from Duke University Press and Finn Arne Jørgensen.

Schivelbusch describes. Instead, time is drawn out, stretched over distance, highlighting the slowness of train travel instead. The four seasons give the viewer a peculiar sense of time passing, but more important is the way new media and geospatial technologies are profoundly intertwined in the presentation of the railway journey from Trondheim to Bodø. The absolute location information enabled by the synchronised GPS data links the four different train rides to each other. When presented as four video feeds on one screen, the train becomes one machine moving through four seasons, four different versions of one place, at the same time.

The accompanying website allowed viewers to choose between the original broadcast, with music, interviews, and some video material from other cameras outside and on the side of the train, the four seasons as individual feeds, and the synchronised version with all four feeds at the same time.[31] A dynamically updated map displays the train's position and allows viewers to click to skip ahead to particular locations. In addition, the website had information about the history of Nordlandsbanen, the playlist for the 77 songs with local artists that played during the broadcast, and an interactive video mixer (in beta), where visitors can create their own video mix between two of the seasons. A link to a very technical write-up about the production documented the actual and time-consuming work that went into creating the show.[32]

As Slow As It Gets? Hurtigruten

As interesting and popular as the two railroad shows were, they cannot compare to what we can only describe as the high point of the NRK slow travel series, an 8,048-minute (five and a half days) live broadcast of Hurtigruten, the Coastal Express, sailing from Bergen on the southwest coast of Norway to Kirkenes in the far north, a total distance of 2,703 kilometres or 1,460 nautical miles. As you might expect, the show was very slow – viewers could see the view from the ship, mixed in with interviews and commentaries on board the ship, all in real time. NRK showed everything live, and a website showed the video stream, paired with a map where you could see the ship move in real time and other information. Furthermore, NRK made downloads of the stream available in full HD as BitTorrent downloads while the show was still on.

The show was a big hit in Norway when it ran in June 2011 – when the show peaked, half of Norway's roughly five million people had watched it. Furthermore, the show was also transmitted live on the internet, where 46% of the viewers came from outside of Norway. Even more interesting were all the people that showed up along the coast, waving from land, cruising around in boats, and also the huge crowds at all the stops. The small places were generally the ones with the most people. My hometown Sortland (with 10,000 inhabitants), for instance, had more people show up at 3:30 at night (although the sun was out since it's above the Arctic circle, as shown in Figure 2.3) than Trondheim (with 175,000 people) had in the middle of the day. It seems like the experience of watching the show took people somewhat by surprise. The premise sounds quite ludicrous, like watching paint dry on live TV, but people initially looked out of pure curiosity and then found it hard to stop. Twitter was full of people who seemed unable to turn off the TV and go to bed at night as Hurtigruten sailed through Vesterålen in the midnight sun. The #Hurtigruten hashtag trended in Norway during the entire week of the show, and many place-names would also appear on the top list of Twitter topics as Hurtigruten sailed into those places. In other words, this was a mediated representation of the coast of an entire nation that really interfaced with people's daily lives. During both the train shows and the Hurtigruten one, the Twitter discussion backchannel was critical to the popularity of the show. This was not a form of armchair travel undertaken alone and in isolation but rather a deeply social event, extended and augmented by digital media.

Figure 2.3 Hurtigruten sailing into Sortland in the midnight sun. Norwegian Broadcasting Corporation, *Hurtigruten: Minutt for minutt*, 2011.

Source: Reproduced by kind permission from Duke University Press and Finn Arne Jørgensen.

The popularity took NRK completely by surprise, even knowing how well the Bergensbanen show had gone. The producers spent a fair amount of time before the show launched, justifying the expenditure of taxpayer money, arguing that "it is probably considerably cheaper than many large sports events, and it may perhaps also connect with people in a deeper way. After all, we are the license-funded Norwegian Broadcasting Corporation. We need to do things like this, because if we don't, no one else will."[33]

I think there are many reasons why the Hurtigruten show struck a chord in Norway. One of them has to do with history and nature. The infrastructural role of Hurtigruten as a critical means of transportation is long past. Once upon a time, it was essential for transporting people, mail, and goods in a reliable way along the coast. It still brings cargo and people, of course, but today there are many other options available. Like many old technologies, Hurtigruten has found new life in new roles.

More than anything else, Hurtigruten is a tourist ship now. But the show also demonstrates how Hurtigruten has become a part of the cultural landscape of coastal Norway and a way of experiencing and taking part in nature. The old infrastructures of travel live on as narratives of bodies in motion through landscapes, but not just any landscape. In the same way that the early trekkers and the Norwegian Trekking Association explored the Norwegian countryside as a way of constructing a new national identity in the 1800s, the tourist experience of sailing along the coast in Hurtigruten is one of experiencing an iconic national landscape. We find similar sentiments expressed in the Norwegian tourist railroads; travelling with these particular transportation infrastructures becomes a way of seeing the best that Norway has to offer as a tourist destination. Both written and digital armchair travel media build upon such interpretations of national landscapes.

The website that NRK made for the show represents a great model for visualising travel in digital media. As we see in Figure 2.4, the site has three main elements: (1) a zoomable map with a red line marking the progress of Hurtigruten and markers for all the stops along the way;[34]

Figure 2.4 The Hurtigruten: Minutt for minutt interactive website. Norwegian Broadcasting Corporation, *Hurtigruten: minutt for minutt*, 2011.

Source: Reproduced by kind permission from Duke University Press and Finn Arne Jørgensen.

(2) a video window showing a live or archived video stream in which clicking anywhere along the red line on the map will show you the video for that spot; (3) an information window that shows you the Hurtigruten, radar data, links to torrent downloads of raw video data in full HD (CC-licensed), and a link to a 3D view in Google Earth. Some of this content clearly targets what we can only describe as enthusiast viewers rather than the mainstream viewer, who would probably be unlikely to download and explore the radar data file.

The Hurtigruten show is not just a successful example of new media armchair travel but also how rich this media can be. It was a slow but deeply mediated experience. When planning the show, NRK tested various ways of integrating place data in augmented-reality-like approaches, such as floating text bubbles that would move with the camera on-screen. They asked people for input on the NRK website – what would they like to see? Suggestions included water temperature, air temperature, humidity, air pressure, accelerometer, compass data, radar and sonar live feed, underwater cameras, engine room sound, GPS coordinates, raw video files with timestamps, and so on. The combination of suggestions hinted at a desire to use various types of sensors and recorders to blend the technology of the ship with the outside landscapes that Hurtigruten sailed through, all presented to the viewer through a digital interface. After the show was over, NRK did not end up releasing all the data they recorded but made the GPS data available in JSON format, as well as around 600 GB of high-quality video files for free download under a Creative Commons license.

NRK announced a competition for the best remixes and mash-ups created with the Creative Commons–licensed material. The perhaps most obvious entries fast-forwarded the video, compressing the 134-hour long journey all the way down to a five-minute speed run of the Norwegian coast.[35] Other entries took screen captures at regular intervals and organised them into gorgeous high-resolution posters that look like they were sorted by colour but that actually visualised the slowly changing light of the Norwegian summer.[36] Going to the other extreme, one viewer extracted the 9,486,520 frames where Hurtigruten was moving and used these to generate one composite image of the "average" view – a blurred grey and flat sea separated from a slightly lighter grey sky by a dark grey horizon – with the white bow of the ship sharply in focus.[37] The winner was probably the most time-consuming and meticulous of all the entries – a massive timetable index of the entire journey, listing events and points of interest, time, location, and a direct link to the location in the archived stream on the NRK website. This indexing job took a total of eight months to complete. While the winner did not use the Creative Commons–licensed video at all, the NRK jury thought that his entry added so much value to the project that they found him a clear winner of the competition.[38] The grand prize was (obviously) a free trip with Hurtigruten.

In the full Hurtigruten show, viewers are presented with what we can describe as an *annotated landscape*, including both recorded geospatial information and highly manual annotations such as those of the remix competition winner. If we think about how we often navigate landscapes now, accessing these invisible digital layers of information about the landscape as we move through it, using a handheld GPS-enabled device (finding out our direction, speed, altitude, routes, weather forecasts, notable attractions and their history, the location of the nearest Starbucks, etc.), we are simultaneously moving in two types of landscapes at once, both the immediate and physical on the one hand, and the digital and distributed on the other. Experiencing and navigating the world around us requires us to circulate between these two categories of knowing.

The Hurtigruten show was an experiment in geospatial visualisation that successfully managed to blend these two views of the world in an appealing and popular manner. It is a fantastic experience, culturally immersive and able to bring the entire country together in a way that few other TV programmes have. But it is important to note that it is without the instant gratification of so much contemporary entertainment. In a way, it can be compared to the slow food movement. It is slow entertainment, meant to be stretched out and savoured.

Conclusion

Armchair travel directs our attention to the mediated character of location and of nature itself. Schivelbusch has been criticised, and in some ways rightly so, for focusing almost exclusively on the phenomenology of train travel, being more concerned with "the making and remaking of world views rather than the contested qualities of world views as modes of reception and representation, with implications for politics and sectional interests," as George Revill writes.[39] The ways in which we experience, navigate, and ultimately know natural environments and landscapes today have become suffused with digital information structures, making armchair travel as dependent on technology as physical travel is. Our mode of transportation as we travel – in body or in armchair – influences the way we view the landscapes we travel through. This insight is one of the broader contributions of Schivelbusch's work beyond transport history. The slow digital travel programmes developed by the Norwegian Broadcasting Corporation point to a convergence of mediating strategies: texts, images, maps, GPS data, video, sound, and even integrating social media into the experience. The result is simultaneously an extension and an update of traditional travel narratives. Highlighting the processes of mediation that take place in the relationship between the experience of being aboard Hurtigruten or a train, experiencing nature first-hand, and watching it on TV is very much in line with Schivelbusch's goal to understand the subjective experience of new technologies. In this sense, mediation is about more than simple representation. As in Schivelbusch's machine ensemble, we have seen how digital media forms a layer between (virtual) traveller and landscape. On the one hand, these mediated relationships create a response from the viewer, evoking and shaping a new experience; on the other, they deepen our understanding of the act of moving through the landscapes they open up for us.

Environmental historians and nature writers alike have, to a large degree, been concerned with close readings of the relationships between particular groups of people and particular places. The nature we meet in these narratives is very often a nature that is experienced through the body, a very physical relationship. Yet our idea of what nature is has expanded quite dramatically as a result of both new scientific instruments and new nature management regimes. The natural world becomes both bigger and smaller at the same time, extending out in space and down into our own bodies. We know from scientific studies that we generally can't know this "nature" directly.[40] This idea of nature is becoming very hard to separate from the digital tools and media we use to observe, interpret, and manage it. Our ideas, our standards, for what is natural are distributed and maintained in digital tools and media like databases, computer models, GISs, and so on. Paul Edwards' massive and prize-winning book on computer modelling and climate change, *A Vast Machine: Computer Models, Climate Data, and the Politics of Global Warming*, is one recent example of studies highlighting this perspective.[41] Such a perspective on nature pulls us in a few different directions, up towards abstraction and global management systems, like Edwards and his vast machines. But also down, out into the field, to the bodily experience of nature. We can call these *distant* and *close* natures, directly borrowing from Franco Moretti's ways of reading literature on different scales.[42] Distant natures, those that are not experienced through the body but distributed through data and media, need different modes of analysis and storytelling. Human interpretation and experience are still relevant, but we need to understand how it is mediated through machines, technologies, models, and database structures.

If we think of technology as a set of relations – social, economic, even epistemological – the digital turn certainly embodies the same kind of relations. Animal-based travel carries a set of relations between bodies, of struggling, tired horses and humans jostled about in carriages or on horseback. The locomotive took away the animal, converting coal and water into steam, smoke, power, and motion. What happens with these relations in the digital? Things never remain the same as we move between media; something is lost and something is gained. Still, if we think of the mediation process as primarily one of representation, then something is definitely lost in translation. Instead, we should think of mediation as the making of connections. Travel narratives demonstrate this clearly – as John Urry argues, "multiple forms of actual and imagined presence that carry connections across and into various kinds of social space."[43] If we focus on the experiential aspect that Schivelbusch was out to capture in his book, we can see how something new is created in this process. New media technologies enable particular relationships between people and the world, and this act of mediation is by no means neutral, in the same way that Schivelbusch's machine ensemble is not neutral. In that sense, mediation is an important way *we are in the world*. Mediation is how we interface with the world, with all that it implies, including the fact that *we have always been mediated*.[44] And if we have always been mediated, we can't assume that the shape and content of this mediation have remained constant over time. But this fact also means that forms of media, old and new alike, are fundamentally entangled with both historical and present human experiences of the world. The forms of digital armchair travel discussed in this article are both mediated and augmented, a communal experience that adds to the physical experience. There is something profound and tremendously powerful at work in slow travel programmes: the articulation of authenticity and meaning. The railroad that Schivelbusch describes as "the annihilator of time and space" is no longer as fast as it once seemed. Now that the railroad is increasingly framed and portrayed as a technology for slow, contemplative travel – for landscapes we observe slowly change as we travel through them – we must ask, what is the difference between our experience of the journey and the subjective experience that Schivelbusch was out to capture? While armchair travel as a genre has become updated and brought into new digital media, the search for meaning in a changing world continues to be a key theme in this genre. This is a place where the history of technology, the environmental humanities, and the digital humanities can and should work with each other. Rich and deep digital media can enable new forms of storytelling and presentation that we can't afford to ignore.

Acknowledgements

I wish to thank the anonymous reviewers (one of whom produced the most awesomely thoughtful, constructive, and helpful review I have ever received), the participants providing feedback at the various events in Europe and the US where I have presented parts of the material in this article, and most of all, Dolly Jørgensen for her valuable comments. I'm also indebted to Wilko Graf von Hardenberg and Kimberly Coulter for making this publication happen in the first place and to Thom van Dooren for his help in the process.

Notes

1 This chapter was originally published in *Environmental Humanities*, vol. 4, 2014, pp. 95–112 www.environmentalhumanities.org. ISSN: 2201–1919 Copyright: © Jørgensen 2014; The chapter is reproduced by kind permission from Duke University Press and Finn Arne Jørgensen.
2 Wolfgang Schivelbusch, *The Railway Journey: The Industrialization of Time and Space in the 19th Century* (Berkeley: University of California Press, 1986).
3 Bernd Stiegler, *Traveling in Place: A History of Armchair Travel* (Chicago: University of Chicago Press, 2013), *Kindle* ebook file, loc. 6.
4 Schivelbusch, *Railway Journey*.
5 In a strict interpretation, you would have to walk barefoot and naked through uncharted land at a time before the Anthropocene, with no goal of returning to civilisation, in order to experience nature unfiltered by technology.
6 Michael North, *Novelty: A History of the New* (Chicago: University of Chicago Press, 2013).
7 Carolyn Marvin, *When Old Technologies Were New: Thinking About Electric Communication in the Late Nineteenth Century* (New York: Oxford University Press, 1988).
8 Frédéric Dimanche and Diane Samdahl, "Leisure as Symbolic Consumption: A Conceptualization and Prospectus for Future Research," *Leisure Sciences* 16, no. 2 (1994): 119–129.
9 Thorstein Veblen, *The Theory of the Leisure Class* (New York: Penguin Books, 1994 [1899]).
10 Tommy Gärling, Dick Ettema, and Margareta Friman, eds., *Handbook of Sustainable Travel* (Berlin: Springer, 2014).
11 Janet E. Dickinson, Les M. Lumsdon, and Derek Robbins, "Slow Travel: Issues for Tourism and Climate Change," *Journal of Sustainable Tourism* 19, no. 3, (2011): 281–300; Janet Dickinson and Les Lumsdom, *Slow Travel and Tourism* (London: Earthscan, 2010).
12 Janet E. Dickinson, D. Robbins, and Les Lumsdon, "Holiday Travel Discourses and Climate Change," *Journal of Transport Geography* 18, (2010): 482–489.
13 Les M. Lumsdon and Peter McGrath, "Developing a Conceptual Framework for Slow Travel: A Grounded Theory Approach," *Journal of Sustainable Tourism* 19, no. 3 (2011): 265–279.
14 Jennie Germann Molz, "Representing Pace in Tourism Mobilities: Staycations, Slow Travel and *The Amazing Race*," *Journal of Tourism and Cultural Change* 7, no. 4, (2009): 270-286.
15 Michael Freeman, *Railways and the Victorian Imagination* (New Haven: Yale University Press, 1999).
16 Brian Dolan, *Exploring European Frontiers: British Travellers in the Age of the Enlightenment* (London: MacMillan, 2000).
17 Jørgen Alnæs, *I eventyret. Norske reiseskildringer fra Astrup til Aasheim* (Oslo: Cappelen Damm, 2008).
18 Schivelbusch, *Railway Journey*, 58.
19 Peter Fjågesund and Ruth A. Symes, *The Northern Utopia: British Perceptions in Norway in the Nineteenth Century* (Amsterdam: Rodopi, 2003).

20 Peter Fjågesund and Ruth A. Symes, *The Northern Utopia: British Perceptions in Norway in the Nineteenth Century* (Amsterdam: Rodopi, 2003).
21 See for instance *Den norske turistforenings aarbog for 1897* (Kristiania: Grøndahl & Sønn bogtrykkeri, 1897), 5.
22 Yngvar Nielsen, *Reisehaandbog over Norge* (Kristiania, 1879). This travel guide was published in a total of 12 editions until 1915.
23 Yngvar Nielsen, *Erindringer fra et halvt aarhundredes vandreliv* (Kristiania, 1909).
24 W. Mattieu Williams, *Through Norway With a Knapsack* (London: Edward Stanford, 1876), 41.
25 David E. Nye, *American Technological Sublime* (Cambridge, MA.: The MIT Press, 1996); David Blackbourn, *The Conquest of Nature: Water, Landscape, and the Making of Modern Germany* (New York: W.W. Norton & Company, 2007).
26 Andrew Utterson, "Destination Digital: Documentary Representation and the Virtual Travelogue," *Quarterly Review of Film and Video* 20, no. 3 (2003): 193–202.
27 Erkki Huhtamo, *Illusions in Motion: Media Archaeology of the Moving Panorama and Related Spectacles* (Cambridge, MA: The MIT Press, 2013).
28 Martin Loiperdinger, "Lumière's *Arrival of the Train*: Cinema's Founding Myth," *The Moving Image* 4, no. 1 (2004): 89–118.
29 Hellmuth Karasek, "Lokomotive der Gefühle," *Spiegel* 52, (1994): 154.
30 News in English.no, "Marathon documentary marks Bergen-Oslo line's 100th year," accessed 22 January 2014, http://www.newsinenglish.no/2009/11/30/marathon-documentary-marks-bergen-oslo-lines-100th-year/.
31 Norwegian Broadcasting Corporation, "Nordlandsbanen: Minutt for minutt," accessed 22 January 2014, http://www.nrk.no/nordlandsbanen/.
32 Norwegian Broadcasting Corporation, "Årstider i sync: produksjonen av Nordlandsbanen minutt for minutt," accessed 22 January 2014, http://nrkbeta.no/2012/12/29/arstider-i-sync-produksjonen-av-nordlandsbanen-minutt-for-minutt/.
33 Anders Hofseth, "Hurtigruten: FAQ – Ofte stilte spørsmål," accessed 22 January 2014, http://nrkbeta.no/2011/06/22/hurtigruten-faq/.
34 The map recently broke, most likely as a result of a Google Maps API update. NRK notified me that they are trying to fix the problem, but this illustrates well the challenges of sustaining digital projects over time.
35 Andreas Doppelmayr, "Hurtigruten In 5 Minutes," accessed 7 May 2014, https://vimeo.com/26214090.
36 Jon Olav Eikenes, "Hurtigruten minutt for minutt" *Flickr* set, accessed 7 May 2014 https://www.flickr.com/photos/jonolave/sets/72157626928644711/with/5873571817/.
37 Geir Bjerke, "'Hurtigruten: Minutt for minutt' in one frame," accessed 7 May 2014, https://www.flickr.com/photos/neonstz/5899253694/in/set-72157627109390926/.
38 Norwegian Broadcasting Corporation, "Hurtigrute-vinneren," accessed 7 May 2014, http://nrkbeta.no/2013/07/05/hurtigrute-vinneren/.
39 George Revill, "Perception, Reception and Representation: Wolfgang Schivelbusch and the Cultural History of Travel and Transport," in Peter Norton, Gijs Mom, Liz Millward, Mathieu Flonneau eds., *Mobility in History. Reviews and Reflections* (Neuchâtel: Éditions Alphil-Presses universitaires suisses, 2012), 43.
40 For example, Sara B. Pritchard, "Joining Environmental History with Science and Technology Studies: Promises, Challenges, and Contributions," in *New Natures: Joining Environmental History with Science and Technology Studies*, ed. Dolly Jørgensen, Finn Arne Jørgensen, and Sara B. Pritchard (Pittsburgh: University of Pittsburgh Press, 2013), 1–18.
41 Paul N. Edwards, *A Vast Machine: Computer Models, Climate Data, and the Politics of Global Warming* (Cambridge, MA: The MIT Press, 2010).
42 Franco Moretti, *Graphs, Maps, Trees: Abstract Models for Literary History* (London: Verso, 2007).
43 John Urry, "Social Networks, Travel and Talk," *The British Journal of Sociology* 54, no. 2 (2003): 156.
44 Sarah Kember and Joanna Zylinska, *Life after New Media: Mediation as a Vital Process* (Cambridge, MA: The MIT Press, 2012).

Sources

Alnæs, Jørgen. 2008. *I eventyret. Norske reiseskildringer fra Astrup til Aasheim.* Oslo: Cappelen Damm.
Bjerke, Geir. 2014. "'Hurtigruten: Minutt for minutt' in one frame." Accessed May 7, 2014. www.flickr.com/photos/neonstz/5899253694/in/set-72157627109390926/.

Blackbourn, David. 2007. *The Conquest of Nature: Water, Landscape, and the Making of Modern Germany.* New York: W. W. Norton & Company.

Den norske turistforening. 1899. *Den norske turistforenings aarbog for 1899.* Kristiania: Grøndahl & Sønn bogtrykkeri.

———. 1987. *Den norske turistforenings aarbog for 1897.* Kristiania: Grøndahl & Sønn bogtrykkeri.

Dickinson, Janet E., and Les Lumsdom. 2010. *Slow Travel and Tourism.* London: Earthscan.

Dickinson, Janet E., Les M. Lumsdon, and Derek Robbins. 2011. "Slow Travel: Issues for Tourism and Climate Change." *Journal of Sustainable Tourism* 19 (3): 281–300.

Dickinson, Janet E., D. Robbins, and Les Lumsdon. 2010. "Holiday Travel Discourses and Climate Change." *Journal of Transport Geography* 18: 482–89.

Dimanche, Frédéric, and Diane Samdahl. 1994. "Leisure as Symbolic Consumption: A Conceptualization and Prospectus for Future Research." *Leisure Sciences* 16 (2): 119–29.

Dolan, Brian. 2000. *Exploring European Frontiers: British Travellers in the Age of the Enlightenment.* London: MacMillan.

Doppelmayr, Andreas. 2014. "Hurtigruten in 5 Minutes." Accessed May 7, 2014. https://vimeo.com/26214090.

Edwards, Paul N. 2010. *A Vast Machine: Computer Models, Climate Data, and the Politics of Global Warming.* Cambridge, MA: The MIT Press.

Eikenes, Jon Olav. 2014. "Hurtigruten minutt for minutt." Accessed May 7, 2014. www.flickr.com/photos/jonolave/sets/72157626928644711/with/5873571817/.

Fjågesund, Peter, and Ruth A. Symes. 2003. *The Northern Utopia: British Perceptions in Norway in the Nineteenth Century.* Amsterdam: Rodopi.

Freeman, Michael. 1999. *Railways and the Victorian Imagination.* New Haven: Yale University Press.

Gärling, Tommy, Dick Ettema, and Margareta Friman, eds. 2014. *Handbook of Sustainable Travel.* Berlin: Springer.

Hofseth, Anders. 2014. "Hurtigruten: FAQ – Ofte stilte spørsmål." Accessed January 22, 2014. nrkbeta.no/2011/06/22/hurtigruten-faq/.

Huhtamo, Erkki. 2013. *Illusions in Motion: Media Archaeology of the Moving Panorama and Related Spectacles.* Cambridge, MA: The MIT Press.

Kember, Sarah, and Joanna Zylinska. 2012. *Life after New Media: Mediation as a Vital Process.* Cambridge, MA: The MIT Press.

Loiperdinger, Martin. 2004. "Lumière's Arrival of the Train: Cinema's Founding Myth." *The Moving Image* 4 (1): 89–118.

Lumsdon, Les M., and Peter McGrath. 2011. "Developing a Conceptual Framework for Slow Travel: A Grounded Theory Approach." *Journal of Sustainable Tourism* 19 (3): 265–79.

Marvin, Carolyn. 1988. *When Old Technologies Were New: Thinking About Electric Communication in the Late Nineteenth Century.* New York: Oxford University Press.

Molz, Jennie Germann. 2009. "Representing Pace in Tourism Mobilities: Staycations, Slow Travel and *The Amazing Race.*" *Journal of Tourism and Cultural Change* 7 (4): 270–86.

Moretti, Franco. 2007. *Graphs, Maps, Trees: Abstract Models for Literary History.* London: Verso.

News in English.no. 2009. Marathon Documentary Marks Bergen-Oslo Line's 100th Year. Accessed January 22, 2014. <www.newsinenglish.no/2009/11/30/marathon-documentary-marks-bergen-oslo-lines-100th-year/.>

Nielsen, Yngvar. 1879. *Reisehaandbog over Norge.* Kristiania.

———. 1909. *Erindringer fra et halvt aarhundredes vandreliv.* Kristiania.

North, Michael. 2013. *Novelty: A History of the New.* Chicago: University of Chicago Press.

Norwegian Broadcasting Corporation. "Hurtigrute-vinneren." Accessed May 7, 2014. nrkbeta.no/2013/07/05/hurtigrute-vinneren/.

———. "Nordlandsbanen: Minutt for minutt." Accessed January 22, 2014. www.nrk.no/nordlandsbanen/.

———. "Årstider i sync: produksjonen av Nordlandsbanen minutt for minutt." Accessed January 22, 2014. nrkbeta.no/2012/12/29/arstider-i-sync-produksjonen-av-nordlandsbanen-minutt-for-minutt/.

Nye, David E. 1996. *American Technological Sublime.* Cambridge, MA: The MIT Press.

Pritchard, Sara B. 2013. "Joining Environmental History with Science and Technology Studies: Promises, Challenges, and Contributions." In *New Natures: Joining Environmental History with Science and Technology Studies*, edited by Dolly Jørgensen, Finn Arne Jørgensen, and Sara B. Pritchard, 1–18. Pittsburgh: University of Pittsburgh Press.

Revill, George. 2012. "Perception, Reception and Representation: Wolfgang Schivelbusch and the Cultural History of Travel and Transport." In *Mobility in History. Reviews and Reflections*, edited by Peter

Norton, Gijs Mom, Liz Millward, and Mathieu Flonneau, 31–48. Neuchâtel: Éditions Alphil-Presses Universitaires Suisses.

Schivelbusch, Wolfgang. 1986. *The Railway Journey: The Industrialization of Time and Space in the 19th Century*. Berkeley: University of California Press.

Stiegler, Bernd. 2013. *Traveling in Place: A History of Armchair Travel*. Chicago: University of Chicago Press.

Urry, John. 2003. "Social Networks, Travel and Talk." *The British Journal of Sociology* 54 (2): 155–75.

Utterson, Andrew. 2003. "Destination Digital: Documentary Representation and the Virtual Travelogue." *Quarterly Review of Film and Video* 20 (3): 193–202.

Veblen, Thorstein. 1994 [1899]. *The Theory of the Leisure Class*. New York: Penguin Books.

Williams, W. Mattieu. 1876. *Through Norway with a Knapsack*. London: Edward Stanford.

3
DEEP WEATHER[1]

Ursula Biemann

Introduction

When factoring climate change into spatial considerations, the concept of border might have to be entirely rethought. The forces that, until recently, were shaping the historical borders on earth are surpassed by infinitely larger, untamable ones that show no respect for human-made boundaries. How does a geocentric framing that remains so outrageously indifferent to political determination affect the topology of borders? If we have been critically thinking about border topologies in terms of their formative social and political histories, we now have to view them in much longer time frames and try to comprehend how the temporalities of the materials and natural conditions that constitute them move across the terrain and transform it in the process.

Becoming Geological

Post-Anthropocenic art operates on the grounds that until recently have stood outside representation, moving on uncharted land, or more to the point, is itself exposed to geological forces. Davis and Turpin (2015, 3) write in their introduction to *Art in the Anthropocene*, "Becoming-geological undoes aesthetic sensibilities and ungrounds political commitments." In other words, the rapid transformation of our physical environment is also urging us to find new textual and aesthetic modes of addressing and perceiving it. It is under these considerations that I'd like to review two remote locations I visited during field trips on opposite sides of the world featuring distinct moving topographies and migrating terrains. Located in frontier spaces, their unstable properties are as much due to their physical vagueness as to the narratives that have attempted to grasp them. The appearance of these places in a recent video essay *Deep Weather* (Bieman 2013) recognises them as bounded yet shifting forms in which time and becoming occur.[2] First, the scarred earth and sulfuric clouds in northern Alberta unfold a highly stratified temporal composition: the geological time of fossil deposits in the Canadian tar sands, the mythic time of First Nations communities whose decisions take into account the well-being of the next seven generations, the local overuse of seasonal freshwater for large-scale tar extraction, and the financial fluctuations of global commodity markets.

The translation between these incongruent tempi relentlessly grinds against each other. The second scene in *Deep Weather* involves masses of people stemming rising sea levels in the Ganges

 DOI: 10.4324/9781003082798-5

delta. The specificity of a place and the geologic and atmospheric forces that violently engage it are generating a dynamic that is increasingly out of sync. As Chambers (2015, 6) recently writes in his beautiful book on borders, "Suspended in a worldly network, the dense immediacy of locality and the powerful resonance of a planetary grammar are compounded in an uneven, even unstable, certainly inconclusive, mix." On these shifting grounds, a videographic perspective cannot possibly be one of stability and explanation. Rather, language, image, and thought have to be mobilised so as to disable the fiction of a fixed sense of dwelling. The moving images of vast landscapes are imbued with a hauntingly physical voice, creating an unsettling incongruence. Following a cyclone that roared over Bangladesh, the video voice-over whispers, "Fluid lands moved further East and large chunks broke off, triggering uncertainty about a transforming living space where land is little more than a fluctuating, mobile mass." As land that defies the geometry of absolute space, the India-Bangladesh boundary running through the mighty river delta needs to be continuously redefined. With the rising sea, arable and urban space is obviously shrinking. The narrative takes up the foreboding calamity of statelessness that gradually sprawls over all continents and seven seas and turns it into an opportunity to recognise water as the territory of citizenship. Here, the extended form of citizenship isn't bound to specific terrestrial definitions but to planet Earth with its expanding oceans.

The two images attendant to this text address planetary border topologies. The first one speaks of the carbon geologies of the tar sands in the midst of the boreal forests of northern Canada, a pristine landscape possessing a long history of fossil fuel extraction (Figure 3.1); the second speaks of the hydrogeographies of the near-permanently flood-threatened Bangladesh (Figure 3.2), requiring *ecotonic* navigations. Two remote and simultaneously occurring scenes are connected through their atmospheric chemistry. The linking of these two landscapes is pursued through two narratives, one about oil, the other about water – vital "ur-liquids" that form the undercurrents of all narrations as they are activating profound changes in the planetary ecology.

Figure 3.1 Tar sand fields in Alberta, Canada.

Source: Video still from *Deep Weather*.

Figure 3.2 Embankment building in the delta of Bangladesh.[3]

Source: Video still from *Deep Weather*

Set in times of epic geological, chemical, and hydrological disorder, *Deep Weather* engages the Earth as a closed system. Climate change, exacerbated by projects such as the Canadian tar sands, puts the life of large world populations in danger. Melting Himalayan ice fields, rising planetary sea levels, and extreme weather events increasingly impose an amphibian lifestyle on the Bangladeshi population. Gigantic efforts are made by the community to build protective mud embankments. Hands-on work by thousands is what climate change will mean for most people in the deltas of the Global South. These are the measures taken by populations who progressively have to live on water when large parts of the land will be submerged.

Conclusion

These planetary relations are of a magnitude that is hard to grasp, all the more as the most significant chemical processes are occurring between locations and are invisible to our eyes. Morton (2013) speaks of global warming as a hyperobject – a very large, diffused object that is permanently present called for significant expansion at this time. To this effect, *Deep Weather* strives to thicken the understanding of these geographies by reaching deep into the interior of the Earth, down to Cambrian layers of carbon deposits, and extending a hundred miles into the atmosphere where particles circulate through rivers in the sky. Such border topologies are three-dimensional, constantly recomposing, exhalable, but no longer omitted. The science-fictional voice-over whispered in the wind activates a time-space that exceeds the localised physical and political reality of borders to plunge into a temporality of deep time where we have to index ourselves anew.

Acknowledgements

Ursula Biemann is grateful to have been invited to visit the tar sands in the context of the Petrocultures conference held at the University of Alberta in Edmonton, published online in special issue 2012 (3–2) of *Imaginations*, guest-edited by Sheena Wilson and Andrew Pendakis.

Notes

1 This chapter is taken from a previously published article in GeoHumanties: GeoHumanities, 2(2) 2016, 373–376 © Copyright 2016 by American Association of Geographers. Initial submission, March 2016; revised submission, March 2016; final acceptance, March 2016. Published by Taylor & Francis Group, LLC.

2 Video link to *Deep Weather* (https://vimeo.com/90098625).

3 Photo by Faisal Akram from Dhaka, Bangladesh, licensed under the Creative Commons Attribution-Share Alike 2.0 Generic license.

Sources

Bieman, U. 2013. *Deep Weather.* Video Essay | 00:08:58 | Switzerland | English | Color | Stereo | 16:9 | HD video. https://vimeo.com/90098625.

Chambers, I. 2015. *Location, Borders and Beyond.* Naples: CreateSpace Independent Publishing Platform.

Davis, H., and E. Turpin. 2015. *Art & Death: Lives between the Fifth Assessment & the Sixth Extinction in Art in the Anthropocene – Encounters Among Aesthetics, Politics, Environments and Epistemologies.* London: Open Humanities Press.

Morton, T. 2013. *Hyperobjects, Philosophy and Ecology after the End of the World.* Minneapolis: University of Minnesota Press.

4

ADDING SPATIAL CONTEXT TO THE 17 APRIL 1975 EVACUATION OF PHNOM PENH

How Spatial Video Geonarratives Can Geographically Enrich Genocide Testimony

Andrew Curtis, James Tyner, Jayakrishnan Ajayakumar, Sokvisal Kimsroy, and Mr Kok-Chhay Ly

Introduction

Genocide testimony is vital in terms of remembering, understanding, prosecuting, and then archiving horrific events (Caswell 2014). Yet while the focus on these testimonies is, understandably, the perspective of the individual, what receives less attention is the detailing of the spatial – specifically, understanding the places of importance and the geographic context in which events occurred. For example, between 1975 and 1979, upwards of two million men, women, and children perished from starvation, disease, exhaustion, inadequate medical care, torture, murder, and execution during the Cambodian genocide (Vickery 1988; Heuveline 1998; de Walque 2006). One of the beginning phases of this genocide was the forced evacuation of Phnom Penh and other cities. Figure 4.1 displays the generalised movement of people away from urban centres under Khmer Rouge rule, and in so doing, it appears to support the perspective of urbicide, which is the deliberate targeting and destruction of urban forms (cf. McIntyre 1996; Coates 2005). Yet this map contains multiple nested spaces and experiences, with variations occurring at every geographic scale and location. The situation between any two urban areas would be different, as would it be between two sectors of the same city or two families in each sector. What is often missing from such representations is a merging of context and spatial detail that would not only inform us with regards to our understanding of the varying geographies at work but also underlying theories regarding process and political and economic intent. Unfortunately, current methods of data collection (through interviews) tend not to adequately capture this mix of context and spatial detail.

Although there have been various technological advances in how testimony is recorded and presented (French 2009; Pinchevski 2012), the extraction and presentation of a geographic perspective are often lacking, which therefore constrains researchers wanting to analyse and visualise events spatially. There have been notable attempts at introducing geographic perspectives into

DOI: 10.4324/9781003082798-6

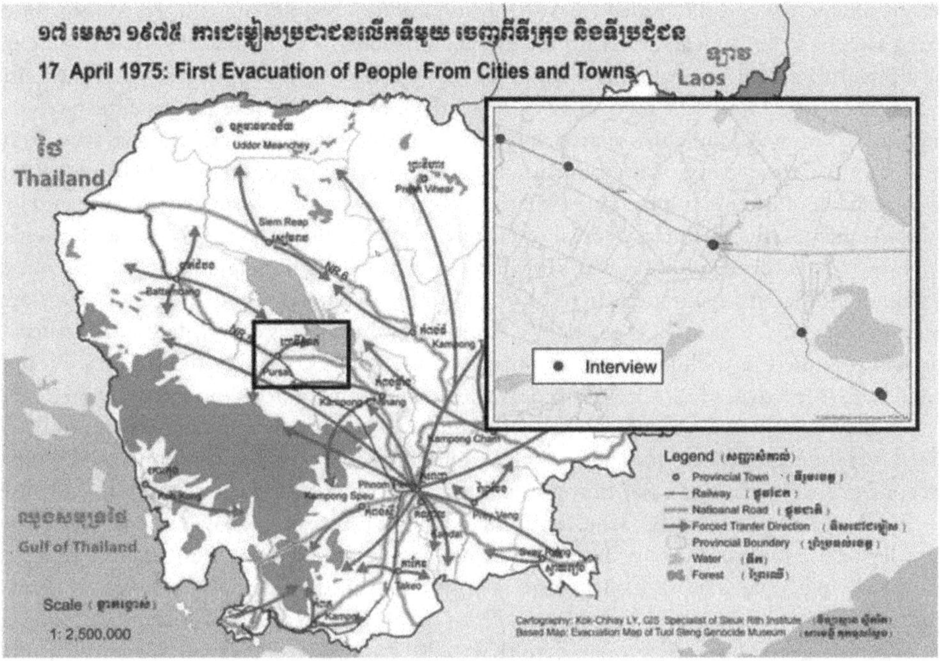

Figure 4.1 A digital (cartographic) enhancement of the hand-painted force transfer maps displayed in the Tuol Sleng Genocide Museum in Phnom Penh. The inset map displays a section of the main train line that was integral in the process and locations where the authors of this paper have conducted interviews.

genocide research (Knowles, Cole, and Giordano 2014; Giaccaria and Minca 2016), such as non-traditional cartographic approaches to capture experience, nuance and temporal fuzziness in existing data (Presner, Shepard, and Kawano 2014; Knowles, Westerveld and Strom 2015), and the conceptual use of thick mapping[1] to combine multiple perspectives (Harris 2016). There is also debate in terms of how researchers can effectively visualise the interwoven complexities of historical, spatial, and emotive data (Jasket, Knowles, Chester Harvey, and Blackshear; Southall 2014). Attention should also be given, we argue, to *inserting the spatial* when new data (in the form of interviews) are being collected, as more attention to geographic detail will propagate a richer thick map with more analytical possibilities. Yet testimony with a richer spatial component opens not only greater possibilities in terms of research but also education. In this paper, we present an example of a spatially framed interview technique that can be used in humanities research to achieve this goal – a spatial video geonarrative (SVG), which is an environmentally inspired interview recorded simultaneously with video and GPS coordinates. These data, in association with the associated bespoke software, allow for the interactive mapping of a transcribed interview supported by video data taken from where each comment is made.

Conceptually, the more detailed the spatial data are as inputs into a thick map, the greater the potential for analysis. If events can be linked to exact buildings and street segments, then the interrelationship between those places can become clearer. Typically, the technology allowing a researcher to explore this type of relationship is a GIS. Yet this software, though having been widely used in humanities – for example, in Holocaust research – has limitations. In particular, this approach can result in an artificial forcing of information into the rigid data structures of the

GIS (Knowles, Cole, and Giordano 2014). The typical GIS consists of linking features (a bridge acting as a choke point in an evacuation) and their attributes (the number of people passing over the bridge) to a map. Researchers using a GIS would have to "reduce" all events into either points (the bridge), lines (the road crossing the bridge), or polygons (the sector of the city where the bridge is found). While this approach works for many topics, it is less effective when trying to capture the complexity of the human experience, including context, different media types (such as video), fuzzy space (meaning experiences cannot be tied to a single location), and multiple time frames. For example, general testimony might include three spatial scales in the same sentence ("This corner of what was known to be a problematic neighbourhood was integral in beginning the city-wide movement of . . ."). Similarly, the temporal scale is often complex and non-sequential ("Seeing people being shot at that location was especially traumatic because I would play there as a child, and even today, when I return . . ."). Again, the GIS, though a useful tool, is less than ideal software to deal with such temporal non-linearity (Gregory 2008).

A related consideration is the data we use as input. Genocide testimony continues to be collected, yet little attention is paid to how the addition of a geographic component could make geocoding easier – in this case, how the places being described can be mapped. This limits the possibility of what can be achieved using any spatial software, most notably at the finest of scales where locations do not have names that can be mined from the text (for example, a trench where people were shot). It is here we diverge from the humanistic debates on how to represent geographic data and instead draw from spatial investigations of social data, especially the uncertain geographic context problem (Kwan 2012a, 2012b). This work suggests that many of the traditional datasets used in research (for example, crime or health data) do not capture the depth or nuance of human experience (the context) surrounding these outcomes. One approach to improve this aspect of data collection is the geonarrative (Kwan 2008; Kwan and Ding 2008) which captures a person's interaction with his/her environment and can lead to a more contextualised and richer geographic description of relationships (Evans and Jones 2011; Mennis, Mason, and Cao 2013). It is here that we frame our work – that is, as a mode of collecting new genocide data while still being cognisant of the limitations of the spatial software approach. In so doing, whether the subject is describing the trauma of living with violence now or in the past, we are, we would argue, more fully able to explore the intersection of place and experience (Kwan 2013).

Spatial Video Geonarratives

While there is a rich literature on how to extract spatiality from fundamentally non-spatial textual sources (for example, see Knowles 2008) and the role GIS can play in genocide studies (Fitchett and Good 2012; Hunter 2016), SVG presents a departure from both these as it is designed to create a richness in a spatial context and locational detail in new data. Comparable approaches in the humanities include spatial ethnography (Kim 2015) and the work of Kawano and colleagues (2016) whose ethnographies, though contributing to a thick mapping approach, do not encode spatial features directly within the narrative. SVG is an environmentally immersive technique as sights, sounds, and even smells trigger memories that are then tied to a geocoded location (Curtis et al. 2015, 2016, 2018). The SVG differs from other immersive techniques in that video is simultaneously collected, meaning that subsequent virtual rides can retrace the interview. In addition, software has been developed that can map what was said to where it was said, as well as provide tools that allow for interactive textual, image, and locational investigation of the narrative. The video can be used as a data source in itself, or at the least it can provide additional spatial accuracy to the narrative by allowing a place being described (such as a building) to be accurately geolocated. The video also allows a team of researchers who did not participate in the original data collection to virtually experience the environment being described. Indeed, SVG has been utilised in various data challenged environments to elicit an understanding of events, processes, and emotions from an individual's perspective. This approach has been used to compare community and police perspectives for the same space (Curtis et al. 2016), capture the thoughts and perspectives of those experiencing recovery after a disaster (Curtis et al. 2015), tap into the institutional knowledge of an environmental health specialist (Krystosik et al. 2017), understand the day-to-day experiences of society's most marginalised (Curtis et al. 2015), or provide a means to display a neighbourhood voice. From a technical perspective, an SVG is an audio interview, a simultaneously collected video that records the environment through which the subject is moving, and a GPS receiver. The resulting interview, once transcribed, can be linked to the video and GPS so that each comment has a corresponding visual and location. Typically, the participant is driven and, with a minimum of interviewer involvement, is asked to describe the environment through which he/she passes. Once collected, the narrative is transcribed and the GPS extracted so that both can be merged together. To do this, specialised software, Wordmapper, has been developed to connect all data inputs by their timestamps. Once the video, GPS and transcription have been merged together, we can begin a variety of different investigations to synergistically add depth to any described event. A typical SVG produces three types of insight: spatially specific, spatially fuzzy, and spatially inspired. Spatially specific comments are tied to a location while in its vicinity:

> Over here. They came here and surrounded this place. They shot people at this corner.

Spatially fuzzy comments describe a more general area without an exact anchor point:

> We could not drive. We pushed them slowly. We could not drive because it was very crowded. I helped my family push the car slowly, and it was very hot in April. It was very hot, and we were thirsty. It was painful. We did not have anything to eat except the packed noodles. We ate them directly without cooking them in hot water. We had stomachache and diarrhoea there.

Spatially inspired comments can come from sight, sound, or smell or maybe a run-on thought from a previous comment, which then reveals new information that has no specific location:

> He was evacuated there, and he died there. He died because he ate human flesh. He dug a human body and grilled it to eat. He ate it. He was a doctor. Then they killed him.

The next challenge is how to visualise and investigate such complex data. As previously mentioned, simply adding attribute columns to a point on a map, as one would in a typical GIS, is too reductionist for such complex, emotionally charged data (Knowles, Westerveld, and Strom 2015). We need to be able to do more than ask, "Show me where this comment occurs." To illustrate how we can more fully understand the spatial (and human) complexities involved using SVG, we will use examples drawn from the forced evacuation of Phnom Penh on 17 April 1975 during the Cambodian genocide.

To show the spatial deficiencies of more traditional interviews, we can return to the main map of Figure 4.1. In this map, a single railway line is visible. The inset map shows a small section of this line with red dots, including stopping points (usually stations) where the authors of this paper have previously collected interviews on the uses of the train, with a focus on any witnessed trauma. This railway served multiple purposes; it was used for transporting people to prisons and then execution sites, moving workers between zones of construction, and even transporting soldiers. For many, the train ride was an unknown as it would be uncertain where the train was going and whether those on board would be killed. As one might expect, this geographic feature became associated with considerable violence, with interviews describing onboard morbidity and mortality. However, while "the train" might be described consistently in interviews as a focal point of trauma, it can also be considered an example of nested spaces and time frames. There were multiple stopping points along the line, where people witnessed events that varied in nature and time period. The following two quotes, extracted from these interviews, illustrate this:

At Veal Renh Station:

> They were taken here. They were arrested from Tik Sap and Sre Chap – everywhere. They were killed here. Soldiers were taken here. They arrived at 6:00 p.m. At first, they took young people, and then they killed elderly people. The children shouted and cried "Grandma!" and "Grandpa!"

At Romeas Station:

> The concrete structure there! People were killed there. Over here! They were killed all over the place. It was a former military base. They were skulls everywhere. We can get inside if you want.

The first of the preceding quotes contains spatial information (the location of the interview, the two origin place-names), but there is no further geographic detail. However, the second quote contains fine-scale specific locations, such as the concrete structure that can be mapped if coordinates had been collected at that time of the interview. The need for such spatial detail becomes even more important when the space involved becomes more complex, such as a major city. The challenge, as described at the beginning of the paper, is how to record these geographies and then how to represent/visualise/investigate them. If we achieve this, then by adding multiple narratives together, we can begin to develop a situational understanding of what happened and its aftermath.

The Forced Evacuation of Phnom Penh

Following their victory on 17 April 1975, the members of the Armed Forces of the Communist Party of Kampuchea (CPK) began forcibly evacuating the capital city. Upwards of three million people – more than half of whom were peasants who had fled the fighting during five years of civil war (1970–1975) and eight years of American bombing (1965–1973) – were relocated onto cooperatives and work camps in neighbouring provinces. Many were forced to walk; others were transported by truck or train. It was apparent that little planning went into the specific procedures of the evacuation (cf. Nhem 2013). There was little coordination among the Khmer Rouge soldiers, and the resultant death toll, while not accurately known, was considerable (Vickery 1984; Chandler 1991).

The evacuation of urban areas, including Phnom Penh, was a long-standing practice of the Khmer Rouge. As early as 1971, Khmer Rouge forces began to systematically burn villages and hamlets that fell under their control as they attempted to "liberate" the country. For example, in 1973, Khmer Rouge soldiers seized half of Kompong Cham City and, in the process, forcibly moved upwards of 15,000 people into the countryside (Kiernan 1985, 371). For many scholars, the evacuation of Phnom Penh and other urban areas constitutes an anti-urban bias and, accordingly, should be understood as a form of urbicide (cf. Bishop and Clancey 2004; Shaw 2004; Coates 2005). Documentary evidence belies this assessment, however, and indicates rather that the CPK understood the necessity of retaining Phnom Penh and other, selected urban areas as critical nodes in an evolving political economy. The purpose of these evacuations was economic. Simply put, the CPK required massive supplies of labour to achieve its economic objectives, namely the rapid increase in agricultural crops for export. More precisely, the CPK required a constant supply of workers to clear forests, build irrigation systems, and grow rice (Tyner 2014, 2017; Tyner and Will 2015; Rice and Tyner 2017). Effectively, the evacuation of urban areas, including Phnom Penh, was initiated for immediate, pragmatic concerns and, for this reason, should demand our attention. As indicated earlier, historical accounts and memoirs detail the lived experiences of men, women, and children during the evacuation. Scholars have detailed, albeit partially, the tactics employed by the Khmer Rouge to affect the evacuation (cf. Nhem 2013). Survivors have recalled the emotional and physical hardships of evacuation (Ponchaud 1978; Ung 2000; Seng 2005). While the Cambodian genocide illustrates the close association between urban geographies and mass violence, we are often left, however, with little spatial detail and analysis, especially at finer (sub-city) geographic scales. SVG can facilitate such comparative investigations by both enriching the testimony through immersive experience and the capturing resulting geographies in a mappable format.

Collecting Spatially Contextualised Interviews

In 2017, seven SVGs were collected in Phnom Penh. The subjects all participated in the evacuation, and each was asked to retrace the exact route while describing the happenings, and places, along their forced march.[2] Data collection followed the same pattern, with a typical SVG setup of GPS-enabled contour +2 cameras mounted on the inside window of the left and right side of a vehicle. Two audio recorders were placed on or around the subject who was sitting in the front seat. Before the ride, the subject was given a brief description of the project rationale and asked for verbal consent in keeping with a bespoke ethics research protocol. Each ride lasted between 60 and 90 minutes. The subject dictated the route to the driver and followed his/her evacuation path as closely as possible. At least one of the researchers in the vehicle was Cambodian and worked previously as a DC-Cam-trained interviewer. He was integral in minimising any language and cultural barriers, conducting the interview in Khmer, and then providing translation. Subjects for this study were drawn from his set of contacts in Cambodia. After collection, the narrative was transcribed and translated into English. Timestamps were inserted preceding each comment. The following is an example:

> [00:23:54] Along the road, patients were abandoned in the fields. I saw them being left alone on the bed. They were in the fields. I guess the medical staff members were ordered to move those patients out of the hospitals, and when they got out the city and did not see or know any relatives of those patients. Then they just abandoned those patients.

The timestamp is the point on the video when the previous comment can be heard. For this quote, the information being recalled describes a traumatic event witnessed along the evacuation route, but it also contains associated environmental information (the fields through which they were walking), though it is not clear whether a specific space is being identified. The participant was describing this event where he remembered it to have occurred, but the haze of memory and a changing landscape made this recall "fuzzy."

After transcription, each narrative was re-read for themes that could guide the subsequent investigation. Reading the narratives was an iterative process, in that while the general theme categories and several sub-themes may be known beforehand (such as trauma and witnessing bodies), the richness of the geonarrative, both contextually and spatially, leads to an expansion of these preconceived themes. The narratives were then analysed and visualised using Wordmapper, which merges the transcription with the GPS path. Wordmapper has been developed with three imperatives: (1) to limit the amount of technical experience needed to run the software, thus making the SVG technique as ubiquitous as possible,[3] (2) to provide data output suitable for qualitative and quantitative analysis beyond the scope of the software, and (3) to move beyond the limitations "of the search box"[4] in the spirit of inductive visualisation, in other words providing the ability to perform iterative and multi-type investigation. In order to map out where each comment has been made, the GPS path is extracted from the video using Contour Storyteller software.[5] In a typical SVG collection there are three possible timestamps; the audio recording, the video recording, and the "official" Greenwich Mean Time (GMT) of the GPS. By matching the audio time with the associated GPS GMT time, we can establish where each word (and the beginning of each comment) was said. Wordmapper does this by interpolating all words between each inserted timestamp. Outputs include a visualisation of the narrative (a word cloud) and maps where each word or comment is located. While a search box for keywords is included, it is expected that this is part of an iterative loop. We initially enter a preconceived search term, we see the results of this search, what was said in connection with that term, and where it was said, and then we refine (or expand) our question. For example, we used the following keywords to capture different experiences of trauma: *body*, *dead*, *death*, *kill*, *shot*, and *shoot*.

Mapped output comprises GIS and Google Earth files. Each word or the beginning of each comment is displayed as a red pin on Google Earth. Queried words (or comments containing the queried word) are identified using a gold pin. In this way, we can map where different traumatic events are mentioned. On Google Earth, the user can read the narrative in the left-hand side table of comments and then zoom to the location by double-clicking on any single comment. The GIS output (as a shapefile) allows for more sophisticated spatial manipulation as the searched-for words are identified in the attribute table. The user can investigate data by text, by map, thematically, graphically, or by referring back to the video, which means this software is similar in spirit to the inductive visualisation approach suggested by Knowles and colleagues (2015). Just as previous examples of this in genocide research have explored geographic and emotional themes using the low-tech flexibility of coloured pens and paper, here our crayons include computer code that allows similar explorations of co-connected maps, graphics, texts, and videos. While we have reduced each word of a powerful and personal memory to a coordinate, it should rather be considered as a spatial index that connects multiple media layers. We can also easily go back to the narrative for additional context, to a summary of the text for co-occurrence, to the map for a greater understanding of where these events are happening, and to the video to further enhance our depth of understanding. We have facilitated the deepening of the testimony rather than reducing it.

Extracting Spatial Insights from the Narratives

Seven SVGs were collected in Phnom Penh in either January (subject A and S21) or June 2017 (subjects 1 through 5) (Figure 4.2). Of these seven, six SVGs followed the evacuation route each took between 17 and 20 April 1975. The seventh interview, S21, so named because the interviewee describes what it was like to be a prisoner in the S21 prison facility, also discussed

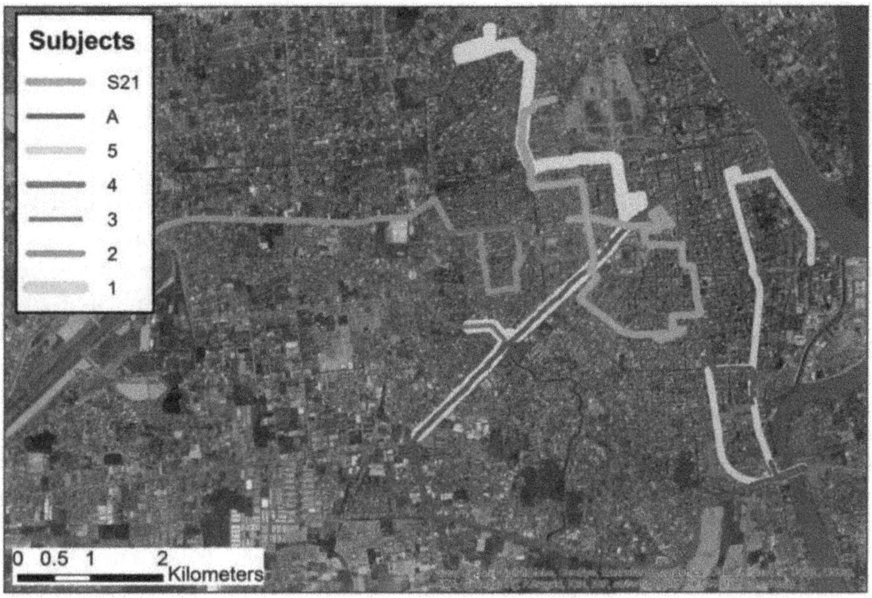

Figure 4.2 Seven mapped SVG routes, six of which show their actual forced evacuation paths.

the evacuation, but his narrative also discussed other events and locations. The S21 SVG will be considered separately as an example of a more temporally complex narrative.

After data collection, a metadata sheet was created for each ride.[6] The GPS path was extracted for each video, and the interview was transcribed and translated, with media timestamps being inserted before each comment. Examples are the following:

> [00:32:29] A: We slept near Chbar Ampov Cinema. We were exhausted and slept right away. When we woke up, we saw one dead body nearby.
>
> [00:32:41] A: We did smell something that night, but we were too exhausted to care about it. The following morning, we saw the body.
>
> [00:32:46] Q: The body might have been there for some time, but then you saw it?
>
> [00:32:48] A: Yes, we did not know when that person had died. The body was badly swollen. I was young and I had never seen a dead body before.

Each narrative was re-read with all salient comments being placed into thematic categories while specific spatial locations were identified, such as where buildings stood, the role they played, or how whole environments had changed from paddy fields into densely packed buildings. In the previous quote, a spatially specific location is identified along the route (where the first night's sleep occurred) along with a traumatic experience that occurred there. Therefore, in our transcribed evacuation, we have not only a specific contextualised location but also an entry into a sub-theme of trauma. Three major themes were identified, the first including events from before or after the evacuation period, including personal (what it was like to live on these streets), social (the ownership of houses and their community roles), and political histories (previous conflicts in Cambodia that had impacted the participant's family). The second set of themes involves the evacuation itself, the events leading up to the Khmer Rouge entering the city (for example, whether the participant experienced the artillery shelling), first encounters, the events around the home, what they were told to do, what did the family then did, when and from where did the evacuation start, and the route itself. While much of this is contextual detail – for example, describing all the activity in and around the home before starting the evacuation – some of it is also explicitly spatial: where was that home located?

The third set of themes concerned the experiences on the march itself; access to food, water, and toilets; where the first night was spent; the presence of and interactions with soldiers; and where trauma was experienced. In addition to these locations, the condition of the individual (exhaustion, sickness) and emotions (fear, loss), as recalled by the interviewees, can also be noted. Spatial questions can be asked within these more emotive themes: Did the physical/emotional experience differ across the city? Was there an association with differing military oversight (varying by cadres)? Did certain sections of the route cause more fear? And what role did the infrastructure (such as bridges) play in these human outcomes?

Wordmapper was run with an input of the transcribed narrative, the extracted GPS path, and an initial trauma-related keyword set for trauma. Figure 4.3 displays the associated word clouds for each of the subjects that followed their evacuation path. While the most dominant words are as expected (human, people), a few other trauma-related terms do arise for some of the subjects (pistol), while others could warrant further investigation (children, afraid). These word clouds give us our first insight into variation between the subjects. To consider what was the physical toll on evacuees and were there any spatially specific features of importance along the route, we can go deeper into the narrative by linking these comments to the maps and video. For example, if we return to the earlier quote describing where patients were left to die, after running Wordmapper we can now see exactly where this comment was made on the evacuation path, and by

Figure 4.3 The frequency of words in comments made by the SVG subjects when various trauma keywords are combined in the search.

Figure 4.4 This map shows where different evacuation streams converge, the first being inside the yellow circle (only one SVG describes this) and then subsequently at the bridge, where three different SVGs comment on the trauma experienced at this choke point.

returning to the video, we can become familiar with the environment that stimulated the memory. We can also return to Wordmapper to change our query to find out where other "patient" references occurred. In effect, we can use a comment as an entry into a thick map to spatially and then topically connect multiple narratives and imagery to that location and/or theme.

The SVG results reveal that the choice of route was left to the evacuees as long as the direction was away from the city. We can visualise this in a GIS using the spatial output from Wordmapper. In the example displayed in Figure 4.4, one SVG subject had been travelling along the blue road (south to north) when his evacuation stream began to merge with another column heading east (the path is not shown as no SVG was collected, but the merging point was around the yellow circle). At this convergence, they were not allowed to turn left, as that would have been heading back into the city. The map illustrates this by showing where the comment was made (the centre of the yellow circle) and where the two streams would have met. These merged evacuation streams would then join other columns of people at the bridge (B) to produce one of the most traumatic landscapes of the evacuation. Interestingly, the route of this SVG looped around the bottom of the city before merging with the second column. This meant the direction was, for a time, counter to the prevailing belief that evacuation routes only went outwards. Interestingly, while the narratives describe how the only direction was away from the city, it is the cartographic representation made possible by the SVG that reveals that this was not always so.

As previously mentioned, the re-reading of the narratives identifies other sub-themes. While the narrative describes the physical and emotional toll associated with trauma, it also conveys how choke points often lead to a worsening of conditions, especially around the bridges:

> We could move very slowly. We got stuck on the bridge until 4:00 or 5:00 p.m. Then we continued. It was very difficult travelling on the bridge. It was hot, and we were

> thirsty. As we got stuck on the bridge, my father went to the river to get water. My father could swim and do any other things for us. He went to pick up water. Then we drank water. Speaking of the Basac River, there were dead bodies floating along the river. This bridge did not exist at that time. There was only one bridge. Yes, speaking of which, people peed and defecated on the bridge, and it smelled.

We know from Figure 4.4 that at least four columns of people merged at the Monivong Bridge, two from the north and the two converging by the yellow circle. Interestingly, we know details of three of these routes through SVG collected along them, but the fourth is only revealed by being mentioned in a narrative. This shows how the richness of these interviews can reveal spatial detail even beyond the route being collected. On the bridge, people were squeezed into a smaller space, which would have accentuated their already deteriorating situation, especially as the bridge was reached for many (as extrapolated from the SVGs) three days into the march when sickness had begun to break out, and the tolerance of the disgruntled soldiers was starting to manifest in violence. To explore the impact of these congestion points further, we changed the keyword in Wordmapper to "bridge"[7] and began to find other mentions of trauma connected with bridges elsewhere in the city – for example, at a smaller crossing point on the Veng Sreng Boulevard:

> After crossing the bridge, I began to see dead bodies along the road. We saw the bodies, but what the elderly people tried to do was to make us walk further and avoid seeing those bodies.

This second bridge also revealed one implication of the initial "trick" (as described by the subjects) by the Khmer Rouge that began the evacuation, where the citizens of Phnom Penh were initially told that they would only be evacuated for three days.[8] When mapping the routes around this bridge (Figure 4.5), we saw that three streams converged here, one (subject 3) swung

Figure 4.5 Route convergence at the bridge on the Veng Sreng Boulevard.

around from the west, and the two others (subjects 1 and A) followed the road southwest from the centre of Phnom Penh. The family of subject 1 stopped in the vicinity, waiting for the three days to pass and the return to order, not wanting to put too much distance between themselves and their home. Eventually, they realised that they would not be allowed to return and so rejoined the column leaving the city:

> To the best of my knowledge, I think my family and others did not want to leave the city too far. They wandered around this area and stayed here for three days. Therefore, I could say it took us three days to reach this point where we are now. However, after three days passed, the Khmer Rouge continued to say or insist on our evacuation. They did not let us go back. We thought and heard that the evacuation was only for three days. And after three days, the Khmer Rouge said they needed five days because three days were not enough. Then they said they would not allow people to return to the city, and they stopped mentioning days. They only said, "Go further and do not return."

As we searched for other interactions in the narratives, we found a more immediate link between the three-day trick and the worsening conditions along the route in that families did not take enough food for a long, forced march on foot:

> We travelled along this road and reached Kien Svay. After staying for a week, we ran out of food. We were too many people, and we had only one bag of rice. We did not prepare well or pack lots of rice because they said that we would leave for only three days.

And:

> [My father] heard the announcement that they needed former workers to return to the city and work for them. At one point, he thought of returning, but he was told not to return. If he had, he would have died. At that time, many people were killed because of such tricks. They said they had people leave the city for three days. Generally, people could not prepare for it, but my father did pack some items and food for us to eat. A few days later, we ran out of food.

A final SVG collected at the same time as the others, subject S21, who also experienced the evacuation, provides an illustration of how a narrative can contain complex temporal sequences. For the other narratives, the described events can be categorised as before, during, and after the evacuation, with the majority of each interview focused on a three-day period. For these subjects, mapping out testimony as different layers on the same map is appropriate. However, re-reading S21's narrative reveals four distinct time periods that all occupied the same general space. The initial evacuation, which though starting in a similar fashion to the other SVGs (where the subject lived during the shelling, where he started his evacuation), differed because the entire route was not followed. The second temporal period was described when the subject was returned to the city by the Khmer Rouge because of his mechanical skills. He was tasked to search the abandoned buildings and find sewing machines, which he then repaired and serviced for the city's textile sector. This period is also spatially specific as the narratives are recorded at the actual locations. For example, consider Figure 4.6, which shows the buildings that were part of the textile sector. While these can be represented as points or polygons on a map of that period,

Figure 4.6 Contour Storyteller software is used to show the buildings described in the SVG as playing an important role in the textile sector. The inset map also identifies where this image was recorded

they can also be thought of as containers enriched with process, history, social and political structure, and emotional interpretation. Indeed, the buildings seen in Figure 4.6 were described in detail in terms of who lived on what floor, how these residents interacted according to rank, and when and what type of social mixing was allowed.

> [00:50:57] The Khmer Rouge lived separately. However, only unit chiefs lived with us.
> [00:51:04] Q: What about the person in charge of this place?
> [00:51:06] There was a person named Kun. He was the big chief.
> [00:51:16] The sewing machines were all here, and I taught them here. I taught them how to fix sewing machines, and it stretched from the corner there to here.
> [00:51:31] Workers lived on the upper floors, and they placed sewing machines on the ground floors. People made clothes here.
> [00:52:16] Wives and husbands were allowed to meet once a month. On the upper floors.

The third period describes his being tricked, then transported to S21, and his arrival and torture. The final period describes the process of leaving S21 as the Vietnamese entered the city. All four periods described by this subject are valuable and add to our understanding of events in Phnom Penh: for him, the beginning part of the evacuation was more violent than what was told in the other SVG routes. The description of the textile sector (and its potential to be mapped) adds detail to a city where little information (and no spatial detail) exists for the period of the Khmer Rouge rule.[9] The description of the ride to S21 adds spatial detail absent in his many other interviews (Mey 2012), showing exactly where he was picked up (and how he was "tricked"), then the chilling wait outside a largely unknown facility, and lastly, the route away from S21 and the revelation of why other prisoners were left behind to be murdered (the guards couldn't find the keys) and that, while 18 left the prison, only 12 would eventually be listed as survivors.

Implications of a Spatially Contextualised Interview Approach

In this paper, we have deepened our understanding of the spatial aspects of the forced evacuation of Phnom Penh in 1975, with an emphasis on the details of the routes taken and the trauma experienced. We have gained new insights into the human perspective of what it was like to walk within these columns of people, the heat, exhaustion, lack of food, etc. Even from these few SVGs, we hear about the on-the-fly decisions that were made for survival, mundane issues such as dealing with human excreta, and how a competitor/comrade tension developed with fellow evacuees. At the same time, we have added to the discourse on how best to apply spatial research to such an emotional topic. To achieve this, testimony was collected in a way that explicitly captured geographic data could be mapped. These additional contextualised spatial details not only improve our understanding of what happened but also call into question some of the more widely believed assumptions. For example, in none of the narratives was there a consistent Khmer Rouge presence lining the paths, shooting their guns in the air and policing the routes as has previously been described. Indeed, for long stretches, the soldiers were absent (though in one SVG, it is described ominously that "they were there"). Decisions like where to get food and water, where to stop and sleep, and where to wander were left to the individual. The routes did vary in terms of experienced trauma, where dead bodies were seen, or acts of violence witnessed. For example, there was variation in when each family started the evacuation, ranging from the day the Khmer Rouge entered the city to almost two days later. With more SVG, we could establish validation and more robustly map out how experiences differed by sector of the city and, therefore, by the cadre in control.

We argue that immersive environmental testimony not only improves our ability to map, analyse, and visualise socio-spatial information at a granular level but also leads to deeper data that can be used to spin off in different directions to more fully contextualise a place and its situation. In this regard, our participant's experiences create a map of places, not spaces (Tuan 1977), and in Wordmapper, we have the type of inductive visualisation tool that can help us investigate this type of data richness. While *representing words as points* might sound reductionist, we are able to explore themes in a non-linear manner, with or without spatial context. Each place contains stories from before, during and after the Khmer Rouge. By collecting more SVGs, we further *deepen* these locations as multiple contexts, emotions, histories, and even the connective tissue that ties the places together begins to be revealed. Rather than being a reduced representation of events, it is a gateway into a deeper experience. The map, which maintains a more traditional structure for easy navigation, manipulation, and analysis, is also just a gateway.

For the broader humanities, Wordmapper is an example of new computer code that can help sort through and interpret spatial data (Cresswell 2015). However, while we are cognisant of more appropriate ways to work with these types of data, it should not be at the risk of limiting users by excessive technology. The development of new software must be done in such a way to allow ubiquitous use; otherwise, we face the same tensions that occurred with the perceived reemergence of positivism in geography through GIS. Not only should new methods be easy to use, but they should allow for the continued evolution of how they work with these data.[10] The evolution will continue as more detail, different research questions, and topical areas emerge requiring different or modified tools. For example, these data should be further investigated for emotional content. While "sentiment analysis" is an important topic of consideration in computer science, being the ability to identify and code for emotions, and we have mentioned throughout this paper how geographers need more sensitive spatial tools when working with such complex and emotionally charged data, we have really only scratched the surface in terms of how to adequately represent *emotionally* contextualised spatial data. In this way, SVG offers us the chance not only to add new insights into different topical fields but also to reinterpret and even challenge existing knowledge.

Acknowledgements

A. Curtis would like to thank the students of the GIS Health & Hazards Lab who have helped with various tasks in and around this project. He would also like to thank the University of Southern California Shoah Foundation and all attendees of the Digital Approaches to Genocide workshop for their valuable comments regarding an earlier presentation of this paper. All authors would like to thank the SVG participants who gave their valuable time. Their insights were extremely informative and moving. We would also like to thank the Cambodian Ministry of Environment (MoE), especially the Department of Geospatial Information Service (DGIS). J. Tyner would like to thank the College of Arts & Sciences at Kent State University for their support.

Notes

1 The "thick map" is a way to combine traditional mapping elements with other layers, such as videos or narratives, that can enhance the experience and insight. This is a particularly relevant approach when different disciplines work together collecting and using a variety of data types, with the map being the connecting tissue allowing the researcher to drill down into what is known or has been witnessed at that location. In this way, we can develop a more comprehensive understanding of what happened geographically for one or multiple periods of time as perceived/experienced/explained by different perspectives.

2 A further two SVGs were collected at the same time, from a survivor from S-21, the notorious prison camp in the centre of the city, and from a rural village chief connected to a Khmer Rouge forced dam-building project.

3 While the ability to code Wordmapper and its different evolving stages does obviously require considerable programming ability, the user version and its interface are extremely intuitive.

4 Search boxes, or GIS queries, tend to be linear in nature as the underlying inflexibility of the data structure means that our investigation is a progression of our own preconception. We query data based on what we expect (or hope) to find. This was raised as a discussion by Todd Presner in an opening address at the centre for Advanced Genocide Research's Digital Approaches to Genocide Studies conference in October, 2017 (https://sfi.usc.edu/cagr/conferences/2017_international/schedule).

5 Recent problems with the Contour company have led the research team to be concerned about the longevity of the storyteller software. As a result, we have written bespoke software to extract GPS coordinates not only from Contour devices but a variety of other GPS-enabled video cameras.

6 This sheet contains the camera name, the quality of the video, audio and GPS, notation regarding anything of interest occurring on the drive, any technical/data collection issues, and maps from each camera. These are vital for future cross-comparison of different SVG and assessing any deficiency in the data collection process.

7 This new query generates a fresh set of word clouds and mapped outcomes. The same type of query could have been run for sleep, food, and sickness – all consistent themes through the narratives.

8 They entered the city at night and fired in the air. In the morning, they made announcement through loudspeaker that people had to move out for three days because they needed to wipe out the imperialist.

9 Despite arguments to the contrary, Phnom Penh (and other urban areas) was not an "empty" city. Rather, Phnom Penh and other key cities served as nodal points in the broader political economy of Democratic Kampuchea (see Tyner et al. 2014; Rice and Tyner 2017).

10 Indeed, in the first version of this paper sent to reviewers, we concluded that the future versions of Wordmapper will have the ability to map and index the transcription according to theme and whether each comment is spatially specific, fuzzy, or inspired. The word cloud will also be spatialised, allowing the researcher to move seamlessly between subsections of the narrative, map, and video. All of these are now available in the current version of the software (Figure 4.4).

Sources

Beorn, W., T. Cole, S. Gigliotti, A. Giordano, A. Holian, P. B. Jaskot, A. K. Knowles, M. Masurovsky, and E. B. Steiner. 2009. "Geographies of the Holocaust." *Geographical Review* 99 (4): 563–74.

Bishop, R., and G. Clancey. 2004. "The City-as-Target, or Perpetuation and Death." In *Cities, War, and Terrorism: Towards an Urban Geopolitics*, edited by S. Graham, 54–74. Malden, MA: Blackwell.

Bodenhamer, D. J. 2010. "The Potential of the Spatial Humanities." In *The Spatial Humanities: GIS and the Future of Humanities Scholarship*, edited by D. J. Bodenhamer, J. Corrigan, and T. Harris, 14–31. Bloomington: Indiana University Press.

Bodenhamer, D. J., J. Corrigan, and T. M. Harris, eds. 2010. *The Spatial Humanities: GIS and the Future of Humanities Scholarship*. Bloomington: Indiana University Press.

Caswell, M. 2014. *Archiving the Unspeakable: Silence, Memory, and the Photographic Record in Cambodia*. Madison: University of Wisconsin Press.

Chandler, D. P. 1991. *The Tragedy of Cambodian History: Politics, War, and Revolution since 1945*. New Haven, CT: Yale University Press.

Coates, J. J. 2005. *Cambodia Now: Life in the Wake of War*. Jefferson, NC: McFarland.

Colls, C. S. 2015. *Holocaust Archaeologies: Approaches and Future Directions*. Cham: Springer.

Cresswell, T. 2015. "Space, Place, and the Triumph of the Humanities." *GeoHumanities* 1 (1): 4–9.

Curtis, A., J. W. Curtis, L. C. Porter, E. Jefferis, and Eric Shook. 2016. "Context and Spatial Nuance Inside a Neighborhood's Drug Hotspot: Implications for the Crime-Health Nexus." *Annals of the Association of American Geographers* 106 (4): 819–36.

Curtis, Andrew, Jacqueline W. Curtis, Eric Shook, Steve Smith, Eric Jefferis, Lauren Porter, Laura Schuch, Chaz Felix, and Peter R. Kerndt. 2015. "Spatial Video Geonarratives and Health: Case Studies in Post-Disaster Recovery, Crime, Mosquito Control and Tuberculosis in the Homeless." *International Journal of Health Geographics* 14 (1): 22.

Curtis, A., C. Felix, S. Mitchell, and P. Kerndt. 2018. "Contextualizing Overdoses in Los Angeles' Skid Row between 2014 and 2016 by Leveraging the Spatial Knowledge of the Marginalized." *Annals of the Association of American Geographers* 108: 1521–36.

de Walque, D. 2006. "The Socio-Demographic Legacy of the Khmer Rouge Period in Cambodia." *Population Studies* 60 (2): 223–31.

Evans, J., and P. Jones. 2011. "The Walking Interview: Methodology, Mobility and Place." *Applied Geography* 31 (2): 849–58.

Fielding, N. G. 2012. "Triangulation and Mixed Methods Designs Data Integration with New Research Technologies." *Journal of Mixed Methods Research* 6 (2): 124–36.

Fitchett, P. G., and A. J. Good. 2012. "Teaching Genocide through GIS: A Transformative Approach." *The Clearing House: A Journal of Educational Strategies, Issues and Ideas* 85 (3): 87–92.

French, B. M. 2009. "Technologies of Telling: Discourse, Transparency, and Erasure in Guatemalan Truth Commission Testimony." *Journal of Human Rights* 8 (1): 92–109.

Giaccaria, P., and C. Minca, eds. 2016. *Hitler's Geographies: The Spatialities of the Third Reich*. Chicago, IL: University of Chicago Press.

Gieseking, J. J. 2013. "Where We Go From Here: The Mental Sketch Mapping Method and Its Analytic Components." *Qualitative Inquiry* 19 (9): 712–24.

Gregory, I. N. 2008. "'A Map Is Just a Bad Graph': Why Spatial Statistics Are Important for Historical GIS." In *Placing History: How Maps, Spatial Data, and GIS Are Changing Historical Scholarship*, ed. A. K. Knowles, 123–49. Redlands: ESRI Press.

Harris, T. M. 2016. "From PGIS to Participatory Deep Mapping and Spatial Storytelling: An Evolving Trajectory in Community Knowledge Representation in GIS." *The Cartographic Journal* 53 (4): 318–25.

Heuveline, P. 1998. "'Between One and Three Million': Towards the Demographic Reconstruction of a Decade of Cambodian History (1970–1979)." *Population Studies* 52 (1): 49–65.

Hornsby, S. J. 2017 *American Pictorial Maps: The Golden Age*. Chicago and Washington, DC: University of Chicago Press with the Library of Congress.

Hunter, R. 2016. "Geographies of the Holocaust." *The AAG Review of Books* 4 (3): 156–58.

Jaskot, P. B., A. K. Knowles, Chester Harvey, and B. Perry Blackshear. 2014. "Visualizing the Archive: Building at Auschwitz as a Geographical Problem." In *Geographies of the Holocaust*, edited by A. K. Knowles, T. Cole, and A. Giordano, 158–91. Bloomington: Indiana University Press.

Jessop, M., 2007. "The Inhibition of Geographical Information in Digital Humanities Scholarship." *Literary and Linguistic Computing* 23 (1): 39–50.

Kawano, Y., A. Munaim, J. Goto, Y. Shobugawa, and M. Naito. 2016. "Sensing Space: Augmenting Scientific Data with Spatial Ethnography." *GeoHumanities* 2 (2): 485–508.

Kiernan, B. 1985. *How Pol Pot Came to Power: A History of Communism in Kampuchea, 1930–1975*. London: Verso.

Kim, A. M. 2015. *Sidewalk city: Remapping Public Space in Ho Chi Minh City*. Chicago: University of Chicago Press.

Knowles, A. K. 2008. *Placing History: How Maps, Spatial Data, and GIS Are Changing Historical Scholarship*. Redlands, CA: ESRI Press.

Knowles, A. K., T. Cole, and A. Giordano, eds. 2014. *Geographies of the Holocaust*. Bloomington, IN: Indiana University Press.

Knowles, A. K., P. B. Jaskot, B. P. Blackshear, M. DeGroot, and A. Yule. 2014. "Mapping the SS Concentration Camps." In *Geographies of the Holocaust*, edited by A. K. Knowles, T. Cole, and A. Giordano, 18–51. Bloomington: Indiana University Press.

Knowles, A. K., L. Westerveld, and L. Strom. 2015. "Inductive Visualization: A Humanistic Alternative to GIS." *GeoHumanities* 1 (2): 233–65.

Krystosik, A. R., A. Curtis, P. Buritica, J. Ajayakumar, R. Squires, D. Dávalos, et al. 2017. "Community Context and Sub-Neighborhood Scale Detail to Explain Dengue, Chikungunya and Zika patterns in Cali, Colombia." *PLoS One* 12 (8): e0181208.

Kwan, M.-P. 2008. "From Oral Histories to Visual Narratives: Re-presenting the Post-September 11 Experiences of the Muslim Women in the USA." *Social & Cultural Geography* 9 (6): 653–69. doi:10.1080/14649360802292462.

———. 2012a. "How GIS Can Help Address the Uncertain Geographic Context Problem in Social Science Research." *Annals of GIS* 18 (4): 245–55. doi:10.1080/19475683.2012.727867.

———. 2012b. "The Uncertain Geographic Context Problem." *Annals of the Association of American Geographers* 102 (5): 958–68. doi:10.1080/00045608.2012.687349.

———. 2013. "Beyond Space (As We Knew It): Toward Temporally Integrated Geographies of Segregation, Health, and Accessibility." *Annals of the Association of American Geographers* 103 (5): 1078–86. doi: 10.1080/00045608.2013.792177.

Kwan, M.-P., and G. Ding. 2008. "Geo-Narrative: Extending Geographic Information Systems for Narrative Analysis in Qualitative and Mixed-Method Research." *The Professional Geographer* 60 (4): 443–65. doi:10.1080/ 00330120802211752.

McIntyre, K. 1996. "Geography as Destiny: Cities, villages and Khmer Rouge Orientalism." *Comparative Studies in Society and History* 38 (4): 730–58.

Mennis, J., M. J. Mason, and Y. Cao. 2013. "Qualitative GIS and the Visualization of Narrative Activity Space Data." *International Journal of Geographical Information Science* 27 (2): 267–91.

Mey, C. 2012. *Survivor: The Triumph of an Ordinary Man in the Khmer Rouge Genocide*. Phnom Penh: Documentation Center of Cambodia.

Mills, J. W., E. Shiau, B. Lowery, D. Sloane, K. Hennigan, and A. Curtis. 2014. "The Prospects and Problems of Integrating Sketch Maps with Geographic Information Systems (GIS) to Understand Environmental Perception: A Case Study of Mapping Youth Fear in Los Angeles Gang Neighborhoods." *Environment and Planning B, Planning and Design* 41 (2): 251–71.

Nhem, B. 2013. *The Khmer Rouge: Ideology, Militarism, and the Revolution That Consumed a Generation*. Santa Barbara, CA: Praeger.

Pinchevski, A. 2012. "The Audiovisual Unconscious: Media and Trauma in the Video Archive for Holocaust Testimonies." *Critical Inquiry* 39 (1): 142–66.

Ponchaud, F. 1978. *Cambodia Year Zero*. Translated by Nancy Amphoux. New York: Holt, Rinehart, and Winston.

Presner, T., D. Shepard, and Y. Kawano. 2014. *HyperCities: Thick Mapping in the Digital Humanities*. Cambridge, MA: Harvard University Press.

Rice, S. and J. Tyner. 2017. "The Rice Cities of the Khmer Rouge: An Urban Political Ecology of Rural Mass Violence." *Transactions of the Institute of British Geographers* 42 (4): 559–71.

Schuch, L., A. Curtis, and Joel Davidson. 2017. "Reducing Lead Exposure Risk to Vulnerable Populations: A Proactive Geographic Solution." *Annals of the Association of American Geographers* 107 (3): 606–24.

Seng, V. 2005. *The Price We Paid: A Life Experience in the Khmer Rouge Regime, Cambodia*. Lincoln, NE: iUniverse.

Shaw, M. 2004. "New Wars of the City: Relationships of 'Urbicide' and 'Genocide.'" In *Cities, War, and Terrorism: Towards an Urban Geopolitics*, edited by S. Graham, 141–53. Malden, MA: Blackwell.

Southall, H. 2014. "Rebuilding the Great Britain Historical GIS, Part 3: Integrating Qualitative Content for a Sense of Place." *Historical Methods: A Journal of Quantitative and Interdisciplinary History* 47 (1): 31–44.
Tuan, Y.-F. 1977. *Space and Place: The Perspective of Experience*. Minneapolis: University of Minnesota Press.
Tyner, J. A. 2014. "Violence, Surplus Production, and the Transformation of Nature During the Cambodian Genocide." *Rethinking Marxism* 26 (4): 490–506.
———. 2017. *From Rice Fields to Killing Fields: Nature, Life, and Labor under the Khmer Rouge*. Syracuse, NY: Syracuse University Press.
Tyner, J. A., S. Henkin, S. Sirik, and S. Kimsroy. 2014. "Phnom Penh during the Cambodian Genocide: A Case of Selective Urbicide." *Environment and Planning A* 46 (8): 1873–91.
Tyner, J. A., and R. Will. 2015. "Nature and Post-Conflict Violence: Water Management Under the Communist Party of Kampuchea, 1975–1979." *Transactions of the Institute of British Geographers* 40 (3): 362–74.
Ung, L. 2000. *First They Killed My Father: A Daughter of Cambodia Remembers*. New York: Harper Collins.
Vickery, M. 1984. *Cambodia, 1975–1982*. Chiang Mai: Silkworm Books.
———. 1988. "How Many Died in Pol Pot's Kampuchea?" *Bulletin of Concerned Asian Scholars* 20: 377–85.

5

NORMALISED ALTERITY

Visualising Black Spatial Humanities[1]

Darius Scott

Introduction

Digitally innovated geospatial tools have arguably come to offer opportunities for more just representations (Crang 2015; Offen 2013). Projects like Motor City Mapping and Detroit Food Map exemplify the purchase of such representations, which are shaped with input from on-the-ground perspectives in defiance of hegemonic map-making traditions. These digital projects support claims that the yet growing practice of creating StoryMaps and other media-embedded sorts democratises the means of making what we consider cartography (Caquard 2013; Corner 2011). What, then, is there to currently say for the cartographic enterprise at large's legacy of racism? Further, what possibilities are there for minding the alterity of Black spatial collectivity given the potentials of digital media beyond the whole of mapping? In the summer of 2016, academics from around the United States gathered to address such questions for the NEH Institute on Space and Place in Africana/Black Studies.

Broadly speaking, we came together at the Institute out of concern for how African and African diasporic spaces might be better represented via digital technology and media. We shared our research and listened to trailblazers who presented projects like the Virtual Harlem Project, which uses immersive virtual reality to represent the Black cultural mecca Harlem in the 1920s–1930s (Carter n.d.; Johnson et al. 2002). With a focus on space and digital technology, conventional geospatial technology took a central place in the collective toolkit of the institute participants. Presenters like Judith Madera, author of *Black Atlas: Geography and Flow in Nineteenth-Century African American Literature* (2015), furthered this theme. As a consequence, one of three weeks was dedicated largely to learning how to better use different GIS technologies. Such a focus on the map reflects a trend in digital humanities undertakings and "an emerging focus on the role that geospatial technologies can have in engaging with the history of race across the African Diaspora" (Kim 2017, 1). However, a focus on GIS gives pause considering how anti-Blackness has been advanced via geospatial representations such as redlining (Lipsitz 2011). Indeed this function of mapping continues as GIS contemporarily empowers violent state terror against Black communities vis-à-vis the likes of predictive crime mapping (Jefferson 2018).

With a critical need for disempowering maps as forces of racial violence and inequity, more critical uses of geospatial technology like those advanced by some institute participants are critical. For instance, the Ward uses digital mapping to enliven the maps in W.E.B. Du Bois'

 DOI: 10.4324/9781003082798-7

The Philadelphia Negro, which demarcated the economic diversity of the city's Seventh Ward, a vibrant Black community ("The Ward Race and Class in Du Bois' Seventh Ward" n.d.). Along-side the maps, the public history project aimed at high school students presents oral histories and a board game, which introduces audiences to Du Bois' rigorous analysis, which itself sought to problematise myopic, oversimplified understandings of Black communities.

The Ward and similar digital mapping projects are important for informing the public of histories and places at risk of being forgotten. However, in this article, I broach the inherent limitations of geospatial technology for visualising narrated and contested sites of Black collectivity even in light of recent critical cartographic engagements with narrative (Caquard 2013; Wood 2013). My analysis emerges from the conclusion of the institute and follow-up workshop that set two tasks: (1) crafting a book project reflecting our collective efforts and (2), more generally, identifying the ground that holds our multidisciplinary work together. We named both "Black spatial humanities." I aim to consider how such a dual intellectual project, Black spatial humanities, might be more critical of geospatial technology and its limitations. I then propose digital animation as one potential countermapping alternative specifically for narrated sites of Black collectivity that have been historically obscured and mismanaged via geospatial technologies.

Background

To substantiate inquiry, I turn to animations created in collaboration with a professional animator. These brief animated clips feature oral histories from rural, historically African American communities in Piedmont, North Carolina, which were the focus of the Southern Oral History Program's Back Ways project. The visualised communities were built around back ways or historic wagon roads that led to and from family farms. Despite their importance, many of the paths were never shown on official road maps. Accounts of them are embedded in oral history interviewees' stories of growing up as well as in passed down genealogical anecdotes. These stories and anecdotes refute the blank space of dominant maps that omit the wagon roads. In critical cartography, a growing interest in the narrative-cartography relationship offers some guidance for reckoning with such oral countermapping (Caquard 2013; Leszczynski 2015; Maharawal and McElroy 2018). However, while this work may offer allied support for Black spatial humanities, the back ways narratives show that objects that counter maps need not be some alternative versions of the maps themselves.

As I hope to make clear, practitioners of Black spatial humanities have an opportunity to clarify the distinction between the scope of representable space and the established boundaries of critical cartographies. Black spatial humanities and its digital representations of space could manifest via means of representing space beyond cartographic visualisations and critically assessing the purchase of cartography. As is well-known in geography, dominant constructions of maps arose in the 1500s to help growing Western empires control wide swaths of territory. Critical cartographers theorise the ongoing role of the map from the scale of global empires to that of local governments (Pickles 2004; Wood, Fels, and Krygier 2010). Indeed, cartographic representations are never neutral but always at the service of the state.

Among critical cartographers and GIS researchers alike, narrative has been identified as one way to decentre seemingly neutral representations of space (Caquard 2013; Kwan 2008; Kwan and Ding 2008). Such work aligns with core suggestions in Black geographies literature, a likely locus of Black spatial humanities thought (McKittrick and Woods 2007). However, there are pertinent differences between critical cartography and Black geographies when it comes to representations of space. While core critiques of cartographic approaches find fault with the dominant maps' normativity (Knowles, Westerveld, and Strom 2015; Wood, Fels, and Krygier 2010), Black spatial humanities has the potential to recognise the normativity of Black spatial representation as a matter of promoting radically different understandings of space – ones where narrated Black collectivity predicates place rather than cartographic positioning. This article examines the potential importance of "regularity." Rather than eschew all order, Black productions "*reconfigure* classificatory spatial practices" (McKittrick and Woods 2007, 5, emphasis added). In meditating on non-cartographic representations of Black spatial productions, this article, therefore, also takes up the task of "embracing the normative" (Olson and Sayer 2009) in consideration of Black spatial humanities.

The argument that I advance begins with the premise that Black life's demarcations of space with narrative have been subject to some normative regulatory forces born out of alterity. The preservation of these narrative demarcations depends on such regulation. As detailed by Black geographies scholars, such as Clyde Woods, Katherine McKittrick, and Angel David Nieves, the critical study of Black space must account for the practical rigidity of humanistic processes such as storytelling to counteract underdeveloped analysis, particularly those that simply enumerate the physical conditions of Black neighbourhoods (Woods 2002).

The Measure of Black Geographies

The interdisciplinary field of Black geographies focuses on the production of space by narrative and lived experience. Its contemporary framework is often traced to the work of Clyde Woods and Katherine McKittrick, both of whom have described their work explicitly as "Black geographies" (McKittrick and Woods 2007). I focus on Black geographies here through the work of Kathryn McKittrick, Clyde Woods, and Sylvia Wynter (2000, 2006), as well as work included in and resolutely followed by their text *Black Geographies and the Politics of Place*. Work in the interdisciplinary field focuses on the collective emplacement of Black people in contexts of disenfranchising dominant and state-led economic or infrastructural development (Inwood 2011; Woods 1998). Such development, like urban renewal and interstate highway building, intensifies uneven participation in modernisation along racial lines (Bullard et al. 2007; McKittrick 2011).

Modernising state development and planning facilitates new rationales for uneven participation or the disproportionate burden of environmental harms. Meanwhile, the metrics of modernisation ignore the vitality of Black communities. The too-frequent result is that Black communities appear suited for unwanted by-products of modernising development, including ultimate demise. This is seen in countless cases of waste facilities plotted in historically Black neighbourhoods (Pulido 1996; Woods 2002). From planners' views, Black communities often appear as uniform sites of dilapidation and pathology rather than places of community, family, and history (Pulido 1996, 2000). Black geographic scholarship provides a less morbid view of these communities and those living in them.

Black geographies foster a growing recognition that historical Black emplacement implicates collective refutation of the West's racial misnamings (Hawthorne 2019). Disseminated traditions, stories, and ways of navigation draw forth an alternative, self-determined understanding of Black identities outside of denigrating representations (McKittrick 2006; Nieves 2007). Black geographies demand we look beyond dominant narratives of victimised communities to see the vitality at stake when the state fails to recognise the ongoing importance of historical narrative and lived experience (Woods 1998, 2002). Rather than translating radical Black geographic spaces into the language of cartography, however radical, we must altogether reconfigure the ways we know spaces to be demarcated and sustained. These ways are hardly outside normative conditions.

Between Place and Narrative

Critical cartographic work with narrative calls for more attention to history, artistic expression, and subjective experience (Bodenhamer, Corrigan, and Harris 2015; Caquard 2013; Peterle 2018; Tally 2014; Wood 2013). One part of this complements humanists' recent reckoning with a historical concern for cartographic representations that have gone without adequate reflection (Offen 2013). Other humanists and cultural geographers have joined long-standing critical cartographic explorations of what digitalisation and increased accessibility mean for more humanistic visualisations of space (Crang 2015; Knowles, Westerveld, and Strom 2015). Following the maxim of maps producing place, critical cartography projects consider how the accessibility of online map interfaces, like Google Maps, might allow laymen to "play" with the territories and places wrought by cartographic visualisations (Corner 2011; Pickles 2004). Concerns with democratisation parallel arguments in history suggesting digital accessibility might usher in a welcomed upset of who gets to say exactly what archives are during their digital renovations (Cohen and Rosenzweig 2006). Alongside these vibrant, transdisciplinary conversations in journals such as *GeoHumanities*, there are others reminding scholars to remain mindful of cartography's fundamental shortcomings even as it attends to more humanistic matters like narratives (Rose 2016).

In *Rethinking the Power of Maps* (2010), "Talking Back to The Map," Wood et al. lament the failure of public participation GIS (PPGIS) to de-hegemonise the business of mapping: "I'd have to say, despite the high idealism and great goodwill of perhaps all its practitioners, that PPGIS is scarcely GIS, intensely hegemonic, hardly public, and anything but participatory" (160). The text goes on to decry the lack of similarities between PPGIS projects and the countermapping work of Debord and the Situationists, who embraced emotion while constructing more complete GISs based on localised subjective experience. The creation of the Situationist maps, for instance, began with *dérives* through the city streets of Paris. Eschewing the order imposed by power broking planners like Le Corbusier, Debord created *The Naked City* map. It was arranged with cutout portions of Parisian maps interspersed with swirling arrows to suggest the subjective and meandering in-and-out flows of *dérives*. The work serves as a reminder that concerns with emotion and subjectivity that are missing from dominant spatial visualisations have not been entirely lost on contemporary geographic visualisation, even as they constitute the margins of that particular analytic and empirical examples.

In cultural geography, there is a substantial number of recent and notable methodological undertakings which follow the tradition of Debord and the Situationists. These are methods empowered by a long-standing reaction to ordering, dominant cartographic representations. They embrace anything but abstract outputs. Analyses by Knowles, Westerveld, and Strom (2015) promote inductive visualisation, which privileges the emotions and narratives of Holocaust survivor testimonies rather than attempting to contort them to fit any sort of conventional GIS visualisation. The visualisations take the shape of two-dimensional pictorial and chart-like timelines with no prescribed form. It follows that these visualisations might avoid conforming to what Wood, Fels, and Krygier (2010) lambast as the "normative goal" of PPGIS to "construe the public monolithically, as a people united about ends, if divided over means" (162). This is taken to include work like Kwan and Ding's (2008), which makes efforts to humanise GIS with oral history and personal accounts.

Considering the tension between these PPGIS projects and abstract work like the inductive visualisation of Holocaust testimonies, I am inclined to question some discursive work surrounding cartography for Black spatial humanities. By seemingly assigning normative legibility and fixedness exclusively to the likes of maps, counter-projects are potentially left as the makings of fatally incomprehensible visual representations of space. In other words, counter-cartography loses its potential to legibly represent. This critique of cartography then runs the risk of assigning already marginalised perspectives or people as being unrepresentable, the spatial equivalent of those in the margins having "names their captors would not recognize" (Spillers 1987, 72). In criticising PPGIS supporters who tout its legibility to politicians, Wood, Fels, and Krygier (2010) says, "[W]hat [the supporters] really mean is that the message has been reframed into the language of regulation" (164). I am inclined to think that for Black spatial humanities, regulation might not be regarded so negatively. Olson and Sayer (2009, 181) argue that much critical geographic work has "become increasingly reticent about making its critiques and their standpoints or rationales explicit, or has softened its critiques, so that in some quarters being critical has reduced to trying merely to 'unsettle' some ideas or to being reflexive." In this sense, "normative" means making evaluative claims via notions of good and bad, flourishing and suffering. I am moved to consider the normative work inherent in the place-charting narratives of the back ways communities and other Black geographies. They have been mobilised repeatedly in efforts to have outsiders readily know of embattled land uses and tenures. In this way, I consider the telling of the narratives countermapping, which problematises the nowhere-at-all-ness in which conventional maps place Black life with family anecdotes and oft-recounted community sentiments.[2]

When I recorded the narratives of the back ways communities, their space-charting qualities were readily apparent. These narratives made the communities at once material and historical, and they have been mobilised in grassroots political fights against local North Carolina governments and in the preservation of the communities themselves. They call for representation that reflects their intelligibility. While visualisations like Debord's are important and undeniably politically engaged, we must not ignore the allure or comprehensibility of dominant cartographic representation as we attempt to counter it. I do not mean to discount the intellectual projects of Knowles, Westerveld, and Strom (2015) and Wood et al. (2010), in teasing out the flattenings and endless ethical quandaries posed by creating visual representations of space within traditional GIS. On the contrary, I agree with such underlying critique and the "intensely hegemonic" fate of PPGIS "as we know it." I am weary of even public GIS projects, about which Woods (2002) and McKittrick (2006, 2011) offer critiques and which raise questions about the empirical, positivist nature of mapping that naturalises, or presents as merely factual, the material conditions of African American neighbourhoods. At the same time, I am aligned with the call of PPGIS projects like those lambasted by Wood, which moves us to assess the social justice impacts of countermapping in albeit normative contexts. Most importantly, however, I recognise intelligibility as an important motivation for Black spatial humanities, though not one for which the holistic alterity of Black productions should be sacrificed.

In the context of the Back Ways interviews, following the edicts of Wood, Fels, and Krygier (2010) might mean over-determining the partiality of some accounts from narrators and failing to mind the ways such accounts are at work to *uphold* totalising views and productions of space. If we accept Woods' (1998) claim that the blues establishes an entire epistemology that challenges a global plantation logic, it stands to reason that it might accommodate worldviews of its own, albeit ones characteristically cast from localised positions (i.e. the Mississippi Delta). Through cadence and melody, the blues configures all it touches through its doubly critical and "just music" work. By committing ourselves solely to partiality and tensions, we fail to account for that which is not in tension per se or that which is creative and unifying rather than confrontational. Such creativity may be subversive yet like the blues or a personal recount of some back way. For the digital productions of Black spatial humanities, dualistic thinking (i.e. legibility vs criticality) distorts and discounts the potential variability of abstraction – that is, the abstract is always posited as most dominant and never subversive but always subverted. I wager that the potential of Black spatial humanities is partly hinged on overcoming the prevalence of this dualistic thinking.

Practical Matters and Representing the Back Ways

By centring oral histories, the Back Ways project draws from the life stories of African Americans who have lived around historic wagon roads in Orange County (NC) through the 20th century and onwards. The interviewees weave long road narratives in their personal histories covering birth, school, work, marriage, and the achievement of old age. Though the work of Black geographies scholarship has improved critical knowledge-making practices of racialised geographies of the American South, we do not know how such sites may be critically conceptualised via digital media. The first-hand accounts provide one way of attending to the interrelated benefits and difficulties of life on the back way.

Telling the stories of formerly obscured and marginalised African American communities in the US South like those of the back ways requires methodologies for accessing previously unrecorded data, along with analysis and presentation approaches that may counter the dehumanisation resulting from many of our whitewashed histories. Doing so advances existing research on the back ways of North Carolina and efforts to develop alternative digital expressions of place and space that better express the concerns of Black geographies. At the 2016 NEH Black Spatial Humanities Institute, I began designing a new digital humanities project to facilitate analysing, curating, and sharing the oral history-recorded experiences of back ways community members. Simply, the work is meant to visualise oral history clips with animation similar in form to common television cartoons. The clips illuminate unique Black geographic information through first-hand accounts of living in the spaces and through passed-down stories of elders doing so. The visualisations illustrate the spatial practices of individual community members, like the chore of drawing water from a creek, along with transformations of the landscape, such as the development of the road. The work is meant to yield more critical and accurate representations of communities formed around the roads.

Orange County, the location of the back ways communities, is the home of the University of North Carolina at Chapel Hill. According to the US Census, it has the highest median household income in the state, and its schools are recognised as being the best in North Carolina. Despite its notable progressive political leaning, Orange County, as described by the interviewees, is also noted for intense interracial tensions that include violence and harassment over the 20th and 21st centuries. One back ways interviewee, for instance, Dr Freddie Parker, recounts the violent transition from attending the all-Black Central High School to the newly desegregated Orange County High School in the 1960s: "It was rough, a lot of bloodshed." His history laments a lack of foresight afforded to his community's demand for desegregation:

> I don't think we really had the foresight to see what it really meant because if you decide that you're going to bring the walls of segregation down, the white students are not coming to your school.

Across shifts like school desegregation occurring in the encompassing interracial Orange County, the rural and historically agricultural back ways communities are characterised as maintaining a sense of accommodating normalcy for its residents, which is, however, as precarious as it is essential to the everyday and historical emplacements for those residents and their families. The back ways, historic wagon roads used by Black farming families, themselves evidence the grounded nature of the communities that emerged around them – communities with histories of land cultivation and inhabited heirs' property. Some residents who contributed their oral histories are as much community historians by living on inherited property along a back way for as long as nine decades and descending from back ways community founders. Indeed, the histories lie with them and not in any official archives. Meanwhile, the narrated coordinates of community boundaries uniquely lie in those histories due to the historical denial of community recognition on the part of local governments. Some back ways communities lie in formally marginalised zones called extraterritorial jurisdictions.[3] In the context of the Back Ways project, all are described with nods to antagonistic county-community relations.

Back ways represent communities' historical exclusion from state transportation mapping, surveillance, and development. In oral history interviews, participants explain that this widespread exclusion is said to have contributed to community and family autonomy from hostile government policies. For those who live along them and use them, the roads are often presented as entangled components of century-long family histories which anchor the community to the physical environment. Recent development and modernisation of these roads through paving and other forms of "improvement" ignore the communities' historical and racialised emplacement. However, road improvements draw forth how erasures arise when the communities are delineated with US Census blocks and natural features of the landscape. Narrative and heritage are considered too messy even when recognised as important factors to consider in such development processes (Louis Berger Group 2001).

Indeed, there is little applied work that minds space-charting accounts of communal subjectivity and historical experiences with the actual impact assessments of communities in local and regional development projects in the US South and elsewhere. It is through such understanding that regulation, which I am interpreting here as the systematised narration of historical Black geographies by those principally residing in them, might be important for representing spaces of Black collectivity. Without doing so, we fail to reckon with the integrity of these real sites of historical and ongoing collectivity. Indeed, these sites have had to be both othered and reliable. They require communities' regulation of knowledge and call for representation that is sufficiently accommodating.

Centring personal accounts facilitates minding the steadfastness of back ways communities like Rogers Road. Population counts and geographic coordinates do not relay their historical depth and intergenerational importance. Without featuring the narratives in spatial representations, the community risks being rendered as an area where Black people have happened to live for some time. The road would not be understood as a binding locus for the families who live there. While the narratives that do provide this information are performed and recited, thus not fleeting or ungraspable, visually representing them is a difficult undertaking. Even so, it is an important one for such legibility and communication.

The inclusion of multimedia animation is somewhat novel in historical accounts of Black life in the US South. My choice of this medium is based on its ability to allow for temporal representations of spatial dynamics, such as a community's formation over the 20th century (Johnson 2002). Further, empirical work in geography has found it to be better suited for promoting course material retention (Crooks, Verdi, and White 2005; Edsall and Wentz 2007), a point that is perhaps especially important to take into account when communicating marginalised histories that have been violently erased from the landscape and our public knowledge. Animation is characteristically familiar and engaging. While the reading and interpretation of maps may be intimidating to viewers, engagement with animation is intended to be approachable while also clearly implying their obvious representative character. Cartoons, as commonly consumed media, are already recognised for being subjective and partial compared to the feigned immutability of maps, however public. This empowers potential involvement to include community members' robust critique of what is being produced rather than acquiescent compliance for fear of getting something wrong or not understanding. As an output, animation stands to be considerably more accessible to diverse audiences. Indeed, spatial work is bound to continually struggle to engage with supposed public-faced digital projects that require a specific literacy, even if they do so out of reluctance to oversimplify.

Because of this ease of access and legibility, the communication of unique spatial information is more likely. This is important as the primary point of the animation is to have people know of Black geographic space singularly demarcated by personal and community narratives. The animations depict life at the scales of the home and the community in the rural back ways enclaves. Having these two scales of animation establishes the historical depth of the farming communities established around wagon roads. The underappreciated space-demarcating practices accorded to Black geographies are too important to toy around with obfuscation. We must be attentive to the robust alterity that Black communities have counted on for generations now.

The Process of Creating Animations

For this research, three animations were created with a professional animator. These clips came from the set of Back Ways interviews. The first step of the process was to isolate three pertinent oral history clips in which interviewees relay some spatial detail of the community's shape and historical presence, with features that emplace people and portray them as dwelling in and interacting with the landscape. The interviewees chosen for these animations were in their 80s and 90s. The clips were taken from a collection of already coded and analysed transcripts. The process involved combing through the pre-coded clips to determine which were most suitable for animation. The criteria used limited clips to accounts of movement through community space (i.e. walking to church) that were succinctly shared in the interest of short animation capability. The clips that were eventually chosen are rich and moving examples of everyday life in the back ways communities. After the clips were selected, they were individually edited with Adobe Premier to improve the quality of the audio and order the narrative if necessary. Editing on Premier sometimes involved rearranging the order information was spoken to account for backtracking and achieve greater clarity of the geographic features and events involved in the narrative. The results of such editing are described in Table 5.1

The editing was essential for giving the animator a clear story to depict. As is the case with the original transcription presented previously, Harold Russell describes several different scenes related to the life of the church when asked about its general history. Illustrating all of the details of his oral history, with the looping and bypassing of time, would have been challenging for the animator due to financial constraints. This, therefore, required limiting the length of animation clips, and not all parts of a coherent narrative could be included in the animation. Each of the three animations was limited to ~30 seconds, which meant that certain portions of the narrative, like Harold's sister being left at the church, had to be removed. Care was given to ensure the clips remained true to the content described in the oral histories throughout the process of animation. No editing occurred to alter the meaning of Harold and the other interviewees' accounts. Nonetheless, it is important to clarify that these representations are not more comprehensive in their data coverage than a cartographic representation of the same space. They are similarly selective, though the types of spatial data that are selected for representation are very different from those that might be selected for cartographic mapping.

Table 5.1 Comparison of Original Transcript Text and Text of Excerpt Edited for Animation.

ORIGINAL TRANSCRIPT	*EDITED FOR ANIMATION*
HR: My parents, my grandparents across the street, and my mother used to walk through the woods from there, across the street, up to that church, about four miles. DS: Wow. And how do you think the roads got in such bad condition? Or do you think it was more just people started driving more and needed to use the roads? HR: I don't think the roads never were in good condition. It never was a through road where actually cars drove through. It was just a road to the church and then out. So, it wasn't a state road that was kept by the state or anything. It was just a road that they created. That's the way I understand it. DS: Okay. And if you know any stories or have any experiences, how did the congregation of the church react to the idea of relocating it initially? HR: I think that they were. This is what I hear. I don't know for sure. DS: Okay. And – HR: I remember going to the old church years ago. But my sister says she remembers going to my great-grandmother's funeral there, and it's a story that she remembers. They forgot her and left her standing out there. DS: Oh no! HR: And it was in the winter. [Laughs] So, they were wondering where she was. I think at that time they were driving. I can look up the date. But they went back and they found her, and she was standing out there crying. DS: Gosh. At the funeral? HR: I heard one story about somebody – they were having service once, and somebody saw a snake come down the wall. [Laughs] So.	I remember going to the old church years ago. It was on an area called Seven Mile Creek. My grandparents, across the street, and my mother used to walk from there, across the street, up to that church – about four miles. They were having service once, and somebody saw a snake come down the wall.

The clips selected for animation communicated vibrant instances of life within three back ways community spaces. Each is taken from a separate oral history interview collected in the summer and fall of 2014. The selected segments depict scenes of everyday life in the historically agricultural Black communities of Orange County. The scenes cover the holistic and encompassing life community members were able to have all within these rural spaces of collectivity and include themes of healthcare and religious observance. As described previously, Harold Russell's clip depicts how his family walked four miles through the woods to reach a wooded church site. Mary Cole describes how her childhood home served as the space for church service and how she had to move the furniture weekly to accommodate the congregation. Gertrude Nunn discusses how her mother sent her to get spring water and mended her brother's leg within the home space after he cut it badly with an axe. These clips were chosen for the vividness of the descriptions and the ease by which I reasoned an animator would be able to depict the words spoken.

Everyday Methods of Collaborating for an Animated Project

The process of hiring a professional animator was facilitated by a website called Upwork.com, which matches freelancing creative professionals, such as animators and sound editors, with job opportunities. I selected this service due to its transparency and reputable standing. Those in need of service can post advertisements for jobs along with a fixed price for the task. The following figure is an image of the call for an animator as it appeared on the website. After posting it, I was able to invite animators to place bids based on their public portfolios, which are also accessible for browsing on the website. Other non-invited animators were able to also place bids for the job. The animator I worked with, Stella Rosen, was invited to undertake the job based on the look and quality of her previous animations. Once invited, Stella accepted the position, and we entered a contract.

After securing the contract, Stella and I corresponded and exchanged media via the Upwork website's messaging feature. I shared the first clip with her and described the scene as it is described in the clip itself to ensure that she identified the key features. I also provided photographs of time-/region-appropriate clothing and scenery from the Yale Photogrammar repository. Finally, I provided some background information about the person speaking, such as age and tenure in the community space, as well as the community space itself (i.e. its status as a family farm). Within a day, Stella delivered a video storyboard of the animation, which is depicted in the following figure. This storyboard provided a rough play of the animation and its contents. Upon receiving feedback, Stella then altered the storyboard and sent an updated version, which is also depicted in the following figure. This process of revising the storyboard occurred with all three clips, with them all going through two or three rounds of storyboard revisions. For example, with the first clip, I requested that the speaker be depicted as a young girl witnessing the story and that her action of running to a spring for water be included, which were not shown on the initial storyboard as shown in the following figure. Having these aspects animated were critical for the overarching goal of the animations being the humanising of long-disregarded rural sites of Black collectivity. Such sites have been historically unmapped and considered merely wooded and meagre. The animations were meant to highlight the evidence of rich livelihoods that occur within the rural spaces themselves, along with the people who have lived within them.

Both of the depictions in Figures 5.1 and 5.2 are taken from the same mark in time. They are shown to illustrate the transformation of the animations' eventual content per the aims of the project, which were to ensure that representations were also populated with the gaze of the creator of the content (i.e. the oral history participant). The process of producing these illustrations was made easier by the responsiveness and talent of the animator and was supported by my clarity when contracting her; I was careful to convey that I intended to show how the communities from which the stories come to exist and make their histories tangible. She was receptive to such an aim, and it showed in the work she was able to produce.

Figure 5.1 The first draft of the clip storyboard.

Figure 5.2 A revised draft of the clip storyboard.

The Final Animations

The animations are colourful, dynamic depictions of everyday life in three different historically Black back ways communities in rural Orange County, North Carolina. They show the actions of community residents against and with the surrounding rural environments to the effect of humanising the often-disregarded landscape. Oftentimes, such populated Black environments are discursively marginalised or altogether elided in dominant representations of space. Indeed, as Price (2004) notes, exclusion of racialised peoples to such discursive unmapping in the wild is critical to the function of Western understanding of place. Such exclusion, in the form of cartographic erasure and otherwise, allows local governments to disregard the robustness and life within the sites of Black spatial collectivity. This then eases the facilitation of harmful land use, like the placement of a landfill in the Rogers Road community, which is the setting of one of the animations. The map then is a historically polarising tool of exploitation and harm for these communities. In light of this, the three animations provide some alternative means of counter-mapping without reinvigorating the potentially hostile function of the map itself.

Animation 1: https://vimeo.com/263541225 (Password: backways)

In the first animation (Figure 5.3), Harold Russell describes the wooded site of his family's historic church. Harold Russell is a community elder who returned to his rural enclave following a career in chemistry. He received his PhD from Cornell University. Harold Russell has taken on the unofficial role of historian for Harvey's Chapel, a church founded by his ancestors and the one he attends today. Part of his historical work has involved going a search for the original church site's land deed and attempting to uncover how the church came to be located in a relatively remote location. The location of the church is the focus of Russel's animation clip.

The clip opens with Harold stating that he remembers going to the church many years ago, which is shown surrounded by trees. Two birds fly across the sky as the screen pans across the mass of greenery before settling on the home of Harold's grandparents as he names the location of the church "near Seven Mile Creek." Harold is then heard recounting how his mother, in her youth, and his grandparents would walk four miles from their home to the church as a regular practice while the animation depicts them strolling through tall grasses and shrubbery. Though simpler than the other two clips in terms of action, this animation illustrates the wide-ranging forested landscape that sets the historic collectivity of Harold's family and community.

The animation concludes with Harold telling how someone once saw a snake slither down the wall of the church. By depicting the woods and the church's emplacement side-by-side, the animation shows how the rural and natural environments are intertwined. It implicates the

Figure 5.3 Animation for Harold Russell's oral history.

ways that the natural environment vis-à-vis the greenery and the snake betray the emplacement rather than the absence of human collectivity vis-à-vis the church. The wilderness, typically depicted as a blank space on the map, is portrayed as a setting for Harold's family mobility and his community's coming together.

Animation 2: https://vimeo.com/263541003 (Password: backways)

In the second animation, featuring Mary Cole (see Figure 5.4), she recounts moving furniture in her childhood home weekly to make room for church services. Today, she is a community elder whose father bought the land that came to be a community epicentre. Including providing space for religious worship, her father's land also accommodates a sizable farm and the residences of some of Cole's relatives. Throughout her oral history, Cole recounts the effort and activities that went into her home serving as a community space – the bubbling kitchen and myriad relations coloured her childhood experiences. Also, the status of her home as a community space involved work on her part, which is recounted in her clip about moving furniture before worship service.

The animation opens with a shot of her family house. The sun replaces the moon to show how the services and need for moving furniture occurred mornings and nights. On Wednesday nights, her family hosted bible study while congregants showed up for worship services on Sunday mornings. Such weekly day and night activity undergirds the status of their home as the designated site for the church. The animation then moves to the inside of the home, where a preacher is shown delivering a sermon.

Mary narrates the scene relaying how different preachers would come to lead the congregation. The scene then shows a crowd of people as Mary recounts how many people would come to attend the services. Such depiction enlivens the historic communal centrality of Mary Cole's family land.

The animation concludes with a young Mary being shown struggling to move a sofa as she recounts having to move the furniture to accommodate the crowd. The animation concludes with a flashing view of the room that held the congregants, now shown as a living space full of

Figure 5.4 Animation for Mary Cole's oral history.

furniture – sofa, vases, end tables, and a coffee table – as Mary recalls vowing to never move her furniture so much again as an adult.

Animation 3: https://vimeo.com/263540643 (Password: backways)

The third animation illustrates an emergency from the childhood of Gertrude Nunn, where her mother sent her to fetch water from a nearby spring to treat her brother's wound (see Figure 5.5). Nunn has spent decades living in the rural community that she currently calls home, Rogers Road. She is a well-known matriarch of Rogers Road, which is named after her father. She has also acted as an advocate for the community – organising and speaking out against the placement of an ill-conceived landfill. She recounts such instances of modernisation and how they have affected life in the community space. Reflecting on earlier times, like the one in her animation, she recalls an aspect of self-sufficiency in times of crisis that may now be gone.

The animation opens with a young Gertrude turning toward a developing pasture scene of cows grazing. Immediately, the agricultural setting is established with the livestock and the Gertrude, recalling the everyday practice of having to take them out to graze. Her brother's injury was a result of his carrying an axe while taking them to do so. At this point, the scene turns to a disembodied axe in the centre of the screen. The animation carries on with Gertrude recounting how the axe fell off her brother's shoulder and badly cut his leg. The animation then depicts the disembodied axe in the centre falling to create an also disembodied wound at the bottom of the screen. As Gertrude recalls blood flowing out vigorously, the screen is filled with a fluid pale red hue. The scene then turns to an alert young Gertrude running from the spring as commanded by her mother with an overflowing pail of water in hand. The healing effect of the water is implicated in what follows. Gertrude recalls her mother cleaning the wound with water, packing it with mud and a felt hat, and then wrapping it with a clean cloth. These actions are depicted one by one.

They are all disembodied. The relationship between the resources of the land – fresh spring water – and the well-being of the community are represented by the animation via the healing

Figure 5.5 Animation for Gertrude Nunn's oral history.

of Gertrude's brother via her mother's knowledge. The animation closes with her remembering how the wound heals, leaving her brother with no complications.

Conclusion

The animations produced here were able to depict stories of life in the back ways communities. By just listening to the recorded audio or reading through the transcripts, it is easy to miss the particular illuminations of space relayed by the oral history accounts. The animations, however, provoke viewers to reckon with the particularities of day-to-day life in the rural Black collectives. At the same time, the animations presented here are not without limitations. One is the limitation of cost. It took specialised skill to create the animation, which I, like most researchers, do not possess. This meant hiring an independent artist for a limited amount of animation. Naturally, the vast bulk of the spatial account contained in the back ways interviews were left out. Relatedly, the need to hire an independent contractor meant the process of creating them had to be done by someone without much knowledge of the research project – Stella is a professional animator who, by no fault of her own, is not knowledgeable about Black geographic and critical cartographic literature or the empirical data that predicates the creation of the three animations.

Future work with animation, like that modelled here, could benefit from more robust partnerships with animators. It could have been useful to have Stella on board at an earlier stage of the project and in thinking through what questions were asked in interviews and what the broad research aims were. Another limitation of animation, here and generally speaking, is the inability to comprehensively represent space. They do not depict how large or populated the communities are. In light of this, it is critical to remain mindful of what scale of space is comparatively represented – that of everyday life, which perhaps makes the lack of comprehensibility a trade-off. With these limitations considered, the animations were still successful in relaying the regularity of occupying the back ways communities as narrated by interviewees.

The regularity of the narratives depicted by the animations is evident in their telling. While Gertrude's daughter was not yet born during the incident, she is heard in the clip, prompting and corroborating the telling of the story. In the portion with Mary Cole, she mentions how she told her kids, as she tells in her oral history, that she vowed to never move furniture in her own home as a result of the previously recounted practice. Harold himself was not yet born when his mother, in her youth, walked with his grandparents to the church; the narrative and its place-illuminating qualities were passed down to him. Also, he recounts the story of the snake, which had been told to him before he told it again. Such is the nature of the narratives, which themselves animate the space of the rural Black communities as historical and lived-in sites of collective self-reliance. To represent such spaces in-depth, we cannot rely on the conventional map. Indeed, such is true for the social depth of all communities.

While cartography provides useful tools for digital humanities and the conduct of Black spatial humanities, the spaces wrought by Black collectivity are likely seldom to find sweeping purchase there. If we take seriously the charge of McKittrick and Woods (2007) that narrative and lived experience determine Black geographic space, we, too, must consider means of representation that accommodate rather than assimilate humanistic matters. In this paper, I invite the reader to consider animation as only one potential means of representing the narratives of individuals from the three Black communities. This means it is undoubtedly incomplete and inadequate to "do the job" of representing the totality of any Black geographic space on its own. We must also consider the possibilities of film, still art, audio, and other sorts, which often are produced from within communities themselves as being representations of space. We, too, must be mindful of the impossibility of the task – representing that which is unfolding and often intently unseen. I hope that this work of aligning the narratives vis-à-vis animations as counter-cartographic and space-demarcating widens the scope of reckoning with such (im) possibilities of alterity represented.

Acknowledgements

The author owes thanks to Angel David Nieves and Kim Gallon, who organised Space and Place in Africana/Black Studies: An Institute on Spatial Humanities Theories, Methods, and Practice for Africana Studies (National Endowment for the Humanities). In addition, the author appreciates the generous feedback of Seth Kotch, Malinda Maynor Lowery, Betsy Olson, Scott Kirsch, Banu Gökarıksel, and the reviewers.

Notes

1 *GeoHumanities*, 00(00) 2021, 1–19 © Copyright 2021 by American Association of Geographers. Initial submission, July 2020; revised submission, February 2021; final acceptance, February 2021. Published by Taylor & Francis Group, LLC.

2 "Nowhere at all" is a construct adapted from Hortense Spillers' 1987 essay, "Mama's Baby, Papa's Maybe: An American Grammar Book."

3 This term is used by governments, in this case, the surrounding city governments, to mark places subject to the authority of their legal power that lie outside of terriorial boundaries. These jurisdictions lack elected political representation.

Sources

Bodenhamer, D., J. Corrigan, and T. M. Harris. 2015. *Deep Maps and Spatial Narratives*. Indiana: Indiana University Press.

Bullard, R., P. Mohai, R. Saha, and B. Wright. 2007. "Toxic Wastes and Race at Twenty 1987–2007." In *A Report Prepared for the United Church of Christ Justice & Witness Ministries*. Cleveland: United Church of Christ.

Caquard, S. 2013. "Cartography I: Mapping Narrative Cartography." *Progress in Human Geography* 37 (1): 135–44. doi:10.1177/0309132511423796.

Carter, B. n.d. "Virtual Harlem." Accessed July 17, 2020. https://scalar.usc.edu/works/harlem-renaissance/index.

Cohen, D. J., and R. Rosenzweig. 2006. *Digital History: A Guide to Gathering, Preserving, and Presenting the Past on the Web*. Philadelphia: University of Pennsylvania Press.

Corner, J. 2011. "The Agency of Mapping: Speculation, Critique and Invention." In *The Map Reader: Theories of Mapping Practice and Cartographic Representation*, 89–101. doi:10.1002/9780470979587.ch12.

Crang, M. 2015. "The Promises and Perils of a Digital Geohumanities." *Cultural Geographies* 22 (2): 351–60. doi:10.1177/ 1474474015572303.

Crooks, S. M., M. P. Verdi, and D. R. White. 2005. "Effects of Contiguity and Feature Animation in Computer-Based Geography Instruction." *Journal of Educational Technology Systems* 33 (3): 259–81. doi:10.2190/NQ6B-3LMA-VMVA-L312.

Edsall, R., and E. Wentz. 2007. "Comparing Strategies for Presenting Concepts in Introductory Undergraduate Geography: Physical Models vs. Computer Visualization." *Journal of Geography in Higher Education* 31 (3): 427–44. doi:10.1080/03098260701513993.

Hawthorne, C. 2019. "Black Matters Are Spatial Matters: Black Geographies for the Twenty-First Century." *Geography Compass* 13 (11). doi:10.1111/gec3.12468.

Inwood, J. F. J. 2011. "Geographies of Race in the American South: The Continuing Legacies of Jim Crow Segregation." *Southeastern Geographer* 51 (4): 564–77. doi:10.1353/sgo.2011.0033.

Jefferson, B. J. 2018. "Predictable Policing: Predictive Crime Mapping and Geographies of Policing and Race." *Annals of the American Association of Geographers* 108 (1): 1–16. doi:10.1080/24694452.2017.1293500.

Johnson, A., J. Leigh, B. Carter, J. Sosnoski, and S. Jones. 2002. "Virtual Harlem." *IEEE Computer Graphics and Applications* 22: 61–67. doi:10.1109/MCG.2002.1028727.

Johnson, N. 2002. "Animating Geography: Multimedia and Communication." *Journal of Geography in Higher Education* 26 (1): 13–18. doi:10.1080/03098260120110331.

Kim, D. J. 2017. "Introductory/Framing Remarks." In *Black Spatial Humanities: Theories, Methods, and Praxis in Digital Humanities (a Follow-Up NEH ODH Summer Institute Panel)*, edited by A. D. Nieves, K. Gallon, D. J. Kim, S. Nesbit, B. Carter, and J. Johnson, 1–2. Montreal: Digital Humanities.

Knowles, A. K., L. Westerveld, and L. Strom. 2015. "Inductive Visualization: A Humanistic Alternative to GIS." *GeoHumanities* 1 (2): 233–65. doi:10.1080/2373566X.2015.1108831.

Kwan, M.-P. 2008. "From Oral Histories to Visual Narratives: Re-presenting the Post-September 11 Experiences of the Muslim Women in the USA." *Social & Cultural Geography* 9 (6): 653–69. doi:10.1080/14649360802292462.

Kwan, M.-P., and G. Ding. 2008. "Geo-Narrative: Extending Geographic Information Systems for Narrative Analysis in Qualitative and Mixed-Method Research." *The Professional Geographer* 60 (4): 443–65. doi:10.1080/ 00330120802211752.

Leszczynski, A. 2015. "Spatial Media/Tion." *Progress in Human Geography* 39 (6): 729–51. doi:10.1177/0309132514558443.

Lipsitz, G. 2011. *How Racism Takes Place*. Philadelphia: Temple University Press.

Louis Berger Group. 2001. *Guidance for Assessing Indirect and Cumulative Impacts of Transportation Projects in North Carolina. Volume I: Guidance Policy Report*. Cary: Louis Berger Group.

Madera, J. 2015. *Black Atlas: Geography and Flow in Nineteenth-Century African American literature*. Durham: Duke University Press.

Maharawal, M. M., and E. McElroy. 2018. "The Anti-Eviction Mapping Project: Counter Mapping and Oral History Toward Bay Area Housing Justice." *Annals of the American Association of Geographers* 108 (2): 380–89. doi:10.1080/ 24694452.2017.1365583.

McKittrick, K. 2006. *Demonic Grounds: Black Women and the Cartographies of Struggle*. Minneapolis: University of Minnesota Press.

———. 2011. "On Plantations, Prisons, and a Black Sense of Place." *Social & Cultural Geography* 12 (8): 947–63. doi:10.1080/14649365.2011.624280.

McKittrick, K., and C. A. Woods. 2007. *Black Geographies and the Politics of Place*. Toronto, ON: Between the Lines.

Nieves, A. D. 2007. "Memories of Africville: Urban Renewal, Reparations, and the Africadian Diaspora." In *Black Geographies and the Politics of Place*, edited by K. McKittrick and C. A. Woods, 82–96. Toronto: Between the Lines.

Offen, K. 2013. "Historical Geography II: Digital Imaginations." *Progress in Human Geography* 37 (4): 564–77. doi:10.1177/0309132512462807.

Olson, E., and A. Sayer. 2009. "Radical Geography and its Critical Standpoints: Embracing the Normative." *Antipode* 41 (1): 180–98. doi:10.1111/j.1467-8330.2008.00661.x.

Peterle, G. 2018. "Carto-fiction: Narrativising Maps through Creative Writing." *Social & Cultural Geography* (January): 1–24. doi:10.1080/14649365.2018.1428820.

Pickles, J. 2004. *A History of Spaces: Cartographic Reason, Mapping, and the Geo-Coded World*. London: Routledge.

Price, P. 2004. *Dry Place: Landscapes of Belonging and Exclusion*. Minneapolis: University of Minnesota Press.

Pulido, L. 1996. "Critical Review of the Methodology Environmental Racism Research." *Antipode* 28 (2): 142–59. doi:10.1111/j.1467-8330.1996.tb00519.x.

———. 2000. "Rethinking Environmental Racism: White Privilege and Urban Development in Southern California." *Annals of the Association of American Geographers* 90 (1): 12–40. doi:10.1111/0004-5608.00182.

Rose, G. 2016. "Rethinking the Geographies of Cultural "Objects" through Digital Technologies." *Progress in Human Geography* 40 (3): 334–51. doi:10.1177/0309132515580493.

Spillers, H. 1987. "Mama's Baby, Papa's Maybe: An American Grammar Book." *Diacritics* 17 (2): 64–81. doi:10.2307/ 464747.

Tally, R. 2014. *Literary Cartographies: Spatiality, Representation, and Narrative*. 1st ed. New York, NY: Palgrave Macmillan.

"The Ward: Race and Class in Du Bois' Seventh Ward." n.d. Accessed July 17, 2020. www.dubois-theward.org/.

Wood, D. 2013. *Everything Sings: Maps for a Narrative Atlas*. 2nd ed. Los Angeles: Siglio.

Wood, D., J. Fels, and J. Krygier. 2010. *Rethinking the Power of Maps*. New York: Guilford Press.

Woods, C. 1998. *Development Arrested: The Blues and Plantation Power in the Mississippi Delta*. London: Verso.
———. 2002. "Life after Death." *The Professional Geographer* 54 (1): 62–66. doi:10.1111/0033-0124.00315.
Wynter, S. 2000. "Beyond Miranda's Meanings: Un-silencing the 'Demonic Ground' of 'Caliban's Woman.'" In *The Black Feminist Reader*, edited by J. James and T. D. Sharpley-Whiting, xiv, 302. Malden, MA: Blackwell Publishers.
———. 2006. "On How We Mistook the Map for the Territory, and Reimprisoned Ourselves in Our Unbearable Wrongness of Being, of Desêtre: Black Studies Toward the Human Project." In *A Companion to African-American Studies*, edited by L. R. Gordon and J. A. Gordon, 107–18. Malden, MA: Wiley-Blackwell.

6

NEW MACHINES IN THE GARDEN

The Digital Environmental Humanities

Charles Travis

> [W]here we are free of our labors
> and joined back to nature,
> [. . .]
> and all watched over
> by machines of loving grace.
>
> – *Richard Brautigan,* All Watched Over By Machines of Loving Grace *(1967)*

Introduction

In the first two decades of the 21st century, the digital revolution and informal age of the Anthropocene have emerged as intimately interwoven phenomena. The former is refiguring scholarship and pedagogy in the humanities of the West, arguably with a similar long-range impact that Johannes Gutenberg's printing press inaugurated in 1440 CE; the latter audaciously posits *Homo sapiens* as a geological force capable of altering our planetary systems. The Oxford neuroscientist Susan Greenfield contends that there are similarities in adapting and mitigating the wicked problem of global warming and addressing sociopolitical disruptions created by 21st-century digital media platforms:

> [T]he human brain will adapt to whatever environment in which it is placed [and] could therefore be changing in parallel, in corresponding new ways. To the extent that we can begin to understand and anticipate these changes positive or negative, we will be able to better navigate this new world.
>
> *(2014, 13)*

The digital revolution is the fruit of transdisciplinary research involving physics, philosophy, logic, computing, linguistics, mathematics, and engineering. Its impact has set silent shockwaves roiling through the halls of the Western academy. Reverberating across its institutional colonial and extractive networks, the revolution has utterly transformed the manner through which data is collected and parsed into information. In turn, it has impacted how information has been

DOI: 10.4324/9781003082798-8

translated into knowledge, and then communicated in the lecture hall, laboratory, peer-reviewed journal and professional conference. As a result, "the scale, diversity, and complexity of the living world come to us through chains of technological mediation and the genres and conventions of screen culture" (Whitelaw and Smaill 2021, 80). Finn Arne Jørgensen (2014, 95) muses that "the idea of nature is becoming very hard to separate from the digital tools and media we use to observe, interpret, and manage it," and John Durham Peters (2015, 8) notes that digital media is giving "new life to age-old practices such as navigating, cultivating, stargazing, weather forecasting, documenting, and fishing."

Milad Doueihi (2013) describes how in a 1956 letter to the United Nations Educational, Scientific and Cultural Organization, anthropologist Claude Lévi-Strauss described the "three humanisms" that shaped Western intellectual history – the rediscovery of Greco-Roman classicism during the Renaissance, the "exotic humanism" of knowledge gained from the "Orient and the Far East," and the ascendancy of "democratic humanism" – and notes that these

> three kinds of humanism are linked to discoveries: in one case that of texts; in others that of cultures and the many ways they are expressed; and finally, that of all human phenomena as a subject of study (myth, oral communication, etc.). In each case, new fields of investigation have resulted both in methods and in the questioning of values associated with documents and cultural and scientific practices.

Following Lévi-Strauss, Doueihi (2013) identifies "digital humanism" as a fourth convergence of the world's complex cultural heritage and technological innovations that are both disrupting and transforming relationships between peoples, terrains, and non-human habitats. Doueihi (2013) asks, "[W]hat is the situation with the anthropology of this new inhabited earth, these new digital territories that are flexible, fluid and constantly moving? How should we think about them, analyze them, [since they] cannot be dissociated from our daily lives?" In this regard, it is salient and complementary to turn to Sylvia Wynter's statement that "I want the West to recognize the dimensions of what it has brought into the world – this with respect to, inter alia, our now purely naturalized modes or genres of humanness. You see? Because the West did change the world, totally" (quoted in McKittrick 2015). Wynter (2003, 260) concludes,

> [T]he struggle of our new millennium will be one between the ongoing imperative of securing the well-being of our present ethnoclass (i.e., Western bourgeois) conceptions of the human, Man, which overrepresents itself as if it were the human itself, and that of securing the well-being, and therefore the full cognitive and behavioral autonomy, of the human species itself/ourselves.

Indeed, despite the United Nations' Intergovernmental Panel on Climate Change's (IPCC) numerous reports, studies, and models – a corpus largely dominated by geoscientists and economists – and suffering a dearth of liberal arts and (digital) humanities scholars, public attitudes in 21st century seem over or underwhelmed, ambivalent or apathetic to the IPCC's dire prognostications on global warming. Evidence promulgated by Western-centric *Homo economicus* narratives composed of a skeletal landscape of statistics, hockey-stick graphs, and CO_2 particle emissions thresholds have led to cap and trade deals in addition to corporate greenwashing campaigns but have failed to inspire the wider breadth of the public imagination in any positive or practical ways to involve themselves in solutions.

Wendy Hui Kyong Chun argues that "the humanities has a duty to model critically informed approaches to interpret the vague and numerically-driven climate visualizations presented to the public" (2015; Gould 2021). Furthermore, Alan Liu (2012) asserts that the digital turn in the humanities has ideally positioned scholars to create, adapt, and disseminate new methods for interacting with and communicating in the public sphere "so that research and teaching organically generate advocacy in the form of publicly meaningful representations of the humanities." In contrast to STEM disciplines, digital methods in the humanities generally emerged in two camps: "literature, history, and philosophy on one side and communication and media studies on the other" (Miller 2012, 2). In 2009, Lev Manovich speculated that the "systematic use of large-scale computational analysis and interactive visualization of cultural patterns will become a major trend in cultural criticism and culture industries in the coming decades" and queried "what will happen when humanists start using interactive visualizations as a standard tool in their work, the way many scientists do already?" (Svensson 2012).

However, Andrew Prescott (2012) counters that if humanities practitioners "focus on modeling methods used by other scholars, we will simply never develop new methods of our own," and concedes that "a lot of this will be ad hoc, will pay little attention to standards, won't be seeking to produce a service, and won't worry about sustainability. It will be experimental." For example, we can see that the practice of hermeneutics, one of the principal methods in humanities scholarship, has digitally shapeshifted into performances of *deformance*, *corpus analytics*, *deep and thick mapping*, and *ergodic, distant, and close readings*, among other liminal methods of interpretation. Prescott (2012) notes that

> the interaction between carver and stone is important in understanding the conventions and structure of different types of inscription. The craft of the scribe affected the structure and content of the manuscript. . . . I write differently when I tweet to when I send an e-mail. Text technologies have a complex interaction with textuality and thus with the whole of human understanding.

Such digital methods have engendered a sense of alienation in some scholars. Phillip Barron (2016) states "for many of us trained in the humanities, to contribute data to such a project feels a bit like chopping up a Picasso into a million pieces and feeding those pieces one by one into a machine that promises to put it all back together, cleaner and prettier than it looked before." Indeed, the philosopher Hannah Arendt acerbically observed that humans: "forever tempted to lift the veil of the future – with the aid of computers or horoscopes or the intestines of sacrificial animals – have a worse record to show in these 'sciences' than in almost any scientific endeavor" (1978, 159). In contrast, Willard McCarthy (2004), in emphasising *poesis* over *positivism*, argues that humanities computational explorations "are better understood as temporary states in a process of coming to know rather than fixed structures of knowledge" and states "for the moment and the foreseeable future, *computers are essentially modeling machines, not knowledge jukeboxes*."

Over the past two decades, such digital approaches have facilitated transdisciplinary encounters between fields as diverse as human cognition, environmental studies, genetics, bioinformatics, linguistics, gaming, architecture, philosophy, social media, cartography, literature, music, painting, and history. Such encounters reflect the dynamic fluidities of environmental media intimated by the heuristic of the Anthropocene, more so than the static, stratigraphic snapshots of the Cartesian human-environmental binary framing of the Holocene (Travis 2018). However, the environmental footprint of digital methods and paraphernalia has created a path, with a long tail that can be traced back to the exploitative practices, extractive industries and social injustices of the latter geological epoch.

New Machines in the Garden

This chapter's epigraph, taken from Brautigan's poem "All Watched Over By Machines of Loving Grace" (1967), provides an idyllic, utopian vision of artificial intelligence in harmonic, cybernetic assemblage with the Edenic garden of nature.

> *I like to think*
> *(it has to be!)*
> *of a cybernetic ecology*
> *where we are free of our labors*
> *and joined back to nature,*
> *returned to our mammal*
> *brothers and sisters . . .*

Yet Donna Haraway (1991, 151) argues, "[T]he cyborg would not recognize the Garden of Eden; it is not made of mud and cannot dream of returning to dust." Both perspectives promote Cartesian human-environmental binaries and obscure the fact that many of the computer components of a scholar's "cyborg" (human-computer) assemblage are indeed harvested from the mud, dust, and geological strata of the earth. It has been argued that cybernetic tools "are rooted in anthropocentric and Western ways of understanding our relationships with and in the world, which maintains myths such as the neutrality of digital technology or linear forms of progress" (Jeong, Sherman, and Tippins 2021). In addition, many humanities digital practitioners "have too often seen their role as being responsible for shaping on-line culture and for ensuring the provision of suitably high-brow material" (Prescott 2012) – in the process eliding wider environmental and social justice concerns.

Bethany Nowviskie has challenged humanities digital practitioners to tackle ecological dilemmas linked to global warming. She argues that the "rhetorical, technological, aesthetic, and deeply personal, sometimes even sentimental, struggles brought into focus by the Anthropocene" are prompting us to "position the work of the digital humanities in time" to explore its scholarly, technological, and environmental ramifications (Nowviskie 2015, i7). Leo Marx's mapping of the 19th-century "psychic landscape" in *The Machine in the Garden*, featuring "striking sensory images of the artifacts of industrial capitalism: canals, steam engines, steamboats, locomotives, the telegraph, looms and factories" (2000 [1964], 370–71), provides such a precedent. Although leaving at times disastrous imprints (slag heaps, rivers on fire, buffalo bone pyramids waiting to be ground into animal feed) on urban and "pastoral" environments, "the rapid expansion of machine technologies ushered in a faith that history itself had become a process of rapid and limitless material progress" (Meikle 2003, 152). Walt Whitman (1861 & 1891), the celebrated 19th-century bard of United States expansion and innovation, declared that "exact science and its practical movements are no checks on the greatest poet but always his encouragement and support." In *Years of the Modern*, Whitman situates the American Poet within the mechanical realms of science and engineering:

> *His daring foot is on land and sea everywhere – he colonizes the*
> *Pacific, the archipelagoes;*
> *With the steam-ship, the electric telegraph, the newspaper, the*
> *wholesale engines of war,*
> *With these, and the world-spreading factories, he interlinks*
> *all geography, all lands.*
>
> *(Whitman 1861 & 1891)*

In addition to these 19th-century mechanistic marvels lauded by Whitman, Charles Babbage's difference engine (1822), Lady Ada Byron's Bernoulli algorithm script (1843), Samuel Morse's first demonstration of coded electrical pulses (1838), and George Boole's *The Laws of Thought* (1854) contributed to the development in the 1940s of the US Army's ENIAC programmable electronic computer and Alan Turing's Enigma cypher-breaking calculating machine – itself a precursor for 21st-century artificial intelligence applications (Turing 2004; Chandra 2013). Through a "steampunk" looking glass, we can see that 19th-century coding, travel, and communication analogues foreshadowed the digital infrastructures girding the World Wide Web. In transforming human cultures, these industrial artefacts functioned as the result of extractive industries that supplied coal, steel, iron, copper, and wood – all assembled in cases by exploited labour.

In *Man and Nature*, George Perkins Marsh observed that the mechanised society emerging in the 19th century had begun to wage "an almost indiscriminate war-fare upon all the forms of animal and vegetable existence" in its aspirational advances towards the progressive utopia of advanced "civilisation" (2003 [1864], 40). Geographically, the scale and extent of warfare in the 19th century increased in size because of a greater number of rifles and ammunition supplied by Industrial Revolution armament factories (Huby 2008, 408). For instance, during the American Civil War, Confederate General Robert E. Lee's invasion of the Northern states of Maryland and Pennsylvania culminated in the Battle of Antietam on 17 September 1962. This single clash between the South and the Union North recorded the highest death toll experienced to that point in United States history, prompting the poet Emily Dickinson to write the following:

The name – of it – is "Autumn" –
The hue – of it – is Blood –
An Artery – upon the Hill –
A Vein – along the Road –
Great Globules – in the Alleys –
And Oh, the Shower of Stain –
When Winds – upset the Basin –
And spill the Scarlet Rain –
(Quoted in Cody 2003, 25)

Dickinson perceived the Civil War as an ecological event that entangled the human body and environment on a savage scale. Evocations of "arteries upon the hills, bodies of stone, winds that make as to devour" in her war poems feature ecological images that "may be far less metaphoric than we assume" (Marrs 2017, 218–19). The conflict between the industrial North and the agricultural South juxtaposes medieval and industrial age ideologies and infrastructures (feudal-like plantations of the enslaved protected by chivalrous Confederate calvary officers-cum-knights versus Union troops transported by railroad and generals communicating by the digital age's analogue, the telegraph). Cody Marrs (2017, 220) describes the military-industrial appetite engendered by this Anthropocene conflict:

To feed the war machine, foundries were erected, forests destroyed, animals slaughtered, mines depleted, railroads extended, and guns and shells and bullets produced en masse – all to sustain massive, locust-like armies that left little in their wake and navies forged for the first time out of iron and powered by steam.

Following the Civil War, rail transportation "interjected" itself between the general public and the landscape. The traveller perceived the landscape as it was filtered through the machine ensemble (Schivelbusch 1986, 24). In America, the Gold Rush of 1849 and the completion of the transcontinental railroad in 1869 metamorphosed the Spanish mission pueblo of San Francisco into the great western terminal of the United States. In 1890, the urban-technological nexus inspired Walter Gilpin's *The Cosmopolitan Railway: Compacting and Fusing Together All the World's Continents*, which imagined a global commercial, transport, and communication network encircling the belly of the earth along an oscillating path traced by Prussian geographer Alexander von Humboldt's isothermal zodiac.

Gilpin's vision obliquely anticipated the expansive global reach of the digital campus-fortresses of Microsoft, Apple, and Google in Silicon Valley, adjacent to the San Francisco Bay region-global port from 1849. Their digital empires span the tax-haven corollaries in the docklands of Dublin, Ireland, and other corporate-revenue-friendly regimes, in addition to the computer/smartphone parts sweatshops operating in the Global South and East. In a sense, such techno-corporate "ecosystem" practices reify for the "digital revolution" the concept of the *Plantationocene*, which stands in contrast to the Western Enlightenment construction of "man" that seems to inform Anthropocene discourses. In this regard, Anna Tsing, employing a neocolonial lens, situates the "plantation" at "precisely the conjuncture between ecological simplifications, the discipline of plants in particular, and the discipline of humans to work on those" (Mittman 2019, 6).

A mechanical framing of nature, inaugurated by the 19th-century Industrial Revolution, focused through the prism of railway travel, provided people with transcendent perceptions of nature as they moved "rapidly from place to place" across the Earth's continents (Merchant 2020, 76). In contrast, the new digital machines of the 21st century permit us to move information precipitously at the speed of light from place to place. This ability is again transforming human perceptions of the indices of time and place as they intersect with the world's regional environments. The coding and mass production of cyberspaces based on the capitalist-Fordist model produced digital trails to virtual landscapes in which people can communicate and interact instantaneously, thus collapsing the structures of clockwork time and labour practices inaugurated during the 19th-century industrial age.

It is easy to imagine that with our "green" digital devices, we access and move effortlessly and in an environmentally friendly fashion through the cyber-ether of the web cloud space. However, the apparatus and paraphernalia of our "new machines in the garden" anchor us by electronic signals and supply chains to the garrisoned spaces of Silicon Valley's digital campuses and internet server farms, themselves tied to extractive and predatory labour practices. Stratigraphic benchmarks indicating the presence of the Anthropocene were created by the prehistoric harnessing of fire, the invention of the 18th-century steam pump that unleashed the Industrial Revolution, and the splitting of the atom and detonation of Fat Boy, the hydrogen bomb, in 1945 at Trinity, New Mexico.

Likewise, the digital revolution is beginning to leave its indelible environmental anthropogenic imprint. The petrochemical industry, in addition to creating materials for plastic bottles, food packaging, and ubiquity of other products, supplies plastics for mobile and smartphones, earbuds, tablets, computers, and screens that are used, disposed, and replaced with every new technological innovation. Consequently, *plastiglomerates* – composite "rocks" formed from melted plastics, beach sediments, basaltic lava, and organic debris – now litter Hawaiian beaches. In addition, the Great Pacific Garbage Patch (twice the size of the US state of Texas) is carried on oceanic currents within the Polynesian triangle.

It and other "*plastigomerate* archipelagoes" now host maritime "neopelagic communities" of shrimp, starfish, anemones, barnacles, and other coastal species, which provide their own unique Anthropocene signals in the gyres of our global oceans (Corcoran, Moore, and Jazvac 2014; Haram et al. 2021). Terrestrially, mining supplies aluminium, potassium, nickel, gold, copper, silicon, lithium, and other elements for the screens, circuit boards, and batteries of our digital revolution accoutrements. However, the extraction of such minerals and precious metals contributes to the 10% of human energy utilisation expended globally by the mining industry, which is also one of the largest consumers of H_2O on earth and, as a consequence, "mining's most common casualty." It has also been estimated that it takes approximately 3,787 gallons of water to sanitise an eight-inch silicon wafer foundation to a level of cleanliness so that 100 computer chips can be constructed. With millions of chips being produced on a yearly basis, billions of gallons of water are consequently being expended (Park and Pellow 2004; Christian 2005, 21–25; Bese 2017; Dudley 2019; *Safe Drinking Water Foundation, 2021*).

In addition to the environmental costs incurred by these industries, exploited workers are shackled in the production chains that assemble our sleek MacBooks and PCs. One of the most egregious cases of human rights abuses connected to the digital revolution is occurring in the Xinjiang region of China, where Muslim Uighurs, detained in internment camps and prisons, undergo "ideological and behavioural re-education." Once "graduated" from the Chinese Communist Party's indoctrination camps, many internees are sent to toil in rare-earth-mineral mines and factories to source materials and manufacture screens, cameras, and fingerprint scanners for suppliers to companies such as Apple and Lenovo, which equip the DEH with its hardware (Kang and Wang 2020).

Eerily, the Uighur persecution resonates with eco-disaster, dystopian narratives of the United States in Octavia E. Butler's *Parable of the Sower* (1993) and its sequel, *Parable of the Talents* (1998), and Philip K. Dick's *Do Androids Dream of Electric Sheep?* (1968). Arendt reflects that science and culture are closely entwined, with prescient insights about emerging technologies emerging in dreams and "in the highly non-respectable literature of science-fiction" (1998, 2). Butler's *Parable of the Sower*, set in 2024, is chronicled in 15-year-old Lauren Oya Olamina's journal, where epigraphical fragments of Earthseed's creed, a religion she is inventing, precede her every entry. Her "designer-eco-faith" proselytises extraterrestrial colonisation as the solution to global social and environmental disasters. Lauren lives in a multi-ethnic middle- and working-class gated neighbourhood near Los Angeles – "a carcass covered with too many maggots" (Butler 2012 [1993], 12) where fresh water is scarce, and the metropolis is threatened by global warming, rising sea levels, and drought. Feral dogs and gangs of homeless addled by a Big Pharma smart drug called pyro, which provides users with a sexual high by committing arson and roaming outside its walled communities. Lauren and her friends dare to venture on a bike trek outside their gates, and Butler depicts a dystopian, semi-feudal, medievalesque landscape:

> Up toward the hills there were walled estates – one big house and a lot of shacky little dependencies where the servants lived. We didn't pass anything like that today. In fact we passed a couple of neighborhoods so poor that their walls were made up of unmortared rocks, chunks of concrete, and trash. Then there were the pitiful, unwalled residential areas. A lot of the houses were trashed – burned, vandalized, infested with drunks or druggies or squatted-in by homeless families with their filthy, gaunt, half-naked children.
>
> *(Butler 2012 [1993], 12)*

Across the United States, fires are rampant and under the administration of President Donner – who eschews science – and police and public schools are being privatised, with municipalities turned into corporate work camps, reminiscent of 20th-century Appalachian coal company towns. Lauren practices shooting with a BB gun, and forced by events, she leads a "migration-pilgrimage" north to the rural, forested region of Humboldt County, Oregon. There Lauren and her flock establish Acorn, a commune of self-deluded "empaths" (individuals who believe they share the feelings of others) to practice the doctrines of Earthseed.

Butler states that "ecology, especially global warming, is almost a character in *Parable of the Sower*" and that she "made a real effort to talk about what could actually happen or is in the process of happening: the walled communities and the illiteracy and the global warming and lots of other things." In its sequel, the *Parable of the Talents*, Butler wants to give her "characters the chance to work on the solutions, to say, 'Here is the solution!'" (Rowell and Butler 1997, 61; Potts and Butler 1996, 336).

Parable of the Talents, set in 2032, finds Lauren, daughter Larkin and husband Taylor, living at Acorn. The United States has engaged in a war with Canada under the "Christian" administration of President Andrew Steele Jarret. A Texan who aims to eradicate other religions and faith communities, Jarrett has a campaign slogan: "Make America Great Again." In company towns, indentured servitude and slavery are enforced with high-tech shock collars. Virtual reality goggles called Dream Masks allow a functionally illiterate populace to experience the illusion of simple life based on a deluded and fantasist reading of the past. In addition, journalism has been reduced to "news bullets" composed of

> flashy pictures and quick, witty, verbal one-two punches. Twenty-five or thirty words are supposed to be enough in a news bullet to explain either a war or an unusual set of Christmas lights. Bullets are cheap and full of big, dramatic pictures. Some bullets are true virtuals that allow people to experience – safely – hurricanes, epidemics, fires and mass murder. Hell of a kick.
>
> *(Butler 1998, 78)*

In *Parable of the Talents*, Acorn is taken over by a Christian paramilitary group named the Crusaders and turned into a "re-education" camp to eliminate the Earthseed faith. Lauren, her family, and her followers submit to rapes and beatings and are forced to wear shock collars. After killing their captors, the Acorn community scatters to hide in the Pacific Northwest wilderness. At the close of the novel, we find Lauren's bible, *Earthseed: The First Book of the Living*, published and the dying octogenarian estranged from Larkin due to her devotion to the religion she created. In her last moments, Lauren gazes at the *Christopher Columbus*, an orbiting starship about to depart from Earth with settlers who will establish the first human extraterrestrial colony. Butler's late-20th-century novels anticipated many of the issues and dilemmas the DEH (and other fields) are currently grappling with. On the cusp of the millennium, discussing anthropogenically created catastrophes, she remarked in an interview:

> We are liable to bring ourselves right up to the brink on one occasion or another. Now we're talking so much about biological warfare that sooner or later someone's bound to try it, just because it's what's popular right now. It's interesting how things come into fashion. . . . Chances are that the more we progress – if that's the word-technologically, the more likely we are to do a lot of harm to the environment. That's not necessarily true; It's possible that computers and computer-related technology, communications technology, will change some of that. I don't know. It's possible.
>
> *(Palwick and Butler 1999, 150–52)*

In turn, Dick's *Do Androids Dream of Electric Sheep?* depicts a post-apocalyptic San Francisco in 1992 ravaged by the dust of nuclear "World War Terminus." Due to extinctions and the loss of global biodiversity, the city is populated by a dwindling society that fetishises and commodifies any existing biotic species:

> Here had been the suburbs of San Francisco, a short ride by monorail rapid transit; the entire peninsula had chattered like a bird tree with life and opinions and complaints, and now the watchful owners had either died or migrated to a colony world. . . . The dust which had contaminated most of the planet's surface had originated in no country. . . . First, strangely, the owls had died. At the time it had seemed almost funny, the fat, fluffy white birds lying here and there, in yards and on streets. . . . Medieval plagues had manifested themselves in a similar way, in the form of many dead rats. This plague, however, had descended from above.
>
> *(Dick 1968, 8)*

Rick Deckard, the *tech-noir bounty hunter* charged in Dick's novel with tracking down artificial intelligence humanoids on the run, ruefully states, "I want to have an animal; I keep trying to buy one. But on my salary, on what a city employee makes" (Dick 1968, 7). In pursuit of six Nexus 6 droids who have escaped slavery from an outer-space mining outpost, Rick asks himself,

> Do androids dream? . . . Evidently; that's why they occasionally kill their employers and flee here. A better life, without servitude. Like Luba Luft; singing Don Giovanni and Le Nozze instead of toiling across the face of a barren rock-strewn field. On a fundamentally uninhabitable colony world.
>
> *(Dick 1968, 83)*

Butler's and Dick's scenarios echo in Amanda Starling Gould's (2016, 14) observation that "our phones, as well as our laptops, tablets, and smart-enabled devices, are part of a vast human- and natural resource-intensive system (digital metabolism)." In particular, Dick noted that *Electric Sheep* aptly reflected the environment of a

> man-made world of machines, artificial constructs, computers, electronic systems, interlinking homeostatic components . . . becoming alive, or at least quasi-alive, and in ways specifically and fundamentally analogous to ourselves."
>
> *(Dick 1995, 183)*

Each digital device begins in the mines, proceeds to a manufacturing plant, and returns to the earth as waste after its deliberately short lifetime. Consequently, "media technologies generate meaning, but also detritus and disease. Their industrial life cycles extend far-flung injuries into natural and bio-physical environments" (Maxwell and Miller 2012, 165).

Conclusion

The DEH can begin addressing questions raised in this chapter by can looking to the ancient myth of Prometheus, which serves as a cautionary tale about the dangers incurred after *Homo sapiens* harnessed fire. The act set in motion the geophysical process of combustion that "facilitated the transformation of much of the terrestrial surface . . . and in the process pushed the parameters of the earth system into a new geological epoch" (Dalby 2018, 721). The geophysicist Michael Mann observes that global warming constitutes an "ethical problem" that places a significant onus on the liberal arts and humanities disciplines to address what is essentially a struggle at the heart of our shared human condition (Holm and Travis 2017, 114). In addition, Chelsea M. Frazier (2016, 44), following Wynter's train of thought on the need to disrupt standard environmental studies tropes, observes,

> "[T]he West" itself – its divisions of space and its rigid notions of the human subject – are insufficient frameworks through which "global warming, severe climate change, and the sharply unequal distribution of the earth's resources" can be effectively addressed.

One of the major divisions in cyberspace power is depicted by French novelist Michel Houellebecq in *The Map and the Territory* (2014). His protagonist, the artist Jed Martin (echoing GIS techniques), superimposes photographic images on Michelin road maps to represent places such as his grandmother's village, Châtelus-le-Marcheix. Another of Martin's works consists of 42 portraits of modern-day occupations, including one titled "Bill Gates and Steve Jobs Discussing the Future of Information Technology," inspired by "the cinnabar greens that give such a magical glow to the forests of California pine descending toward the sea" (Houellebecq 2014, 75). As digital age barons, Gates and Jobs dominate the means that provide the general public access to the cybersphere. Umberto Eco (1994) draws a playful but salient analogy between the two respective operating systems the pair represent and the 16th- and 17th-century theological-ideological cleavage created by the European Reformation and Counter-Reformation:

> The fact is that the world is divided between users of the Macintosh computer and users of MS-DOS compatible computers. I am firmly of the opinion that the Macintosh is Catholic and that DOS is Protestant. Indeed, the Macintosh is counter-reformist and has been influenced by the *ratio studiorum* of the Jesuits. It is cheerful, friendly, conciliatory; it tells the faithful how they must proceed step by step to reach – if not the kingdom of Heaven – the moment in which their document is printed. It is catechistic: The essence of revelation is dealt with via simple formulae and sumptuous icons. Everyone has a right to salvation. DOS is Protestant, or even Calvinistic. It allows free interpretation of scripture, demands difficult personal decisions, imposes a subtle hermeneutics upon the user, and takes for granted the idea that not all can achieve salvation. To make the system work you need to interpret the program yourself . . . with the passage to Windows, the DOS universe has come to resemble more closely the counter-reformist tolerance of the Macintosh. It's true: Windows represents an Anglican-style schism, big ceremonies in the cathedral, but there is always the possibility of a return to DOS to change things in accordance with bizarre decisions: When it comes down to it, you can decide to ordain women and gays if you want to. . . . One may wonder whether, as time goes by, the use of one system rather than another leads to profound inner changes. Can you use DOS and be a Vande supporter? And more: Would Celine have written using Word . . .? Would Descartes have programmed in Pascal? And machine code, which lies beneath and decides the destiny of both systems (or environments, if you prefer)? Ah, that belongs to the Old Testament, and is Talmudic and cabalistic.

Eco's shrewd allusion to the "environments of code" presciently anticipated themes of concern to the theory and practice of the DEH. To address the wicked problem of global warming, to quote John Durham Peters, a "true humanist would also be a naturalist, one who produces knowledge about things that are, were, and are to come." (2015, 28). In addition, Alan Liu (2012) states that digital scholars "can most profoundly advocate for the humanities by helping to broaden the very idea of instrumentalism, technological, and otherwise." However, the DEH can be viewed as a Janus-faced phenomenon. On the one hand, the ubiquity of computing, smartphone, gaming, tablets, devices, and infrastructures employed in DEH performances are imbricated in destructive, unjust, and unethical environmental and social practices. The digital revolution, in the words of Wynter (2003, 261), facilitates "the dynamic of overconsumption on the part of the rich techno-industrial North paralleled by that overpopulation on the part of the dispossessed poor, still partly agrarian worlds of the South) – these are all differing facets of the central ethno-class Man vs. Human struggle." In a biotech trope that "reboots" Mary Shelley's vision in *Frankenstein – or the Modern Prometheus* (1819), carbon atoms harvested from the DNA of the human genome have been used to "grow" graphene computer-chip semiconductor transistors to act as "synapses" in the "brains" of our DEH tools and devices (Abate 2013; Sokolov et al. 2013).

On the other hand, the humanities can be expanded by the DEH to operate on widely interactive and multiple modalities and dimensions of the human relation to the environment, incorporating textual, tactile, visual, and auditory mediations in the pursuit and creation of knowledge. Such methods are the fruit of explorations and experimentations with proprietary and open-source music, art, geo and network mapping software, and multidisciplinary collaborations, providing a shift from the single, siloed scholar model to one that embraces eclectic research partnerships and teams.

The DEH digitally braids strands from philosophy, linguistics, history, literature, and geography with other disciplinary threads in the humanities, arts, and computing and natural sciences. By doing so, the DEH holds the potential to weave millennial mythologies, narratives, and heuristics; contribute tools and methods to promote "out of the box" thinking; and promote agencies to address the ethical-technical-environmental dilemmas we are facing in the 21st century. Indeed, the development and use of tools have been part of humanities scholarship for centuries. As Prescott observes (2012), the alphabetisation of biblical extracts in Peter of Capua's 11th-century *Distinctiones Theologicae* paved the way for the first concordance to the scriptures, compiled under the supervision of the Dominican Hugh of St Cher between 1235 and 1249 ce at the monastery of St Jacques in Paris:

> [W]ith these new alphabetical tools, the cultivation of memory became less important and it was the ability to manipulate these new knowledge systems which counted . . . the distinctiones and concordances altered the way in which man explored his relationship with God changed; they changed conceptions of what it meant to be human.
>
> *(Prescott 2012)*

In spite of a double-faced disposition juxtaposing a dystopian environmental footprint with the utopian possibilities of research and pedagogy, perhaps the DEH can be integrated with alternative and Indigenous codings of human-environmental-cosmic relations. And in a manner not unlike the medieval concordance of the scriptures, in what Wynter deems an "Augustinian turn" which involves "the taking and revising of an existing system of knowledge, in order to create that which is imperatively emancipatorily new" (McKittrick 2015), the DEH will provide humanities (and other) scholars with the means to digitally plot balanced and sustainable paths which transcend the bounds of our limited Western-centric environmental consciousness to transform what it means to be ethically and globally human in the 21st century.

Sources

Abate, Tom. 2013. "Stanford Scientists Use DNA to Assemble a Transistor from Graphene." *Stanford Engineering*. http://engineering.stanford.edu/news/stanford-scientists-use-dna-assemble-transistor-graphene.

Arendt, H. 1978. *The Life of the Mind*. New York: Harcourt Brace, Jovanovich.

———. 1998. *The Human Condition*. 2nd ed. Chicago and London: University of Chicago Press.

Barron, P. 2016. "Putting the 'Humanities' in 'Digital Humanities.'" www. insidehighered. com/views/2010/11/04/barron.

Bese, M. 2017. "10 Incredible Mining Facts, 3D Perspectives from." *Dassault Systèmes*, June 25, 2017. https://blogs.3ds.com/perspectives/10-incredible-mining-facts/.

Brautigan, R. 1967. "All Watched Over By Machines of Loving Grace." In *American Dust, Richard Brautigan's Life and Writing*. Accessed June 8, 2021. www.brautigan.net/machines.html.

Butler, Octavia, E. 1998. *Parable of the Talents: A Novel*. Vol. 2. New York: Seven Stories Press.

———. 2012 [1993]. *Parable of the Sower: Volume 1*. New York: Iconic EBooks: Open Road Media.

Chandra, V. 2013. *Geek Sublime: Writing Fiction, Coding Software*. London: Faber & Faber.

Christian, D. 2005. "Bridging the Two Cultures: History, Big History, and Science." *Historically Speaking* 6 (5): 21–26.

Chun, W. H. K. 2015. "On Hypo-Real Models or Global Climate Change: A Challenge for the Humanities." *Critical Inquiry* 41 (3): 675–703.

Cody, D. 2003. "Blood in the Basin: The Civil War in Emily Dickinsonis' 'The Name of it is Autumn.'" *The Emily Dickinson Journal* 12 (1): 25–52.

Corcoran, P. L., C. J. Moore, and K. Jazvac. 2014. "An Anthropogenic Marker Horizon in the Future Rock Record." *GSA Today* 24 (6): 4–8.

Dalby, S. 2018. "Firepower: Geopolitical Cultures in the Anthropocene." *Geopolitics* 23 (3): 718–42.

Dick, Philip, K. 1968. *Do Androids Dream of Electric Sheep?* New York: Doubleday.

———. 1995. "The Android and the Human." In *The Shifting Realities of Philip K. Dick*, edited by Lawrence Sutin, 183–210. New York: Pantheon Books.

Doueihi, M. 2013. "About Digital Humanism | Umanesimo Digitale." *E-Zine, R.A.N.K.E.D.* Accessed August 2015. www.rebelalliance.eu/e-zine/digital-humanism-umanesimo-digitale.

Dudley, B. 2019. "BP Statistical Review of World Energy." In *BP Statistical Review*. London: British Petroleum.

Eco, Umberto. 1994. "La bustina di Minerva." *Espresso*, September 30.

Frazier, C. M. 2016. "Troubling Ecology: Wangechi Mutu, Octavia Butler, and Black Feminist Interventions in Environmentalism." *Critical Ethnic Studies* 2 (1): 40–72.

Gilpin, W. 1890. *The Cosmopolitan Railway: Compacting and Fusing Together All the World's Continents*. San Francisco, CA: The History Company Publishers.

Greenfield, Susan. 2014. *Mind Change: How Digital Technologies Are Leaving Their Mark on our Brains*. London: Penguin.

Gould, Amanda Starling. 2016. "Restor (y) ing the Ground: Digital Environmental Media Studies." *Networking Knowledge: Journal of the MeCCSA Postgraduate Network* 9 (5).

———. 2021. "Anthropocene Digital Humanities." Accessed June1, 2021. https://amandastarlinggould.com/anthropocenedh/.

Haram, L. E., J. T. Carlton, L. Centurioni, et al. 2021. "Emergence of a Neopelagic Community Through the Establishment of Coastal Species on the High Seas." *Nature Communications* 12 (6885). https://doi.org/10.1038/s41467-021-27188-6.

Haraway, D. 1991. "A Cyborg Manifesto: Science, Technology, and Socialist Feminism in the Late Twentieth Century." In *Simians, Cyborgs and Women: The Reinvention of Nature*, 149–81. New York: Routledge.

Holm, Poul, and Charles Travis. 2017. "The New Human Condition and Climate Change: Humanities and Social Science Perceptions of Threat." *Global and Planetary Change* 156: 112–14.

Houellebecq, Michel. 2014. *The Map and the Territory*. New York: Random House.

Hupy, Joseph P. 2008. "The Environmental Footprint of War." *Environment and History*: 405–21.

Jeong, Sophia, Brandon Sherman, and Deborah J. Tippins. 2021. "The Anthropocene as We Know It: Posthumanism, Science Education and Scientific Literacy as a Path to Sustainability." *Cultural Studies of Science Education* (April). https://doi.org/10.1007/s11422-021-10029-9.

Jørgensen, F. 2014. "The Armchair Traveller's Guide to Digital Environmental Humanities." *Environmental Humanities* 4: 95–1112.

Kang, D., and Y. Wang. 2020. "Gadgets for Tech Giants Made with Coerced Uighur Labor." *AP News*, March 5, 2020. https://apnews.com/article/ap-top-news-international-news-apple-inc-weekend-reads-china-clamps-down-3f9a92b8dfd3cae379b57622dd801dd5.

Liu, A. Y. 2012. "Where Is Cultural Criticism in the Digital Humanities?" In *Debates in the Digital Humanities*, edited by K. Gold Matthew, 490–509. Minneapolis, University of Minnesota Press. https://dhdebates.gc.cuny.edu/projects/debates-in-the-digital-humanities.

Marrs, Cody. 2017. "Dickinson in the Anthropocene." *ESQ: A Journal of Nineteenth-Century American Literature and Culture* 63 (2): 201–25.

Marsh, George Perkins. 2003. *Man and Nature*. Seattle: University of Washington Press.

Marx, L. 2000 [1964]. *The Machine in the Garden*. Oxford: Oxford University Press.

Maxwell, Richard, and Toby Miller. 2012. *Greening the Media*. Oxford: Oxford University Press.

McCarty, W. 2004. "Modeling: A Study in Words and Meanings." In *A Companion to Digital Humanities*, edited by S. Schreibman, R. Siemens, and J. Unsworth. Oxford: Blackwell. www.digitalhumanities.org/companion.

McKittrick, Katherine, ed. 2015. *Sylvia Wynter: On Being Human As Praxis*. Chapel Hill: Duke University Press. ProQuest Ebook Central. http://ebookcentral.proquest.com/lib/utarl/detail.action?docID=1884075.

Meike, J. L. 2003. "Review: Leo Marx's 'The Machine in the Garden.'" *Technology and Culture* 44 (1): 147–59.

Merchant, C. 2020. *The Anthropocene and the Humanities: From Climate Change to a New Age of Sustainability*. New Haven: Yale University Press.

Miller, Toby. 2012. *Blow Up the Humanities*. Philadelphia: Temple University Press.

Mitman, G. 2019. "Reflections on the Plantationocene: A Conversation with Donna Haraway and Anna Tsing." *Edge Effects* 12.

Nowiskie, B. 2015. Digital Humanities in the Anthropocene. *Digital Scholarship in the Humanities*, 30 (1). Also see: Bethany Nowviskie, *digital humanities in the anthropocene*, 10 July 2014 <https://nowviskie.org/2014/anthropocene/>

Palwick, S., and O. Butler. 1999. "Imagining a Sustainable Way of Life: An Interview with Octavia Butler." *Interdisciplinary Studies in Literature and Environment*: 149–58.

Park, L. S., and D. N. Pellow. 2004. "Racial Formation, Environmental Racism, and the Emergence of Silicon Valley." *Ethnicities* 4: 404–24.

Peters, John Durham. 2015. *The Marvelous Clouds: Toward a Philosophy of Elemental Media*. Chicago, IL: University of Chicago Press, 3.

Potts, S. W., and O. E. Butler. 1996. "'We Keep Playing the Same Record': A Conversation with Octavia E. Butler." *Science Fiction Studies*: 331–38.

Prescott, A. 2012. "Making the Digital Human: Anxieties, Possibilities, Challenges, presented at the Digital Humanities Summer School, Oxford University." In *Digital Riffs: Extemporizations, Excursions and Explorations in the Digital Humanities*. http://digitalriffs.blogspot.co.uk/2012/07/making-digital-human-anxieties.html.

Rowell, C. H., and O. E. Butler. 1997. "An Interview with Octavia E. Butler." *Callaloo* 20 (1): 47–66.

Safe Drinking Water Foundation. 2021. Water Consumption. <https://www.safewater.org/fact-sheets-1/2017/1/23/water-consumption>

Schivelbusch, W. 1986. *The Railway Journey: The Industrialization of Time and Space in the 19th Century*. Berkeley: University of California Press.

Shelley, M. 1819. *Frankenstein or The Modern Prometheus*. London: Lackington, Hughes, Harding, Mavor, & Jones.

Sokolov, A. N., F. L. Yap, N. Liu, K. Kim, L. Ci, O. B. Johnson, H. Wang, M. Vosgueritchian, A. L. Koh, J. Chen, and J. Park. 2013. "Direct Growth of Aligned Graphitic Nanoribbons from a DNA Template by Chemical Vapour Deposition." *Nature Communications* 4 (1): 1–8.

Steffen, W., J. Grinevald, P. Crutzen, and J. McNeill. 2011. "The Anthropocene: Conceptual and Historical Perspectives." *Philosophical Transactions of the Royal Society A: Mathematical, Physical and Engineering Sciences* 369 (1938).

Svensson, P. 2012. "Envisioning the Digital Humanities." *Digital Humanities Quarterly* 6 (1).

Tolstoy, L. 1869. *War and Peace* (*Война и миръ*). Moscow: The Russian Messenger.

Travis, C. 2018. "The Digital Anthropocene, Deep Mapping, and Environmental Humanities' Big Data." *Resilience: A Journal of the Environmental Humanities* 5 (2): 172–88.

Turing, A. M. 2004. *The Essential Turing*. Oxford: Oxford University Press.

Whitelaw, Mitchell, and Belinda Smaill. 2021. "Biodiversity Data as Public Environmental Media: Citizen Science Projects, National Databases and Data Visualizations." *Journal of Environmental Media* 2 (1): 79–99.

Whitman, W. 1861 & 1891. *The Walt Whitman Archive*. Edited by Matt Cohen. Gen. ed. Folsom and Kenneth M. Price. https://whitmanarchive.org/published/LG/1867/poems/7.

Wynter, S. 2003. "Unsettling the Coloniality of Being/Power/Truth/Freedom: Towards the Human, after Man, its Overrepresentation – An Argument." *CR: The New Centennial Review* 3 (3): 257–337.

PART II

Voicing Indigeneity

7

FROM LOCALISED RESISTANCE TO THE SOCIAL DISTANCE POWWOW

Movements in the World of Indigenous Americans

J. Albert Nungaray

Introduction

With the hundredth anniversary of Indigenous citizenship in the United States, the question rose in my mind of how we original "Americans" got here. Today, we see a strong activist movement, cultural revitalisation, and even the first Indigenous woman US Secretary of the Interior, Deb Haaland. Children are learning their traditional dances, languages, and stories at levels we have not seen since before colonisation. There has been amazing growth, especially in the last 20 years, culminating in the digitally enabled Social Distance Powwow platform and community.

But where did this story arc begin? How did Indigenous Americans go from being a threat to the nation worthy of extermination to holding positions of political power, including as a member of the US presidential cabinet in that very nation? How are the Indigenous peoples of the Americas resisting continued injustice and reclaiming their identity? What if I told you I was going to connect the Laguna Pueblo Secretary of the Interior Haaland to the historic late-19th-century worldwide sensation and *Wild West* showman extraordinaire, Buffalo Bill (William Cody)? No, I am not implying they were related in any way. However, I will argue that Indigenous American activist resistance has followed a trajectory of engaging entertainment, broadcast, media, and digital platforms and technologies to move from isolated local resistance movements to digitally networked global communities of activism, resilience, and power.

Fair warning, my writing style may supply a more intimate type of narrative than academia is accustomed to. However, I assure you it is done with purpose. Culturally, I need to start on a personal note, as it is my responsibility to put a little of myself into this story. When I first moved to the Dallas-Fort Worth (DFW) metroplex to attend Texas Christian University (TCU) for my education, I did not know how important this history would be to my life. I was isolated from my home, alone in a city I did not know. By luck, the salvation of my sanity came in the form of a radio broadcast – *Beyond Bows and Arrows Radio* – on the local station, KNON. Hearing the tribal drums, that powwow music I love so much, and inside jokes from the disc jockeys once a

DOI: 10.4324/9781003082798-10

week for one hour, I felt at home. At that moment, much like those who listened to *Radio Free Alcatraz* might have felt (as will be discussed later), I was reminded that I was not alone. Soon, I was connected to the Urban Inter-Tribal Center of Texas, university student organisations, and the wonderful urban Indian population of North Texas. Though I am of the Tewa, Pueblo people, I am not a registered member of my tribe. And because I do not have a tribal identification card – which is much like possessing an American Kennel Club dog or racehorse breeding certification – I have often been considered "not Indian enough" outside the tribal core of my family and friends. However, here, in the DFW urban community, I was welcomed with open arms. Because of these connections, I was successfully able to assist in the passage of Indigenous Peoples' Day proclamations and inaugurate celebrations in Fort Worth, Tarrant County, Dallas, and the State of Texas (*Red Handed Warrior Society* 2021). I was able to establish a Native student association at TCU, my undergraduate university, and restructure Indigenous cultural representations at several local historical sites in the area. In addition, I was even able to push forward on my path to a doctoral programme in history at the University of Texas, Arlington. These would not have happened without digital technologies and mediums of communication, in addition to the lifetimes of work by those who came before me. Professionally, I may be a historian, but at my core, I am an Indigenous storyteller. So in terms of the story, we will start by simply stating that the path taken from the days of *Buffalo Bill's Wild West* "show" to the strong Indigenous leadership we see today in the top circles of United States power is amazing.

Though I am beginning my story in the late 19th century, Indigenous Peoples of the Americas had been facing extermination campaigns for several centuries. As the century was closing, these efforts had been taken to new heights. Whereas in the 17th and 18th centuries, alliances and agreements between the British, French, and Spanish – before the "Americans" in 1776 – kept violence more evenly distributed, the westward expansion of the United States and the associated concept of manifest destiny escalated violence to previously unseen and genocidal levels. After all, where the British, French, and Spanish had each other to worry about, the Americans had the destiny of God's preordained mission of expanding their nation from sea to shining sea on their minds, regardless of who may be in the way of that providential undertaking. Enter *Buffalo Bill's Wild West* show (a term Cody hated, as he wished to portray the *real* Wild West). From the arenas of world fairs to the floors of political conventions, Buffalo Bill and his show travelled the world showcasing Indigenous Americans in full regalia. In a land where it had become illegal to practice their religion, hold their rites of passage, or teach their language to their children, Indigenous Americans were paraded in front of awestruck audiences in every corner of the United States and Europe (see Figure 7.1).

Rebellion and combat are not the sole means of resistance. For better or worse, *Buffalo Bill's Wild West* show could be considered one of the first acts of what we could recognise as "modern" Indigenous activism. Because by participating in this show, Indigenous Americans were able to interact with people of other tribes. This included famed leadership figures like Sitting Bull of the Hunkpapa Sioux. While they earned a small profit for their performances and escaped violence and life on the reservation, Indigenous Americans were able to share their cultures and customs, lobby for rights, and keep their ways alive in manners they otherwise may not have had the opportunity to do so. For over 30 years, *Buffalo Bill's Wild West* show and others like it allowed for the preservation of tribal cultures – albeit for the purposes of entertainment and spectacle – in addition to affording a place of refuge in a time when Indigenous Americans were considered an enemy of the United States.

In 1924, less than a decade after Cody's passing, Indigenous American people adorned in full regalia successfully lobbied for citizenship on behalf of all tribal societies in the United States. Welcomed to Washington, DC, to advocate for their rights, Indigenous Americans even posed

Figure 7.1 Buffalo Bill's Wild West Show, 1890, in Rome, Italy (Wikipedia Commons).

for photographs on the White House lawn with President Coolidge. These acts of resistance did not go away with *Buffalo Bill's Wild West* show. Half a century later, the American Indian Movement (AIM) continued the traditions of Indigenous activism, albeit in much different ways. In the 1970s, AIM occupied the island prison of Alcatraz in San Francisco Bay, raided the Bureau of Indian Affairs in Washington, DC, and engaged in an armed standoff against federal agents at Wounded Knee on the Pine Ridge Reservation in South Dakota. American Indigenous peoples possess long memories and have fought racist tropes and practices, political and social injustices, appropriation, and abuse for over six centuries. In 2019 and 2020, when the National Football League's Washington Redskins, Major League Baseball's Cleveland Indians, and Land O' Lakes Butter manufacturer decided to respectively retire the team names, the Chief Wahoo mascot, and the image of the Native American woman MIA from its packaging, there was a public outcry. People asked, "Where was this resistance before?" Well, the answer is that it had been there all along, just not in a space where people noticed it.

Paths of Resistance

It is within this space that this chapter will now focus on. It must be recognised that Indigenous timelines are not like Western timelines. Rather than temporising in straight chronologies, we are cyclical and thematic. As stated previously, I am an Indigenous storyteller first. As such, this story needs to circle back a little. Where one path of resistance evolved with direct action, causes, and conflict, another evolved with education and creating connections. The two sides of this story are exemplified on the one hand by *Buffalo Bill's Wild West* show and AIM's campaigns. On the other hand, they are illustrated by the path of *healthways* and education. While medicine and healthways may seem to be unrelated tangents to the topic of resistance, they are core to opposition and revitalisation campaigns throughout the centuries.

The portrayals and perceptions of Indigenous cultures, healthways, and sociopolitical inequities were not simply left behind when the United States was established or when the Mexican

Revolution expelled Spanish control from Mesoamerica. Policies put in place by such polities to control Indigenous cultures still have impacts well into the 21st century. In spite of this, healthway practices, once labelled as witchcraft, hocus-pocus, old wives' tales, or hippy stuff, have persisted. Although medicine and politics are not generally considered interrelated, in Indigenous American culture, they are very much connected and serve as a daily part of spiritual and community life. Be it physically or psychologically, prayer, bathing, food, herbs, and smoke are all considered medicinal and healthways to healing. Part of the subjugation of Indigenous Americans were the political and legal controls established to erase healthway practices and confirm the "superiority" of Western medicine. As laws and systemic oppressions were established, Indigenous American religions were outlawed. Medical historian Francisco Guerra calls this process "medical colonisation" and argues this was a purposeful and methodical part of the subjugation of Indigenous peoples, concluding that

> the religious denominations of the colonizing powers in America, both Catholics and Protestants, had a considerable influence upon the development of medicine in the New World, and, furthermore, gave to the practice and to the present-day institutions distinctive characteristics that evolved from the colonial period.
>
> *(Guerra 1963, 154)*

While this again draws on colonial United States and Mexican history, these practices of control and erasure persisted well into the 20th century. Speaking with elders, examples of child separations during the residential school era and before the implementation of the Indian Child Welfare Act were rampant and enforced for reasons like "poverty" or "poor health." This included practising Indigenous medicine rather than going to a certified Western physician because traditional healthways were not considered effective or respectable (Larney 2017; Davis 2001, 20–22). Charges of alcoholism, abuse, or threats to "the moral good" were often used with or without evidence in order to force children into boarding schools and adoption (*Second Judicial Circuit Court South Dakota* 2019). In 1891, compulsory schooling and residential schools were officially established to assimilate Indigenous children into the United States and eliminate all traces of their tribal cultures. While family separations started decades earlier, hundreds of thousands of children were taken by force to over 300 schools in the United States and Canada, separating them from their cultures and traditions.

Though seeming like an issue relegated to the distant past – Indigenous children from the late 19th to well into the mid-20th century (cases were not uncommon even in 1952) could be bought by White families for as little as five to ten dollars (Smith 2013, 17). Such practices were born of a "kill the Indian, save the man" mentality (the motto of the Carlisle Indian Industrial School) to promote the forced assimilation of Indigenous peoples. When speaking of mental health – even in light of the massacres, broken treaties, and poverty, practices of family and cultural separation remains one of the darkest historical traumas in Indigenous American memory. It is estimated that by the mid-20th century, one in four Indigenous children were still being removed when their families were deemed "unfit" (*NICWA.org* 2019). A full decade after the 1964 Civil Rights Act, Indigenous American religions were officially legalised, and child separations were legally ended with the American Indian Religious Freedom Act and Indian Child Welfare Act in 1978, as reports of intentional and unintentional oppression were brought to light (*NICWA.org* 2019). Within this context, activists in tribal communities came of age – so to speak – and addressed issues both through direct action and through education. I will discuss the direct action first, returning to the story arc of *Buffalo Bill's Wild West* show.

The American Indian Movement

To understand how contemporary movements like the digitally enabled Social Distance Powwow bring the Indigenous past into the present in a new way, we need to examine the groundwork of a few of the largest and most successful resistance and revitalisation campaigns in the North American Indigenous world. Although this chapter has argued that the first "modern" Indigenous cultural and political activism in the United States can be traced to *Buffalo Bill's Wild West* show, it was the American Indian Movement (AIM) in the mid-20th century that took resistance and activism to the next level. Between 1953 and 1969, the US government put in place policies which superficially were purported to end the reservation system. However, such policies had more damaging impacts and sparked deeper and unanticipated resistance. Part of the "Indian Termination Policies" was the *Indian Relocation Act* of 1956, which aimed to relocate adults and their families to urban centres and away from reservations. The act provided dedicated resources for job training and transportation from the reservations to urban areas, and even instituted programmes for initial housing and healthcare. These do not sound horrible at first glance. However, though their purpose was to end reservation system, in practice they dispersed and assimilated Indigenous peoples into urban populations. What those relocated found instead was more poverty, little to no government support, and initial isolation. From an Indigenous perspective such policies can be easily seen as yet another attempt in a long line of stratagems to eliminate tribal cultures and practices. As Steven L. Pevar observes,

> Nothing else that Congress can do causes tribal members to lose more of their rights than termination. Termination is the ultimate weapon of Congress and ultimate fear of tribes. Despite its drastic effect, the Supreme Court has held that Congress has the power under the Commerce Clause to terminate a tribe
>
> *(Pevar 1983, 68).*

Still, while sweeping and detrimental, it could be argued that these policies backfired. In practice, they led to the development of heterogeneous urban Indigenous communities which like those who participated in *Buffalo Bill's Wild West* show, began to spread their cultures, practices and traditions pan-tribally. Indigenous American issues which had previously been relegated to isolated communities on reservations were suddenly cast across the cityscapes of the United States. Urban centres like the Dallas-Fort Worth Metroplex, San Francisco, Phoenix, and Oklahoma City became mixing-places and hotbeds for Indigenous American congregations. While the Indian Relocation Act was not a good thing for tribal continuity, as many people were cut off from their families (adding to continuing inter-generational experiences of colonial and cultural trauma) the new connections formed in these urban communities were beneficial in their own way. Resulting in stronger and farther reaching social and political activism, the urban facilitation of community connections and networks, contributed to the establishment, diversity and strengthening of AIM. Although the structures in place within these urban centres and in the greater United States as a whole were not built for Indigenous communities, their dispersion led to several iconic events in "modern" American Indigenous history, including the Occupation of Alcatraz, the "Second" Wounded Knee, the seizing of the Mayflower replica in 1970, and the occupation in Washington, DC, of the Bureau of Indian Affairs offices. The first two acts of resistance hold particular importance and precedent for the DEH due to their unique scope and use of media and technology.

As word of mouth and tribal connections can only get you so far, the Occupation of Alcatraz from 1969 to 1971 used the mass communication technology of the era to broadcast Indigenous activism and resistance to its fullest effect. Whereas acts of resistance prior to the 1950s, 1960s, and 1970s were largely relegated to single and often isolated tribes, the Occupation of Alcatraz commenced with Indigenous college students who had been gathering at the San Francisco American Indian Center (Chaat Smith 1996; Hickey 2020). Activists used universities as forums, and by attracting news coverage, and establishing their own pirate radio station, were able to swell the protest from a handful of students to between 600 and 1000 campaigners. Knowing fully what they were doing and fully tongue-in-cheek, the activists offered to buy Alcatraz for $24.00 in beads and cloth (Chaat Smith 1996, 24). To the general public that amount might not hold any significance. However, Indigenous Americans have long-term memories, and it is common knowledge among tribal communities this was the price paid to the Lenape people for the island of Manhattan by the Dutch in 1626. For tribal peoples from all over the country who were being moved to urban centres and intermingling for the first time in large numbers, Alcatraz was a cathartic moment for many (Kelly 2009; Various 2017). When John Trudell spoke on *Radio Free Alcatraz* during the Occupation, it was like the voice of their people finally breaking free from the reservation. It created a moment not just for individual Lakota, Navajo, Iroquois, Pueblo, Ojibwe, Muwekma Ohlone or any of the other 600 and more tribes in America. It was about *all* Indigenous peoples. With the entire apparatus of the United States power structure skewed against them, in terms of everything from water rights and pipelines to courts and governmental institutions, Trudell's broadcast spoke for Indigenous people, and *to* Indigenous people, in a way few had ever done so before (Needham 2016).

Although Alcatraz was eventually re-taken by United States authorities, following the Occupation, Richard Nixon (1970) acknowledged that "The time has come to break decisively with the past and to create the conditions for a new era in which the Indian future is determined by Indian acts and Indian decisions." In the 19 months of freedom afforded by the Occupation, pan-tribal attitudes and practices were forged, and created far-reaching impacts that can still be witnessed to this day at powwows across the United States and Canada.

Soon after, other direct actions of occupation began. AIM became a thorn in the side of the US government, showing up in DC, Boston, and Wounded Knee in North Dakota – where one of the most significant and most highly publicised events of Indigenous resistance took place. Wounded Knee was the site of one of the most horrific single events in US history. On the freezing morning of 29 December 1890, the US Army's Seventh Cavalry encircled an encampment at Wounded Knee Creek of Lakota Sioux, who were about to surrender and accept reservation life. Part of this surrender from seasonal nomadism to forced permanent settlement was to be the disarmament of the remaining Sioux hunters and warriors.

Unfortunately, no one told the Sioux about this until the soldiers were demanding their weapons. Elders say that Black Coyote, a deaf man, did not understand the commands being given to him and resisted. Others say that the soldiers were angry about the deaths of fellow Seventh Cavalry soldiers killed along with General George Custer in Wyoming Territory at the Battle of Greasy Grass/Little Bighorn in 1876. Still others say it was out of fear of the Ghost Dance, a religious revival that centred around a prophesied expulsion of white colonizers. Regardless of why, a rifle went off and a massacre commenced. The Sioux encampment was attacked with rifles, small arms, and rapid-fire Hotchkiss guns. Between 250 and 300 men, women, and children were killed. Between 25 and 30 cavalrymen died, mostly by friendly fire. The remains of tribal members were then denied a proper burial, left to freeze, and tossed into a mass grave. Twenty cavalrymen received the American Medal of Honor for this action. As one can guess, this left a lasting and sour memory. When AIM gained traction in the 1970s, the memory of the massacre was far from forgotten. In 1973, a dispute concerning corrupt leadership among the Oglala Sioux at the Pine Ridge Reservation sparked an armed occupation of a church near

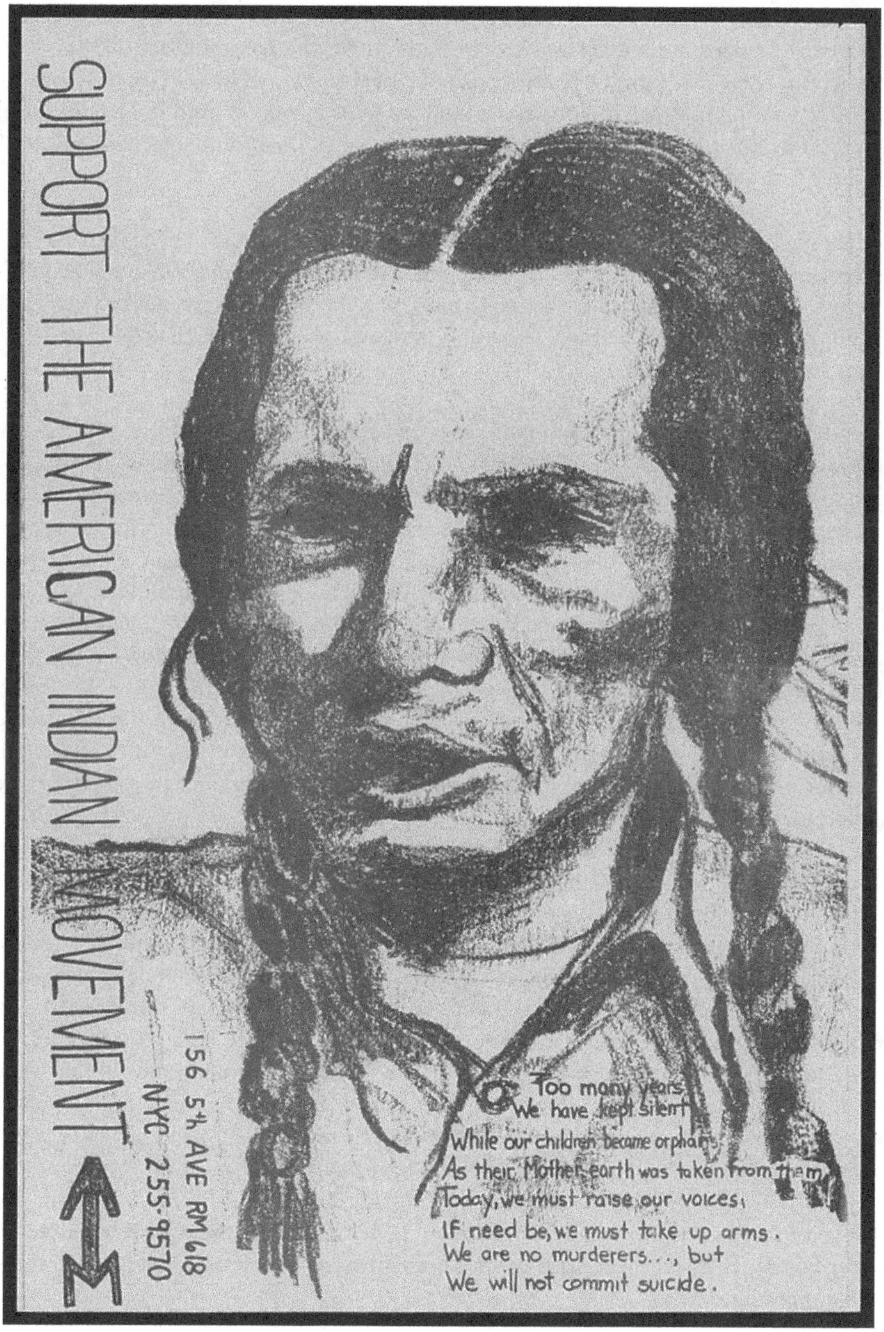

Figure 7.2 1960 poster depicting a portrait of a Native American to raise awareness for the American Indian Movement (Wikipedia Commons).

the 1890 massacre site at Wounded Knee. Members of AIM, along with a party of Oglala who opposed tribal leadership they felt was crooked and under the control of the US government, entrenched themselves in a prolonged siege. From 27 February to 8 May 1973, the party resisted tribal police who supported tribal chairman Richard Wilson, agents from the Bureau of Indian Affairs, the FBI, the US Marshall's Office, and other agencies. According to John Sayer (1997), the government response was overwhelming and brutal:

> [T]he equipment maintained by the military while in use during the siege included fifteen armored personnel carriers, clothing, rifles, grenade launchers, flares, and 133,000 rounds of ammunition, for a total cost, including the use of maintenance personnel from the National Guard of five states and pilot and planes for aerial photographs, of over half a million dollars.

All this to stop a band of around 200 men, women, children, and elderly. Still, because of this occupation, AIM leaders like Russell Means and Dennis Banks became household names among Indigenous American households around the country. The adroit use of national television coverage gained attention for their wider causes, not only for the Oglala but for treaty rights of Indigenous tribes all over the United States. Their broadcast media campaign was hugely successful, with public sentiment swaying in their favour and public outcry at multiple levels. Other minority groups like the Congressional Black Caucus and members of the Chicano Movement were vocal in backing AIM's causes. Even in Hollywood and country music circles, the actor Marlon Brando and singer Johnny Cash, respectively, voiced support (Riches 1997, 159) Sadly, like so many other events, the 1973 Siege at Wounded Knee ended with the loss of life and the US government back in control. In the decades since, Indigenous resistance has manifested in many forms. Until the advent of the internet, most of these resistance movements remained highly localised.

The media coverage of the Wounded Knee Siege and broadcasts of *Radio Free Alcatraz* were much more broadly viewed and heard than any Indigenous resistance campaigns before their time; they were still limited in scope to those watching specific television stations or within radio signal radii. However, as Indigenous American rights became more solidified and termination policies began to end, methods of broadcast technology learned from Wounded Knee and Alcatraz contributed to revitalisation and resistance campaigns, movements and causes becoming more visible and gaining traction with the general American public. The protection of Indigenous children in 1978 with the Indian Child Welfare Act was a feature of this. In the 1990s, the Native American Languages Act was passed, finally allowing tribes to teach their children their own language in schools, followed by the Native American Graves Protection and Repatriation Act, which protected sites, bodies, and artefacts from grave robbers and the antiquities trade. One by one, laws which had been in place to eliminate Indigenous American cultures for 250 years began to fall. As the year 2000 rolled around, Indigenous activists were ready to engage digital technologies in the next steps to create forms of resistance and to revitalise and foster resilient communities.

Indigenous Digital Resistance and Resilience in the New Millennium

Now, not all is doom and gloom. Indigenous Americans are resilient. Attempts across the Western Hemisphere utilising digital technologies and other methods are working to both preserve and resurrect Indigenous medicine, healthways, and cultures. Indigenous peoples in the United

States were not the only ones to suffer from European colonisation and settlement. Most Indigenous nations in the Americas have struggled with the same issues of genocide and oppression. Moving beyond the borders of the United States, digital technologies and the interconnected nature of the 21st-century internet of things comes into play. In Peru, for example, people like Dr Marta Villar and organisations like Misha Rastrera are working with the World Health Organization (WHO) to re-cultivate traditional medicines and adapt their use to complement Western medicine.[1] Misha Rastrera's digital platform remediates flora, botany, herbs and other natural products from Andean-Amazonian environments for global circulation and consumption, creating a world-wide market to ensure their sustainable cultivation. As Pedro Amasifuen, a farmer of medicinal plants, states "to have these medicinal plants is to save our Indigenous world" (Machiaro 2019). Misha Rastrera's attempts to bring access to traditional medicines through digital pathways is seeing growing success, especially as supplements to Western medicine. And they are not alone, as the WHO reports similar movements around the globe with Indigenous populations of colonised nations disseminating traditional knowledges, practices and flora through the World Wide Web and social media platforms (WHO 2019).

In North America, Indigenous sweat lodges and healing ceremony practices are finding their way through similar knowledge systems transmissions into Western medicine.[2] This is especially true in the treatment of post-traumatic stress disorder for returning military veterans. Whereas before, it was literally illegal to conduct a sweat lodge in public or as "medicine," the acknowledgement of their healing properties is the result of Indigenous educators and medical practitioners advocating such healthways. Such practices are being used to treat individuals suffering from mental health issues in prisons, the elderly in hospices, military veterans, and first responders. Because of advocacy and perseverance, where once was an underground practice of healing through ceremony, herbs, and sweats is now a widely accessed practice gaining respect among the medical communities they serve.

Such healthways would not have survived without elders willing to break the law to keep them alive and are now being promulgated through digital platforms and networks. In Canada, the efforts of Indigenous doctors like Dr Evan Adams (widely known for his role as an actor in the film *Smoke Signals*), changes are being made within and outside of the Canadian healthcare system. After cases of forced chemotherapy and other involuntary treatments were discovered, Adams, employing digital and other forms of media, advocated for more holistic approaches and medical autonomy for Indigenous populations. Speaking to the *Canadian Medical Association Journal*, he stated,

> Our health indicators say we are making a difference. . . . People are very clear they don't want their newly reformed health system to be a carbon copy of the Western health care system.
>
> *(Vogel 2015, E10)*

While the system is far from perfect, as distrust of the government and hospitals still leads many to avoid treatment altogether, improvements are being made. One such improvement is the permission of healers to *smudge* (ceremonially burn sacred herbs) in hospitals across Canada. While doctors and laymen alike still debate whether any improvement in patient condition is a result of the psychological benefit of these practices or some physiological response to a substance in the smoke, it has been shown that patients receiving this care generally do show improvement. This simple gesture, allowing an ancient practice to take place in a patient's room, has brought hope and joy to the Native American community. Dr Adams used the media platform gained from film to advocate for his people, and he is not alone. Indigenous actors, musicians, artists, social media influencers, and designers use their broadcast and social media platforms to shift perceptions and call attention to issues in a way that direct action like protests and occupations cannot.

After the announcement of these policy changes in Toronto and Ottowa in 2017, social media was flooded with well-wishes, thank-you messages, and shows of respect. Sadly, the story in the United States is much different. Indigenous protesters, activists, and healers have been arrested for smudging in multiple cities and states. In one widely circulated story from 2016, Josie Valadez Fraire of Denver was arrested (and subsequently released) for attempted vandalism for smudging at a counter-protest outside a Trump rally. Officers stomped out her sage and claimed she was trying to start a fire (Nicol 2016). Still, we continue to carry on these same practices regardless.

In 2016 and 2017, activists in support of the Standing Rock Sioux were arrested as they prayed, sang, and smudged in resistance to the Dakota Access Pipeline that would run through their reservation, in violation of the Fort Laramie Treaty (1868). *The Native Knowledge 360 Treaties Still Matter – The Dakota Access Pipeline* website illustrates how Indigenous activists at Standing Rock continue the practices of harnessing the media and entertainment platforms of the age to organise resistance and social and environmental justice campaigns.[3] Echoing the events at Wounded Knee in 1890 and 1973, US governmental response to the protest was fully militarised, and sacred cultural items were confiscated, and peaceful actions – like burning sage

Figure 7.3 Protesting the Dakota Access Pipeline: We can't drink oil! #NoDAPL (Wikipedia Commons/ Creative Commons – [CC BY-SA 4.0]).

and chanting – were misconstrued as hostile. But unlike the previous two conflicts, images of these "policing" actions circulated on digital and social media, bringing the acts of Indigenous resistance, the acts of these Water Protectors, into global consciousness. A similar standoff by the activist group Mauna Kea Anaina Hou, at Mauna Kea, on the island of Hawaii, where a 30-metre telescope was scheduled to be built at the top of a sacred mountain, went online in July 2019 with a digital petition calling for "The Immediate Halt to the Construction of the TMT Telescope" posted on Change.org, the activist website. By the end of the month the petition had gathered more than 278,057 signatures globally (Wu 2019). In contrast to the Standing Rock protests, police response at Mauna Kea was much more peaceful and respectful, but again elders with smudge bundles in their hands were the first to be arrested.

Still, despite all the negativity and conflict of the Standing Rock and Manua Kea protests, one beautiful thing has emerged. The rise of the internet has brought about a budding Indigenous renaissance. Because of social media and independent digital press like *Indian Country Today*, the Indigenous world is more interconnected than ever before.[4] With this worldwide communication, support to and from tribal communities has been astounding. Beyond the specific moments of resistance to the respective Dakota Access, Keystone XL, and Transmountain pipelines through tribal lands and across sacred waterways, direct action at the US national monument at Mount Rushmore, and the telescope at Mauna Kea, the sharing of information and support in cyberspace contributes to continental and supra-national global diffusions of Indigenous resistance campaigns, and traditional knowledge, including medicinal healthways and recovery of cultural heritages (see Figure 3).

Indigenous adaptations to the digital world can be seen in many ways, especially after the worldwide COVID-19 pandemic began. Support for Indigenous movements was no longer relegated to reservations or the locations of direct action. Such events became global knowledge as they were covered internationally on social media and by the independent digital press (Earhart 2018).

A prime example can be found in Brazil, where Indigenous peoples such as the Matsés and Acaté have been in the middle of a catastrophic struggle since 2016. Despite efforts to aid researchers and healers globally, their Indigenous ways of life and sacred rainforests have come under fire (literally, not figuratively), leaving these tribes in regions of the Peruvian and Brazilian Amazon safeguarding their knowledge with a little outside help from digital and social media attention. With the right-wing Brazilian nationalist regime of President Jair Bolsonaro in power and public anti-Indigenous sentiment spreading, often violently, these projects and cultural revitalisation efforts by the Matsés and Acaté peoples are under threat.

But thanks to communication with Indigenous scholars and allies at universities and activist groups online, tribal members and allies from as far away as Canada and New Zealand flocked to the Amazonian region when government forces came to burn villages and the surrounding forest. Through the use of digital and social media, a societal spotlight illuminated issues the Matsés and Acaté peoples face, and direct and international action was able to be taken. They have since developed an Indigenous encyclopedia of Amazonian medicine, with over 500 pages of traditions, plants, descriptions, photographs, and illustrations. Dr Christopher Herndon states in an interview with the Yale School of Medicine,

> With the medicinal plant knowledge disappearing fast among most indigenous groups and no one to write it down, the true losers in the end are tragically the indigenous stakeholders themselves. . . . The methodology developed by the Matsés and Acaté can be a template for other indigenous cultures to safeguard their ancestral knowledge.
> *(Blair 2016)*

Sadly, while still being monitored and discussed on digital and social media, Bolsonaro's regime remains in power, stoking anti-Indigenous feelings, leaving Indigenous projects and cultural revitalisation movements in the Amazon rainforest in danger.

The Social Distance Powwow

When the COVID-19 pandemic started, the world transitioned to a new reality. Nowhere was this more evident than among the Indigenous community in the United States. No, it is not that the pandemic spread more quickly or there were more deaths. While there were racial and ethnic disparities, and the support from the US government to reservations was not exactly stellar, that is not what I am speaking of. In the Indigenous community, the livelihoods of many are dependent on the powwow circuit. The crafts and competitions sold and hosted at these events throughout the year are a dependable and often generational source of income that completely disappeared seemingly overnight. However, out of this grim environment, a wonderful thing sprang out. As suddenly as COVID-19 appeared, so did the Social Distance Powwow and other digital mediums for activism, culture, and markets expanded far beyond reservations.

Some existed before, with online stores and markets not being a new phenomenon. What was new was the widespread visibility and utilisation of these online mediums in the Indigenous community. Unlike the Standing Rock, Brazil, or Mauna Kea actions, which utilised social media to spread the news of in-person events, the Social Distance Powwow was born entirely digital. Co-founded by Whitney Recountre, Stephanie Hebert, and Dan Simonds, the Social Distance Powwow gained so much attention that they began selling branded merchandise (almost as a joke to begin with) and starting secondary pages like the Social Distance Powwow Prayer Group and the Social Distance Powwow Marketplace. Within six months of the start of the pandemic, the Facebook page grew to over 250,000 members and became an active and thriving platform for indigeneity, culture, and community to hold powwows in digital space. Users could upload videos of their dancing, singing, and/or drumming for cash prizes sponsored by various tribes, families, and organisations. People who would normally be making their living selling their crafts were given a space and audience to sell their wares on the web without setting up their own online store or fussing with advertising. Shut down by the COVID-19 pandemic, the powwow circuit simply moved on to the internet.

The Social Distance Powwow quickly became a source of community news, activist organisation, and a cultural outlet. When the Washington Redskins announced the retirement of the racially charged mascot, the Social Distance Powwow exploded with posts. Similarly, when protests erupted at various locations around the Americas, live video streamed from the Social Distance Powwow to the masses. As the pandemic continued, more and more people began to take notice, and the visibility of the Social Distance Powwow went international. It became a common thing to see Maori and Hawaiians along with tribes from Mexico, Chile, and Brazil represented on the page. The Social Distance Powwow was not alone, however. Social apps like TikTok and Instagram witnessed an influx of dancers, singers, and Native inside jokes. Through the use of meme formats, trending skits, and dances, Indigenous TikTokers and influencers spread awareness of cultural issues and customs. Dozens of Indigenous musicians and artists like Supaman, Dallas Goldtooth, Northern Cree, and A Tribe Called Red successfully streamed their music, comedy, and videos on a wide variety of platforms. This was nothing new, as famous tribal leaders like Sitting Bull toured with *Buffalo Bill's Wild West* show, and Geronimo appeared at the St Louis World's Fair in 1904. Native musicians and actors even used similar platforms to communicate with white audiences at the turn of the 20th century and spread awareness and lobby for support, such as the US citizenship campaign for Indigenous Americans. For example, Sonya Blackstone (Creek/Cherokee), a World War I veteran, toured with composer Charles Wakefield Cadman to sing arias and solos, then speak about issues concerning reservations and allotments. Some of these leaders were so vocal in their efforts that they successfully had the head of the Bureau of Indian Affairs removed from office (Troutman 2013). Originating in late-19th-century saloons and opera houses to 20th-century Hollywood and 21st-century digital mediums, these Indigenous-shaped spaces became platforms for activism, cultural revitalisation, and pride which the US government tried so hard to destroy.

It has not all been jubilant, however. Sadly, in late May of 2021, the speed of which news could spread digitally was illustrated after the Canadian government announced the discovery of the remains of at least 215 children buried at the site of a former Indian residential school in Kamloops, British Columbia (Davies 2021). Following this, in July 2021, the Cowessess First Nations discovered the remains of 751 bodies at the site of the former Marieval Indian Residential School in the Saskatchewan province. Most remains were Indigenous children, and "some former students of the schools have described the bodies of infants born to girls impregnated by priests and monks being incinerated" (Austen and Bilefsky 2021). The last residential school in Canada closed in the 1990s, and in 2015, the Truth and Reconciliation Commission of Canada stated that residential schools were "an integral part of a conscious policy of cultural genocide" established to separate Indigenous youths from their families and "indoctrinate children" into the Anglo-Quebecois culture of Canada (Davies 2021).

Whereas before the digital revolution, the story might have probably stayed in Western Canada or even more so to the isolated Tk'emlúps te Secwépemc and Cowessess First Nations, news of the mass burials spread virally across the globe via the conduits of social media. Within hours, Indigenous pages from the Social Distance Powwow, to TikTok, to *Indian Country Today* were posting condolences, calls to action, and prayers for the children and their families. News spread beyond the Indigenous community to other activist communities and political forums, and the resulting outcry resulted in the national government quickly calling for the Canadian flag to immediately be flown at half-mast in mourning. Always ready to show resilience and cultural pride, the recovered remains have been repatriated by caravans of relatives who welcome the children and take them back home in ceremony and finally in peace. Although it is difficult and emotional, the tribal communities are pushing forward to try and get every child home. With the digital world at our disposal and the means to digitise records for greater scrutiny and employ geospatial and ground radar, search and repatriation of the lost children will continue for the foreseeable future.

Conclusion

So what does this say about the future of activism and resistance in the Indigenous community? With Haaland becoming the first Native American Secretary of the Interior in the US, social media presence expanding, and activist victories, digital spotlights are focused on Indigenous community and leadership more than ever before. Because of digital media and methods, Indigenous peoples that otherwise would have been isolated are communicating and organising protests and sharing their healthways on wider and broader scales. While the members of *Buffalo Bill's Wild West* show and the American Indian Movement worked tirelessly to keep their cultures alive, even helping establish many of the pan-tribal practices and styles we know today, I can only wonder what they could have done with the tools and techniques of the digital sphere at their disposal. Digital media has contributed to highlighting equity and social justice issues for Indigenous peoples but has not magically fixed every social-political-cultural problem shared by so many in my community. However, platforms such as the Social Distance Powwow certainly helped many of us to psychologically survive the pandemic.

I cannot say that the digital world is going to solve all the problems of the Indigenous world in the near future. What I can say with absolute confidence, however, is that Indigenous resistance is not going to disappear any time soon. Although Indian termination policies tried to end the US reservation system to fully assimilate Indigenous peoples into "American" culture, local resistances found that entertainment, broadcast, and digital mediums could blossom their efforts onto larger stages and more expansive venues. From Wounded Knee to Standing Rock, from *Buffalo Bill's Wild West* show to the Social Distance Powwow, Indigenous cultures have adapted to the worlds and mediums around them. The digital world is simply a continuation of this path. Removing relics of the past like the Washington Redskins, the Land O' Lakes Girl, and Chief Wahoo is part of a multigenerational resistance that has always been there. Now, unlike previous generations, we have the digital technology and audiences to make our voices as activists and scholars, as artists and politicians, as *people* heard beyond the silos of our small communities (Guiliano and Heitman 2017). In 2021, the US Poet Laureate and Pulitzer Prize winners for Poetry and Fiction were all Indigenous women. Sterlin Harjo's Indigenous produced Hulu series *Reservation Dogs* is one of the breakout streaming television hits of the year. There are Indigenous tribal members in Congress and Hollywood and Indigenous social media influencers. Speaking to the tribal community, our elders, I promise the fight is bigger than the Rez now, and the commonly heard rallying cry of "respect our existence or expect our resistance" is growing stronger and stronger with every shared social media post. We say it loud and proud that our existence is our resistance, our resilience, and our hope for the future. The Indigenous world has been here on Turtle Island since time immemorial.[5] It is only fitting that we make our presence known in this new and ever-evolving digital world.

Notes

1 Misha Rastrera (www.misharastrera.com).
2 The use of sweat lodges, huts, and saunas have also been found in Gaelic and Scandinavian cultures.
3 The Native Knowledge 360: *Treaties Still Matter – The Dakota Access Pipeline* (https://americanindian.si.edu/nk360/plains-treaties/dapl).
4 *Indian Country Today* (https://indiancountrytoday.com), a leading Native owned and operated online publication.
5 *Turtle Island* is an Indigenous name for North America, used in the United States and Canada, by Indigenous storytellers and activists. It also signifies the Earth and is based on a shared North American Indigenous creation story.

Sources

Austen, Ian, and Dan Bilefsky. 2021. "Hundreds More Unmarked Graves Found at Former Residential School in Canada." *New York Times*, June 24, 2021.

Blair, Jenny. 2016. "An Encyclopedia of Medicine from the Amazon." *Yale Medicine* 54 (2) (Winter): 8–9.

Chaat Smith, Paul. 1996. *Like a Hurricane: The Indian Movement from Alcatraz to Wounded Knee*. New York: The New Press.

Davies, Guy. 2021. "215 Bodies Discovered at Former Residential School for Indigenous Children in Canada." *ABC News*, May 29, 2021. Online.

Davis. J. 2001 "American Indian Boarding School Experiences: Recent Studies from Native Perspectives." *OAH Magazine of History* 15 (2) (Winter): 20–22.

Earhart, A. E. 2018. "Digital Humanities Within a Global Context: Creating Borderlands of Localized Expression." *Fudan Journal of the Humanities and Social Sciences* 11 (3): 257–369.

Government of Canada Half Masting Notice for the Discovery of Remains at the Kamloops Indian Residential School. 2021. "Government of Canada." May 31. www.canada.ca/en/canadian-heritage/services/half-masting-notices.html.

Guerra, Francisco. 1963. "Medical Colonization of the New World." *Medical History* 7 (2): 147–54.

Guiliano, J., and C. Heitman. 2017. "Indigenizing the Digital Humanities: Challenges, Questions, and Research Opportunities." In *DH 2017-ddhh2017.adho.org*. https://dh2017.adho.org/abstracts/372/372.pdf.

Hickey, Alanna. 2020. "Poetic Resistances and the Indian Occupation of Alcatraz." *American Literary History* 32 (2) (Summer): 273–300.

Indian Relocation Act of 1956. Public Law 84–956. United States 84th Congress public statutes at large 70 Stat. 986.

"Indigenous Leaders, Experts Call for Protection of Sites of Former Residential Schools." *CBC News*. British Columbia, Canada. May 30, 2021.

Kelly, C. R. 2009. *The Rhetoric of Red Power and the American Indian occupation of Alcatraz Island (1969–1971)*. University of Minnesota Digital Conservancy. https://hdl.handle.net/11299/54605.

Larney, Peggy. 2017. Interview with author.

Machiaro, Veronica. 2019. "Medicina Ancestral: Plantas Curativas en Perú." *DW Español* 26 (July). video.

Morgan, T. J. 1891. "Report of the Commissioner of Indian Affairs." *Office of the United States Secretary of the Interior*, October 1, 1891. Washington, DC.

National Indian Child Welfare Association. 2019. "About IWCA." Web. Portland, Oregon. NICWA.org.

Needham, Andrew. 2016. *Power Lines: Phoenix and the Making of the Modern Southwest*. Princeton: Princeton University Press.

Nicol, Emily. 2016. "Indigenous Woman in US Arrested for Burning Sage at Trump Protest Rally." *National Indigenous Television. Australia*, July 6, 2016.

Nixon, Richard. 1970. *Special Message on Indian Affairs*. Washington, DC: United States Congressional Address.

Peltier, Leonard. 2000. *Prison Writings: My Life Is My Sun Dance*. New York, NY: Macmillan.

Pevar, Steven L. 1983. *The Rights of Indians and Tribes: The Basic ACLU Guide to Indian and Tribal Rights*. Carbondale, IL: Southern Illinois University Press.

Red Handed Warrior Society. 2021. "Texas Governor Greg Abbott signs Indigenous People's Day and Indigenous People's Week Resolution." *Indian Country Today*, June 21, 2021. Online.

Riches, William T. Martin. 1997. "Ripples from the Pond." In *The Civil Rights Movement: Struggle and Resistance*. New York, NY: Palgrave Macmillan.

Ryan, Casey. 2009. *The Rhetoric of Red Power and the American Indian Occupation of Alcatraz Island (1969–1971)*. Minneapolis, MN: University of Minnesota.

Sayer, John. 1997. *Ghost Dancing the Law: The Wounded Knee Trials*. Cambridge, MA: Harvard University Press.

Second Judicial Circuit Court, South Dakota. 2019. "M.W.D et al v. the Catholic Diocese of Sioux Falls et al – Complaint." Accessed August 2, 2019.

Smith, Andrea. 2013. *Indigenous Peoples and Boarding Schools: A Comparative Study*. February 2010. New York, NY: Secretariat of the United Nations Permanent Forum on Indigenous Issues.

Social Distance Powwow, Facebook Pages and Community Groups. www.facebook.com/groups/832568190487520/.

Troutman, John W. 2013. *Indian Blues: American Indians and the Politics of Music, 1879–1934*. Norman, OK: University of Oklahoma.

Various Authors. 2017. "Voices from Alcatraz Island." *Indian Country Today*, September 2, 2017.

Vogel, Lauren. 2015. "Broken Trust Drives Native Health Disparities." *CMAJ Group* 187 (1) (January 6, 2015).

World Health Organization. 2019. *WHO Global Report on Traditional and Complementary Medicine*. Geneva. Licence: CC BY-NC-SA 3.0 IGO.

Wu, Nina. 2019. "Online Petition Demanding Halt to Thirty Meter Telescope Project Collects 100K Signatures." *Honolulu Star-Advertiser*, July 18, 2019.

8

COUNTERMAPPING PLANTS AND INDIGENOUS LIFEWAYS IN NORTH AMERICA

A Case Study of Tending to Turtle Island

Mickey Dennis, Kelli Hayes, Claudia Berger, Jiyoung Lee, Chris Alen Sula, and Blair Talbot

Introduction

Tending to Turtle Island (Talbot et al. 2020) is a digital mapping project created as part of a graduate-level course in digital humanities in the fall of 2020. Through three different maps, we explore plants in relation to histories of settler colonialism, alongside Indigenous knowledge and culture:

- "Visualizing a World Network of Trees" connects plants native to Lenapehoking (the land of the Lenape people, which spans from Western Connecticut to Eastern Pennsylvania and the Hudson Valley to Delaware, with Manhattan at its centre, from which we write) to a global network of plant transfer and displacement.
- "Native Plants of the High Line" examines native plants in a small, present-day park in New York City and invites reconsideration of familiar, day-to-day landscapes.
- "Body as Botany: Reconnecting the Body to the Land" explores plants, bodies, and stories across Turtle Island, the name that many Indigenous peoples, especially Algonquian- and Iroquoian-speaking peoples, use to describe the land otherwise known as North America.

In presenting these maps here, we consider prospects and limitations for anti-colonial and decolonial countermapping, offer critical reflections on the linguistic imperialism present in scientific databases, and discuss the colonial and positivist logic embedded in many GIS technologies, including ArcGIS, which was used to create these maps. This chapter does not intend to provide any easy answers to these questions or assert to resolve our predicament as settler scholars. Rather, our aim is to bear these complexities in mind while examining the movement of plants and plant knowledge across the continent and globe and, more broadly, to trace the contours of colonialism and settler colonialism along these lines.

We begin by situating this project within the larger framework of digital environmental humanities (DEH) and noting how the field should centre Indigenous peoples and their

DOI: 10.4324/9781003082798-11

knowledge and lifeways in considerations of ecology, nature, and the environment. In doing so, we hope to make space for alternative ways of knowing and understanding the landscapes we all call home.

Centring Indigenous Studies within the Digital Environmental Humanities

The environmental humanities have emerged in the 21st century as a varied terrain of scholarly activities (Emmett and Nye 2017) that inhabit "a difficult space of simultaneous critique and action" (Rose et al. 2012, 3). Central to this movement is the recognition that environmental humanities "must avoid becoming a handmaiden to environmental science" (Bergthaller et al. 2014, 268) and instead pose "fundamentally different questions, questions of value and meaning informed by nuanced historical understanding of the cultures that frame environmental problems" (Nye et al. 2013, 28). Such questions concern the very concepts of human, bodies, species, and the power relations among them, including "questions of racism and coloniality, gender and sexual difference, poverty, social exclusion, and other ethical domains," and open new possibilities for alternative conceptions of space, time, and interdependence (Neimanis, Åsberg, and Hedrén 2015, 79).

The growth of the digital humanities has added new dimensions to the questions and tactics of the environmental humanities. Digital interfaces offer imaginative, experimental, and collaborative environments for reading (Posthumus and Sinclair 2014), touring landscapes (Jørgensen 2014), envisioning space (Travis and Holm 2016), and stewarding Indigenous knowledge (Christen 2018; Risak 2020), including knowledge of the environment (Senier 2014), among many other projects (for examples, see Adamson 2018). While the digital humanities have been keen to adopt various technologies for scholarly purposes, critics within the field have called for greater attention to the histories, embedded logic, and environmental impact of those technologies (Liu 2012; Drucker 2012; Gabrys 2013; Sinclair and Posthumus 2017; Posthumus, Sinclair, and Poplawski 2018), as well as to differential access to resources across the globe (Gil and Ortega 2016; Risam 2018). Similarly, while making frequent use of technologies in this project, we also raise critical questions about those technologies, especially colonial legacies of mapping.

As settler scholars writing on the occupied land of Lenapehoking, we place special focus here on the Lenape and other Indigenous peoples and their knowledge and lifeways – recognising that a still broader analysis would include animals, insects, fungi, and other kingdoms in addition to plants. Our approach aligns with others who have pursued DEH from an anti- or postcolonial perspective (Bergthaller et al. 2014, 269–70), which is found in even the earliest calls to action in the field (Rose and Robin 2004; Griffiths 2007). Though we arrived at this focus by tracing the colonial history of plants and the knowledge systems surrounding them, Indigenous studies are central to concepts of human relationship to nature (Kimmerer 2013; Salmón 2020) and therefore merit greater attention within the (digital) environmental humanities.

The environmental humanities are inextricably spatial: questions about nature, habitats, and ecologies are fundamentally questions about *land* (and water and air). Set against histories of colonialism and settler colonialism, these are also questions about *whose* land – not in the sense of ownership, but rather of stewardship across generations. Who have been and who are the caretakers of these lands? How do these caretakers conceptualise land, nature, the environment, and human relationships to it? More broadly, how can questions of borders, territories, ownership, and resources be conceptualised and reconceptualised – and not just about land but also about other spaces, including digital ones?

This work follows DeLoughrey, Didur, and Carrigan's call to situate "environmental humanities with a firm grounding in the significance of the ongoing histories of imperialism" (2015, 3). In the case of Turtle Island, this ongoing history is marked both by external colonialism – understood to include the expropriation of natural resources, living organisms, and people, whether through conscription, enslavement, or other means (Tuck and Yang 2012, 4) – and by internal colonialism, or settler colonialism[1] – understood to include "spatial removal, mass killings, and biocultural assimilation" in settled lands (Wolfe 2006, 403). Importantly, colonialism has both tangible and intangible effects on bodies and minds, including appropriation and erasure of Indigenous language, knowledge, and culture (Jensen et al. 2009, 43).

While acknowledging the ongoing history of settler colonialism, we also recognise the damage-centred approach present in much of settler colonial studies (Tuck 2009) and the importance of placing Indigenous studies alongside discussions of settler colonialism. As Kauanui notes, "any meaningful engagement with theories of settler colonialism . . . necessarily needs to tend to the question of indigeneity. Settler Colonial Studies does not, should not, and cannot replace Indigenous Studies" (2016). Centring Indigenous peoples and their knowledge and lifeways offers possibilities for "environmental imaginaries," including "everyday practices within non-Western cultures and in pre, post- or non-capitalist contexts" (Neimanis, Åsberg, and Hedrén 2015, 82).

Relatedly, we do not here adopt the framework of the Anthropocene, which serves as a point of departure for much of the literature on environmental humanities. As some critics have noted, there are differential responsibilities for climate change among people across the globe and, even within countries in the Global North, among people from different social strata, particularly the most privileged (Cuomo 2011; Chakrabarty 2012). Moreover, human communities have lived for tens of thousands of years without causing the type of environmental degradation seen since the Industrial Revolution – and now its digital manifestations (Travis and Holm 2016). The Anthropocene is bound to the ongoing history of capitalism, itself tied intimately to colonialism and extraction. Alternative framings, such as the Capitalocene (Moore 2015; Altvater et al. 2016) and the Plantationocene (Haraway 2015; Haraway et al. 2016; Davis et al. 2019), especially in the context of plants and the "entangled triad structure of settler-native-slave" (Tuck and Yang 2012, 1), seem a better fit for this project – though even these replicate the harm-based narratives previously discussed in connection to settler colonial studies.

For this reason, we draw inspiration from Haraway's concept of the Chthulucene (2015), which honours Indigenous cosmologies[2] and offers a new way of thinking about human relationships with the land. The Chthulucene reconceives history and temporality by unseating humans as the principal actors in our contemporary geological age and reimagines our role as co-inhabitants within a multispecies ecosystem in a world on the brink of environmental collapse. Such thinking answers Fawcett's (2000) call for alternative conceptions of time, space, and interdependence and typifies what Randolph refers to as ethical imagining, a cultural practice of imagining new futures that map potential paths out of our current sociopolitical and ecological crisis (2007, 68).

In the following section, we discuss the three maps we created through this project, prefacing each with critical reflections on mapping, data, and visualisation tools. The making of these maps reveals common problems with information and representation – in some cases insurmountable – and presents strategies that other digital environmental humanists may use in approaching similar datasets and inquiries. Many of our conclusions come in the form of further questions and provocations rather than solutions, as is common with critical making in the digital humanities.

Mapping, Countermapping, and Power

Maps are often regarded as neutral entities that reflect common, agreed-upon understandings of the world. This characterisation ignores the inherently *political* nature of mapmaking and cartography and the means by which maps mediate power (Wood and Fels 1992; Pickles 1995; Wood 2010). In the case of settler colonialism, maps have been and are still used to divorce people from land, erect borders that confine and exclude, empower and enrich empires, and damage or destroy relationships to land, home, and history: "As soon as lines were drawn on maps by European hands, Indigenous place-names, which are intricately connected with Indigenous history, stories, and teachings, were replaced . . . erasing Indigenous presence from the lands" ("Native Land" 2019). Entire cosmologies that once expanded outward from one's ancestral home and helped situate oneself in time, space, and community were upended through the imposition of colonial maps and notions of land *ownership* – that land is material property to own or to steal, to extract resources from, and to profit from as an exchangeable commodity in a marketplace – in contrast to Indigenous conceptions of land *stewardship* – that land is an entity in its own right, to coexist with and to care for, connected to ancestral origin stories and communal responsibilities (Small and Sheehan 2008). This colonial ideology worked in tandem with the task of removing Indigenous peoples from their lands and, in many cases, severed Indigenous peoples from a spiritual connection to nature.

Because maps reflect the ideologies and power structures of those who make them, they are also potent sites for critical interrogation: their "absences, their exclusions and omissions, along with the difficulty of actually realising the lived experience of the spatial knowledge that maps aim to convey, open up possibilities for resisting geographies of power and for a re-mapping of the landscape on other terms" (Hunt and Stevenson 2017, 376). This framing invites a reimagining and reclaiming of mapping practices in ways that open new possibilities for knowing and interrogate the politics of "discovery." Some Indigenous communities, as well as scholars, have attempted to use the same mapmaking processes that robbed Indigenous peoples of their lands to counter colonial power and further the aims of redistributive, transformative, and restorative justice (Kidd 2019).

Broadly construed, countermapping refers to a range of methods used to map against power structures in service of anti-authoritarian goals (Huggan 1989; Perkins 2004). Critical cartography, which countermapping practices complement and are often embedded within, focuses more generally on spatial power and maps as sites of power (Huggan 1989; Crampton and Krygier 2005; Perkins 2004; Allen and Queen 2015; Pavlovskaya 2016). Countermapping practices are generally subversive in that they seek to disrupt dominant narratives and (re)surface knowledge and stories that have been silenced.

Indigenous countermapping, in particular, examines both "historic and spatial violence" and contests the concept that people and their relationship to land can ever be neutral (Hunt and Stevenson 2017, 373). Projects in this area may be anti-colonial – in the sense that they make visible and challenge the ongoing history of colonialism – or part of decolonial practices that take backspace (or land or resources) or restore Indigenous knowledge and lifeways (Iralu 2021; de Leeuw and Hunt 2018; Segalo, Manoff, and Fine 2015). Many countermaps do both, and some Indigenous peoples do not refer to their work as countermapping at all, seeing any form of mapping as perpetuating colonial frameworks (Remy 2018).

In developing our project on plants, we consulted many examples of countermapping and critical cartography, paying special attention to work representing Indigenous peoples, lands, and native flora and fauna. We considered how these projects record, encode, and visualise data. We looked critically at binaries, such as land/people, body/earth, and Native/non-Native, which are created and reinforced by Eurocentric mapping practices (O'Brien 2002; DeLoughrey, Didur, and Carrigan 2015). We approached maps with critical questions in mind: Who is creating the maps? Who is compiling the data being used? Whose claims count?

The Native Land project (https://native-land.ca) was central to our work. Started in 2015 by a settler hailing from the Okanagan territory, the project is currently in the stewardship of an Indigenous-led not-for-profit (Native Land Digital) and seeks to unsettle ways of orienting the North American territory. The map presents Indigenous lands, languages, and treaties, rather than colonial methods or metrics, and invites users to reconsider their perceptions of land, territory, people, and statehood. Borders and territories in Native Lands are multiple, overlapping, indeterminate, and porous (Sula and Daniell 2019), rendering the continent in new ways for many viewers, who are asked to search their address, click around, and think critically about the map. Taking inspiration from Native Land, we sought to create a map that invites new understandings of the landscape we call home, specifically in relation to histories of colonialism. We began by examining datasets on flora in New York City, ultimately settling on trees as a focus of inquiry.

"Visualizing a World Network of Trees" Map

Colonizers carried with them more than maps and notions of land; they also carried plants. Physically uprooting and relocating plants across oceans, situating these plants in manufactured environments, cataloguing them in endless detail – all these were exertions of imperial power on the natural world. "Visualizing a World Network of Trees" was intended to provide a broad perspective of colonialism and its hand in shaping the landscape. Recognising our own positionality and situatedness in New York City, we focused on tree species tracked through the NYC Street Tree Census conducted by NYC Parks & Recreation (2015) and made available by NYC Open Data. From over 600,000 individual trees recorded in the census, a sample of 130 trees was chosen, each one representing a single species in the dataset. We then researched each

Figure 8.1 "Visualizing a World Network of Trees" presents 130 trees, the approximate location of origin of their species around the country or globe, and their relocation to New York City.

species to determine its approximate location of origin, using online sources, such as the Missouri Botanical Garden Plants Finder, the Morton Abortorium, the Gymnosperm Database, and the American Conifer Society, among others. Finally, we created a network map using the XY line tool in ArcGIS, connecting tree origin locations to their destination site in NYC. Users can click on a point to view details on each tree (Latin name, common name, approximate origin, latitude and longitude in NYC), and the accompanying narrative asks them to consider why certain categories, such as Latin name, are represented and why other categories are currently omitted, such as the Native name for the tree in its country of origin.

Trees tend to cross geopolitical boundaries, making it difficult in many instances to identify any one country as the original location for a particular species. Moreover, the distribution of trees across any region changes over time, and widespread, systematic data on historical patterns is lacking. Nevertheless, GIS programmes require precise points or boundaries to display on a map, and our workaround was to choose the first origin country listed as an approximate source of each tree. Even this required interpretation on our part, as some sources listed regions without precise definition or location, such as "Northern China" or "Central Europe." In most cases, we selected a city located in that region to represent the tree's place of origin.

Though imprecise, this map helps to raise awareness of the global network of trees and invites new consideration of familiar landscapes. A curious pedestrian might stop to wonder how a tree known as the Japanese maple or the Siberian elm came to shade the street they walk down. The question of Native names for trees also serves to complicate our everyday understandings: How does our relationship to a dogwood tree change when referred to by any other name – or more specifically, when referred to as a *tuwchalakw*? These questions of language and knowing reverberate throughout our maps and, in turn, invite greater scrutiny of the data sources used here and the long history of botanical information, itself intimately bound to colonialism.

Surfacing Knowledge Structures and the Naming of Plants

The 17th and 18th centuries witnessed an explosion of interest in cataloguing the natural world. Alongside the expansion of imperial power, a frenzied attempt was made to gather plants from across the globe and prune them into a newly invented taxonomic nomenclature. In 1623, about 6,000 known plant species were recorded by Caspar Bauhin; by 1800, over 50,000 had been catalogued by Georges Cuvier (Schiebinger 2004, 194). Most famous in this area is perhaps Carl von Linné (commonly known as Carl Linnaeus, as he renamed himself in Latin), an 18th-century Swedish botanist and physician who is often unironically regaled as the father of taxonomy. His *Systema Naturae* (1768/1758) developed a method of binomial taxonomic nomenclature, the classification schema for minerals, plants, and animals still in use today (in an expanded form).[3]

Key to this burgeoning information communication system was an international network of botanical gardens (Crosby 1972, 1986; Brockway 1979; Schiebinger 2004; Schiebinger and Swan 2016). By the end of the late 18th century, Europeans had established 1,600 botanical gardens throughout the world along the tentacular contours of imperial expansion. These were not, as Schiebinger notes, "idyllic bits of green intended to delight city dwellers, but experimental stations for agriculture and way stations for plant acclimatization for domestic and global trade, rare medicaments, and cash crops" (2004, 11). Botanical gardens are uniquely situated within the history of plants and colonialism, both as repositories of plant data and as institutional sites of homogenisation, invested in the business of gaining profit and power through the exploitation of natural resources and local knowledge of colonised territories (Brockway 1979, 192).

Botany, like other natural sciences, "began as a *technoscope* – a way to visualize at-a-distance – but, at the end of the 18th century, it was already a *teletechnique* – a way to act at-a-distance"

(Lafuente and Valverde 2011, 140). Through scientific illustrations, nomenclature, and schema, early botany established a form of biopower and a network through which knowledge objects could circulate. The project of fitting the global natural world into a tightly controlled vocabulary in the learned language of the European elite is faulty for many obvious reasons, including the disregard for local herbalist practices and histories, the perpetuation of the notion of plant species as stable and static objects that can be defined independently of their cultural and ecological contexts, and the fact that the obsessive taxonimisation of the natural world is a prelude to extractive capitalism. This scientific project contributed to the erasure of Indigenous knowledge and cultures and appropriated that knowledge for commercial ends.

Recognising this entangled relationship between colonial and Indigenous knowledge systems and colonial power, we resolved to use Indigenous sources wherever possible and to remain critical of other data sources. In practice, this meant committing to the use of Indigenous names for plants wherever possible and focusing our work on native plants and their Indigenous uses. Both of these tasks proved challenging.

"Unnaming" plants is difficult, in part because the act of erasure (of local history, tradition, and language) itself was utilised as a very effective tactic of settler colonialism. This task is further complicated by the diversity of languages and dialects. In the case of Lenapehoking, there are two languages (Unami and Munsee, both branches of the larger Eastern Algonquin family of languages) and many dialects within each language that have their own unique names for different plant species and components. In addition, these languages evolved significantly during and after the forced relocation of many Lenape people to Oklahoma, Kansas, Wisconsin, and elsewhere. In the present day, our ability to access Indigenous names for a single plant is greatly limited by how each language has been recorded – or not – over time.

When recorded, these principally oral languages have invariably been transliterated differently by each transcriptor. Native speakers of varying locations, time periods, and mother dialects and tongues (e.g. Southern Unami, Oklahoma Lenape, Munsee) might pronounce or spell the same spoken word in different ways, just as the various settler linguists of Swedish, English, or French origin across the 18th, 19th, and 20th centuries also transliterated the same spoken word differently. These linguistic structures are themselves influenced by disparate ideas about naming, classification, and the very structure of plants within each culture: Where does a cedar tree begin, and where does it end? Does a tree encompass the roots that extend below it or smoke that extends above it when burned? Is a forest contained in a single seed? Different languages have different answers to these questions. Issues of naming persist well beyond the decision to de-emphasise Latin and English names for plants and point to the need for greater attention to Indigenous concepts of the environment.

Our research into the plant life of Lenapehoking led us to the Lenape Center and its co-director and co-founder Curtis Zuniga, who spoke with us about Lenape connections to the land. In these tellings, the Creator gave the Lenape language, knowledge, and guidance to develop customs and lifeways for their existence. The land has a spirit, and the Lenape have an affinity toward land as a life-giving power that is far greater than any human. Animal spirits would guide the Lenape and tell stories about which plants to use and which ones to avoid. Often, these plants were native to the area, although some were transplanted from other locations, both from within Turtle Island and from abroad.

As another source, we consulted uses of plants recorded in the Native American Ethnobotany Database (NAEB) (https://naeb.brit.org), an extensive online database compiling Indigenous knowledge of and uses for plants as medicine, food, ceremonial objects, fibre, and dye. The first iteration of the NAEB dates back to the mid-1970s in punch-card format. Today, it exists as both an online database as well as a 927-page print reference text (Moerman 1998). Over 44,000 discrete uses for plants, 4,260 plant species, and 291 Native American tribes are recorded in the database. Users are able to search and cross-reference the indices of both the online and print formats according to any combination of tribe, plant, or recorded use.

While NAEB data proved important for our project, our use of it was not without hesitation or critique. We are especially sceptical of the intentions of many settler scientists in the 19th and 20th centuries who compiled the source material collated in the NAEB. When undertaken by outsiders, ethnobotany (the study of human interactions with plants) can be seen as reinforcing colonialist worldviews that position Indigenous people and their traditions as objects of study rather than as makers and collaborators in their own right (Baldauf 2019). Projects like the NAEB, though rich in information, may "reassert [Eurocentric] epistemic authority while simultaneously flattening out its colonial pasts and legacies" under the "depoliticized valence" of science (Foster 2019, 3).

Using this database as a tool rather than a touchstone, we were careful not to include any plant uses that could be considered sacred knowledge, especially uses marked as ceremonial in the database. We also focused on local contexts around present-day New York City and oral histories of native plants as a counterpoint to NAEB data.

"Native Plants of the High Line" Map

Our second map visualises a subsection of plants grown on the High Line, a small Manhattan park that had a history as an elevated train track before being abandoned for decades and eventually converted to a park. This portion of our project maps plants that were not only native to the region but, according the Welikia Project (https://welikia.org), were likely to have been growing on Mannahatta pre-European contact.

At its heart, "Native Plants" is a data curation project that links a variety of sources, including NAEB data, Welikia, and plant lists from Friends of the High Line, to tell a fuller history of native plants. Though Latin scientific names were key to relating data across these sources, our map uses the Lenape term for each plant, where possible, relying on sources like the Lenape Talking Dictionary (www.talk-lenape.org), one of the only online oral history resources available for the

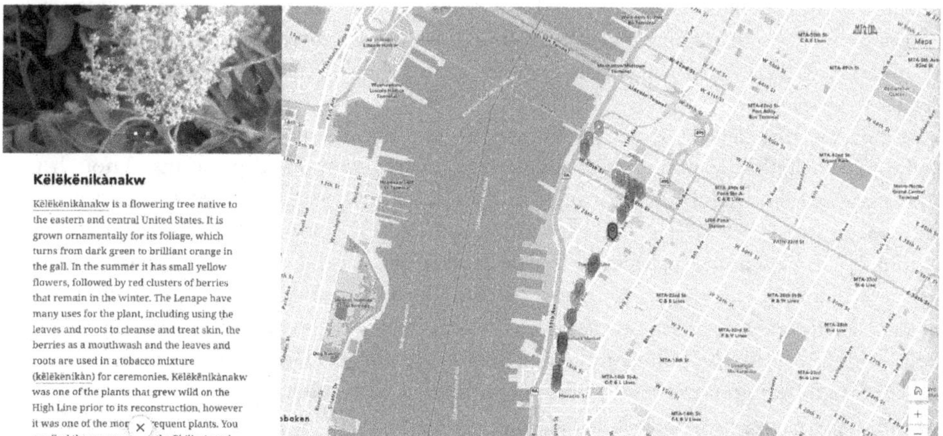

Figure 8.2 "Native Plants on the High Line" focuses on 48 native plants located along the High Line Park, including Lenape names for these plants and describing Indigenous uses of them.

Lenape. Unfortunately, we could only identify Lenape names for 9 of the 48 plants on the map, defaulting to English common names for the others, while acknowledging that English also has a history as a colonial and colonising language. We gave Lenape terms visual authority on the map by capitalising them, linked to pronunciations, and discussed Indigenous plant uses, native ranges, and key characteristics of each plant.

Since the goal of this map was to prompt viewers to reconsider familiar landscapes, we used ArcGIS StoryMaps and a left-side image gallery to the viewer's attention. When the user selects a plant, the image is enlarged, and users can scroll through multiple pictures of the plant in various stages of growth. StoryMaps also allowed us to write fuller biographies based on the data we had collected, inviting users to spend more time with each plant rather than quickly scanning a table for information. Working with StoryMaps required us to manually place each point of data, but this also forced us to decide the order in which plants would appear in the gallery and how we might curate tours through the park. While users may not find the plant in the park at the precise point it appears on the map,[4] this friction creates an interesting opportunity for visitors to explore and study the plants around them.

Making with (and Breaking) GIS Tools

While our maps set out to uplift Indigenous stories and work against colonial systems and structures, these attempts at "critical settler cartography" (Fujikane 2021) would be incomplete without acknowledging the origins of GIS. Supported by government agencies in the United States and Canada, GIS was used by departments of land and wildlife management to document and regulate the lands they control. GIS technology also depends on the GPS, intimately linked to militarist and capitalist concerns in the 20th century (Kaplan 2006).

Though open-source GIS tools exist, we chose to use the proprietary ArcGIS suite for this project, in part because our university has a site license and also because the suite has a number of tools and features that support the different directions of our three maps: the XY line tool for the tree network, StoryMaps for the High Line map, and Experience Builder for the body map (which we will come to in the next section). The basic features of ArcGIS were easy to learn and allowed us to publish and embed our maps within contextual essays. Together, these benefits let us focus on data, design, research, and representation. While we recognise that proprietary tools generally serve as barriers against those who cannot afford a license, even open-source GIS tools replicate certain colonial values associated with the technology generally (Gieseking 2018), two of which we consider in the following paragraphs: precision and alternative spatialities.

At the most basic level, GIS tools require latitude and longitude coordinates to position items on the map, whether as points or as lines or boundaries composed of points. Though point-based maps can be useful, they do not always reflect how people experience or think about land, space, or place (Murrieta-Flores, Donaldson, and Gregory 2016). The very metaphor of "pinning" – as in pinning a specimen for study, display, or preservation – was not lost on us in this project, and the degree of precision required by GIS software was at odds with much of our data. Plants exist over ranges of space, crossing boundaries and borders and making it difficult to identify any one point or even an area for any plant: Does a plant end with its visible surface? Should we count its roots, often commingled with other plants? What about its pollen and the many routes by which it circulates? The question of where any plant begins and ends is deeply informed by culture, an indeterminacy in tension with the positivist assumptions of GIS. Though one could, in practice, use a GPS device to mark locations of plants, this technical solution elides the deep cultural and conceptual issues at play with plants (and other things), a case of GIS requiring "scholars to change their methods to suit technology, rather than making the technology work for them" (Kemp and Mostern 2001).

More fundamentally, GIS tools reflect certain assumptions about space (and time, as well). Precise points are set against the grid of one of many projection systems, long recognised for their varying distortions and prizing of some areas of the globe over others (Mulcahy and Clarke 2001). Still, there remains a fundamental assumption that space is objective – shared by all observers and measurable as such – and that time is ordered and continuous when it is represented at all. But what if land and water and air are not discrete entities but rather viewed in relation to human beings and other living things? What if humans, too, exist in relation to their ancestors and to generations to come – and in ways that are not easily modelled on linear time? We wondered whether and how such views of space and time might be represented using GIS tools developed within Western contexts.

For our third map, we drew inspiration from the A:shiwi (Zuni) countermapping project (https://emergencemagazine.org/story/counter-mapping), which seeks to reconnect the present generation of A:shiwi with their past and their land, again emphasising the role of maps in positioning people to the world. This project resurfaces the ancestral knowledge and memories imbued in the A:shiwi environment and cosmology, reasserting the importance of experience and stories in visualising time and space. A second, visual reference came from an e-literature project called "High Muck A Muck" (http://highmuckamuck.ca), created by a Vancouver art collective in 2014. This interactive poem explores Chinese immigration to the west coast of Canada – "into which Asian immigrants enter but are never fully allowed to arrive" – using a series of watercolour maps and illustrations, which link to text and video. The main background features an outline of a human torso superimposed on a map of Western Canada, with waters, mountains, and trees giving texture to the body. Visually, the display centres on people and reasserts that land and body are one, even when dislocated through diaspora and colonising forces. Drawing on these concepts, we set out to create a body map of plants and Indigenous peoples.

"Body as Botany: Reconnecting the Body to the Land" Map

Each Indigenous culture has its own creation stories about the beginning of the world; how land formed; how crops began to grow; relationships with animals; movements of the sun, moon, and stars; and more. In "Body as Botany," we wanted to take a closer look at these stories, their connection to land, and the plants that grow on it. We also wanted to rebuff the colonial concept that the only useful map is a snapshot of the earth pinned with information. We began by trying to reimagine a map of Turtle Island along the lines of a human body. Specifically, we examined alternative projection systems that might accept standard coordinate data but represent them in novel ways, much like cartogram maps warp areas based on value. A subsequent idea was to create "fake," or placeholder, longitudes and latitudes for various plants to recreate the shape of a human body on a map of Turtle Island, building on previous work mapping non-spatial data using concepts and metaphors (Old 2001; Xin, Ai, and Ai 2018). Still, we struggled in representing the circular/cyclical connections of land, plants, and people found in many Indigenous cultures (O'Sullivan 2020). The very idea of a body map brought a slew of questions: Would we use one map for the whole continent, one map per tribe, multiple maps per location? (How) Would we represent sex and gender for this body, or even cardinal direction and orientation? Would our countermapping efforts fail to account for concepts of place and body that are not familiar to us as settlers?

With these complexities in mind, we began researching Indigenous creation stories associated with geographic features (e.g. lakes, mountains) and with body parts, using tribal web resources

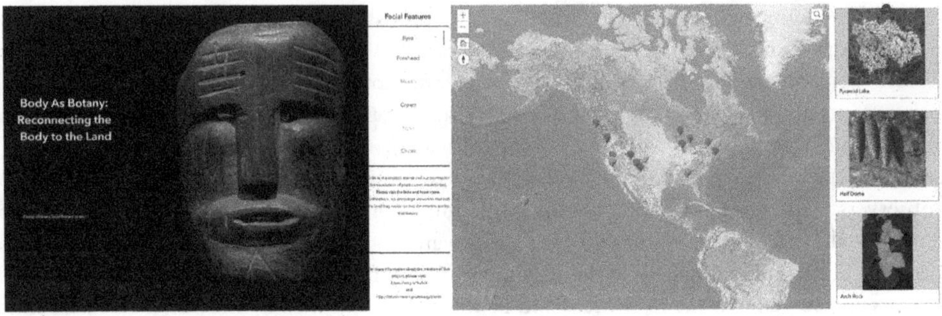

Figure 8.3 In "Body as Botany," users are asked to click on a facial feature of a Mesingw mask, which leads them to an Indigenous creation story from a tribe that used a specific plant as medicine for that body part.

as much as possible – though many of these sites do not appear in the top Google search results (or at all). With each story, we identified the tribe that tells the story, the land where the geographic feature is located, and the native plants used by that tribe for the body part mentioned in the story. For example, a Paiute creation story tells that Chi-ui Pah (Pyramid Lake) was formed from the tears of Stone Mother, thus connecting this story to the eyes. The Paiute use a strained decoction of leaves from *tosi-tonig* or *wada'a-kwasi'* (western yarrow, or *Achillea millefolium*) as drops for sore eyes, linking the plant back to Pyramid Lake. Some connections surfaced quickly, while others required more creativity, such as a plant that stimulated the appetite of a giant who ate too much. With 20 or more sets of creation stories, lands, and plants identified – mostly about the head – our vision of the body map manifested as a facial feature map, rendered using a Lenape mask of Mesingw, a powerful medicine spirit who maintains the balance of nature.

A screenshot from the "Body as Botany" web interface showing the home page on the left with the text "The Body as Botany: Reconnecting the Body to the Land" and the Mesingw face mask, a middle panel contains a list of facial features with eyes highlighted, and the right panel shows a map of North America with location points related to the eyes selected. On the far right of this panel are three squares depicting plants. These are titled, from top to bottom, "Pyramid Lake," "Half Dome," and "Arch Rock."

Using ArcGIS Experience Builder, we attempted to create interactivity and fluidity between the face, native plants, creation stories, and geographic features. We chose pictures of native plants in the wild rather than a taxonomy specimen photograph or a botanical illustration associated with colonial enterprises. The initial image of the face previews the creation stories that await while also problematising notions of space by having the same facial feature associated with multiple sites across the entire continent. Despite their geographic distance on the continent, plants, creation stories, and people are linked spiritually on this map, presenting an alternative view of the objective, spatially accurate maps we often see.

Though we attempted to use the Indigenous name of the plant corresponding to each tribe's use and story, further research is needed here, given the number and complexity of languages involved. In conversation with Curtis Zuniga, we imagined the potential for a fuller version of this map in dialogue with the many peoples whose stories appear here, as well as others. While acknowledging the essential role of outreach in projects like this one, we also note the significant time (perhaps hundreds of hours in this case) and resources (including fair compensation for Indigenous peoples participating in this work) that such engagement would require – far beyond what was available to us in one academic semester. At best, we hope this map and the project as a whole serve as a model that others might learn from, build upon, and use to direct attention and resources toward projects that centre Indigenous people and knowledge.

Conclusion

As non-Native occupants of unceded Lenapehoking, we decided that our approach should avoid historical narratives that cast white settlers in the leading role of the drama of colonisation and again force Indigenous peoples and their rich and complex cultures to the periphery. We aimed to uproot the history of plants from the historiography of colonialism by de-emphasising retellings of harm and instead foregrounding Indigenous stories and lifeways. In some instances, this case study reveals the availability and discoverability – or not – of Indigenous knowledge resources, especially those about Indigenous languages. In others, it offers the messiness of plants and difficult heritage (Macdonald 2010) as examples that elude the assumptions of GIS technologies and perhaps databases more broadly (Posner 2016).

As Guiliano and Heitman note, the circulation and use of Indigenous data collected through colonial processes – including, we would add, colonial tools – can be both generative and destructive: "The ethical, and we argue the only path forward is through slow, thoughtful, inclusive, and collaborative practices that recognize and privilege Indigenous-centric research practices and ways of knowing" (2019). In this spirit, we offer the following steps as crucial to the task of developing critical, socially and ecologically responsible DEH projects:

- Committing to the overarching goal of decolonisation and the repatriation of land to Indigenous peoples: no "decolonizing perspectives" or "anticolonial methods" stand in for the overdue return of land to Native people – "no phraseology can be a substitute for reality" (Fanon 1963, 45).
- Working to protect and repatriate native plants and Indigenous resources.
- Critiquing the imperial history of Western science and the tools and technologies used in the DEH.
- Remaining critical of and actively resisting the extractivist goals and transactional nature that much of the environmental sciences, including GIS, are bound to.
- Supporting and collaborating with Indigenous scientists, scholars, and communities when designing, implementing, and disseminating projects.
- Including Indigenous languages in taxonomic nomenclature and databases (Gillman and Wright 2020).
- Incorporating Indigenous epistemologies and ontologies when organising knowledge about the environment, especially where it concerns dynamic conceptions of what constitutes a lifeform and the interspecies relations amongst lifeforms/subject-object relations.
- Learning from Indigenous science and the embedding of storytelling, history, language, and vision-building within it.
- Helping to preserve Indigenous languages, cultures, and knowledge and in ways desirable for Indigenous communities (Christen 2018; Snipp 2016)
- Cultivating self-critical practices as settlers when working with Indigenous knowledge.
- Building new methodologies and digital technologies that facilitate the overarching project of decolonisation.
- Visualising space in a way that respects Indigenous knowledge and culture.

Critical to the task of ethical imagining in this project was acknowledging the ways in which academic research is always-already structured by a legacy of positivist epistemology, which simultaneously delimits our understanding of the world and delegitimises Indigenous ways of knowing. By interrogating these epistemologies, questioning what counts as knowledge, and returning sovereignty to Indigenous peoples and their knowledge and lifeways, we can accomplish larger shifts in and through the DEH. And there is no easier place to start than with the plants around us.

Acknowledgements

We acknowledge the Lenape people, the original caretakers of the land on which Pratt Institute sits and on which most of our project work has occurred. In particular, we wish to thank Curtis Zuniga of the Lenape Center and the Delaware Tribe of Indians for a dialogue about Lenape people, their culture, and their relationship to the environment. We also acknowledge the many Indigenous peoples of Turtle Island, whose stories and lifeways have informed this project. We also wish to thank Prof. Dan Moerman for help with the Native American Ethnobotany Database. We are grateful to Prof. Nancy Smith for suggesting many readings about plants and the environment at the start of our project and to the team at Pratt SAVI (Spatial Analysis and Visualization Initiative), who provided guidance in formatting our data and using ArcGIS. Finally, we acknowledge members of the Pratt community, as well as editors of this collected volume, for their feedback on our work.

Notes

1 While placing special focus on settler colonialism here, we also recognise that not all settlers "benefit equally from the settler-colonial state," due to differential positions in oppressive structures such as white supremacy, hetero-patriarchy, capitalism, and especially slavery, which brought settlers to these lands against their will (Jensen et al. 2009, 11). Garba and Sorentino (2020) offer a forcible critique of how settler colonial theory tends to diminish the historical role and experiences of Black people in the colonisation of the Americas. For example, while Tuck and Yang's well-circulated article names the settler-Native-slave triad as such, most of their discussion centres on the settler-Native dyad. Subsuming the distinct experiences of Native and Black Americans into a monolithic category, ignoring the unique position of forcibly relocated enslaved Africans and their descendants, and skimming over the foundational role that chattel slavery played in settler colonialism are all commonly reproduced pitfalls within settler colonial theory.

2 The Chthulucene takes its name from the soil-dwelling spider *Pimoa cthulhu*: *Pimoa*, meaning "big legs" in the language of the Goshute people of Utah, and *chthulu*, a purposeful respelling of the taxonomist's nomenclature ("cthulhu") that reinserts the *ch*thonic into the soil-dwelling, tentacularly limbed spider. As a boundary crosser between death and life, two worlds divided by the soil underfoot, she is a close relative to the Diné's Spider Woman (Na'ashjé'íí Asdzáá), the Hopi's Spider Grandmother (Kokyangwuti), the A:shiwi's Water Spider (K'yhan'asdebi), and the Pueblo people's Thought Woman (Tsichtinako), all important life-giving figures in their respective cosmologies.

3 Linnaeus also developed a schema for classifying humans along oppressive and heavily reductive lines of racial and sexual difference, which aided the work of colonialism.

4 The Friends of the High Line dataset does not give specific locations of plants, only sections of the park where they appear. The High Line is a very narrow park, averaging 30–50 feet in most areas, and each section is only a few city blocks long. Given this small area, we used approximate locations on our map to indicate where a plant might be found. In principle, the location of each plant could be marked using a GPS device. However, deeper problems of precision persist where plants are concerned, which we discuss in the next section.

Sources

Adamson, Joni. 2018. "Introduction: The HfE Project and Beyond: New Constellations of Practice in the Environmental and Digital Humanities." *Resilience: A Journal of the Environmental Humanities* 5 (2): 1–20.

Allen, Tania, and Sara Queen. 2015. "Beyond the Map: Unpacking Critical Cartography in the Digital Humanities." *Visible Language* 49 (3): 79–98.

Altvater, Elmar, Eileen C. Crist, Donna J. Haraway, Daniel Hartley, Christian Parenti, and Justin McBrien. 2016. *Anthropocene or Capitalocene? Nature, History, and the Crisis of Capitalism*. Oakland, CA: PM Press.

Baldauf, Cristina. 2019. "From the Colonialist to the 'Autobotanical' Approach: The Evolution of the Subject-Object Relationship in Ethnobotanical Research." *Acta Botanica Brasilica* 33 (2): 386–90. https://doi.org/10.1590/0102-33062018abb0343.

Bergthaller, Hannes, Rob Emmett, Adeline Johns-Putra, Agnes Kneitz, Susanna Lidström, Shane McCorristine, Isabel Pérez Ramos, Dana Phillips, Kate Rigby, and Libby Robin. 2014. "Mapping Common Ground: Ecocriticism, Environmental History, and the Environmental Humanities." *Environmental Humanities* 5 (1): 261–76. https://doi.org/10.1215/22011919-3615505.

Brockway, Lucile H. 1979. "Science and Colonial Expansion: The Role of the British Royal Botanic Gardens." *American Ethnologist* 6 (3): 449–65. https://doi.org/10.1525/ae.1979.6.3.02a00030.

Chakrabarty, Dipesh. 2012. "Postcolonial Studies and the Challenge of Climate Change." *New Literary History: A Journal of Theory and Interpretation* 43 (1): 1–18. https://doi.org/10.1353/nlh.2012.0007.

Christen, Kimberly. 2018. "Relationships, Not Records: Digital Heritage and the Ethics of Sharing Indigenous Knowledge Online." In *The Routledge Companion to Media Studies and Digital Humanities*, edited by Jentry Sayers, 1st ed., 403–12. New York, NY: Routledge.

Crampton, Jeremy W., and John Krygier. 2005. "An Introduction to Critical Cartography." *ACME: An International Journal for Critical Geographies* 4 (1): 11–33.

Crosby, Alfred W. 1972. *The Columbian Exchange: Biological and Cultural Consequences of 1492*. Westport, CT: Greenwood Press.

———. 1986. *Ecological Imperialism: The Biological Expansion of Europe, 900–1900*. 1st ed. New York: Cambridge University Press.

Cuomo, Chris J. 2011. "Climate Change, Vulnerability, and Responsibility." *Hypatia* 26 (4): 690–714.

Davis, Janae, Alex A. Moulton, Levi Van Sant, and Brian Williams. 2019. "Anthropocene, Capitalocene, . . . Plantationocene? A Manifesto for Ecological Justice in an Age of Global Crises." *Geography Compass* 13 (5): e12438. https://doi.org/10.1111/gec3.12438.

DeLoughrey, Elizabeth, Jill Didur, and Anthony Carrigan. 2015. *Global Ecologies and the Environmental Humanities: Postcolonial Approaches*. New York, NY: Routledge.

Drucker, Johanna. 2012. "Humanistic Theory and Digital Scholarship." In *Debates in the Digital Humanities*. University of Minnesota Press. https://dhdebates.gc.cuny.edu/read/untitled-88c11800-9446-469b-a3be-3fdb36bfbd1e/section/0b495250–97af-4046–91ff-98b6ea9f83c0#ch06.

Emmett, Robert S., and David E. Nye. 2017. *The Environmental Humanities: A Critical Introduction*. Cambridge, MA: MIT Press.

Fanon, Frantz. 1963. *The Wretched of the Earth*. New York, NY: Grove Press.

Fawcett, Leesa. 2000. "Ethical Imagining: Ecofeminist Possibilities and Environmental Learning." *Canadian Journal of Environmental Education (CJEE)* 5 (1): 134–49.

Foster, Laura. 2019. "Critical Perspectives on Plants, Race, and Colonialism: An Introduction." *Catalyst: Feminism, Theory, Technoscience* 5 (2). https://doi.org/10.28968/cftt.v5i2.32309.

Fujikane, Candace. 2021. *Mapping Abundance for a Planetary Future: Kanaka Maoli and Critical Settler Cartography in Hawai'i*. Durham, NC: Duke University Press.

Gabrys, Jennifer. 2013. *Digital Rubbish: A Natural History of Electronics*. Ann Arbor, MI: University of Michigan Press.

Garba, Tapji, and Sara-Maria Sorentino. 2020. "Slavery Is a Metaphor: A Critical Commentary on Eve Tuck and K. Wayne Yang's 'Decolonization Is Not a Metaphor.'" *Antipode* 52 (3): 764–82. https://doi.org/10.1111/anti.12615.

Gieseking, Jen Jack. 2018. "Where Are We? The Method of Mapping with GIS in Digital Humanities." *American Quarterly* 70 (3): 641–48. https://doi.org/10.1353/aq.2018.0047.

Gil, Alex, and Élika Ortega. 2016. "Global Outlooks in Digital Humanities: Multilingual Practices and Minimal Computing." In *Doing Digital Humanities*, edited by Constance Crompton, Richard Lane, and Ray Siemens, 58–70. Routledge. https://doi.org/10.4324/9781315707860-12.

Gillman, Len Norman, and Shane Donald Wright. 2020. "Restoring Indigenous Names in Taxonomy." *Communications Biology* 3 (1): 1–3. https://doi.org/10.1038/s42003-020-01344-y.

Griffiths, Tom. 2007. "The Humanities and an Environmentally Sustainable Australia." *Australian Humanities Review* 43. http://australianhumanitiesreview.org/2007/03/01/the-humanities-and-an-environmentally-sustainable-australia/.

Guiliano, Jennifer, and Carolyn Heitman. 2019. "Difficult Heritage and the Complexities of Indigenous Data." *Journal of Cultural Analytics* 4 (1). https://doi.org/10.22148/16.044.

Haraway, Donna. 2015. "Anthropocene, Capitalocene, Plantationocene, Chthulucene: Making Kin." *Environmental Humanities* 6 (1): 159–65. https://doi.org/10.1215/22011919-3615934.

———. 2016. *Staying with the Trouble: Making Kin in the Chthulucene*. Durham and London: Duke University Press.

Haraway, Donna, Noboru Ishikawa, Scott F. Gilbert, Kenneth Olwig, Anna L. Tsing, and Nils Bubandt. 2016. "Anthropologists Are Talking – About the Anthropocene." *Ethnos* 81 (3): 535–64. https://doi.org/10.1080/00141844.2015.1105838.

Huggan, Graham. 1989. "Decolonizing the Map: Post-Colonialism, Post-Structuralism, and the Cartographic Connection." *ARIEL: A Review of International English Literature* 20 (4): 115–31.

Hunt, Dallas, and Shaun A. Stevenson. 2017. "Decolonizing Geographies of Power: Indigenous Digital Counter-Mapping Practices on Turtle Island." *Settler Colonial Studies* 7 (3): 372–92. https://doi.org/10.1080/2201473X.2016.1186311.

Iralu, Elspeth. 2021. "Putting Indian Country on the Map: Indigenous Practices of Spatial Justice." *Antipode* 53 (5): 1485–502. https://doi.org/10.1111/anti.12734.

Jensen, Derrick, Andrea Smith, Waziyatawin, Dee Brown, Ward Churchill, Elizabeth Martinez, and Denise Breton. 2009. *Unsettling Ourselves: Reflections and Resources for Deconstructing Colonial Mentality*. University of Minnesota. https://unsettlingminnesota.files.wordpress.com/2009/11/um_sourcebook_jan10_revision.pdf.

Jørgensen, Finn Arne. 2014. "The Armchair Traveller's Guide to Digital Environmental Humanities." *Environmental Humanities* 4 (1): 95–112. https://doi.org/10.1215/22011919-3614944.

Kaplan, Caren. 2006. "Precision Targets: GPS and the Militarization of U.S. Consumer Identity." *American Quarterly* 58 (3): 693–713. https://www.jstor.org/stable/40068389.

Kauanui, J. Kēhaulani. 2016. "'A Structure, Not an Event': Settler Colonialism and Enduring Indigeneity." *Lateral* 5 (1). https://doi.org/10.25158/L5.1.7.

Kemp, Karen K., and Ruth Mostern. 2001. "Spatial Vagueness and Uncertainty in the Computational Humanities." In First COSIT Workshop on Spatial Vagueness, Uncertainty and Granularity, Ogunquit, Maine, quoted in Matthijs Kouw, Charles Van Den Heuvel, and Andrea Scharnhorst, "Exploring Uncertainty in Knowledge Representations: Classifications, Simulations, and Models of the World." In *Virtual Knowledge: Experimenting in the Humanities and the Social Sciences*, edited by Paul Wouters, et al., 89–126 Cambridge, MA: MIT Press, 2013.

Kidd, Dorothy. 2019. "Extra-Activism: Counter-Mapping and Data Justice." *Information, Communication & Society* 22 (7): 954–70. https://doi.org/10.1080/1369118X.2019.1581243.

Kimmerer, Robin Wall. 2013. *Braiding Sweetgrass: Indigenous Wisdom, Scientific Knowledge and the Teachings of Plants*. Minneapolis, MN: Milkweed Editions.

Lafuente, Antonio, and Nuria Valverde. 2011. "Linnean Botany and Spanish Imperial Biopolitics." In *Colonial Botany: Science, Commerce, and Politics in the Early Modern World*, edited by Londa Schiebinger and Claudia Swan, 134–47. University of Pennsylvania Press. https://digital.csic.es/handle/10261/32575.

Leeuw, Sarah de, and Sarah Hunt. 2018. "Unsettling Decolonizing Geographies." *Geography Compass* 12 (7): e12376. https://doi.org/10.1111/gec3.12376.

Linné, Carl von. 1768. *Systema Naturae: Per Regna Tria Natura, Secundum Classes, Ordines, Genera, Species, Cum Characteribus, Differentiis, Synonymis, Locis*. Ed. 12, Reformata. Vol. 3. Holmiae: Impensis direct. Laurentii Salvii. www.biodiversitylibrary.org/item/137477.

Liu, Alan. 2012. "Where Is Cultural Criticism in the Digital Humanities?" In *Debates in the Digital Humanities*, edited by Matthew K. Gold, 490–509. Minneapolis, MN: University of Minnesota Press. http://dhdebates.gc.cuny.edu/debates/text/20.

Macdonald, Sharon. 2010. *Difficult Heritage: Negotiating the Nazi Past in Nuremberg and Beyond*. New York, NY: Routledge.

Mattern, Shannon. 2015. "Gaps in the Map: Why We're Mapping Everything, and Why Not Everything Can, or Should, be Mapped." *Words in Space*, September 18, 2015. https://wordsinspace.net/2015/09/18/gaps-in-the-map-why-were-mapping-everything-and-why-not-everything-can-or-should-be-mapped/.

Moerman, Daniel E. 1998. *Native American Ethnobotany*. Portland, OR: Timber Press.

Moore, Jason W. 2015. *Capitalism in the Web of Life: Ecology and the Accumulation of Capital*. Brooklyn, NY: Verso Books.

Mulcahy, Karen A., and Keith C. Clarke. 2001. "Symbolization of Map Projection Distortion: A Review." *Cartography and Geographic Information Science* 28 (3). https://login.ezproxy.pratt.edu/login?url=https://search.ebscohost.com/login.aspx?direct=true&db=edsgao&AN=edsgcl.78393275&site=eds-live&scope=site.

Murrieta-Flores, Patricia, Christopher Donaldson, and Ian Gregory. 2016. "GIS and Literary History: Advancing Digital Humanities Research through the Spatial Analysis of Historical Travel Writing and Topographical Literature." *Digital Humanities Quarterly* 11 (1).

"Native Land." 2019. https://native-land.ca/resources/teachers-guide/.

Neimanis, Astrida, Cecilia Åsberg, and Johan Hedrén. 2015. "Four Problems, Four Directions for Environmental Humanities: Toward Critical Posthumanities for the Anthropocene." *Ethics and the Environment* 20 (1): 67–97. https://doi.org/10.2979/ethicsenviro.20.1.67.

NYC Parks & Recreation. 2015. *NYC Street Tree Census*. New York: NYC Open Data. http://media.nycgovparks.org/images/web/TreesCount/Index.html.

Nye, David E., Linda Rugg, James Fleming, and Robert Emmett. 2013. *The Emergence of the Environmental Humanities*. Stockholm: MISTRA (Swedish Foundation for Strategic Environmental Research). www.mistra.org/wp-content/uploads/2018/06/Environmental-Humanities-Background.pdf.

O'Brien, Susie. 2002. "The Garden and the World: Jamaica Kincaid and the Cultural Borders of Ecocriticism." *Mosaic: An Interdisciplinary Critical Journal* 35 (2): 167–84.

Old, L. John. 2001. "Utilizing Spatial Information Systems for Non-Spatial-Data Analysis." *Scientometrics* 51: 563–71. https://doi.org/10.1023/A:1019603321216.

O'Sullivan, Megan. 2020. "Indigenous Ethnobiology of the Upper Midwest." *ArcGIS StoryMaps*. October 18, 2020. https://storymaps.arcgis.com/stories/82229bebffe0470e9b200e48d5cd6312.

Pavlovskaya, Marianna. 2016. "Digital Place-Making: Insights from Critical Cartography and GIS." In *The Digital Arts and Humanities*, edited by Charles Travis and Alexander von Lünen, 153–67. Springer Geography. Cham: Springer International Publishing. https://doi.org/10.1007/978-3-319-40953-5_9.

Perkins, Chris. 2004. "Cartography – Cultures of Mapping: Power in Practice." *Progress in Human Geography* 28 (3): 381–91. https://doi.org/10.1191/0309132504ph504pr.

Pickles, John. 1995. *Ground Truth*. New York: Guilford.

Posner, Miriam. 2016. "What's Next: The Radical, Unrealized Potential of Digital Humanities." In *Debates in the Digital Humanities*, edited by Matthew K. Gold and Lauren F. Klein. University of Minnesota Press. https://dhdebates.gc.cuny.edu/read/untitled/section/a22aca14-0eb0-4cc6-a622-6fee9428a357.

Posthumus, Stephanie, and Stéfan Sinclair. 2014. "Reading Environment(s): Digital Humanities Meets Ecocriticism." *Green Letters* 18 (3): 254–73. https://doi.org/10.1080/14688417.2014.966737.

Posthumus, Stephanie, Stéfan Sinclair, and Veronica Poplawski. 2018. "Digital and Environmental Humanities: Strong Networks, Innovative Tools, Interactive Objects." *Resilience: A Journal of the Environmental Humanities* 5 (2): 156. https://doi.org/10.5250/resilience.5.2.0156.

Presner, Todd, and David Shepard. 2015. "Mapping the Geospatial Turn." In *A New Companion to Digital Humanities*, edited by Susan Schreibman, Ray Siemens, and John Unsworth, 199–212. Chichester: John Wiley & Sons, Ltd. https://doi.org/10.1002/9781118680605.ch14.

Randolph, Jeanne. 2007. *Ethics of Luxury: Materialism and Imagination*. Toronto: YYZ Books.

Remy, Lola. 2018. "Making the Map Speak: Indigenous Animated Cartographies as Contrapuntal Spatial Representations." *NECSUS* 7: 21.

Risak, Sam. 2020. *The Ubume Challenge: A Digital Environmental Humanities Project*. Orange, CA: Chapman University. https://digitalcommons.chapman.edu/english_theses/15.

Risam, Roopika. 2018. "Decolonizing the Digital Humanities in Theory And Practice." In *The Routledge Companion to Media Studies and Digital Humanities*, edited by Jentry Sayers. New York: Routledge. https://digitalcommons.salemstate.edu/english_facpub/7.

Rose, Deborah Bird, Thom van Dooren, Matthew Chrulew, Stuart Cooke, Matthew Kearnes, and Emily O'Gorman. 2012. "Thinking Through the Environment, Unsettling the Humanities." *Environmental Humanities* 1 (1): 1–5. https://doi.org/10.1215/22011919-3609940.

Rose, Deborah Bird, and Libby Robin. 2004. "The Ecological Humanities in Action: An Invitation – AHR." *Australian Humanities Review* 31–32. http://australianhumanitiesreview.org/2004/04/01/the-ecological-humanities-in-action-an-invitation/.

Salmón, Enrique. 2020. *Iwígara: American Indian Ethnobotanical Traditions and Science*. Portland, OR: Timber Press.

Schiebinger, Londa. 2004. *Plants and Empire: Colonial Bioprospecting in the Atlantic World*. Cambridge, MA: Harvard University Press.

Schiebinger, Londa, and Claudia Swan. 2016. *Colonial Botany: Science, Commerce, and Politics in the Early Modern World*. Philadelphia, PA: University of Pennsylvania Press.

Segalo, Puleng, Einat Manoff, and Michelle Fine. 2015. "Working with Embroideries and Counter-Maps: Engaging Memory and Imagination within Decolonizing Frameworks." *Journal of Social and Political Psychology* 3 (1): 342–64. https://doi.org/10.5964/jspp.v3i1.145.

Senier, Siobhan. 2014. "Decolonizing the Archive: Digitizing Native Literature with Students and Tribal Communities." *Resilience: A Journal of the Environmental Humanities* 1 (3): 69–85.

Sinclair, Stéfan, and Stephanie Posthumus. 2017. "Digital ? Environmental: Humanities: Digital Environmental Humanities." In *The Routledge Companion to the Environmental Humanities*, edited by Ursula K. Heise, Jon Christensen, and Michelle Niemann, 369–78. London: Routledge. https://dig-eh.org/deh-routledge/.

Small, Garrick, and John Sheehan. 2008. "The Metaphysics of Indigenous Ownership: Why Indigenous Ownership Is Incomparable to Western Conceptions of Property Value." In *Indigenous Peoples and Real Estate Valuation*, edited by Robert A. Simons, Rachel Malmgren, and Garrick Small, 103–19. Research Issues in Real Estate. Boston, MA: Springer US. https://doi.org/10.1007/978-0-387-77938-6_6.

Snipp, C. Matthew. 2016. "What Does Data Sovereignty Imply: What Does It Look Like?" In *Indigenous Data Sovereignty*, edited by Tahu Kukutai and John Taylor, Vol. 38, 39–56. Toward an Agenda. Canberra: ANU Press. www.jstor.org/stable/j.ctt1q1crgf.10.

Sula, Chris Alen, and Rachel Daniell. 2019. "Mapping and Countermapping Borders." HASTAC 2019 Conference. Unceded Musqueam (xʷməθkʷəy̓əm) Territory. Vancouever, UBC Vancouver.

Talbot, Blair, Claudia Berger, Jiyoung Lee, Kelli Hayes, Mickey Dennis, and Chris Alen Sula. 2020. *Tending to Turtle Island: Indigenous Peoples, Settler Colonialism, and Plants in North America*. Pratt Institute. https://studentwork.prattsi.org/plants/.

Travis, Charles, and Poul Holm. 2016. "The Digital Environmental Humanities – What Is It and Why Do We Need It? The NorFish Project and SmartCity Lifeworlds." In *The Digital Arts and Humanities: Neogeography, Social Media and Big Data Integrations and Applications*, edited by Charles Travis and Alexander von Lünen, 187–204. Springer Geography. Cham: Springer International Publishing. https://doi.org/10.1007/978-3-319-40953-5_11.

Tuck, Eve. 2009. "Suspending Damage: A Letter to Communities." *Harvard Educational Review* 79 (3): 409–28. https://doi.org/10.17763/haer.79.3.n0016675661t3n15.

Tuck, Eve, and K. Wayne Yang. 2012. "Decolonization Is Not a Metaphor." *Decolonization: Indigeneity, Education & Society* 1 (1): 1–40.

Wolfe, Patrick. 2006. "Settler Colonialism and the Elimination of the Native." *Journal of Genocide Research* 8 (4): 387–409. https://doi.org/10.1080/14623520601056240.

Wood, Denis. 2010. *Rethinking the Power of Maps*. New York, NY: Guilford Press.

Wood, Denis, and John Fels. 1992. *The Power of Maps*. New York, NY: Guilford Press.

Xin, Rui, Tinghua Ai, and Bo Ai. 2018. "Metaphor Representation and Analysis of Non-Spatial Data in Map-Like Visualizations." *ISPRS International Journal of Geo-Information* 7 (6): 225. https://doi.org/10.3390/ijgi7060225.

9

THE DOUBLE DATA MOVEMENT TOWARDS THE ECOLOGICAL PLURIVERSE

The Case of the Native Land Information System

Aude K. Chesnais

> For every act of oppression, there is an act of resistance.
>
> – *Stephen Small*

Introduction

As a commitment to the Sustainability Development Goals (SDGs), initiatives are emerging to scale digital innovation for sustainability. This is reflected in the recent formation of the Coalition for Digital Sustainability (CODES) as part of the United Nations Secretary General's Roadmap for Digital Collaboration. While this may be a positive step towards incorporating wider perspectives in the Western-centric epistemologies that inform most international decision-making, it will take a consort of similar efforts to resolve the profound historical inequality embedded in knowledge production. Indeed, producing data is never neutral and is the product of our socio-ecological worldviews. In considering digital data design to support ecological transitions, we first need to reposition data production in its political-economic context, as a vector of change enabling worldviews and tangible realities.

For millions of Indigenous peoples worldwide, this reality has been the systematic disappearance of their land driven and justified by the use of Western-centric data. Indeed, data is at the heart of the colonial process, employed as a historical tool to instrumentalise land dispossession and inform policymaking to structure exclusionary systems. Geographical data systems have been particularly central to organising the Western colonial enterprise. According to Frantz Fanon, observing these data systems can empower powerful systemic change:

> [T]he colonial world is a world divided into compartments. . . . Yet, if we examine closely this system of compartments, we will at least be able to reveal the lines of force

DOI: 10.4324/9781003082798-12

> it implies. This approach to the colonial world, its ordering and its geographical layout will allow us to mark out the lines on which a decolonized society will be reorganized.
>
> *(Fanon 1963)*

More particularly, the commodification of land through colonial land tenure has served as the base for the capitalist project, which has precipitated our species into what some call the Anthropocene. Land tenure is literally about putting lines on the land in order to create separation. In the capitalist development process, it has structured the privatisation and commodification of land in order to feed and sustain agricultural extraction and industrial development – in other words, the means of production that sustain capitalist modes of production. The decolonial process largely consists in identifying and deconstructing these colonial relations to land, and such a process is anchored in the specificities of local power dynamics (Tuck and Yang 2012). In United States Native land, two colonial patterns have intertwined to create secrecy and impede on the exercise of sovereign land management:

1. The historical mismanagement of tribal land through the passing of acts that do not hold Native interests in priority and, on the contrary, benefit non-Natives.
2. A pattern of concealing existing data or not collecting it altogether.

Indeed, the land tenure of Native land overseen by the Bureau of Indian Affairs (BIA) has been the backbone of the establishment of the United States as we know it. Deprived of their homelands and forced onto land reservations set aside in the most undesirable parts of the country, Native nations underwent a process of slow genocide, ethnocide, ecocide, and epistemicide that continues to this day. Far from being random, this exclusionary process, which forms the base of the United States economy, was accompanied by theological, cultural, and legal underpinnings structured by data systems.

In a fast-paced data-driven world increasingly led by digital technologies which purpose to solve global socio-environmental planetary challenges, it becomes essential to question both the uses and the epistemological source of digital innovation as it more broadly relates to data and knowledge production. Accordingly, the DEH is becoming a key interdisciplinary framework to critically understand the profound societal changes resulting from this millennial trend, which should, in turn, inform better-applied research. As a contribution, this chapter retraces and links the role of data in the colonial history of land dispossession – largely responsible for the Anthropocene – to contemporary tokens of Indigenous data production which use digital innovation to enact alternative sustainable outcomes for Native land. Here, I particularly highlight the role of data as "maker of worlds" and the need to clearly identify and link data production to the ontology it serves, whether by maintaining or rupturing certain worldviews.

Dispossessing Land through Data

Shortly after Columbus set foot in the New World, the doctrine of discovery – a 1493 papal bull authorising Christians to seize non-Christians' property in the name of God – set a moral allowance for conquest. The "exploration" of new lands, or invasion of Native territory, relied on a series of maps and early scouting, which established the first boundaries upon which to define the new empire. Despite the occasional use of the word "peace" across that period, such exclusionary worldviews and cultural projects could, by essence, not coexist with surrounding Indigenous ontologies, which were presented with two choices: assimilate or perish.

Over the following centuries, and after years of conflict between settlers and Native nations largely under- and misrepresented by history books, the signature of unilateral treaties and executive orders based on the cataloguing of explored territories confined the remaining nations into what is today known as American Indian reservations. While peoples' movements had been restrained, their ways of life remained and threatened the very project of the "American Dream" – a White Christian, patriarchal, nuclear-family-oriented lifestyle, where nature as a subservient external entity to mankind is to be tamed through a strong work ethic guided by conformity to the group's values. As Max Weber's (1920) famous analysis so clairvoyantly examined, the capitalist project was born.

The Dawes Act of 1889 and subsequent legislative acts have done nothing to Native land but ensure that the remaining nations conform with the set goal of the American Dream. After partitioning Native lands into individual parcels attributed to male heads of households, the BIA appointed itself to determine for Native peoples their right to use these lands through organising them in a fee or trust status, starting a land apartheid system which continues to this day. The process of cataloguing, distributing, lease managing and record-keeping of Native lands by the BIA is a well-documented massive historical failure which has shaped land management and development on Native lands (Anderson and Lueck 1992; McKean, Taylor, and Liu 1995; Gregg and Cooper 2010; Palmer 2011; Palmer and Rundstrom 2013).

The simple irony of wanting to serve Native peoples by leaving their land management to a federal organisation created in 1824 with the purpose of civilising and assimilating Native populations should speak for itself. But recent archival work bears witness to a colonial data system that enshrined the dispossession of Native land into law and buried it in secrecy. For instance, GIS planning by the BIA has served the colonial agenda by monitoring land transactions in "Indian Country" and opening them to settler industries, thus "acting as forward scouts for exploitative industry" while marginalising the people it purposed to serve (Madsen 1995, 223; Palmer and Rundstrom 2013).

The federal prevalence over data collection and management contributed to making Native peoples and issues invisible. For instance, whereas their land was still being managed by federal entities, Native populations were not counted as official citizens of the United States by the Census until the 1924 Indian Citizenship Act. This is a perfect example of the more subtle impacts of data colonialism. By controlling what, when, and how data was collected, analysed, and interpreted, the federal government has thereby largely controlled the visibility and thus the public existence of Native peoples or what was then seen as the "Indian problem."

This pattern has continued to this day, even into the recent progressive digitisation of data by federal agencies. Indeed, while data digitisation holds the potential to support greater emancipation and support tribal sovereignty, the BIA still oversees the release of land tenure data, and other federal agencies usually do not release suitable data for analysis at the reservation level (Rodriguez-Lonebear 2016; Palmer and Rundstrom 2013; Guzman 1992). In the era of digitisation, where digital information is required for management, the structural issue of data colonialism on US Native lands has created a situation where Native land management is impaired comparatively to US land management, which fully benefits from the myriad of datasets available for planning.

Additionally, while the data collected often does not reflect tribal priorities, tribes still need to use data in order to maintain their legitimacy. This is because their land rights are characterised by a dependency relationship with the federal government that dates back to the treaty era, which coerces tribes into reporting data in certain ways to justify federal funding. Consequently, "tribes must grapple with the task of building strong nations while utilizing data that have been collected to advance the aims of other governments" (Rodriguez-Lonebear 2016, 254). The impact of discriminatory data practices extends beyond issues of development and planning. In fact, it relates to ontological struggles and the prevalence or extinction of worldviews which enact different versions of their relations to nature.

Establishing the "One World" View: Data as Epistemicide and World-Making

Controlling data processes is not solely about controlling land but is equally important in controlling worldviews. By defining the validation of knowledge processes and installing Western scientific methods as the sole source of reliable knowledge, the colonial process commits epistemicide – the extinction and marginalisation of alternative worldviews to a dominant one. Decolonial scholars argue that the linear and exclusionary theological and cultural base embedded in the Western scientific model has positioned it worldwide as a powerfully hegemonic ontology, described as the "One World" view – making it particularly hard for competing worldviews to coexist into a balanced multiplicity of views, or pluriverse (Querejazu 2016; Escobar 2016).

For instance, the majority of knowledge taught internationally is presented as a supposed neutral knowledge base, however led by a Western-centric ontology. Although knowledge originates from various places, from the known Arab mathematics to the direct democratic models practised by the Iroquois Confederacy, it has been compacted into a Western-centric cluster, where sources and places seem to be systematically replaced by Western- and usually white-male-sounding voices. Most disciplines are still taught with this disproportionate weight on Western sources worldwide, accompanied by affirmations of a supposedly more objective and scientifically sound Western knowledge. For instance, while most people think of astronomy as an eminently Western discipline overseen by mystified entities like NASA and perceived through a Western cosmology, who has learned in school of Lakota star knowledge or Mayan cosmology, to name but a few?

The idea of the superiority of Western knowledge has evolved since the doctrine of discovery. With globalisation, it traded the cloak of claimed colonisation for the cloak of developmentalism, where an objectified Western knowledge base is presented as the result of more evolved forms of human development yet unachieved by other civilisations. Within the development criteria, which are presented as objective and universal, other world regions are seen and analysed through the Western lens. By keeping this idea of superior knowledge and continuing to erase alternatives, the One World view maintains a cultural hegemony which prevents the deep restructuring of the economic benefits of its mode of production (an international racial division of labour, global land base, Global North–Global South economic flows, etc.). We could refer to this globalised knowledge system as the colonial division of knowledge – a system by which injustice gets manufactured globally through data systems informed by a hegemonic cultural project.

Although dominant today, the One World view is widely considered to be a historical anomaly and an illusion resulting from the Western colonial process which puts a veil on historical world alternatives (Capra and Luisi n.d.; Querejazu 2016). By contrast, most Indigenous worldviews present similarities of more relational and embedded ways of inhabiting the earth (Goodchild 2021). Yet contrary to how they are often presented, non-Western worldviews are far from being homogenous. They result from a myriad of diverse cultures that emerged in a different time and space yet present more relational man-nature models. This tells us that while the capitalist mode of production is currently hegemonic in terms of representation and economic domination, we have to remove the veil of the colonial division of knowledge and reposition it within the larger timespan of human existence and cultural diversity to see it appear in stark ontological contrast from other worldviews.

Firstly, this historical conflict places the data sovereignty struggle into an issue of cognitive justice purposed to restore a pluriverse by toning down the colonial division of knowledge and creating space for other ways of knowing and envisioning the world (De Sousa Santos 2014). Yet beyond the issue of ontological fairness, the colonial division of knowledge also bears a major weight in provoking climate change by generalising worldwide a mode of relating to nature as a distinct subordinate object serving human systems, which forms the ideological base for global land commodification and an inherently unsustainable mode of production. This worldview reflects separation by design and struggles to consider and comprehend non-human interests, which makes it fundamentally insufficient to design sustainable futures (Cajete 1999). Instead, it has mastered the art of offering technical solutions to existential crises such as climate change by failing to question its own ontology, which explains why it still rewards the economic integration of climate adaptation over more profound cultural shifts. How can this awareness inform the way we reflect on data design and the effective ecological transition we wish to produce? How can digital technologies enable this process? By understanding how the One World view reproduces commodified relations to natural resources through data systems, we can begin to look at the data processes supportive of decolonised and thus more sustainable worlds.

Indigenous Data Sovereignty: A Double Movement towards the Pluriverse

Opposition and resistance are natural properties found in earth and human systems. The absence of visibility over data sovereignty and ontological justice does not mean it does not exist. In fact, the struggle over the coexistence of knowledge systems has been the backbone of Indigenous survival struggles, which makes indistinguishable the struggles towards data sovereignty and towards establishing a pluriverse. Indigenous data sovereignty debates have developed across the world and are gaining visibility through the democratisation of digital communication and social media (Kukutai and Taylor 2016).

In the United States, the National Congress for American Indians established guidelines suggesting regulations for data management: "Tribes exercise Indigenous data sovereignty through the interrelated processes of decolonizing data and Indigenizing data governance . . . data are the building blocks of good governance" (National Congress of American Indians 2018). Debates are mainly structured around two points, which reflect the two historical patterns previously expressed: (1) access and decolonisation of externally collected data and (2) definition of locally defined and culturally appropriate data.

Indeed, on the one hand, "tribes have still very little access to the data collected by external agents about their citizens, lands, and resources, which underscores the need for tribal protection, ownership and application of tribal data" (National Congress of American Indians 2018). But such data is crucially needed to inform all types of tribal planning and conform to the legal requirements to extend their sovereignty – for instance, to get Census challenges or Integrated Natural Resource Management Plans (IRMPs) approved (Schultz and Rainie 2014). It is also necessary to defend tribal interests coveted by extractive industries, who already have access to such data.

On the other hand, the longer goal is to deeply transform data systems so that they represent Native worldviews, which are about justice and epistemology: "Information, data, and research about our peoples – collected about us, with us, or by us – belong to us and must be cared for by us" (United States Indigenous Data Sovereignty Network n.d.). This goal is utterly important as

Figure 9.1 Double data movement towards the pluriverse.

Source: Aude K. Chesnais.

it helps bring the pluriverse back to life by promoting the impact of Indigenous worldviews on global decision-making while coercing Western worldviews to step down from their dominion into an equal place. By making space for Indigenous ontologies, we also hold space for more relational human-environment systems to inform the profound ecological shifts of our time.

This presents a critical challenge, as we have seen that linear Western knowledge is mutually exclusive with pluriversal worldviews such as Indigenous knowledge systems, which are more relational, integrative of their environment, and technically more visual, spatial, and kinesthetic (Cajete 1999). To support these two goals, a double data movement is needed: the first towards using available data to dismantle the colonial data systems currently in the service of land dispossession and the second about defining what Indigenous and more circular data systems by design look like today and promote their impact locally and globally.

Fitting Squares into Circles to Fight Colonial Oppression: The Example of the Native Lands Information System

The democratisation of GIS technology and data-processing tools is bringing change to the picture of Native land sovereignty at an unprecedented rate. Throughout the world, Indigenous scholars are increasingly using and developing data tools to support the broader assertion of land sovereignty and sustainable land management. In the United States, a momentum is building in the wake of the path set forth by Native sovereignty movements. While Native land sovereignty has been widely defined by Native scholars, a new array of researchers and activists are bridging Western science and Indigenous knowledge systems to build stronger tools to uncover the past and support the sovereign transformation of their land (Mutua and Swadener 2004; Bartlett, Marshall, and Marshall 2012; Johnson et al. 2015; Whyte, Brewer, and Johnson 2016).

The first movement towards Indigenous data sovereignty is thus one of data hybridisation in order to shed light on structural land oppression and inequality and protect Native lands' interests: "The tribal data revolution demands new approaches, new warriors, new structures and new partnerships to meet the contemporary challenges of tribal data governance in the twenty-first century" (Rodriguez-Lonebear 2016). The data outcomes produced by these hybrid systems have been shown effective in supporting Native land claims in legal trials, as seen in the relief gained by the Standing Rock Sioux Tribe Trial over the passage of the Dakota Access Pipeline (DAPL) on its territory. It can also produce innovative land management practices, as exemplified by the ongoing legal process to endow rights to rivers or forests in many parts of the world.

However, although this first movement is a necessary step, it does not yield data which fully represent Indigenous worldviews and is thus referred to here as "fitting squares in circles," in reference to the process of using linear-based data, datasets and data processes to solve issues within communities functioning under more circular ontologies. This section addresses some of the technical and epistemological challenges inherent in data hybridisation through the examples of breakthrough Native land research.

The task to put together the puzzle of Native land oppression in the United States is massive. While most localised oppression is known and remembered by the peoples' collective memory and teachings and increasingly shared to rewrite a more accurate version of history, that knowledge is yet to be consolidated into a nationwide and chronologically consistent picture powerful enough to shatter the foundational myths of the United States of America. Digital innovation is revolutionising this process, particularly in GIS, which is opening new doors for Native land research, for the first time enabling us to clearly quantify the breadth of Native land oppression in the history of the United States.

The last Plenary Session of the Indigenous Peoples Specialty Group at the Association of American Geographers' Annual Meeting gathered Native scholars Dr Brewer, J. Mysel, D. Bartecchi, and myself to present some of the research cases discussed here. But this GIS momentum is being built by a growing base of other Native scholars and activists, among which I could mention Dr K. Whyte and his team and the team at Native Land Digital.[1] Here, I focus on the data processes I know best, which have been developed by the Native Lands Advocacy Project within the Native Land Information System (NLIS), the largest repository for nationwide Native land use data in the United States.[2] This project was born of 20 years of dedicated work and partnership between the non-profit Village Earth and the Indian Land Tenure Foundation, a respected Native-led organization aiming at putting back "native lands in native hands."

The premise behind the NLIS was simple; since most public datasets were released in unusable format for Native geographies except for those with analytical skills, could GIS and digital tools be used to present this data in a more usable format to tribal users? The NLIS was born; this dedicated online platform processes publicly available data crucial to natural

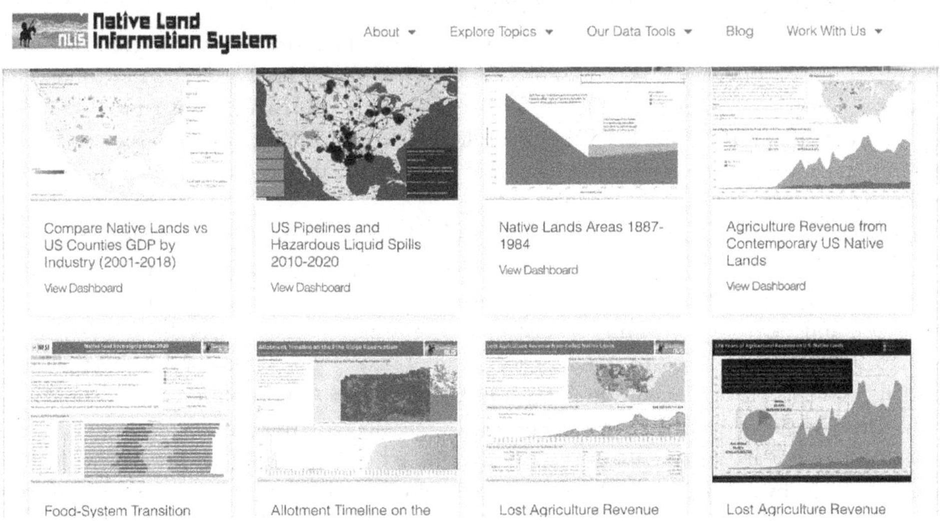

Figure 9.2 Extract of the NLIS site data dashboards.

resource management, advocacy and planning, such as the Census of Agriculture for American Indian Reservations, the Cropland Data Layer (CDL), and the National Land Cover (NLCD), and derives special calculations that help critically assess and monitor the state of Native land tenure and land use to support local food systems. The idea is to use digital tools such as GIS and data visualisation software like Tableau to aggregate and present data for all and each reservation and contextualise it so it can be used by tribes to counteract the damage done through Westerncentric linear data models. The power of visual data representation is enhanced through the use of the latest technologies and curated in one hosting website for ease of use.

Key outputs include the Lost Agricultural Revenue Dashboard, or LARD (an acronym referring back to a Lakota historical description of white people as taking the best cut/fat of the meat), which for the first time reconstitutes the historical picture of agriculture revenue generated on Native land. Another output of the NLIS is the Food Systems Transition Index, an aggregate measure gathering 20 indicators to assess and support healthy food systems on Native land. It relies on existing datasets aggregated at the reservation level and processed in particularly novel ways. Firstly, its design started from a meta-analysis of the meanings of Indigenous food sovereignty, which constituted an epistemological base to choose and process indicators.

After feedback from Native food practitioners, indicators were constructed to provide monitoring tools that would embody some baselines of healthy and sovereign Native food systems in terms of land tenure, agriculture and land use type, climate impact, human health, and so on. While it cannot represent the depth and nuances of Native food systems, this hybrid design enabled the construction of a new tool to assess, for the first time, interconnected dimensions of sustainable food systems using linear datasets. Among key indicators, it features one measuring Native land sovereignty through inequality in the Native land tenure system, the ecological impact of grown crops, and another that uses the Cropland Data Layer to flag monoculture.

Feedback on the NLIS has been very encouraging, and some of the data dashboards were designed specifically for particular Native organisations and their campaign – for instance, the US Pipeline and Hazardous Liquid Spills dashboard and the more recent dashboard looking at the racial distribution of farm debt and its impact on Native agricultural revenue. The NLIS's success is only a witness to the huge gap that needs to be filled to support sovereign and quality data access on US Native lands. The project is currently preparing to enter a new phase, with a wider set of partnerships with Native-led organisations, which will aim to use this digital data tool to support the creation of integrated resource management plans, a necessary legal step in order for tribes to manage their natural resources as they see fit without the oversight of the BIA.

This case study is one of many innovative uses of digital technologies currently happening to advance Native land research. While these data systems are not adequate to fully represent Indigenous ontologies, they are efficient for Native communities to deconstruct and fight land oppression and advocate for solutions to Native land issues. Combining archival research, GIS, and data visualisations is allowing a new generation of Native land researchers across the United States to move forward to reconstitute the full history of land oppression from the reservation era to this day. Such prowess is greatly enabled by the democratisation of digital technologies. However, because they adapt Western tools and use externally produced linear datasets, these data designs are, by essence, shaped in reaction to colonial worldviews. Whereas they are crucial to redress structural inequality, they are limited in representing the full depth of Indigenous worldviews. What would such data designs look like?

Weaving Kinship Knowledge Systems to Support the Pluriverse and the Ecological Transition

The second movement towards Indigenous data sovereignty is about defining Indigenous data systems. This work in progress relies on alternative worldviews and data systems to the One World, which already exist as counter-epistemologies (De Sousa Santos 2014) but are not considered globally legitimate. "Our people have always been data gatherers," claims Rodriguez-Lonebear (2016, 254), giving the example of winter counts, a set of traditional stories collected by some tribes over the winter as pictograms usually painted on a piece of leather or fabric to record a community's life and events.

The core of this second data movement is thus not about creating Indigenous data systems but about reviving and making space for them within the pluriverse. This challenge is nested in decolonial resistance (Brown and Strega 2005; Meyer 2014; Escobar 2007) and joins a more global resistance against the One World view: "By interrupting the neoliberal globalizing project of constructing One World, many Indigenous, Afrodescendant, peasant, and poor urban communities are advancing ontological struggles" (Escobar 2016, 20).

But making space for these alternative ontologies also becomes essential to support deep ecological design. As we have explained, Indigenous worldviews are multiple and are able to coexist with diverging ontologies due to their more integrated view of nature and marriage between human and non human worlds: "Anthropocentrism has no place here, because humans do not have a superior status within their environment. They do not dominate nature, but as any other non-human, they are care-takers" (Querejazu 2016, 9). Indigenous knowledge systems are reflective of many worlds and many natures (Inoue and Moreira 2016) but are anchored in land, art, language, and culture (Cajete 1994; Rodriguez-Lonebear 2016). They are relational in essence and rely on methods like storytelling (Windchief and San Pedro 2009) to perpetuate the long-term integration of human beings within their environment.

If you listen carefully to any knowledge taught within an Indigenous framework, whether Native American, First Nations, Australian Aboriginal, Sami, or South or West African, data is always contextualised, and the object can thus organically not isolate human beings from their environment, which in turn impacts natural resource planning and the shape of the entire built environment. Escobar exemplifies this relationship between ways of "knowing-feeling the earth" and ways of organising natural resources by referring to the cognitive impossibility for Indigenous worldviews to conceive a system like slavery plantations based on a colonial division of labour and commodification of nature: "plantations are unthinkable from the relational perspective of forest-worlds" (Escobar 2016, 20). All elements of an ecosystem, including human beings, are tied within relationships which bind human action to their consequences on a space-time continuum. As such, resulting knowledge systems could be described as circular or kinship-based.

This relational pattern ties the entire way of knowing to practical environmental realities and livelihoods – for example, the health of a stream or the defence of a particular land use. In fact, kinship knowledge systems make environmental health indistinguishable from human health. This is why Lakota storytelling assimilates the disappearance of land to the disappearance of the people (Schusky 1980) or Standing Rock activists protesting the Dakota Access Pipeline have called themselves water protectors to honour the kinship they entertain with water/*mni*, considered as a relative. This type of integrative storytelling creates tangibility and gives shape to alternative life projects which are not based on human-nature separation (Blaser 2014).

Kinship knowledge systems cannot be brainstormed in a public conference. They are learnt through individual ties to place and their dependencies on other living entities. In other words, they are not manmade but instead circumstantially woven into being. Indeed, kinship relations develop on a particular land on which human and non-human group members rely collectively for subsistence, which over time inform stories to relay information in more integrative ways. Relational knowledge is constructed by the realisation of interdependencies between systemic elements, which is inhibited by the illusion of separation largely triggered in commodified land systems. The way we relate to the world defines the way we describe it and is thus reflected in the structures of data systems. In relational data systems, the process is more important than the result, which makes the journey of learning more important than the destination, but also cultivates a better awareness of interdependencies and thus a more interconnected understanding of the world which structurally results in more sustainable outcomes.

In this framework, data as an output does not really make sense. This is why talking about data production in terms of methods or techniques cannot be the foundation for designing solutions to local and global issues. Instead, the emphasis is on the process which determines the shape of innovation. Of course, data production can serve the overall process; it just does not have the same centrality as in the One World view. For instance, the NLIS Pipeline Spill Dashboard is an example of a particular demand from an Indigenous activist organisation because they recognise that digital visual tools can help assess and spread awareness of the severity of pipeline issues on Native land. But the output itself is not simply serving a project or an organisation but a different worldview that relates to water in a completely different manner. In this framework, the role of digital innovation can only be secondary, subject to scrutiny and employed in the service of conscientised kinship relations in particular territories.

By contrast, Western-centric ways of knowing tend to be linear and go from a point A to a point B, looking at an overall target or milestone, which prioritises the outcome over the process. This focus on the outcome is a pattern enabled by the One World view. Because its knowledge system is considered universal and its epistemological tenets stand unquestioned, Western knowledge producers tend to ignore the ontological framework in which their knowledge is being produced, which actually forms the baseline of scientific testing. The illusion of neutrality empowers knowledge producers to replace process by outcome. Even in the social sciences, where process is questioned, the academic institution tends to prioritise outputs and outcomes over process. A "good" academic is determined by how much they publish in how many reputable journals, as any project is assessed by measures collectively understood to quantify success.

This has a tremendous impact on data systems and their planning and timeline and explains, for instance, why Western innovation and development is usually planned over several years. In Native land planning, temporality tends to be longer and anchored in intergenerational impact. This explains why many grassroots projects plan their actions over seven generations, which affects design into a more integrated and regenerative shape. Additionally, because they are not anthropocentric, kinship knowledge systems truly allow for the integration of environmental insights because humans are not perceived as sole holders of knowledge, which triggers a practical form of biomimicry, as Goodchild (2021, 96) states, "the river teaches us."

Although we are increasingly seeing more circular or regenerative data systems sprouting from Western knowledge centres, I would like to highlight here an important difference. Through the same mechanism of separation between ontology and innovation, those models are often presented as new innovations originating from modern thought, another product of the Western scientific superiority, instead of giving credit to the entities and the long line of traditions that resulted in a particular innovation. This apolitical and acultural version of circular thinking continues to reify the One World view and impedes the emergence of the pluriverse.

Another undermined and yet essential feature of kinship data systems is their integration within ceremony, consistently with the meaning-making inherent in relational epistemologies (Wilson 2008). The absence of compartmentalisation between man and nature also reconciles the practical and the sacred, human and non-human worlds. Knowledge becomes an existential and spiritual endeavour to make sense of diverse yet coexisting realities. In such a framework, the spiritual realm exists in complementarity with the earthly realm, as one reality does not neglect the other. In fact, spiritual ceremony becomes the cement that enables and perpetuates relational knowledge. In Goodchild (2021), a discussant describes how the sacred opening ceremony of an academic gathering with prayers and smudging sage for purification changed the atmosphere in the room, giving the impression of "enter[ing] a sacred lodge" and impacting the outcome of the event.

Additionally to characterising Indigenous relational ontologies, these observations of kinship knowledge systems hold tremendous potential for deep ecological design. By transforming these lessons into epistemological shifts, researchers and practitioners alike from various cultural contexts can integrate or reintegrate the alternative relational worldviews needed to break away from the human-nature separation.

Practical Tips for Relational Knowledge Integration

The key part towards the recovery and encounter of the pluriverse is the word "encountering" (Querejazu 2016). In other words, the process is fundamental and requires brutal honesty to unlearn separative behaviours and reflexes. These processes of knowledge-seeking have been described by many Native scholars as "[r]egenerative, braiding, bridging, circle of relationships, insurgent, exercise in humility" (Goodchild 2021). This exercise in humility is a clear break from the cult of the *ego* that so often informs knowledge production.

The first step towards more relational knowledge systems is thus a move away from the *ego* to encounter the other. This process might be uncomfortable but necessary. It is accompanied by a process of eye-opening, which starts with a responsibility to inform ourselves about the weight and power of data. For instance, it is fundamental to demystify the concept of raw data. Raw data does not exist; it is, in fact, decontextualised data, which appears neutral but is in fact located in Western knowledge production and methods sprouting from the illusion of separation from nature that isolates objects from whole and participates in designing unsustainable worldviews.

Upon this realisation, researchers and practitioners often begin to deeply question their positionality and consider and accept other worldviews. This shift needs to be followed by a reconnection of data to its immediate and long-term consequences on all environmental interdependencies, which inspires us to insert a form of deep precautionary principle into all knowledge production. Perhaps a really uncomfortable piece for Western knowledge producers is that the true integration of this connection does not come from the mind but from the heart and relies on the felt parts of the human-nature relations so often dismissed by Western knowledge systems. Developing a sense of the social field and place in which kinship is lived and felt will slowly change our relation to our environment and thus to knowledge and data systems. The goal is to recreate a personal and collective covenant with knowledge, embedded in meaning-making and in the service of all kinship relations.

Translation plays a key role in supporting kinship knowledge systems. It can occur practically through the reinterpretation of visual models to accommodate Indigenous worldviews. One practical example was given by the translation of Kate Raworth's "Doughnut Economics" graph into a Maori version consistent with their worldview. Digital technologies, especially visual data systems such as GIS, are key tools to support Indigenous data sovereignty. For instance, the platform *TERRASTORIES* is offering a customisable and visual data mapping tool supportive of Native languages and is available offline for maximum data protection.[3] When guided by pluriversal principles, digital technology can fully support Indigenous worldviews and co-design the ecological transition.

Conclusion

For Indigenous peoples, the stake of reviving and making space for their knowledge systems is "crucial in the resuscitation of practices and intellectual life outside of settler ontologies" (Tuck and Yang 2012). Because they are nested within the inherently colonial struggle for land and ontological existence, supporting Indigenous data sovereignty is akin to supporting the emergence of a pluriverse away from the One World view, which maintains a fundamentally unsustainable mode of production and restrains deep ecological design. The DEH hold a tremendous potential for change and are being taken up to support Indigenous efforts towards data sovereignty.

The data struggle towards the pluriverse can be characterised by a double movement: the first towards transforming and reducing harm caused by linear Western knowledge systems, referred to as "fitting squares into circles," and the second towards designing data systems reflective of alternative worldviews and thereby truly enabling a sustainable pluriverse, referred to here a "weaving kinship knowledge." While the second movement is essential to establish the pluriverse and an ecological transition based on other principles than linearity and the illusion of man-nature separation, the first movement is complementary as a practical movement of data resistance to stop and reverse the harm caused by Western-centric data systems. Real solutions impose this two-way answer or two-eyed seeing (Goodchild 2021).

Because of their unique positionality, Indigenous scholars are already in this seminal in-between space. They have acquired the capacity to function in both or many worlds and understand their distinctions along with the dangers inherent in the One World view. People with these hybrid capacities are vital to the design of the ecological transition but are often silenced within the colonial division of knowledge. Because of their involvement in knowledge production, researchers and practitioners have a particular moral responsibility to learn about and deconstruct the colonial harm inherent in the One World view and participate in enabling the pluriverse by making space for Indigenous worldviews and voices. By incorporating best practices from Indigenous worldviews, such as deconstructing the cult of the ego, acknowledging kinship, recreating a sense of place, and engaging in knowledge translation, all knowledge producers can help shape pluriversal data systems that together need to mirror our repaired relation with the Earth. In this journey in service of relational ontologies, the wide applications and interactivity of digital tools and their democratisation bring about the new potential to empower Native land research and Indigenous sovereignty.

Notes

1 Native Land Digital (www.native-land.ca).
2 Native Land Information System (www.nativeland.info).
3 TERRASTORIES (https://terrastories.io).

Sources

Anderson, T. L., and D Lueck – Property Rights and Indian Economies. 1992. "Agricultural Development and Land Tenure in Indian Country." *Books.Google.Com*. https://books.google.com/books?hl=en&lr=&id=dwk8HPl1g04C&oi=fnd&pg=PA147&dq=Agricultural+Development+Land+Tenure+Indian+Country+Anderson+Lueck+-+Property+rights+and+Indian+economies&ots=EDxLfMt-F4&sig=0J8bfR_X3MmZREJ27W8Gs5hJtzw.

Bartlett, Cheryl, Murdena Marshall, and Albert Marshall. 2012. "Two-Eyed Seeing and Other Lessons Learned within a Co-Learning Journey of Bringing Together Indigenous and Mainstream Knowledges and Ways of Knowing." *Journal of Environmental Studies and Sciences* 2 (4): 331–40. https://doi.org/10.1007/s13412-012-0086-8.

Blaser, Mario. 2014. "Ontology and Indigeneity: On the Political Ontology of Heterogeneous Assemblages." *Cultural Geographies* 21 (1): 49–58. https://doi.org/10.1177/1474474012462534.

Brown, Leslie Allison, and Susan Strega, eds. 2005. *Research as Resistance: Critical, Indigenous and Anti-Oppressive Approaches*. Canadian Scholars' Press. https://books.google.fr/books?hl=en&lr=&id=Nbf300AIjbEC&oi=fnd&pg=PP1&dq=Brown,+L.+%26+Strega,+S.+(Eds.)+(2005).+Research+as+Resistance:+critical,+Indigenous,+%26+antioppressive+approaches.Canadian+Scholars'+Press&ots=U7S2Qzzya0&sig=vhq0bFPUROO20rbygumWH.

Cajete, Gregory A. 1994. *Look to the Mountain : An Ecology of Indigenous Education*. Kivakí Press. https://eric.ed.gov/?id=ED375993.

———. 1999. "The Native American Learner and Bicultural Science Education." In *Next Steps: Research and Practice to Advance Indian Education*, 27, Charleston: ERIC/CRESS.

Capra, Fritjof, and Pier Luigi Luisi. n.d. "The Systems View of Life A Unifying Vision."

Congress, NCAI. 2018. "NCAI Resolution # MOH-04–026 Support of US Indigenous Data Sovereignty and Inclusion of Tribes in the Development of Tribal Data Governance Principles." *NCAI 2018 Mid-Year Publication* mid-year: 3.

Escobar, Arturo. 2007. "Worlds and Knowledges Otherwise: The Latin American Modernity/Coloniality Research Program." *Cultural Studies* 21 (2–3): 180–210. http://eds.b.ebscohost.com.ezproxy2.library.colostate.edu/ehost/pdfviewer/pdfviewer?vid=4&sid=635db27c-a436-4f51-b3f1-43a22a9a64ac%40sessionmgr104.

———. 2016. "Thinking-Feeling with the Earth: Territorial Struggles and the Ontological Dimension of the Epistemologies of the South." *AIBR Revista de Antropologia Iberoamericana* 11 (1): 11–32. https://doi.org/10.11156/aibr.110102e.

Fanon, Frantz. 1963. *The Wretched of the Earth*. Vol. 1. Grove Press. www.google.fr/books/edition/_/M0xvW6B-f8UC?hl=en&sa=X&ved=2ahUKEwjY2IzL_drwAhUO8BQKHTYyC-cQre8FMAB-6BQgDEIEB.

Goodchild, Melanie. 2021. "Relational Systems Thinking: That' s How Change Is Going to Come, from Our Earth Mother." *Journal of Awareness-Based Systems Change* 1 (1): 75–103. https://doi.org/10.47061/jabsc.v1i1.577.

Gregg, Mathew T., and D. Mitchell Cooper. 2010. "The Political Economy of American Indian Allotment Revisited." *Journal of Business & Economics Research* 8 (5): 89. http://search.proquest.com/openview/54e33d802df1889468d5b09485b7a56f/1?pq-origsite=gscholar&cbl=54879.

Guzman, Jesus Villegas. 1992. "Soliloquio de Medianoche." *Revista Canadiense de Estuidos Hispanicos* 16 (3): 411–23.

Inoue, Cristina Yumie Aoki, and Paula Franco Moreira. 2016. "Many Worlds, Many Nature(s), One Planet: Indigenous Knowledge in the Anthropocene." *Revista Brasileira de Política Internacional* 59 (2). https://doi.org/10.1590/0034-7329201600209.

Johnson, Jay T., Richard Howitt, Gregory Cajete, Fikret Berkes, Renee Pualani Louis, and Andrew Kliskey. 2015. "Weaving Indigenous and Sustainability Sciences to Diversify Our Methods." *Sustainability Science*. https://doi.org/10.1007/s11625-015-0349-x.

Kukutai, Tahu, and John Taylor. 2016. *Indigenous Data Sovereignty: Toward an Agenda*. Australian National University. www.ands.org.au/working-with-data/sensitive-data/Indigenous-data.

Madsen, W. 1995. Protecting indigenous peoples' privacy from "eyes in the sky." In Proceedings of the Conference on Law and Information Policy for Spatial Databases, ed. H. Onsrud, 223–31. Orono, ME: National Center for Geographic Information and Analysis.

McKean, John R., R. Garth Taylor, and Wen Lin Liu. 1995. "Inadequate Agricultural Database for American Indians?" *Society and Natural Resources* 8 (4): 361–66. https://doi.org/10.1080/08941929509380928.

Meyer, Manulani Aluli. 2014. "Indigenous and Authentic: Hawaiian Epistemology and the Triangulation of Meaning." In *Handbook of Critical and Indigenous Methodologies*, edited by Norman K. Denzin, Yvonne S. Lincoln, and Linda Tuhiwai Smith, 217–32. https://doi.org/10.4135/9781483385686.

Mutua, Kagendo, and Beth Blue. Swadener. 2004. *Decolonizing Research in Cross-Cultural Contexts: Critical Personal Narratives*. SUNY Press. https://books.google.com/books?hl=en&lr=&id=l3jl-ObBxHQC&pgis=1.

Palmer, Mark H. 2011. "Sold! The Loss of Kiowa Allotments in the Post-Indian Reorganization Era." *American Indian Culture and Research Journal* 35 (3): 37–57. https://doi.org/10.17953/aicr.35.3.ag57542426n1v58q.

Palmer, Mark H., and Robert Rundstrom. 2013. "GIS, Internal Colonialism, and the U.S. Bureau of Indian Affairs." *Annals of the Association of American Geographers* 103 (5): 1142–59. https://doi.org/10.1080/00045608.2012.720233.

Querejazu, Amaya. 2016. "Encountering the Pluriverse : Looking for Alternatives in Other Worlds." *Revista Brasileira de Política Internacional* 59 (2): 16. https://doi.org/10.1590/0034-7329201600207.

Rodriguez-Lonebear, D. 2016. "Building a Data Revolution in Indian Country." In *Indigenous Data Sovereignty: Towards an Agenda*, 253–74. oapen.org. www.oapen.org/download?type=document&docid=624262#page=277.

Schultz, Jennifer Lee, and Stephanie Carroll Rainie. 2014. "The Strategic Power of Data: A Key Aspect of Sovereignty." *International Indigenous Policy Journal* 5 (4): 3. https://doi.org/10.18584/iipj.2014.5.4.1.

Schusky, E. L. 1980. *Political Organization of Native North Americans*. University Press of America. http://books.google.com/books?id=Rxo_AQAAIAAJ.

Sousa Santos, Boaventura De. 2014. *Epistemologies of the South: Justice against Epistemicide*. London and New York: Routledge.

Tuck, Eve, and K. Wayne Yang. 2012. "Decolonization Is Not a Metaphor." *Decolonization: Indigeneity, Education, & Society* 1 (1): 1–40.

United States Indigenous Data Sovereignty Network. n.d. "United States Indigenous Data Sovereignty Network." Accessed December 16, 2019. https://usIndigenousdata.org/.

Weber, M. 1920. "The Protestant Ethic and the Spirit of Capitalism. New York (Scribner's) 1920." https://opus4.kobv.de/opus4-Fromm/frontdoor/index/index/docId/29064.

Whyte, Kyle Powys, Joseph P. Brewer, and Jay T. Johnson. 2016. "Weaving Indigenous Science, Protocols and Sustainability Science." *Sustainability Science* 11 (1). https://doi.org/10.1007/s11625-015-0296-6.

Wilson, Shawn. 2008. *Research Is Ceremony: Indigenous Research Methods*. Fernwood Publishing. https://eduq.info/xmlui/handle/11515/35872.

Windchief, Sweeney, and Timothy San Pedro, eds. 2009. *Applying Indigenous Research Methods: Storying with Peoples and Communities*. Routledge. https://books.google.fr/books?hl=en&lr=&id=fzmDDwAAQBAJ&oi=fnd&pg=PP1&dq=Tuck,+E.,+%26+Yang,+K.W.+(2019)+Series+Editor+Introduction.+In+S.+Windchief+%26+T.+San+Pedro+(Eds.),+Applying+Indigenous+Research+Methods:+Storying+with+Peoples+and+Communities.+Rout.

10

GROUNDWORKS

Re-storying Northern California with Emplaced Indigenous Media

Ian Garrett,[1] *Desirae Harp, Ras K'Dee, L Frank, Tiśina Parker, Kanyon Sayers-Roods, Bernadette Smith, and Rulan Tangen*

Introduction

Groundworks is a multifaceted media collaboration exploring the concept of "re-storying" the land, similar to the idea that "digital media provides the most complete contemporary platform to challenge geographical borders as well as reconsider transnational contexts" (Weidner, Braidotti, and Klumbyte 2019, 16). This project was organised through a collaboration between Dancing Earth, a dance company with a history of ongoing Indigenous collaborations, and Toasterlab, a mixed-reality performance collective. The lead artists, and many of this chapter's co-authors, are Ras K'Dee (Pomo), Desirae Harp (Wappo), Bernadette Smith (Pomo), Kaynon Sayers-Roods (Ohlone), and L Frank (Tongva). Through a number of residences with Pomo, Wappo, Ohlone, and Tongva communities, the collaborators developed a library of immersive content to provide a unique exploration of issues important to the collaborators' communities. This includes live site-specific performance, short 360VR films, a full-length documentary, and a mobile application that is still in development.

Our intention has been to bring attention to contemporary Indigenous life in what is now recognised as Northern California through a limited Indigital geographic information network (iGIN) that highlights the cartographic encounters (Palmer 2012) of twice-colonised California. The project deals with land management, water rights, food security, infrastructure and planning, and the recognition of California's First Nations. These issues are of concern for all Californians, especially in an age of climate change. But they are particularly acute in Indigenous communities that have called these lands home for millennia. These communities work hard to remain resilient despite centuries of colonisation and marginalisation. Their efforts have led to the growing recognition of the traditional stewards of the land with respect and reciprocity. The practices of the artists involved with *Groundworks* are important examples of how traditional knowledge is bridged with contemporary reality. The authors of this chapter share the creative process and practical execution of bonding contemporary artistic practices and traditional ceremony-inspired dance and music of Indigenous collaborators with the land through the project's use of immersive located media. And it discusses the work of connecting artists,

DOI: 10.4324/9781003082798-13

Figure 10.1 Collaborators take a seat on Mount St Helena/Kanamota featured (left to right): Sophie Traub, Michael Jaguar, Desirae Harp, Kenny Ray Ramos, Tiśina Parker.

Photo credit: Ian Garrett

their communities, and extended reality technologies to collapse time and space, complicating relationships to each place for the artists and their future audiences.

Dancing Earth

Many of the collaborators on this project have long relationships with Dancing Earth, whose mission is "to create and support contemporary global Indigenous dance and related arts, to encourage and revitalize awareness of bio-cultural diversity through artistic expression, for the education and wellness of all peoples" (Dancing Earth Creations n.d.). The company was founded in 2004 by Rulan Tangen, who had previously danced for companies including Michael Mao Dance, Peridance Ensemble, Karen Jamieson Dance, Littleglobe, Marin Ballet, Catskill Ballet Theater, Redwood Empire Ballet, and the New York Grand Opera. She is also experienced in Northern Plains traditional powwow dancing through her adopted Lakota family. After years of professional dance practice and teaching, Tangen desired to create opportunities for aspiring performers. Surviving cancer led her to discover her leadership purpose and her work

> values movement as an expression of plurality of ancestral and futuristic worldviews, interpreted through dance as a functional ritual for transformation and healing, and the energetic connection with all forms of life on earth. Of heritage including Kampampangan/Pangasinan of Luzon Island, Philippines, and Norsk/Eire Europe, she has

> recruited and nurtured new generations of innovative cultural dancers and holds the belief that "to dance is to live, to live is to dance."
>
> *(Dancing Earth Creations n.d.)*

Dancing Earth is based in Ogaa Po Ogeh, occupied Tewa territory known as Santa Fe, New Mexico, and Yelamu, occupied Ohlone territory known as San Francisco, California. The company has a history of working with Bay Area Indigenous artists. The *Groundworks* project was conceptualised as an act of reciprocity to shift focus to the Indigenous collaborators and their communities. Early in discussions about the project, the creation of a mobile app to help people understand the history of the land became central. But while the company has a history of working with video and stage technology for their performances, a mobile application was something it had never engaged.

Toasterlab

Toasterlab is a mixed-reality performance collective whose core members are Ian Garrett, Justine Garrett, and Andrew Sempere. It was founded in 2015 to formally support the production of the collective's first large-scale project *Transmission*:

> Toasterlab creates place-based extended reality experiences that promote deeper engagement with history, community, and imagination. Toasterlab combines expertise in storytelling, theatrical and media production, and the development of new technology to produce both original work and partnerships.
>
> *(Toasterlab 2017)*

The collective grew out of a combination of ecological approaches to art-making, interactive technology in performance, and site-specific performance. It began with inquiry into the effective creation of archives for site-specific performances for a dance project called *500 Miles, 500 Stories* by the DC-based Dance Exchange. In this project, the company walked from their studio to coal mines in West Virginia –the source of the electrical power the studio used. Along the way, they created many site-specific performances about the social and environmental impacts of the company's electrical usage. This led to questions about a way to more intrinsically link such performances to the locations in which they were created and executed. In a discussion about how to archive this work, a question arose – what if we could link these dance and music works created by populations defined by place to places after they became uninhabitable? Ever since, the objective of Toasterlab's work has been the creation of technology to "haunt" locations with performance-based artwork to address such issues.

This is done through a combination of geolocation, mobile devices sensors, and augmented reality (AR). This "haunting" allows the audience/user to locate and view recorded site-specific, performance-based artwork in the same context and orientation that it was created and intended to be experienced. This is meant to "time-shift" the experience of a live performance, making it accessible at a later time while maintaining an intrinsic relationship to its original location.

Toasterlab's first major project *Transmission* was imagined as the movie *Arrival* (Villeneuve 2016) combined with the geolocated, AR game *Pokemon Go*. It was an immersive mixed-reality theatrical production that told the story of two sisters selected to join a mission to meet our celestial neighbours. Their story was told through a live show at the 2017 Edinburgh Festival Fringe in Scotland, as part of the FuturePlay festival, a podcast, and several site-specific AR scenes that are linked to specific locations throughout Edinburgh. A mobile app delivered the geolocation and access to the related location-based content to audience members as they wandered the city. Subsequently, Toasterlab, following the successful run of *Transmission*, sought to develop more explicitly environmental work. Keen to support a project that incorporated Indigenous "ancestral and futuristic worldviews," such as the type which Rulan Tangen created, Ian reached out to see if she might be interested in collaborating on a project which used Toasterlab's technology. Serendipitously, Dancing Earth had just begun ideating the *Groundworks* project.

Lead Collaborating Artists

The collaborating companies provided the organisational framework to handle the production logistics of the project. Five key artists, each with established relationships to Dancing Earth provided leadership for the project's artistic vision. Its recording and performance content was collectively devised based on the work of these artists. Ras K'Dee is Pomo, with ties to multiple bands in Sonoma and Mendocino Counties. He is an accomplished musician, producer, and core member of Audiopharmacy, an international touring band described as a "world hip-hop/ electronic" ensemble. As the editor for *Snag Magazine*, Ras K'Dee is building the Nest, an arts and community facility in Forestville, California, using traditional techniques.

Desirae Harp is a member of the Mishewal Wappo tribe from the central coast of California and a descendant of the Diné Nation from the North American Southwest. As a singer/ songwriter, cultural bearer/activist, and teacher, Desirae sings with Audiopharmacy and uses her music as a teaching tool to facilitate workshops for youth on cultural survival, social justice, and environmental justice across the country. She is the founder of the Mishewal Ona★staTis language revitalisation programme and works with the Run4Salmon campaign to restore California waterways, salmon runs, and Indigenous ways of life.

Bernadette Smith is a Pomo singer, musician, and playwright from the Point Arena Manchester Band of Pomo Indians. She is an activist leader involved with Missing and Murdered Indigenous Women and is currently working on reclaiming land traditionally used by her tribe for their acorn harvest, a place currently occupied by a decommissioned United States Air Force base.[2]

Kanyon Sayers-Roods is a multidisciplinary Ohlone artist from Indian Canyon, a sovereign Indian nation outside of Hollister, California, which provides ceremonial ground for groups without their own land base. She continues the work started by her mother to maintain and expand land and water access as the area surrounding sovereign and ceremonial ground is converted to vineyards.

L Frank (L. Frank Manriquez) is a Tongva-Acjachemen artist based in Santa Rosa, California. She is a writer, tribal scholar, cartoonist, and Indigenous language activist, contributing to the recovery of Tongva language. She is an important keeper of knowledge related to Indigenous craft, building techniques, traditional foods, agriculture, and land management. In addition to activism to reclaim language, L Frank has led the first rebuilding of many generations of Tongva canoes through traditional means.

Many more culture bearers and artistic contributors have also been involved in the project, including the mentors of these lead artists. Ann-Marie Sayer is a Mutsun Ohlone elder who has protected Indian Canyon and is Kanyon Sayers-Roods' mother. Gregg Castro (*t'rowt'raahl* Salinan/Rumsien and Ramaytush Ohlone) has been involved in the preservation of his cultural heritage for over 30 years and provides mentorship to Kanyon. TekTekh Gabaldon is a Mishewal Wappo traditional culture bearer and is Desirae Harp's mother. Clarence Carrillo leads language revitalisation efforts with the Point Arena Manchester band of Pomo Indians and mentors Ras K'Dee. A number of artists affiliated with Dancing Earth have made contributions by generating music, text, and choreography. This includes poet turned director and television writer Tazbah

Figure 10.2 L Frank discussing rediscovering language and building a new Tongvan canoe.

Photo credit: Teni Brandt

Rose Chavez (Bishop Paiute Tribe, from the Nüümü, Diné, and San Carlos Apache tribes), interdisciplinary artist Esme Olivia, and much of Audiopharmacy. The project is ultimately held together by the production management and community liaison work of Tiśina Parker (Southern Sierra Miwuk of Yosemite, Mono Lake Kucadikadi Paiute, and Kashia Pomo tribes).

The Collaboration

The critical idea in the *Groundworks* collaboration is to use Toasterlab's approach to technology to reclaim the history of the land through devising site-specific performance media using Dancing Earth's approach. The idea is to re-story these places and bring the stories of California's original caretakers back into relationship with these lands using accessible technology – in this case, the ubiquitous smartphone. The mobile application is the genesis of the project, but a number of additional media and interactive technology elements have been developed. This includes a site-specific performance on Alcatraz Island in San Francisco Bay (site of the 1969–1971 American Indian Movement Occupation) and a television documentary. It has also led to the development of elements of the touring stage production of *BTW US – Between Underground & Skyworld* and the streaming performance *Indigenous Futurities*.[3]

The goal of *Groundworks* was to share complex understandings of contemporary Indigenous community life through performances that engaged cutting edge technology. In seeking to create a technological system of reciprocity with the artists, the project, through its stage productions and digital streams, asked audiences to be in an active relationship with the site, the performance, and the community. The collaboration between artists and audience aimed to re-story the land and make that which has become invisible become visible again – as opposed to bringing the work into fixed presentation spaces. Project performances and streams offered a means to collaboratively create a counter-narrative of place, in contrast to how as Dylan Robinson describes, in

> museums across the globe, glass vitrines display cultural belongings of the Northwest coast First People. . . . While such displays are offered to members of the general public primarily for their aesthetic contemplation, for Indigenous people the experience of such displays can often be traumatic and triggering.
>
> *(2020, 86)*

The initial development of the content for this project began in 2017 and evolved through a series of intensive residencies that were focused on community building and knowledge exchange between project partners that led up to two key dates. The first date, 8 October 2018 marked the first time the City of San Francisco observed Indigenous People's Day by replacing Columbus Day. Though this primarily changed a statutory holiday, it was a significant sign of change that a day named for Christopher Columbus – who many contend was the catalyst for the genocide of the Native peoples of Turtle Island (the Indigenous name for North America) – is becoming a day to celebrate peoples have been erased by the holiday. The second date, 9 October 2019, commemorated the 50th anniversary of the Indians of All Tribes' Occupation of Alcatraz Island, led by Mohawk activist Richard Oakes. As the origin of the Indigenize the Bay movement, one of the aims of the Occupation was to make the Indigenous history of the California Bay region visible again.

In addition to time spent in San Francisco, residencies brought the collaborators to a variety of locations within two hours of the city, including Point Arena, Manchester, Gualala, Forrestville, Santa Rosa, Santa Cruz, Indian Canyon, and others. Locations were selected based on their importance to the artists with regards to issues they wanted to raise or based on the artistic vision of the media.

The project is rooted in the ethics of Dancing Earth with its history of work with Indigenous contemporary performing arts. This collaboration engages Indigenous aesthetic values that disrupt settler-colonial notions of discrete genres. This represents a commitment to indigenising settler "business as usual" practices. Significant attention was paid to carefully and partially sharing any traditional knowledge. The methodology was co-created with culture carriers from diverse First Nations, which have varying internal and external restrictions around knowledge-sharing. The collaborators on the project have received permission to share vulnerable tribal knowledge because they offer it in the coded, symbolic language of contemporary performance.

The project's mobile application, based on the previous work of Toasterlab, uses an authoring device, the MapTool. Built to manage immersive experiences by combining content such as 360VR video, binaural and ambisonic audio, volumetric performance capture, and interactive digital media, MapTool integrates these modes with locative data on mobile devices. This allows the content developed to be paired with specific places and be oriented to these sites. The resulting effect is to provide a window into the recorded events through the screen of the user's device. Geolocation provides the ability to locate the performance, and this application of AR provides a window into the past after an event has occurred and been recorded. Ronald Azuma describes AR as

> a variation of Virtual Environments (VE), or Virtual Reality as it is more commonly called. VE technologies completely immerse a user inside a synthetic environment. . . . In contrast, AR allows the user to see the real world, with virtual objects superimposed upon or composited with the real world. Therefore, AR supplements reality, rather than completely replacing it.
>
> *(1997, 356)*

As GPS allows technology to create links based on location, AR allows content to be superimposed to share physical space with virtual objects when viewed through a device like a contemporary smartphone or tablets. Such devices contain receivers to use GPS, three-dimensional position accelerometers, and high-resolution cameras. Such technologies offered the AR performance system the means to allow participants to find the place where a performance had previously taken place and experience it in relation to the present physical environment, providing an ability "to think outside human speed and scale" (Cohen and Lemenager 2016, 341).

The *Groundworks* project follows the trend of an emerging field of located mixed-reality artwork. John Craig Freeman's (2013) use of geolocation and AR in a public art project concerning migrant workers who died along the US-Mexico border marks the locations where their human remains were recovered. *Broadway Augmented* (2014), curated by Shelly Willis and Rachel Clarke, is a virtual public art project created by a dozen artists that was superimposed over the cityscape of Sacramento, California. With regards to performance content, dance artist and technologist Jacob Niedzwiecki (2019) developed *Jacqueries* and the forthcoming *Henry G20*, an AR performance, adapting William Shakespeare's historical drama *Henry V*, set in 2010 during the Group of Twenty (G20) intergovernmental summit in Toronto, Canada (*Henry G20* n.d.).[4]

The use of AR and geolocation has also become a tool in Indigenous projects. Wikiupedia by Adrian Duke and the Vancouver Native Housing Society places Indigenous stories on the Vancouver landscape (Bridges 2017). NativeLand.ca and its companion app reveal community contributed Indigenous land identification.[5] Indigital is a start-up working with aboriginal communities in Australia to create mixed-reality holograms of themselves talking about their stories in their own language.[6] Taking inspiration from these previous works, *Groundworks* guides the user through Northern California to reveal an interactive contemporary Indigenous view of the region.

In addition to orientation and temporal shifting, the *Groundworks* app allows the user to engage with that content in unique ways. For instance, some content may only be accessible when an audience member is actually standing at the coordinates of the original event, requiring them to have a real-life experience of the place specified. The project also integrates original languages, requiring the user to speak words in Pomo or Ohlone to access elements of content using basic voice recognition technology. This creates a reciprocal, active relationship between the audience, the artists, and the site.

The ultimate goal of this performance system, best described by Simon, Paolantonio, and Clamen (2005), is the effect of coming in contact with a ghost, in that it changes you to become more aware of the living reality of the present. This intrinsically links content to place but also has the effect of archiving the experience of being in that place. A forest after a fire, the change of seasons, irreversible climate change, and other environmental shifts come into conversation with the performance after it is recorded at a specific time, thus constantly asking the audience to reconsider the context.

Intellectual Property and Community Consultation

In addition to the creative and technical work for the project, *Groundworks* has generated, through an Indigenous lens, a framework for respecting the intellectual property of all contributors. Jane Anderson and Kim Christen point out, "As part of the colonial collecting endeavor, Indigenous peoples' lives and cultural practices were often documented and recorded to a remarkable degree. Framed as the 'subjects' of these works, not as their authors and owners, Indigenous people and communities have had no legal rights to determine how and when this documentary material should be accessed or by whom – that is, they cannot just 'chuck a copyright on it'" (Anderson and Christen 2013, 106). Both US and Canadian copyright laws automatically assign the rights to a piece of media, such as the content generated in *Groundworks*, to the creator of that content. However, this is not assumed in many Indigenous communities. Having knowledge shared with someone, recorded or not, does not entitle the person receiving that knowledge to share it on without the permission of the person who has shared it with them before. Therefore, for the purpose of respect for the dissemination of knowledge, songs, language, and so on by the Indigenous contributors to the project, a memorandum of understanding was developed and reviewed by York University's Research Ethics Board following Guidelines for Research Involving Aboriginal/Indigenous Peoples, which devolved the assumed copyright under US and Canadian law back to the contributor except for explicit and agreed usages. It outlined the obligations of each of the partners towards each other (Toasterlab 2018).

This has led to ongoing and constant affirmative consent from the collaborators to counteract the prevailing extractive model of much documentary work in the United States and Canada. The project can only use recorded material as agreed with a limited license for explicitly specified uses. Additional uses must seek the consent of those recorded, and the contributor or community can withdraw their participation. It applies principles of ethical social science research to the intellectual property used in an artistic project and requires that any permanent use, such as the broadcast documentary, involves a new release for the specific content.

Media and Equipment

Groundworks uses a variety of content types, but the primary format is 360VR video. We used a variety of specialised cameras to record monoscopic and stereoscopic 360-degree video content based on the scenarios presented by the recorded events. This allowed for the recording of a variety of immersive experiences for emplacement. Recent advancements in 360 image capture have streamlined the recording and stitching of multiple wide-angle lenses to create a seamless, spherical 360-degree image or video though such techniques have existed for over a century (Magnor et al. 2015). This spherical content is then stored in a flat format as though it were a globe being rolled out, or projected as a map. This video sphere is then easily viewed as an immersive VR video using many applications that support 360 content, such as YouTube, where the positional sensors of the device allow the user to change their view of the content by moving the device.

In Toasterlab's earlier work, 360VR video had been used as an accessible alternative to true AR content. This was done to work around technical challenges of turning performance content recorded with real humans into AR virtual objects and the computational limitations of older mobile devices. By combining this with geolocation, two events can be collapsed into one mixed-reality experience – the presence of the user at a specific location and a recorded immersive video. By orienting the recorded event to match the experience of the site in the present, the device acts as a window into another point in time for the same view of the same place (Garrett 2017).

Both 360VR and true AR rely on numerous sensors which track the position of a device. Toasterlab's unique process makes use of other sensors as well. A GPS antenna allows the device to track the geolocation of the device. The accelerometer measures the acceleration of a device across multiple axes to determine orientation and changes in position. Using these sensors, a device can accurately track virtual objects in spatial relationship to the device. With access to the device's camera, these virtual objects can be composited with the camera's view to make the virtual object appear to be stationary in real space.

For those familiar with Janet Cardiff and George Bures Miller's series of *Walks* or Rimini Protokol's *Situation Rooms*, the effect will be similar. In Cardiff and Miller's work, audio is recorded using binaural microphones, and video is recorded with the intended orientation of the audience (Nedelkopoulou 2011). The experience of these walks, in particular the recent *Night Walk in Edinburgh*, like *Transmission*, is meant to overlap and guide the viewer in their real-life experience. Protokol's *Situation Rooms* provides iPads and headphones to 20 audience members, and the recorded, on-screen experience guides them through a number of rooms (Schwanecke 2017). Toasterlab's work differs in two unique ways. First, it uses 360VR video in place of fixed "flat" content, which allows the viewer to reorient their point of view freely. Second, it uses location data to make progress through the experience interactive and audience-driven.

For *Groundworks*, three different cameras were used to capture these experiences. In the early residencies, as the collaborators were devising their original ideas, the primary camera used was the prosumer Vuze Camera. Vuze, created by Human Eyes Technology, uses four pairs of lenses, each at a right angle to the next and spaced at an assumed pupil distance from its companion, to record 4K stereoscopic footage. Once a number of scenes had been planned, the professional Insta360 Pro camera was rented for higher resolution capture. This camera uses six wide-angle lenses positioned around a spherical body to record 6K stereoscopic footage. To record impromptu footage in the field, we used the pocket-sized 360 action camera Insta360 ONE. This allowed the project to be flexible with recording conditions. And though 360VR video is the primary media type, other media content types are also used. This includes conventional flat video and volumetric performance capture. Volumetric capture, a more recent recording technique which overcomes earlier challenges in Toasterlab's work, uses an array of different types of cameras inwards to record a performance from multiple angles concurrently and creates a 3D video model (Alloway 2019).

In addition to behind-the-scenes footage, the project expanded to include documentation of longer interactions between collaborators and their community mentors. At first, this documentation was for the benefit of the collaborators, so they would have recordings of interactions with their mentors; this subsequently turned into its own documentary project. It was also used to create a short film based on Kanyon Sayers-Roods telling of *How Turtle Got the Cracks on His Back*, which has been an official selection at the American Indian and Poppy Jasper Film Festivals. Immersive audio was captured using both binaural and ambisonic field recorders. These recordings provide audio-only mixed-reality experiences. Binaural recordings consist of left and right stereo channels, which are recorded using two microphones placed a similar distance apart as a person's ears. The slight difference in the arrival time of sound at each of these microphones creates the illusion of localised sound by recreating the way sound arrives in a person's ears. Ambisonic audio records and playback, effectively an audio sphere, which, like 360VR video, can retain its orientation as the listener moves their head.

Locations and Content

The purpose of this extensive recording is to emplace each piece of content at a location which is significant to the artists. When they are collected in the mobile application, this provides a navigation tool for a specific region centring contemporary Indigenous thinking about place. California has been colonised twice. It was first colonised by the Spanish and later signed over to the United States through treaty. But the region has been home to Indigenous communities for thousands of years. Under the Spanish, many Indigenous people were brought into the mission system and were pushed further out of traditional territories with the western expansion of the United States, a belief in manifest destiny, and white supremacy. For hundreds of years, there have been efforts to erase Indigenous peoples in these places. This informs the experience of most California Native people, but the experience of this displacement has been uneven. Some communities are federally recognised, while some are not. Some have been able to revitalise original languages, while others have not. Some have a land base, while some do not. Access to locations with significant connections to food, water, and ritual varies across sovereign, public, and private land (U.S. National Park Service n.d.).

The project is centred on the San Francisco Bay Area, which may also be referred to as Yelamu referring to an independent tribe of the Ramaytush Ohlone whose traditional territory was very similar to the boundaries of San Francisco County (Cordero n.d.). The city served as a hub for all of the *Groundworks* project's activities and a location for many rehearsals and presentations of the work in progress, particularly *Dance Mission Creations* in the San Francisco's Mission District. Excerpts from the project were presented in the rotunda of San Francisco City Hall and at Yerba Buena Gardens, a popular cultural centre. In between residencies, many collaborators were involved in climate marches and events in September 2018 in the city which are included in the project's content. Similarly, nearly all collaborators attended the San Francisco's appeals board hearings on the removal of the controversial Early Days statue outside of city hall. This monument "depicted a fallen American Indian cowering at the feet of a Catholic missionary who points to heaven and a Spanish cowboy raising his hand in victory" (Blei 2018), and excerpts from the recorded hearing are included in the project. Elements created in the city, such as the short film *How Turtle Got the Cracks on His Back*, led by Kanyon Sayers-Roods, are included in project media and have gone on to have a life of their own at festivals. This short piece combined Sayer-Roods' traditional storytelling with visuals gleaned from across the city.

Beyond the San Francisco peninsula, the project pays special attention to Alcatraz Island as the site of the live performance at the culmination of its planned residencies. Alcatraz was used as a staging ground for repressing Indigenous peoples by the US Army, and the military prison built on the island incarcerated many Indigenous leaders alongside soldiers. After the prison was closed in 1963, the land became surplus government property. Many plans to redevelop the Island were proposed, but in November of 1969, Indians of All Tribes began the 19-month Occupation of Alcatraz, which redefined the federal relationship with Indigenous populations across the United States. The island is now managed by the US National Park Service, which guides tourists through the prison, maintains breeding spaces for migratory birds, and supports commemoration of the Occupation. Twice a year, the Occupation is acknowledged by sunrise ceremonies on Indigenous Peoples' Day and on Thanks-taking/Thanksgiving Day (U.S. National Park Service n.d.). On the first official Indigenous Peoples' Day for the City of San Francisco, the site-specific performance component of *Groundworks* was shared after the annual sunrise ceremony. It led attendees from the ceremony grounds to the loading dock of the island, with performance offerings developed over the course of the project. Moving north along the coast, we worked our way into Pomo territory. This included a regular stop at the Nest to document its build progress. We moved to the territory of the Kashaya Pomo tribe and Point Arena Manchester Bands of Pomo Indians. Here we created 360VR pieces related to traditional Pomo dance, seaweed harvesting, the impact of the purple spiny sea urchin on abalone population, and the development of Bernadette Smith's dance/theatre performance about the threats to the Tanoak acorn.

Inland residencies focused around the city of Santa Rosa between devastating forest fire seasons. Desirae Harp's mother, TekTekh Gabaldon, shared traditional uses of Indigenous plants such as the use of dogbane for rope and Manzanita berry tea. Another day started at the Old Faithful Geyser of California, asking the private proprietor to allow access to local Indigenous people for ceremonial purposes. After the geyser, we hiked to the peak of Kanamota (Mount St

Figure 10.3 Esme Olivia poses in the waterfall in Indian Canyon.

Photo credit: Ian Garrett

Helena), the Wappo's sacred mountain, through the charred remains of recent forest fires (see Figure 10.1). The peak, a place traditionally used for connecting with ancestors, is now the location of a television broadcast aerial.

In later visits to Santa Rosa, we were guests in L Frank's back garden. It has become a location for working with traditional building techniques and growing many of the plants that Gabaldon uses in her demonstrations. L Frank led conversations about the recovery of the Tongva language. The poem she wrote while working on language revitalise – visible in Figure 10.2 – was integrated into the music for *Groundworks*.

In the opposite direction, to the south of Yelamu, is Ohlone Territory. Indian Canyon is the only land continuously held by the Ohlone people as well as the only federally recognised "Indian country" along coastal Northern California between Santa Barbara and Sonoma. Kanyon Sayers-Roods grew up here, and her mother, Anne Marie Sayers, is Tribal Chair of Indian Canyon. Once also known as Indian Gulch, this protected enclave has served as a refuge for Indigenous people avoiding interactions with settlers. It now sits tucked behind land used for viticulture. To protect this land and the water access essential to the off-grid utilities of the Canyon, Sayers had it designated as agricultural land by herding pygmy goats. Virtual reality experiences were documented along the mile-long canyon, including a dance for the waterfall that feeds into the Harlan Creek at the southern edge of the Canyon (Figure 10.3), smudging in the arbour areas, the sharing of songs by the Canyon's healing pole, and an extended conversation with Gregg Castro, one of Sayers-Roods' mentors.

Mobile Application

The future of the *Groundworks* project is focused on the development of a mobile application which will guide users through the region and lead them to interact with the content. Many of these experiences will be freely available to play within the application, but a key feature is the integration of various access barriers to content which require activity by the user to "unlock." This process, known in game design as gating, is "where game designers can prevent players from progressing through a narrative until they have completed a given objective, performed a specific action, developed new skills, or acquired a special item" (Solarski 2017, 38). This is intended to require acts of reciprocity between the user in accepting knowledge and the artist/culture bearer to respectfully engage such experiences by limiting access through associate tasks. These are cultural checks in digital heritage stewardship (Christen 2018). The tasks can be reading or listening to contextual media, learning an original place-name or word which the device's vocal recognition can decipher, or simply arriving at the content's location. As articulated through the project's approach to intellectual property, it is not appropriate to freely share the content at all times, and these "gates" are developed as a way to encourage respectful exchange.

Many Toasterlab projects exist as web applications, which are easily accessible to most users because they run in the included mobile browser.[7] Mobile browsers are able to access the GPS data from a device and can playback many common media types. However, they do not currently support 360VR video playback. This is typically handled by sending the user to another application like the YouTube app. Further, using the browser on a mobile device requires an active data connection to stream content. Based on the locations of this project, many of the sites are not covered by cellular data service appropriate for accessing the content; nevertheless, "like freeways before them . . . wireless networks hold out the promise to spatially liberate the citizen by connecting the city without undermining the autonomy of the individual citizen" (Varnelis 2008, 151).

Tracking the data about what a user has or has not accomplished is best accomplished with a dedicated app. Based on previous experiences with limited network bandwidth, a system of packaging-optimised content, both media files and map data, to be pre-downloaded while still on an appropriate network has been built into the MapTool to eliminate the dependency on an active data connection. This also requires a dedicated app and the time to develop it. However, dedicated apps are not without their own challenges beyond the time required to programme them. For instance, while GPS signal is free to access, its accuracy can be highly variable. Mapping applications filter data to best approximate the device's location. In areas with extensive data coverage, navigation apps also factor in cellular and visible wireless networks. These can assist the device with increasing the accuracy of the location it reports. Our MapTool has evolved to include a variety of methods of filtering locational data as well.

With all of these considerations, the MapTool and our ability to create mobile apps have become well refined, but what works in concept will always encounter challenges in the field. An essential part of the process is extensive testing of the app across devices and conditions. Extremely specific locations require onsite analysis to optimise the app to account for variable conditions. Topography and architecture can affect GPS reception, scattering recording locations or causing consistent misidentification.

Project Trajectory

The last time the collaborators met together was in October 2019. Dance Mission in San Francisco presented the work in progress of Dancing Earth Creations' production of *BTW US – Between Underground & Skyworld*.[8] Before the technical rehearsals, the collaborators gathered to review progress and discuss the potential of the mobile application. On 27 October 2019, as part of the Reindigenize: Bay Area culture sharing event, Toasterlab shared the video content on Oculus Headsets with community members in attendance. At the premiere of *BTW US – Between Underground & Skyworld* at Arizona State University's ASU Gammage auditorium on 25 January 2020, Toasterlab shared the 360VR content as part of the pre-show events for this performance. Toasterlab has been unable to travel back to California since March 2020 due to COVID-19 restrictions, while Dancing Earth's company members have had mixed ability to travel depending on their locations. Many collaborators have also focused their attention appropriately on supporting their communities through this crisis. This has meant that two essential elements for the next steps of the project have been indefinitely delayed – ongoing community consultation has not been possible (with limited ability to work on shorts and projects, such as the presentation of *How Turtle Got the Cracks on His Back* at film festivals in partnership with Sayers-Roods) and the field testing of technology. Through hard-learned lessons, we are unwilling to compromise about onsite testing. At this writing, we are waiting for public health restrictions to lift to allow us to proceed. As such, the earliest launch date for this project is likely the fall of 2023. Accounting for collaborators' schedules, development timelines, and anticipating testing, this may still be changed.

Even though the realisation of this project in its final form may be delayed due to COVID-19, additional components of this project and related collaborations have continued with positive reciprocity. The broadcast documentary connected to the project moves forward in post-production. And in June 2020, the available Dancing Earth company members who were to tour with *BTW US – Between Underground & Skyworld* worked with Toasterlab to present a new live streaming performance called *Indigenous Futurities* with each of the cast members in their homes. So while we could not come together for *Groundworks*, we did manage to connect across eight cities in three countries (United States, Canada, and New Zealand).

Conclusion

In a clip of Gregg Castro's conversation with Kanyon Sayers-Roods used in the soundscape of the live *Groundworks* performance on Alcatraz Island, Castro describes a conversation about the difference between dances performed in eastern and western parts of Turtle Island. While one group dances in a clockwise direction, the other dances counterclockwise. When someone asked why they moved in different directions from each other, the answer was that it was to balance the world. *Groundworks* is as much a media project as it is a process of laying foundational relationships, the groundwork, for collaboration. And the act of re-storying through this process is akin to that act of balance. In addition to revealing the stories and history of California Native communities, the approach to logistics, funding, intellectual property rights, and the uneven distribution of technology to support the creative work of the collaborators, as this chapter has outlined, reconsiders relationships that may otherwise be limited by default by colonial systems that have resulted in the marginalisation of Indigenous people and environmental degradation in California.

The six-page memorandum of understanding that devolves the copyright back to a collaborator and their community is necessary because it undoes the assumed default rights position that sees the receiver of knowledge as the owner, as though using a camera was to extract a resource. This rationale for why this project approaches rights in the way it does is also an explanation as to why the project focuses on accessible free technology. Re-storying is about restoration and relationships for a shared future. These efforts problematise many assumptions about intellectual property and technology through a lens of reciprocal responsibility. It is interesting to note that the first component to be imagined when the first connections were made may be the last known component to be completed. Even once there is a mobile app for release, it may not be appropriate to consider the project complete. It is intended that additional experiences could be added to the app in the future. The infrastructure and relationships that have been built between collaborators, communities, land, and technology will certainly continue. Which prompts the question – why should we not continue to create interjections into the history and geography of California, or beyond, that continue to expand understanding of these locations and their narratives through the sharing of emplaced stories?

Notes

1 An important note: It is important to note that the lead author of this chapter is a white cisgender male settler in Canada who is in a tenured faculty position and benefits from significant systemic and institutional privilege. It is the responsibility of someone in this position of privilege to work as an ally for those who do not benefit from the same privilege or who have experienced oppression as a result of this privilege. The project described in this chapter has taken efforts to ensure that it is done in a way that acknowledges and, at times, takes advantage of this privilege to work with reciprocity, respect, and equity. This project attempts to work against and undo a history of extractive documentation and other predatory Indigenous/settler interactions. But it is also not without its challenges and controversies, often stemming from the oppressive colonial systems within which the project is executed. The authors would like to acknowledge the various territories they have had the pleasure to work within and be welcome to. Included in the co-authors of this chapter are representatives of Pomo, Wappo, Ohlone, Sierra Miwok, and Tongva communities. It is with respect and working in a good way that each is welcome into the other's traditional lands. Additionally, as lead author, I would also like to acknowledge the caretakers of the land where I am based and have the pleasure of working; the land I am standing on today is the traditional territory of many nations, including the Mississaugas of the Credit, the Anishnabeg, the Chippewa, the Haudenosaunee, and the Wendat peoples, and is now home to many diverse First Nations, Inuit, and Métis peoples. Tkaronto, known by its colonial name as Toronto, is covered by Treaty 13, signed with the Mississaugas of the Credit. It is here where I serve as Associate Professor of Ecological Design for Performance at York University.

2 Murdered & Missing Indigenous Women (www.nativewomenswilderness.org/mmiw).

3 *Indigenous Futurities* (*IF*), Dancing Earth in CyberSpace (https://fac.coloradocollege.edu/connect/indigenous-futurities-dancing-earth-in-cyberspace).

4 Henry G20 (www.henryg20.com).

5 Native Land Digital: Our home on native land (https://native-land.ca).

6 Indigital (https://indigital.net.au).

7 Toasterlab (https://toasterlab.com).

8 *BTW US – Between Underground & Skyworld* (https://dancingearth.org/between-underground-and-skyworld).

Sources

Alloway, Meredith. 2019. "FROM ALL ANGLES." *Filmmaker* (Summer). Music & Performing Arts Collection.

Anderson, Jane, and Kimberly Christen. 2013. "'Chuck a Copyright on It': Dilemmas of Digital Return and the Possibilities for Traditional Knowledge Licenses and Labels." *Museum Anthropology Review* 7 (1–2): 105–26.

Azuma, R T. 1997. "A Survey of Augmented Reality." *Presence: Teleoperators and Virtual Environments* 6 (4): 355–85.

Blei, Daniela. 2018. "San Francisco's 'Early Days' Statue Is Gone. Now Comes the Work of Activating Real History." *Smithsonian Magazine*, October 4, 2018. www.smithsonianmag.com/smithsonian-institution/san-francisco-early-days-statue-gone-now-comes-work-activating-real-history-180970462/.

Bridges, Alicia. 2017. "Saskatchewan Man Creates Indigenous 'Wikiupedia' with New Phone App | CBC News." *CBC*, February 17, 2017. www.cbc.ca/news/canada/saskatoon/adrian-duke-wikiupedia-phone-app-1.3988502.

Christen, Kimberly. 2018. "Relationships, Not Records: Digital Heritage and the Ethics of Sharing Indigenous Knowledge Online." In 1st ed., Vol. 1, 403–12. New York: Routledge.

Clarke, Rachel, and Shelby Wilis. 2014. *Broadway Augmented.* Augmented Reality.

Cohen, Jeffrey Jerome, and Stephanie Lemenager. 2016. "Introduction: Assembling the Ecological Digital Humanities." *PMLA/Publications of the Modern Language Association of America* 131 (2): 340–46.

Cordero, Jonathan. n.d. "Who Are the Original Peoples of San Francisco and of the San Francisco Peninsula?" *Ramaytush Ohlone.* Accessed April 30, 2021. www.ramaytush.com/original-peoples-of-san-francisco.html.

Dancing Earth Creations. n.d. "About Dancing Earth." *Dancing Earth Creations.* Accessed May 2, 2021a. https://dancingearth.org/about.

———. n.d. "Artistic & Founding Director, Rulan Tangen." *Dancing Earth Creations.* Accessed May 2, 2021b. https://dancingearth.org/rulan.

Freeman, J. C. 2013. "Border Memorial: Frontera De Los Muertos." *Public Art Dialogue* 3 (1): 129–31.

Garrett, Ian. 2017. "Technological Haunting for the Time Shifting of Performance." *CSPA Quarterly* 16 (Spring): 34–28.

"Henry G20." n.d. *Henry G20.* Accessed September 12, 2021. www.henryg20.com.

Madley, Benjamin. 2019. "California's First Mass Incarceration System: Franciscan Missions, California Indians, and Penal Servitude, 1769–1836." *Pacific Historical Review* 88 (1): 14–47.

Magnor, Marcus A., Christian Theobalt, Olga Sorkine-Hornung, and Oliver Grau. 2015. *Digital Representations of the Real World: How to Capture, Model, and Render Visual Reality.* London: CRC Press LLC.

Nedelkopoulou, Eirini. 2011. "Walking Out on Our Bodies Participation as Ecstasis in Janet Cardiff's Walks." *Performance Research* 16 (4): 117–23.

Niedzwiecki, Jacob. 2019. "Jacqueries: Mind Games, Street Action, and the Art of the Heist." *Canadian Theatre Review* 178 (March): 26–31. https://doi.org/10.3138/ctr.178.005.

Palmer, Mark. 2012. "Theorizing Indigital Geographic Information Networks." *Cartographica: The International Journal for Geographic Information and Geovisualization* 47 (2): 80–91.

Robinson, Dylan. 2020. *Hungry Listening.* University of Minnesota Press. www.jstor.org/stable/10.5749/j.ctvzpv6bb.

Schwanecke, Christine. 2017. "Mobile People, Weapons, and Data Streams; Mobile Audiences and Theatre Spaces: Rimini Protokoll's Situation Rooms as a Globalised Theatre Experience." *Journal of Contemporary Drama in English* 5 (2): 358–71.

Simon, R. I., Mario Di Paolantonio, and Mark Clamen. 2005. "Remembrance as Praxis and the Ethics of the Interhuman." In *The Touch of the Past: Remembrance, Learning, and Ethics*, edited by Roger I. Simon, 132–55. New York: Palgrave Macmillan US.

Solarski, Chris. 2017. *Interactive Stories and Video Game Art: A Storytelling Framework for Game Design.* Natick: CRC Press LLC.

Toasterlab. 2017. "About." *Toasterlab*, January 24, 2017. https://toasterlab.com/about/.

———. 2018. "Groundworks Partnership Memorandum of Understanding." *Toasterlab.*

US National Park Service. n.d. "Article Series (U.S. National Park Service)." Accessed May 1, 2021. www.nps.gov/articles/series.htm.

Varnelis, Kazys. 2008. *The Infrastructural City: Networked Ecologies in Los Angeles.* Barcelona: Actar.

Villeneuve, D. 2016. *Arrival.* Hollywood: Paramount Pictures.

Weidner, Chad, Rosi Braidotti, and Goda Klumbyte. 2019. "The Emergent Environmental Humanities: Engineering the Social Imaginary." *Connotations* 28: 1–25.

Willis, S. and Clarke, R. 2014. *Broadway Augmented.* Sacramento: Robert T. Matsui Gallery. http://www.broadwayaugmented.net/.

11

DATAFICATION, DIGITISATION, AND THE NARRATION OF AGRICULTURE IN MALAWI

From Productivity Measures to Curated Folklore

Dumisani Z. Moyo and Deborah P. Dixon

Introduction

The DEH offers a useful framework for (1) a critical engagement with the ways in which a "data colonialism" allows for governments, supranational agencies, NGOs, economists and environmental sciences to *datafy* and *digitise* Global South agriculture in the form of aggregated farming practices and outputs, and the farmer as an agent of production and consumption; and (2) a critical reckoning with how various forms of digitalisation can help to "decolonise" such articulations, offering alternate ways of knowing how to farm. To datafy is to locate and collect information on activities and events such that quantified data is produced; such data can be monitored, tracked, analysed, and optimised, allowing for a range of policies and programmes to be designed, evidenced, and justified. As numerous scholars have pointed out, such data shapes views on people and place, as well as views on what is possible and impossible to achieve and who is best placed to make such judgements (e.g. Escobar 2016; D. Moyo et al. 2016; B.H.Z. Moyo and Moyo 2017; Mbembe 2017; Eriksen 2007; Krätli 2008). Digitisation is the conversion of data into a computer-readable format, allowing for the digital representation of text, image, sound and so on, and its analysis and transformation via software. While the digitisation of datafied information has certainly further congealed existing power relationships, particular forms of digital practice have also become significant as alternate, valued forms of knowing and narrating the world that, moreover, have the capacity to enrol other publics with attendant effects.

At a broad scale, humanities-focused work brings to the fore cultural and ethical – as well as political – questions around the process and impacts of a data-driven knowledge building, questions that are relevant for sustainable futures in the face of unprecedented economic, technological, and social change (Weidner, Braidotti, and Klumbyte 2019). What a digital, environmentally focused humanities can offer more specifically is an attentiveness to how the digitisation of datasets further congeals established forms of knowledge production but can also enable new

DOI: 10.4324/9781003082798-14

forms of environmental storytelling and attendant effects to emerge from the intimate scale of the farmed field to the "world stage" of state agricultural reports. In the midst of debates around the aims and practice of a decolonialism – wherein colonialist forms of knowledge production are acknowledged as such and provincialised and are critically interrogated as to their work in the world, while Indigenous knowledge (IK) production is acknowledged not as marginal or silent but as marginalised and unattended to in Western academe – questions arise as to how digitisation might be used (though not unproblematically) to undermine what are well-entrenched articulations for farmers and farming in the Global South.

In what follows, we briefly outline the agricultural situation in Malawi to provide context for Section 3, which focuses on how farming practices are currently datafied and digitised as part of state-led governance of this sector and the power relations inherent to this. Drawing on the research of Dumisani Z. Moyo, the section outlines how data is collected from farmers in the field and uploaded such that digitised data can be produced in a range of forms for various purposes and readerships. Such efforts form a counterpoint to the ongoing project of digitising folklore in Malawi; in Section 4, we outline this a project that promises to offer another form of narration that situates people and place. And yet, as Dumisani's research on this project goes on to note, unless the digital humanities of this alternate datafication and digitisation is accorded adequate attention, the result may be a further entrenching of a colonial view of people and place.

Agriculture in Malawi

Agriculture is the most important sector of sub-Saharan Africa's Malawian economy. It "contributes to about 40% of the GDP, accounts for more than 90% of export earnings, offers employment to more than 80% of the population and supplies over 90% of the food consumed in the country" (Government of Malawi 2006, 1). Colonial Malawi (1889–1964) was built on plantation agriculture largely in the southern region, where vast areas of seemingly uninhabited land were alienated; less so in the central region and much less so in the north (Vaughan 1982; Prowse 2013; Ng'ong'ola 1986). Under British occupation, "colonialism fuelled capitalism by arrogating to the settlers the means of economic production and by reducing the Africans to a labouring class or a rural peasantry" (Ng'ong'ola 1986, 240). In this system, settler-owned estates grew crops in response to global markets. Cash crops for the export and internal market and food crops for the internal market were emphasised (Ng'ong'ola 1986). While export crops (produced initially, exclusively by white settlers) generated much needed foreign currency, food crops (mostly produced by African peasants) sustained the production base locally. The principal export crops were coffee for a very short period and tobacco, tea, and cotton for most of the colonial period (Ng'ong'ola 1986; Quinn 1994; Vaughan 1982).

In this estate-based agricultural production and market system, the Indigene was framed as not intelligent enough to participate at the same level of freedom of contract as the settler (Ng'ong'ola 1986, 243; Vaughan 1982; Peters 1997). Such a system allies with what Achille Mbembe (2003) would call a necropolis – effected here by disturbing Indigenous systems and efforts at progress via repressive, coercive, and paternalistic land and land use, labour, and educational and market policies and regulations (Ng'ong'ola 1986; Vaughan 1982; Peters 1997). Indigenes were mainly peasants relegated to supplying estate labour (i.e. mostly male adult household members, but sometimes entire families) and some export crop production on their own farms (to supplement settler interests). Economic practices, notably European merchandise and tax systems including hut tax and the infamous *thangata* labour system, were used to coerce Africans into labour supply. Hut tax was a revenue stream for the colonial government, charged to everyone who owned a hut, poor or rich (Kwengwere 2011). It is reported that many Indigenes could not afford it, forcing them into supplying estate labour even at the expense of their own farms; the hut tax thus entrenched a poverty cycle and trap of repeated, effectively coerced estate labour (Ng'ong'ola 1986; Kwengwere 2011). *Thangata* was similarly legislated but more informally governed by estate owners who collected "rent" from workers they provided with land for settlement and cultivation – a minimum of two month's labour supply comprising a payment in lieu of the hut tax for the one month, plus one month's *thangata* labour that was oftentimes exploitatively extended to as long as five months by the estate owners (Kwengwere 2011). The colonial agricultural system was very much predicated on the establishment, maintenance, and evolution through time of a record-keeping system that firmly tied particular social structures to the organisation and shaping of the environment under agriculture. As Lamm et al. note, it was during the colonial era, for example, that an agricultural extension service was designed and established (in 1907), as the colonial government trained a new cohort of farming experts with the goal of compelling farmers to adopt new kinds of agricultural techniques: unsurprisingly, this "extension service delivery was top-down, with a strong emphasis on cash crop production" (Lamm et al. 2021, 1387).

Following independence, the economy remained largely dependent on primary agricultural exports, with cane sugar joining the pre-existing (colonial) league of key crops. What is more, following independence, it was deemed imperative that a proper agricultural education system would be set up. This formed a key impetus for the establishment of Bunda College of Agriculture in 1966 and the Natural Resources College in 1969; these organisations would supply trained agricultural extension workers who then mostly move on into employment in heavily donor-dependent and donor-driven government and (increasingly) civil society systems, as well as an influential private sector comprising mostly supranational agricultural companies. Some of the power relations within which extension workers operated, and which provided a context for the collection and dissemination of data on farm productivity, but also on purported farmer malfeasance, are noted in the Ministry of Agriculture and Food Security's 2006 report, which observes,

> The extension approaches that have been used over the years include Coercion – where farmers were forced to follow recommended practices, otherwise those that did not comply were either fined or jailed; Individual approach – this included use of master farmers and extension agents through individual visits; Group approach – that included use of farmer clubs and cooperatives for input supply, commercial crop production, dairying and marketing.
>
> *(Government of Malawi 2006, 2)*

It was not until the 2000s that the top-down model of agricultural extension work was substantially changed (on paper):

> In contrast to the colonial era, decentralization emphasized bottom-up approaches to extension delivery, which promoted a demand-driven, diffuse knowledge from the formal agricultural education system in which farmers requested specific extension services based on their needs.
>
> *(Lamm et al. 2021, 1387)*

As of 2019, Malawi had close to 1,700 agricultural extension workers intended to undertake outreach with close to four million farmers (*Nyasa Times*, October 8, 2019). The work undertaken by agricultural agents provides a significant stream of data into a "digital ecology" of Malawi farming, wherein information on farming and farmers is collected, datafied, and digitised. Data is also collected by other agencies, however, and in the next section, we explain in more detail how this process is undertaken. Following this, we look at how an alternate form of digitisation – the collection and curation of Indigenous folklore – has been undertaken. To be sure, such a method presents a very different kind of storytelling about what are largely farming communities, but as a *decolonial* alternative, it falls short.

Creating Agricultural Data

As Heeks and Shelkhar summarise, the goals and activities of the United Nations sustainable development programmes have helped trigger a step-change in how the agricultural sector has been datafied. This datafication "can be described in terms of a growing volume, velocity, variety and visibility of data, with greater use of new forms and streams of data in decision-making." A positive reading of datafication reads this as

> essential to both delivery and measurement of the Sustainable Development Goals. Specifically, it argues for a set of particular development benefits from datafication: improving agricultural productivity though better advice for farmers, helping stop spread of diseases through better charting of their diffusion, improving accountability of government through greater openness of public sector decisions, etc.
>
> *(Heeks and Shekhar 2019, 993)*

In Malawi presently, the monitoring and evaluation (M&E) system of the National Agriculture Policy (Government of Malawi 2016) effectively provides the backbone and the framework for agricultural datafication and digitisation in the country. This system is designed to leverage existing data systems within government, as well as those of development partners, civil society, the private sector (including consulting firms and individuals for operational support), and similarly largely donor-driven projects at academic and research institutes. As a sub-component of the Ministry of Agriculture, the Department of Agriculture Extensions Services is also at the centre of the country's annual Agricultural Production Estimates (APES) – arguably the major agricultural survey in the country, with data feeding into major global datasets, including the databases of the World Bank and the Food and Agriculture Organization (FAO) of the United Nations. Under the management of district councils, extension workers collect and collate data from the farm level, through the various levels of the government extension system, to national level estimates of agricultural output. Similarly, in other agricultural surveys, extension agents are central; they influence the design of research questions, especially sampling design and protocols, as well as directly supply quantitative or qualitative data.

M. Jerven (2014) notes that there are political and technical inadequacies in compiling the APES, including an entrenched data falsification culture at all levels. Comprehensive and rich on the face of it, a DEH approach remains attentive to how people and places are being narrated in particular ways that are impactful via datafication; the impacts including major decisions pertaining to policy and programme/project implementation. Extension workers and other researchers collect primary agricultural data on incomes, production levels, land allocations, husbandry practices, and interpretations or mediations of the same. Process-wise, a core research team (many times, consultants) will be commissioned to manage a research project. They will frame the questions to be asked, many times recycling questions asked before (and elsewhere). The problematics of this recycling, including a blindspot around IK of farming, are discussed in ample detail in the literature (see, for example, D.Z. Moyo 2012; M. Jerven 2009; Briggs and Moyo 2012; Escobar 2016; Mignolo and Escobar 2010; Escobar 1995; Chambers 2008; D. Moyo et al. 2016; B.H.Z. Moyo and Moyo 2017; Howitt, Havnen, and Veland 2012). The research questions will be translated into data collection protocols and tools such as semi-structured questionnaires and checklists – printed into hard copy or presented in digital format. This would be a month's work or so. Yet the core research team often has too many commitments to collect data from the farmer. And so a team of enumerators, with (much) lower qualifications and experience (and usually little, if any, interest in the validity of the data) will be engaged, trained for two or three days, and deployed. From this point there are significant variations between the collection of quantitative and qualitative data.

Quantitative data normally comprises collecting a lot of quantifiable data within a short span of time. In this practice, it is expected that an enumerator will take an hour with a farmer. This one hour is supposed to capture a representative and valid snapshot of the farmer's farming and non-farming livelihoods covering minimally an agricultural year, usually several years. The enumerator will normally sit with the farmer under some shade, removed from the farm being discussed. The farmer, on the other hand, is now used to interviews, has evidently generated mental template responses, and will normally answer to meet the enumerators' expectations unless one probes and questions. For more detail on this snapshot setting, or really, rapid appraisal setting, see Chambers (2008) and his discussion of development tourism, as well as Briggs, Badri, and Mekki (1999).

After this collection, the data reverts to the core team or, as is increasingly the case, to a separate data manager/analyst. For hard copies, a separate team will be engaged to enter the data. The data manager/analyst will then run analysis protocols generating tables for interpretation and representation by the core team. It is this highly mediated information, processed through multiple hands with loose quality control measures that are featured in reports and briefs, that is translated (selectively) into policies, projects, and actions.

Qualitative data often involves a smaller number of interviews/discussions per research project (and receives closer attention from the core team) but usually faces similar pressures for time and resources, as well as the mediation challenge, where enumerators are engaged. One major set of differences obtains where ethnographic or anthropological methodologies have been deployed, with the principal investigator(s) or similarly interested co-investigators themselves collecting the data from the farmers.

Rarely core investigators closely monitor quantitative (and qualitative) data collection in the form of repeat interviews, listening in on enumerators at work, and more/less real-time monitoring of data when captured through computer-assisted interviews (essentially, questionnaires in digital format and variants of the same) – with a similarly real-time feedback system to the data collection teams. A case in point would be a recent data collection exercise Dumisani Z. Moyo followed as part of his fieldwork. The data collection at issue is arguably highly important work as it informs a major plant breeding programme in the country. Part of the research was a choice experiment where farmers were asked to state their preferences for selected traits of a particular legume. Upon following one enumerator, it was found that a question intended to be dropped from the exercise had been mistakenly included, and data on this was collected and entered. Similarly, when visual aids of plant varieties were presented to respondents to aid a discussion of leaf colour, the articulation of the experiment questions suggested mistakenly that some of these varieties were indeed part of the plant breeding experiment. Finally, the core team found that where farmers were supposed to be asked for their actual experience with actual varieties (thus revealing a preference) in the interview preceding the experiment, the mistaken impression was given that it was the potential, hypothetical varieties that were under discussion. Once recorded, analysed, and represented (the digitisation process, in turn facilitating an often unquestioning credulity toward the representations), there is hardly any way these inaccuracies can be identified, let alone corrected, until the wrong varieties appear in the field in three year's time.

Digitising Folklore

Decolonisation explores ways of de-linking from the colonial legacies of knowledge production outlined previously, in a form of direct action called epistemic disobedience, drawing on, among other things, alternative forms of knowledge, including IK to challenge both the epistemic and material foundations of the historical European power projection (Weidner, Braidotti, and Klumbyte 2019). DEH is productive here in that it directs us to forms of storytelling that are digitised but counter, in some form, the datafication outlined previously. That is, digital practices that present a very different account of people and place. Yet it must be asked, are such examples of a radical DEH a departure from what has been outlined previously, or might they become complementary narrations?

As D. Moyo and Dixon (2021) remark, folklore has been promoted as a space of ontological, teleological, and epistemological escape/freedom from colonial/imperial negativities. Indeed, the study of Indigenous folklore has recently benefited from a heightened impetus. UNESCO, in particular, has signified the importance of this with two key documents: the *Recommendation on the Safeguarding of Traditional Culture and Folklore* (UNESCO 1989) and the *Convention for the Safeguarding of the Intangible Cultural Heritage* (UNESCO 2003). In the Global South, the United Nations (through its agencies including UNDP and UNESCO) is partnering with national government agencies and philanthrocapitalism to research, document, and digitise folklore, with the ostensible aim of conserving, protecting and promoting cultural heritage. In the same vein, digital storytelling has been gaining traction over time in agricultural development practice. More recently, these case studies are being captured as audiovisuals as well – even for agricultural extension purposes. Indeed, we see the rise of digital extension methodologies that include the capturing of stories in digital, audiovisual format and airing them on radio and television.

In this section, we focus on the UNESCO-supported *Malawi Folktales and Folksongs Project*, which makes available select, curated, digitised folklore. Implemented in 2011 and ongoing, this project was designed to be concerned mainly with collecting folktales and folksongs throughout Malawi for educational purposes. It has evolved into a composite of six projects (the National Library Service, the Timveni Child and Youth Media Organization, Music Crossroads Malawi, and the Tumaini Letu and Nanzikambe Arts Development Organization) jointly implemented by government agencies, the civil society, and the private sector. A quote from a leading scholar of Malawian folklore, Boston Soko, Professor of Oral Literature, University of Mzuzu is captured on the Malaw Folktales Project's website and elucidates the relevance of the project to environmental management:

> The emphasis is on respect for tradition as well as nature in general. The respect for tradition goes along with the belief that everything, according to the elders' vision of the world, trees, animals, rivers, stones, mountains, are endowed with life, hence the interaction of humans and non-humans in the folktales. Mountains, trees or stones were believed to be the abode of the spirits. Because today respect for these has disappeared, we see the wanton cutting down of trees, the destruction of sacred places and the disinterest in oral traditions.
>
> *(Sony 2022)*

Dumisani was granted access to and reviewed the unpublished version of the archive; the publication process is underway. Furthermore, he held key informant interviews with key staff on the project at managerial and operational levels. According to these key informants, the selection of folklore for digitisation was based on geography, ethnical/cultural distribution, and similarities among entries. That is, folklore was selected to come from the three administrative regions of the country, covering as many districts as feasible whilst avoiding reinventing the wheel in districts that had benefitted from significant similar digitisation efforts previously. Particular attention was given to capturing the cultural diversity of the country, defined in terms of ethnic groupings. Finally, entries considered repetitive of folklore already captured were left out. An interesting observation is that there was a significantly subjective angle to the process. Notably, one informant remarked, "In some cases, . . . you find that some entries are just nonsense. . . . Some were so explicit you wouldn't want to promote them, as it were."

Further, the key informants observed that a major factor in deciding if a particular collected entry would eventually be published was functionality, educational value and appropriateness, quickly acknowledging that these were quite subjective processes. Entries from *chinamwali* (a local initiation ceremony for girls), for example, were considered damaging and inappropriate for primary and secondary school learners. As Wynter (1997) argues, the blanket demonisation of such practices has strong, demonstrable ties with white supremacy. "You wouldn't want to have such material for primary and secondary schools," remarked the participant in a manner that said to me, "You should know [this]; it goes without saying!" Functionality included "the Malawianness" of the entries, another substantially subjective consideration with glaringly missing criteria. "It is a very subjective process, we know," one of the key informants was quick to add. Out of this subjective process, the project ends up with a collection for publication that noticeably does not include folklore antagonistic to colonialism, coloniality, and the country's one-party system and its associated vices. "The entries are mostly neutral . . . [and] folktale themes are universal," observed one of the informants.

Having reviewed a sample of the audiovisuals captured, there was hardly any that introduces the student/learner to decoloniality by highlighting the colonial oppression and struggles which were continued by the one-party regime. Such key teachings as "Learn their ways but neither reveal your ways nor lose them – it will give you an advantage over them!" have been long lost (Moyo, BHZ, in personal communication). There is neutrality to the collected folklore that, in effect, yields a blindspot to the important colonial history of the country, especially in the light of evidently ongoing postcolonialities.

A critical question with regard to such online archives is, what is left out? Key informant interviews, for example, noted a deliberate suppression of dances like *Gule Wamkulu* during the colonial era, similar to songlines considered antagonistic to Christianity. These "antagonistic" songs are hard to find in the collection, with the key informants not sure if the collection includes them. "We had collected them in some other programme, but we never got to publishing them. They are just lying [unused] somewhere." "The entries are mostly neutral . . . folktale themes are universal . . . the focus is on such issues as internal discipline in communities – issues of corruption for example. . . . The songs mostly address such issues as how to live in a community; informal education including addressing social ills." Herein is the trouble, in that the dynamics that characterise the interaction of communities, not just interactions within communities, are key to understanding the colonisation and underdevelopment of a people by others. A collection that is silent on those dynamics is thus dangerously apolitical; this blindspot to decolonial IK in folklore digitisation very much recalls the blindspot to IK in agricultural datafication as outlined in the preceding section.

Conclusion

Departing from Mbembe's elucidation that coloniality has historically been cultural, seeping into practically every sphere of life, it is not far-fetched to see a common colonial thread here. In both of the cases outlined in this chapter – agricultural datafication/digitisation and folklore datafication/digitisation – there is the absence of IK that might become the basis for a decolonial critique. For instance, the collection held by the folklore project that Dumisani reviewed serves to preserve locally produced material that is considered politically neutral. In a similar vein the national seed policy evidently recognises and collects information on local crop varieties, but only as material marked for replacement by improved varieties and not as a source of useful genetic material and such. This is an observation that corroborates the findings of Stevens (2004), and Tribe (2004), where seemingly neutral, objective actions were found to subtly help sustain and propagate colonial agendas.

It is not mere semantics we are dealing with here. Indeed, "[t]he critique of life as a critique of language is then, precisely what the term 'Africa' invites us to undertake" (Mbembe 2017, 53). A fuller understanding of the knowledge production spaces in which coloniality is nested is arguably a key ingredient to any meaningful, effective, efficient, productive, and sustainable decoloniality project. Colonialism and decoloniality are, by definition, highly politically charged. Yet the political conflict does not vanish with the shutting closed of the eyes, ears, mind, and spirit; neither does change come or emerge by mere wishful thinking. There is a passiveness, we submit, that not only does not get the work of decoloniality/decolonialism done but actually militates against any progress or potential progress at decoloniality. For an agricultural economy like Malawi, where farming is still significantly based on IK, the linkages between a well-established, state-led agricultural data collection and an emerging folklore digitisation need to be critically assessed if radically different narrations of people and place are to be designed, valued, and disseminated. It is towards a decolonial DEH that we must direct our efforts.

Sources

Baker, C. 1975. "Tax Collection in Malawi: An Administrative History, 1891–1972." *International Journal of African Historical Studies* 8 (1). Accessed May 30, 2016. http://www.jstor.org/stable/217485,

Brennert, Kai T. 2019. "Malawi Projects: Folktales, Folksongs and Storytelling 2011–2019." Evaluation Report. REI Foundation Limited & Malawi National Commission for UNESCO.

Briggs, J., M. Badri, and A. M. Mekki. 1999. "Indigenous Knowledges and Vegetation Use among Bedouin in the Eastern Desert of Egypt." *Applied Geography* 19: 78–103.

Briggs, John, and Boyson Moyo. 2012. "The Resilience of Indigenous Knowledge in Small-Scale African Agriculture: Key Drivers." *Scottish Geographical Journal* 128 (1): 64–80.

Chambers, R. 2008. *Revolutions in Development Enquiry*. London: Earthscan.

Eriksen, C. 2007. "Why Do They Burn the 'Bush'? Fire, Rural Livelihoods, and Conservation in Zambia." *The Geographical Journal* 173 (3): 242–56.

Escobar, A. 1995. *Encountering Development: The Making and Unmaking of the Third World*. Princeton: Princeton University Press.

———. 2016. "Thinking-Feeling with the Earth: Territorial Struggles and the Ontological Dimensions of the Epistemologies of the South." *Revisita de Anthropologia Iberoamericana* 11 (1): 11–36.

Government of Malawi. 2006. *The District Agricultural Extension Services System Implementation Guide*. Lilongwe: Ministry of Agriculture and Food Security.

Government of Malawi. 2016. *National Agriculture Policy*. Lilongwe, Malawi: Ministry of Agriculture, Irrigation and Water Development.

Heeks, R., and S. Shekhar. 2019. "Datafication, Development and Marginalised Urban Communities: An Applied Data Justice Framework." *Information, Communication & Society* 22 (7): 992–1011.

Howitt, R., O. Havnen, and S. Veland. 2012. "Natural and Unnatural Disasters: Responding with Respect for Indigenous Rights and Knowledges." *Geographical Research* 50 (1): 47–59.

Jerven, M. 2009. "The Relativity of Poverty and Income: How Reliable Are African Economic Statistics?" *African Affairs* 109 (434): 77–96.

———. 2014. "The Political Economy of Agricultural Statistics and Input Subsidies: Evidence from India, Nigeria and Malawi." *Journal of Agrarian Change* 14 (1): 129–45.

Krätli, S. 2008. "What Do Breeders Breed? On Pastoralists, Cattle and Unpredictability." *Journal of Agriculture and Environment for International Development* 102 (1/2): 123–39.

Kwengwere, P. 2011. "Inequality in Malawi." In *Tearing us Apart: Inequalities in Southern Africa*, edited by H. Jaunch and D. Muchena. Johannesburg: Open Society Initiative for Southern Africa, South Africa.

Lamm, K. W., F. Masambuka-Kanchewa, A. J. Lamm, K. Davis, S. Nahdy, and M. A. Oyugi. 2021. "A Case Study Analysis of Extension Service Provision in Malawi." *African Journal of Agricultural Research* 17 (11): 1386–92.

Mandala, E. 1982. "Peasant Cotton Agriculture, Gender and Inter-Generational Relationships: The Lower Tchiri (Shire) Valley of Malawi, 1906–1940." *African Studies Review* 25 (2/3): 27–44.

Mbembe, A. (2003). Necropolitics. *Public Culture* 15 (1): 11-–40.

———. 2017. *Critique of Black Reason*. Durham and London: Duke University Press.

Mignolo, Walter D., and Arturo Escobar. 2010. *Globalization and the Decolonial Option*. New York and London: Routledge.

Moyo, B. H. Z., and D. Z. Moyo. 2017. "Indigenous Knowledge Perceptions and Development Practice in Northern Malawi: Lessons from Small-Scale Farmers' Agricultural Practices." In *Handbook of Research on Social, Cultural, and Educational Considerations of Indigenous Knowledge in Developing Countries*, edited by P. Ngulube. Hershey, PA: IGI Global.

Moyo, D., and D. Dixon. 2021. "'Digitising Geographies of Indigenous Folklore in the Global South: Colonial and Decolonial Praxis' Conference Session Abstract, Royal Geographical Society-Institute of British Geographers Annual International Conference 2021, 31 August to 3 September.

Moyo, D., A. K. Edriss, L. Mapemba, and B. Moyo. 2016. "Agricultural Output Aggregation at a Crossroads: Insights from the Interface of Quantitative Analysis, Agricultural Modernization and Indigenous Knowledge, 1961–2005." In *Improving Rural Livelihoods: Case Studies from Malawi*. Norway: CCAB-MAC, LUANAR and Norwegian University of Life Sciences.

Moyo, D. Z. 2012. "Agricultural Resilience According to Indigenous Knowledge-Based Case Studies and Economic Quantitative International Production Studies: Divergent Realities or Divergent Representation?" (MSc thesis).

Ng'ong'ola, C. 1986. "Malawi's Agricultural Economy and the Evolution of Legislation on the Production and Marketing of Peasant Economic Crops." *Journal of Southern African Studies* 12 (2): 240–62.

Nyasa Times, Malawi Government to Employ 400 Workers this Year, October 8 2019. Accessed at Malawi government to employ 400 extension workers this year | Malawi Nyasa Times – News from Malawi about Malawi.

Peters, Pauline E. 1997. "Against the Odds: Matriliny, Land and Gender in the Shire Highlands of Malawi." *Critique of Anthropology* 17 (2): 189–210.

Prowse, M. 2013. "A History of Tobacco Production and Marketing in Malawi, 1890–2010." *Journal of Eastern African Studies* 7 (4): 691–712.

Quinn, V. J. 1994. "A History of the Politics of Food and Nutrition in Malawi: The Context for Food and Nutritional Surveillance." *Food Policy* 19 (3): 255–71.

Rodney, W. (1972). *How Europe Underdeveloped Africa*. London: Bogle-L'Ouverture Publications.

Sony. 2022. *Malawi Folktale Project*. Tokyo: Sony Group Corporation. https://www.sony.com/en/SonyInfo/csr/ForTheNextGeneration/malawi/.

Stevens, Robert. 2004. *University to Uni: The Politics of Higher Education in England Since 1944*. London: Politico's.

Tembo, F. 2003. "Multiple Identities, Representations and Categorisations: Experiences in the Study of People's Life-Worlds in Rural Malawi." *Singapore Journal of Tropical Geography* 24 (2): 229–41.

Tribe, Keith. 2004. "Educational Economies." *Economy and Society* 33 (4): 605–20. https://doi.org/10.1080/0308514042000285314.

Tuck, E., and K. W. Yang. 2012. "Decolonization Is Not a Metaphor." *Decolonization: Indigeneity, Education & Society* 1 (1).

UNESCO. 1989. "Records of the General Conference, 25th session, Paris, 17 October to 16 November 1989, v. 1: Resolutions." https://unesdoc.unesco.org/ark:/48223/pf0000084696.page=242 (date accessed: 10 May 2022).

———. 2003. "Text of the Convention for the Safeguarding of the Intangible Cultural Heritage." https://ich.unesco.org/en/convention (date accessed: 10 May 2022).

Vaughan, M. 1982. "Food Production and Family Labour in Southern Malawi: The Shire Highlands and Upper Shire Valley in the Early Colonial Period." *Journal of African History* 23 (3): 351–64.

Weidner, C., R. Braidotti, and G. Klumbyte. 2019. "The Emergent Environmental Humanities: Engineering the Social Imaginary." *Connotations: A Journal for Critical Debate* 28: 1–25.

Wynter, S. 1997. "Columbus, the Ocean Blue, and Fables that Stir the Mind: To Reinvent the Study of Letters." In *Poetics of the Americas: Race, Founding, and Textuality*. In *Poetics of the Americas: Race, Founding, Textuality,* edited by B. Cowan and J. Humphries, 141–64. Baton Rouge: LSU Press.

12

SPATIAL VIDEO GEONARRATIVES

Digitising Indigenous Folklores in Urban Flooding Lived Experiences

Josephine Zimba

Introduction

Walking interviews have increasingly been used in geographical research. This type of interview is a form of a mobile, or "on the move," research method, which may be researcher-led or go-along (Kusenbach 2003). In the former, the researcher chooses the routes depending on the research objectives, while in the latter, the researcher follows the participants in their day-to-day activities. The latter approach, also known as the hands-off approach (Evans and Jones 2011, 851), is often preferred for its ability to empower the participants and modify the power relations between the researcher and participant. Scholars who prefer walking interviews over sedentary interviews often view discussion as easier to generate when walking than in a sedentary situation (Kinney 2019, 175), with the natural pauses due to walking less awkward than silence in an interview room. In addition, such interviews give the researcher the opportunity to walk in the interviewee's shoes and share thoughts and emotions in relation to the sites visited (D'Errico and Hunt 2019).

The relevance of environmental features in informing discussions cannot be overemphasised. As Hitchings and Jones noted in their work on people-plant encounter, "walking in place triggered conversations" (2004, 9), and participants easily expressed both present and past attitudes and feelings towards the environment as they moved around in the botanical gardens, the environment of reference. Hence, the major strength of mobile interviews lies in their ability to generate more contextualised and deeply insightful interviews (Evans and Jones 2011). However, this data collection technique has been faulted for several reasons. To start with, not everyone is comfortable being seen giving interviews. A case in point is Muslim women for whom their cultural and faith-based concerns, at times, limit their participation in mobile interviews (Warren 2017).

Nevertheless, regarding enriched analysis of walking interviews, spatial transcripts (Jones and Evans 2012) are a valuable technique. The technique involves geo-referenced transcripts of interviews generated by linking GPS coordinates of the route taken with the transcripts of the recorded interview. This integration of transcripts and geographical data "provides a geographic context that facilitates interpretation and understanding of the lived experiences of the research participants" (Kwan and Ding 2008, 458). Hence, the approach essentially ensures that narratives are spatially located for better data visualisation and interpretation.

DOI: 10.4324/9781003082798-15

Malawi, a developing country in Southern Africa, has, of late, experienced an increase in the number and intensity of extreme weather events associated with a changing climate. While studies and discourses around the impacts of climate change, particularly in regions/countries whose economies are predominantly driven by the agricultural sector, have hitherto focused on rural areas, urban areas have also experienced an increase in extreme weather events. Similarly, studies to understand the role of Indigenous knowledge systems in responding to climate change are predominantly rural-focused. This trend, however, is not of Malawi alone. Researchers in different geographical contexts have investigated how communities respond to climate change impacts. In such endeavours, the importance of local or Indigenous knowledge in the management of environmental hazards and disasters has been extensively foregrounded (Lin and Chang 2020; Setten and Lein 2019).

Indigenous knowledge systems are "distinctive understandings, rooted in cultural experience, that guide relations among human, non-human, and other-than-human beings in specific ecosystems" (Bruchac 2014, 3815), often shared and preserved among generations through folklores and cultural practices. Rather than viewing it as an even unified knowledge system, Indigenous knowledge is often uneven and fragmented within communities, with differences based on various socio-demographic factors such as gender, age, employment status, and religious beliefs (Ndlela, Mkwanazi, and Chimonyo 2021). There is a general concentration of Indigenous knowledge studies in low- and middle-income countries, a situation that reinforces the Western science–Indigenous knowledge divide among scholarship (Briggs 2005, 102). This apparent concentration of studies in the Global South may be due to the historical association of Indigenous knowledge systems with "primitive societies," "the poor," or "underdevelopment" unlike scientific knowledge systems associated with modernity and developed societies (Nakata 2002, 282; Tsuji and Ho 2002, 333–34).

A recent study in Malawi found evidence of a strong divide between Western and local knowledge, which culminates in the marginalisation of local knowledge in disaster risk management practice (Šakić Trogrlić et al. 2021). Although studies have been undertaken in different geographical contexts, there is a clear emphasis on the use of Indigenous knowledge systems for agricultural productivity and biodiversity conservation in rural settings (Kosoe, Adjei, and Diawuo 2020; Mamun and Pavel 2014; Pareek and Trivedi 2011). Further, such research has often used surveys (largely quantitative), sedentary interviews and focus group discussions as the main data collection methods. While these suffice for the identification and documentation of Indigenous knowledge systems, collecting such information on the move in the study site could provide an opportunity to enrich the visualisation and interpretation of Indigenous knowledge systems.

The literature abounds with research on Indigenous knowledge and climate change adaptation in Africa. In Kenya, for instance, agropastoralists, albeit in minority, adopt the planting of drought-resistant crops and early maturing varieties when their Indigenous-based indicators forecast the occurrence of drought in the coming season (Speranza et al. 2010). In Zimbabwe, the adaptation involves the shift from planting maize to millet and wheat, in addition to the adoption of *mujogo*, a practice akin to mulching (Mugambiwa 2018), and the use of post-disaster Indigenous-knowledge-based measures, such as the construction of *amazibuko* (temporary footbridges) using local materials and traditional skills (Dube and Munsaka 2018). Despite this extensive research, there is a dearth in the literature on how Indigenous knowledge and practices are used in responding to climate change in urban areas (Petzold et al. 2020). This research, therefore, focuses on understanding how Indigenous knowledge can be used in responding to climate change and its effects in urban areas in Malawi, a country in Southern Africa. The current chapter, therefore, proceeds by introducing spatial video geonarrative (hereafter SVG) as a method detailing how it has been used in this and previous studies before detailing the processes followed in employing SVG to digitise Indigenous knowledge and disucssing the ethical and practical challenges associated with this methodology.

The Spatial Video Geonarrative: A Brief Introduction to the Method

The spatial video geonarrative (SVG) is a semi-structured mobile interview which comprises the collection of GIS coordinates of the interview route, the interview audio recording and a video of the route and its surroundings. The video is important as a data source itself which may be used by researchers absent during the actual interview to experience the environment in which the interview was conducted (Curtis et al. 2019, 389). It may be archived or indeed split into still images for further analysis. The video, which is the visual component, is, therefore, the main component differentiating this technique from traditional geonarratives, spatial transcripts, or mobile audio interviews. Insights from this method are either spatially specific, spatially fuzzy or spatially inspired comments (Curtis et al. 2019, 389–90). While spatially specific insights concern a specific location within the study area, spatially fuzzy comments are about the whole area in general, and spatially inspired comments arise through memories triggered by the sight, smell, or sound of something bringing forth information not specific to any location.

SVG has previously been used to geographically contextualise forced evictions during the Cambodia Genocide of the 1970s (Curtis et al. 2019); map out micro spaces of drug activity in Los Angeles Skid Row (Curtis et al. 2018); enrich explanations of outbreaks of diseases such as dengue, chikungunya, and Zika in Cambodia (Krystosik et al. 2017); enrich police service data with community understandings of crime hotspots in Ohio (Curtis et al. 2016); and understand microscale spatial patterns of post-disaster recovery in New Orleans (Curtis, Duval-Diop, and Novak 2010). Recently, scholars have been developing Wordmapper (Ajayakumar et al. 2019; Ajayakumar 2019), a software that would be used to handle all three forms of data used in SVG to ease the data management load associated with SVG. Save for a few exceptions from Cambodia and Tanzania, most of the studies employing this approach have hitherto been conducted in high-income countries. Being a relatively technology-demanding approach compared to traditional sedentary interviews, there is, therefore, a need to employ an adjusted/adapted SVG and elucidate the practical implications shaped by sociocultural contexts in low-income countries like Malawi.

DEH literature has often interrogated how digital tools and techniques are developed and applied to understand human-environment relations (Sinclair and Posthumus 2017). There have been calls to include local knowledge in environmental management practices, including climate adaptation interventions (Green and Raygorodetsky 2010). However, there have also been concerns of a threat to Indigenous knowledge practices due to "cultural erosion" driven by social, political, economic, and ecological forces. To address this challenge, Flor highlights the import of digital tools:

> It has been an established fact that indigenous peoples have a wealth of knowledge on biodiversity. However, these may be characterized as tacit rather than explicit. This knowledge should be made available to others through a system powered by information and communication technology.
>
> *(2002 n.p.)*

In this sense, the use of digital tools to curate heritage is instrumental to "revitalise endangered cultures, improve the economic independence and sustainability of Indigenous communities and to increase community-based involvement in planning and development" (Hunter 2005, 109). Additionally, there have been calls within the digital humanities scholarship to experiment and interrogate the compatibility of digital tools such as GIS with Indigenous knowledge systems (Palmer 2012; Robbins 2003). It is in line with these concerns that I embarked on the project to digitise Indigenous knowledge used in responding to urban floods. This chapter shares a methodology I used to digitally capture and systematically analyse the Indigenous knowledge systems in Malawi, as part of a broader PhD research. I intended to use SVG as a methodology to capture Indigenous knowledge systems and practices used in responding to urban flood risks, a methodology that has not been used within the DEH scholarship. Since SVGs can be used to map the institutional knowledge of public health experts or professionals mostly for the purposes of archiving (Curtis et al. 2015, 7–8), the current study contributes to the DEH scholarship by leveraging this capability to spatially capture and map the Indigenous knowledge practices and experiences of residents of informal settlements responding to climate change. This chapter particularly highlights the benefits and challenges of the method to digitise Indigenous knowledge systems foregrounding ways in which these systems simultaneously lend themselves to and escape digitisation. I believe that this methodology brings to the fore multiple nuances relevant to understanding the humanistic perspective in human-environment interactions.

The SVG methodology employed in this project, a participant-led walking interview, was largely based on that by Curtis, Duval-Diop, and Novak (2010), with minor modifications due to equipment availability and the terrain of the study area. In previous projects, researchers have used GPS-enabled video cameras (Ajayakumar et al. 2019; Curtis et al. 2015), which were unavailable for this study; instead, the researcher used a GPS recorder to collect GIS coordinates of the interview route. While some projects (Curtis et al. 2015; Ajayakumar et al. 2019) use driving as a form of mobility, in this study, the researcher walked with the participant as the terrain of the study area did not allow for driving. Being an informal settlement, the road network is mainly of footpaths with narrow roads. Nevertheless, walking allowed for the interviews to be fully mobile, which allowed access to micro spaces which would otherwise be inaccessible. Cognisant that traditional custodians of Indigenous knowledge institutions such as Chiefs and elders (Kosoe, Adjei, and Diawuo 2020) were often rural based and either absent or with minimal influence in upholding and preserving Indigenous knowledge and practices in Malawi's urban areas, I, therefore, leveraged the presence and proximity of features to the interviewees to prompt discussions on the Indigenous knowledge practices used in adapting to climate change in urban areas. In the process, I highlight how features in the environment prompted the discussions and influenced the responses.

This study was conducted in Salisbury Lines, an informal settlement in Mzuzu City, Malawi. The unique socio-economic and disaster profile of Mzuzu made it an ideal case study area. Mzuzu is the third-largest city with a population of 221,272 and has a surface area covering 146 square kilometres (National Statistical Office 2019). The city is the fastest growing city in Malawi, with an intercensal annual growth rate of 5.4%, almost double the national intercensal annual growth rate. By 2030, Mzuzu City is projected to have a population of about 365,638. One of the drivers of such a population growth is migration. Among all local government areas, Mzuzu City has the highest proportion of migrants and the second-highest proportion of in-migrants from outside Malawi at about 1.7%. Further, Mzuzu City has experienced an increase in the frequency and intensity of floods since 2002. The worst flood event occurred in 2016, affecting 19,000 people in 15 settlements (Kita 2017b), including Salisbury Lines.

Salisbury Lines, one of the largest informal settlements in Mzuzu, was particularly chosen for this study due to its high vulnerability to annual floods as it is situated on a low-lying wetland. This is compounded by a lack of access to municipal services as informal settlements are considered illegal and therefore not officially recognised. This "illegal" status leaves residents of Salisbury Lines least prioritised in various government projects, including those aimed at managing urban floods. With limited support from the local authority, residents often depend on endogenous intangible resources "influenced by previous generations' observations and experiment" (Nyong, Adesina, and Osman Elasha 2007, 792) to negotiate such environmental hazards. As such, the high immigration levels from both within and outside Malawi into Mzuzu present a unique scenario where cultural contacts and engagements among people from different ethnic groups could facilitate the exchange of experiences and information regarding Indigenous practices relevant to their livelihoods including flood management.

Digitising Indigenous Knowledge: The Process

Like all research involving human subjects, this study required and was granted ethical approval from my institution, the University of Glasgow. Key ethical issues specifically related to this project concerned the need for valid written and informed consent, data protection, and arrangements for the offering of anonymity and confidentiality. Considering that the study was conducted during a period of political tension, guaranteeing confidentiality to research participants was fundamental not only to support participant recruitment but to also protect the research participants from potential repercussions such as being excluded from participating in or benefitting from development-related programmes, and even more so as the influence of partisan politics in disaster risk management activities in Malawi is well-known (Kita 2017a). Ensuring confidentiality, particularly with audio and video being captured, was the biggest challenge. While the approach does not involve filming the participant as the camera faces away from the participant capturing their view of the surroundings, the issue was more the possibility of capturing other people's faces during the process. This was addressed by setting the camera at a low angle to capture the landscape and then blurring the faces of people that were unintentionally captured to prevent identification. However, just like in traditional walking interviews, it was difficult to fully maintain anonymity/confidentiality as participants are seen with the researcher during the interview. Although draft interview protocols/guides were submitted during the ethical application process, finalisation of the same was made later following the testing of the tool in the field. This guide laid out the broad questions that would steer the interview. Since this was part of a broader PhD research work, I present here, only the question related to Indigenous knowledge systems including Indigenous knowledge-based interventions, relevant for the current chapter:

1 How are you affected by climate change? Take me to the places in the area where the effects are mostly felt (the hotspots). (Who is most affected? Have the effects changed over time? If yes, what changes are there in terms of intensity or frequency?)
2 Are there any Indigenous-knowledge-based signs they look out for to know when the rains will start or whether they will experience floods that year? What are these signs?
3 What are the interventions taken to address the impacts of climate change? Would you share any Indigenous-knowledge-based interventions implemented in the community to address the impacts? Take me to the places where the interventions are. Are these the interventions you need? Are they working?

Before the actual data collection, a trial of the tools and how they worked was conducted, including noting the power lifespan of the camera. This helped in scheduling the interviews and avoided running out of power during the interview process, as did trialing the positioning of the voice recorder with a wind guard to allow for easy recording even in noisy and windy environments.

Ten interviews were conducted in this study in the period between November 2019 and April 2021. The participants included four members of the Ward Civil Protection Committee (WCPC), a committee responsible for disaster risk management at the ward level. Other participants included community leaders and community members. Due to the need for knowledge about the study area and Indigenous knowledge systems in relation to responding to floods, the purposive sampling technique was used to select and recruit participants. For the purposes of this study, participants needed to have lived in the area for a period of not less than five years to ensure participants had experienced the annual floods, including those of 2016, the worst to hit Mzuzu City since 1991 (Kita 2017b). Being fluent in all three languages used in this study (i.e. English, Chichewa, and Chitumbuka), I did all the translations of information sheets, consent forms, interview guide and transcripts. This minimised the risk of information distortion or misunderstanding, which comes when there is a language barrier or an external translator. At least three days before the scheduled interview, participants were informed what the research was about, why it was being conducted, what their participation would involve, and how the data would be used. This was also detailed to all participants in an information sheet in either Chichewa or Chitumbuka language to facilitate informed decision-making regarding their participation. A list of the main questions for the interview was also provided. On the day, participants were asked to select a route that they felt was most appropriate to respond to the questions, and they were encouraged to take as much time as they wanted while on the route and pause the interview if they wished.

The average length of the time taken per route was 36 minutes. The shortest track took 22 minutes, while the longest interview and track took 46 minutes to complete. The relatively short interviews could be attributed to the political atmosphere at that time; most (eight) of the interviews were conducted following the heavily contested elections of May 2019. Participants were uneasy about being seen moving around the communities for fear of being mistaken for campaign teams or rival political groups. However, the length of a track has no significant bearing on the depth or richness of the discussion (Emmel and Clark 2009). During the interview, the video, the audio, and the GPS recording were done simultaneously. Due care was taken to make sure that the starting point of all three was matched, and the GPS was set to record a position every 30 seconds.

The data collection generated three major sets/types of data. The first one is the audio recording of the interview. This audio recording was translated from Chichewa and Chitumbuka (the key local languages used in the study area) to English, transcribed and coded based on the recurring themes in the discussion. The transcription was done at 30-second intervals and saved as an excel file which had a time column, the transcript itself, and thematic codes. The second set of data is the GPS track. The GPS file, which was originally in a GPS Exchange (.gpx) format, was converted into a comma-separated values (.csv) file using the GPSBabel software. Thereafter, the transcript and the thematic codes were copied and pasted into the .csv file in line with the corresponding times. At this point, the .csv file had information regarding what was said (transcript and the code) and where (GPS coordinates), a spatialised transcript. The final set of data was the video. The video was processed using MPEG Streamclip 1.2 to create still images every 30 seconds of play. The still images were converted to and saved as a .csv file. This list was then copied onto the earlier .csv file containing time-stamped transcripts and GPS coordinates. At this point, a 30-second narrative had a corresponding image and location. In that way, the transcripts and images were ready to be referenced to the route using QGIS 3.16.4.

Locating the Experiences

Based on the transcripts and the dominant themes from the analysis of the transcripts, I identified six codes through which to code the entire dataset: Indigenous knowledge indicators, Indigenous knowledge response, hotspot, intervention, distraction, and walking. "Hotspot" code was assigned to all discussions relating to areas or places most affected by a flooding event, including the extent of damages and losses. "Intervention" covered all discussions relating to general responses to floods in the area, both structural and non-structural measures. As in any mobile interview, the interviews in the study were not uninterrupted. Any discussion outside the interview questions, such as greeting a community leader or a friend, was coded as "distraction." Further, natural pauses from navigating the terrain in during the interview were coded as "walking." While the rest of the codes are more obvious, I further coded and mapped instances of "distraction" and "walking" to foreground the real practicalities of using a hand-held approach as opposed to vehicle-mounted systems used in most similar studies. Table 12.1 shows the frequency count of the codes across all ten participants.

The low frequency of Indigenous-knowledge-related codes suggests few instances where participants discussed Indigenous knowledge issues. In contrast, most participants constantly directed the discussion to areas most impacted by floods and the interventions needed or currently in place. Interventions, in this case, were understood as any activity undertaken to reduce the impacts of floods at the community and household levels. This disparity may suggest the extent to which Indigenous knowledge systems are devalued in urban settings. This could be consistent with Maweu's assertion that Indigenous knowledge is often taken as primitive and subjective and viewed as "a body of relatively old information that has been handed down from generation to generation essentially unchanged, hence dismissed as obsolete" (2011, 37). This view was evident in the responses of some participants in the study, as one participant said,

> You're asking about how we use Indigenous knowledge to predict the weather? No, these days we do not use those ones. We listen to the information from the Department of Climate Change and Meteorological Services. Those ones are for our great-great-grandparents! These days we get weather forecasts from the radio.

Table 12.1 Code Frequency Count.

Participant	*Code frequency count*					
	IK Indicators	*IK Response*	*Hotspot*	*Intervention*	*Distraction*	*Walking*
A	4	2	4	2	4	7
B	1	0	11	3	2	0
C	1	2	7	1	8	10
D	2	0	7	3	2	0
E	1	1	8	6	4	5
F	1	0	5	2	0	3
G	1	0	5	7	1	0
H	1	1	2	4	2	3
I	2	1	5	2	0	4
J	2	2	0	5	1	1
Total	**16**	**9**	**54**	**35**	**24**	**33**

(*Source:* Author)

On the one hand, such a response signifies the potential devaluation of Indigenous knowledge in urban areas. On the other hand, it is not entirely surprising given that mainstream narratives in addressing climate change have often externalised Indigenous knowledge systems. As such, and being a researcher affiliated to a Western institution – a community outsider, in this case – such respondents may have been engendered by a cautious scepticism, which Dutta avers makes Indigenous people "say things just to please or at least not to offend the outsiders" (2019, 5). However, despite some evidence of devaluation among some participants, Indigenous knowledge has not been abandoned by all. On the contrary, other participants in the study acknowledged using Indigenous knowledge most of the times as they neither have access to forecasts by the meteorological department, nor do they trust their reliability. And yet again, others who use both knowledge systems to inform their actions in flood risk management. As one participant who prefers Indigenous knowledge said, "I do not trust forecasts on the radio. They [officials from the meteorological department] are not God!" This is unsurprising as communities are known to rarely depend on one "source" of knowledge or information when responding to environmental changes (Mpandeli et al. 2017; Orlove et al. 2010; Speranza et al. 2010). I mapped the occurrence of the codes with each participant. Figure 12.1 and Figure 12.2 show the incidences of particular codes on the route of each SVG.

Based on the responses of the participants who acknowledged using Indigenous knowledge systems in flood risk management, the Indigenous knowledge systems are mostly used for early warning. Most of the participants reported the use of *kotcha* (temperature) and *mphepo* (wind) as some of the indicators used to predict weather patterns. Much as these may be well-known scientific indicators, communities do not use instruments to ascertain their predictions. Based on personal experiences over time, people are able to predict how much rain they will receive

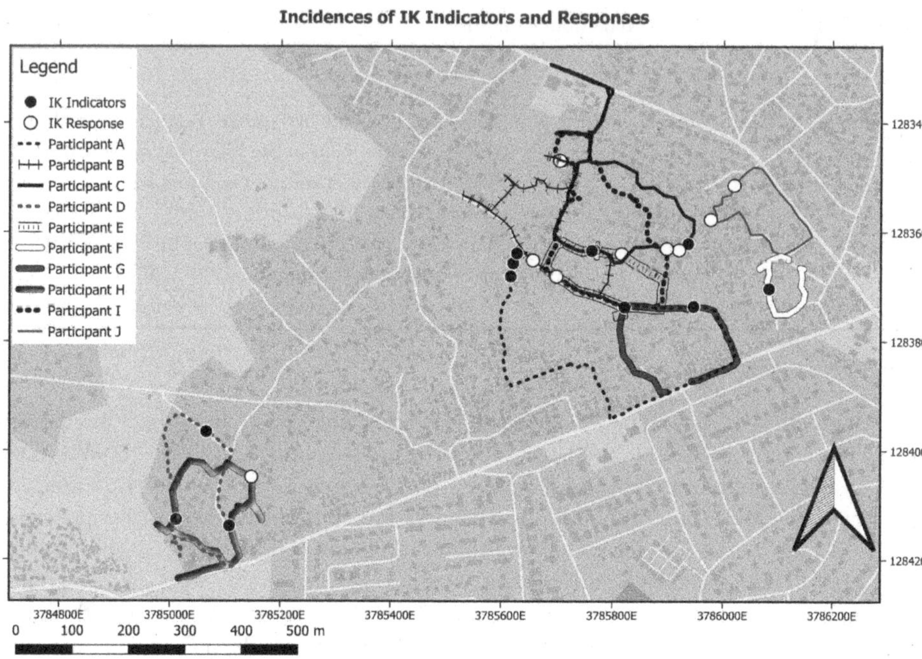

Figure 12.1 Incidences of IK indicators and response.

Source: author (own production)

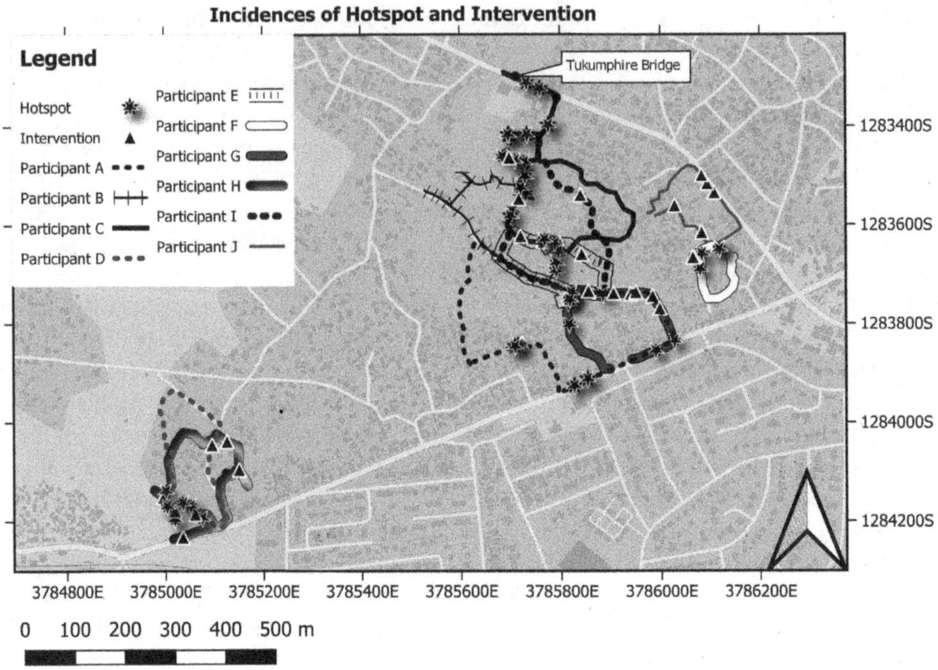

Figure 12.2 Incidences of hotspot and intervention.

Source: author (own production)

Table 12.2 Elements for Weather Predictions Using IK.

Element	*Characteristic*	*Interpretation*
Temperature	Maximum temperatures	The hotter the hot-dry season (August to October), the heavier the rains in the following rainy season.
Wind	Speed	The occurrence of strong winds predicts the occurrence of heavy rains
Birds	Presence and number	The sighting of a large number of birds of a particular species signifies the imminence of rainfall.
Frogs	Croaking	When frogs croak, it signifies the imminence of rainfall.

(*Source:* Author)

based on how hot the hot-dry season was and the occurrence of strong winds. Besides using such meteorological indicators, biological indicators, such as birds and frogs, are also used to forecast weather conditions. Table 12.2 contains the Indigenous-knowledge-based indicators, the characteristics of the indicator, and interpretation as used in predicting weather patterns.

As observed in Table 12.2, the people in Salisbury Lines draw from their Indigenous knowledge to predict not only the occurrence of extreme weather events such as heavy rainfall but also determine the timing of weather events. These findings are consistent with those of Kalanda-Joshua et al. (2011), who found that, in responding to climate change in Malawi, Indigenous knowledge is often used to predict the occurrence of weather events. However, these indicators are often for shorter-term predictions, with some (e.g. birds) used to predict daily weather conditions and others (e.g. temperatures during hot-dry season) used to predict rainfall patterns for the imminent rainfall season. Consistent with experiences from communities in Uganda and Kenya (Okonya, Ajayi, and Mafongoya 2017; Speranza et al. 2010), Indigenous knowledge systems in Mzuzu City are often used for daily and seasonal weather forecasting and never to predict changes in longer time frames, such as decades.

From the interviews, all participants mentioned one main flood risk adaptation strategy used in Salisbury Lines: the use of unlined stormwater drains to manage floodwaters. The preference for such drains by municipal authorities is because of their associated low initial costs since no cement, concrete, or stone is required to have the drains in place. However, their main flaw is the requirement for frequent maintenance or clearing drain growth, which is exacerbated by the fertile soil and high water table in wetland areas like Salisbury Lines. This is the point where Indigenous knowledge plays a role. The prediction of when and how much rainfall to expect using the aforementioned meteorological and biological elements helps people to plan when to start clearing the drains in preparation for the rainy season. When they experience significantly high temperatures during the hot-dry season, community leaders know that they will receive heavy rainfall during the following rainfall season. As such, they plan and engage the municipal authorities through their local councillors for support in drain construction and clearing, mobilise community members to clear existing drainage channels around their compounds, and open new ones where needed. These activities help to lessen the impact of floods which occur as a result of heavy rainfall as the drainage system is better able to manage the stormwater during the rainfall event.

Geolocating the participant's experiences, however, it was noted that the responses were either spatially inspired or spatially fuzzy. As can be seen from Figure 12.1, most of the discussion on Indigenous knowledge indicators occurred in more watery places. One such response from participant C and a visual of their surroundings is shown in Figure 12.3 and is illustrative of spatially inspired responses made as it was as we passed through a watery place:

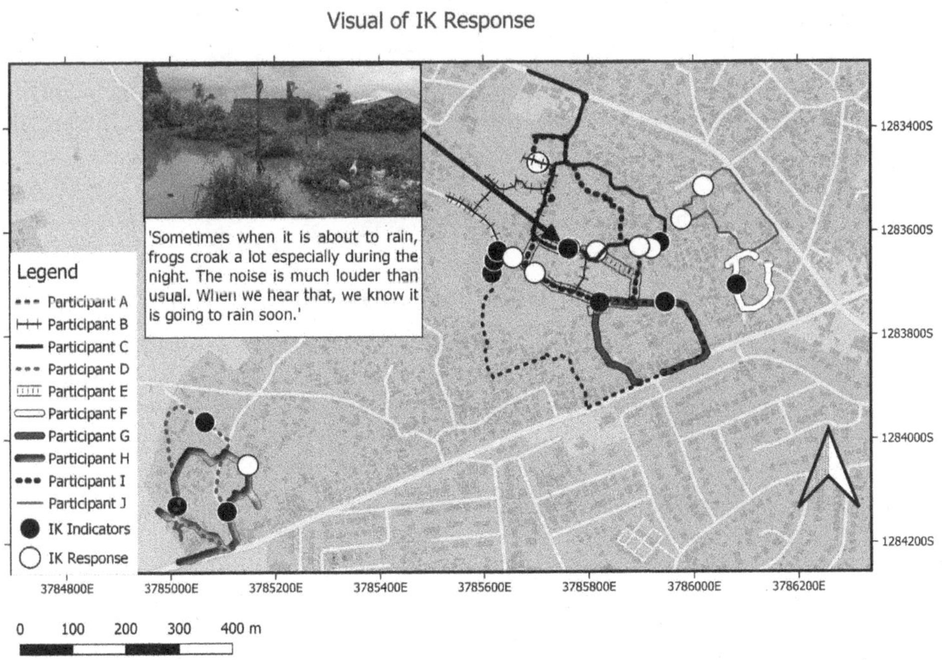

Figure 12.3 A spatially inspired response.

Source: author (own production)

Such a watery place resembles *dambos*, shallow wetlands suitable habitats for anurans (Bittencourt-Silva 2019). Hence, much as the description of indicators was not spatially specific, it may be argued that it was cued by the environment where the narration was given in. Additionally, participant D's response illustrates a spatially fuzzy discussion on Indigenous knowledge indicators:

> The way it was hot the past few weeks, we knew that is just a sign that this month it's going to rain heavily. We knew that even if it rained for just three days, we were going to feel it!

Although data from such a discussion can be located on the map, it does not make reference to a specific location within the area. Nevertheless, such insights are still pertinent as they espouse the complexity in the mapping of such multifactorial knowledge systems. Further, they enrich our understanding of the extent and breadth of Indigenous knowledge systems in urban environments. In this case, though the place is used to stimulate discussion, the narrative cannot be precisely tied to a specific location. This is mainly because most of the elements/indicators are in motion and, at times, intangible (such as wind and heat). These observations are substantiated by more spatially specific comments by the same participants when discussing flood hotspots and interventions. Participant D's following comment illustrates this point:

> In the past, water used to pass this way. Now they put bags of sand and cement. And another place which is problematic is over there! . . . So, from the upper part, all drains from the hotel and the rest of that area direct the water here. So when this place is full of water, depending on the amount it receives, it bursts. The water reaches that level, even brings this down. . . . Now you see this stream is calm, but it gets angry! This same stream roars when it rains!

Therefore, in employing SVG to digitise such knowledge systems, the investigation ought to go beyond mapping. Regarding Indigenous knowledge and practices used in responding to urban flooding in one of the increasingly flooded informal settlements in Mzuzu required that the investigation include interweaving various insights and the visuals collected from the video data to comprehend the experiences of the communities.

Beyond Locating Experiences: Insights from Geonarratives

Using SVG to understand the experiences of floods in this study also brought to the fore other aspects of the experiences. One critical aspect is the psychological distress associated with the flood events. Participant E said while pointing at a flooded compound in a hotspot area within the settlement,

> The impacts [of floods] are now greater than in the past. See that compound, looking like a pig's kraal, is that peace? You'll see that the whole neighbourhood is like that, is that peace? . . . As it is, it seems it's going to rain again this evening. We look happy during the day but seeing a possibility of rains in the evening makes us fearful and not have peace.

The walking interview and analysis of the geonarratives, therefore, accentuate our understanding of how deep the experiences of flood events are. Drawing from the walking interview method as one "that allows *explicit connection* between an interviewee's narrative and the places" (Harris et al. 2013, 350, emphasis added), the addition of the visual element helps understand the depth of the experience for the participants, "being in a place is likely to evoke a richer array of emotions than non-situated approaches" (Stals, Smyth, and IJsselsteijn 2014, 742). Much as I would not claim that I fully shared the emotions of participants as in "temporarily 'live' participants' lives or even inhabit their bodies" (King and Woodroffe 2017, 13), the walking interview, however, led to an empathic understanding. I discerned that their experiences of floods are beyond material losses, experiences that can neither be eyed nor physically located.

The process further revealed how some members of the communities attribute their experiences to the shunning of Indigenous knowledge practices in preference to modern practices. One participant who has lived in the area for over five decades narrated how floods in the 1970s and 1980s did not lead to collapsing of housing units. According to the participant, this was because the houses were built using the traditional *yomata* (wattle and daub) building technique. These are often round-shaped houses with mud and bamboo walls, common in sub-Saharan Africa. Such houses had a stronger structural form than their contemporary rectangle-shaped counterparts (Ngoma and Sassu 2004, 2). Observing the structures that have been rebuilt following their collapse in 2016, most of them are built using unbaked bricks and mud mortar. This partial pursuit of modern and resilient structures (built using baked bricks and cement mortar), therefore, not only reproduces but also worsens the impacts of the floods on the communities.

Insights from the Video

During the walking interview, a common thing among the interviewees regarding responses to floods was the use of drains. Most participants indicated that is the *only* thing they individually or collectively do to manage floods. At this point, the video analysis becomes advantageous in my data analysis. The interweaving process involved in the SVG brings to the fore possible adaptation/adjustment of Indigenous knowledge practices to respond to flood challenges. I use three illustrations to demonstrate how the video was used in the interweaving process regarding how residents in Salisbury Lines use local practices in response to floods. During the interviews, most participants reported challenges with the drainage system and the frequent need for maintenance due to plant overgrowth and waste. However, I observed in the video data the presence of live hedges lining drainage systems, particularly in the hotspot areas. Further probing on this revealed that people have resorted to using live hedges, which were initially used to demarcate compounds and restrict animal movement in traditional compounds as waste management structures. Figure 12.4 shows an example of such hedges. The hedges are planted along the drains to trap wastes from the compound to avoid blockages and reduce the risk of overflooding of drains.

The local communities have also adopted other local ways of living with floods. Residents of Salisbury Lines have not abandoned the traditional agricultural practices common in African homesteads. Regardless of the size of the land, most compounds had a garden with different crops planted in one garden. Common crops planted included maize, beans, sugarcane, sweet potatoes, and tomatoes. Figure 12.5 shows one such garden planted with groundnuts and sweet potatoes. Intercropping is a traditional practice among locals in Northern Malawi, unlike monocropping, which is based on Western knowledge (Moyo and Moyo 2014).

Further, residents in the informal settlement do not "live with floods" by merely having to fight against the negative consequences the floods bring. Residents also take advantage of these opportunities; the most apparent was the use of the drainage channels as a source of irrigation water (Figure 12.6). In the videos, particularly those undertaken during the dry season, I noticed

Figure 12.4 Hedges along the drainage system.

Source: author (own production)

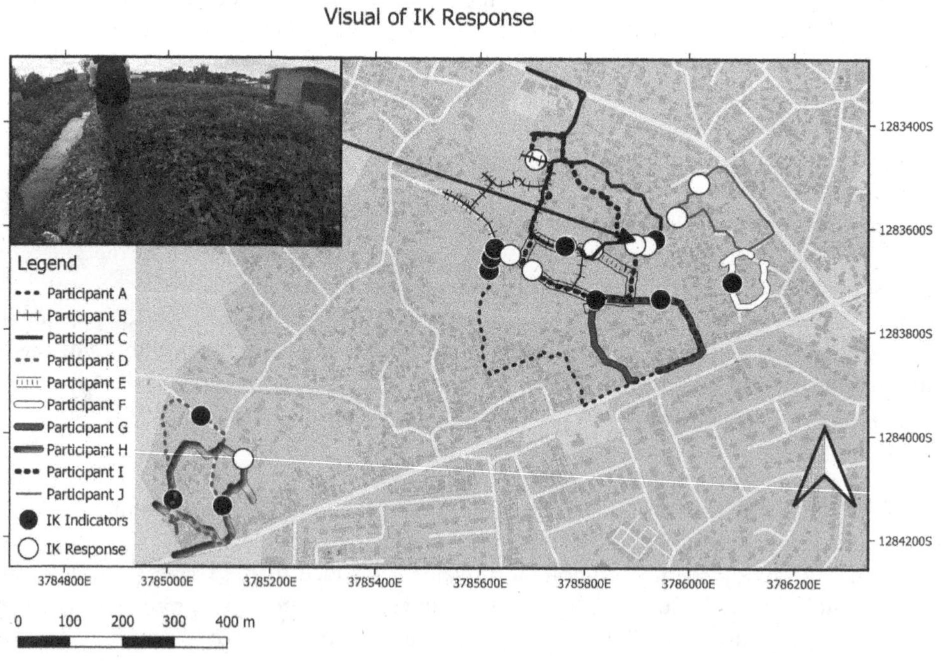

Figure 12.5 Intercropping as an adaptation strategy.

Source: author (own production)

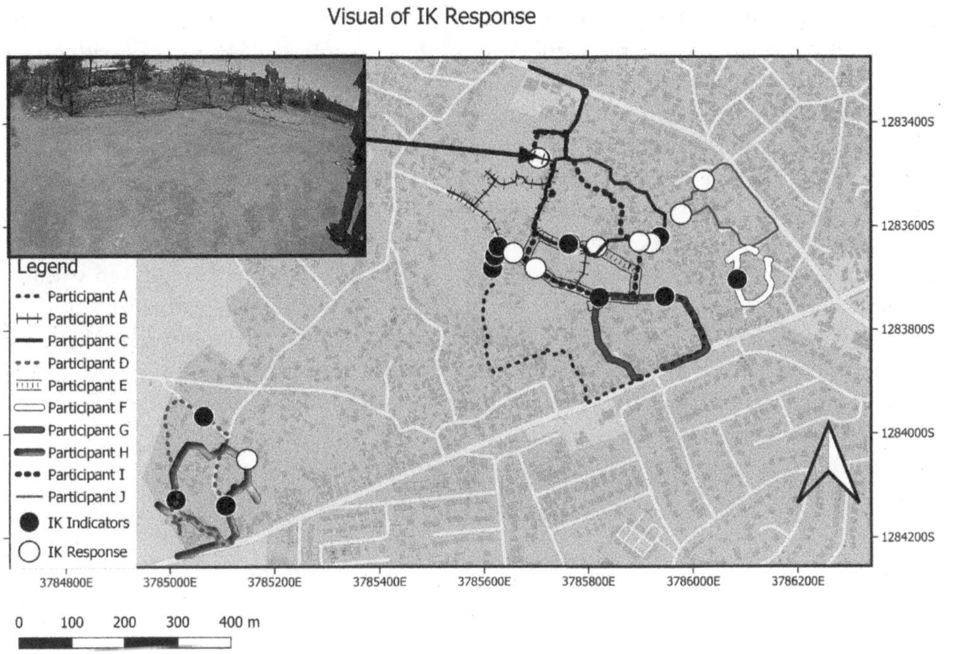

Figure 12.6 Irrigation as an adaptation strategy.

Source: author (own production)

gardens with green maize and beans almost at maturity. This observation from the video clearly helped me understand that though floods would be perceived negatively at a glance and from interview responses, amidst the flood challenge, residents of Salisbury Lines view floods as an opportunity to enhance food production and earn their livelihoods.

A final illustration is of the use of possible Indigenous knowledge–Western science hybrid practices in responding to floods. This is particularly important because Indigenous knowledge is neither pristine nor static (Balay-As, Marlowe, and Gaillard 2018; Hilhorst et al. 2015;), and nor are local practices used in people's interactions with the environment. With this understanding, further such practices were observed in the video. These include local engineering approaches, such as sand filling and the construction of bridges using planks. Such kinds of interventions have also been observed among other Indigenous communities in Zimbabwe and Nigeria (Dube and Munsaka 2018; Fabiyi and Oloukoi 2013).

Ethical and Practical Challenges with the Methodology

Local Politics

A number of modifications were made to address practical challenges in the field. Ideally, the SVG approach often involves mounting the camera on the participant to capture the participant's view of the surroundings during the interview. However, some part of the data collection was undertaken during a time when political tensions were high in Malawi. It was after the highly contested elections of May 2019, which the opposition asked the courts to nullify. Between October and November 2019, the highly publicised court proceedings were underway, and people, particularly from cities, including Mzuzu, were still protesting the results of the elections through street protests. As such, the participants were not comfortable being seen with cameras, which resulted in the camera being mounted on the researcher instead.

The prevailing political context also influenced participant recruitment as community leaders ensured that participants came from different parts/blocks of the informal settlement to allow for geographically diverse insights and representation in the study. While the research treated the settlement as one study area, the community leaders (block leaders) view it as a sum of different blocks (sub-units of the neighbourhood), and so no participant would take me around the whole community unless the block leader allowed. This led to shorter routes being taken within the settlement than anticipated. However, the arrangement empowered the participants, including the community leaders, as partners in the research, thereby moderating power relations between the researcher and participants. Further, the representation from participants from diverse blocks gave the researcher the chance to widen the possible areas of focus by the community to avoid domination from a specific block.

Sociocultural Factors

The challenge of walking may also have contributed to the low responses on Indigenous knowledge related responses during the interviews. Just like in other African societies such as Ghana (Kosoe, Adjei, and Diawuo 2020, 1066), the main custodians of Indigenous knowledge are elders, for whom walking may be a challenge, particularly in the muddy terrain of the informal settlement. The terrain also affected the flow of the interview, as evidenced by Figure 12.7, with several instances of "walking" code.

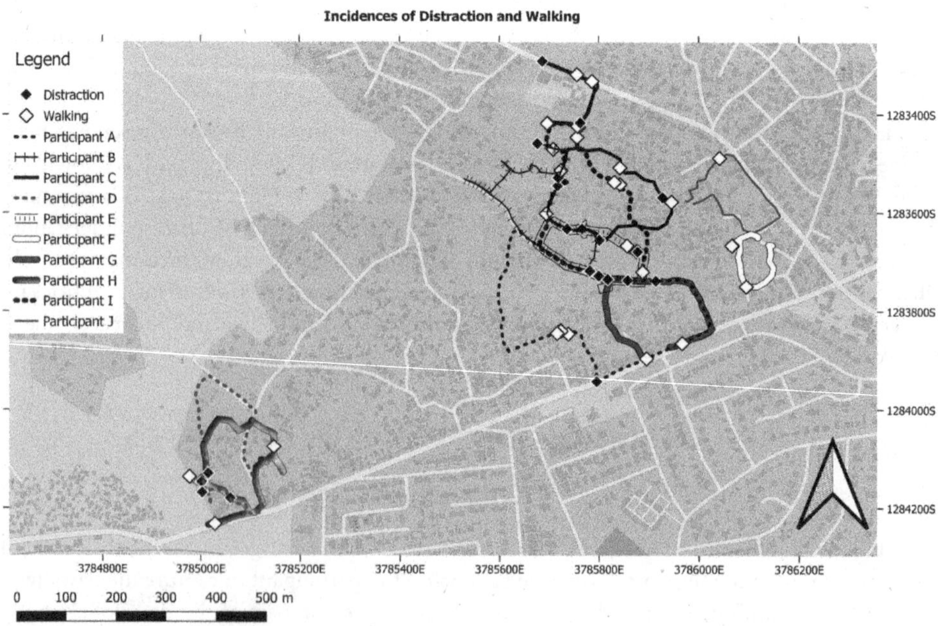

Figure 12.7 Incidences of distraction and walking.

Source: author (own production)

This effect is not entirely detrimental to the research process as it offered the researcher the opportunity to explore some of the community's experiences in place, such as the everyday mobility challenges faced during the wet season and the resultant use of local engineering responses to floods. Besides offering natural breaks during the interview, walking-only bits of the process enriched the engagement with places and participants.

Weather

The other practical concern was weather. To maximise my observation of lived experiences in the likelihood of a flood event, I conducted the data collection during the rainy season. While there is no consensus on the effect of weather on walking interview processes in the literature (Evans and Jones 2011; Clark and Emmel 2008), the weather slightly affected the data collection exercise. Not only did we have to reschedule some walks, which was problematic from a scheduling perspective (D'Errico and Hunt 2019), but sometimes participants had to choose a slightly different route which was passable in muddy conditions. However, out of ten walks, only once did we have to significantly change the route due to the conditions, while in most cases, small alterations were all that was required to access the most critical locations the participant intended to draw our attention to.

Conclusion

Using SVGs to digitise Indigenous knowledge practices used in flood-affected areas enriched the discussions on experiences of urban flooding with an additional visual component for analysis. While most of the Indigenous knowledge practices were in relation to early warning purposes, further analysis of the visuals revealed evidence of adapted Indigenous knowledge practices in responding to floods such as irrigation, intercropping, the presence of hedges close to drains to reduce flooding, and other local engineering interventions. Further, due to the nature of the research and its focus on Indigenous knowledge, most of the insights gained from the SVG processes were to a greater degree spatially inspired or spatially fuzzy than spatially specific. This could be attributed to the mobile or intangible nature of some elements in the Indigenous knowledge systems used by the communities. However, this also evidences the ways in which Indigenous knowledge systems inherently "resist" digitisation. While most resistance to digitisation of Indigenous knowledge often borders ethical issues such as open access and rights to privacy (Manžuch 2017), using SVG to digitise Indigenous knowledge practices used in responding to climatic extremes reveals a mundane form of resistance through inherent spatial fuzziness of the weather monitoring practices. As with other ethnographic research methods, ethical and practical considerations need to be foregrounded when undertaking SVGs. These include critical reflections on how weather and prevailing sociocultural contexts could necessitate marginal adjustments of the method to achieve the research goal.

As a digital capturing method, the SVG is essential in spatially capturing human-environment interactions. Its flexibility (in terms of how one can analyse and visualise the data) and focus on micro spaces give it an edge in capturing nuances in generalised narratives offering a powerful tool to understand how humans interact and negotiate environmental challenges. The current research, therefore, has demonstrated the extent to which Indigenous knowledge practices employed in responding to climate extremes simultaneously render and resist digitisation in mundane ways. Cognisant of the current work to develop an app that combines all forms of data and enhances analysis, it remains highly likely that a video camera, GPS device, and voice recorder for the data collection will remain in use for some time. This is particularly true for areas where access to internet connection is significantly low owing to high data charges coupled with low network coverage. For researchers working in such areas, offline data collection techniques remain fundamental to successful use, particularly regarding the potential use of the methodology to digitise folklore on experiencing climate change in rural settings. Further, while for the purposes of this work, I intend to produce further outputs such as story maps, there is a need to develop offline dynamic story maps which would be widely accessible, most importantly for the researched communities as well. At a time when scholars and some custodians of Indigenous knowledge worry about the erosion of Indigenous knowledge practices (Batibo 2013, 162), the use of offline dynamic story maps will serve as archives for place-specific Indigenous knowledge practices accessible for generations to come.

Sources

Ajayakumar, Jayakrishnan. 2019. "Context in Geographic Data: How to Explore, Extract and Analyze Data from Spatial Video and Spatial Video Geonarratives." Kent State University. https://rave.ohiolink.edu/etdc/view?acc_num=kent1560165020968485.

Ajayakumar, Jayakrishnan, Andrew Curtis, Steve Smith, and Jacqueline Curtis. 2019. "The Use of Geonarratives to Add Context to Fine Scale Geospatial Research." *International Journal of Environmental Research and Public Health* 16 (3). https://doi.org/10.3390/ijerph16030515.

Balay-As, Marjorie, Jay Marlowe, and J. C. Gaillard. 2018. "Deconstructing the Binary between Indigenous and Scientific Knowledge in Disaster Risk Reduction: Approaches to High Impact Weather Hazards." *International Journal of Disaster Risk Reduction* 30: 18–24. https://doi.org/10.1016/j.ijdrr.2018.03.013.

Batibo, H. M. 2013. "Preserving and Transmitting Indigenous Knowledge in Diminishing Bio-Cultural Environment: Case Studies from Botswana and Tanzania. (Special Issue: Vitalizing Indigenous Knowledge in Africa.)." *African Study Monographs* 34 (3): 161–73. http://jambo.africa.kyoto-u.ac.jp/kiroku/asm_normal/abstracts/pdf/34-3/batibo.pdf.

Bittencourt-Silva, Gabriela B. 2019. "A Herpetological Survey of Western Zambia." *Amphibian and Reptile Conservation* 13 (2): 1–28.

Briggs, John. 2005. "The Use of Indigenous Knowledge in Development: Problems and Challenges." *Progress in Development Studies* 5 (2): 99–114. https://doi.org/10.1191/1464993405ps105oa.

Bruchac, Margaret M. 2014. "Indigenous Knowledge and Traditional Knowledge." In *Encyclopedia of Global Archaeology*, edited by C. Smith, 3814–24. New York: Springer. https://doi.org/10.1007/978-3-030-30018-0_10.

Clark, Andrew, and Nick Emmel. 2008. "Walking Interviews: More than Walking and Talking ?" Presented at 'Peripatetic Practices': A Workshop on Walking (London) March.

Curtis, Andrew, Jacqueline W. Curtis, Lauren C. Porter, Eric Jefferis, and Eric Shook. 2016. "Context and Spatial Nuance inside a Neighborhood's Drug Hotspot: Implications for the Crime-Health Nexus." *Annals of the American Association of Geographers* 106 (4): 819–36. https://doi.org/10.1080/24694452.2016.1164582.

Curtis, Andrew, Jacqueline W. Curtis, Eric Shook, Steve Smith, Eric Jefferis, Lauren Porter, Laura Schuch, Chaz Felix, and Peter R. Kerndt. 2015. "Spatial Video Geonarratives and Health: Case Studies in Post-Disaster Recovery, Crime, Mosquito Control and Tuberculosis in the Homeless." *International Journal of Health Geographics* 14 (22): 1–15. https://doi.org/10.1186/s12942-015-0014-8.

Curtis, Andrew, Dominique Duval-Diop, and Jenny Novak. 2010. "Identifying Spatial Patterns of Recovery and Abandonment in the Post-Katrina Holy Cross Neighborhood of New Orleans." *Cartography and Geographic Information Science* 37 (1): 45–56. https://doi.org/10.1559/152304010790588043.

Curtis, Andrew, Chaz Felix, Susanne Mitchell, Jayakrishnan Ajayakumar, and Peter R. Kerndt. 2018. "Contextualizing Overdoses in Los Angeles's Skid Row between 2014 and 2016 by Leveraging the Spatial Knowledge of the Marginalized as a Resource." *Annals of the American Association of Geographers* 108 (6): 1521–36. https://doi.org/10.1080/24694452.2018.1471386.

Curtis, Andrew, James Tyner, Jayakrishnan Ajayakumar, Sokvisal Kimsroy, and Kok-Chhay Ly. 2019. "Adding Spatial Context to the 17 April 1975 Evacuation of Phnom Penh: How Spatial Video Geonarratives Can Geographically Enrich Genocide Testimony." *GeoHumanities* 5 (2): 386–404. https://doi.org/10.1080/2373566x.2019.1624186.

D'Errico, Danila, and Nigel Hunt. 2019. "Place Responsiveness: IPA Walking Interviews to Explore Participants' Responses to Natural Disasters." *Qualitative Research in Psychology*. https://doi.org/10.1080/14780887.2019.1604929.

Dube, Ernest, and Edson Munsaka. 2018. "The Contribution of Indigenous Knowledge of Indigenous Knowledge to Disaster Risk Reduction Activities in Zimbabwe: A Big Call to Practioners." *Journal of Disaster Risk Studies* 10 (1): 1–8. https://doi.org/10.4102/jamba. v10i1.493.

Dutta, Uttaran. 2019. "Digital Preservation of Indigenous Culture and Narratives from the Global South: In Search of an Approach." *Humanities* 8 (2): 68. https://doi.org/10.3390/h8020068.

Emmel, Nick, and Andrew Clark. 2009. "The Methods Used in Connected Lives : Investigating Networks, Neighbourhoods and Communities." NCRM Working Paper Series 06/09. www.ncrm.ac.uk.

Evans, James, and Phil Jones. 2011. "The Walking Interview: Methodology, Mobility and Place." *Applied Geography* 31 (2): 849–58. https://doi.org/10.1016/j.apgeog.2010.09.005.

Fabiyi, O., and J. Oloukoi. 2013. "Indigenous Knowledge System and Local Adaptation Strategies to Flooding in Coastal Rural Communities of Nigeria." *Journal of Indigenous Social Development* 2 (1): 1–19.

Flor, Alexander G. 2002. *Ethnovideography: Digital Video-Based Indigenous Knowledge System*. Los Baños: SEAMEO SEARCA.

Green, D., and G. Raygorodetsky. 2010. "Indigenous Knowledge of a Changing Climate." *Climatic Change* 100 (2): 239–42. https://doi.org/10.1007/s10584-010-9804-y.

Harris, Edmund M., Deborah G. Martin, Colin Polsky, Lillian Denhardt, and Abigail Nehring. 2013. "Beyond 'Lawn People': The Role of Emotions in Suburban Yard Management Practices." *Professional Geographer* 65 (2): 345–61. https://doi.org/10.1080/00330124.2012.681586.

Hilhorst, Dorothea, Judith Baart, Gemma van der Haar, and Floor Maria Leeftink. 2015. "Is Disaster 'Normal' for Indigenous People? Indigenous Knowledge and Coping Practices." *Disaster Prevention and Management* 24 (4): 506–22. https://doi.org/10.1108/DPM-02-2015-0027.

Hitchings, Russell, and Verity Jones. 2004. "Living with Plants and the Exploration of Botanical Encounter within Human Geographic Research Practice." *Ethics, Place and Environment* 7 (1–2): 3–18. https://doi.org/10.1080/1366879042000264741.

Hunter, Jane. 2005. "The Role of Information Technologies in Indigenous Knowledge Management." *Australian Academic and Research Libraries* 36 (2): 109–24. https://doi.org/10.1080/00048623.2005.10721252.

Jones, Phil, and James Evans. 2012. "The Spatial Transcript: Analysing Mobilities through Qualitative GIS." *Area* 44 (1): 92–99. https://doi.org/10.1111/j.1475-4762.2011.01058.x.

Kalanda-Joshua, Miriam, Cosmo Ngongondo, Lucy Chipeta, and F. Mpembeka. 2011. "Integrating Indigenous Knowledge with Conventional Science: Enhancing Localised Climate and Weather Forecasts in Nessa, Mulanje, Malawi." *Physics and Chemistry of the Earth* 36 (14–15): 996–1003. https://doi.org/10.1016/j.pce.2011.08.001.

King, Alexandra C, and Jessica Woodroffe. 2017. "Walking Interviews." In *Handbook of Research Methods in Health Social Sciences*, edited by P. Liamputtong, 1–22. https://doi.org/10.1007/978-981-10-2779-6_28-1.

Kinney, Penelope. 2019. "Walking Interview Ethics." In *The SAGE Handbook of Qualitative Research Ethics*, edited by Ron Iphofen and Martin Tolich, 174–87. SAGE Publications Ltd. https://doi.org/10.4135/9781526435446.n12.

Kita, Stern Mwakalimi. 2017a. "'Government Doesn't Have the Muscle': State, NGOs, Local Politics, and Disaster Risk Governance in Malawi." *Risk, Hazards and Crisis in Public Policy* 8 (3): 244–67. https://doi.org/10.1002/rhc3.12118.

———. 2017b. "Urban Vulnerability, Disaster Risk Reduction and Resettlement in Mzuzu City, Malawi." *International Journal of Disaster Risk Reduction* 22 (March): 158–66. https://doi.org/10.1016/j.ijdrr.2017.03.010.

Kosoe, Enoch Akwasi, Prince Osei Wusu Adjei, and Francis Diawuo. 2020. "From Sacrilege to Sustainability: The Role of Indigenous Knowledge Systems in Biodiversity Conservation in the Upper West Region of Ghana." *GeoJournal* 85 (4): 1057–74. https://doi.org/10.1007/s10708-019-10010-8.

Krystosik, Amy R., Andrew Curtis, Paola Buritica, Jayakrishnan Ajayakumar, Robert Squires, Diana Dávalos, Robinson Pacheco, Madhav P. Bhatta, and Mark A. James. 2017. "Community Context and Sub-Neighborhood Scale Detail to Explain Dengue, Chikungunya and Zika Patterns in Cali, Colombia." *PLoS One* 12 (8): 1–25. https://doi.org/10.1371/journal.pone.0181208.

Kusenbach, Margarethe. 2003. "Street Phenomenology: The Go-along as Ethnographic Research Tool." *Ethnography* 4 (3): 455–85. https://doi.org/10.1177/146613810343007.

Kwan, Mei Po, and Guoxiang Ding. 2008. "Geo-Narrative: Extending Geographic Information Systems for Narrative Analysis in Qualitative and Mixed-Method Research." *The Professional Geographer* 60 (4): 443–65. https://doi.org/10.1080/00330120802211752.

Lin, Pei Shan Sonia, and Kai Min Chang. 2020. "Metamorphosis from Local Knowledge to Involuted Disaster Knowledge for Disaster Governance in a Landslide-Prone Tribal Community in Taiwan." *International Journal of Disaster Risk Reduction* 42 (July 2019): 101339. https://doi.org/10.1016/j.ijdrr.2019.101339.

Mamun, Md Abdullah Al, and Muha Abdullah Al Pavel. 2014. "Climate Change Adaptation Strategies through Indigenous Knowledge System: Aspect on Agro-Crop Production in the Flood Prone Areas of Bangladesh." *Asian Journal of Agriculture and Rural Development Journal* 4 (1): 42–58.

Manžuch, Zinaida. 2017. "Ethical Issues in Digitization of Cultural Heritage." *Journal of Contemporary Archival Studies* 4 (4): 1–17.

Maweu, Jacinta Mwende. 2011. "Indigenous Ecological Knowledge and Modern Western Ecological Knowledge: Complementary, Not Contradictory." *Thought and Practice* 3 (2): 35–47. https://doi.org/10.4314/tp.v3i2.

Moyo, Boyson Henry Zondiwe, and Dumisani Zondiwe Moyo. 2014. "Indigenous Knowledge Perceptions and Development Practice in Northern Malawi." *Geographical Journal* 180 (4): 392–401. https://doi.org/10.1111/geoj.12056.

Mpandeli, S., P. Maponya, S. Liphadzi, and G. Backeberg. 2017. "Indigenous Knowledge Systems for Manging Climate Change in South Africa." In *Indigenous Knowledge and Climate Change Management in Africa*, edited by P. L. Mafongoya and O. C. Ajayi, 255–76. Wageningen: CTA.

Mugambiwa, Shingirai S. 2018. "Adaptation Measures to Sustain Indigenous Practices and the Use of Indigenous Knowledge Systems to Adapt to Climate Change in Mutoko Rural District of Zimbabwe." *Jamba: Journal of Disaster Risk Studies* 10 (1): 1–9. https://doi.org/10.4102/jamba.v10i1.388.

Nakata, Martin. 2002. "Indigenous Knowledge and the Cultural Interface: Underlying Issues at the Intersection of Knowledge and Information Systems." *IFLA Journal* 28 (5–6): 281–91. https://doi.org/10.1177/034003520202800513.

National Statistical Office. 2019. "2018 Malawi Population and Housing Census Main Report." https://doi.org/10.1097/01.gim.0000223467.60151.02.

Ndlela, Sithembile Z., Mbusiseni V. Mkwanazi, and Michael Chimonyo. 2021. "Factors Affecting Utilisation of Indigenous Knowledge to Control Gastrointestinal Nematodes in Goats." *Agriculture* 11 (2): 160. https://doi.org/10.3390/agriculture11020160.

Ngoma, Ignasio, and Mauro Sassu. 2004. "Sustainable African Housing Through Traditional Techniques and Materials: A Proposal for a Light Seismic Roof." In Proceedings of the 13th World Conference on Earthquake Engineering, August 1–6, Vancouver, Canada, Paper No. 170. www.researchgate.net/publication/258052911%0Ahttp://dx.doi.org/10.1016/j.jascer.2013.01.002%0Ahttp://eprints.uthm.edu.my/351/1/STUDY_ON_THE_DYNAMIC_CHARACTERISTIC_OF_COCONUT_FIBRE_REINFORCED_COMPOSITES.pdf%0Awww.degruyter.com/view/books/97.

Nyong, A., F. Adesina, and B. Osman Elasha. 2007. "The Value of Indigenous Knowledge in Climate Change Mitigation and Adaptation Strategies in the African Sahel." *Mitigation and Adaptation Strategies for Global Change* 12 (5): 787–97. https://doi.org/10.1007/s11027-007-9099-0.

Okonya, J. S., O. C. Ajayi, and P. L. Mafongoya. 2017. "The Role of Indigenous Knowledge in Seasonal Weather Forecasting and Planning of Farm Activities by Rural Crop Farmers in Uganda." In *Indigenous Knowledge Systems and Climate Change Management in Africa*, edited by P. L. Mafongoya and O. C. Ajayi, 239–54. Wageningen: CTA.

Orlove, Ben, Carla Roncoli, Merit Kabugo, and Abushen Majugu. 2010. "Indigenous Climate Knowledge in Southern Uganda: The Multiple Components of a Dynamic Regional System." *Climatic Change* 100 (2): 243–65. https://doi.org/10.1007/s10584-009-9586-2.

Palmer, Mark. 2012. "Theorizing Indigital Geographic Information Networks." *Cartographica* 47 (2): 80–91. https://doi.org/10.3138/carto.47.2.80.

Pareek, Aparna, and P. C. Trivedi. 2011. "Cultural Values and Indigenous Knowledge of Climate Change and Disaster Prediction in Rajasthan, India." *Indian Journal of Traditional Knowledge* 10 (1): 183–89.

Petzold, Jan, Nadine Andrews, James D. Ford, Christopher Hedemann, and Julio C. Postigo. 2020. "Indigenous Knowledge on Climate Change Adaptation: A Global Evidence Map of Academic Literature." *Environmental Research Letters* 15 (11). https://doi.org/10.1088/1748-9326/abb330.

Robbins, Paul. 2003. "Beyond Ground Truth: GIS and the Environmental Knowledge of Herders, Professional Foresters, and Other Traditional Communities." *Human Ecology* 31 (2): 233–53. https://doi.org/10.1023/A:1023932829887.

Šakić Trogrlić, Robert, Melanie Duncan, Grant Wright, Marc van den Homberg, Adebayo Adeloye, Faidess Mwale, and Colin McQuistan. 2021. "External Stakeholders' Attitudes towards and Engagement with Local Knowledge in Disaster Risk Reduction: Are We Only Paying Lip Service?" *International Journal of Disaster Risk Reduction* 58 (February): 102196. https://doi.org/10.1016/j.ijdrr.2021.102196.

Setten, Gunhild, and Haakon Lein. 2019. "'We Draw on What We Know Anyway': The Meaning and Role of Local Knowledge in Natural Hazard Management." *International Journal of Disaster Risk Reduction* 38 (May): 101184. https://doi.org/10.1016/j.ijdrr.2019.101184.

Sinclair, Stefan, and Stephanie Posthumus. 2017. "Digital? Environmental: Humanities." In *The Routledge Companion to the Environmental Humanities*, edited by Ursula K. Heise, Jon Christensen, and Michelle Niemann, 369–77. Oxfordshire and New York: Routledge.

Speranza, Chinwe Ifejika, Boniface Kiteme, Peter Ambenje, Urs Wiesmann, and Samuel Makali. 2010. "Indigenous Knowledge Related to Climate Variability and Change: Insights from Droughts in Semi-Arid Areas of Former Makueni District, Kenya." *Climatic Change* 100 (2): 295–315. https://doi.org/10.1007/s10584-009-9713-0.

Stals, Shenando, Michael Smyth, and Wijnand IJsselsteijn. 2014. "Walking & Talking: Probing the Urban Lived Experience." In Proceedings of the NordiCHI 2014: The 8th Nordic Conference on Human-Computer Interaction: Fun, Fast, Foundational, 737–46. https://doi.org/10.1145/2639189.2641215.

Tsuji, Leonard, and Elise Ho. 2002. "Traditional Environmental Knowledge and Western Science: In Search of Common Ground." *Canadian Journal of Native Studies* 22 (2): 327–60.

Warren, Saskia. 2017. "Pluralising the Walking Interview: Researching (Im)Mobilities with Muslim Women." *Social and Cultural Geography* 18 (6): 786–807. https://doi.org/10.1080/14649365.2016.1228113.

PART III

Geopoetics and Performance

13

EXPLORING SENSIBLE VIRTUAL IMMERSIVE SPACES THROUGH DIGITAL GEORAMAS

Pablo Mansilla-Quiñones, Juan Carlos Jeldes Pontio, and Andrés Moreira-Muñoz

Introduction

The geographical imaginaries about colonial territories has been disseminated by the artefacts of cultural consumption, such as books, photographs, films, atlases, and other media that narrate geographical explorations of overseas territories under colonial rule. In Europe, during the 19th century, at the apogee of the imperialism-colonialism of France, Great Britain, and other Western empires, various types of immersive geographical paraphernalia, such as panoramas, dioramas, and georamas were created. By reproducing landscapes of distant territories, through analogous media, such geo-constructs brought the experience of unknown places and territories as a spectacle aimed at the inhabitants of the big cities of these European empires. From a decolonial perspective, in the geohumanities and digital humanities, these geo-artefacts can be subjected to critical questioning. As the postcolonial theorist Edward Said (2018, 27) observes, imperial cultural and aesthetic representations contributed to narratives of symbolic power upon which the domination of colonial peoples and territories was built. As Said notes,

> in narratives, stories, tales of travels and explorations, consciousness was represented as the main authority, as a source of energy that gave meaning not only to colonizing activities, but also to geographies and exotic peoples.
>
> *(2018, 27)*

Thus, spatial representations contained in various types of panoramas continue to be problematic since they remain embedded in power relations. The colonial production of spatial images designed landscapes on which colonial geographic imaginaries are sustained.

Such relationships have been studied by Edward Said and later by the critical geographer Derek Gregory (1994) to explore the ways in which colonial geographical imaginaries are produced as actions of negative radical alterity. Geographical imaginaries arise from discursive representations contained in scientific and artistic materials and other forms of symbolic expression, which have recreated the particular perspectives of spaces under colonial rule. These imaginary

DOI: 10.4324/9781003082798-17

geographies have allowed the construction of images of otherness, which Said (2013) contends refers to the representations of the East generated from Europe:

> The imaginary geography that extends from the vivid portraits found in *Inferno* to the prosaic pigeonholes of the *Bibliothèque orientale*, by d'Herbelot, legitimizes a vocabulary and a universe of discourse peculiar to and representative of the discussion and understanding of Islam and the Orient.
>
> *(2013, 43)*

Within this context, the immersive experiences of georamas and panoramas accompanied the symbolic representation of European geopolitical power in this imperial phase of the modern world system, where the geographical expansion and control of overseas territories contributed to the political and economic sustenance of these Western hegemonies. Georamas and other types of colonial cultural artefacts were claimed to be scientific and neutral during this period. An example is the "human zoos" installed in the acclimatisation gardens of Paris, which correspond to the symbolic devices of power deployed in the second half of the 19th century to configure representations of the colonial geocultural and political domain. In such manners, the coloniality of power becomes effective and manages to remain until the present time as a social project that creates a new social intersubjectivity, a new geoculture that affects the way of seeing and acting in the world (Quijano 2000). Producing a negative "otherness" that denies the way of seeing the other, Indigenous, black woman and her ontological forms of relationship with the territory – which is presented as nonexistent – provides colonists with the moral imperative to bring Western development to the colonised territories (Quintero-Weir 2016; Mansilla-Quiñones, Quintero-Weir, and Moreira-Muñoz 2019). Various representations of distant territories emerge from such geocultural imaginaries, like the notions of orientalism, tropicality, and australity, through which places of conquest are described, justifying practices of colonialism as positive actions to promote the development of societies and territories considered "backward." These colonial geographic imaginaries are part of the symbolic violence through which social consent is obtained to justify colonial rule. Its negative impacts end up affecting colonial subjects and their ways of living, which in turn erodes the territorial ontological basis of the existence of Indigenous peoples, transgressing their productions of life, knowledge, social practices, bodies, imaginaries, and meanings about the world they inhabit (Mansilla-Quiñones, Quintero-Weir, and Moreira-Muñoz 2019). This coloniality also extends to representations of nature and to the multiple organisms that cohabit this planet, on which the modern effects of the coloniality upon nature are demonstrated. For example, in the colonial imaginaries of the Caribbean, Amazon, and Patagonia, among others, nature is represented as a negative "exteriority" that must be dominated. In the face of an exhausted monist vision and rhetoric established by modernity, it becomes necessary to scrutinise the production of colonial geographical narratives and knowledge rooted in territory and in nature. Doing so contributes constructively to the design of alternative ways out of a world in crisis (Escobar 2003; Haraway 2015). A reformulation of the representations of nature consists of a search for immersive geographic experiences that, given contemporary digital tools, can contribute to dialogues of knowledge and searches for experiences of coexistence to construct other possible worlds and allow us to consider the possibility of living on our common planet in a different way. Raising critical questions about "ways of seeing" and the production of modern, decolonial geographical images, Donna Haraway and other feminist scientists in the 1980s inaugurated strong debates about the point of view. While promoting a monistic perspective of knowledge, critics focused on the male, white, Eurocentric, and anthropocentric perspectives that prevailed in science and the humanities. In her writings on situated knowledge, Haraway (1990) questioned the "oculocentrism" of the sciences:

> Eyes have been used to signify a perverse capacity, refined to perfection in the history of science – related to militarism, capitalism, colonialism, and male supremacy – to distance the knowing subject who is to be known from everyone and everything in the interest of unfettered power.
>
> *(Haraway 1990, 188)*

From such a perspective, science and modern reason have been based on the primacy of the human eye in the production of knowledge. Within the context of a fragmented modernity, dichotomies have emerged to separate body/mind or nature/culture, creating other binary distinctions that order good/bad and superior/inferior (Mansilla and Imilan 2020). Thus, Haraway instigated scientific writing from the perspective of somatography away from the sight of the male gaze: "we need to reclaim that sense to find our way through all the visualizing tricks and the powers of the sciences and modern technologies that have transformed the debates on objectivity" (1990, 189). This is accomplished by promoting a partial point of view, which questions the objectiveness and pretensions of neutrality. Isolated in our gaze, we do not deepen our contemplative perspectives in order to "denaturalize" the ways in which we have been taught to see and feel about nature. Therefore, it is urgent to seek new ways of perceiving through sensible spaces of immersion (Freitag et al. 2020). It can be noted that

> Deleuze offers a fresh line of flight with the potential to deterritorialise the discourse surrounding concept mapping, thus widening its applicability and increasing its accessibility to researchers who do not necessarily share the same arborescent concept mapping heritage.
>
> *(Kinchin and Gravett 2020, 1)*

In this sense, from the current perspective of DEH and geohumanities, it is important to reflect on the devices and representations of power imbricated in the production of the geographic images embedded in panoramas, dioramas, and georamas. In this chapter, we explore the relevance of spatial representations and immersive experiences generated during the 19th century through various formats such as panoramas, georamas, dioramas, which were European inventions to showcase distant colonial and other territories, with everyday landscape scenes of these places (Jørgensen 2014). We also propose a sensible reappropriation of these devices of geographical representation through the production of prototypes that encourage co-creation and dialogues of knowledge rooted in spatial images. Digital humanities are increasingly engaged with the creation of new visual strategies for the presentation of data, and it is necessary to incorporate critical perspectives on the new ways of seeing that are in play in this field.

This includes the manners through which digital media enable dialogues of knowledge between ways of seeing the world and opens avenues to the pluriverse – a world where multiple representations of the world coalesce (Escoba 2003; Blaser and Marisol de la Cadena 2018). We adopt the word "sensible" in defining its political agency:

> [W]hen a philosopher like Jacques Rancière writes about the "*partage du sensible*," we understand that this passivity is only apparent: our sensitivity results from an activity of partition and of partaking. Things don't just project their images upon the blank

> screen of senses: we, humans, actively categorize them. We filter them, we select some and reject others, we classify them, according to complex mechanisms of distinction that are both socially constructed over time, and individually reconducted each time we sense anything. . . . We, people of the 21st century, are therefore fully entitled to feel good (about ourselves) when we "feel well," i.e., when we do our best to "become sensitive" to the existence, sufferings and rights of all the creatures (women, colonial subjects, gays, and battery hens) that previously fell outside of the *partage du sensible* experienced by our barbarian ancestors.
>
> *(Citton 2013, 2)*

In this chapter, by adopting deep mapping strategies, we will explore sensible, virtual, immersive spaces and the devices that "detonate" the experiences of space in contemporary digital georamas.

Digital Georamas: Representing the Common Home

The first panoramas appeared in the early 19th century as large circular paintings that could be viewed from a central point in a panoptical perspective. According to Belisle (2016), the name "panorama" was coined by Robert Barker from the Greek words *pan* ("all") and *horma* ("view"), who created a series of canvases depicting the cities of London and Westminster. Visible from a central platform, panoramas provided a sensory impression of being "inside the painting" (Belisle 2016, 316). As Jørgensen notes,

> panoramas offered viewers immersive landscape paintings of close and distant places. The panoramas could take their audience to exotic and scenic locations, often far away, without the inconvenience, hardship, and expense of traveling.
>
> *(Jørgensen 2014, 101)*

Panoramas were based on large-format installations mounted inside pavilions, consisting of cylindrical rooms inside which paintings of a landscape or scene were installed on curved, continuous canvases. In this way, spaces were created that accommodated a number of attendees, allowing them to look at a landscape from the perspective of a 360-degree view. Robert Barker's patent 1787 lists his invention as a circular building to expose a great cylindrical painting together with a central platform at a certain height and distance for observation. Baker's enclosure manifested in diverse styles of immersion, such as the georama, cosmorama, mareorama, and diorama (Hernández-Barbosa 2017).[1]

As noted in the Research in Image and Sound Design (RISD) project at the Universidad de Buenos Aires, the diorama is a technical invention in which it is possible to "see through" a three-dimensional installation of a scene, composed of scale objects, background paintings and lighting.[2] In dioramic scenes, the aim was to create a sensation of spatial depth by recreating landscapes or historical situations, generally situated in big cities. The first diorama was built in Paris in 1822 by Louis Daguerre. Its objective was to give the viewer the feeling of being in another place. The diorama's rooms were entered through a camera obscura so that the senses of the audience were deceived and, via their imagination, were immersed and transported to another place. Dioramas were popularised in the late 19th and early 20th centuries by Frank Chapman, an associate of the American Museum of Natural History and, in the 21st century, are consolidated under the Panorama Council (https://panoramacouncil.org) (Asociación Belenista de Bizkaia 2021; International Panorama Council 2021).

For each of these dioramic scenes, a high level of technical skill was required to produce the audience's immersion experience. The main component consisted of a contraption constructed with a large cloth or curtain placed within a calculated curve on which the landscape scene was painted. Dioramas used techniques based on false perspectives, transparencies, and overlapping planes, framing the two-dimensional painting so that it was able to provoke a sensation of depth and a three-dimensional perception of the objects represented on the canvas. Besse (2013) highlights the immersive paradox that panoramas confront us with, creating a geographical illusion in order to re-territorialise our spatial experience:

> We need to be immersed in the most strong illusion to be introduced more directly to the reality itself. We need to forget our actual reality to have an access to the virtual reality of the external world that is presented on the painting. The panorama is a paradoxical space, but the georama too is a space of that kind
>
> *(2003, 3).*

In contrast, georamas appear as a variation of painted canvases, specifically to give an immersive sensation of the Earth as such. Besse (2003) points out that the georama allows having an all-encompassing perspective of the planet representing the world through an image of a map scaled to a large size, 1:1,000,000, projected upon an edifice. The georama is an inverse geographical device presented to the populations of large metropolises, promoting a geographical imaginary and particular scientific vision where an image of the Earth is projected in such a large size to give the impression of a malleable world. This was to achieve a rapport with viewers, imparting the expanding spheres of global communications, the telegraph and its growing relationship between empires and industries, and the introduction of standardised measurements such as the metre (Belisle 2016). The first recognised georama consisted of a sphere 12 metres in diameter, built in Paris in 1826 by Charles Delangard, who

> emphasized that the Georama was especially valuable for displaying geographical information because it could be analyzed at different visual scales; it "allow[ed] the spectator either to examine a single place minutely, or to take a *coup-d'oeil* to the full extent of his visual angle." For Delangard, the Georama's ability to express information across various scales allowed it to communicate "a volume of information brought together, which could not be collected by any other means." This helped overcome the "great obstacle to the study of Geography" namely, "the difficulty of managing the voluminous details.
>
> *(Belisle 2016, 318)*

Besse (2003) points out that the georama was much less popular than other types of "oramas" of the period since it only "taught" a mute map of the world, despite being situated as a pedagogical device to influence global imaginaries: "Its claim is to present itself as a scene of the geographical knowledge. Its claim is to convey in a popular way the scientific knowledge given by the geographers of the time." Hidden under this mantle of scientific neutrality was the colonial logic of modernity. This influenced Eurocentric geographic epistemology, which, on the one hand, provided the power of knowledge for the colonial enterprise and, on the other, eliminated geographic narratives of the colonised peoples and territories from the map.

The Prussian geographer Alexander von Humboldt (1769–1859), in his work *Cosmos: A Sketch of a Physical Description of the Universe* (1845–1862), stated that the georama presented the possibility of representing "an overview of the universe" at a glance (Besse 2003). Humboldt visited Delangard's georama several times and claimed he had managed to correct several of the sphere's interpretations and dimensions due to his knowledge of cartography and maps. Another geographer inclined to the possibilities of the georama was anarchist geographer Eliseo Reclus (1830–1905), who conceived an exhibit for the 1900 Universal Exposition in Paris, which never materialised.

> Now, at a time when every . . . newspaper brings us news from all parts of the world; when every one of us . . . is fed and clothed with productions of all continents and seas; . . . the moment has come for us to have grand representations of our common home, and not to satisfy ourselves with petty spheres. . . . Now Globes must be temples themselves, as well by the magnificence or proportions as by the beauty of workmanship and the scrupulous care of scientific drawing. In sight of such constructions, people must feel grave and respectful, not only because those monuments consecrated to science will partake of its majesty, but also because they will belong to all men, without any privilege for race or nationality, and will help to strengthen within us the feeling that we are one and the same family.
>
> *(Belisle 2016, 320)*

Belisle (2016) notes that Reclus drew "on the sanctity of science to elevate this sense of connection from the vulgar reality of capitalism to a 'grave and respectful' reverence for the world as a 'common home.'" Panoramas, georamas, and dioramas artificially created the illusion of a landscape at a scale that left the individual inside and "immersed" in the exhibit's images, designed to shape the imagination of the spectator. As a type of 19th-century-society entertainment, such exhibits were constructed as pavilions and in buildings specially designed as centres of attraction.

Commensurate with the emergence of photography and film, and though precursors to cinema, these types of visual-spatial displays were taken up by museums, world fair exhibits, and later in the 20th century, Disney World (Kamcke and Hutterer 2015). It is interesting to note that all these forms of representation of other places preceded cinema and tended to disappear once the techniques of modern cinema emerged, as in the case of the Phono-Cinéma-Théâtre and the Théâtroscope. In the present day, augmented reality has been engaged to create digitally enhanced dioramas, such as in the exhibits featured at the Carnegie Museum of Natural History in Pittsburgh, Pennsylvania (Jørgensen 2014; Hernández-Barbosa 2017; Harrington et al. 2019).

From Panoramas to Augmented Reality

As the panorama was based on an objective vision of reality, its similarities with today's virtual reality (VR) and augmented reality (AR) devices are evident, although not so obvious. Both mediums pretend that every observer is able to have a similar immersive sensation from different vantage points. In the 20th century, we had a more complex conception of reality, which was reflected in the greater challenges of achieving similar experiences in different audiences with distinctive life histories and singular degrees of integration with technologies (Mansilla-Quiñones, Manríquez, and Moreira-Muñoz 2021).

Since the time of 19th-century georamas and dioramas, technology has advanced exponentially, to the point that digital, virtual mapping, and AR techniques, integrated into the form of immersive cybernetic spaces, have applications in fields as diverse as geoinformatics, biogeocultural heritage urbanism, astronautics medicine, social sciences, journalism, and certainly art, in close relation to geohumanities (Barazzetti, Previtali, and Scaioni 2020; Gwozdz 2020; Meenar and Kitson 2020; Pavlik 2020; Basu, Bannova, and Camba 2021; Casanova et al.

2021; Mansilla-Quiñones, Manríquez, and Moreira-Muñoz 2021; Rousell, n.d.). In particular, new platforms, labelled with the term "geomedia," have been designed to provide links between electronic media, the internet, geolocation technologies, and AR. As Lapenta (2011, 14) observes, geomedia platforms are inaugurating "a new mode of digital composite imaging, data association and socially maintained data exchange and communication." These platforms go hand in hand with substantial advances in GIS and emerging VR geolocation technologies engaged in the digital humanities, applications in geohistory, and now geospatial humanities (Panecki 2015; Vila, Albalat, and Pi 2016; Maluly 2017; Cura et al. 2018; Gribaudi 2018; Bruckmann et al. 2019; Murrieta-Flores and Martins 2019). Currently, hybrid research-action spaces shared between the geohumanities and urban studies are emerging with "the co-creation of a cartographic network that can be entered, activated, and extended along a multiplicity of trajectories, opening the inquiry process to more-than-human ecologies of participation" (Rousell n.d.). While immersive spaces have existed for at least a decade (e.g. Reality Deck at Stony Brook University; see Belisle 2016), AR is becoming increasingly ubiquitous and available at everyone's fingertips via smartphones and other emerging digital applications (Rakkolainen et al. 2016; Belisle 2020).

Deep mapping, which links digital and analogue data sources and methods, is an emerging subfield in the digital humanities in which cartographers are invited to immerse themselves

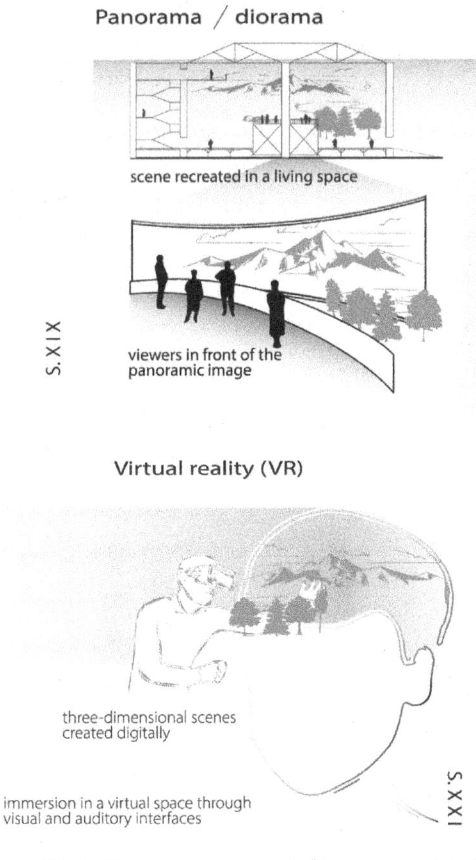

Figure 13.1 From panoramas and dioramas to virtual reality.

in the depth of a map from ethnographic and "platial" perspectives. As Roberts (2016) notes, deep mapping can be conceived as "a space in which an almost unlimited range and quantity of sources can be included, interrogated, manipulated, archived, analyzed and read." Charles Travis (2013, 13) observes,

> "Deep mapping" attempts to unravel narratives of the timespace that are difficult to apprehend, represent and transmit through traditional geographic methods and tools. For instance, the ability to iterate spatial and temporal scales with techniques adopted from the arts and humanities provides a powerful research tool to pursue what can be called . . . "Performative," and "Immersive" engagements of space-time modelling in GIScience.

By integrating GIS technologies with other devices that can geo-reference multiple digital records (photographs, video, audio, etc.), deep mapping facilitates the plotting of spatial stories with techniques that overcome the limitations of traditional maps (Bodenhamer, Corrigan, and Harris 2015; Roberts 2016).

Digital Georamas Integrating Narrative Time-Spaces

Spatial narratives express actions that territorialise geographic space, and visualisations of territorial memory are woven by an emplaced human group from collectively significant images of places. This presupposes a relation between image and experience through territorialisation processes, contextualised by time and place. What emerges is the spatial-territorial mark of the group incorporated materially and symbolically in their collective memory with strong implications for community-making. The means of registering the images/experiences of a group's territorial memory is through elaborations of a narrative of the symbolically constructed "platial" experience. Within these stories, symbolic elements fix place/time appropriation processes and their material or symbolic importance for deployment or exercise of the groups' territoriality. At the same time, novel spatial narratives propose a relational perspective, recognising open dialogues among human and non-human actors, through listening and the exchange of communications that unfold with the territorial expressions of forests, rivers, birds, and animals with which an ontological dialogue is maintained (Inoue and Moreira 2016; Ortiz 2017). Such spatial narratives open pluriverses for creating a new convivial human condition and build on an open dialogue between diverse forms of human and non-human life, which promote the permanence, transmission, and fertilisation of territorial existence (Figure 13.1) (Ortiz 2017; Gahman, Greenidge, and Team 2020; Wise and Noble 2016).

Our collective experience with local communities span different territories and biocultures along the Americas, from la Guajira towards Patagonia, including spatial narratives (Jamonnak et al. 2020), related to participatory mapping in biosphere reserves (Leguía et al. 2021); depopulation and re-territorialisation (Mansilla-Quiñones et al. 2021); hydrosocial metabolism (Panez-Pinto, Mansilla-Quiñones, and Moreira-Muñoz 2018); and Indigenous dispossession, cosmovision, and cosmopolitics (Mansilla-Quiñones and Imilan 2020). Our Digital georama project contemplates the creation of a medium, a device that tells a geographic story. One that critically explores any territory, including not just the visual characteristics but the corporalities, feelings, and effects of subjects when faced with territorial representations of geohistorical space in which there is a conflict over the use and significance of such a space.

Digital Georama Prototype Seeking Immersive Spaces

With the aim of investigating a reappropriation of the "georama" from the contemporary perspective of the DEH, we propose the construction of a prototype called the digital georama, through which deep mapping techniques are integrated in an innovative way. This prototype includes 3D printing techniques of models of the territory, on which projections of the digital georama's spectators-actors are generated in real time, selecting images of their silhouettes to interact with the surrounding landscape.

To produce this interactive illusion, an analogue-digital version of the pepper effect is used, through which the viewer sees the figure of their body located inside the three-dimensional space of the digital georama.

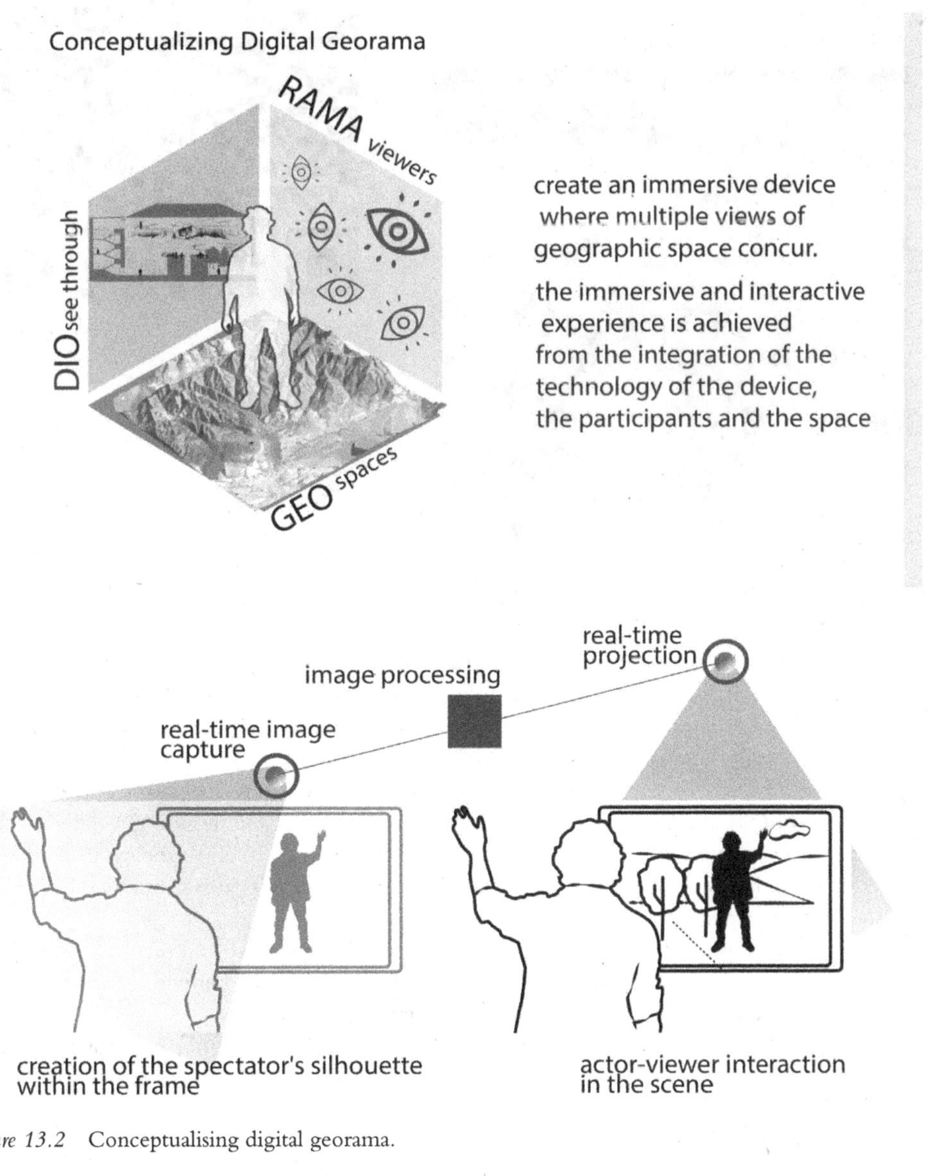

Figure 13.2 Conceptualising digital georama.

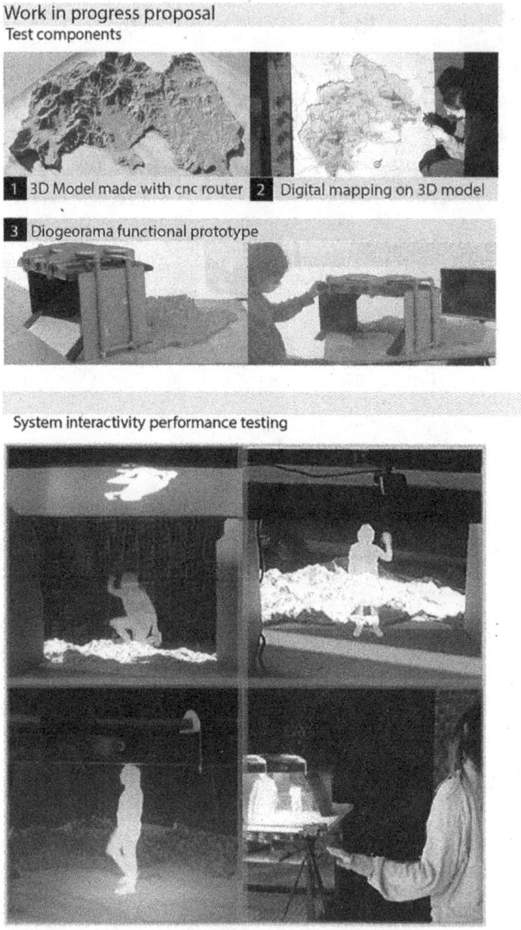

Scan this code to access a youtube video explaining the details of the digital georama prototype.

Figure 13.3 Work in progress proposal digital georama.

These digital georamas are used in territories where there are conflicting representations of nature and culture, in contexts of modern colonial geographic representations and imaginaries. The intention of the digital georama is for people to communicate their territorial representations through bodily languages and performative acts. One aspect that stands out in this prototype is that, contrary to traditional georamas, people are not mere spectators but rather have the ability to unfold and see themselves immersed in the landscape, building a different form of alterity. At the same time, another aspect to highlight is that in this prototype, people can interact with the landscape, leaving parts of their geographical narratives on the landscape from a constructivist perspective.

We propose the use of digital georamas as implicitly demonstrative and inclusive devices that facilitate sensible immersions in nature, in which the co-creation of knowledge emerges *in situ* that scrutinises the territorial and environmental community memory.

The technical proposal of the prototype is composed of three immersive projection techniques that are reformulated from contemporary technological tools:

- ***Digito-physical superposition***

This is very similar to AR but without the need for external body devices, such as glasses or gloves. Through the use of projections on transparent surfaces, digito-physical superposition generates before the eyes of spectators, an interactivity between virtual and physical elements to compose a complete, composite image. In addition, this method allows the experience to be lived collectively since the composite digital reality is not impeded by AR/VR devices, achieving transparent feedback between the participants themselves and their experiences.

- ***Pepper effect/augmented reality***

This adapts an optical illusion technique used in mid-19th-century theatres to simulate ghosts, allowing them to "interact" with actors on stage. Modern holograms are able to "bring to presence" a digital object through VR, with a specific arrangement between projected light and the surface that refracts it, thus generating a three-dimensional image. This effect is the basis for the development of prototypes to meet objectives defined for the digital georama in a synchronous use of digital audiovisual materials and three-dimensional geographical representations of the place to be exhibited.

- ***Silhouetting***

A present challenge in the development of our proposal points towards the integration of the spectators in the project in roles of co-authority. By establishing a flow of dialogue when showing the place to be exhibited, we can generate an interactive response from spectators, making them part of the scene. With this, the question "What do we collect from the participants?" is explored by focusing simultaneously on the essence of each person and their silhouette. This formal representation of people incorporates them into the project with a progressive co-construction, allowing the viewer to become a participant in the exhibition, of a digital georama that is constituted for every participant.

Conclusion

The production of time-space representations through technological devices, including geomedia and VR, provides a horizon of possibilities for critical political engagement in "sensible immersive virtual spaces." While discussing the possibilities of digital georamas in the current context of the DEH and geohumanities, it is unavoidable to reflect on such devices and representations of power. In this sense, the relevance of time-space visualisations and immersive experiences generated during the 19th century are worthy of revisitation and reinvention through digital virtual mapping and AR techniques. This deserves a deep discussion of the reappropriation of the devices of geographical representation by the creation of prototypes that encourage the co-creation and dialogues of knowledge derived from spatial images, in the sense of deep mapping. We are testing our digital georama devices on parallel tracks: one in the city and the other in an impoverished rural setting, where water and memory have been stolen.

The DEH is increasingly engaged with the creation of new visual strategies for the presentation of data, and it is necessary to incorporate critical perspectives on these new ways of "digital seeing." Through a territory-based approach, our digital georama contributes to the challenges of interdisciplinary dialogues in the DEH between design, geography, and local knowledge. With our "convivial" approach to the use of digital technologies, we seek to promote the co-creation of spatial narratives in geographical contexts where frictions between technologies, culture, and nature are found in order to promote instances of reflection and attitudes that

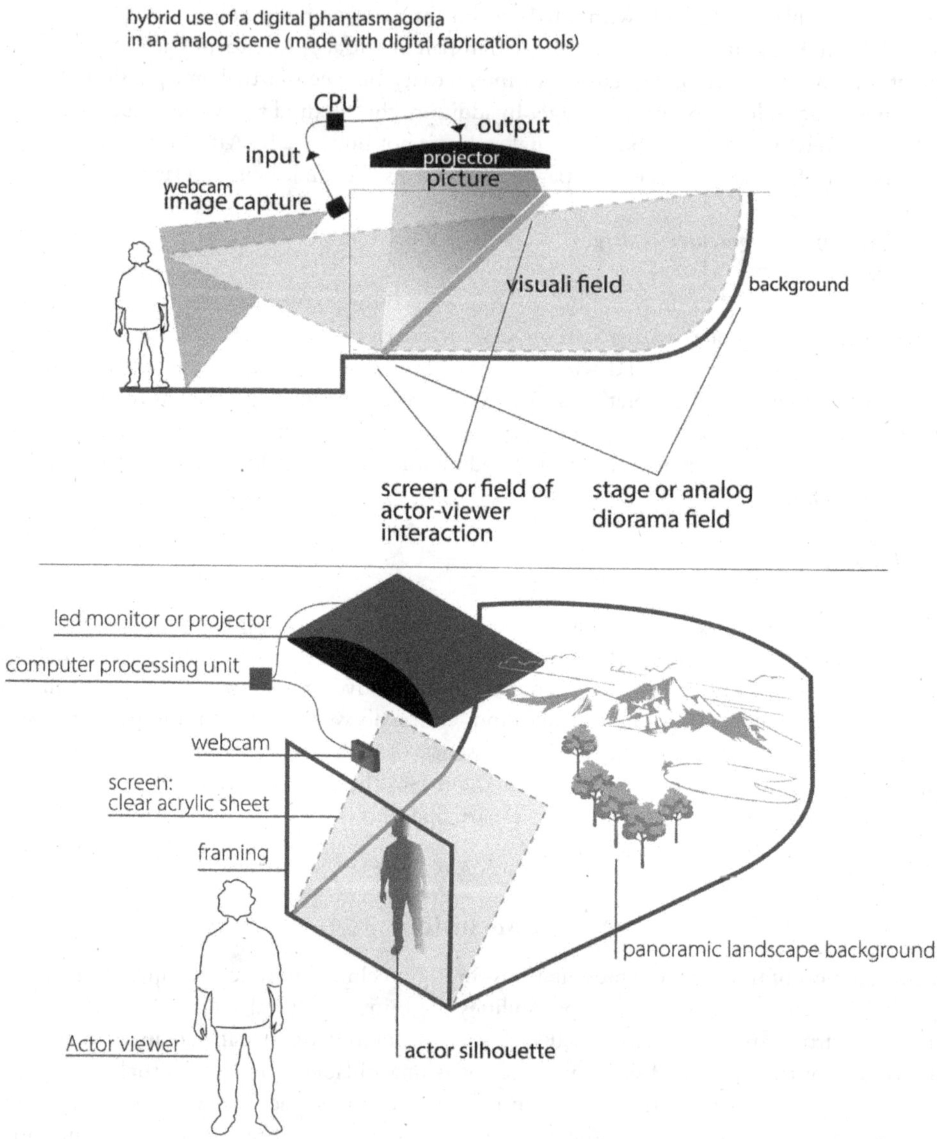

Figure 13.4 Detailed explanation of the technical proposal of the digital georama.

contribute to change. Our DEH explorations seek "other ways of seeing" beyond the lenses of modern, colonial, and scientific "oculocentrism" to map out new forms of re-territorialisation for a world in crisis.

Acknowledgements

The authors would like to thank Antonia Gallardo and Jaime Morales, research and design assistants of the digital georama prototype; the ANID FONDECYT project n°11181086 "Uninhabiting the extremes: New ways of inhabiting the rural in Magallanes"; and the BioGeoArt project,

ANID SOC 180040, "GeoHumanities and Creative (Bio)Geographies addressing sustainability and co-conservation through 'Rhizomatic Immersion.'"

Notes

1 IDIS (http://proyectoidis.org/ilusiones-de-movimiento).
2 IDIS (https://proyectoidis.org/propuesta).

Sources

Asociación Belenista de Bizkaia. 2021. "Historia del diorama." http://abelenbizkaia.com/articulos/historia-del-diorama/.

Barazzetti, Luigi, Mattia Previtali, and Marco Scaioni. 2020. "Procedures for Condition Mapping Using 360 Degrees Images." *Isprs International Journal of Geo-Information* 9 (1). https://doi.org/10.3390/ijgi9010034.

Basu, Tamalee, Olga Bannova, and Jorge D. Camba. 2021. "Mixed Reality Architecture in Space Habitats." *Acta Astronautica* 178: 548–55. https://doi.org/10.1016/j.actaastro.2020.09.036.

Belisle, Brooke. 2016. "Nature at a Glance: Immersive Maps from Panoramic to Digital." *Early Popular Visual Culture* 13 (4): 313–35. https://doi.org/10.1080/17460654.2015.1111590.

———. 2020. "Whole World within Reach: Google Earth VR." *Journal of Visual Culture* 19 (1): 112–36. https://doi.org/10.1177/1470412920909990.

Besse, Jean-Marc. 2013. "Embrasser la terre d'un seul coup d'œil: The First Parisian Georamas." *Maps and Society*. France. ffhalshs-00113279f.

Blaser, Mario, and C. de la. 2018. "Pluriverse: Proposals for a World of a Many Worlds." In *A World of Many Worlds*, edited by Edited by Mario Blaser and Marisol de la Cadena De. Durham: Duke University Press.

Bodenhamer, D., J. Corrigan, and T. Harris. 2015. *Deep Maps and Spatial Narratives*. Edited by 1. Indiana: Indiana University Press.

Bruckmann, Laurent, Antelie Amanejieu, Maurice Olivier Zogning Moffo, and Pierre Ozer. 2019. "Geo-historical Analysis of Flood Risk Spatio-Temporal Evolution and Its Management in the Urban Area of Douala (Cameroon)." *PHYSIO-GEO* 13: 91–113. https://doi.org/10.4000/physio-geo.8038.

Casanova, Morgane, Anne Clavreul, Gwenaelle Soulard, Matthieu Delion, Ghislaine Aubin, Aram Ter Minassian, Renaud Seguier, and Philippe Menei. 2021. "Immersive Virtual Reality and Ocular Tracking for Brain Mapping During Awake Surgery: Prospective Evaluation Study." *Journal of Medical Internet Research* 23 (3). https://doi.org/10.2196/24373.

Citton, Yves. 2013. "Political Agency and the Ambivalence of the Sensible." In *Jacques Rancière. History, Politics, Asthetics*, 120–39. Durham, NC: Duke University Press.

Cupples, Julie, Marcela Palomino-Schalscha, and Manuel Prieto. 2019. *The Routledge Handbook of Latin American Development*. New York and London: Routledge.

Cura, Remi, Bertrand Dumenieu, Nathalie Abadie, Benoit Costes, Julien Perret, and Maurizio Gribaudi. 2018. "Historical Collaborative Geocoding." *ISPRS International Journal of Geo-Information* 7 (7). https://doi.org/10.3390/ijgi7070262.

Escobar, A. 2003. "Mundos y Conocimientos de Otro Modo." *Tabula Rasa*. www.cecs-argentina.org/web2015/wp-content/uploads/2015/05/Escobar-Mundos-y-conocimientos-de-otro-modo.-El-programa-de-investigacion-de-modernidad-colonialidad-latino.pdf.

Freitag, Florian, Céline Molter, Laura Katharina Mücke, Helena Rapp, Damien B. Schlarb, Elisabeth Sommerlad, Clemens Spahr, and Dominic Zerhoch. 2020. "Immersivity: An Interdisciplinary Approach to Spaces of Immersion." *Journals.Openedition.Org/Ambiances* (December). https://doi.org/10.4000/AMBIANCES.3233.

Gahman, L, A Greenidge, and Julian Cho Society Youth Planning Team. 2020. "This Present Relationship and Its Beauty . . . Indigenous Youth Activism and Desire-Based Research in the Postcolonial Caribbean." *Antipode Online* 23 (202) (October): 1–7.

Gregory, Derek. 1994. *Geographical Imaginations*. Oxford: Blackwell.

Gribaudi, Maurizio. 2018. "Cassini's Map: Roads and Landscapes in 18th Century France." *Quaderni Storici* 53 (2): 475–506.

Gwozdz, Andrzej. 2020. "Thinking Bauhaus . . . Legacy of the Art of Light in Contemporary Projection Performances in Painting." *Sztuka I Dokumentacja-Art & Documentation* 23: 51+. https://doi.org/10.32020/ARTandDOC/23/2020/8.

Hamilton, Jennifer Mae, and Astrida Neimanis. 2018. "Composting Feminisms and Environmental Humanities." *Environmental Humanities* 10 (2): 501–27. https://doi.org/10.1215/22011919-7156859.

Haraway, Donna. 1990. *Simians, Cyborgs, and Women: The Reinvention of Nature.* New York: Routledge.

———. 2003. "Situated Knowledges: The Science Question in Feminism and the Privilege of Partial Perspective in Feenberg." In *Turning Points in Qualitative Research: Tying Knots in a Handkerchief*, edited by Yvonna S. Lincoln and Norman K. Denzin, 21–46. Oxford, UK: Altamira.

———. 2015. "Anthropocene, Capitalocene, Plantationocene, Chthulucene: Making Kin." *Environmental Humanities* 6 (1): 159–65. https://doi.org/10.1215/22011919-3615934.

Harrington, Maria C. R., Markus Tatzgern, T. O. M Langer, and John W. Wenzel. 2019. "Augmented Reality Brings the Real World into Natural History Dioramas with Data Visualizations and Bioacoustics at the Carnegie Museum of Natural History." *Curator-The Museum Journal* 62 (2): 177–93. https://doi.org/10.1111/cura.12308.

Harris, Trevor M. 2017. "Deep Mapping and Sensual Immersive Geographies." In *International Encyclopedia of Geography: People, the Earth, Environment and Technology*, 1–13. John Wiley & Sons, Ltd. https://doi.org/10.1002/9781118786352.wbieg1042.

Hernández Barbosa, Sonsoles. 2017. "Beyond the Visual: Panoramatic Attractions in the 1900 World's Fair." 32 (4): 359–70. https://doi.org/10.1080/1472586X.2017.1288071.

International Panorama Council. 2021. https://panoramacouncil.org/en/what_we_do/fields_of_activities/panoramas/.

Jamonnak, Suphanut, Ye Zhao, Andrew Curtis, Shamal Al-dohuki, Xinyue Ye, Farah Kamw, and Jing Yang. 2020. "GeoVisuals: A Visual Analytics Approach to Leverage the Potential of Spatial Videos and Associated Geonarratives." *International Journal of Geographical Information Science*: 1–21. https://doi.org/10.1080/13658816.2020.1737700.

Jørgensen, Finn Arne. 2014. "The Armchair Traveller's Guide to Digital Environmental Humanities." *Environmental Humanities* 4 (1) (May): 95–112. https://doi.org/10.1215/22011919-3614944.

Kamcke, Claudia, and Rainer Hutterer. 2015. "History of Dioramas." *Natural History Dioramas: History, Construction and Educational Role* (January): 7–21. https://doi.org/10.1007/978-94-017-9496-1_2.

Kinchin, I. M., and K. Gravett. 2020. "Concept Mapping in the Age of Deleuze: Fresh Perspectives and New Challenges." *Education Sciences* 10 (3): 82.

Lapenta, Francesco. 2011. "Geomedia: On Location-Based Media, the Changing Status of Collective Image Production and the Emergence of Social Navigation Systems." 26 (1): 14–24. https://doi.org/10.1080/1472586X.2011.548485.

Leguia-Cruz, Marcelo, Colectiva Tejer-Nos, Natalia Ortiz-Cubillos, Pablo Mansilla-Quiñones, and Andrés Moreira-Muñoz. 2021. "Biocultural Resistance and Re-Existence through a Dialogue of Knowledges and Citizen Art in a Threatened Biosphere Reserve." *Eco.Mont – Journal on Protected Mountain Areas Research and Management* 2: 79–84.

Maluly, Vinicius Sodre. 2017. "'Finding Paths{'} in the Eighteenth Century Cartography." *Boletin Goiano De Geografia* 37 (2): 175–91. https://doi.org/10.5216/bgg.v37i2.49150.

Mansilla-Quiñones, Pablo, Hermann Manríquez, and Andrés Moreira-Muñoz. 2021. "Virtual Heritage: A Model of Participatory Knowledge Construction Toward Biogeocultural Heritage Conservation." 75–94. https://doi.org/10.1007/978-981-15-4956-4_5.

Mansilla-Quiñones, Pablo, Susana Cortés-Morales, and Andrés Moreira-Muñoz. 2021. "Depopulation and Rural Shrinkage in Subantarctic Biosphere Reserves : Envisioning Re-Territorialization by Young People." *Eco.Mont – Journal on Protected Mountain Areas Research and Management* 2: 76–81.

Mansilla-Quiñones, Pablo, and Walter Imilan Ojeda. 2020. "Coloniality of Power, Urban Development and Mapuche Dispossession: Urbanization on Mapuche Land in Chilean Araucania." *Scripta Nova-Revista Electronica De Geografia Y Ciencias Sociales* 24 (630).

Mansilla-Quiñones, P., J. Quintero-Weir, and A. Moreira-Muñoz. 2019. "Geografía de las ausencias, colonialidad del estar y el territorio comosustantivo crítico en las epistemologías del Sur." *Utopia y Praxis Latinoamericana* 24 (86): 148–61.

Meenar, Mahbubur, and Jennifer Kitson. 2020. "Using Multi-Sensory and Multi-Dimensional Immersive Virtual Reality in Participatory Planning." *Urban Science* 4 (3). https://doi.org/10.3390/urbansci4030034.

Mires Ortiz, A. 2017. "La Tierra Cuenta. Oralidad, Lectura y Escritura En Territorio Comunitario." *Revista Interamericana de Bibliotecología Medellín* 40 (1): 95–103. https://doi.org/10.17533/udea.rib.v40n1a09.

Murrieta-Flores, Patricia, and Bruno Martins. 2019. "The Geospatial Humanities: Past, Present and Future." *International Journal of Geographical Information Science* 33 (12): 2424–29. https://doi.org/10.1080/13658816.2019.1645336.

Panecki, Tomasz. 2015. "The Evaluation of Archival Maps in Geohistorical Research." *Miscellanea Geographica* 19 (4): 72–77. https://doi.org/10.1515/mgrsd-2015-0027.

Panez-Pinto, Alexander, Pablo Mansilla-Quiñones, and Andrés Moreira-Muñoz. 2018. "Agua, Tierra y Fractura Sociometabólica Del Agronegocio." *Bitacora Urbano Territorial* 28 (3): 153–60. https://doi.org/10.15446/bitacora.v28n3.72210.

Pavlik V, John. 2020. "Drones, Augmented Reality and Virtual Reality Journalism: Mapping Their Role in Immersive News Content." *Media and Communication* 8 (3): 137–46. https://doi.org/10.17645/mac.v8i3.3031.

Prádanos, Luis I. 2019. "Environmental Humanities: Ecocriticism and Cultural Decolonization." *Revista de Teoria de La Literatura y Literatura Comparada* 21: 9–14.

Quijano, Aníbal. 2000. "Colonialidad Del Poder, Eurocentrismo y América Latina." In *La Colonialidad Del Saber: Eurocentrismo y Ciencias Sociales. Perspectivas Latinoamericanas*, edited by CLACSO. Buenos Aires. http://biblioteca.clacso.edu.ar/clacso/sur-sur/20100708050100/11_quijano.pdf.

Quintero-Weir, José. 2016. "El Sentipensar Añuu y Sus Palabras Claves. En Torno a La Configuración Añuu de Su Sentipensar." *Revista de Ciencias de La Educación, Docencia, Investigación y Tecnologías de La Información CEDOTIC* 1 (1).

Rakkolainen, Ismo, Roope Raisamo, Matthew Turk, and Tobias Höllerer. 2016. "Casual Immersive Viewing with Smartphones." *AcademicMindtrek* 16 (October): 1–5. https://doi.org/10.1145/2994310.2994314.

Roberts, Les. 2016. "Deep Mapping and Spatial Anthropology." *Humanities* 5 (1): 5. https://doi.org/10.3390/h5010005.

Rousell, David. n.d. "A Map You Can Walk Into: Immersive Cartography and the Speculative Potentials of Data." *Qualitative Inquiry*. https://doi.org/10.1177/1077800420935927.

Said, Edward. 2013. *Orientalismo*. España: Penguin Random House Grupo Editorial España.

———. 2018. *Cultura e Imperialismo*. Barcelona: Penguin Random House.

Travis, Charles. 2014. "Transcending the Cube: Translating GIScience Time and Space Perspectives in a Humanities GIS." 28 (5): 1149–64. https://doi.org/10.1080/13658816.2013.829232.

Tunnicliffe, Sue Dale, and Annette Scheersoi. 2015. "Natural History Dioramas: History, Construction and Educational Role." *Natural History Dioramas: History, Construction and Educational Role* (January): 1–289. https://doi.org/10.1007/978-94-017-9496-1.

Vila, M., D. Albalat, and R. Pi. 2016. "Geological Mapping for the Urban Area of Tarragona." *Environmental Earth Sciences* 75 (5). https://doi.org/10.1007/s12665-015-4987-1.

Wise, Amanda, and Greg Noble. 2016. "Convivialities: An Orientation." *Journal of Intercultural Studies* 37 (5): 423–31. https://doi.org/10.1080/07256868.2016.1213786.

Yumie Aoki Inoue, Cristina, and Paula Franco Moreira. 2016. "Many Worlds, Many Nature(s), One Planet: Indigenous Knowledge in the Anthropocene." *Revista Brasileira de Politica Internacional* 59 (2): e009.

14

THE DIGITAL POETICS OF LOST WATERSCAPES IN COIMBATORE, SOUTH INDIA

Shanmugapriya T. Priya and Deborah Sutton

Introduction

How can DEH allow for new iterations of social, physical and cultural landscapes? Our project, Digital Innovations in Water Scarcity, Coimbatore, South India, responds to this question by examining the transformed waterscapes of Coimbatore, South India, across 150 years, using a range of data, including historical maps (archived in the Map Reading Room of the National Library of Scotland [NLS]), current satellite imagery, and interviews with a range of local stakeholders: farmers, water experts, writers activists, and NGOs. How can the capacities of digital technologies help us to rethink waterscapes that have been shaped by colonisation, using data extracted from the colonial archive? How can these histories be connected to current water scarcities but also to contemporary cultures and quotidian experiences of place? We are particularly keen to explore the capacity of creative digital interfaces to push forward research that is grounded in data from the global south. The project aimed to reflect carefully on the structural imbalances generated by the colonial history with which it concerns itself and that is embedded in the inequalities between the majority and minority worlds, between which the authors collaborate.

Amidst the ongoing COVID-19 pandemic, our engagement with digital technologies as a means of recording, archiving, manipulating and sharing data has become both more urgent and enterprising. In fact, the pandemic has made the project almost entirely dependent upon assemblages of digital iterations of water: maps, statistics, interviews, texts. The project aims to harness this assemblage and create creative digital visualisations that challenge the colonial denotation of water as a taxable resource and the disaggregation of water from living landscapes. The digital poetry text "Lost Water! Remainscape?" is one of the key outputs of the project and draws on the competency of digital technologies to generate heterogeneous, kinetic images and texts, graphic designs, videos, and other interactive components. The project uses creative, poetic visualisations to reimagine water histories in Coimbatore in the living and literary landscape, and to think about what has been lost, what can be retained or even regained.

Digital humanities (DH) and environmental humanities (EH) both help form the backdrop to this project. As Posthumus and Sinclair (2017, 370) point out, while the former is characterised by innovative methodological structures without thematic cohesion, the latter is

 DOI: 10.4324/9781003082798-18

"thematically more coherent but perhaps lack methodological cohesion". A tactical merging of the two – digital environmental humanities (DEH) – they argue, is a response to the challenges of the Anthropocene and the continued unfolding of a digital revolution. In a similar vein, Travis and Holm coined the term "Digital Anthropocene" to describe the entwined currents of "digital revolution, human-induced climate change, and the historical strands of sociopolitical agency and conflict" (2016, 189). They postulate that the deployment of technology "can function to mitigate global environmental change, allow humans to adapt to new environments, and create sustainable forms of existence on the planet" (Travis and Holm, 2016, 189).[1]

Our approach holds that digital literature (DL) is one of the drivers of this digital revolution and can be effectively employed to create meaningful interventions in ongoing environmental crises. These creative interventions are characterised by the layering of data and media drawn from a diversity of archives and framed by perspectives that reflect the experiences of those most profoundly affected by environmental stress. DL originated as an experimentation with digital creativity and literary text in the mid-20th century (Funkhouser 2007, 1). For example, Christopher Strachey's love letter generator and Theo Lutz's "Stochastische Texte" are the first machine literary works created in the mid-20th century (Roberts 2017; Funkhouser 2007, 37). Such electronic literary works have been emerging with advanced computing technology (Electronic Literature Collection, n.d.; Shanmugapriya and Menon 2019b, 70). Subsequently, DL innately possesses interactive digital elements that consist of linear, non-linear, and kinetic texts, interactive interfaces and graphics, kinetic images, audios, and videos. Such advanced digital components can be deployed in environmental research projects to augment awareness about the impact of environmental degradation. It has the potential to ignite conversation about environmental issues in a manner that brings a number of disciplines and diverse (and even disparate) perspectives together. For example, this project draws on maps and statistics generated by an imperial bureaucracy that was antagonistic towards local populations and sceptical of the management of water resources. The project also works to mitigate the complexity of colonial place-names that combine a variety of both sequential and co-extant transliterations. The project aims to make these materials both a way of informing contemporary understandings of water activism and readily available to a range of activists as tools. More broadly, in this chapter, we argue that DL as a method can enhance and interpret the data generated in a DEH approach, allowing for a wider reach of outputs and thus cognisance of environmental issues among both academic and non-academic audiences.

In what follows, we discuss the place of visualisations in DEH and propose and theorise DL as a method to amplify the concern about environmental issues. Finally, we describe the digital poetry developed from our research on waterscapes in Coimbatore, South India. We employ digital poetry as a method to visualise selected attributes and themes from the resources collected, including interviews, historical maps and texts and literature. Visual poetry is an attempt to re-narrate specific questions, concerns, and information about water scarcity. The project, as it continues and develops, will use these visualisations as a methodology to begin new conversations about water scarcity and to develop and co-create new versions of itself.

Visualisation in the Digital Environmental Humanities

There is significant literature on the potential role of creative visualisation in environmental advocacy (see Sheppard 2005; Mirzoeff 2014; Metze 2020). Visualisation is "the representation of an object, situation or set of information in a diagram, photograph, or other sort of image, as well as forming a mental image" (Metze 2020, 745). Visualisations are increasingly nuanced in order to represent data that contains numbers and languages that can be understood by various audiences. Innovative digital tools, software, and algorithms can enhance both the analysis and explication of complex data. Visual stories bring inquisitiveness, creativity, and play to environmental issues that often attract more technical and catastrophising approaches. In the DEH, creative and information visualisations are of paramount importance in telling stories in a meaningful and compelling way, revealing patterns and relationships and decision-making by deploying digital tools and technologies to exhibit environmental challenges and issues. As Metze demonstrates, visualisation has a pivotal role in "data-communication, influences decision-making, public perception, public participation, and knowledge cocreation" (2020, 745). What is more, styles and forms of visuals can transcend language and cultural barriers to enable knowledge participation and co-creation (2020, 754).

Ben Shneiderman writes, "Humanities researchers who adopt visual analytical tools are likely to find new ways to support passionately held theories and make creative leaps that advance their scholarship" (in Ferster 2013, xi). However, visualisations in the humanities bring their own conventions and paradigms. Conventional visualisation forms, such as graphs, charts, and maps, are borrowed from the natural sciences, social sciences, and business applications (Drucker 2018, 249). Johanna Drucker points out that these models are limited in the "application to interpretative practices in the humanities" (2018, 249). Insofar as they meant to provide information rather than engage the audience in a series of interpretations.

Similarly, George Lakoff suggests that we do not merely provide "numbers and material facts without framing them so their overall significance can be understood. Instead find general themes or narratives that incorporate the points" we "need to make" (2010, 79–80). EH, in which both environmental and social components are intrinsic, requires creative visualisations that do not merely emulate the linear model system of scientific communication for knowledge integration. Instead, these visualisations must reflectively recognise their re-narration of, for example, the colonial and state-scientific archives and be a means of actively dismantling the authoritarian environmental paradigms from which they were generated.

Digital Literature as a Method

Digital literature – or electronic literature, as these artefacts were initially called – originated in the mid-20th century (Shanmugapriya and Menon 2018a, 70). Later, this genre was consolidated and evolved by a broadening institutional landscape of funding schemes, teaching programmes and scholarships such as National Endowment for the Humanities Digital Start-Up Grant, courses on electronic literature in various universities across the world, and ELO Research Fellowships (Electronic Literature Organization, n.d.). ELO defines electronic literature as "works with important literary aspects that take advantage of the capabilities and contexts provided by the stand-alone or networked computer" (Electronic Literature Directory n.d.). This definition can be extended to include digital communication technology (iPhone, Android, and notebooks, etc.), which can play a pivotal role in creating and disseminating literature and creating new audiences (Shanmugapriya and Menon 2018a, 170).

DL is composed of an unprecedented amalgamation of heterogeneous media, containing kinetic texts, kinetic images, videos, graphical designs, and sounds. It is fluid and has the capability to blur the traditional boundaries between artistic expression, artefact, creator, and reader. The creator(s) can produce a digital literary artefact that invites its reader to play, read, explore, and even manipulate. The reader, then, ultimately becomes part of the narrative. DL is a resource that can simultaneously make evident the imprints of one or more readers and retain elements of both its original form and meaning. It is this dynamic interface that this project seeks to explore as a counterpoint to the convictions of state resource management. The materials of colonial and postcolonial state science have yielded much data on which the creative visualisations rely. DL provides a format which can pull apart and reassemble this data. Many digital artists and creators employ electronic literature as an agency to explore and question contemporary issues. For example, Pereira discusses how the digital literary works of J.R. Carpenter's *The Gathering Cloud* and *This Is a Picture of Wind* and Scott Rettberg's *Toxi•City: A Climate Change Narrative* use digital artefacts to encapsulate environmental issues (Pereira 2020).

The creative media practice and platforms of DL have an affinity with DH, which endeavours to blend software-led remote methods of data retrieval, orchestration, and analysis with the qualitative, intuitive methods of humanities research. This confluence was explored by the panel Intersectional Scholarship in Electronic Literature and Digital Humanities, at the Association of Digital Humanities Organizations conference 2018. Élika Ortega, O'Sullivan, and Grigar, for example, proposed that electronic literature offers a model for DH praxis in terms of exploring and addressing "the effect of digital media as it has modified – and continues to propose a modification of – reading and writing practices as well as modes of abstracting, encoding, and communicating information" (Ortega, O'Sullivan, and Grigar 2016). Digital environmental humanists can adopt the material composition of electronic literature in order to extend and augment, as well as intensify, the outreach of DH projects. For example, the You and CO_2 project employed interactive literature to engage school students with climate change, carbon futures, and social justice. The project provided a dynamic platform through which young people wrote and to place themselves in an alternative future (Rudd, Horry, and Skains 2020, 230–33).

Innovative visualisations and narrativisations can contain multiple layers and incorporate nonfiction and fictional entities. For instance, in the ELO 2019 annual conference, Richard Carter, with his panel members Tina Escaja and Paulo Silva Pereira, explores the "intersection between digital creativity and ecological thematics, dynamics, and materialities"(2020). The emergent field of digital rhetorics invites the reader to inscribe their own experience of the environmental crisis. At the same time, Metze points out a crucial lacuna in the current creative visualisation of EH, which is the lack of participation and collaboration of "stakeholders, citizens, and decision-makers in the creation of new models, and visualizations" (2020, 753). The technological capacities of DL as a method for the DEH can bring together researchers, artists, citizens, and decision-makers to make new narratives of people and place.

Digital Innovation in Water Scarcity in Coimbatore, India

According to a report by the World Resources Institute, India ranks 13 among 17 countries facing extreme high-water stress (Hofste and Schleifer 2019). Coimbatore, a semi-arid region in Southern India, has experienced frequent and severe droughts in the past four decades. The region's water crisis reflects the complex environmental and political legacies of imperial and Indian state-science interventions along the course of the Kaveri river, which traverses four states in Southern India and has been the subject of significant hydrological interventions and fractious, inter-state political disputes. The Coimbatore district was part of the Madras Presidency under British India (1799–1947) and was subsequently divided into five districts in 1979. An acute water crisis has resulted from climate change overlaid and preceded by decades of poor management and unplanned development. The region was classified as drought-prone as early as the 1970s (Priya et al. 2011, 448). Many lakes and tanks have been destroyed or are near-empty in and around the city of Coimbatore and in Erode, Tirupur, and Karur districts. What is more, the condition of the water bodies in these districts is poor due to mismanagement, climate change, and pollution.

Our research project focused on, firstly, drawing together a large digital corpus of graphic and textual information about the history of water in the region and, secondly, working with local activists to design dynamic visualisations and narrations based on that corpus. The Survey of India maps of Southern India (1916–1945) held by the National Library of Scotland have been digitised as part of the project. These archived maps are open-access on the NLS website (https://maps.nls.uk/india/survey-of-india). We have used GIS and ArcGIS software to create georeferenced historical maps that chart the transformation of waterscapes using features such as transparency, spy and side by side (see Figure 14.1). These features allow anyone to explore the past and cartographic presence of water bodies over the past hundred years. The interactive maps are open-access and available to scholars, NGOs and other audiences. For example, the collaged screenshots of georeferenced maps show that part of the Ukkulam tank has been transformed into a government bus stop now located in Coimbatore. Similarly, the users can explore the transformed water bodies, noting how many are now just dry lands and how many have become concrete lands and roads.

In the preliminary phase of our project, we identified ten disappeared tanks and 15 shrinking water bodies. The disappeared tanks are all relatively small and have been replaced by either houses or agricultural lands. The larger ones are shrunken by the gradual encroachment of buildings and farming around the tanks. From the beginning of the project, we were aware that the maps and other sources on which we rely for data are, in many senses, remote from the local communities resident there. Colonial survey maps were created by a colonial bureaucracy suspicious of the instability of Indian riverine systems and the supposed indifference of local communities to the production potential of water resources (Indian Irrigation Commission 1903). Meanwhile, present-day satellite images represent data that is ordered according to the categories and scales amenable to state science. For example, the government of India Bhuvan geospatial initiative is a significant attempt to make geospatial planning data available, but its format follows and reiterates the bureaucratic order of the state (https://bhuvan.nrsc.gov.in/home/index.php).

Our intention was to redeploy this information that quite deliberately detached water, in terms of scale, categories, and access to data, from local communities and to create visualisations that restored water bodies as dynamic and proximate resources. This reassemblage of data relating to water within the localities from which it was abstracted was carried out through a series of reflective stages. Following the digitisation of the NLS maps, we relied upon a "breaking up" of these to create smaller visualisations framed by the concerns of local activists and communities. Our aim here was to resituate the disembodied corpus of textual and graphic materials within the everyday experiences of water scarcity via poetic visualisations free of the totalising and authoritative presumptions of colonial cartographies.

This ambition to reframe data from the colonial cartographic archive meant that interactions about the history of local water bodies, water scarcity, and management with local farmers, activists, writers and NGOs are key to our analysis and visualisations. These interactions allow us to document local water narratives. These narratives are the means by which our analysis and visualisations can meaningfully respond to and reflect lived experiences of the water crisis in the region. Although inhibited by the COVID-19 pandemic, our interviews with local stakeholders provided narratives about specific water bodies and about materials near and associated with water: pumps (old and new, hand and electric, common and private), wells, tanks, and lithic epigraphy that documents historic dedication of particular tanks and draws attention to the long-standing relationship between water and secular and devotional authority.

Nostalgia for lost water was a prominent theme in local narratives and became a key idea in connecting our datasets of maps and texts with contemporary scarcity. Specific ponds and tanks

Figure 14.1 Georeferenced maps of the 19th-century Survey of Maps of India.

Image credit: National Library of Scotland

are remembered in these narrations, and waterscapes are remembered as an integral part of a larger, flourishing (arguably halcyon) village ecosystem. The idea of absent water is contained both in the narratives and the colonial ordinance maps, albeit in very different ways. Memories return depleted water to a landscape as an expression of the loss of something that is remembered as once immanent and available. The digitised maps, produced as an expression and effect of the colonial government's presumed control of water bodies, provide visual evidence of the same lost and depleted water sources. This connection drew our attention to the contradiction that lay at the heart of our project. The survey maps and much of the textual and statistical information we collected and digitised not only belonged to but played an important role within the colonial and postcolonial state regimes of hydrological management that created the conditions of the water shortage. The visualisations, therefore, seek to both reflect and invert the environmental agenda contained in imperial cartography.

Local narratives of integrated, accessible water systems are partially the expression of nostalgia for larger and profounder losses associated with the transformation of the agrarian economy and landscape. But there is no question that groundwater based water resources were disrupted, marginalised, and eventually replaced from the early 20th century onwards. Local water management systems in villages, known as *maramatthu*, were abandoned after the introduction of many bore wells and tap water systems. This shift from a reliance on the surface to groundwater led to the neglect of local tanks. Small tanks were converted into wasteland, real estate, and a few converted into agricultural lands. The small water paths or streams that carried surface water to the bigger tanks were no longer needed and became blocked by concrete roads, weeds, muds, and construction. This led to two consequences. First, during the rainy season the small streams, with no route to the tanks, flood the villages. Second, the parched tanks gradually became dumping grounds for rubbish. It is these narratives and disappearance and shrinking water bodies that we next sought to capture in digital poetry through various heterogeneous entities, such as kinetic texts, non-texts, maps, graphics and images.

Digital Poetry: "Lost Water! Remainscape?"

The digital poetry text "Lost Water! Remainscape?" was created using Blender, Adobe Animate CC, Python, and HTML5 and is intended to offer a reimagining and revisitation of the lost waterscapes and a digital conduit that flows between the past and the present. The written text is in both Tamil and English. The balance and relationship between the languages are of particular significance to the authors. English dominates both the colonial archive and DEH scholarly networks. Tamil, spoken as a mother tongue by the first author, is the language of the region and of the interviews with local activists, educators, and communities. The poetry, as well as the other information about water bodies, was written by the first author of this paper, Shanmugapriya, in collaboration with Jagadeesh, a local activist and author who mediated a great deal of the project's fieldwork with local communities.

The digital poetry contains five sections which are titled "Instructions," "Historical Map," "3D River," "3D Water Tanks," and "Photo Animation" (see Figure 14.2). The first one provides detailed information on how to navigate the visuals and graphics to read the poetry and other information. The second has the screenshots of the historical maps from the Survey of India maps of Southern India, depicting the disappeared and shrinking tanks in the Coimbatore region and satellite imagery providing the base layers for the poetry and other information. As shown in Figure 14.3, water tanks are highlighted in shiny white elements. Poetry and explanatory text are implanted in the arrow images (see Figure 14.4). The explanatory texts describe the information about some of the pivotal historical tanks that disappeared and are shrinking currently. They will pop up when the user/player moves the cursor near to them.

The third, 3D River, represents the rivers in the British India Coimbatore region. The 3D digital animations embody features of the waterscape, such as flowing water, fish, butterflies, and trees (see Figure 14.5). These animations were created based on the narrative collected from the interviews. For example, Periyakannan, one of the interviewees, told us that the river Noyyal, which originates in the western gates flows through Coimbatore, was once a robust waterscape and provided many uses, such as transport, recharging groundwater, and food. The animation also captures alternate imaginaries and topographies of the water. For example, the Cauvery and Bhavani Rivers meet at Kooduthurai in the Erode district. The interviewee N. Aruchamy recounted a series of narratives in which the rivers become sentient agents, sensitive to the landscape, to each other and to calendrical time. In these water stories, the river Cauvery would cry if Bhavani did not reach her during a particular festival in the month of August. Another river, called Amirtha Nathi, co-joined with the Cauvery and Bhavani Rivers beneath the water's surface in Kooduthurai. These poetics offer a confluence of water as cultural, devotional, and socio-economic resource and, in doing so, enriches and deepens our understandings of the

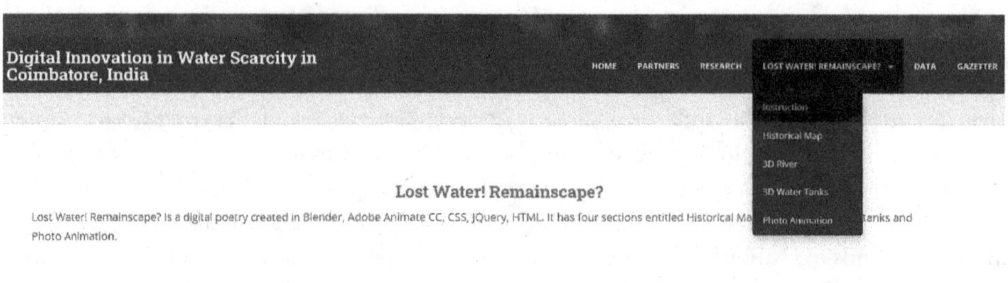

Figure 14.2 Interface of digital poetry "Lost Water! Remainscape?"

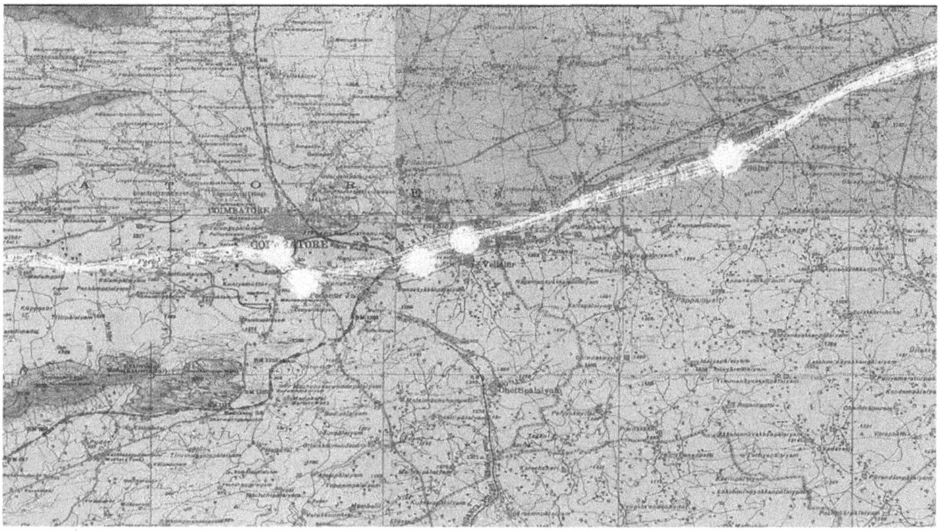

Figure 14.3 The Noyyal River and its tanks are represented by shiny elements.

Image credit: National Library of Scotland

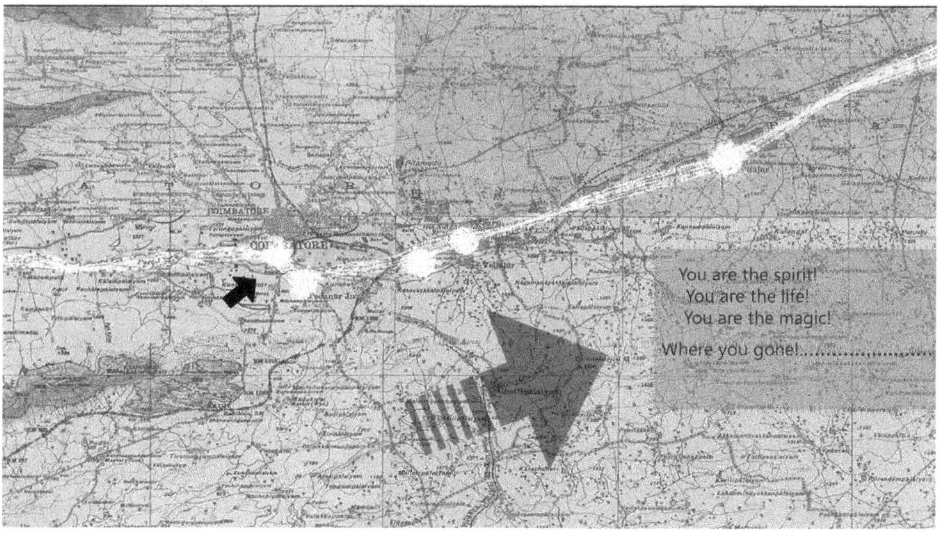

Figure 14.4 Poetry is implanted in the arrow image.

toponymies that exist on maps and government reports. The digital poetry text is designed as an effective digital rhetoric, a deliberate poetic intervention through images and text. The layering of digital information provides the means to represent and explore the complex cultural knowledge of water that linear, static cartesian cartographies exclude.

The fourth, 3D Water Tanks, allow the user to explore water tank systems in the precolonial period. It was created using data from the interviews, literature, and historical texts. For

Figure 14.5 3D animation of the waterscape of a river.

Figure 14.6 The screenshots navigating the scenes in 3D Water Tanks.

example, the 30 historical tanks and 23 anicuts of Noyyal River were created during the Chola period to store its surplus water and to mitigate flooding in the region while maintaining groundwater levels (see Figure 14.6). This visualisation responds to the nostalgia contained in local narratives relating to a precolonial past and emphasises the reliance and focus of precolonial water engineering on surface water rather than groundwater. The visualisation is a deliberate attempt to unsettle the linear trajectory of decline and fragmentation of the recent past. The poetry attempts to reflect the tank systems' significance as part of a local, customary landscape. Most of the local Hindu festivals begin and end with the extraction of water from these tanks. The interviewee Saravanan pointed out that the water scarcity and dry tanks and channels create both productive and cultural precarity.

The last photo animation contains photos that were taken and aggregated during the field visits to the rivers, channels, and tanks. These pictures display the current condition of the water bodies. Most of the tanks and channels in rural places are either dry or occupied by weeds. Many water bodies in the urban and semi-urban places function merely as a wasteland to dump wastes or are used as drainage. For example, Figure 14.7 shows Panjapatti Lake, which was constructed in 1911 during the British India period. It was once a major source for drinking and farming of 18 villages and has been dry for 16 years due to climate change and mismanagement. When the user moves the cursor across the names of the tanks and channels that float on the page, then the

Figure 14.7 Panjapatti Lake at Karur.

poetry and explanatory text pop up. The text will disappear once the reader moves the cursor away from the photos. The details include the information about that particular water body collected from the interview with local people.

Conclusion

DEH provides an opportunity for humanities scholars to experiment with the potential of digital literature through interdisciplinary methods. Such approaches rely upon interactions across a range of perspectives, not only in terms of academic interdisciplinarity but also in the foregrounding of activist and local stakeholder voices, which continue to be vigilant of those inequalities and in pursuing DL as a method for addressing them. In our project, we work closely with local environmental activists Kaviyarasu, Jagadeesh, and Saravanan; students and scholars of our partner institution, Kongunadu Arts and Science College, Coimbatore; authors and journalists Elangovan and Velayutham; and a few NGOs, such as OSAI Environmental Organisation and Diminished Pond Security Merger. The endeavour to produce collaborative works offered an exciting means to discern the proficiency and insights of each other's works and disciplines. At times, our own project struggled to coalesce the very different idioms and preferences of our partners and collaborators. Any research project that draws data from the colonial archive is profoundly aware of the systemic silencing and marginalisation of agency as "informant" in that archive. Our project was also aware of its place within the contemporary inequalities that structure academic work conducted between the minority and majority worlds. Although informed by a range of historical and ethnographic research, the visualisations are synthetic, creative works that are authored by Shanmugapriya T. In the subsequent development of the visualisations, therefore, and in the continuation of the project as the COVID-19 pandemic recedes, the project will endeavour to explore the potential of DL to create collaborations and networks that deliberately offset and to renegotiate these inequalities. The digital poetry "Lost Water! Remainscape?" will be disseminated to students, scholars, activists, and the general public through our previously mentioned academic and NGO partners and local schools and colleges. Feedback and some of the interviews conducted will be made available via the project website: www.lancaster.ac.uk/fass/digital-india.

Funding

This research was supported by the Arts and Humanities Research Council (AHRC), which sponsors the project Digital Innovation in Water Scarcity in Coimbatore, India (Project Reference: AH/T011580/1).

Acknowledgement

We are grateful to Jagadeesh, who wrote the poem in Tamil, and we thank Dharanraj, Mohanapriya, and Naveen Kumar for their technical help and for the creative work. We also deeply thank the editor Deborah P. Dixon, whose reviews and comments helped to improve the article.

Note

1 Given the benefit of digital technologies in examining environmental issues, digital technologies themselves create carbon footprints. Studying the disposal of digital technologies is one of the important aspects of the DEH (Posthumus and Sinclair 2017, 372).

Sources

Carter, R. A. 2020. "Electronic Literature in the Anthropocene." *Electronic Book Review*. https://doi.org/10.7273/rt06-ts14.

Drucker, Johanna. 2018. "Non-Representational Approaches to Modeling Interpretation in a Graphical Environment." *Digital Scholarship in the Humanities* 33 (2) (June): 248–63. https://doi.org/10.1093/llc/fqx034.

Electronic Literature Collection. n.d. "Electronic Literature Organization." https://collection.eliterature.org/.

Electronic Literature Directory. n.d. "Electronic Literature Organization." https://directory.eliterature.org/.

Electronic Literature Organization. n.d. "Electronic Literature Organization." https://eliterature.org/2021/08/call-for-elo-research-fellows-2022/.

Ferster, Bill. 2013. *Interactive Visualization: Insight through Inquiry*. Cambridge, MA: MIT Press.

Funkhouser, Chris. 2007. *Prehistoric Digital Poetry: An Archeology of Forms, 1959–1995*. Tuscaloosa, AL: University of Alabama Press.

Hofste, R., and L. Schleifer. 2019. *17 Countries, Home to One-Quarter of the World's Population, Face Extremely High Water Stress*. World Resource Institute. www.wri.org/insights/17-countries-home-one-quarter-worlds-population-face-extremely-high-water-stress.

Krause, A., and E. P. Bucy. 2018. "Interpreting Images of Fracking: How Visual Frames and Standing Attitudes Shape Perceptions of Environmental Risk and Economic Benefit." *Environmental Communication* 12 (3): 322–43. https://doi.org/10.1080/17524032.2017.1412996.

Lakoff, George. 2010. "Why it Matters How We Frame the Environment." *Environmental Communication* 4: 70–81. https://doi.org/10.1080/17524030903529749.

Lutz, T. 1959. *Stochastische Texte*. Karlsruhe: Center for Art and Media. https://zkm.de/en/artwork/stochastic-texts.

Metze, Tamara. 2020. "Visualization in Environmental Policy and Planning: A Systematic Review and Research Agenda." *Journal of Environmental Policy & Planning* 22: 745–60. https://doi.org/10.1080/1523908X.2020.1798751.

Mirzoeff, Nicholas. 2014. "Visualizing the Anthropocene." *Public Culture* 26: 213–32. https://doi.org/10.1215/08992363-2392039.

Ortega, E., J. O'Sullivan, and D. Grigar. 2016. "Intersectional Scholarship in Electronic Literature and Digital Humanities." Digital Humanities 2016: Conference Abstracts. Jagiellonian University & Pedagogical University, Kraków, 82–85.

Pereira, Silva Paulo. 2020. "Greening the Digital Muse: An Ecocritical Examination of Contemporary Digital Art and Literature." *Electronic Book Review*. https://doi.org/10.7273/v30n-1a73.

Posthumus, S., and S. Sinclair. 2017. "Digital? Environmental: Humanities." In *Routledge Companion to the Environmental Humanities*, edited by J. Christenson, U. Heise, and M. Niemann, 369–77. London: Routledge.

Priya, Jennifer, G., G. Thankam, S. Thankam, and M. Mathew. 2011. "Monitoring the Pollution Intensity of Wetlands of Coimbatore, Tamil Nadu, India." *Nature Environment Pollution Technology* 12 (3): 447–54.

Report of the Indian Irrigation Commission, 1901–1903. London. 1903.

Rettberg, Scott. 2016. "Electronic Literature as Digital Humanities." In *A New Companion to Digital Humanities*, edited by S. Schreibman, R. Siemens, and J. Unsworth, 127–36. Chichester: Wiley Blackwell.

Roberts, Siobhan. 2017. "Christopher Strachey's Nineteen-Fifties Love Machine." *The New Yorker*, February 14, 2017. www.newyorker.com/tech/annals-of-technology/christopher-stracheys-nineteen-fifties-love-machine.

Rudd, J. A., R. Horry, and R. L. Skains. 2020. "You and CO2: A Public Engagement Study to Engage Secondary School Students with the Issue of Climate Change." *Journal of Science Education and Technology* 29 (2): 230–41. https://doi.org/10.1007/s10956-019-09808-5.

Shanmugapriya, T., and N. Menon. 2018a. "Locating New Literary Practices in Indian Digital Spaces." *MATLIT: Materialities of Literature* 6 (1): 159–74. https://doi.org/10.14195/2182-8830_6-1_11.

———. 2019b. "First and Second Waves of Indian Electronic Literature." *Journal of Comparative Literature and Aesthetics* 42 (4): 63–71.

Sheppard, S. R. J. 2005. "Landscape Visualisation and Climate Change: The Potential for Influencing Perceptions and Behaviour." *Environmental Science and Policy* 8 (6): 637–54. https://doi.org/10.1016/j.envsci.2005.08.002.

Travis, C., and P. Holm. 2016. "The Digital Environmental Humanities – What Is It and Why Do We Need It? the NorFish Project and SmartCity Lifeworlds. Edited by C. Travis and A. von Lünen." In *The Digital Arts and Humanities*, 187–204. Cham: Springer Geography. Springer. https://doi.org/10.1007/978-3-319-40953-5_11.

15

RELATIONALITY IN THE ONLINE LITERARY JOURNAL *SPIRAL ORB*

Eric Magrane and Wendy Burk

Introduction

We write as founding editor of the online poetry journal *Spiral Orb* (spiralorb.net) (Magrane) and as a production editor and guest editor (Burk). From 2010 to 2019, *Spiral Orb* published 15 issues. The journal's online format and design are intended to encourage a particular kind of reading, a hypertextual experience akin to early ideas of the internet. That is, rather than take the form of a simple translation of a print journal construct onto a web format, *Spiral Orb* is designed with the form of a hypertextual web in mind. Excerpts from all works published in an issue are composted into an entry poem that serves as the table of contents for that issue. Readers navigate by clicking on hyperlinks embedded in the entry poem; once a reader arrives at a poem, they find additional links embedded in the work to other poems from the issue. The resulting digital ecology of authorship, screen, text, and reading offers what Magrane (2010) called "an experiment in permaculture poetics," referencing *Spiral Orb*'s systems focus and the multiple functions that each work published in an issue serves through its hypertextual relationships with the rest of the journal.

In this chapter, we discuss and reflect on the organisation and structure of *Spiral Orb* as a digital ecology and environment. Jørgensen (2014) notes, "If we think of technology as a set of relations – social, economic, even epistemological – the digital turn certainly embodies the same kind of relations" (109). In the context of *Spiral Orb* and this chapter, we mean for our use of the terms "ecology" and "systems" to similarly inflect the DEH as a set of relations, an approach that applies to ecosystems both physical and metaphorical.[1] We use the term "environment" in this chapter with two inflections. First, we address the environment in the sense of *surroundings*. For example, the relationships among the works in an issue of *Spiral Orb* represent a kind of ecology or ecosystem that exists within the broader environment (surroundings) of the journal and of the Web. Second, we note that many of the individual poems and issues of *Spiral Orb* address environmental concerns in their content, such as species protection, loss of biodiversity, and the effects of human impact. The terms "ecology" and "environment" are often intertwined and linked in the environmental humanities, as in Rose et al.'s (2012) claim that the environmental humanities are an approach "that rejects reductionist accounts of self-contained, rational, decision-making subjects. Rather, the environmental humanities positions us as participants in lively ecologies of meaning and value" (2). The relational approach we take here also echoes

 DOI: 10.4324/9781003082798-19

feminist scholarship and practices of "becoming with" and kinship (Haraway 2008, 2016). *Spiral Orb*, as structured and presented online, allows its poems to become with others. An individual poem is more than a self-contained poem-object; it is a vital energy-construct interacting within the environment of *Spiral Orb*.

In what follows, we briefly summarise the emergence of the journal before contextualising the conceptual framework of permaculture poetics and how this concept is embodied in the journal's layout and design. Then we discuss a series of special issues that the journal published: two poetic/literary inventories and three collaborative curation issues. Inventories include "A Poetic Inventory of Saguaro National Park" (issue 5) and "A Literary Inventory of Organ Mountains-Desert Peaks" (issue 15) and feature a total of 135 contributors who wrote poetry and prose addressed to species who live in Saguaro National Park and Organ Mountains-Desert Peaks National Monument (OMDP) in the Southwestern United States. The collaborative curation issues (7, 10, and 13) featured a distributed curatorial process in which Burk invited contributors to invite other writers to participate in the issue.

Since its inception in 2011, *Spiral Orb* has been a small DIY-style journal and a labour of love. Magrane came up with the initial concept, design, and structure; he and Burk are the only editors of the journal. Designed with Adobe Dreamweaver and hosted by GoDaddy (godaddy.com), the site takes in no revenue and has no advertisements. Submissions were managed over e-mail until issue 8 when the journal began using Submittable, a common submission platform for literary journals and presses. Magrane made the editorial decisions on what to publish for open issues and on revision requests. In general, about 5 to 10% of open submissions were accepted. On average, each regular issue of *Spiral Orb* contained 14 poems, of which two were solicited from invited writers and twelve were accepted through the open submissions process. (The poetic/literary inventory issues and the collaborative curation issues were edited differently, as we describe later in this chapter.) The journal published an eclectic mix of emerging and established poets and has been listed or featured in magazines and websites geared to professional writers, including *Poets & Writers*, *NewPages*, and *Duotrope*. As of 2021, *Spiral Orb* is on hiatus from publishing new issues,[2] giving us time and space to reflect on its run in the context of DEH.

A brief explanatory text at the foot of *Spiral Orb*'s home page describes the journal as "an experiment in juxtaposition, interrelationships, and intertextuality – a cross-pollination." After 15 issues of the *Spiral Orb* project, we find that the ideas of juxtaposition, interrelationship, and intertextuality continue to encapsulate the conceptual and formal expression of the journal. Accordingly, in this chapter, we describe and reflect on the *Spiral Orb* project as an example of how relationality, linkages, formal experimentation, and de- and re-composition can be integral to DEH practices.

Permaculture Poetics, Relational Systems, and Stacked Functions

The concept of stacked functions, or multifunctionality, in which each element of a system provides multiple functions, is key to the practice of permaculture (Holmgren 2002). As an example, in Tucson, Arizona (where we lived at the time of *Spiral Orb*'s founding), we plumbed the greywater from our washing machine to a basin by the laundry shed, where we planted a citrus tree. Every time we did laundry, we were also watering the tree. As the tree grew, its shade mitigated the searing desert heat, the reuse of greywater reduced our overall water footprint, and we had juicy oranges to eat for most of the winter.

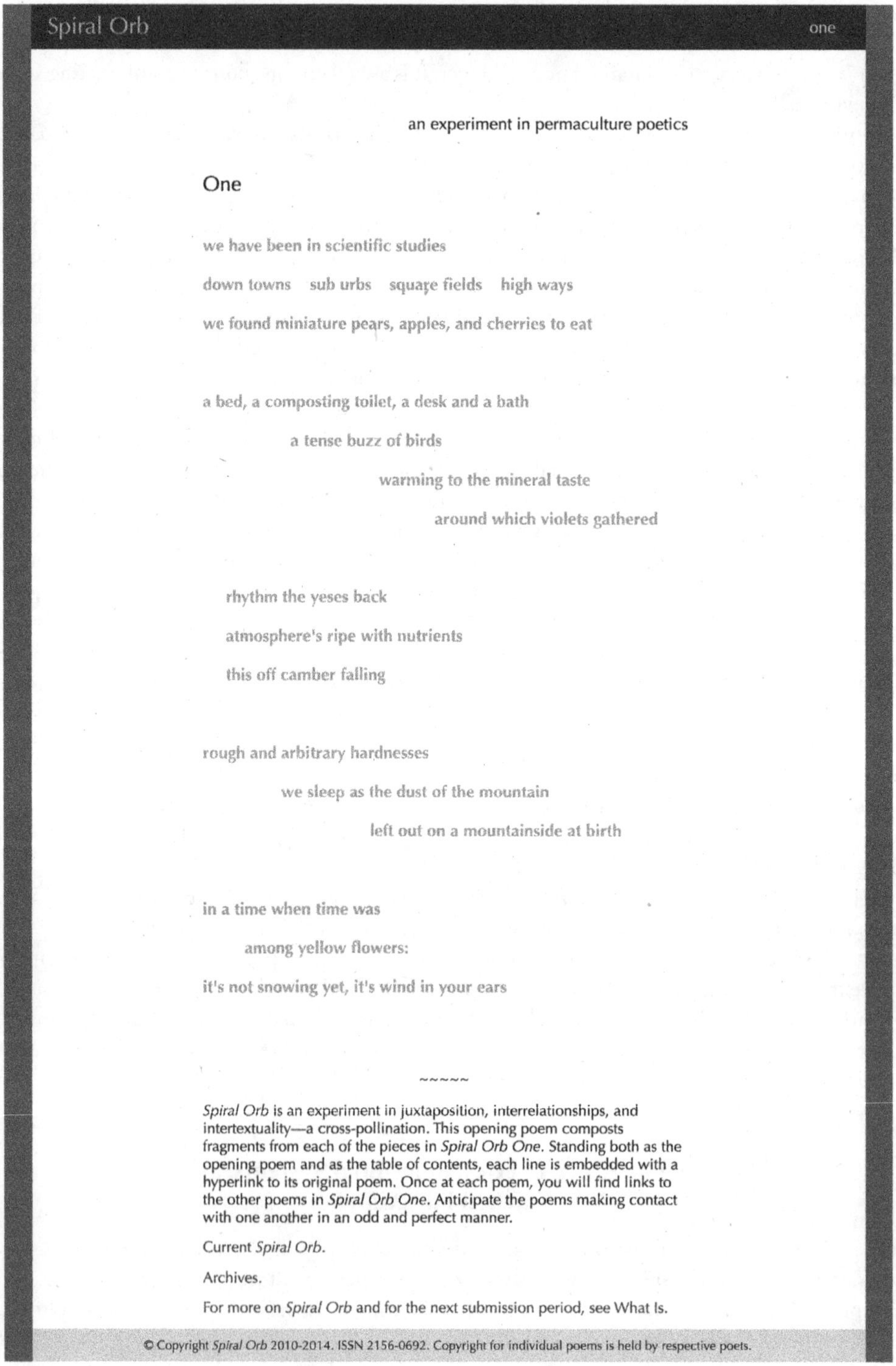

Spiral Orb one

an experiment in permaculture poetics

One

we have been in scientific studies
down towns sub urbs square fields high ways
we found miniature pears, apples, and cherries to eat

a bed, a composting toilet, a desk and a bath
a tense buzz of birds
warming to the mineral taste
around which violets gathered

rhythm the yeses back
atmosphere's ripe with nutrients
this off camber falling

rough and arbitrary hardnesses
we sleep as the dust of the mountain
left out on a mountainside at birth

in a time when time was
among yellow flowers:
it's not snowing yet, it's wind in your ears

~~~~~

Spiral Orb is an experiment in juxtaposition, interrelationships, and intertextuality—a cross-pollination. This opening poem composts fragments from each of the pieces in *Spiral Orb One*. Standing both as the opening poem and as the table of contents, each line is embedded with a hyperlink to its original poem. Once at each poem, you will find links to the other poems in *Spiral Orb One*. Anticipate the poems making contact with one another in an odd and perfect manner.

Current *Spiral Orb*.

Archives.

For more on *Spiral Orb* and for the next submission period, see What Is.

© Copyright *Spiral Orb* 2010-2014. ISSN 2156-0692. Copyright for individual poems is held by respective poets.

Figure 15.1 Entry poem.
~~~~~

Magrane (2010) gave *Spiral Orb* the byline "an experiment in permaculture poetics" in reference to the concept of stacked functions as a metaphorical framework for the journal's design.[3] Each poem in an issue, for instance, contributes a line or phrase to the entry poem, and it links to other poems within the issue. The multiple functions for works published in the journal reflect the idea that each issue represents a digital relational ecosystem rather than a collection of discrete poem-objects. The entry poem also embodies this idea. Rather than differentiating between titles and authors as a traditional table of contents would, it places the poems in relation to each other as a meeting place, where lines and fragments combine to create new resonances, frictions, and intertextual readings. It can be said that, through the entry poem, the works published in an issue of *Spiral Orb* are in a sense reading each other, as well as reading us as editors. The reading relationship is decentred from author-text-reader to be more multi-directional, and the texts are performative as much as or more than they are representational (Crang 2015).

The use of compost is another important element of permaculture (Holmgren 2002) and is a key conceptual framework for *Spiral Orb*. At its base, composting is the recycling of matter: starting with organic scraps, then adding water, heat, and aeration to produce rich soil for new growth. Our editorial and curatorial process of selecting fragments and lines from poems in *Spiral Orb* and remixing them into a new work represents a recycling of poem-matter, hence a composting practice. In this practice, Magrane (or Burk, for the issues she guest-edited) reviews the page proofs for the individual poems to be published in an issue, selecting lines or fragments of lines that stand out for their striking use of language and their potential resonance (or, in some cases, assonance) with other selected lines. These lines are arranged in a blank document and ordered and reordered until the internal logic and music of a poem are apparent. As compost is turned and mixed into new matter, so too do the lines of individual poems undergo several reorganisations and recombinations on their way to becoming a coherent entry poem.

The metaphor of poetry as compost is an ecopoetic and geopoetic notion (Rasula 2002; de Leeuw and Magrane 2019) in which poetic practice can be attuned to ecological and geographical concerns. Here, poetics as making might be considered a recycling of matter, growth and decay, rotting, and de- and re-composition. To borrow Olson's conception of a poem as a "high-energy construct" ([1950] 1997, 240), the de- and re-composition that takes place in *Spiral Orb*'s entry poems is a form of energy transformation. The energy that a particular fragment or line exhibits in the context of the original poem changes through its interaction with other fragments in the entry poem. We suggest that the re-composed poetry in *Spiral Orb* and its articulation in the form of the online journal-object are instances of "vibrant matter" (Haraway 2008; Bennett 2010; Peacock 2012). We are certainly present as editors in the curatorial choices that we make by selecting lines and fragments for the entry poem and the links between poems. Nevertheless, we believe that the issues have their own vitalism outside of our editorial and curatorial decisions. This vitalism is lodged in the intertextual relationships enacted across *Spiral Orb*'s online presentation, as a reader interacts with the journal and as the poems interact with each other.

Design Simplicity and *Spiral Orb* as "Deformance"

Spiral Orb has a purposefully stripped-down design that has remained consistent throughout the journal's run: a simple off-white reading page set in front of a grey background; text in Garamond or Optima font, dependent upon browser; and black, green (to indicate links), or red (for hovering over a link) text colour. Continued simplicity in design has helped to spotlight the journal's primary hyperlink organisational structure rather than foregrounding web design trends. The design is meant to hearken back to the early possibilities of the internet and hyperlinked reading. Through *Spiral Orb*'s design simplicity, readers are encouraged to engage with an issue in a manner akin to a "choose your own adventure" reading experience. Each click leads to multiple possibilities and pathways for further movement through the issue. Because most readers' initial encounters with an issue occur through the entry poem – which deliberately omits titles, authors' names, and other attributions – the traditional notion of authorship recedes. Beyond the entry poem, which links to anywhere from 12 to more than 80 works, each poem leads to two other poems within the same issue, each of these poems links to two more poems, and so on until the reader comes full circle. When the reader clicks on a line from the entry poem to access other works in the issue, additional resonances emerge in response to the reader's individual strategy of navigation. The possibility of a front-to-back or hierarchical ordering does not exist. Each engagement with an issue leads to a new immanent order, bringing new possibilities for interpretation. We liken this multiplicity of navigation to how McGann and Samuels (2001) work with Emily Dickinson's idea of reading a poem backwards to posit *deformance* as an act of critical literary interpretation:

> [T]he critical and interpretive question is not "what does the poem mean?" but "how do we release or expose the poem's possibilities of meaning?" Dickinson's reading proposal has nothing to say about "meaning" at all, new or old. Her thought, her *idea*, is not a reimagined meaning but a project for reconstituting the work's aesthetic form, as if a disordering of one's senses of the work would make us dwellers in possibility.
> *(McGann and Samuels 2001, 108)*

While they apply this deformative approach to individual poems by Stevens and Coleridge, it strikes us that our editing process for *Spiral Orb* might also be considered one of deformance. Although the individual poems themselves appear unchanged, the act of excerpting fragments to include in the entry poem is also a kind of deformance. McGann and Samuels (2001) go on to describe the procedures of deformance: "A deformative procedure puts the reader in a highly idiosyncratic relation to the work . . . deformance sends both reader and work through the textual looking glass" (116). In our function as editors of *Spiral Orb*, we are also active readers: our choice of lines and fragments to juxtapose and reconstitute into the entry poem emerges from our close reading of and engagement with the issue's contributions.

Literary Inventories

Issues 5 and 15 of *Spiral Orb* (published in 2014 and 2019) featured "A Poetic Inventory of Saguaro National Park" and "A Literary Inventory of Organ Mountains-Desert Peaks National Monument." In these issues, contributors wrote poems or short prose pieces addressed to species who live in Saguaro National Park in Tucson, Arizona, and OMDP in Las Cruces, New Mexico. Eighty writers contributed to "A Poetic Inventory of Saguaro National Park," while 55 writers contributed to "A Literary Inventory of Organ Mountains-Desert Peaks National Monument."

The literary inventory issues were connected with BioBlitzes held at Saguaro National Park and OMDP in October 2011 and May 2019, respectively. These were large-scale biological survey events sponsored by the National Geographic Society and the US National Park Service, in which citizen scientists joined researchers in documenting and inventorying species in the parks. The idea for a literary inventory focused on US public lands grew out of Magrane's (2011) work on an art planning committee for the Saguaro National Park BioBlitz:

> Leading up to the 2011 National Park Service and National Geographic Society Bio-Blitz at Saguaro National Park, I asked poets and writers to write pieces based on species in the park. Mirroring the inventory form of the BioBlitz, in which the public joined scientists in doing species inventories within the park, the Poetic Inventory took another view at biodiversity: how do we, as Homo sapiens – one species among many – relate with other species? The project's contributors used various modes to address their species. Some wrote poems taking the voice of their species; some wrote celebrations of their species; some wrote to their species, addressing them in the form of an ode or asking questions; some wrote playful lyrics; some followed the human name of the species into a poem, letting language be a species itself; some created new fairy tales.
>
> *(Magrane 2011)*

Public reading events featuring contributors to the literary inventories took place on the public lands during the BioBlitzes. Collaborations with other organisations, including the University of Arizona Poetry Center and the Las Cruces Museum of Nature and Science, led to additional public events featuring work from the issues. The Poetic Inventory of Saguaro National Park was further developed into a book project, *The Sonoran Desert: A Literary Field Guide* (Magrane and Cokinos 2016), which inspired other literary field guide publications in the bioregional model (Malone 2013; McLarney, Street, and Gaddy 2019; Magrane 2020).

These two issues of *Spiral Orb* are the ones that have most explicitly engaged with a bioregional model for community environmental writing. While, in general, contributors to *Spiral Orb* hail from diverse locations worldwide, and the journal's guidelines for open submissions place no restrictions on subject or theme, all of the contributors to the literary inventories had a physical connection to Saguaro National Park or OMDP – most of them living in the communities adjacent to these public lands – and all of the works published in issues 5 and 15 focused on species living within the parks. "A Poetic Inventory of Saguaro National Park" was built on Magrane's experience as a hiking guide and naturalist in the Sonoran Desert and his longstanding ties with the literary community of Tucson. On the other hand, "A Literary Inventory of Organ Mountains-Desert Peaks" was a way for Magrane (2019) to get to know a community where he had newly arrived:

> As I recently moved to Las Cruces, New Mexico to take a position in the Department of Geography at New Mexico State University (NMSU), I have approached this Literary Inventory of Organ Mountains-Desert Peaks as a means for me to begin to get to know the community here – both the human and the more-than-human communities. As a geographer, I think of this project as a public geohumanities project, a multi-vocal expression and gathering of how a human community knows, gets to know, and represents the other species with whom they share this place.
>
> *(Magrane 2019)*

The hyperlinked form of *Spiral Orb* is particularly suited to the literary inventory issues. The links from one species-piece to another mirror the interwoven ecological relationships that make up a bioregion, as well as reflecting affinities in content, language, or tone between the literary works. For example, Amaris Feland Ketcham (2019), a participant in the OMDP literary inventory writing about the Scott's oriole, describes the yellow-and-black desert bird as "tying the yucca's loose ends." This phrase from Ketcham's poem refers to the Scott's oriole's close association with yuccas, which are desert plants known for their loose cascades of long, slender leaves. As published in *Spiral Orb* 15, the phrase is embedded with a link to Andrea Blancas Beltran's (2019) poem for the Soaptree yucca: an editorial choice that underscores the ecological relationship between the bird and the plant. When a reader clicks on the words "tying the yucca's loose ends" and is transported to Beltran's poem, they encounter poetic images that resonate with Ketcham's work, including a memorable description of yucca plants that "lean / into sundry directions . . . across / artificial borderlines" (Beltran 2019). Each literary inventory issue is a web of relations, a multispecies poetic ecology.

Collaborative Curation

Issues 7, 10, and 13 of *Spiral Orb* (published in 2014, 2015, and 2017) were a linked series centred on a collaborative curation process. For issue 7, subtitled "Marks, Lines, and Lineage," guest editor Wendy Burk invited a group of authors whose work she admired to contribute a text to the issue and also asked them to invite another author to contribute. The published issue included the authors who accepted Burk's invitation and the authors invited by those authors. The work was presented in the same format as other issues of *Spiral Orb*, with a composted entry poem

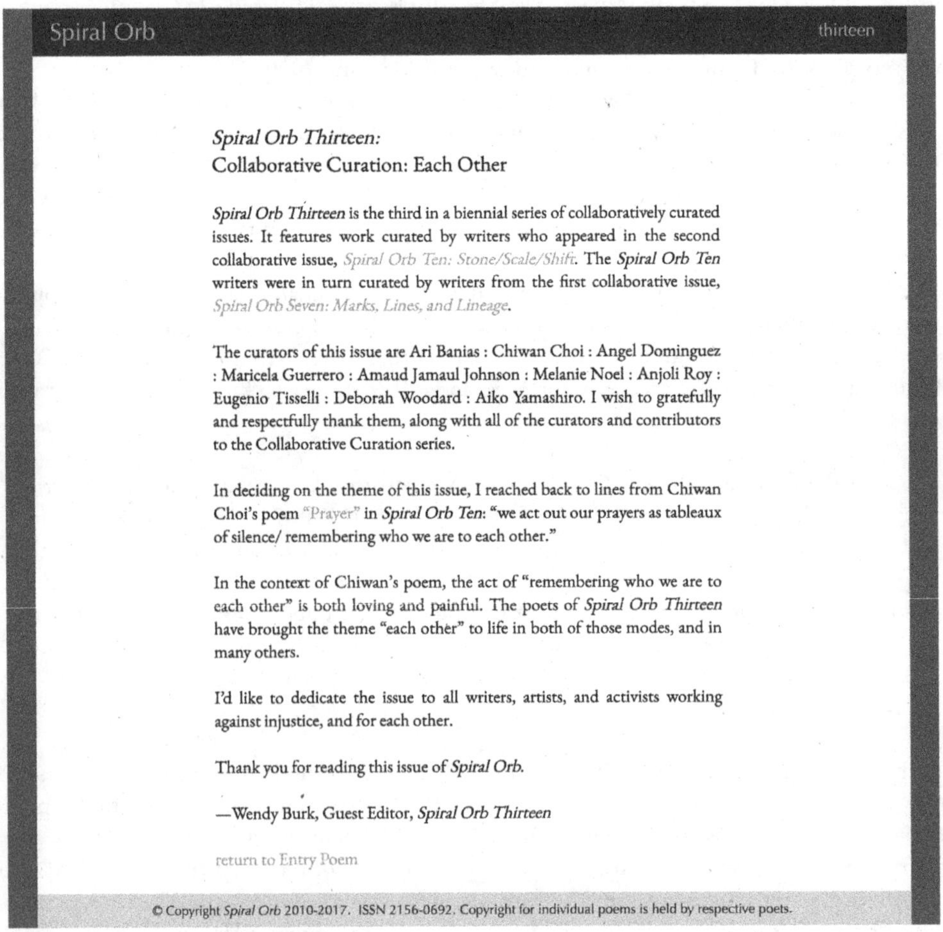
Spiral Orb

thirteen

Spiral Orb Thirteen:
Collaborative Curation: Each Other

Spiral Orb Thirteen is the third in a biennial series of collaboratively curated issues. It features work curated by writers who appeared in the second collaborative issue, *Spiral Orb Ten: Stone/Scale/Shift*. The *Spiral Orb Ten* writers were in turn curated by writers from the first collaborative issue, *Spiral Orb Seven: Marks, Lines, and Lineage*.

The curators of this issue are Ari Banias : Chiwan Choi : Angel Dominguez : Maricela Guerrero : Amaud Jamaul Johnson : Melanie Noel : Anjoli Roy : Eugenio Tisselli : Deborah Woodard : Aiko Yamashiro. I wish to gratefully and respectfully thank them, along with all of the curators and contributors to the Collaborative Curation series.

In deciding on the theme of this issue, I reached back to lines from Chiwan Choi's poem "Prayer" in *Spiral Orb Ten*: "we act out our prayers as tableaux of silence/ remembering who we are to each other."

In the context of Chiwan's poem, the act of "remembering who we are to each other" is both loving and painful. The poets of *Spiral Orb Thirteen* have brought the theme "each other" to life in both of those modes, and in many others.

I'd like to dedicate the issue to all writers, artists, and activists working against injustice, and for each other.

Thank you for reading this issue of *Spiral Orb.*

—Wendy Burk, Guest Editor, *Spiral Orb Thirteen*

return to Entry Poem

© Copyright *Spiral Orb* 2010-2017. ISSN 2156-0692. Copyright for individual poems is held by respective poets.

Figure 15.2 Collaborative curation.

and links between poems, and with the addition of an editor's note explaining the concept of the issue. For issue 10, "Stone/Scale/Shift," all of the authors from issue 7 were asked to invite an author to contribute to issue 10. Thus, none of the authors published in issue 10 was directly invited by Burk. The same process was followed for issue 13, "Each Other," whose authors were invited by the contributors from issue 10.[4]

For each *Collaborative Curation* issue, writers were asked to contribute a single text of their own choosing, of any length, style, or theme, written in any language or in more than one language. Burk requested that authors include in their text one or more of the words from the issue's subtitle (such as "mark," "line," or "lineage" for issue 7). Many authors included one or more of the words directly in their text; other authors included variations on the words or chose to align their text thematically with one of the words. Burk accepted and published the texts as submitted by the writers. Her curatorial decision-making over the course of the three issues was limited to the selection of a theme for each issue, the selection of the initial group of authors who comprised half of issue 7, and the writing of an editor's note for each issue.

Burk thought of the *Collaborative Curation* series as an extension of *Spiral Orb*'s focus on interrelationships. In a curation process guided by a single editor or group of editors, a more or less cohesive relationship arises among the works published in a literary journal, mediated by the worldviews, tastes, identities, and affiliations of the editors. Burk (2014) was seeking "alternative ways of generating [physical and digital] networks." In her editor's note, she described her interest in "art that grows and changes thanks to a changing group of creators" (Burk 2014).

Burk hoped to see the *Collaborative Curation* issues evolve from the varied interrelationships between authors inviting other authors. As an example, one of the authors invited for issue 7 published their own text in the issue and was also the translator of another author's text. As another example, also drawn from issue 7, one author invited a second author whose work was translated by a third author; all three of the authors went on to invite contributors to issue 10. Authors invited their students and their teachers; authors dedicated their work to other authors published in the series. Thus, the *Collaborative Curation* series is not the product of a unified editorial aesthetic, but neither does it represent a depersonalised or objective process. Like the Web itself or like a stripped-down social network, the series represents an array of purposeful and subjective yet also chance-driven linkages: "a system of non-linear lineage" (Burk 2014).[5]

The title of Manuel Fihman's (2014) poem from issue 7, "Juego en Evolución/Evolving Game," embodies the way in which each *Collaborative Curation* issue functions on its own but also evolves from the previous issue. From the editor's standpoint, initiating a collaborative curation process caused Burk's literary concerns and interpretations to evolve as she followed threads from the authors of one issue to another. A lack of curatorial direction did not result in a lack of investment. Rather, the surprises and singularities generated by not controlling the curatorial process fostered Burk's engagement with and appreciation of the texts published in the *Collaborative Curation* series. The distributed agency across the *Collaborative Curation* issues resulted in a digital environment in which the special issues' expression evolved from the concerns of Burk and contributing curators into something more: something with its own vitality.

Conclusion

Spiral Orb's relationality is crucial to understanding the journal as a DEH project. At the conceptual and design levels, each issue is a relational hyperlinked experience. When reflecting on the journal as a digital ecology and environment, we return to the idea that the individual pieces that make up the journal are also made into something else in their "becoming with" other pieces of the journal. Through curatorial and editorial practices of de- and re-composition and deformance, the hyperlinked design lends vibrancy and performativity to *Spiral Orb*, one that is not centred on individual works published by the journal but on the juxtapositions and interrelations that are enacted and presented.

The design simplicity and hyperlinked system have also allowed us to experiment with place-based community environmental writing projects, such as the literary inventories, and strategies of distributed curation, such as the collaborative curation issues, and present them in a manner that links form to content. In particular, as evidenced by the special issues discussed in this chapter, editing the journal has been a relational and community-engaged experience. The editing process is about building relationships as much as it is about building an issue. *Spiral Orb* is an example of how DEH journals can be considered social practices and a means to develop relationships with contributors or to extend relationships further.

At a basic level, the ecological and environmental crises of the current moment are founded on off-kilter and broken relationships: between humans, other-than-humans, and forms of matter and between humans and ecological systems. It seems to us that a goal of DEH practices can be the fostering, resetting, and even deforming and recomposing of some of these relationships. This goal was, in many ways, the goal of *Spiral Orb* – in its form, in its content, and in its practice.

Notes

1 We also recognise cautions against uncritical use of ecological and environmental metaphors in the DEH, especially in relation to the energy infrastructure and carbon footprint of the cloud (Carruth 2014). As with any website, *Spiral Orb* does have an energy footprint, although its simple Web 1.0 design style keeps its footprint relatively small. Based on an analysis on websitecarbon.com on 13 September 2021, *Spiral Orb* produces 0.38 kilograms of CO_2 equivalent per year, which the carbon calculator notes is "cleaner than 99% of web pages tested."

2 The last issue of *Spiral Orb* was published in 2019. Like many small literary journals, *Spiral Orb* is edited by a handful of people (in our case, the two of us). Because of other commitments and projects, we are currently not planning to publish any new issues; however, that may change in the future.

3 The permaculture poetics of *Spiral Orb* is, in its primary sense, a theoretical and practical framework for the journal's organisation and embedded relationships. For an in-depth approach to permapoesis as a living and making practice, see Patrick Jones' project of permapoesis as "the portmanteau for permanent making; making that comes from permaculture living practices" (2013, ix). Jones also contributed a slow-text to the first issue of *Spiral Orb*.

4 A full list of the curators/contributors for *Spiral Orb* 7, 10, and 13 (in alphabetical order): Juana Adcock, Jamaica Baldwin, Ari Banias, Rocío Carlos, Chiwan Choi, Don Mee Choi, Donovan Kūhiō Colleps, Angel Dominguez, Joshua Jennifer Espinoza, Manuel Fihman, Hugo García Manríquez, Maricela Guerrero, Yona Harvey, Jen Hofer, Amaud Jamaul Johnson, Douglas Kearney, Hannah Kezema, Rajiv Mohabir, Tracie Morris, Melanie Noel, Óscar de Pablo, G.E. Patterson, Craig Santos Perez, JD Pluecker, Frances Richard, Cristina Rivera Garza, Lester Robles, Anjoli Roy, Lauren Russell, Danez Smith, Simon Seisho Tajiri, Eugenio Tisselli, Jennifer Tseng, Sara Uribe, Ellen Welcker, Deborah Woodard, Aiko Yamashiro, Maged Zaher, Lila Zemborain, and Samantha Zighelboim.

5 Here, we would also like to note Ortega's (2019) arguments in "*Zonas de Contacto*: A Digital Humanities Ecology of Knowledges," particularly "the self-reflexive capacity of knowledge production as a social practice to modify its own operations" (para. 8) and "the process of creating horizontal platforms, and thus hetero-referentiality" (para. 18) in the digital humanities. The collaborative curation process fostered a plurality of voices and poems, including poems in English and Spanish and visual poems, and we believe that Burk's (2014) conception of the collaborative curation issues as "a system of non-linear lineage" does some of this contact work as well.

Sources

Beltran, Andrea Blancas. 2019. "*Yucca elata*: Soaptree Yucca." *Spiral Orb* 15. https://spiralorb.net/fifteen/beltran.

Bennett, Jane. 2010. *Vibrant Matter*. Durham, NC: Duke University Press. https://doi.org/10.1215/9780822391623.

Burk, Wendy. 2014. "*Spiral Orb Seven*: Collaborative Curation: Marks, Lines, and Lineage." *Spiral Orb* 7. https://spiralorb.net/seven/about.html.

Carruth, Allison. 2014. "The Digital Cloud and the Micropolitics of Energy." *Public Culture* 26 (2) (Spring): 339–64. https://doi.org/10.1215/08992363-2392093.

Crang, Mike. 2015. "The Promises and Perils of a Digital Geohumanities." *Cultural Geographies* 22 (2) (April): 351–60. https://doi.org/10.1177/1474474015572303.

de Leeuw, Sarah, and Eric Magrane. 2019. "Geopoetics." In *Keywords in Radical Geography:* Antipode *at 50*, edited by the *Antipode* Editorial Collective, 146–50. Hoboken, NJ and Oxford, UK: Wiley-Blackwell. https://doi.org/10.1002/9781119558071.ch26.

Fihman, Manuel. 2014. "Juego en Evolución/Evolving Game." *Spiral Orb* 7. https://spiralorb.net/seven/fihman.html.

Haraway, Donna. 2008. *When Species Meet*. Minneapolis: University of Minnesota Press.

———. 2016. *Staying with the Trouble*. Durham, NC: Duke University Press. https://doi.org/10.1215/9780822373780.

Holmgren, David. 2002. *Permaculture: Principles and Pathways Beyond Sustainability*. Hepburn, Victoria, Australia: Holmgren Design Services.

Jones, Patrick. 2013. "Walking for Food: Regaining Permapoesis." DCA Diss, University of Western Sydney.

Jørgensen, Finn Arne. 2014. "The Armchair Traveller's Guide to Digital Environmental Humanities." *Environmental Humanities* 4 (1) (May): 95–112. https://doi.org/10.1215/22011919-3614944.

Ketcham, Amaris Feland. 2019. "*Icterus parisorum*: Scott's Oriole." *Spiral Orb* 15. https://spiralorb.net/fifteen/ketcham.

Magrane, Eric. 2010. "Spiral Orb One." *Spiral Orb* 1. https://spiralorb.net/one/.

———. 2011. "*Spiral Orb Five*: A Poetic Inventory of Saguaro National Park." *Spiral Orb* 5. https://spiralorb.net/poeticinventory.html.

———. 2019. "*Spiral Orb Fifteen*: A Literary Inventory of Organ Mountains-Desert Peaks National Monument." *Spiral Orb* 15. https://spiralorb.net/omdp.html.

———. 2020. "Literary Field Guides and Poetic Inventories in the Extended Rocky Mountain Region." In *The Rocky Mountain West: A Compendium of Geographic Perspectives*, edited by Michael Keables, 72–76. Washington, DC: American Association of Geographers.

Magrane, Eric, and Christopher Cokinos, eds. 2016. *The Sonoran Desert: A Literary Field Guide*. Tucson: The University of Arizona Press.

Malone, Charles, ed. 2013. *A Poetic Inventory of Rocky Mountain National Park*. Fort Collins, CO: Wolverine Farm Publishing.

McGann, Jerome and Lisa Samuels. 2001. "Deformance and Interpretation." In *Radiant Textuality: Literature After the World Wide Web*, 105–35. New York: Palgrave Macmillan.

McLarney, Rose, Laura-Gray Street, and L. L. Gaddy, eds. 2019. *A Literary Field Guide to Southern Appalachia*. Athens: University of Georgia Press.

Olson, Charles. [1950] 1997. "Projective Verse." In *Collected Prose*, edited by Donald Allen and Benjamin Friedlander, 239–49. Oakland: University of California Press.

Ortega, Élika. 2019. "*Zonas de Contacto*: A Digital Humanities Ecology of Knowledges." In *Debates in the Digital Humanities 2019*, edited by Matthew K. Gold and Lauren F. Klein. Minneapolis: University of Minnesota Press. https://dhdebates.gc.cuny.edu/read/4805e692-0823-4073-b431-5a684250a82d/section/aeee46e3-dddc-4668-a1b3-c8983ba4d70a#ch15.

Peacock, Laurel. 2012. "SAD in the Anthropocene: Brenda Hillman's Ecopoetics of Affect." *Environmental Humanities* 1 (1) (May): 85–102. https://doi.org/10.1215/22011919-3609985.

Rasula, Jed. 2002. *This Compost: Ecological Imperatives in American Poetry*. Athens: University of Georgia Press.

Rose, Deborah Bird, Thom van Dooren, Matthew Chrulew, Stuart Cooke, Matthew Kearnes, and Emily O'Gorman. 2012. "Thinking Through the Environment, Unsettling the Humanities." *Environmental Humanities* 1 (1) (May): 1–5. https://doi.org/10.1215/22011919-3609940.

16

CHEMO CREATURES IN A DIGITAL OCEAN!

The Making of a Speculative Ecosystem

Lucy Sabin

Introduction

Sounds of the sea fill the expectant darkness of the gallery. A screen illuminates. The establishing shot depicts a rugged shoreline. Rock pools fringed with tendrils of macro-algae dominate the low angle shots, intimating a non-human perspective. Something here is "waiting" and "listening," announces a largo voice-over. The camera tracks forward, pulling the viewer into this amphibious geography. A roaring wave comes into focus. It engulfs the lens in a profusion of bubbles, then a calmer montage of drifting seaweed. The audio dampens, reminding bodies of the pressing weight of water on eardrums. Gradually, the location shooting dissolves into a Stygian, computer-generated simulation architected around porous rocks with crevices that glow eerily. Extreme close-ups reveal the sources of this luminescence: pulsating organisms crowned, like sea urchins, with shimmering spicules. These bottom feeders are, it transpires, grazing on a blackened bloom of algae, using its toxicity to paradoxically curb their volatile (cancerous) growth. Each specimen's fluctuating mass is expressed as ephemeral dots of light set to a tinny diegetic score.

This chapter seeks to uncover the interdisciplinary and multimedia processes that are present in, yet exceed, the polished final work, *In Search of Chemozoa* (boredomresearch 2020a). What follows is a textual "making of," or behind-the-scenes exposé. I have drawn primarily on an interview and follow-up correspondence with digital artists Vicky Isley and Paul Smith, known collectively as boredomresearch.

While tracing the evolution of the Chemozoa project, I examine the ways in which digital media are used by boredomresearch to set in motion an artistic experiment and affective space for rethinking health in more-than-human terms. First, in "Modelling and Making Worlds," I outline how boredomresearch work with data in expressive ways that transcend the representational requirements of scientific modelling. Second, "A New Model Organism" homes in on the Chemozoa as an artistic approach to modelling cell behaviour (Posthumus and Sinclair 2014, 269). Third, "Restless Balance" is a meditation on the emergent and generative software effects that give each Chemozoa a complex and poetic relationship with their contaminated environment. The final section, "The Language of the Documentary," analyses how cinematic conventions and innovations weave together organism and environment into a narrative form.

 DOI: 10.4324/9781003082798-20

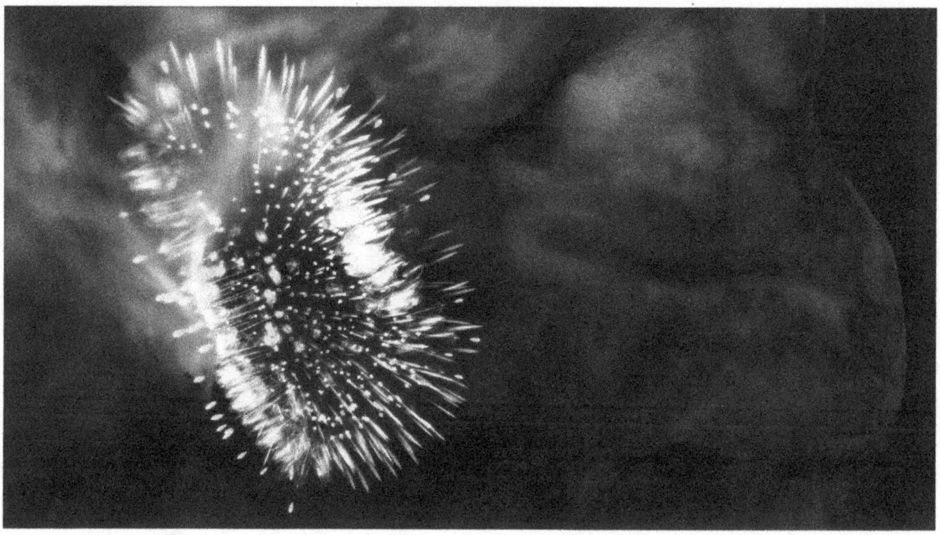

Figure 16.1 A Chemozoa on a rock. Still from *In Search of Chemozoa*.

Credit: boredomresearch, 2020

The following analysis seeks to foreground underlying processes of creative experimentation. As formative elements of the project, technological and aesthetic details are central to this ecology of ideas (Dixon, Hawkins, and Straughan 2012), along with other "embodied *practicalities* of knowing" (Despret 2013, 69, my emphasis). The aim is to indicate where digital modalities, environmental concerns, and the humanities might intersect in practice. So this chapter puts practice before theory as its rule of thumb; think of it as a process-oriented inquiry that attempts to make tacit knowledge available for further discussion. Salient themes of methodological relevance to the nexus of DEH include art-science collaborations, data modelling, affect, and more-than-human storytelling.

Modelling and Making Worlds

Arizona Cancer Evolution Center has an established "ArtSci" programme. Previous projects have aimed to explore cancer in novel ways using artistic methods. For instance, researchers in the Maley Lab, which investigates cancer in relation to evolutionary biology, have developed a software programme that generates musical dissonance to evoke cellular deviance. And former artist-in-residence, Susan Beiner, created intricate ceramic sculptures with repeated textures to emulate metastasis through tangible and three-dimensional forms. (Miniature "metastatised" replicas have been exhibited in different locations.) As these examples illustrate, the assemblage of media that an artist works within and through may, by virtue of material and aesthetic qualities, lend itself to unique ways of thinking about a less perceptible phenomenon.

Isley and Smith specialise in programming speculative ecosystems, and they use experimental combinations of "new media" to do so. Each of their projects proposes its own digital Anthropocene (Travis 2018) – in a non-anthropocentric way – wherein viral vectors and toxic exposures are played out in more-than-human fictions (e.g. boredomresearch 2016, 2018). These dynamic worlds, with their coded variables and biological themes, attempt to do what scientific test systems cannot: to

Figure 16.2 Environment shot of incoming waves. Still from *In Search of Chemozoa.*

Credit: boredomresearch, 2020

explore the semiotics of data modelling as an activity carried out by living, breathing researchers. While scientists are trained to streamline data to avoid any kind of messy entanglement that would render the output scientifically useless – that is, not directly comparable with other abstract results – boredomresearch proactively "look for the mess" (Isley, interview with author, December 17, 2021). By embracing states of entanglement (for want of a better word) as ontological co-dependence without flattening the specificity of each relation, boredomresearch incorporate into their digital worlds the kinds of dynamic dimensions that scientists might systematically discard or not have access to, such as landscapes, emotions, or speculative fictions (Haraway 2016).

Seeking out the discarded or overlooked details of scientific research is a step toward offering "something different from the science" but equally "robust" (Smith, interview with author, December 17, 2021). In this respect, boredomresearch differentiate between artistic and scientific ways of knowing. Both are fictions, by the way, that relate to "an idea of truth", according to the artists. "And what does truth mean in a scientific context?" Smith questioned, "Is that the same idea as truth in an artistic context?" Speaking about a previous project, AfterGlow (boredomresearch 2016), a computer-generated real-time artwork about malaria transmission, he stated, "We wanted to capture the truth of the visual complexity of a disease like malaria as it would exist in a landscape if we were able to see that." Being true for the artists is an additive as opposed to a subtractive empiricism (Latour 2016) that relates to the intuition of composition in aesthetics or the lesson in a fable. There is, simultaneously, profound resonance and openness of interpretation.

To make clear the distinction between representational models or data visualisations and their artistic worlds, boredomresearch refer to their work as "expressions." The onus is on translating "the feeling more than the science" (Smith, ibid.). For example, feelings of melancholia seem to pervade throughout their oeuvre to date. Isley puts the melancholy down to the "fragility" of the natural systems they look at, as well as the unpredictability of software development, "You experience fragility when something can easily collapse or become noise, so when we're programming something, you see that emergent behaviour and then you experience loss, in a way" (on loss, see High 2021). Computer modelling is a mode of artistic expression here. And "if you're creating an artistic expression of something, you must feel something" (Smith ibid.).

A New Model Organism

The Chemozoa are an artistic and affective expression of the analytic work taking place at ACE. The concepts for *In Search of Chemozoa* were developed gradually as the artists immersed themselves in the scientific context. By conducting exploratory interviews with the cancer researchers and being a "fly on the wall" in the laboratories, Isley and Smith absorbed ideas from the two interconnected laboratories at the Center: the Maley Lab (or evolutionary biology lab) and the Cooperation and Conflict Lab, where researchers use systems thinking from social psychology to examine why some cells work together while others appear to "cheat the system" (see Aktipis 2020). Before delving into the creation of the Chemozoa, I first outline a scientific concept and case study that were integral to the conceptualisation of this digital species.

Some of the scientific research at ACE involves observing a select group of invertebrates under different laboratory conditions to better understand their apparent resilience to cancer. The laboratory animals are model organisms; their tissues are recruited as part of a biological test system with potential insights for cancer care. Since the early 1900s, model organisms have traditionally denoted a reductive handful of species that now serve as empirical emblems for cell biology. Yet with the advent of new technologies that speed up gene sequencing, there is a resurgent enthusiasm to make, as it were, *new model organisms* on the basis of each species' attributes, as opposed to any precedents for working with that species (e.g. Goldstein and King 2016; Russel et al. 2017). For example, researchers at ACE move between wet and dry labs to construct and study model organisms with elevated regenerative attributes.

Out of their own considerations of the scientists' question, *how to live with cancer*, Isley and Smith developed a fictitious model organism – the Chemozoa – that lives *as* cancer (on the monsters of BioArt, see Dixon 2008). They describe the Chemozoa as the "digital nemesis" of the Placozoa (lit. "flat animal"), one of the model organisms at ACE, which has the simplest structure of all known animals. While the Placozoa is tested for its resilience to high-energy radiation (Fortunato et al. 2020), the Chemozoa has a cancerous mechanic programmed into its cells, each of which glows with the eery radiance of underwater nuclear reactors (Cherenkov effect). While the Placozoa has been extracted from a sample of algae to be observed under laboratory conditions, the Chemozoa heralds algal toxicity within an ocean habitat. As a speculative system for thinking and feeling with, the Chemozoa evinces artistic licence in its ability to imaginatively leap across scientifically uncharted territory and imagine otherwise.

Imagining otherwise extends to the digital milieu that boredomresearch built into a game engine, which is layered with under and above water location shooting in the video. The setting for the film seems to play upon the contrast between artificial laboratory conditions and the natural habitats of the Placozoa. The scientists' attempts to replicate the latter in the wet lab tangentially inspired boredomresearch's digital ocean habitat. To emulate "calm water areas with hard substrates like mangrove tree roots, rocks, corals" (Schleicherová et al. 2017), the scientists set up tanks with special aeration systems and rocks imported from Egypt, believed to contain a Goldilocks combination of minerals and microbes (boredomresearch 2020b). Correspondingly, craggy rocks are a leitmotif throughout boredomresearch's experimental film; the artists scanned an actual rock and imported its textures into their virtual environment via photogrammetry (digital as opposed to physical importation). The rocks in *In Search of Chemozoa* take on a crucial significance in the narrative. Unlike the existing

Figure 16.3 Angelo Fortunato looking down a microscope. Still from *In Search of Chemozoa*.

Credit: boredomresearch, 2020

model organisms at the Center, Chemozoan cell regulation does not depend on capacities that a certain organism is believed to possess in isolation but on symbiotic dynamics that extend inextricably across this speculative ecosystem.

To then situate the organism within a recognisable environment while also simulating cell behaviour, it proved necessary to exaggerate the scale of the computerised organisms in relation to their setting. As Smith put it, "we wanted to create something that had screen presence, but a maximum cell count of about a thousand cells, so the cells had to be big!" (ibid.). Isley remedied that the exaggerated proportions turned out to be a benefit in the eyes of the scientists, who can only observe creatures like Placozoa under a microscope as opposed to in their natural habitat. This question of scale surfaces in a particular sequence of *In Search of Chemoza* when a mid-shot of a scientist in a white lab coat peering into a microscope cuts to an ocean view framed by a peephole, connecting the microcosm with the macrocosm. In composing their own realm of experimentation, the artists overcame some of the scalar limitations faced by evolutionary biologists studying microorganisms.

At the Cancer Evolution Center, pragmatic questions such as "Which rocks and algae need to be in the tank to keep the Placozoa alive?" must be answered before scientists can begin to ask, "How do Placozoan cells protect against radiation?" Contrastingly, for boredomresearch, details about the constructed environment in which Placozoa are studied opened a world of possibilities. While the scientists were necessarily more concerned with controlling environmental conditions to produce a repeatable and comparable method for gathering reliable data, the artists delved into the messy entanglements between the research subject and its milieu. *In Search of Chemozoa* traces and probes relations rather than numbers. Freed from the pressures of science to design conditions with the objective of obtaining a categorical or numerical response (Stengers 2018, 62–63), the artists emphasise the chaotic complexities of organisms that recursively change and are changed by their environment. A frond of seaweed or a rock is never just that.

Figure 16.4 Close-up of Placozoa tank at ACE.

Credit: boredomresearch, 2019

Restless Balance

In Search of Chemozoa sets in motion a body-world relationship that analogises chemotherapy as well as more extensive rhythms of care and intensities of exposure within toxic environments. boredomresearch refer to this paradoxical state of dependence on toxicity as "restless balance"; the oxymoron became the title of their exhibition at the ASU Art Museum (5 December 2020–30 May 2021). Inspired by epidemiology and ecology, restless balance describes the dynamic continua between bodies and their worlds. The poetic phrase refers to seeking harmony in motion, "searching for some sense of stability but recognising change and the awk wardness that that creates" (Smith, ibid.). For the introduction label to the exhibition at ASU, Isley and Smith wrote,

> With the first recognition by Hippocrates that human health is subject to environmental factors we now find ourselves increasingly conscious of a destabilised natural order. Aware that our own actions are contrary to those that improve our position, a desire for an increasingly elusive solid ground, sought as an essential basis for stability, has become a restless pursuit for balance. . . . To be sought but never found.

Chemozoa embody restless balance. The pullulating mobilities of their cellular communities "lit up like Christmas lights" evoke the micro-cinematographic aesthetic of live-cell imaging (Landecker 2013). Encoded inside a game engine before being captured with a wide-angle lens, each organism's cellular reproduction and death are visible as emergent effects relating to their feeding habits; "as they're feeding, they'll grow bigger but, also, you'll see this mechanism of apoptosis. Then the Chemozoa shrink" (Isley, ibid.). The Chemozoa rely on "toxic algae" in

Figure 16.5 Extreme close-up of Chemozoan "cells," including the red dots of toxic algae. Still from *In Search of Chemozoa.*

Credit: boredomresearch, 2020

their environment for curbing their growth. Survival requires a recursive rhythm of carefully timed doses of algae to "manage the divergent clones" in their cell tissue (Smith, ibid.). These exposures are integral to the organism's metabolic and reproductive cycles (on toxicity as "distributed reproduction," see Murphy 2013). When ingested, the algae become an endosymbiotic nucleus of fiery embers inside the body of each organism.

The Chemozoa are "effectively giving themselves their own chemo dosage" (Isley, ibid.). Relying on these calculated exposures performs the almost paradoxical logic of chemotherapies: treating with a poison that also cures in certain concentrations (Stengers, discussed in Kirksey 2017). Chemozoan behaviour enacts chemotherapy by restlessly balancing relative toxicities, relative presuppositions of harm caused by a substance when encountered by a body. This tension is reinforced by the oxymorons that pepper the voice-over description: "harvesting a *bittersweet* coating of *nutritious contamination*," these beings are "*stillness* in *motion* . . . *progression arrested* . . . searching without advance or resolution" (boredomresearch 2020a; my emphasis). Chemozoan chemotherapy is timed, but it also exists outside linear time. There is no life without cell death.

In boredomresearch's biomedical imaginary, the trials and tribulations of chemotherapy are not a drastic attempt to obliterate abnormalities. *In Search of Cheomzoa* is not a depiction of an all or nothing "fight" against cancer (Sontag 1983 [1978]). Nor are the doses based on abstract measurements. This is a story about *adapting to* and *living via* toxicity through embodied knowledge of the environment. The analogy of chemotherapy is thus extended to encompass notions of environmental health, from one "chemical regime" to another (Murphy 2008). Shifting the dominant narrative of illness from the individual body to its relations with the environment, the Chemozoa debunk persistent myths of purity or immunity in worlds of ubiquitous (yet unevenly distributed) carcinogenic, endocrine-, and metabolic-disrupting chemicals (see Barry 2017; Romero et al. 2017; Shapiro and Kirksey 2017).

During research and development, boredomresearch investigated how blooms of microalgae, provoked by climate change and anthropogenic run-off, lead to low-oxygen dead zones (boredomresearch, e-mail to author, 22 March 2021). In the film, the "sickening algae" first materialises as an inky plume, carrying with it the loaded symbolism of an oil spill at sea. The blackened bloom is a harbinger of the Chemozoa, ocean wanderers who go in search of toxic tides. "Queer survivors" (Murphy 2013) of late industrial pollution, their bodies have made bioavailable the toxicants that persist and bioaccumulate in their food chain. Through harvesting the blooms, then, the Chemozoa are agents of bioremediation, restlessly balancing their own health with that of their environment. Care in a "permanently polluted world" is an everyday chore, never finished (Liboiron, Tironi, and Calvillo 2018).

The Language of the Documentary

In order to mobilise care and curiosity, boredomresearch have used filmmaking conventions to bring together the ideas covered throughout this chapter in a "low resistance way" (Smith, ibid.). In particular, the artists were inspired by the genre of documentary filmmaking, the conventions of which have historically mixed and blurred scientific and artistic knowledge and techniques. During our interview, the artists volunteered that they followed certain conventions from the "familiar language of the documentary such as the establishing shot, where you establish an idea of a location and then you have a journey that takes you from an idea of a place to a particular kind of situation in that place." In this sense, the use of landscape "made itself necessary" by giving context to a "situation where we can experience a creature and have an introduction" (Smith, ibid., see also Haraway's "situated knowledges," 1988).

While the above-water opening scene was shot on location in Asturias, Northern Spain, and the underwater shots of turbidity were filmed in Mar Menor Lagoon, Murcia, Southern Spain (where the artists researched toxic algae), the scenes in which we encounter the Chemozoa are computer-generated animations built with game engine software. The compositing between landscape and digital models feels seamless in the final cut, thanks to the sense of going on a journey, hence the title of the artwork. As Isley put it, "every camera angle transports you further in this search." Accordingly, "the [digital] environment was set up with certain shots in mind, such as panning around a rock to see the Chemozoa." An element of chaos, due to the generative nature of the animation as it renders in real time (during production), made this search feel more real to the artists; sometimes, a Chemozoa would ignore its cue to stay next to the rock! Isley and Smith experienced "weird moments" like this during production; "we felt as though we were out in nature, trying to document these beings" (Isley, ibid.).

In our interview, boredomresearch were resistant to labels such as science fiction. They were also reluctant to call *In Search of Chemozoa* a pseudo-documentary, even though this term has been used in internal and external communications by commissioners and curators. Limitations of labels notwithstanding, perhaps there might be a parallel to tentatively draw between this digital artwork and the emerging genre of the speculative documentary, which embraces "perpetual uncertainty, contamination, contestation, befoggedness and messiness" in its "engagement with, and . . . creation of, multiple and mutable realities" (Dienderen et al. 2019). A heterogeneous genre, the speculative documentary resembles the "design fiction" (Dunne and Raby 2013, 89–100) in its use of familiar signifiers to build plausibility, allowing the audience to contemplate a slightly altered reality. So, when the otherworldly Chemozoans appear and the location-based cinematography shifts to *in silico*, the embodied viewer enters into a fabulated world that is framed within more recognisable coordinates.

As Jamie Lorimer holds, "moving images *should* open thinking spaces for a micro-politics of curiosity in which we remain unsure as to what bodies and images might yet become" (2015, 138; my italics). Lorimer claims that such experimental media are led by a "logic of curiosity,"

Figure 16.6 Oblique close-up of the custom-labelled keyboard that boredomresearch used for producing *In Search of Chemozoa*.

Credit: boredomresearch, 2020

Figure 16.7 Multi-channel video installation at Aspex Gallery. All three screens show different views of Chemozoa.

Credit: boredomresearch, 2021

enlisting the surrealist wildlife documentary, postmodern animal art, and experimental video (133). *In Search of Chemozoa* certainly calls into question the mainstream experience of viewing nature on screen, perhaps more through the curiosity of artistic experimentation than an obligation for the filmmakers to open a particular "thinking space." This disruption is partly achieved by the cyclical format of the screenplay, which rolls backwards and forwards as the camera bobs in and out of the water; the 13-minute video is designed to be watched from any point in its loop so passers-by in the gallery can join at any stage. This downplaying of beginning and end reinforces the idea that we are seeing an ecosystem *in media res*. There is no certainty as to what bodies and images might yet become because they are perpetually becoming.

The amphibious camerawork and non-linear editing of *In Search of Chemozoa* piques curiosity in a manner reminiscent of Jean Painlevé's surrealist wildlife documentaries of the mid 20th Century (see Lorimer 2015, 133–34). Viewed within the history of underwater exposés, *In Search of Chemozoa* is part of an historical tradition of using technological innovations to mediatise the ocean as a volumetric setting for dramatic happenings (Cohen 2019). As media theorist Nicole Starosielski observes, the way we visualise the ocean is of increasing importance, being rooted in socio-historical contexts, which often involve exploitation and inequity (2012). Present in our biological makeup, watery media spawn an imaginary space for uncanny encounters with ourselves, including our evolutionary and maternal origins (Neimanis 2016). Plunging into the sea, physically or imaginatively, allows us to viscerally relive the interiority and interfaces of bodies, tissues, and cells (see Jue on Cousteau 2020, 34–70), as well as naturecultures writ large. Intimacy and vastness co-exist here.

The voice-over guides this quest to find Chemozoa, all the while inviting audiences to perhaps reflect upon their own embodiment and the worlds in which they participate. The cyclical script for the voice-over brings together elements of interviews that boredomresearch conducted with over 20 scientists, creating a collective narrative. In transposing these insights, Isley and Smith chose to use poetic rather than scientific language "to capture some of the rich emotional value that both underlies and motivates the research" (boredomresearch, ibid.). So while the commentary follows the wildlife documentary convention of being off-screen and therefore disembodied, the script is received less as a master narrative from a position of disconnected omniscience and more as a fable being passed on with care. Voice-over artist Lara Parmiani was directed to perform "with weariness and pausing for reflection," to "seem wise but without . . . any sense of superiority," and "to have a touch of melancholy and fragility, at times overcome by a fascination and subtle joy with the curious nature of the world" (boredomresearch, ibid.)

Figure 16.8 Making a field recording for *In Search of Chemozoa* by River Test, Southampton, UK.

Credit: boredomresearch, 2020

To capture oceanic sounds, boredomresearch made multi-sited field recordings with a hydrophone in the UK and Spain. Making the "voice" of the Chemozoa was less straightforward. It involved elaborating on the backstory of their speculative organism. Initially, Isley and Smith held many conversations with scientists both at the Arizona Cancer and Evolution Center and at Barts Cancer Institute in the UK about "trying to find a way to sonify an organism as though we could hear its cells and maybe the chemical signalling" (ibid.). As inspiration, the artists referenced the Hyena project at the Maley Lab, where researchers are "working on giving music cancer" by "trying to . . . recreate the mechanics of cancer within a piece of music" (Smith, ibid.). The Hyena application analogises musicians in a symphony to the cells of a body, "working together to produce a living, breathing person."[1]

In a similar vein, the voice of the Chemozoa became, in itself, an artistic exercise in simulating cancer and interpreting data artistically. Towards the end of the production process, the artists developed a library of both acoustic and synthesised sounds that might respond to each stage in a specimen's development. From a delicate ticking to sirenic song, Isley and Smith classified the sounds according to their "level of discord" and "complexity of energy," which were matched to the visual content and composition of each shot. The soundscape immerses audiences in this digital ecosystem. At one crescendo, when "more mature" Chemozoa are crowding around a centre-framed rock, "the sound is more electrical and charged as if they are processing their environment on an almost industrial level" (boredomresearch, ibid.). The soundtrack's blend of digital and analogue, machinic and creaturely sounds, is a musical analogy for not just cellular health but also the hybrid concept of biotechnology itself.

Conclusion

Having traced the evolution of this experimental film, I dwell here on two insights that have emerged from this practice-based analysis. First, I briefly suggest an extra-disciplinary approach that might be described beyond the particulars of this project as *art at the ends of science*. By "ends" or "edges," I mean that which lies outside certainty, as well as the limitations that are associated with scientific methods in constructing what is presumed to be known. The world that boredomresearch set in motion began with questions about the constructed nature of scientific frameworks. The work of scientists presented edges in the eyes of the artists that spliced open possibilities for subversive imaginaries with multiple interpretations and affective relations. boredomresearch saw how scientists made model organisms, and they experimented with their own speculative, digital version to star in an alternative narrative: a poetic, dynamic, and normalised account of living as cancer.

Second, I close on the need to *document methods* across the digital environmental arts to better understand the processual evolution of ecological imaginaries as they emerge from a particular context. The trans- or post-disciplinary labour described previously was essential to the digital arts methods developed by boredomresearch for this project. New media techniques were innovated to express *the feeling more than the science*. Analysed together, these methods accumulatively propose a digital ecology that interweaves arts and sciences, wetware and soft/hardware, rocks and life, human and non-human (Posthumus and Sinclair 2014, 270). In so doing, the film invites audiences to expand and de-compartmentalise environmental and medical imaginaries towards a future-oriented "critical posthumanities" (see Neimanis, Åsberg, and Hedrén 2015). *In Search of Chemozoa* is a quest, after all. The journey in the film, from the familiarity of the shoreline to the depths of the digital ocean, analogises the evolution of the project itself, as well as an urgent move towards narrating queer ecological relations.

Acknowledgements

Lucy Sabin wishes to thank Deborah P. Dixon for her invaluable edits. Thanks also to Charles Travis for providing timely guidance throughout the writing and editing process. The author is grateful to Vicky Isley and Paul Smith, a.k.a. boredomresearch, for being incredibly forthcoming and thoughtful throughout the researching, writing, and editing of this chapter. Their experimental film *In Search of Chemozoa* (boredomresearch 2020a) was commissioned and funded by the Arizona Cancer Evolution Center at the Biodesign Institute, Arizona State University, and produced in partnership with Aspex, Portsmouth, UK, and supported by the National Lottery through Arts Council England. The artwork was developed whilst boredomresearch were in residence at the Arizona Cancer Evolution Center and during their PONToon residency at Aspex from 2018 to 2019. The artists wish to thank the following individuals: Athena Aktipis and the Cooperation and Conflict Lab; Aspex Portsmouth; Cristina Baciu, finance manager; John Crozier, film location coordinator; Angelo Fortunato, featured scientist; Carlo Maley and the Cancer and Evolution Lab; and Lara Parmiani, film narrator, with invaluable support from Pamela Winfrey, scientific research curator and film producer.

Note

1 https://cancer-insights.asu.edu/2020/05/capturing-cancer-with-music/.

Sources

Aktipis, Athena. 2020. *The Cheating Cell: How Evolution Helps us Understand and Treat Cancer.* Princeton: Princeton University Press.

Barry, Andrew. 2017. "Manifesto for a Chemical Geography." Inaugural lecture, Gustave Tuck Lecture Theatre, UCL, January 24. www.ucl.ac.uk/anthropocene/sites/anthropocene/files/andrew_barry_manifesto_for_a_chemical_geography.pdf.

boredomresearch. 2016. *AfterGlow.* Computer generated real-time artwork. Berlin: Lumen Prize Exhibition.

———. 2018. *The Ultimate Fate of Jeremy Fisher.* 3D animation. Cumbria: Wray Castle.

———. 2020a. *In Search of Chemozoa.* Three-channel video installation. Tempe: Arizona State University (ASU) Art Museum.

———. 2020b. *For We Are but a Single Cell.* Making-of documentary. Tempe: Arizona State University (ASU) Art Museum.

Cohen, Margaret. 2019. "The Underwater Imagination: From Environment to Film Set, 1954–1956." *English Language Notes* 57 (1): 51–71. https://doi.org/10.1215/00138282-7309677.

Despret, Vinciane. 2013. "Responding Bodies and Partial Affinities in Human – Animal Worlds." *Theory, Culture & Society* 30 (7–8): 51–76. https://doi.org/10.1177/0263276413496852.

Dienderen, An van, Michiel De Cleene, Max Pinckers, and Thomas Bellinck. 2019. "A Manifesto: An Invitation from the School of Speculative Documentary." *Critical Arts* 33 (1): 113–14. https://doi.org/10.1080/02560046.2019.1581240.

Dixon, Deborah P. 2008. "The Blade and the Claw: Science, Art and the Creation of the Lab-Borne Monster." *Social and Cultural Geography* 9 (6): 671–92. https://doi.org.uk/10.1080/14649360802292488.

Dixon, Deborah P., Harriet Hawkins, and Elizabeth Straughan. 2012. "Of Human Birds and Living Rocks: Remaking Aesthetics for Post-Human Worlds." *Dialogues in Human Geography* 2 (3) (November): 249–70. https://doi.org/10.1177/2043820612468692.

Dunne, Anthony, and Fiona Raby. 2013. *Speculative Everything: Design, Fiction, and Social Dreaming.* Cambridge, MA and London, UK: MIT Press.

Fortunato, Angelo, Alexis Fleming, Athena Aktipis, Carlo C Maley. 2020. "Radiation Resistance in Placozoa: *Trichoplax Adhaerens* Upregulates DNA Repair Genes and Extrudes Cells after Exposure." *bioRxiv.* https://doi.org/10.1101/2020.12.24.424349.

Goldstein, Bob, and Nicole King. 2016. "The Future of Cell Biology: Emerging Model Organisms." *Trends in Cell Biology* 26 (11): 818–24. https://doi.org/10.1016/j.tcb.2016.08.005.

Haraway, Donna. 1988. "Situated Knowledges: The Science Question in Feminism and the Privilege of Partial Perspective." *Feminist Studies* 14 (3): 575–99. https://doi.org/10.2307/3178066.

———. 2016. *Staying with the Trouble: Making Kin in the Chthulucene*. Durham, NC: Duke University Press.

High, Casey. 2021. "The Nature of Loss: Ecological Nostalgia and Cultural Politics in Amazonia." *In Ecological Nostalgias: Memory, Affect and Creativity in Times of Ecological Upheavals*, edited by Olivia Angé and David Berliner, 84–106. New York: Berghahn Books.

Jue, Melody. 2020. *Wild Blue Media: Thinking through Seawater*. Durham, NC: Duke University Press.

Kirksey, Eben. 2017. "Caring as Chemo-Ethnographic Method." *Member Voices, Fieldsights*, November 20. https://culanth.org/fieldsights/caring-as-chemo-ethnographic-method.

Landecker, Hannah. 2013. "The Life of Movement: From Microcinematography to Live-Cell Imaging." *Journal of Visual Culture* 11 (3): 378–99. https://doi.org/10.1177/1470412912455622.

Latour, Bruno. 2016. "Foreword: The Scientific Fables of an Empirical La Fontaine." Foreword to *What Would Animals Say if We Asked the Right Questions?* edited by Vinciane Despret, translated by Brett Buchanan, vii–xiv. Minneapolis, MN: University of Minnesota Press.

Liboiron, Max, Manuel Tironi, and Nerea Calvillo. 2018. "Toxic Politics: Acting in a Permanently Polluted World." *Social Studies of Science* 48 (3): 331–49. https://doi.org/10.1177/0306312718783087.

Lorimer, Jamie. 2015. *Wildlife in the Anthropocene: Conservation after Nature*. Minneapolis, MN: University of Minnesota Press.

Murphy, Michelle. 2008. "Chemical Regimes of Living." *Environmental History* 13 (4): 695–703. www.jstor.org/stable/25473297.

———. 2013. "Distributed Reproduction, Chemical Violence, and Latency." *S&F Online* 11 (3) (Summer). https://sfonline.barnard.edu/life-un-ltd-feminism-bioscience-race/distributed-reproduction-chemical-violence-and-latency/.

Neimanis, Astrida. 2016. *Bodies of Water: Posthuman Feminist Phenomenology*. London, UK: Bloomsbury Academic.

Neimanis, Astrida, Cecilia Åsberg, and Johan Hedrén. 2021. "Four Problems, Four Directions for Environmental Humanities: Toward Critical Posthumanities for the Anthropocene." *Ethics and the Environment* 20 (1) (2015): 67–97. https://doi.org/10.2979/ethicsenviro.20.1.67.

Posthumus, Stephanie, and Stéfan Sinclair. 2014. "Reading Environment(s): Digital Humanities Meets Ecocriticism." *Green Letters* 18 (3): 254–73. https://doi.org/10.1080/14688417.2014.966737.

Romero, Adam M., Julie Guthman, Ryan E. Galt, Matt Huber, Becky Mansfield, and Suzana Sawyer. 2017. "Chemical Geographies." *GeoHumanities* 3 (1): 158–77. https://doi.org/10.1080/2373566X.2017.1298972.

Russell, James J., Julie A. Theriot, Pranidhi Sood, Wallace F. Marshall, Laura F. Landweber, Lillian Fritz-Laylin, Jessica K. Polka, et al. 2017. "Non-Model Model Organisms." *BMC Biology* 15 (55). https://doi.org/10.1186/s12915-017-0391-5.

Schleicherová, Dáša, Katharina Dulias, Hans-Jűrgen Osigus, Omid Paknia, Heike Hadrys, and Bernd Schierwater. 2017. "The Most Primitive Metazoan Animals, the Placozoans, Show High Sensitivity to Increasing Ocean Temperatures and Acidities." *Ecology and Evolution* 7: 895–904. https://doi.org/10.1002/ece3.2678.

Shapiro, Nicholas, and Eben Kirksey. 2017. "Chemo-ethnography: An Introduction." *Cultural Anthropology* 32 (4): 481–93. https://doi.org/10.14506/ca32.4.01.

Sontag, Susan. 1983. *Illness as Metaphor*. Harmondsworth: Penguin.

Starosielski, Nicole. 2012. "Beyond Fluidity: A Cultural History of Cinema Under Water." In *Ecocinema Theory and Practice*, edited by Stephen Rust, Salma Monani, and Sean Cubitt, 161–80. New York and Abingdon: Routledge.

Stengers, Isabelle. 2018. *Another Science Is Possible: A Manifesto for Slow Science*. Translated by Stephen Muecke. Cambridge: Polity Press.

Travis, Charles. 2018. "The Digital Anthropocene, Deep Mapping, and Environmental Humanities' Big Data." *Resilience: A Journal of the Environmental Humanities* 5 (2): 172–88. muse.jhu.edu/article/698346.

17

INNOVATIVE AND CREATIVE GEOGRAPHIES

The Shifting Boundaries of Inside, Outside, Real, and Imagined Spaces

William J. Mackwood and Gwenyth H. Dobie

Introduction

Rallentando: *A Gradual Slowing Down*

The Challenge of Urban Life

For the last 20-some years, as co-creators, we have sought to make meaningful work to present to a live-theatre audience. Whether through our small theatre company, Out of the Box Productions, or in our jobs teaching in the School of the Arts, Media, Performance, and Design at York University in Toronto, we continually search out the elusive muse of artistic relevance. Like many working in live performance, we cycle through the ever-evolving methodologies, our work inexorably moving towards the digital: using advanced emerging technologies to immerse our audiences in imaginative environments or, more recently, adding interactive feedback or "play" through performance installations.

One of our earlier projects, *Butterfly: a study interactive* (international tour 2014–15), was pivotal in setting a new direction for our future work. *Butterfly* incorporated an infrared motion-tracking camera and self-programmed, dedicated applications. Our animator-performer, either Gwenyth or a keen volunteer audience member, would visually become a butterfly floating through the forest while their movements generated a melodic soundtrack. By tracking body-core movements (tilt and bow), they were able to control their flight path while simultaneously using their hand movements (tracked in three dimensions) to play two virtual musical instruments (fixed to a predetermined scale). The ability to physically inhabit and affect digitally created natural environments in real time excited us tremendously. Yet there was another more reflective and sobering experience in touring the work. While presenting *Butterfly* to various universities and theatre groups around the world, we experienced life in some of the world's most densely populated cities, and it left us deeply perplexed by the conditions under which so many of the world's population live. Having always lived in areas of Canada where nature was found by simply walking out our door, or maybe down the street, or at worst a short drive away, we then

DOI: 10.4324/9781003082798-21

considered the lives of millions who, for much of their life, may have little or no access to nature. Further, even for those who have access to natural settings, might there be restorative benefits in creating a space where the inhabitants are immersed in nature, digitally created through the use of advanced technology.

At this point, it would be good to consider what we mean by "nature" or "natural," words freely tossed about by artists, scientists, and those who want to sell you something. For at least the last 100 years, researchers have been confirming the positive effects of nature on our immediate (and long-term) mental and physical health. As humans, we can assess the environments we experience on a scale of locations in which the original has been completely eradicated by human activity (think cement, steel and glass), all the way to locations which show imperceptible impact from human activity (imagine sitting on an isolated beach looking out at the ocean). In this chapter, when we speak of nature or natural environments, we are referring to locations that offer the effect or physiological result of locations that are closer to the latter, including immersive environments which are digitally created.

An Imagined Escape

Upon our return from the international tour, our research endeavours pivoted toward an exploration of those immersive digital environments and the possible positive benefits they present for those who, for various reasons, are not able to benefit from an actual immersion in nature. The concept of forest bathing originated in Japan, and with the release of Dr Qing Li's book *Forest Bathing: How Trees Can Help You Find Health and Happiness* (2018), the concept quickly became trendy in California, British Columbia, and other parts of the world. Different from hiking, forest bathing is a slow and contemplative journey through the forest, using one's senses to absorb and be mindful of the experience. For all of our lives, when we needed to get away, to clear our minds, to heal, to create, we would instinctively head for whatever natural environments were available to us. Discovering the concept of forest bathing and reading the associated research only confirmed what we intuitively knew: time spent immersed in nature healed and inspired us. This idea that we might offer the benefits of forest bathing through digitally created environments was the driving force behind our compelling Toronto project, *Rallentando* (described in detail later in this chapter). As we considered the next phase of our creative lives, we simultaneously found ourselves drawn to the natural settings found on the Southern Gulf Islands on the west coast of Canada. Not surprisingly, after a lifetime of creating for the stage, the incessant pull of theatre remained as strong as ever, and we began to consider how we might bring these two pervasive drives into a harmonious purpose. We reflected on the reciprocal nature of the relationship between artists, their creative environment, and the art they produce. Additionally, we knew we wanted to offer opportunities to other artists as well, and so we developed an artist residency programme on Canada's west coast (Salt Spring Island), within the territories of the Coast Salish peoples, where the artist finds a sanctuary to breathe, dream, experiment, create, and play.

In what follows, we discuss the benefits of artist residencies found in natural settings and the process through which our artist residency was developed. In addition, we look at our creative work, especially projects where digitally created environments offer the performer and participant similar benefits to forest bathing.

Art, Residencies, and the Environment

Residencies are one of the key forms of engagement between artist and environment, and artists seeking inspiration through nature is certainly not a new phenomenon. In his book *Artists on*

Figure 17.1 The creation space.

Photo: William J. Mackwood

the Edge: the Rise of Coastal Artists' Colonies, 1880–1920, Brian Barrett explains that coastal settings offered artists "freedoms to explore new avenues of interest, personally, and away from the narrow confines of the academic curriculum" (Barrett 2010, 104). The artist colony movement (that eventually spawned the Arts and Crafts movement) in the United States was born out of an "underlying utopian theme: preservation of the simple life, nostalgia, and a set of values threatened by industrialization" (Aldrich 2008, ii). It may still be true that artists seeking residencies outside urban areas, as much as being drawn to the natural setting, are pushing away from the distractions and interruptions of modern life. In addition, there can be no doubt that many artists are attempting to reconnect with nature. Today, the organisation Res Artis, of which we are a member, promotes close to 600 artist residence centres in over 70 countries around the world, with almost half of those being in a rural setting, while a further 90 boast a natural setting as a component (Res Artis 2021).

There exists little quantitative research exploring the factors fostering creativity at what is perhaps the most quintessentially creative space – the artist residency – and virtually no work exploring the interface of such residencies and the natural environment, despite the long association between the two. Yet in the study "Effects of Interruptions on Creative Thinking," the investigators found that "one's creative thinking could profit from intermittent interruptions of low-cognitive resource requirements. However, when encountering interruptions that consumed excessive cognitive resources, one's creativity was hindered" (Wang, Ye, and Teo 2014, 7). In his article, "The Restorative Benefits of Nature: Toward an Integrative Framework," Stephen Kaplan points to the "significant role that directed attention, a key psychological resource, plays in coping with challenges. From this perspective, the role that natural environments play is a powerful one. Experience in natural environments can not only help mitigate stress; it can also prevent it through aiding in the recovery of this essential resource" (Kaplan 1995, 173). His argument would indicate that people heading for residencies in natural settings may be doing so to simply restore their ability to focus. Kaplan goes on to identify components of a restorative environment:

- *Being away*: most often meaning a natural setting, even if that natural setting is found locally.
- *Fascination*: in particular, soft fascinations (clouds, sunsets, etc.) that hold attention but leave ample room for other thoughts.
- *Extent*: a restorative environment must be of sufficient scope to engage the mind, to take up a substantial portion of the available room in one's head. Even a small area, well designed, can provide a sense of extent.
- *Compatibility*: for many people, the natural environment is experienced as high compatibility, as if there is a special resonance between a natural setting and human inclinations (Kaplan, 174).

Researching Art and Environment through Artist Residencies

In the summer of 2018, we received funding to visit a selection of Canadian artist residencies situated in natural settings, with the research objective of better understanding that relationship. An inspiring example for us was Fogo Island Arts and its associated artist residency. With the collapse of the Newfoundland in-shore fishery and the threat of forced relocation in the 1960s, Memorial University's Extension Department invited the National Film Board of Canada to interview those affected, and the Challenge for Change programme emerged. Through still image and film, the stories of the people and their communities found a political voice ("How filmmakers and fishers saved Fogo Island," CBC Radio, 2018). Subsequently, in the 1980s, Fogo Island Arts was established with the objective of supporting artistic exploration, especially through their uniquely situated art studios. The four artist residency studios designed by architect Todd Saunders are off-grid, self-sustaining and minimise their impact on the environment.

During our visit to Fogo Island in 2018, we had the opportunity to interview Ieva Epnere, a Latvian multimedia artist working in Long Studio. As we interviewed her at her workstation, we looked out over the rocky Newfoundland shoreline and witnessed the awesome power of the North Atlantic Ocean. She generously spoke to the amazing transformative qualities of a residency in nature. For example, in the year previous to our visit, Ieva had taken advantage of geology hikes offered by the "geologist in residency program." The hikes increased her curiosity in rocks and their textures which further fueled her photography work. But as she states, "it's not only that I am interested in the texture of the rocks, but how environment influences people." Inspired by the film *The Children of Fogo Island* (Low 1967), she wanted to capture images of the island children. "The children that grow up here are completely different than children in the cities, how they act and how they talk about their place." Upon returning home that year, she made costumes by printing the photographed rock textures onto silk, then returned the year of our visit to photograph the children of the island wearing her designed costumes in the landscape where the original photos were taken. For her current exhibition, which we were able to attend, she wanted to show "a merging; that people are so much integrated into nature that sometimes they dissolve there." Her exhibition, *On Water, Wind And Faces Of Stone*, spoke to us of the relationship between people and place, specifically how geography defines community.

For Ieva, one of the main advantages of the Fogo Island residency is the expansiveness of the studio setting. As mentioned, the studio looks out over the ocean, providing an uncluttered view, "you can just follow the horizon and think and think. Everything becomes more relaxed." She adds that "it's more after-effect, when you go back to the city, then you feel how much energy you have saved [up] here" (Epnere 2018). We also discussed how the natural movement of water was similar to the natural flow of wind in the leaves of a forest, particularly how this movement, as in Kaplan's component "fascination," was engaging to observe yet allowed much space for thought.

This intersection between artist residencies as creative environments and resident artists attuned to and proactively concerned with the environment resonates with the broader thematic of the environmental art movement. Since the 1990s – and building on the work of artists such as Betty Beaumont (*Ocean Landmark* 1978–80), Andy Goldsworthy (*Pinfold Cones* 1981–85), and Agnes Denes (*Wheatfield, a Confrontation* 1982) – the environmental art movement has brought attention to the concerns of human impact on our planet. Art is intended here to change the way in which we see and think about the climate change crisis, and our role in it. Renée Phillips, founder of the Healing Power of Art & Artists, states, "The creators of environmental art help us to understand nature, the ecosystems, the environmental forces and materials to be aware of, and the damaged environmental areas of concern" (Phillips 2021).

As we began to envision our return to the west coast and the establishment of a residency programme, we knew that the design of the space must take advantage of the forest, specifically the Douglas fir ecosystem found on our property, offering an opportunity to forest-bathe year-round. In fact, we wondered why we couldn't build a glass-walled structure, offering protection from the elements while being visually surrounded by this natural resource. This was beyond our financial means, however, and created as many problems as it solved. Although we would be, as Henry David Thoreau suggested, creating a space "as open and manifest as a bird's nest" (Thoreau 1888, 243), it was only that and offered nothing in the way of creative privacy or control of light. There are valid reasons why black-box theatres are ubiquitous. The driving question became, how do we build a space that offers the inhabitants the ability to be inclusive of the forest setting in which it is placed and the capability to transport the creative inhabitants to environments inspired by their imagination? We also realised that before we could make final design decisions, we needed to consider the end-user, both ourselves and visiting artists.

In addition to creating a space in which to devise our own performance pieces, we wanted to make the space available and inspiring for others. As teachers, we are fully aware of both the challenge of making a living in the live performing arts and the insatiable appetite young people have for this art form. Whether through our roles as professors at York University or as co-artistic directors of Out of the Box Productions, mentoring emerging artists seemed a natural and necessary part of our process. As we contemplated how to better offer assistance to artists seeking growth and development opportunities, we turned our attention to conceiving an artist residency studio that takes advantage of the surrounding natural environment. We knew our newly acquired property, Woodland Farm, was the perfect setting.

Having let go of the glass-wall concept, we once again let our imaginations run. What if the walls could go away when the intended artistic objective and weather conditions agreed? We drew sketches for an open concept 24-by-36-foot hipped-roof barn, with opposing doors that are 16 feet wide by 10 feet high, that when open create a breezeway. One side offers a view onto the gardens and the other into our lush west-coast forest. But more than offering contrasting views of the tamed and natural world, this concept turned out to have a major advantage over the original concept of glass walls. The opening of the doors allows the sounds and smells of

Figure 17.2 Outside/inside/outside.

Dancer: Gwenyth H. Dobie

Photo: William J. Mackwood

the gentle west-coast forest to flow through the building. The pine tongue-and-groove ceiling soars to a full 19 feet, offering room for lofty thoughts (and, of course, to hang all the necessary digital design equipment). Further, the floor space was to be uncluttered, without such annoying things as supporting posts or interior shear walls. It turns out that you can, in fact, achieve these things, but only with considerably complex engineering, incurring many challenges and significantly over-budget expenses.

Still, the final product more than fulfils our original expectations. Sitting inside, with the breezeway doors folded back, offers the best "inside while outside" experience imaginable. What was immutable and silent suddenly transforms into a vibrant environment, filled with shifting light and the sounds of the surrounding forest.

Outside/Inside/Real/Imagined

As the doors swing open, the various depths of view – foreground, middle ground, and background – are distinctly outlined by the massive door frames, with each level equally and harmoniously enticing. For example, one can sit under the vast canopy of an ancient maple tree that borders the cultivated agricultural space of our garden while enjoying the framed interior view of a staged performance supported by the latest in digital technologies, which is in turn backgrounded by a second-framed view into the natural splendour of the west-coast forest. Even on cooler days, the many windows offer a constant view of the surrounding beauty. Our goal of building a technologically advanced performance space that reflects and informs the occupant with its natural setting has been fully met.

The responses to our first open call for artist residencies at Woodland Farm demonstrated the desire artists have to create, not just surrounded by nature but in concert with and inspired by those surroundings. The following are a few samples from residency applications of the benefits artists perceived as they looked forward to their time here:

- "With the confined reality of COVID-19, the act of emerging from spaces that simultaneously create a sense of safety and isolation intrigues me. The constant conversation between land, sea and sky on islands such as Salt Spring is an inspiring dialogue I wish to engage with fully."
- "The residency in Salt Spring Island and the work in the farm is, thus, a chance to revitalize the land (whether it being psychic or corporeal) further exploring the correlation between language, memory and corporeal geography, as well as how singularity can add markers to one's unsettled borders."
- "The Farm's mission of providing a naturally immersive experience in which to clear the mind for creation and reflection is exactly in line with my artistic practice and graduate thesis. I especially love the requirement that resident artists must contribute to the care of the land in order to feel connected and clear-headed. Additionally, I am very interested in indigenous philosophies of land stewardship, so the proximity to the Coast Salish communities is exciting."

Real vs Imagined Environments

Creating Possibilities

Why, then, in this new, specially designed setting, and with the splendour of the west coast environment immediately accessible to us, would we further invest much money and effort into the possibilities offered by creating digital environments? We believe that Kaplan's third component of a restorative environment, "extent" (the idea that even a small area, well-designed, can offer a "sufficient scope to engage the mind"), offers a rich area of exploration. In other words, while forest bathing offers a key element to the residency (and our own creative process), we realised that it limits creative possibilities. Environments created digitally, on the other hand, are only limited by the imagination of the creators, the available technology and the technical skills to realise the vision. With advanced technologies, lighting, sound, and the projected image can be designed and manipulated, often interactively, to effortlessly transport us through time and space, and offer the same effect and physiological benefits to the participants. We also recognise that the latest science would indicate that with climate change, the future might offer less and less opportunity for people to immerse themselves in nature: could digital environments offer an alternative?

All of the works we have devised, designed, and presented with Out of the Box Productions over the years incorporated digital environments, using various approaches to frame or blend the projected image into the intended world of the story. The strategies for integrating digitally mediatised content often begin with solving framing issues. For many, the power of cinema, with its ubiquitous rectangular screen, has held the position of dominant media for decades. Indeed, the creators of live performance are, or should be aware of, the self-defeating use of the moving projected image in direct competition with live performers. When integrating digital environments, how do we decidedly separate *this* from *that* without creating two competing worlds? Or alternatively, how do we soften the frame to offer a gradual transition from *this* to *that*, as if *this* is *that* or *that* is an extension of *this*? Depending on the needs of the work, there are many strategies we have used over the years.

In current theatre practice, there are various techniques used to transport the audience into the world of the play. From the traditional fourth wall viewing port (commonly referred to as the proscenium arch) to totally immersive works where audience and performer mingle and interact, the variations in how to present the work are as diverse as the stories and the creators themselves. In our work, we have continually experimented with the actor-to-audience relationship, and most of the challenges come from solving the transition to or the blending from *this* to *that*. Ever advancing technology: powerful video processors, digital projectors, and projection mapping software now allow us to control the edges down to the individual pixel. This, in turn, has allowed us to: soften the edges, blend overlapping edges to create vast panoramas, or map onto any number or shape of natural surfaces found in the world of the play.

The space we have designed at Woodland Farm takes into account all we have learned over the many projects. Cityscapes, landscapes, or imaginary escapes, we have used and will continue to use digital technology to manipulate light and sound, creating the worlds in which the characters live or in which we immerse our audience. In the following section, we describe three projects of particular significance on our research journey. In *Sound in Silence*, we offered our audience the imagined landscape inside a deaf artist's mind and memories. *Disrupting Solitude* explored the tensions created by social interactions through a digitally mediatised environment. Lastly, *Rallentando* represents our first attempt at offering a journey through fully immersive digitised natural settings, with a focused lens on the perceived physiological effects on the participants.

Sound in Silence *(Victoria [2008]; Toronto [2009])*

Inspired by Dr Norman Doidge's book *The Brain that Changes Itself*, our production of *Sound in Silence* offered Gwenyth an opportunity to explore neuroplasticity in relation to her life-long challenge with hearing loss (Doidge 2007). Both the performers and audience inhabited Gwenyth's "brain," experiencing memory flashbacks, traumatic, and restorative neural events. The use of multiple projectors throwing images onto and filtering through numerous layers of hanging gauze strips placed above and between the inhabitants of the "brain" created the perfect balance between *this* and *that*, the real and the remembered. Attended equally by the hearing and deaf community, the show successfully navigated the complexity of neuroplasticity and the loss of function.

In a feature article, award-winning west-coast writer Linda Rogers described her experience of attending the work: "Random seating in an environment bombarded with sensation and divided by transparent mauve curtains gave hearing audience an opportunity to understand, and deaf participants the opportunity to confront their loss and appreciate the mind and body's ability to compensate. During the performance, I felt as if someone I loved had died, a grey directionless ache. It wasn't rocket science that led me to understand that I was grieving my own hearing, the insults ('Are you deaf or stupid?' a musician asked me when I mis-heard) and deficits a hearing-impaired person negotiates in daily life" (Rogers 2008, 8). The deaf and hard-of-hearing audience were fully included through the use of technology, as a live-feed video of our ASL translator was integrated into the projections. Bringing hearing and deaf audience members into the imagined geography of Gwenyth's mind resulted in an empathetic understanding for both.

Disrupting Solitude *(Toronto [2017])*

Disrupting Solitude premiered in the Dance Department Incubator Festival, an annual interdisciplinary exploration in technology, movement, sound, design, and performance at York University. For this installation piece, a cylindrical, partially translucent screen was hung slightly above and between the participant movers/dancers. Through the use of body-tracking and four opposing projectors, the dancers' avatars fused on the screen. Similar to Bill T. Jones' *Ghostcatching*, but different in that the participants and their avatars are created in real time rather than adding the artwork in post-production (Jones, Kaiser, and Eshka 1999). Thus, the participants danced a duet with their opposite, both in the physical world and digitally. The dancers' hands were tracked in 3D and, through the use of musical sequencing software, created their own melodic accompaniment. Thus, with a tension formed, the dancers could look directly across at their creative dance partners (as in a duet) or look up to see their avatar merged into a dance of light, colours blending, shapes constantly morphing in time to the music that they themselves were creating through their improvised choreography.

Ultimately, *Disrupting Solitude* pondered the agency of the human in an increasingly digitally mediatised existence. We invited participants to artistically explore the dynamic relationship, tension, and potential that exist between people as mediated through technology and the invasive seduction by technology in contemporary life. We questioned the impact of a virtually mediated relationship while your potential partner exists, in the flesh, across the room.

Rallentando *(Toronto [2016])*

Without a doubt, though, *Rallentando* remains our most ambitious attempt to immerse the audience into a digitally created "natural" environment. It was an installation piece based on the Japanese practice of *shinrin-yoku* (forest bathing) and, as talked about earlier, was created in consideration of the millions of people in the world who do not have easy access to nature. Gwenyth, the creative driving force behind this project was also inspired in turn by artist Olafur Eliason, in particular his installation *The Weather Project* at the Tate Museum (2003); author Milan Kundera's reflections in *Slowness* ("the secret bond between slowness and memory"; Kundera and Asher 1996); and ancient Roman philosopher Seneca's spectacular treatise *On the Shortness of Life* (Seneca 2005).

Gwenyth's preparatory research mined a wealth of findings that confirmed there was a consistent pattern of rapid recovery from stress upon exposure to "forest medicine." Specifically, the results from a comprehensive study demonstrated that "forest environments promote lower concentrations of cortisol, lower pulse rate, lower blood pressure, greater parasympathetic nerve activity, and lower sympathetic nerve activity than do city environments" (Park et al. 2009, 18). Of significance for our work, psychologist Deltcho Valtchanov at the University of Waterloo found that immersion in a computer-generated virtual reality natural environment triggered the same kind of responses as when walking in a real-world natural setting: a decrease in levels of both perceived and physiological stress (Valtchanov et al. 2010, 503). Sue Thomas, writer and digital pioneer, confirmed for us in her article "Technobiophilia: We surf the net, stream our films and save stuff in the cloud. Can we get all the nature we need from the digital world?" that "there is increasing evidence that we respond very similarly to a 'natural' environment, whether it's real or virtual, and research confirms that even simulated nature experiences can be remarkably powerful" (Thomas 2013). To be sure, there are many researchers deeply interested in these inquiries, and their work offered the creative team insights into the effects of immersion in nature, whether real-world or digitally created, on our physical and mental health. *Rallentando* would be the performance installation, and laboratory, through which we would explore the possibilities. Inside the *Rallentando* installation, the audience experienced a gradual slackening of tempo, leaving behind the distractions of contemporary urban life. It was a fully immersive environment that created calming effects through changes in the nervous system – in the same way as exposure to nature has been proven to do. We did not want to simulate nature but rather create an immersive environment that exemplified the essence of nature.

In developing *Rallentando*, we used saturated colours of greens and blues: images of trees, water, sky, insects, and birds. In recognition of the calming effect of natural movement (Kaplan's concept of "fascination"), we needed to create animation wherever possible in the transitioning still images. Through the use of an image manipulation application programmed by William, the still images we used were brought to life; the waves rolled onto the shore, leaves fluttered in the breeze, and birds flew through the sky. In addition, the idea of experiencing this piece as a collective, as a gathering of people in a shared space rather than using isolating technology such as VR goggles, stemmed from our interest in the ongoing debate on the correlation between social isolation and technology.

During *Rallentando*, we took our audience on a 20-minute (12-hour) journey from sunrise through sunset and four distinct locations: cityscape, forests, beach, and finally mountainscape. We needed to know if a digitally created environment could soothe our audience's urban angst (the theatre was situated in downtown Toronto) in a similar manner to the proven benefits of forest bathing in a natural environment. Projected, animated environments completely surrounded the audience. A soothing aural soundscape created by a live DJ mixed natural sounds with lovely melodic lines while dancers (fauns) wove through the space, interacting with the digital environment. We used infrared tracking cameras that allowed the fauns to play with visual objects in the projected environment. For example, there were seed pods that floated at random throughout the projected space, and when "touched," soothing thoughts in the form of poetry floated off through the forest. Select audience members were offered bio monitors as they entered. They were able to watch a visual representation in the form of a floating sprite that reflected their bio rhythms as they experienced the Rallentando journey, offering a soft feedback loop that only they were aware of. In response to the post-show survey question, "What were your thoughts when leaving the space?" many commented on the shift in their state of being; the following are two examples:

- I wanted to go back or immediately crawl into bed and allow the relaxation to take me to sleep or to start doing a long and meditative yoga sequence.
- The piece has wonderful potential, especially in terms of expanding the interactive components. I also reflected on the beautiful "cycle" of using technology to create a relaxing oasis of nature within a city, in a society that often blames technology for removing us from the natural world.

Whether it's sitting in someone's brain (*Sound in Silence*), or one's avatar meeting another through movement (*Disrupting Solitude*), or finding the benefits of forest bathing through a fantastical, immersive journey in nature (*Rallentando*), we fully recognise the awesome creative possibilities offered through digital technology. To be sure, the creation space we have developed on Salt Spring Island, complete with open access to the surrounding forest and a fully equipped digital laboratory (the latest in interactive lighting, projection, and sound technologies), will allow us to continue this exciting work, to move easily between inside and outside and between the real and the imagined

On the Precipice

The Great Pause

This past year has been both a frustration and an opportunity. As the world takes a momentous pause for COVID-19, our work has continued. The creative space at Woodland Farm, now completed, awaits the arrival of our first artist residents. We are brimming with hope and creative energy for what will transpire in the space. We know that we will continue to explore and develop our use of digitally created environments, equally inspired by the forest setting of our studio and our replenished imaginations. We also know that visiting artists, both established and emerging, will inspire us with their work and creative energy. Most importantly, we know there is a certain weightiness to the opportunity we have been given. While the world works its way through the challenges of the current pandemic, there remains a much larger challenge that must be faced: a climate crisis. It may be, with so many of the world's natural environments undergoing rapid changes (e.g. coral reefs and the Amazon jungle) that in the not-too-distant future, the health benefits of forest bathing may be available to even less of the world's population. In the words of Henry David Thoreau, "In society you will not find health, but in nature" (Thoreau 1842, 20). We will most certainly continue to explore the possibilities offered by digitally created natural environments.

Salt Spring Island is one of 13 major islands (along with 450 smaller islands) in the Salish Sea. It is impossible to visit here without immediately being made aware of the constant tension

Figure 17.3 Real/imagined.

Concept: Co-authors

Photo: William J. Mackwood

between the push for more commercial development and a powerful push back to protect the unique nature of these islands. The islands make up a significant portion of the coastal Douglas fir zone, a precious and, due to climate change, threatened ecosystem. Many islanders, in collaboration with the Coast Salish Indigenous peoples, are doing everything they can to preserve and protect the gift that has been entrusted to them. Transition Salt Spring, a non-profit organisation supported by local government, just released its Climate Action Plan 2.0. It offers an amazing 250 recommendations on what needs to happen to ensure a sustainable future for the Island. Perhaps to be expected in our world driven by STEM (science, technology, engineering, and mathematics), this seemingly comprehensive report offers nothing on the role of the arts or artists (Transition Salt Spring 2021).

The benefits of forest bathing, whether in a natural environment or a well-constructed digitally created environment, offers benefits that extend beyond the well-being of the individual participant. In addition to the freedom to create, simultaneously drawing inspiration from nature while having the digital tools available to realise their performance visions, our residency requires that artists spend time each day in the forest or the garden, helping to tend to the land. The opportunity for artists to immerse themselves corporeally in the natural environment, to touch and be touched by the raw beauty of the west coast of Canada, offers benefits to the larger world through the work they will create.

As demonstrated by the environmental art movement, artists can and do affect the way we think about the natural world in which we live. At this critical time, when it seems every scientific indicator points to an impending climate disaster, creativity and innovation are at a premium. It is imperative that artists and their audiences are given the opportunity to immerse themselves in natural environments (even digitally created ones) and, similar to their role in the interactive worlds we create through technology, come to realise they have a part to play in the protection of our very precious and fragile natural world. To remain passive is no longer an option.

Sources

Aldrich, Jennifer L. 2008. "Artist Colonies in Europe, the United Sates, and Florida." Master's Thesis, University of Florida. scholarcommons.usf.edu/etd/115.

Amabile, Teresa. 1988. "A Model of Creativity and Innovations in Organizations." *Research in Organizational Behavior* 10: 123–67.

Barrett, Brian Dudley. 2010. *Artists on the Edge: The Rise of Coastal Artists' Colonies, 1880–1920.* Amsterdam: Amsterdam University Press.

Doidge, Norman. 2007. *The Brain That Changes Itself: Stories of Personal Triumph from the Frontiers of Brain Science.* New York, NY: Viking.

Eliason, O. 2003. *Weather Project.* London: Tate Museum.

Epnere, Ieva (multimedia artist). In discussion with the co-authors, June 2018.

"How Filmmakers and Fishers Saved Fogo Island | CBC Radio." 2018. *CBCnews. CBC/Radio Canada,* July 25, 2018. www.cbc.ca/radio/ideas/how-filmmakers-and-fishers-saved-fogo-island-1.4447208.

Jones, Bill T., Paul Kaiser, and Shelley Eshka. 1999. "Ghostcatching." Video. www.youtube.com/watch?v=x-7Mo3cg9jw.

Kaplan, Stephen. 1995. "The Restorative Benefits of Nature: Toward an Integrative Framework." *Journal of Environmental Psychology* 15 (3): 169–82.

Kundera, Milan, and Linda Asher. 1996. *Slowness.* 1st ed. New York: HarperCollinsPublishers.

Li, Qing. 2018. *Forest Bathing: How Trees Can Help You Find Health and Happiness.* London: Penguin Life.

Low, Colin. *The Children of Fogo Island.* National Film Board of Canada, 1967. www.nfb.ca/film/children_of_fogo_island/.

McCoy, Mitchell Janetta, and Gary W. Evans. 2002. "The Potential Role of the Physical Environment in Fostering Creativity." *Creativity Research Journal* 14 (3–4): 409–26.

Out of the Box Productions. Accessed April 27, 2021. www.outoftheboxproductions.ca/.

Park, Bum Jin, Yuko Tsunetsugu, Tamami Kasetani, Takahide Kagawa, and Yoshifumi Miyazaki. 2009. "The Physiological Effects of Shinrin-Yoku (Taking in the Forest Atmosphere or Forest Bathing): Evidence from Field Experiments in 24 Forests across Japan." *Environmental Health and Preventive Medicine* 15 (1): 18–26. https://doi.org/10.1007/s12199-009-0086-9.

Phillips, Renée. 2021. *What is Environmental Art.* The Healing Power of Art & Artists. Accessed April 15, 2021. www.healing-power-of-art.org/what-is-environmental-art/.

Res Artis, Worldwide Network of Artist Residencies. Accessed April 14, 2021, https://resartis.org/.

Rogers, Linda. 2008. "The Sound in Silence." *Focus*, August.

Seneca, L. A. 2005. *On the Shortness of Life.* Translated by Charles Desmond Nuttall, Costa, and Lucius Annaeus Seneca. New York: Penguin Books.

Thomas, Sue. 2013. "Can We Get All the Nature We Need from the Digital World? – Sue Thomas: Aeon Essays." *Aeon. Aeon,* September 24, 2013. https://aeon.co/essays/can-we-get-all-the-nature-we-need-from-the-digital-world.

Thoreau, Henry David. 1842. "Natural History of Massachusetts." www.walden.org/web/viewer.html?file=https%3A%2F%2Fwww.walden.org%2Fwp-content%2Fuploads%2F2016%2F03%2FNaturalHistoryMassachusetts.pdf.

———. 1888. *Walden.* Walter Scott.

Transition Salt Spring. 2021. Accessed April 2021. https://transitionsaltspring.com/.

Valtchanov, Deltcho, Kevin R. Barton, and Colin Ellard. 2010. "Restorative Effects of Virtual Nature Settings." *Cyberpsychology, Behavior, and Social Networking* 13 (5): 503–12. https://doi.org/10.1089/cyber.2009.0308.

Wang, X., S. Ye, and H. H. Teo. 2014. "Effects of Interruptions on Creative Thinking." Proceedings of the 35th International Conference on Information Systems, Auckland, New Zealand.

18

THE SOUND OF ENVIRONMENTAL CRISIS

Silence as/and Eco-Horror in *A Quiet Place*

Tatiana Konrad

Introduction

This chapter examines the role of sound in John Kasinski's horror film *A Quiet Place* (2018). The film is set in a post-apocalyptic world invaded by monstrous creatures. Hypersensitive to sound, these creatures easily identify humans as they are talking or using any objects that make sounds – and murder them. Hence, in order to survive, humans have to adapt to the new reality and find different ways to exist, interact with the environment, and communicate with each other. In the film, silence is the key to survival. This chapter argues that, through silence, *A Quiet Place* provides a powerful commentary on the current environmental crisis. On the one hand, silence in the film signifies the destruction of the world as we know it, with humans being almost extinct and the few survivors unable to interact as they used to. On the other hand, silence is a metaphor for the lack of sufficient action taken to minimise the effects of current global environmental degradation, including climate change. The chapter views *A Quiet Place* as a distinct example of "eco-horror" that, through *silence*, effectively *communicates* the tragedy of our environmental crisis. This chapter thus pays close attention to the film's soundscape and examines its role in transmitting these environmental concerns. Scholars note that approaches to the landscape reveal an overt interest in the visual, while acoustic dimensions are often neglected (Hedfors and Berg in Farina 2014, 2). This chapter foregrounds the role of a filmic soundscape (i.e. a combination of sounds that formulate a film) and considers the soundscape of *A Quiet Place* as a primary means through which the film's environmental messages are transmitted to the viewer. Sound, as the film suggests, can be used as a unique instrument to generate sympathy in the audience, emphasising inaction as a problem and provoking pro-environmental action. Through sound (silence and quietness), *A Quiet Place* turns into a unique example of *Ecocinema*, cinema that, in the words of Paula Willoquet-Maricondi (2010, 9–10),

> overtly engage[s] with environmental concerns either by exploring specific environmental justice issues or, more broadly, by making "nature," from landscapes to wildlife, a primary focus . . . [as well as] compel[s] us to reflect upon what it means to inhabit this planet: that is, to be a member of the planetary ecosystem . . . and . . . to understand the value of this community in a systemic and nonhierarchical way.

DOI: 10.4324/9781003082798-22

To be more specific, *A Quiet Place* is a piece of eco-horror as it "deals with our fears and anxieties about the environment" (Tidwell 2018, 115). Davina Quinlivan (2012, 1) claims that in film "sound serves to stimulate our perception beyond what is visible on screen." The inability to make sounds, the unusual volume of sound, and at times, the entire absence of sound, as can be experienced while watching *A Quite Place*, effectively stimulate audience perceptions of the world and raise eco-awareness in ecologically precarious times. Alexa Weik von Mossner (2014, 14; 1) foregrounds "affect and emotion" as crucial elements in the process of watching *Ecocinema*; for her, affect is "our automatic, visceral response to a given film or sequence" and emotion is "our cognitive awareness of such a response." Through its complex application of sound, *A Quiet Place* works with affect and emotion, making the audience acutely aware of the current environmental crisis and revealing the uncomfortable and scary truth about the consequences of humanity's criminal exploitation of the environment.

Sound in Film

Since the release of the first sound film *The Jazz Singer* in 1927, sound has been a prominent characteristic of cinema (Fairservice 2001, 203). The inclusion of sound in films has not only technologically transformed cinema but also impacted the ways films communicate certain messages to audiences and how films affect viewers. Sound in cinema includes, among others, monologues and conversations between characters, sound effects that characterise certain objects (a driving car, a ringing phone, etc.) or subjects (a barking dog, a crying child, etc.), and music. In order to understand the effects of omitting sound, as *A Quiet Place* does, this section focuses on the role of sound in cinema in general and the advantages of using sound in film.

Except for characters' lines, sound is perhaps most prominently present in cinema through music. Inclusion of music in films is an expected choice, for music has always been a source of "popular entertainment" (Cooke 2008, 4). Music in films performs "three major functions": it "interprets and adds meaning," "aids memory," and "engages the audience" (Cohen 2014, 101). There is a direct connection between image and sound, and music is largely used to intensify the meaning of the visual. Annabel J. Cohen (2014, 102; 110) argues that music directly impacts the way the audience *views* a film; moreover, she emphasises that the more unrealistic a portrayal is, the more music is needed to keep the audience's attention (as is, for example, the case with animation films). Additionally, music connotes emotional messages of a film and functions as "a signifier of emotion itself" (Nagari 2016, 40). Sound supports image, whereas image supports sound in film; each element is used to develop the meaning of the other. To borrow from Noël Carroll and Patrick Carroll (1986, 79), "If adding music to the movie enhances one's expressive control over the action, it is also the case that the movie imagery intensifies the impact of the music by particularizing its affective resonance." Benjamin Nagari (2016, 32) outlines a distinct connection between sound and visualisation and argues that sound can not only help illustrate certain images and stir the imagination of the viewers; sound *is* image. Nagari (2016, 32) studies the psychological effects of hearing and perceiving sounds and emphasises that sound is sonic imagery that can "start emotive dynamics in the psyche"; once an individual begins to recount a specific sound to someone else, they transform sound as image into a "conscious" category. In film studies, sound is divided into *diegetic* and *nondiegetic*, depending on the relevance of sound to narrated events. Thus, everything that is directly related to a scene shown at a specific moment is *diegetic* sound, whereas sound that characterises people or objects that one cannot view in the scene is *nondiegetic* (Nagari 2016, 34).

Michel Chion's theoretical considerations of sound provide a more detailed interpretation of sound in film (see Nagari 2016, 34–35). Yet his concept of *transsensoriality* is particularly valuable in the context of my analysis, and it supports Nagari's claim about the interconnection between sound and image (Nagari 2016, 35). The concept of *transsensoriality* suggests that "hearing may not take place solely through the ears and . . . seeing may not take place solely with the eyes" (Nagari 2016, 35). Gilles Deleuze argues that "all the sound elements, including music, including silence, form a continuum as something which belongs to the visual image" (quoted in Kielian-Gilbert 2014, 504). Scholars thus emphasise the multimodality of sound and image. Certainly, sound and image as such are not the only driving agents in film: "the selection of the right people, the right faces, the right objects, the right actions, and the right sequences, out of all the equally possible selections within the circumstances of a given situation" is equally important to create a successful product (Eisenstein quoted in Buhler 2014, 190).

Other important characteristics of sound in film are that it "can bear particular cultural and ideological values in a film, . . . can fit into or resist the general filmic system of meaning, and . . . reflects larger social and ideological pressures" (Buhler 2014, 220). In this process, sound functions as a mediator between a specific cinematic example and the audience, inviting viewers to ponder certain meanings and generate their own interpretations. Kathryn Kalinak foregrounds the crucial role of sound (and music, in particular) in film, contending that it "control[s] connotation and position[s] the audience to respond" (quoted in Kielian-Gilbert 2014, 501). In other words, sound both forces the audience to *listen* and draws, to various degrees, audience attention to specific scenes.

In horror films – a genre within which *A Quiet Place* operates – sound plays a special function. Lee Barron and Ian Inglis (2009, 187) provide a helpful explanation of how meaning-making is produced in horror films, foregrounding the following means: "rising levels of noise, reduced levels of noise, tonal distortion, accelerated or decelerated rhythms, turbulence and disorder, irregular lyrical contours, heightened pitch, and the juxtaposition of calm and chaos." The scholars add, "What unites these components is that they are all, in one way or another, 'unsettling.' Indeed, a jarring musical soundtrack has been perceived as one of the crucial ways in which the horror film achieves its psychological impact" (Barron and Inglis 2009, 187). Rebecca Coyle (2009, 213) stresses the importance of suspense in horror films, outlining the intersection of sound and image in its creation:

> All horror movies use suspense techniques to create tension and/or excitement and play with the device of building up through suggestion, then delivering acts, images and sounds of graphic fright or horror. Some films are explicit in their horrific elements, and rely on frequent and/or prolonged use of shock scenes. Other films are more suggestive, relying primarily on the imagined rather than the evident and/or the continual deferral of the explicit.

In the creation of suspense, sound – and specifically its absence – plays a crucial role. It is the absence of sound that signals to the audience that a scary moment should happen soon. Such a silent or quiet moment helps raise tension and is hence crucial in creating a moment of horror. *A Quiet Place*, as this chapter argues, omits sound to create suspense and make the audience expect something terrible to happen at any moment. In doing so, the film intensifies tension to the extent that it makes the audience uncomfortable and fully aware of horror as a *reality* (rather than a limited moment). Never resolving tension, *A Quiet Place* uses sound (or rather its absence) to communicate the permanent horror of the new reality displayed in the film – the reality that is the result of an environmental collapse. Philip Hayward (2009, 2) argues that music's "capacity to create tension and shock [is] *supplementary* to narrative" and foregrounds "visual design" as particularly important in horror films. While the image can indeed play a crucial role in horror, sound, as *A Quiet Place* vividly illustrates, is a potent instrument through which horror can be conveyed, too.

Silence in *A Quiet Place*

A Quiet Place tells a story of Lee Abbott (John Krasinski), his wife Evelyn (Emily Blunt), and their three children – the deaf daughter, Regan (Millicent Simmonds), and the sons Marcus (Noah Jupe) and Beau (Cade Woodward). The family struggles to survive in a post-apocalyptic world invaded by monstrous creatures. These creatures are blind, yet they can acutely hear sounds. In order to avoid a deadly meeting with the creatures, humans thus have to stay quiet. Quietness in the film relates to both not speaking and not making any sounds through actions or movements or with the help of other objects.

The film opens with a scene in which the family explore an abandoned supermarket for food, medication, and other necessary items. The youngest child, Beau, finds a toy, which he wants to keep. The toy is too dangerous because, powered through batteries, it can be activated, and the sound from the toy can attract the creatures. From its very beginning, *A Quiet Place* introduces a unique soundscape in which human silence/quietness is crucial, thus emphasising its interest in the world that goes *beyond* the human. Regan allows her brother to keep the toy without the batteries, yet Beau also grabs batteries. On their way, Beau, who is walking slightly behind his family, activates the toy. The terrified family turns to him, Lee runs to help the child, yet he is too slow and a suddenly appearing creature murders Beau. Over a year passes after the tragic accident, Evelyn is now pregnant, and the family continues to survive in their new world.

An important part of survival in *A Quiet Place* is to stay silent. Being quieter or speaking in a whisper is not enough because the creatures can easily detect even the most minor sounds. The American Sign Language that the family use to communicate with the deaf daughter, Regan, becomes an important means to survive. *Communication* among family members thus takes place on a regular basis; *speaking* is part of their daily activities, yet *sound* is what the characters have to avoid. The danger of sound in the new world is effectively conveyed through several scenes. For example, when Lee brings his son Marcus to a waterfall and explains to him that here they can speak as loud as they want to; they can even scream – the water blocks the sound that they can produce, and thus, the creatures cannot hear them. In a later scene, Lee and Marcus encounter a man in a forest, who, evidently unable to live in the new, dangerous world anymore, screams in order to attract the creatures; with the help of sound, the man thereby commits suicide. In both scenes, the interaction between humans and the environment is conveyed through the filmic soundscape. The power of nature over humanity is reinforced through the sounds of the loud waterfall, whereas the vulnerability of humans is emphasised through the characters' screams that in the earlier scene remain inaudible whereas, in the later scene, they lead to death.

Toward the end of the film, when Lee, Regan, and Marcus have to confront a creature, screaming is used as a weapon: it saves some characters while making others more vulnerable. Thus, as the creature attacks Lee, Marcus tries to help his father. The boy gets out of a car that he and Regan use as a shelter and screams, thereby distracting the creature from Lee. When the creature, however, gets on top of the car, shaking and hitting it, Lee realises that the only way he can save his children is by distracting the creature from the car. Lee drops the axe that he uses to protect himself, thus demonstrating his willingness to sacrifice himself for his children, and screams. The creature attacks Lee, whereas Marcus starts the car and, leaving the place, saves his sister and himself.

What does the film attempt to communicate through silence as a survival technique? This chapter argues that silence in *A Quiet Place* can be interpreted in several ways. I interpret the post-apocalyptic setting in the film as an outcome of environmental degradation and argue that *A Quiet Place* attempts to comment on the problem of the environmental crisis that humanity faces today. The collapse of the world as we know it, the emergence of a new, precarious, and dangerous world, the monsters that invade it – these are all the result of nature's exploitation, abuse, and ultimate mutation.

There is an intricate connection between place/space and sound. While the landscape and the soundscape can be examined separately, the two, in fact, dramatically inform one another. Eckehard Pistrick and Cyril Isnart (2013, 504) argue, "Sound (as well as vision and smell) and space mutually reinforce one another in our perception." In *A Quiet Place*, the connection between place/space and sound can be perceived in two ways: first, how the characters perceive their surroundings through silence and, second, how the audience perceives the world that the film imagines and the transformed lives of the human characters through silence and loud sounds. The involvement of the viewer in the process of seeing and perceiving the new world is particularly important to achieve the film's eco-activist goal. Berys Gaut foregrounds *identification* that takes place when audiences watch a film, singling out several ways in which it happens:

> To identify perceptually with a character is to imagine seeing what he sees; to identify affectively with him is to imagine feeling what he feels; to identify motivationally is to imagine wanting what he wants; to identify epistemically with him is to imagine believing what he believes; to identify practically with him is to imagine doing what he does; and so on.
>
> *(Quoted in Ingram 2014, 30)*

Through silence and quiet and loud sounds, *A Quiet Place* forces the viewer to understand the landscape – in the film and in reality – as both existing with and beyond the soundscape. Place, according to Pistrick and Isnart (2013, 504), can be "experienced" both "sensually and bodily," and sound plays a crucial role in this process, "appropriating and humanizing space, turning it into a place, a site of human intervention and sociocultural practice." Through sound, the human both shapes and perceives the environment as a *human* place. This is exactly the trope that *A Quiet Place* employs in order to recreate an eco-horror – once devoid of sound, place becomes a precarious space in which human existence has a contingent nature.

While silence can signify danger, it can also background the anthropocentric view of the world. In *A Quiet Place*, the characters have to remain quiet or silent in order to survive. But such a state of quietness/silence can also help one hear and listen to the non-human world. This reinforces the fluidity of the sound-place relationship, for as Pistrick and Isnart (2013, 506) claim, sounds can be "placed" and "exist beyond place." Through quietness/silence, the film also reminds the characters and the human audiences that they are not the only ones who shape the landscape through sound. The environment is largely formulated through non-humans that inhabit it; even more than that, the environment as such is a being that has a sound materiality of its own. Jonathan Sterne contends that, through sound, one can deal with "big questions about the cultural moments and crises and problems of [the] time" (quoted in Clement 2016, 350). *A Quiet Place*, in particular, addresses the problem of environmental degradation and calls for pro-environmental action by silencing humanity. Sara Kay and François Noudelmann (2018, 2) emphasise how important it is "to go beyond the human voice – and even the human ear – as measure(s) of what sound is" to understand the true nature of sound. This is exactly what *A Quiet Place* does by choosing to put the volume of the human voice down.

This chapter directly connects silence in the film to environmental issues. Silence performs several functions in *A Quiet Place*. First, it is a potent tool that the horror film uses to emphasise the inevitable, dramatic change that is the result of an environmental crisis. The inability to communicate in the way that the characters without hearing loss are used to symbolically stands for the changing status of humans. It deprives them of agency and thus accentuates their vulnerability in the new world – humans are no longer powerful abusers; they are vulnerable subjects that can easily turn into victims.

Second, the film uses silence to broadly comment on the lack of action that humans take in order to prevent the climate crisis and global environmental crisis more generally. The emphasis on being silent is employed to communicate the tragedy of choosing such a trajectory today. In times of crisis, humans and non-humans can die (hence, be silenced) if humanity remains silent or quiet (i.e. passive and neglectful) about the environmental degradation that is occurring right now. Finally, silence in the film is used to create suspense and reconstruct the true horror of today's environmental situation. Sound is used in multiple ways in the film. There are, indeed, moments when suspense created through silence or quietness is resolved through louder sounds. Nevertheless, when considered generally, silence largely invades the film, helping create tension that, in principle, is too hard to resolve. The viewer realises that this tension is the permanent reality, and there is no action that the characters can take to solve the problem. Hence, through silence, the film emphasises the horrifying stage at which humanity finds itself today – an era of anthropogenic environmental degradation that can lead to environmental collapse.

What effect does *A Quiet Place* try to achieve through silence? This chapter argues that the film promotes environmental activism through silence; it chooses a strategy that some might consider paradoxical, yet instead of direct, loud speeches for the audience, the film chooses to be as quiet as possible and, in doing so, thus says much about the problem. Through an unusual turn to silence and quietness, the film forces the viewer to be more attentive and thereby works as a form of environmental activism. According to Carroll and Carroll (1986, 75), sound (and music more specifically) "modifies" films. One way it does so is through the transformation of the visual. But sound also engages the viewer in a specific way: it makes one *listen* to the film. Marianne Kielian-Gilbert (2014, 503) argues that listening is "an act of attention, of an effort to hear toward affect." To make the viewer *listen* is one crucial way to spread eco-awareness. Playing with sound has proved to be an effective and frequently used method in environmental activism. For example, the artist Jana Winderen, through her sound-works that help the audience hear and listen to underwater ecosystems tries to foreground "the importance of the inaudible, . . . that which lies outside our senses and our possibility of perception" (quoted in Gilmurray 2017, 36). Another artist, Andrea Polli, emphasises the power of sound to communicate important issues, including environmental degradation:

> I think that sound is a very visceral thing and I think that if people can really feel the potential difficulties, the potential discomfort, but more than just uncomfortable, actual problems that will result from global warming, maybe in some way they will be convinced to think more seriously about the issue.
>
> *(Quoted in Gilmurray 2017, 36)*

Silence in films, including silence and quietness in *A Quiet Place*, is, of course, a very relative phenomenon. Mervyn Cooke (2008, 1) foregrounds the fact that even in silent cinema, silence was not characteristic of the full process of showing and perceiving films: the audience directly participated in the film by creating noise, and thus, silent cinema was no longer silent – even Andy Warhol's silent movies created in mid-20th century relied on the audience participation. Other scholars stress the power of music in silent films, which broke the silence of those films and detracted audience attention beyond the visual only (Buhler and Neumeyer 2014, 18).

Similarly, *A Quiet Place* is neither fully silent (after all, the film includes scenes where characters talk as loud as the audience would observe in any other film, and communicate in whispers and screams), nor does it exclude audience participation. By generating tension and an atmosphere of horror, the film forces the audience to be acutely aware of the reality reconstructed on the screen and, through its emotional involvement, participate in the film. Film as a medium relies on the audience's emotional involvement, but the *forced* absence of sound (i.e. the characters can make sounds, but they must not if they want to survive) in *A Quiet Place* effectively reaches the viewers and generates sympathy in response. Cooke (2008, 3) draws on Alfred Hitchcock's film *The Birds* (Hitchcock et al. 1963) to illustrate the use of "a threatening silence," such as "when a car is driven away in complete silence at the end of *The Birds*, the same vehicle having demonstrated its noisy engine in a previous scene," with the effect "unsettling." Cooke (2008, 3) concludes that "the sudden cessation of music when the latter is expected to be continuous can have an enormous dramatic impact on an audience." *A Quiet Place* employs a similar technique – it uses silence in the moments when the audience would not conventionally expect silence as well as creates various levels of silence and quietness, thereby making the audience uncomfortable and emphasising the unpleasant and dangerous nature of the new reality reconstructed in the film.

One of the most powerful scenes in *A Quiet Place* is when Evelyn, being alone at home, is in labour. As her water breaks, Evelyn tries to calm herself down and slowly goes to the basement. Yet walking down the stairs, she steps on a nail. While Evelyn manages to keep quiet, she drops a photograph that she has been carrying, and the frame loudly shatters into multiple pieces. The woman switches on the red light – an emergency signal that she sends to her family. Soon Evelyn realises that she is not alone – one of the creatures has heard the sound of the breaking frame and is now searching through the house. Evelyn tries to fight both the fear of the approaching creature and the pain from the onset of labour, keeping herself quiet and calm and breathing heavily. As she hides in the dark basement, the audience can hear only the sounds produced by the creature and Evelyn's breathing. The creature hears the sound of a timer – a trap set by Evelyn – and leaves the room, which gives Evelyn a moment to escape the corner where she has been hiding and move to a bathroom. As the woman lies down in a bathtub, blood running between her legs, the audience hears the creature slithering toward the bathroom. Evelyn is unable to control herself anymore, yet at that moment, Marcus ignites fireworks to distract the creature, and Evelyn begins to scream. She and the baby survive and the family reunites, having experienced yet another moment of horror. The labour scene effectively illustrates a soundscape of environmental crisis and relations between humans and the planet in times of such a calamity. Evelyn is a metaphor for our planet in this scene – like Mother Earth, she can give birth to a new life, but she is also in danger. Evelyn is sweating, her face is distorted because of the pain that she is feeling, yet her pain remains inaudible to the audience. The monster could arrive at any second and kill her and her unborn baby; however, no matter how much she wants to scream for help, she cannot do so. The filmic soundscape imitates a "silenced planet" that is being slowly but steadily destroyed by humanity and that, just like Evelyn in labour, remains quiet in this deadly new reality.

Evelyn's pregnancy is symbolic in the film. It gives hope for humanity's survival. Yet the birth scene, despite its happy end, illustrates how precarious the new conditions are in which humans find themselves. The silence of the birth scene is forced; moreover, the audience realises how hard it is for Evelyn to remain silent and to keep her baby silent. It recognises how difficult it is for Lee to not cry loudly as he runs into the house and, unable to find his wife and seeing only blood in the bathtub, believe that she is dead. And lastly, the audience comprehends how challenging it is for Lee not to scream with happiness after he discovers both Evelyn and the baby safe and sound. Forcing people to be quiet, the film redirects attention from humans to what is happening around them, to the non-human world. Environmental humanities scholars emphasise the importance of recognising the non-human world to better understand not only the environment that surrounds us but also our role on the planet, the responsibility that we bear, and the consequences of our actions. Timothy Morton (2010, 1) coins the term "the ecological thought" to emphasise that "everything is interconnected," and the current crisis perhaps most vividly illustrates the bond between the human and the non-human worlds. According to Morton (2010, 1), "the more we consider it ['the ecological thought'/the bond between the human and non-human worlds], the more our world opens up."

Jane Bennett (2010, ix–xiv), in her influential book *Vibrant Matter: A Political Ecology of Things*, urges humanity to recognise "the nonhuman powers circulating around and within our bodies" and generate "a cultivated, patient, sensory attentiveness to nonhuman forces." Understanding the world *with* but also *beyond* humanity can help us recognise the diversity and complexity of the world that surrounds humankind, the effects of its destructive, anti-environmental actions, and the ramifications of environmental crises. Working through senses, such as hearing, can be an effective and affective way to carry out this intricate task. David Abram (1996, 65) argues, "As we return to our senses, we gradually discover our sensory perceptions to be simply our part of a vast, interpenetrating webwork of perceptions and sensations borne by countless other bodies." Through our senses, humanity can experience the environment on new levels and try to understand its complex nature. Or in words of Abram (1996, 65), humans can recognise themselves in a new role, that of "the attentive human animal who is entirely a part of the world that he, or she, experiences." And this practice has a profound pro-environmental effect. Stacy Alaimo (2010, 2) contends that

> thinking across bodies may catalyze the recognition that the environment, which is too often imagined as inert, empty space or as a resource for human use, is, in fact, a world of fleshy beings with their own needs, claims, and actions.

A Quiet Place invites the audience to experience something that we might not be able to see or might not want to see. The film engages sound to do that and, as a result, communicates dimensions of the problems and threats of environmental collapse.

Conclusion

We live in the era of environmental degradation. It is vitally important that humanity address the problems and challenges of today's world – one that humans built with the help of cheap energy by exploiting the environment and treating nature as an inexhaustible well. Numerous cinematic examples draw the film audience's attention to the ongoing environmental crisis, forcing viewers to see the ramifications of their actions on the environment. *A Quiet Place* is one such example. By imagining a post-apocalyptic world in which humans are vulnerable subjects and survival is possible only if the characters do not make any sounds, the film emphasises the transformation of the world as we know it into a precarious, dangerous, and unpredictable place. *A Quiet Place* uses silence to reinforce the horror of the environmental crisis, illustrating how a lack of sufficient action can lead to the full destruction of an environment that is safe for humans and non-humans, with the emergence of a new, menacing world. The film's soundscape thus becomes crucial in transmitting our current environmental crisis and emphasising the urgency with which we must address it. Through the characters' inability to speak as loud as they want to, behave as they wish, and live the life in the way they choose, the film warns the audience about the serious consequences of environmental collapse, which questions the survival of humans and non-humans.

Sources

Abram, David. 1996. *The Spell of the Sensuous: Perception and Language in a More-Than-Human World*. New York: Vintage Books.

Alaimo, Stacy. 2010. *Bodily Natures: Science, Environment, and the Material Self.* Bloomington: Indiana University Press.

Barron, Lee, and Ian Inglis. 2009. "Scary Movies, Scary Music: Uses and Unities of Heavy Metal in the Contemporary Horror Film." In *Terror Tracks: Music, Sound and Horror Cinema*, edited by Philip Hayward, 186–97. London: Equinox.

Bennett, Jane. 2010. *Vibrant Matter: A Political Ecology of Things*. Durham: Duke University Press.

Buhler, James. 2014. "Ontological, Formal, and Critical Theories of Film Music and Sound." In *The Oxford Handbook of Film Music Studies*, edited by David Neumeyer, 188–225. Oxford: Oxford University Press.

Buhler, James, and David Neumeyer. 2014. "Music and the Ontology of the Sound Film: The Classical Hollywood System." In *The Oxford Handbook of Film Music Studies*, edited by David Neumeyer, 17–43. Oxford: Oxford University Press.

Carroll, Noël, and Patrick Carroll. 1986. "Notes on Movie Music." *Studies in the Literary Imagination* 19 (1): 73–81.

Clement, Tanya E. 2016. "When Texts of Study Are Audio Files: Digital Tools for Sound Studies in Digital Humanities." In *A New Companion to the Digital Humanities*, edited by Susan Schreibman, Ray Siemens, and John Unsworth, 348–57. Hoboken: John Wiley & Sons, Ltd.

Cohen, Annabel J. 2014. "Film Music from the Perspective of Cognitive Science." In *The Oxford Handbook of Film Music Studies*, edited by David Neumeyer, 96–130. Oxford: Oxford University Press.

Cooke, Mervyn. 2008. *A History of Film Music*. Cambridge: Cambridge University Press.

Coyle, Rebecca. 2009. "Spooked by Sound: The Blair Witch Project." In *Terror Tracks: Music, Sound and Horror Cinema*, edited by Philip Hayward, 213–28. London: Equinox.

Fairservice, Don. 2001. *Film Editing: History, Theory and Practice: Looking at the Invisible*. Manchester: Manchester University Press.

Farina, Almo. 2014. *Soundscape Ecology: Principles, Patterns, Methods and Applications*. Dordrecht: Springer.

Gilmurray, Jonathan. 2017. "Ecological Sound Art: Steps towards a New Field." *Organised Sound* 22 (1): 32–41.

Hayward, Philip. 2009. "Introduction: Scoring the Edge." In *Terror Tracks: Music, Sound and Horror Cinema*, edited by Philip Hayward, 1–13. London: Equinox.

Hitchcock, A., E. Hunter, S. Pleshette, S. Taylor, J. Tandy, T. Hedren, and M. D. Du. 1963. *The Birds*. Los Angeles, CA: Alfred J. Hitchcock Productions.

Ingram, David. 2014. "Emotion and Affect in Eco-films: Cognitive and Phenomenological Approaches." In *Moving Environments: Affect, Emotion, Ecology, and Film*, edited by Alexa Weik von Nossner, 23–39. Waterloo: Wilfrid Laurier University Press.

Kay, Sarah, and François Noudelmann. 2018. "Introduction: Soundings and Soundscapes." *Paragraph* 41 (1): 1–9.

Kielian-Gilbert, Marianne. 2014. "Listening in Film: Music/Film Temporality, Materiality, and Memory." In *The Oxford Handbook of Film Music Studies*, edited by David Neumeyer, 500–25. Oxford: Oxford University Press.

Morton, Timothy. 2010. *The Ecological Thought*. Cambridge: Harvard University Press.

Nagari, Benjamin. 2016. *Music as Image: Analytical Psychology and Music in Film*. London: Routledge.

Pistrick, Eckehard, and Cyril Isnart. 2013. "Landscapes, Soundscapes, Mindscapes: Introduction." *Etnográfica: Revista do Centro em Rede de Investigação em Antropologia* 17 (3): 503–13.

A Quiet Place. 2018. Directed by John Krasinski. Performances by Emily Blunt, John Krasinski, Millicent Simmonds, and Noah Jupe. Hollywood: Paramount Pictures.

Quinlivan, Davina. 2012. *The Place of Breath in Cinema*. Edinburgh: Edinburgh University Press.

Tidwell, Christy. 2018. "Ecohorror." In *Posthuman Glossary*, edited by Rosi Braidotti and Maria Hlavajova, 115–17. London: Bloomsbury.

Weik von Mossner, Alexa. 2014. "Introduction: Ecocritical Film Studies and the Effects of Affect, Emotion, and Cognition." In *Moving Environments: Affect, Emotion, Ecology, and Film*, edited by Alexa Weik von Nossner, 1–19. Waterloo: Wilfrid Laurier University Press.

Willoquet-Maricondi, Paula. 2010. "Introduction: From Literary to Cinematic Ecocriticism." In *Framing the World: Explorations in Ecocriticism and Film*, edited by Paula Willoquet-Maricondi, 1–22. Charlottesville: University of Virginia Press.

PART IV

Species, Systems, Sustainability

19

GENOTYPE, PHENOTYPE, PHOTOTYPE

Digital Photography, Biological Variety, and Excessive Overpopulation of Types

Ana Peraica

> Of the parts of animals, some are simple: to wit, all such as divide into parts uniform with themselves, as flesh into flesh; others are composite, such as divide into parts not uniform with themselves, as, for instance, the hand does not divide into hands nor the face into faces.
>
> – *Aristotle,* History of Animals *(350 BCE), book 1*

Introduction

In ancient times species were vanishing in major natural changes accidents, in sync with climactic or astronomic accidents (Kolbert 2014). Human sciences have mapped five such extinctions of species occurring to the present day. Besides the sciences, we also have these extinctions recorded in major cultural narratives. One such narrative, elaborating on the disappearance of species, may be found in the Bible, in the story of Noah's ark. In the wake of the apocalypse, Noah constructs a boat to save both female and male specimens of each animal kind from a flood catastrophe. The narrative did not specify animal species included. However, many medieval visual representations depict the number of animal species known to humans in ancient times as limited to domesticated animals and a few dangerous species in the wild.

Only from today's perspective, in which science recognises millions of species, the architecture of "that 'kind of boat' or 'vast floating building'" seems impossible (Damisch 2016). Although based on the narrative of the biblical version of creation, Noah's ark projected quite a scientific biological formula of salvation; it defined a database of live genetic material that would, hopefully under some new circumstances, procreate again and adapt its biological characteristics according to need. However, the idea that species adapt and vanish if they cannot adapt did not emerge for many centuries. Charles Darwin's *Origin of Species* (1859), the first to advocate the non-creationist theory of species, also proposed the idea of the slow disappearance of species that were unable to compete with other species or adapt to their environments.

DOI: 10.4324/9781003082798-24

Today we are witnessing the combination of extinctions by external force and a slow competition-based one. The present so-called Sixth Extinction of species is, on the one hand, massive as the previous five extinctions (Kolbert 2014). However, significant climate or astronomic events do not drive these events, but rather, Darwinian species competitions are the main drivers. A new competition is deeply grounded in the human state of affairs – the competition in the market economy has had fatal consequences for many lifeforms since the start of contemporary capitalism (Moore 2016). In such a system, humans compete only with themselves while other species either disappear as material tools and vehicles of such competition or simply vanish by denial of their right to exist. Since the birth of contemporary capitalism, humans have been entirely focused on themselves and have been competing with their inventions. Recently deceased meteorologist and atmospheric chemist Paul Crutzen first defined our period as the Anthropocene – the long-term geological period initiated by the invention of the steam engine in 1786. The Anthropocene unfolded as an age of substantial human impact on its habitable environment (Crutzen 2002). Pollution caused by the massive exploitation of coal and fossil oils and their derivates has made the world chemically, atmospherically, and meteorologically unstable and thus unliveable. Progressing slowly, over 200 years, the Anthropocene has reached the point where, according to the Convention of Biological Diversity, 150 living species are lost on a daily basis. With this reduction in genetic variation and species, we must keep in mind the estimated nearly 9 million species living on the planet, and the human sciences have indexed only 1.6 million species, and many may become extinct before being documented (University of Turku 2020). On the other hand, images of some species going extinct have been recorded and archived. So for example, today, we know the dodo, the Honshu wolf, the ivory-billed woodpecker, the huia, the passenger pigeon, the thylacine, and the grey whale by their photographic black-and-white images. Fortunately, the invention of the technology of photography went hand-in-hand with the initiation of the Anthropocene.

Photography, invented only 55 years after the steam engine, which initiated the fatal and massive exploitation of coal and fossil fuel, has thoroughly recorded the processes of the Anthropocene, for which I propose a conception of the *Photographocene* (Peraica 2021a). Although sounding like yet another neologism, my concept is intended to mark knowledge of global environmental changes as conditioned by the mediation processes of photography. For example, comparing historical photographs with current planetary conditions can identify significant anthropogenic environmental changes, such as permafrost thawing and deglaciation. In addition to the slow changes occurring in the landscape, photographers, since the inception of the craft and technology, have been documenting species, including ones that once inhabited our planet. This chapter focuses on the visual documentation of species and the changes such images have undergone with the medium's technological evolution to today's digital mediums and more unhuman like manifestations (Zylinska 2017). Extensive visual archives of species construct this field and computation methods peculiar for the biological use of photographs or mimicking natural reproduction processes (rather than technological processes of the medium). My central questions are as follows: What changes in computational neural networks are introduced, and what is their capacity for generating images of extinct species? Are these changes in any way comparable to genetic computation, or are they merely a simulation? If changes are comparable in any way, how do we approach them and define this new field?[1]

Photogenetics

Photography of species precedes the formation of libraries of genetic material we know today. Although it records only the visual appearance of the biological material, the existence of photography in biology, or more precisely genetics, is undeniable. Therefore, it is useful to define and map this emerging field of *photogenetics* and recognise its presence since the invention of photographic technology (Peraica 2021b; *in print*). It must be recognised that the first attempts to assemble visual databases of species were through piling drawings. Since the Neolithic period, humans have drawn various species, yet systematic documentation was not initiated until the age of discovery and the Enlightenment, between the 15th and 18th centuries, when Westerners started travelling and discovering places outside Europe and the Mediterranean basin. Hand-drawn animal atlases captured biodiversity before photography (Davidson 2017). For example, James Audubon (1785–1851) painted and created an archive of species, his most famous work being a colour-plate atlas *The Birds of America* (1827–1839) Indeed, *speciesism*, paralleling different other forms of chauvinism, like racism, brought many specimens to court collections. However, it was Henry Fox Talbot (1800–1877), one of the inventors of the Stabile photographic image, who was the first to employ the term *photogenetic drawing*. What he meant by the term was twofold: that the picture originated in the light (by process of photo-genesis) and that the use of this technology halts certain biological artefacts and processes.[2] Photographing animals soon become a widespread practice in addition to recording the images of exotic animals. This "provided science with an epistemological tool that produced flattened and manageable copies of animal bodies" and "furnished the practice of transiting animals into discourse through a new sophisticated limiting and flattening process" (Aloi 2018, 161). Talbot was the first to create experimental prints of botanical specimens using light-sensitive salts on paper (Burnett-Brown et al. 2000). His close friend, the botanist Anna Atkins, pioneered the method of *cyanotypes* and continued the methodical documenting and cataloguing of British algae and foreign fauna. It took a while before portable cameras could be taken into the field to record live animals. One of the oldest images of this kind was contained in the collection of Conte de Montizon, featuring a hippopotamus at a zoological garden in 1852. With the popularisation of travel, new images of species were recorded more frequently. By the end of the 19th century, the camera was also used in a specific type of hunt – the photo-hunt, whose mission was object-driven – yet the new type of trophy was the image – a "photo-trophy." In many cases, a photo-trophy accompanied the actual animal corpse. The process thus documented the animalistic human need to take the life of another species.[3]

A new photographic genre of wildlife was promoted by magazines like *Nature* and *National Geographic*, respectively established in1868 and 1888. Existing today, these magazines formed a specific genre of wildlife photography, creating many specialists in the field. For example, Todd R. Forsgreen is known for photographs of animals trapped in nets, Katherine Wolkoff for her taxidermic silhouettes, and J.J. Woodward and Susan Derges for bird images, while Sanna Kanisto produces catalogues of flowers.

Although their images were not initially meant to carry messages of environmental tragedies, today's photographs of wildlife are today becoming more than just aesthetic curiosities. With the planet's loss of biodiversity, these images reverberate with the connotation of the "requiem for species" (Hamilton 2015). Plenty of authors and photographers recording animals shoot the last members of a species, or the so-called endlings, to raise consciousness on current extinctions. These include Tim Flach, Joel Sartore, Susan Middleton, David Littschwager, and Gregory Colbert.[4] Their photographic hunts focus on recording the "rarest of the rare" to preserve a specific type of genetics – at least in its visual form (Ackerman 1997).

Such images are uploaded to databases, becoming new forms of Noah's ark, but now with the dubious capacity to procreate in new circumstances. As the number of images in databases indexing biodiversity on Earth grows, so does species extinction.

Databases

As already mentioned, the human sciences have catalogued about 1.8 million out of nearly 9 million species. Some images in the Biodiversity Heritage Library originate in the 15th century (Ebert 2020). There are also other databases, such as Arkive.org, the Barcode of Life, the Catalogue of Life, Encyclopaedia of Life, Global Biodiversity Facility, Consortium for Conservation of Nature, and the Red List of Extinct Species.[5] Among these databases, two types can be distinguished; one depicts extinct species, and the other represents existing ones. As the Sixth Extinction progresses, the albums of extinct species grow more significant and more extensive than the albums of biodiversity. Ursula Heise (2016, 65) describes two motivations behind building these massive collections:

> Global digital biodiversity databases, then, can be understood to emerge from the conjunction of two tendencies: an encyclopaedic, centripetal impulse that reaches back to the Enlightenment and seeks to inventory the entire known world, and the hyperlinked, centrifugal architecture of the Internet, which seeks to approximate a representation of this world through the constant movement between data sites.

A third motivation can be added to Heise's description – the logic of the medium of photography as original biotechnology. Whereas in the 19th century, photographs were organised in archives, until the end of the 20th century, most images were scanned into chaotic databases. Today, databases act as dynamic datasets, in which an individual image is not networked but engaged in the production of new images. This practice of computing "genetic visual appearance" is not new. The relationship between photography and genetics draws us back to Francis Galton, who introduced, in his treatise *Human Faculty* (1883), the concept of eugenics and related it directly to photographic experiments. Galton was a close relative to Charles Darwin, with whom he exchanged many letters and manuscripts (Gillham 2009). The significant impact of Darwin's thesis is visible in Galton's works *Hereditary Talent and Character* (1865), *Hereditary Genius* (1879), and *Natural Inheritance* (1889). However, the most significant impact, it seems, was in the implementation of photography as a basis of scientific material and evidence. Photography played an important part in Darwin's *Expressions of Emotions in Man and Animals* (1872), the first book ever illustrated by photography (Prodger 2009). While his cousin Darwin used photos to document species, Galton invented a process for making composite portraits, which revolutionised the field of photography.[6] In the article "Composite Portraits, Made by Combining Those of Many Different Persons into a Single Resultant Figure" (1879) Galton described how he overlayed several portraits by making holes in sitters' eyes on the negative, and then sticking negatives onto pins to fuse ideas before re-recording them to produce a composite image.[7]

Using this method, he computed genetic resemblances within one family, social group, nation, or race. Additionally, he compared the medical conditions of patients suffering from tuberculosis, phthisis, and alcoholism, among other ailments. Galton employed his method to show the relation of a subject's visual appearance with a certain (invisible) genetic quality to frame within period concepts of genetics. Galton's method posited that certain visible features could be computed to make conclusions about genetic dispositions by using photographic technologies. To understand Galton's perspective, a brief overview of the concepts of genotype and phenotype may be helpful. The former is a genetic contribution that is often "determined by the environmental factor," while the latter is a visual trace of someone's genetics that can be observed but also recorded (Taylor and Lewontin 2021). Alternatively, the genotype can only

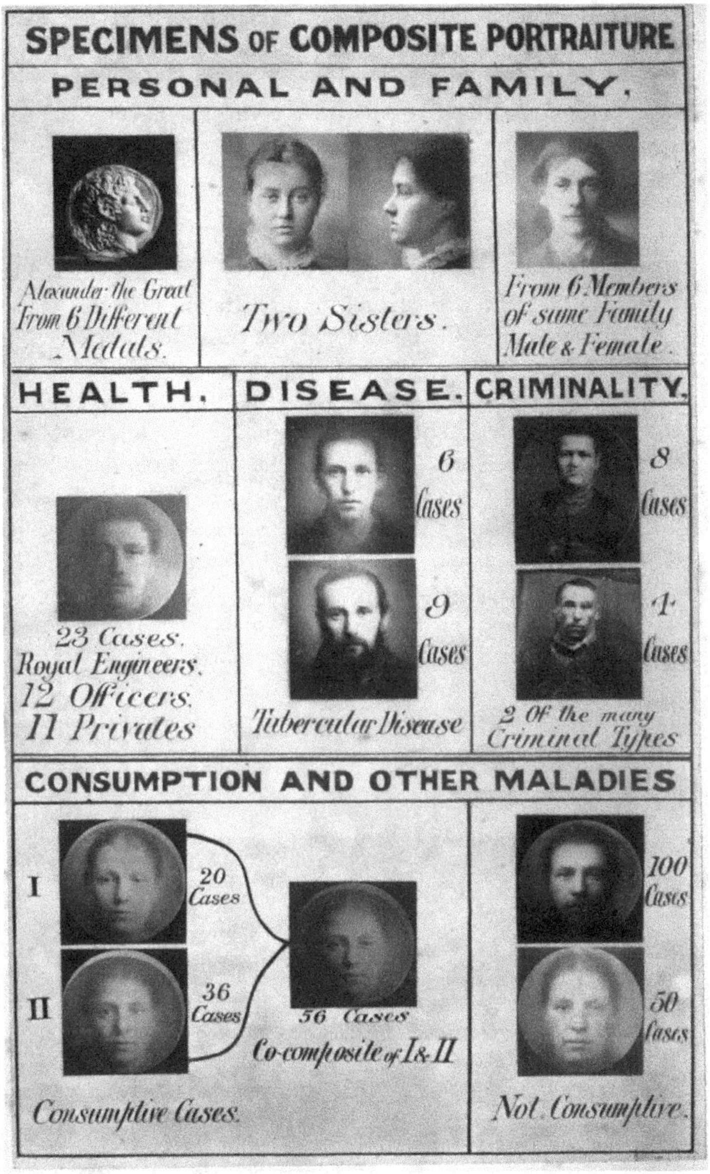

Figure 19.1 Sir Francis Galton 1883. *Inquiries into Human Faculty and Its Development*, p. 7 (Wikimedia archive: the work in the public domain).

be visualised, while phenotype is visible (Nelkin 1996). Galton contended the genotype could be determined from a visual analysis of phenotype. With computer assistance, such calculations become more precise.

Computed photography, or what Daniel Rubinstein calls posthuman photography, is defined as a concern "with the photographic image that is based not on the patriarchal politics of identity and subject-object dualism but on establishing the multiversal: rhizomatic assemblage fragments

[0] + [1] repetition, that when taken together form a picture of what it means 'to be' in the digital age" (2018, 4). As such, it was developed in advance of contemporary generative photography. Artists David Trood and Lillian Schwarz have computed more elements than Galton did originally. Yet the most considerable advancement comes from Nancy Burson, who created software that can reach beyond the appearance of the photographic image and show processes, such as ageing (Buselle 1994). Anne Collins Goodyear prophetically noted that Burson's innovative work on

> portraiture has long reflected the impact of scientific and technological advances on perception of human identity. With the recent proliferation of digital media and the deciphering of human genome, this historic link has reasserted itself
>
> *(2009, 28)*

Technology, and more precisely advanced photographic technology, allows us to test genetic combinations between humans, see how someone's children might look alike, and cross species that are vanishing. Thus, photographic technology relates genotype permutation with phenotype appearance by recording it into photographs. To compute complex visual data, today, it is no longer necessary to pin negatives and rephotograph them, as Galton did in the 19th century. Neural networks, or more precisely generative adversarial networks (GANs), are doing it in competition between two machines – the generator, which produces the image, and the discriminator, which accepts or denies the image as representative of some group. These systems, such as the projects This Person Does Not Exist by Philip Wang or Face Generator by Greg Surma illustrate, compute images representing faces of humans that appear lifelike yet have never existed biologically. GANs are not restricted to computing only "virtual humans" but can freely

Figure 19.2 Philip Wang: This Person Does Not Exist, 2019. www.thispersondoesnotexist.com.

act to create new combinations. Such is the case with GANimals platform designed by the computer systems company NVIDIA.[8] In GANimals, the user can upload an image of their pet to select various cross-species morphings while monitoring genetic mutations in places where the human sciences forbid it. In addition to documenting existing species, new genera are created. However, the problem with digital photography technologies that generate faces of humans or animals out of extant photographic material goes beyond the playfulness of *GANimals* and is twofold. First, the photographic images look like living beings (or they seem to share what is considered a living phenotype), while their genotypes cannot be biological; second, they are made out of images of live, organic beings.

"Empty" Phenotypes

Although some of the images produced by generative networks seem to have phenotypes, there is no genotype behind these images; nevertheless, the idea of genetic permutation does remain. Moreover, what exists behind the observable phenotype is not a genetic material but a photograph. This paradox was already recognised by Eylat Van Essen (2019, 198), who initially pointed to the tense relationship between the medium of photography and genetics, writing that "polemics characterises current photography between . . . total fragmentation and abstraction of reality and . . . affinity with the natural substance to which the biological concepts of genotype and phenotype can be applied." Van Essen (2019, 170) also asserts a relationship between photography and genotype in "subjects photographic genome" recorded by the photographic image. To define the problem of the missing genotype or the "empty" phenotype, I propose to take a step further and define a prototype, the *phototype*, which can be defined as the smallest photographic unit that serves the techno-genetic paradigm of creation, assigning special powers to human technologies. It is a piece of information representing a visual appeal in the technical medium. In most practices of recording living beings, phototypes are indistinguishable from phenotypes. Employing the concept of the phototype, connecting visible phenotypes with existing genotypes, we explore different photographic phenomena – how some unrelated people look alike in photographs and how some people do not look alike in pictures. Alternatively, and even more paradoxically, a phototype becomes more relevant and salient when there is only an image of a particular species left.

In cases of species that are extinct or vanished, photographs have a significant importance. For example, the recently cloned Przewalski's horse was compared to an archival black-and-white photograph showing the horse in the wild in order to prove its successful cloning. When analysing the image of the horse (as it once was in the wild and as it looks cloned), we are faced with biological types that are reproduced outside of photographs and with photographic styles that are repeating and can be autonomously reproduced. Thus, the contemporary photography of species is framed by an archive of phenotypes and its capacities to go a step further and compute something beyond the appearance of an image – the genotype.

In the new digital archives, genotype, phenotype, and phototype meet. In their coordinated action, they promise us a digital capacity of re-programming images and fusing photography and genetics into a hybrid field. With this technology, images from the 19th-century administrative type of archive to the 20th-century database (in which everything is deponed yet nothing is seen) and to 21st-century activated datasets can all be integrated into bases of knowledge and information. This fusion can help us to understand forms of life at a new level and outside the "bureaucracy of death," which marks the indexes of planetary species. To have this hope, we need to recognise that the whole history of photography marks the basin of the phototype. However, the realisation that algorithms and computational neural networks can endlessly generate archives and databases still brings us to a series of questions on the faith of the medium of excessive computation. We can then ask questions on whether we can imagine a way images from databases can be enlived and made back into life in a process reverse to a current transfer of into a database. Would "image bank" deposits ever have the status of the banks of frozen embryos and seeds or other biological banks? If so, can we talk about the excessive human reproduction continuing in digital space and the translation of the problem from "natural" areas into new ones? Would "new species" be neglected in digital space by human self-competition? And finally, what are our obligations in regards to the overpopulation of digital space?

Notes

1 This essay was partially presented at the Art + Anthropocene: Culture, Climate and Changing Planet virtual seminar on 2, 9, 16 and 23 March 2021.

2 Talbot's concept of the photogenic transformed through time and apparently become very popular in the context of film in 1920s (see Rosenblatt 1998). Different from that of the beginning of the 20th century, today's use of the concept is more oriented to visual appeal, so that is why, for example, beauty competitions have the distinct category of Miss Photogenic.

3 According to John Berger, our need to relate to animals in these mediated forms comes as compensation for the life we do not share anymore, proving the Darwinian theme of our evolvement and assuring us in our powers (see Berger 2009).

4 Some projects emphasise the disappearance of life "into the image." *Population by Pixel* was an award-winning 2008 print campaign for WWF Japan by Hakuhodo C&D, relating the number of species to the number of pixels. Each image has an inscription that this number (of pixels or members) is not enough. Another exciting project is *JJSmooth4*, which visualises animals in pixels, addressing the number of members left more directly.

5 Arkive.org (https://icwb.com/one-life); the International Barcode of Life (https://ibol.org); the Catalogue of Life (www.catalogueoflife.org); Encyclopaedia of Life (https://eol.org); Global Biodiversity Information Facility (www.gbif.org); Consortium for Conservation of Nature (www.iccaconsortium.org/index.php/international-en/governance-en); IUCN Red List of Extinct Species (www.iucnredlist.org/search?redListCategory=ex); one of the albums of extinct species is an online album of extinct flora and fauna (www.salisburyjournal.co.uk/news/11054755.online-album-of-extinct-flora-and-fauna).

6 Charles Darwin even forwarded a letter by A.L. Austin addressed to him personally, elaborating on stereophotography. Galton included this letter integrally into his address to the Anthropological Institute (See Galton 1879, 173). In this letter, Austin proposes using stereophotography to compare humans with animals.

7 The paper was delivered to the Anthropological Institute of Great Britain and Ireland in 1898.

8 GANimals (https://ganimals.media.mit.edu).

Sources

Ackerman, Diane. 1997. *The Rarest of the Rare: Vanishing Animals, Timeless Worlds*. New York: Vintage books.

Aloi, Giovanni. 2018. *Speculative Taxidermy: Natural History, Animal Surfaces, and Art in the Anthropocene*. New York and Chichester, West Sussex: Columbia University Press.

Berger, John. 2009. "Why Look at Animals." In *About Looking*, edited by John Berger, 3–28. London: Penguin.

Burnett-Brown, Anthrony, Russel Roberts, and Mark Hawroth-Booth. 2000. "Specimen and Marvels: William Henry Fox Talbot: The Invention of Photography." *Aperture* 161 (Specimen and Marvels: William Henry Fox Talbot and the Invention of Photography): 1–80.

Buselle, Rebecca. 1994. "A Defining Reality: The Photographs of Nancy Burson." *Aperture* 136 (Summer – Metamorphoses: Photography in the Electronic Age): 73–75.

Crutzen, Paul. 2002. "The 'Anthropocene.'" *Journal of Physics IV France* 12. doi:10.1051/jp4:20020447.

Damisch, Hubert. 2016. *Noah's Ark: Essays on Architecture*. Cambridge and London: MIT Press.

Darwin, Charles. 1859 (2001). *On the Origin of Species*. Edited by Jim Manis. The Pennsylvania State University.

———. 1872. *The Expression of the Emotions in Man and Animals*. London: John Murray.

Davidson, Katleen. 2017. *Photography, Natural History and the Nineteenth-Century Museum: Exchanging Views of Empire (Science and the Arts since 1750)*. London and New York: Routledge.

Ebert, Grace. 2020. "150,000 Botanical and Animal Illustrations Available for Free Download from Biodiversity Heritage Library." *Collosal*, January 31, 2020. www.thisiscolossal.com/2020/01/biodiversity-heritage-library-free-download/.

Galton, Francis. 1865. "Hereditary Talent and Character." *Macmillan's Magazine* 12: 157–66 + 318–27.

———. 1869. *Hereditary Genius*. London: Palgrave Macmillan.

———. 1879. "Composite Portraits, Made by Combining Those of Many Different Persons into a Single Resultant Figure." *The Journal of the Anthropological Institute of Great Britain and Ireland* 8: 132–44.

———. 1883. *Inquiries into Human Faculty and Its Development*. Palgrave Macmillan.

———. 1889. *Natural Inheritance*. Palgrave Macmillan.

———. 1909. *Essays in Eugenics*. London: The Eugenics Education Society.

Galton, Sir Francis. 1874. *English Man of Science*. Palgrave Macmillan.

Gillham, Nicolas Wright. 2009. *A Life of Sir Francis Galton: From African Exploration to the Birth of Eugenics*. Oxford and New York: Oxford University Press.

Goodyear, Anne Collins. 2009. "Digitization, Genetics, and the Defacement of Portraiture." *American Art* 23 (2): 28–31.

Hamilton, Clive. 2015. *A Requiem for Species: Why We Resist the Truth About Climate Change*. Sidney: Allen & Unwin.

Heise, Ursula K. 2016. *Imagining Extinction: The Cultural Meanings of Endangered Species*. Chicago: University of Chicago Press.

Kolbert, Elizabeth. 2014. *The Sixth Extinction: An Unnatural History*. London: Henry Holt and Co.

Moore, Jason W., ed. 2016. *Anthropocene or Capitalocene: Nature, History, and the Crisis of Capitalism*. Oakland: Kairos Pm.

Nelkin, D. 1996. "The Gene as Cultural Icon: Visual Images of DNA." *Art Journal* 55 (1): 56–61.

Peraica, Ana. 2021a. "Photographocene: The Past, Present and Future in the Photography of the Environment." *Philosophy of Photography* 11 (1): 99–111.

———. 2021b. "Migration of Species into Images and Databases." Cited in Isabelle Gapp. *Virtual Seminar Series: Art + Anthropocene: Culture, Climate and Our Changing Planet*. East Lansing, MI: H-Environment.

———. In print. "Photogenetics and Generative Adversarial Networks." In *Genetic Histories and Liberties: Eugenics, Genetic Ancestries and Genetic Technologies in Literary and Visual Cultures*, edited by Christina Lake and Helen Thomas. Gender and the Body Series. Edinburgh: Edinburgh University Press.

Prodger, Phillip. 2009. *Darwin's Camera: Art and Photography in the Theory of Evolution*. Oxford and New York: Oxford University Press.

Rosenblatt, Nina Lara. 1998. "Photogenic Neurastenia: On Mass medium and Medium in the 1920." *October* 86 (Autumn): 77–62.

Rubinstein, Daninel. 2018. "Posthuman Photography." In *The Evolution of the Image*, edited by Marco Bohr and Basia Sliwinska, 100–12. New York: Routledge.

Taylor, Peter, and Richard Lewontin. 2021. "The Genotype/Phenotype Distinction." In *The Stanford Encyclopedia of Philosophy*, edited by Edward N. Zalta (Summer 2021 Edition). https://plato.stanford.edu/archives/sum2021/entries/genotype-phenotype/.

University of Turku. 2020. "New Species Described in 2020." *ScienceDaily*, July 1, 2020. Accessed December 6, 2021. www.sciencedaily.com/releases/2020/07/200701100030.htm.

van Essen, Eylat. 2019. "From Photographic Representation to the 'Photographic Genotype.'" In: *Fragmentation of the Photographic Image*, edited by Daniel Rubinstein, 83–100. New York and London: Routledge.

Zylinska, Joanna. 2017. *Nonhuman Photography*. Cambridge: MIT Press.

20

(INTER)NATIONAL CONNECTIONS

Linking Nordic Animals to Biodiversity Observation Networks

Jesse Peterson, Dick Kasperowski, and René van der Wal

Introduction

Seeking to mitigate and redress biodiversity loss in the last few decades, institutions and researchers have developed biodiversity observation networks (BONs). Having been described as a "relatively loose affiliation of organisations that agree to create value by collaborating towards a common purpose while retaining their mandates, resources, and management," such networks are perceived as a necessary form for structuring and synthesising biological observation in order to address "the sheer scale" needed for monitoring biodiversity around the globe as well as to mitigate biodiversity loss and improve the quality of life for people (Walters and Scholes 2017, 6–7). For instance, systems ecologist Robert J. Scholes and colleagues framed the need for an international BON in this fashion: "The problem lies in the diversity of the data and the fact that it is physically dispersed and unorganised. The solution is to organise the information, to unblock the delivery pipeline between suppliers and users, and to create systems whereby data of different kinds, from many sources, can be combined" (Scholes et al. 2008, 1044). Additionally, the Organization for Economic Co-operation and Development (OECD) recommended that a BON be established and supported by its members to reduce costs and labour, advance science, and contribute to sustainable economic development and improve people's quality of life.

Named the Global Biodiversity Information Facility (GBIF), the OECD recommended that GBIF "compile electronically available data about living organisms and ecosystems" as its primary objective (OECD 1999, 2–3). Now located just west of Universitetsparken in Copenhagen, Denmark, the GBIF Secretariat manages, coordinates, and operates a database on biodiversity around the globe. It collects opportunistic data – much of which comes from museum and natural history collections and terrestrial and marine data platforms operated by other users (Pereira et al. 2017, 86; Costello et al. 2017, 148). Much of GBIF's data originates from previously collected material by network partners, which means gathering data in various ways.

One of the most significant data sources for GBIF gets gathered through citizen science methods, with "close to 50% of all species occurrence records in GBIF . . . published from sources that already publish data collected through [citizen science] projects" (Chandler et al.

DOI: 10.4324/9781003082798-25

2017, 214). As of March 2021, GBIF has over 1.6 billion records, which positions GBIF in a leading role for defining and delineating what can be known about the distribution and presence of animals, plants, fungi, and more through time around the globe, including species targeted for conservation, preservation, restoration, or other forms of management (e.g. invasive or "alien" species control). Though BONs demonstrate the move from "the once-obvious tendency of computers to centralise information, and hence power . . . to the looser concepts of networking and dispersion," networks like GBIF have generated access to a wealth of observational data which are spread around the globe and can be accessed en masse (Clarke 1988, 500). Though some social science studies on databases in biology (namely, genomics) exist, most research regarding BONs is typically written to improve and refine these particular networks and point out strengths and weaknesses provided by using different information technology infrastructures (Walters and Scholes 2017; Duffy et al. 2013; Brenton et al. 2018, 67–69). However, research has yet to consider the specific challenges that come to the fore when BONs incorporate non-human organisms as data.

Consequently, this chapter asks what it takes for an occurrence record to appear on the internet? How did the bird we saw a month ago in Sweden end up as a data registry point in GBIF, and what happens to it to do so?[1] What happens if we continue our birdwatching practice through the digital realm? Though such questions could be explored otherwise, this paper attempts a materialist narrative of the journey of a single biodiversity observation, highlighting several nodes of flow and transfer as well as those who assist this observation on its way. As such, this article aims to complement other materialist studies related to environmental big data (Hogan 2015; Gabrys 2014).

Borrowing methodological inspiration from the practices of following things, objects, actors, and data, this narrative describes the flow of data from field observation to the international level of a BON in order to characterise aspects of these networks' facilities and the information pathways that connect the multi-scalar operations at work in these endeavours (Cook 2004; Cook and Harrison 2007; Czarniawska-Joerges 2014, 57–65; Adams and Thompson 2016, 33–40; Akbari 2020). Due to COVID-19 and the difficulties in following digital media, we depend less upon the multi-sited ethnographic component of follow-the-thing and more upon its reporting strategy that invites readers to make their critical knowledge by way of learning about the "messiness" of commodity chains through the practices of juxtaposition and montage (Cook 2004, 642). Though observations of living creatures recorded in BONs are, in most cases, not commodities in that these networks do not monetise them, we suggest that the formal organisation of a commodity chain as "a network of labour and production" may be helpful to describe the activities of a BON (Hopkins and Wallerstein 1986, 159). We do so partly because the observations and derivative data products aggregated and produced by BONs as a "scientific commodity" are intended to be consumed in some fashion by researchers, government officials and policymakers, and the general public (Leonelli 2014, 2). With this in mind, it is crucial to recognise that data – as made evident by geographer Azadeh Akbari in her summary regarding data as a commodity – "repeatedly enters and leaves the commodity cycle . . . It has the potential to cause tremendous profit or to vanish in the vast universe of useless data" (Akbari 2020, 410–14). Thus, she argues that to accommodate for data's seemingly inherent slipperiness, one ought to explore its use value and meanings. Methodologically, actor-network theory suggests that this exploration can be undertaken by following data's traces through "associations and transformations" (Latour 2007, 190; Akbari 2020, 423–24).

Hence, our modest contribution to following data consists of a case study that explores these traces of observation data through physical and virtual site visits and interviews: from its production through human–non-human encounters to one of many possible endpoints.[2] Specifically, we follow the observation of a northern lapwing (*Vanellus vanellus*) on the shoreline of Fysingens Naturreservat just north of Stockholm and its journey from an agricultural field to the GBIF databank. As such, this paper assists in meeting the perceived need for humanities and social science research that seeks to understand data-centric efforts aimed at staying abreast of current trends and the mitigation or management of environmental changes viewed as detrimental (Benson 2016, 9).

Animal

palearctic wader – staging
sensing seasonal shifts
wanders
along generational routes
touching grassland
turned to farmland
reduced kind
fewer kin
less spots
on which to alight, wade, fish, mate
in spring – passage
not visitation
wings wide as a plough
acrobat over a frozen lake
its legs, torso, beak, head
unflappable recursive crest
(Snow and Perrins 1997;
Thorup 2004;
Petersen et al. 2009, 8–14)[3]

Observation

At the top of the birdwatching tower, the frozen lake below, sun glinting off its surface, we point out a bird to the north to our companion. Upright, active, and commanding, he names for me what we see – a northern lapwing. Trying to focus our binoculars on the bird seems an impossible task. The bird is dark and muddy, blurry to our eyes. We drop the binoculars back down and then raise them again in a last-ditch effort to will these binoculars to work. Our companion notices and tells us that the binoculars would work better if we removed the right lens cover from the objective lens instead of just the left one. Curiosity overpowers our embarrassment, so we do so, and this time, the field of vision becomes much clearer. The lapwing moves between the frozen surface of the lake and the grass and reeds that line the shoreline. We see the long feathers that constitute its crest and its other markings. For once, we see a bird that we could theoretically identify with the right field guide. Unlike us, my companion has been showing his adept skill, gained through countless hours of being with birds; scanning branches, tufts of grass, and other typical places where birds might rest; listening to their shrieks, cries, and twitters; and learning the names that accompany such experiences. So far, in addition to the lapwing, he has named for us many birds who have crossed our path: robin, Eurasian wren, greylag goose, Canadian goose, common crane, great tit, marsh tit, long-tailed tit, great spotted woodpecker, lesser spotted woodpecker, Eurasian skylark, European starling, greater white-fronted goose, hooded crow, wood dove, rock dove, Eurasian nuthatch, Eurasian treecreeper, and reed bunting.

Sunlight, dappled by the oak leaves, creates irregular lighting, making it challenging to see the phone screen. Squinting slightly, pushing down his glasses, he jabs his finger at the screen again and again and drags it up and down. He makes selections regarding what we have observed. He uses a programme called Checklista, which saves data to the Swedish Species Observation System (Artportalen), run by the Swedish Species Information Centre (Artdatabanken) located at the Swedish University of Agricultural Sciences (Sveriges lantbruksuniversitet, SLU). Unlike the development of scientific fields such as movement ecology, Artportalen was built out of shared interest between government officials at the Swedish Environmental Protection Agency (Naturvårdsverket) and local and regional birding organisations. Eventually, control for the platform was given over to Artdatabanken. Since its inception, Artportalen has relied upon contributory citizen science in which citizens collect data (Bonney et al. 2009a, 2009b, 11, 17–18; Miller-Rushing, Primack, and Bonney 2012, 286). Seen as "an increasingly integral part of contemporary scientific research, particularly in terms of data acquisition," Artportalen – like many other citizen science endeavours – faces unique challenges, such as maintaining user relationships (e.g. recruitment and retention) and data quality measures.

Nevertheless, here, in the field, Checklista (a web application accessed through an internet browser) functions better on mobile devices than Artportalen's leading submission platform. Its functionality is user-friendly because its interface moves and fits different screen sizes, whereas Artportalen's does not. To have made Artportalen's interface responsive would have been more labour-intensive and costly than building this entirely new web app for recording observations. Hosting this web app online also means that it is less costly to maintain, as building a dedicated app in iOS or Android would require more frequent updates. By building a new web app, the developers also made the collection of observations in this way distinct from recording observations in Artportalen. Instead of recording only individual sightings, Checklista provides the means to make occurrence records of whole lists of species that tend to frequent the area in question. What we record, however, is minimal compared to what we could potentially observe and record. First, we filter out all other living organisms from our list, opting only to receive a checklist of birds. Second, not all the birds we observe will be recorded as positive occurrences; we will report some of the birds we observe as null occurrences. In this way, we do not record everything we experience and observe. Nevertheless, for that which we do record, we must provide four obligatory inputs: time, location, species, and observer.

As we watch him fill in these required inputs or fields, we realise that it is at this moment when our encounters, now digitised, become something else. They are reduced to the act of identification: what, where, when, and by whom. The watching of the lapwing carousel over the frozen lake has somehow vanished. The "peewit" call of the lapwing, a sound like a fingernail scratched quickly across seatbelt vinyl, disappears. No longer is our record iridescent, green, black, or brown. No longer do we experience swooping shadows. It no longer names our desire for connection – the reaching for binoculars even though we have already named the lapwing before spotting it. It is no longer the cold breath of spring wind over the frozen water. No longer orange and peach shining over and through the trees, mingling with the clouds above the horizon. This reality all disappears where flesh meets pixels proffered by the electronic sheen of the screen: the submit button.

Storage

Once the submit button gets pressed, the observation does not get saved as a single computer file stored somewhere on his phone. Instead, these bits of information get transmitted through the internet to one or more hard drives located further north of our position. The many databases used by Artdatabanken and which contain the data reported in Artportalen (and their other web applications) physically occupy digital storage space on several servers at SLU. These servers, surrounded by other servers running different databases, sit inside the server room at this university, which measures approximately 20 metres long and 10 metres wide. When asked about visiting this space, several interviewees remark that the place resembles any other server room that can be seen on Google image search and is not worth the time or energy to visit. It is just "racks and racks and racks of hardware" with "fire protectants and UPS power supplies."

We are assured on several occasions that there is no point in visiting this place. This room, somehow, by being so ordinary, invites its dismissal as a place of importance. It is a means to an end, with nothing seemingly signifying any intrinsic worth or quality here. Cold. Hum and static. Concrete, aluminium, and plastic. Blacks, greys, greens, blues, and whites. Blinking lights and cables jutting in and out of ports. The unsmelled oils and fragrance of carpet, fabric, and dust. Such characteristics invite no interest beyond the instrumental for those whose jobs revolve around and depend upon these apparatuses, embodying instead a mundane, ancillary aspect that these networking computers hold. This nest egg. The repository where hundreds of gigabytes of biodiversity data sit dormant and electrified.

Artdatabanken used to own their hardware and kept it themselves, but they no longer do so. Now, they pay the SLU IT department to house and host their programming. This department ensures the lapwing as data exists. The jovial, bespectacled man with a round face, sporting a moustache and goatee, likes it this way. He walks to stacks and sits at his desk, monitoring the hardware. He tells us that researchers who buy their hardware, including servers, are the norm at Swedish universities. Because the researchers get the money, they often buy cheaper hardware solutions, relying upon their university affiliation to get "free" service from the IT department when their equipment fails in some capacity. It does not help if someone creates their own "fancy storage solution," because it often becomes the IT department's problem.

On the other hand, renting space – becoming an IT "tenant" – on the servers allows the IT department to provide greater customisation for their customers' needs, including Artdatabanken. Thus, he sets up "virtual machines," or servers whose specifications can be modified, to best serve Artdatabanken's momentary hardware and internet requirements. In this way, IT staff facilitate the storage of observation data through the configuration of hardware, allocation of memory and storage, and purchasing of database licenses. Here, data is granted the illusion of permanency, given life as an inexhaustible good, like a jug of water that will never run dry once filled by individual drops of rain.

Though Artdatabanken's rent is "fixed," he hopes to change that. Many "tenants" use the servers, and they all pay the same flat rate. Nevertheless, the needs of these tenants differ. Artdatabanken, for one, uses around 30 virtual machines, and sometimes they use them at double or more the capacity of others. He often negotiates with Artdatabanken staff, seeking solutions for optimising their capacity to transfer data quickly and efficiently. He tells us that the flexibility in the design of Artportalen creates the possibility for searches that are intensive and "nasty for the environment." Indeed, "a weird enough query" can take time and resources, mainly because most searches have to go through all 80 million observations. The only solution in his judgment – to rewrite the whole programme – is impossible. A change such as this is so significant that the invisible gains (a better functioning system) beguile the high level of investment in labour and cost that it would take to accomplish. In any case, he wants to move to a cost per performance model, which will inevitably raise Artdatabanken's rent (while lowering it for other users). Such would raise the threshold for the main limiter that prevents Artdatabanken from scaling up their efforts: price.

Moreover, as the database grows, the need for more storage and memory grows. The subscribed database provider, Microsoft, runs different database editions. As the storage and data needs push against the limits of the current standard edition, Artdatabanken faces a hefty sum for upgrading to the "enterprise" edition. Data content, its representation of the lapwing, has little value at this stage. Instead, the lapwing data is valuable as a transferable presence and as potentiate relationality to other data already in the system, with their meaning lodged in the number of bytes the data occupy and how much energy it takes to sift through it all.

Databases

Though SLU IT maintains the hardware, staff at Artdatabanken assist in ensuring the databases run as smoothly as possible. An operations manager – also with glasses, short hair, and a goatee – tells us that the whole system can be described as a "layer cake." From the bottom to top, each layer can be described in the following: hardware, operations software, database management software, web servers, and visualisation programmes that make everything look nice. He ensures the basic functionality of the whole system by managing how the data gets stored and maintaining the integrity of the servers and databases so that they function according to Artdatabanken's wishes. Doing so is complex because the system carries a history of code objects cobbled together from independent development, open sources produced by third parties, and proprietary software.

To him, humans record their observations as discrete fields through various software applications, and these fields then get transferred to one or more Artdatabanken databases, including a relational database that serves as the primary location for occurrence records made through Artportalen and the other applications Artdatabanken run. Describing the database as a record-keeping tool, he shows us this database, which has many different spreadsheets and data tables that hold many fields. However, the data in this database does not necessarily "stay put." Fields within this database may be unique or copies of data, meaning that the fields may or may not be present in the various other databases and data tables run by Artdatabanken. Subject to being copied, the observation records become data doubles, different recombinations of "discrete informational flows which are stabilised and captured according to pre-established classificatory criteria" and which "serve institutional agendas" (Ericson and Haggerty 2006, 4).

Serving these agendas includes the many data tables created by software developers that house data and its doubles in different ways. The result makes them potential independent repositories that can perform different functionalities and how different relationships between data can get made and through which different analytical results can get extracted. Hence, removing a data table can be like "removing a page from a book"; that is, essential information may get lost if any table gets removed from the system. Thus, each possible field in our record of the lapwing becomes information that can be copied and moved to one or more data tables in one or more databases, including databases not specific to Artportalen: "Data from species portal is transformed and stored in other software databases . . . you omit some information, and maybe you add some information to it . . . one observation might be recorded in various database tables."

In essence, Artportalen has several databases that copy, borrow, and feed information back and forth to each other. For instance, automatic processes in the database add several other fields to our lapwing observation that we did not record ourselves. The record on Artportalen shows added fields regarding the location and a "vulnerability" status from the International Union for Conservation of Nature (IUCN) Red List. It also tags the record as unvalidated. In many ways, therefore, data accumulation is not linear in Artportalen; it accelerates. Data becomes viral, copying and nestling itself in different virtual ecologies that satisfy the niche requirements defined by those who run the system. Neither is data any longer purely what the observer records. The fields of information that go into making up an observation become individualised to establish other relationships. The observation is no longer just itself. It accrues new relationships with other data that get added to it by the system managers and other users. It is put to work through amplification, modification, and duplication, with differing versions and duplicates being distributed into digital realms within the database system as well as onto databases run by other institutions who utilise this data for their own purposes.

As these observations proliferate and gather more data within Artdatabanken's system, they become functional for use. The system is not designed only to store data but to extract it as well. However, as data increasingly take up storage and memory, the system's design begins to show cracks. The manager transports us by the web to a monitoring platform with various measures displayed as graphs and charts in white, blue, and black. One of these graphs shows how users may request data, and in so doing, their queries cause the system to "time out." Time-outs represent the database's inability to return a user request within an allotted time. For Artportalen, the manager has set a time-out to 30 seconds, meaning that he determines what constitutes an acceptable level of functionality in the system.

Consequently, he watches over both users and data, following how many users are logged onto the system and how many time-outs occur. These two variables relate to each other. More users generally imply more time-outs, evidenced by increased volumes of time-outs over weekends when more users make records or search the database (Knape et al. 2022). Therefore, time-outs serve as one form of regulator that provides or denies access to the data in the system.

The entire architecture that supports Artportalen's data needs to be updated, maintained, and replaced. As IT software becomes outdated or specific tools no longer become functional or valuable, systems need to be updated while maintaining the same functionality that characterised the early system. As he told me, "IT is a moving thing." In addition, while data accumulates more than 450 gigabytes – not just from citizen scientists logging their observations but also through the program's internal mechanisms that expand, replicate, read, and find data – the operations become more costly, which delimit what kinds of software can be used. Their database license through Microsoft allows them to conduct business, but once their needs supersede what the license affords, their operations may become much more expensive.

Thus, Artportalen faces an "all pain, no gain" scenario. This situation may force the use of more open-source database software and a move away from reliance upon proprietary software. However, this shift would entail a great deal of labour over many years to come to replicate the working conditions they have now. So for now, this headache is ignored while he focuses on optimising the response rate of the entire system.

Transfers

Observation data also gets transformed through a selection and restructuring process, which occurs when data is prepared for transfer. Artdatabanken, for instance, does not only collect data through Artportalen. County municipalities in Sweden desire more than just what Artportalen can offer, so Artdatabanken has sought to be the sole provider for all of these data records. Therefore, they harvest data from various other web applications and separate projects run by different organisations and researchers, including 16 separate databases brought together by a different entity, the Swedish Biodiversity Data Infrastructure (SBDI). The information harvested from these different databases must be kept separate from Arportalen's data because the data do not share the same information structure. The data provided by these databases may be restructured to be combined and transferred to other network members, including GBIF. In order to do so,

IT personnel must combine the data in some general-purpose model that meets the specific needs of those requesting it. As such, the data from all these projects occupy their own space but must be transformed to be made compatible with the disparate systems operating them.

The lapwing becomes challenging to see, further displaced from its origins as it gets spatialised within the digital realm. Nevertheless, making these transformations is not necessarily intuitive. "How should one cut the parts of something that is collected as individual observations . . .? How [does one] split the elephant into small parts?" To wit, data recorded to Artportalen is not necessarily compatible with other systems in the network. Nevertheless, restructuring data to combine it comes with trade-offs; combining data is only "perfect" for combining it. Artportalen relies upon different standardisation methods that mould and shape data in ways contingent upon the needs for whom the data gets transferred.

In the case of the observation records of the lapwing at Fysingen moving from Artportalen to GBIF, the data recorded in Artportalen must be restructured to meet the "transfer format" requirements of the Darwin Core standard used by GBIF (Wieczorek et al. 2012). Described to us as "a big box with small boxes in it," fitting data into Darwin Core represents "some kind of a deal on how [one] should use the information." However, this use only comes after being provided for in its specific manner. In that sense, the potential use for data equals what and how the data is provided. As a format different from Artportalen's own, some data will not fit or will not be "good" to convert to this format, so it can be hard to make data representable when transferred to GBIF. For example, one of the trade-offs for using Darwin Core is that it "does not allow to link measurements and facts to both events and occurrences in the same dataset" (GBIF 2018). Unlike Artportalen's database, which appears to constantly "move" from additions and modifications as if a seamless stop-motion film, Artportalen's contribution to GBIF moves similarly but much more slowly, with longer stopgaps so that it appears to stutter. This difference results from less frequent updates being made to the data in GBIF. Part of this reason is that certain biodiversity data, such as observations on animals, plants, and fungi, require less updating. Another aspect is that Artportalen cannot send consistent updates and must instead rely upon sending their entire database as a batch transfer, which can only happen a couple of times each year. The storage size during this situation is immense. Once the batch transfer is made, the GBIF secretariat extracts the data, which then gets recontextualised into this new environment and becomes a searchable occurrence record at their end for anyone to find.

Challenges

The northern lapwing on GBIF is in many respects a different being altogether than its counterpart on the shores of Fysingen. From agricultural field to relational database, the pathway we followed does not imply this is the end for the lapwing nor that this is the only path it took. What we did find, however, was that in order to make this particular journey, the lapwing required many people and their assistance, time, knowledge, skills, and tools. Hence, we can describe a BON solution for monitoring biodiversity as activities that amass and make available observation data on non-human organisms. The possibility to achieve these ends entails significant labour practices and materials that alter the nature of that observed through the various stages of its journey, such as through data recording, storage, dispersal, modification, restructuring, and transfer, as well as through their efforts in building capacity for redundancy and flexibility in respect to different analytical schemes. The lapwing, as it gets placed into a relationship with the different actors and materials that constitute the BON – like a bird, observation fields, dataset, and more – these mediations give and take away specific properties from the lapwing through a bidirectional chain of transformation (Latour 1999, 69–79). Similar to the construction of data from biological objects, the lapwing gets "flattened" in ways that make it suitable for travel through computers and networks (Stevens 2013, 117).

Table 20.1 Translations to Transformations Table.

Translations	*Point of access*	*Actors*	*Operation platform*	*Transformations*
Lapwing	Lake	Bird, observer, birding tools	Place, senses	Intimate encounter
Metadata	Phone, notebook	Recorder	Web applications	Made communicable, categorisation, digitisation
Observation	Server, computer	Data managers, internal protocols	Databases	Copies, metadata additions and removals
International record	Server, computer	Data scientist, Darwin Core	Databases, batch files	Standardisation, aggregation, cooperation, competition

Its "data journey" showcases how the lapwing is made subject to decontextualisation, recontextualisation, and reuse (Leonelli 2014, 3–6). Such help takes money, effort, and energy, for the lapwing in all its manifestations does not merely signify a certain level of biodiversity on its own; it also challenges and tests the limits of the network and its infrastructure. In addition, the process which turns the experience of a lapwing into data suppresses how the data accrue, as lapwing data expands into bird data as well as observer data. Following the movement of a lapwing onto the GBIF database suggests several factors that shape and influence BONs and their efforts.

First, the lapwing challenges the BONs in at least two ways. It does so by bringing material considerations to the fore. Though the cost and ability to store data do not pose any real problem or challenge, the accrual of observation records and developments in IT "age" the Artportalen database, posing challenges for how the database gets used and developed in the future. Also, the ability of data to describe reality or to be truthful and trusted becomes a top priority at all stages in this process. In linking the various activities that assist in producing scientific knowledge, science studies scholar Bruno Latour notes that "the succession of stages must be traceable, allowing for travel in both directions. If the chain is interrupted at any point, it ceases to transport truth – ceases, that is, to produce, to construct, to trace, and to conduct it." By extension, the qualia of this truth change with each transformation of data loss or gain between locality or universality, materiality or abstraction, particularity or standardisation (Latour 1999, 69–73).

Hence, following this chain is significant; for instance, as the lapwing moves from the frozen shore and towards GBIF, this data becomes less dependent upon its originary context. As digital humanities scholar Rita Raley notes, "the value of data does not depend on its connection to an actual person until expedience requires that a claim be made for the truth of that data" (Raley 2013, 127–28). This situation implies that we find the truth of the lapwing with respect to global biodiversity loss through the removal of its ecological particularity and place-specific parameters (e.g. the lapwing we saw at that lake on that day).

Following biodiversity, observations that highlight certain stages in this chain receive greater scrutiny than others. The longer this chain becomes, the greater the potential to destabilise what data stands for. Each link added in this chain of transformation creates more possibilities for rupture or destabilisation of the lapwing as objective data. At each juncture in this journey, as intimacy slides from organic to digital and context slips from a place to space, one might form differing perspectives on what these subtle shifts mean, to the point of making data seem biased or even meaningless.

BONs also represent resources for data on people and not just on non-human life. Like many social media companies, including Google (1998) and Facebook (2004), national and international BONs and other online repositories of biodiversity data begin to be established around the turn of the 21st century. To consider the development of BONs as separate from this broader social context would ignore how BONs' complex networks of storage, duplication, transfer, and exchange mirror and exemplify the drive for exhaustive data collection and monitoring. Though digital studies scholar Jennifer Gabrys notices that "the configurations of environmental data can raise rather different issues" than "studies on Big Data" related to social media or other online repositories about people, the concepts and methods used in these studies offer fruitful ground for application to studies on environmental data (Gabrys 2016, 2.). For instance, BONs contribute to datafication through "the transformation of social action [of non-human life] into online quantified data" as well as the social activities of human beings who cooperate in these practices (Cukier and Mayer-Schoenberger 2013, 29, 34–35; Van Dijck 2014, 198). Biodiversity data is most often viewed as data on non-human others when, in fact, it also provides data on those doing the reporting.

Typically, when data reveals the social factors inscribed within them, these factors represent data bias or deficiencies in data collection. For instance, citizen science biodiversity data can vary both spatially and temporally as a result of how it gets collected. Many databases have more records on non-human animals that come near roads and other human-accessible areas, and reporting practices can display alterations resulting from seasonal shifts, weekends and holidays, or weather variables (van der Wal et al. 2015, S595; Knape et al. 2022). Rather than a detriment, such pieces of evidence show that we can learn about many people's practices using these platforms, though few actors in and out of academia have made use of BONs for these purposes

(Kasperowski and Hillman 2018). By contributing to "a legitimate means to *access, understand* and *monitor* people's behaviour," the datafication of non-human species observation has more or less escaped this "revolutionary research opportunity" to study its users (Van Dijk 2014, 198; italics original). Instead, data with apparent social features get filtered out or modified in some way in order to improve and ensure data quality concerning content.

Lastly, data for a BON database such as GBIF shows how "flattening" occurs in this specific context. The many actors we encountered in this process show a clear distinction between the roles of citizen scientists and those who have access to raw data. The lapwing data means different things in different stages and must be shepherded in specific ways to fulfil its many functions. Most of this is automated, but the automation itself requires both labour and expense (Clarke 1988, 501). For Artdatabanken, those who receive remuneration in this process do not identify as researchers (Artdatabanken technically employees only two researchers) but as analysts. Hence, BONs illustrate one research area in which the emergence of data specialists or scientists has come to fruition (Ribes 2019, 515–17; Benson 2016, 3; Arts et al. 2013).

Nonetheless, their specialisation requires others, such as citizen scientists, who support and become the rationale for the data scientist's expertise. The relationship between non-human life, observer, data scientist, and data invites consideration that BONs do more than monitor biodiversity. They may engage in surveillance and "dataveillance" – a situation defined as "the systematic use of personal data systems in the investigation or monitoring of the actions or communications of one or more persons" as well as "continuous surveillance through the use of (meta)data" that allows for "a single unit [to be] identified consistently across a range of data sets with a primary key" (Clarke 1988, 499; Raley 2013, 124; Van Dijck 2014, 198). This argument resembles claims made about tracking animals by other means, such as radio collars and tags, as forms of surveillance (Bergman 2003, 82; Worster 1994, 18; Haraway 2013, 108; Mitman 1996, 117–43; Lewis 2003, 107; Benson 2010, 13). But as the historian of technology Etienne Benson points out, radio-tagging was not only used for surveillance because "total control was unachievable for both political and technical reasons" (Benson 2010, 14).

Instead, he argues, radio-tagging also brought scientists into "intimate" relationships with those they studied (Benson 2010, 15). By introducing fully automated tracking systems and making data "open," scientists (wildlife biologists) became "enablers of intimacy with wild animals rather than its sole possessors; they became specialists who produced connections rather than experts who monopolised authority" (Benson 2010, 26). However, in the case of BONs, intimate encounters occur but not necessarily by those running the show. By faithfully digitising their observations, citizen scientists become intermediaries, and their intimate encounters can be accessed. However, they can only come into play if the citizens themselves are contacted and can prove that they saw what they recorded. Making data shareable, abstractable, and digitised also invites biosecurity and surveillance issues to the fore. In these respects, by having to rely upon autonomous users freely sharing data with institutions, BONs supersede monitoring efforts and engage in dataveillance because they forego "monitoring for specific purposes" in favour of "the continuous tracking of (meta)data for unstated preset purposes" (Van Dijck 2014, 205). Moreover, we can view dataveillance as the addition of IT products to surveillance and those practices that these infrastructures make possible. Raley points out that dataveillance functions as "the disciplinary and control practice of monitoring, aggregating, and sorting data." As such, she argues, "dataveillance . . . is not simply descriptive (monitoring) but also predictive (conjecture) and prescriptive (enactment)" (Raley 2013, 124). In agreement with this characterisation, security studies scholar Sara Degli-Esposti argues that dataveillance has interests in "behavioral manipulation" of people and non-human others that go through or make up part of the supply chain. As she states, "there is an indiscriminate application of dataveillance along the entire supply chain: inanimate objects and animate subjects are treated as interchangeable parts of the same optimisation function" (Degli Esposti 2014, 212). Though our observation of the lapwing does not alter its behaviour in the short term, its introduction into the BON makes it and other lapwings subject to specific forms of human control.

Using this record and others to model the lapwing species' use of habitat, its spatial occurrence over time or additional analyses in order to prescribe recommendations or actions for it constitute grounds for ethical inquiries into these practices. We consider that non-human beings do not or may not provide consent to people who record their presence and activities. Moreover, animals and humans may engage in forms of "countervailance" by hiding or refusing to report vulnerable information (e.g. the location of an eagle's nest) (Raley 2013, 131). Nevertheless, because the willingness of non-human life to participate in these activities cannot be entirely judged, it may be more ethical to allow biodiversity data only to be used for the benefits of non-humans rather than the humans who collect and depend upon this data. However, this is not necessarily the case. For instance, a small number of observations of a vulnerable species in a forest may or may not prevent the forest from being clear-cut by individual property owners or industries. Though a single record of this vulnerable species ought to prevent any part of the forest from being logged by law, additional records of this species in other vicinities may displace the relative importance of these observations, allowing governments and industries to permit certain parts of the forest to be cut down (Sténs and Mårald 2020, 7–9). To no longer use biodiversity data for human interests and agendas would challenge scientific and governmental intentions and the hobbyist naturalists who use these systems for their purposes.

Moreover, creating ways to stimulate citizens to contribute data also functions as a kind of manipulation. Because Artdatabanken relies upon citizen scientists to collect data, they develop Artportalen with certain functionalities that serve the observers more than the scientific intentions of the platform. For example, they satisfy observers' competitive urges with lists that rank observers by how many different species they can record each year.

Sharing data with GBIF and others also leads to cooperation, competition, and discrepancies. Artdatabanken has needed to compete with other biodiversity databases for government funding and other resources. And just as Artdatabanken harvests data from other databases, other databases make use of data from Artdatabanken. GBIF, as a beneficiary of Artportalen's data, functions as one competitor – as it, too, competes for funds made available through organisations such as the European Union. Additionally, since GBIF provides citations for all observation records gathered from other members in the network, this practice places database providers in a potential conflict in terms of scientific standing by making them beholden to how scholastic performance gets measured through citation metrics. Discrepancies are also created, not just because of restructuring data to fit transfer formats but also because national regulations indicate how specific data – such as that on vulnerable species – can be handled and stored. Such considerations consist of several ways a lapwing observed upon a frozen lake can become part of a BON. As the lapwing alters throughout the various stages of this journey, these networks highlight that as they measure biodiversity, they also mediate relationships between localised place and abstractable space. As an occurrence record on GBIF, the lapwing we experienced becomes almost indetectable. Rather than representing a lapwing, the occurrence record on GBIF provides an opportunity for telling a story about this specific form of mediating nature. Tracing this journey assists through "different modes of analysis and storytelling" in order to make vivid how "distant natures, those that are not experienced through the body but distributed through data and media . . . is mediated through machines and technologies, models and database structures" (Jørgensen 2014, 109). Reflecting on the transition from an intimate encounter with a lapwing to its registration within multiple databases assists in understanding the scientific and practical challenges BONs face.

Acknowledgement

René van der Wal received support from the European Commission through Horizon 2020 SwafS-15-2018–2019 grant number 872557 (EnviroCitizen).

Notes

1 The authors have chosen to use the first-person plural to describe experiences, even if such experiences were not experienced by all authors.
2 In addition to published sources, the account that follows is based on conversations, e-mail exchanges, and site visits where possible. The lead author acknowledges those who generously discussed their work with him. Any errors in fact or interpretation are his own.
3 These references and their contents were used in the writing of this poem.

Sources

Adams, Catherine, and Terrie Lynn Thompson. 2016. *Researching a Posthuman World*. London: Palgrave Macmillan.

Akbari, Azadeh. 2020. "Follow the Thing: Data: Contestations over Data from the Global South." *Antipode* 52 (2) (March): 408–29.

Arts, Koen Antonius Johannes, Gemma Webster, Nirwan Sharma, Yolanda Melero Cavero, Christopher Stuart Mellish, Xavier Lambin, and Rene Van Der Wal. 2013. "Capturing Mink and Data: Interacting with a Small and Dispersed Environmental Initiative over the Introduction of Digital Innovation." Framework for Responsible Research and Innovation in ICT. Univetsity of Aberdeen.

Benson, Etienne. 2010. *Wired Wilderness: Technologies of Tracking and the Making of Modern Wildlife*. Baltimore: Johns Hopkins University Press.

———. 2016. "Trackable Life: Data, Sequence, and Organism in Movement Ecology." *Studies in History and Philosophy of Science Part C: Studies in History and Philosophy of Biological and Biomedical Sciences* 57 (June): 137–47.

Bergman, Charles. 2003. *Wild Echoes: Encounters with the Most Endangered Animals in North America*. Champaign, IL: University of Illinois Press.

Bonney, Rick, Heidi Ballard, Rebecca Jordan, Ellen McCallie, Tina Phillips, Jennifer Shirk, and Candie C Wilderman. 2009a. *Public Participation in Scientific Research: Defining the Field and Assessing Its Potential for Informal Science Education. A CAISE Inquiry Group Report*. Washington, DC: Institute of Education Sciences, ERIC.

Bonney, Rick, Caren B. Cooper, Janis Dickinson, Steve Kelling, Tina Phillips, Kenneth V. Rosenberg, and Jennifer Shirk. 2009b. "Citizen Science: A Developing Tool for Expanding Science Knowledge and Scientific Literacy." *BioScience* 59 (11) (December): 977–84.

Brenton, Peter, Stephanie von Gavel, Ella Vogel, and Marie-Elise Lecoq. 2018. "Technology Infrastructure for Citizen Science." In *Citizen Science: Innovation in Open Science, Society and Policy*, edited by Susanne Hecker, Muki Haklay, Anne Bowser, Zen Makuch, Johannes Vogel, and Aletta Bonn, 63–80. London: UCL Press.

Chandler, Mark, Linda See, Christina D. Buesching, Jenny A. Cousins, Chris Gillies, Roland W. Kays, Chris Newman, Henrique M. Pereira, and Patricia Tiago. 2017. "Involving Citizen Scientists in Biodiversity Observation." In *The GEO Handbook on Biodiversity Observation Networks*, edited by Michele Walters and Robert J. Scholes, 211–38. Cham: Springer International Publishing.

Clarke, Roger. 1988. "Information Technology and Dataveillance." *Communications of the ACM* 31 (5): 498–512.

Cook, Ian. 2004. "Follow the Thing: Papaya." *Antipode* 36 (4): 642–64.

Cook, Ian, and Michelle Harrison. 2007. "Follow the Thing: 'West Indian Hot Pepper Sauce.'" *Space and Culture* 10 (1) (February 1): 40–63.

Costello, Mark J., Zeenatul Basher, Laura McLeod, Irawan Asaad, Simon Claus, Leen Vandepitte, Moriaki Yasuhara, et al. 2017. "Methods for the Study of Marine Biodiversity." In *The GEO Handbook on Biodiversity Observation Networks*, edited by Michele Walters and Robert J. Scholes, 211–38. Cham: Springer International Publishing.
Cukier, Kenneth, and Viktor Mayer-Schoenberger. 2013. "The Rise of Big Data: How It's Changing the Way We Think About the World." *Foreign Affairs* 92 (3): 28–40.
Czarniawska-Joerges, Barbara. 2014. *Social Science Research: From Field to Desk*. London and Thousand Oaks, CA: Sage Publications Ltd.
Degli Esposti, Sara. 2014. "When Big Data Meets Dataveillance: The Hidden Side of Analytics." *Surveillance & Society* 12 (2) (May 9): 209–25.
Duffy, J. Emmett, Linda A. Amaral-Zettler, Daphne G. Fautin, Gustav Paulay, Tatiana A. Rynearson, Heidi M. Sosik, and John J. Stachowicz. 2013. "Envisioning a Marine Biodiversity Observation Network." *BioScience* 63 (5) (May 1): 350–61.
Ericson, Richard V., and Kevin D. Haggerty, eds. 2006. *The New Politics of Surveillance and Visibility*. Green College Thematic Lecture Series. Toronto: University of Toronto Press.
Gabrys, Jennifer. 2014. "Powering the Digital: From Energy Ecologies to Electronic Environmentalism." In *Media and the Ecological Crisis*, edited by Richard Maxwell, Jon Raundalen, and Nina Lager Vestberg, 3–18. London: Routledge.
———. 2016. "Practicing, Materialising and Contesting Environmental Data." *Big Data & Society* 3 (2) (December): 2053951716673391.
GBIF. 2018. *Best Practices in Publishing Sampling-Event Data*, version 2.2. Copenhagen: GBIF Secretariat. https://ipt.gbif.org/manual/en/ipt/2.5/best-practices-sampling-event-data.
Haraway, Donna J. 2013. *Primate Visions: Gender, Race, and Nature in the World of Modern Science*. London: Routledge.
Hogan, Mél. 2015. "Data Flows and Water Woes: The Utah Data Center." *Big Data & Society* 2 (2) (December 27): 205395171559242.
Hopkins, Terence K., and Immanuel Wallerstein. 1986. "Commodity Chains in the World-Economy Prior to 1800." *Review (Fernand Braudel Center)* 10 (1): 157–70.
Jørgensen, Finn Arne. 2014. "The Armchair Traveller's Guide to Digital Environmental Humanities." *Environmental Humanities* 4 (1) (May 1): 95–112.
Kasperowski, Dick, and Thomas Hillman. 2018. "The Epistemic Culture in an Online Citizen Science Project: Programs, Antiprograms and Epistemic Subjects." *Social Studies of Science* 48 (4): 564–88.
Knape, Jonas, Stephen James Coulson, René van der Wal, and Debora Arlt. 2022. "Temporal Trends in Opportunistic Citizen Science Reports across Multiple Taxa." *Ambio*, March 29.
Latour, Bruno. 1999. *Pandora's Hope: Essays on the Reality of Science Studies*. 1st ed. Cambridge, MA: Harvard University Press.
———. 2007. *Reassembling the Social: An Introduction to Actor-Network-Theory*. Clarendon Lectures in Management Studies. Oxford: Oxford University Press.
Leonelli, Sabina. 2014. "What Difference Does Quantity Make? On the Epistemology of Big Data in Biology." *Big Data & Society* 1 (1) (July 10): 205395171453439.
Lewis, Michael L. 2003. *Inventing Global Ecology: Tracking the Biodiversity Ideal in India, 1945–1997*. Vol. 5. Hyderabad: Orient Blackswan.
Miller-Rushing, Abraham, Richard Primack, and Rick Bonney. 2012. "The History of Public Participation in Ecological Research." *Frontiers in Ecology and the Environment* 10 (6) (August): 285–90.
Mitman, Gregg. 1996. "When Nature is the Zoo: Vision and Power in the Art and Science of Natural History." *Osiris* 11: 117–43.
OECD. 1999. *Final Report of the OECD Megascience Forum Working Group on Biological Informatics*. Global Science Forum. Paris: Organisation for Economic Co-operation and Development, January.
Pereira, Henrique M., Jayne Belnap, Monika Böhm, Neil Brummitt, Jaime Garcia-Moreno, Richard Gregory, Laura Martin, et al. 2017. "Monitoring Essential Biodiversity Variables at the Species Level." In *The GEO Handbook on Biodiversity Observation Networks*, edited by Michele Walters and Robert J. Scholes, 211–38. Cham: Springer International Publishing.
Petersen, Bo Svenning, and Betrand Trolliet. 2009. "European Commission, and European Union." *European Union Management Plan 2009–2011: Lapwing – Vanellus Vanellus*. Luxembourg: Office for Official Publications of the European Communities.
Raley, Rita. 2013. "Dataveillance and Countervailance." In *"Raw Data" Is an Oxymoron*, edited by Lisa Gitelman, 121–47. Cambridge, MA: The MIT Press.

Ribes, David. 2019. "STS, Meet Data Science, Once Again." *Science, Technology, & Human Values* 44 (3) (May): 514–39.

Scholes, Robert J., G. M. Mace, W. Turner, G. N. Geller, N. Jürgens, A. Larigauderie, D. Muchoney, B. A. Walther, and H. A. Mooney. 2008. "Toward a Global Biodiversity Observing System." *Science* 321 (5892): 1044–45.

Snow, David, and Christopher M. Perrins, eds. 1997. *Birds of the Western Palearctic: Concise Edition*. London: Oxford University Press.

Sténs, Anna, and Erland Mårald. 2020. "'Forest Property Rights under Attack': Actors, Networks and Claims about Forest Ownership in the Swedish Press 2014–2017." *Forest Policy and Economics* 111 (February): 102038.

Stevens, Hallam. 2013. *Life out of Sequence: A Data-Driven History of Bioinformatics*. Chicago: The University of Chicago Press.

Thorup, Ole. 2004. *Breeding Waders in Europe 2000*. Thetford, Norfolk, UK: Wader Study Group.

Van Dijck, Jose. 2014. "Datafication, Dataism and Dataveillance: Big Data between Scientific Paradigm and Ideology." *Surveillance & Society* 12 (2) (May 9): 197–208.

Wal, René van der, Helen Anderson, Annie Robinson, Nirwan Sharma, Chris Mellish, Stuart Roberts, Ben Darvill, and Advaith Siddharthan. 2015. "Mapping Species Distributions: A Comparison of Skilled Naturalist and Lay Citizen Science Recording." *Ambio* 44 (4) (November 1): 584–600.

Walters, Michele, and Robert J. Scholes, eds. 2017. *The GEO Handbook on Biodiversity Observation Networks*. Cham: Springer International Publishing.

Wieczorek, John, David Bloom, Robert Guralnick, Stan Blum, Markus Döring, Renato Giovanni, Tim Robertson, and David Vieglais. 2012. "Darwin Core: An Evolving Community-Developed Biodiversity Data Standard." *PloS One* 7 (1): e29715.

Worster, Donald. 1994. *Nature's Economy: A History of Ecological Ideas*. Cambridge: Cambridg University Press.

21

A SHARK IN YOUR POCKET, A BIRD IN YOUR HAND(HELD)

The Spectacular and Charismatic Visualisation of Nature in Conservation Apps

Lauren Drakopulos, Eric Nost, Roberta Hawkins, and Jennifer J. Silver

Opening Vignettes

Eric: I pull up the eBird website and proceed to record the robin I saw outside my window.[1] I will admit that I am not a birder; plant identification is more my thing. Nevertheless, so far, nothing on eBird says I have to be a birder to use the platform, and I am encouraged to contribute to this large-scale scientific enterprise. I load up an interactive map with bright red pins showing the many birding "hotspots" in and around Guelph, Ontario, Canada. Several of these appear to be municipal landmarks, so I decide to look up how eBird defines and measures hotspots. That brings me to an FAQ tab where it is made clear that if you are new to birding, you should start with a different app to hone your identification skills. Oops. The FAQs also suggest that once you become more proficient in bird identification, you take an eBird essentials course to educate yourself with the platform. Finally, it is made clear that eBird is not the place you go to report that robin you saw out your window the other day. Instead, it is for those serious-minded folks who are ready to do science by downloading a checklist, head out into the "field" (or at least to hotspots), and report what they see. I return to my eBird homepage and am sunken to see my stats – no species observed or photographed; no checklists completed. I have my work cut out for me.

Well, maybe "lazy me" can at least check in on what birds my neighbours have reported. I pull up the eBird species map and zoom into Guelph.[2] This is unfamiliar territory because I first have to enter a specific species rather than see birds that others have observed in the area. I enter "American Robin." I get shades of purple, revealing the frequency of that species across the world. Darker shades indicate areas with frequently observed American robins. I can confirm that American robins have been reported in most if not all parts of the oceans. The presence of these robins appears grey on the map, streaking across the oceans and transnational shipping lanes and tipping off those sailors who took time to complete an eBird checklist on the high seas. I try for a different bird: the omnipresent Canada goose.[3] Zooming into Guelph, loads of blue pins fill up my screen. I am struck by how many people have taken the time to pull out their phones and report having seen this most common of the city's avians.

DOI: 10.4324/9781003082798-26

I think about the bigger picture – what does all this free labour contribute? I head to the "Science" section of eBird's website and focus on the Canada goose. I click on an animated weekly abundance map for the bird and am enthralled. The map shows how the geese, en masse, travel across North America throughout the year in shades of yellow and purple. The map does not show specific birds or flocks and is far less invasive than wildlife tagging and tracking. However, given the precision that birders enter their observations, the yellows and blues take on rough, irregular shapes while forming a clustered pattern – a swarm or flock itself, if you will. The flock flies from the far north in the summer to the southern United States and Mexico in the winter. Of course, there are at least some geese in Guelph at any time of the year. The visualisation invites me to imagine the travels of birds that I regularly see. Where these birds may have come from and where they may be going. I know full well that what I am looking at is the result of modelling by the eBird team at Cornell University, but I also know these models use data that my neighbours gather. So I begin to get a sense of the reward.

Roberta: I open the shark tracker app on my phone, and the first thing I see is a map of eastern North America, the Caribbean, the northern region of South America, and all the ocean spaces in between (Figure 21.1). At first glance, this map is utterly overwhelming. About 30 blue circles overlap with one another. Most have a shark icon in their centre, although some have numerical labels – 12, 4, 22. Many of the circles are pulsing – growing bigger and smaller as I look at them, giving me an eerie feeling that they are breathing. There is also a pulsing red circle with an anchor in the middle and several green circles buried underneath the blue ones. My first impression is "Holy s—, that is a lot of sharks!" In order to make any sense of this, I need to zoom in. When I do, the circles that had numbers turn into individual circles with shark icons, many of them pulsing. In the centre of the map is the red circle with an anchor icon. Once I click on it, I see a research ship – the *MV OCEARCH* docked outside of somewhere called Morehead City, North Carolina, USA.

Clicking back to the map again, I see that there are several sharks close to the ship. So I pick a circle at random and click. I am taken to a kind of bio-page. At the top is an underwater picture of a shark that seems to come from the OCEARCH research platform. Under that is the shark's name: "Martha." A caption indicates that Martha is a female juvenile white shark tagged near Massachusetts in 2020 and named after Martha's Vineyard. She weighs 184 pounds and is 7 feet long. Martha's "latest ping" was just a couple of days ago at 11:34 p.m.

Underneath Martha's info page, the app invites me to leave a comment. To my surprise, there are hundreds of comments. What would people have to say about Martha? The most recent comment is from an hour ago, and it says "OMG Queen" with a crown emoji. There are several more from today: "Martha, my love! Bless me with your grace [heart emoji]," "go Marthaaaaa," "OMG honey, you're back," or "OMG bestie, I missed you." I am surprised at how overwhelmingly positive the comments are – not what I am used to on the internet! I scroll down further to a few days ago and see a different type of message: "Ms Martha, please ping," "Martha come back," "Martha, you good girl?" "Martha girl, where r u?!" People were worried about Martha.

All this concern over Martha makes me want to check on my shark. Miss Costa is a shark from OCEARCH that I have been researching and following for over a year. So I head back to the shark tracker map and use the search function to find her. I am immediately brought to her bio-page and see an image of her lying out of the water on the OCEARCH platform with a black towel draped on her face and a man crouching down, measuring her body with a tape measure (Figure 21.1). It is an image that I have seen before, and it still makes me uncomfortable. Scrolling down, I see that she is also a white shark. She is a subadult female, weighing 1668 pounds and measuring 12 feet, 5 inches. Her name came from a corporate partner: Costa sunglasses.

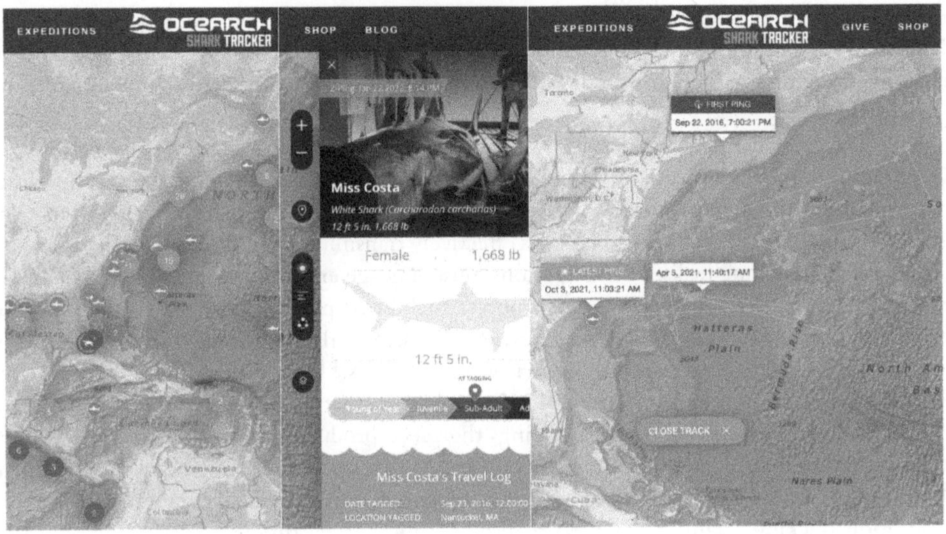

Figure 21.1 Images from the OCEARCH phone app: Miss Costa's profile, map of shark tracker activity, and Miss Costa's tracks map.

I am relieved when I see that Miss Costa has pinged recently – just yesterday at 10:43 a.m. When I click on the "show my track" button, I see yellow dots with a thin yellow line connecting them (Figure 21.1). Over the last four and a half years, Miss Costa has travelled so far! I feel strangely proud of her as I zoom in to examine the map. She has gone from Cape Cod around the Florida Panhandle and up into the Gulf of Mexico several times. She has visited Key West, the Bahamas, and at one point made a trip *way* out into the Atlantic Ocean. After clicking on specific dots for a while, seeing the date and time she was in each location, and wondering what to do with this information, I head back to her bio-page. I scroll down to the comments. The most recent ones are talking about how much Miss Costa travels. Scrolling down a day or two, I see more positive expressions of love with heart and kiss emojis. Older messages are similar to what I saw on Martha's page – people begging Miss Costa to ping, teary-face emojis, and messages saying how much they love her and wish she would return. It is a strange outpouring of emotion here, but I can relate to it. I am glad Miss Costa is still pinging and comforted a little to know she is still out there swimming.

Introduction

Rapid environmental and technological change is transforming human-environment interactions (Travis and Holm 2016, 187–89). Digital platforms used to monitor, track, map, and visualise non-humans and the environment, have become critical tools for engaging the public in conservation practice. We draw on two examples of public conservation monitoring platforms – the OCEARCH app, which monitors sharks with tracking devices, and the eBird app, which crowdsources data for habitat conservation – to demonstrate their distinct visualities and consider how they may reshape nature-society relations. We suggest that DEH can inform deeper understandings of these technologies and the visualisations they produce as meaning-making objects and practices centred on nature. Drawing on aspects of *vignette* as a literary form, we describe our experiences encountering our case study technologies and spatial visualisations as researchers, users and audiences. Doing so allows us to illustrate broader observations about the platforms by focusing on small but significant moments of our engagement, foregrounding our emotional responses and relationships with the natures they represent through maps and other visualisations.

Maps and other data visualisations are a form of world-making that create emotional realities. We often think of data visualisation as a primarily rational endeavour – a matter of symbolising data and designing interfaces in a way that ensures the designer's message about the facts of an issue (e.g. COVID-19 rates, sea level rise) is effectively transmitted and received. Nevertheless, as cartographers have long realised, visualisations must "engage emotion to engage understanding" (Field 2015). Many DataViz creators incorporate such principles in their work, aiming not just to teach the facts but engage "affective knowledge," particularly as a mechanism to elicit behavioural or societal change in response to environmental crises.[4] Describing a particularly effective climate change visualisation, Houser (2017, 366) observes that it "ultimately privileges effective ways of knowing, suggesting that the feelings the piece produces are tantamount to – or even more important than – grasping the science." Beyond just scientific representation, when maps integrate into digital platforms, they create "platform affects" or affective experiences enabled by location tracking technologies used to produce digital real-time maps (Leszczynski 2019, 207–10). Therefore, an approach that understands peoples' interactions with and responses to nature as mediated through technology and emotion provides an insightful way to make sense of eBird, OCEARCH, and other new conservation tracking platforms. In other words, we could think about these platforms in terms of scientificity, evaluations of data credibility, and the effectiveness of data visualisations. However, we are more interested in the question of how they create and enrol audiences. To understand that, we have to assess how they mobilise – intentionally or otherwise – visions of nature to engage emotion.

DEH provides an approach and framework for understanding how technology shapes peoples' emotional responses to nature while also examining the production of new (digital) natures in visual storytelling through data. We can investigate the "spectral aspects of human-nature relations" such as memories, commitments, hopes, dreams, and anticipated futures (Bergthaller et al. 2014, 268) and how these responses are made differently meaningful through technology (Travis and Holm 2016, 188–90). Digital narratives about places and environments told through data and the various affordances of technological platforms and devices make those environments known to the audience. They also direct the audience's emotional experience of place – narratives tell us about an environment and how we should *feel* about that environment. Digital mediation of the environment is then best understood as representation and building human–non-human connections. In the words of Jørgensen (2014, 109),

> [d]istant natures, those that are not experienced through the body but distributed through data and media, need different modes of analysis and storytelling. Human interpretation and experience is still relevant, but we need to understand how it is mediated through machines and technologies, models and database structures.

This chapter argues that digital conservation platforms engender new emotional relations between people and the environment. Platform design and functionality encourage users to visit and connect affectively with the world and non-humans around them. Here we make relations and meanings through repeated encounters, especially with spectacular visualisations and digital non-human charisma. Building on our opening vignettes, we develop our arguments by comparing our case study platforms and highlighting two key observations. Our first one focuses on how our case study platforms educate their users and the kinds of environmental and conservation outcomes they affect. Although both platforms intend to have an educational component rooted in conservation, nature is primarily accessible in a spectacular form through images. Their maps and data visualisations encourage repeated engagement with the platforms without necessarily providing a broader context. Our second observation concerns the way these platforms engage with scale. Conservation platforms tack between individual data points and aggregated datasets – between birds and flocks, sharks and shivers, precision and pattern – and between single moments in time and years. All this requires audiences and users to pivot their thoughts about the spaces and scale of conservation objects and subjects.

Monitoring Spectacularised Nature

Digital environmental technologies are tools for both producing and sharing environmental knowledge. At the same time, they can be used to generate emotional and behavioural responses to environmental phenomena (Verma, van der Wal, and Fischer 2015, 648–49). Technologies offer a window (or "microscope," see Verma, van der Wal, and Fischer 2015, 652–55) into the ordinary beings and actions of the non-human world. For example, tracking devices make the intimate geographies of animals knowable, and species identification platforms guide human perception of a particular species' key traits or characteristics. However, apart from geolocative affects such as trust (see Leszczynski 2019, 211–12), conservation platforms also have the power to create spectacular visions of nature (Adams 2019, 342–43; Igoe 2010, 380–85). This chapter focuses on how platforms leverage non-human charisma to create emotional responses in their human users (Altrudi 2021, 137–39; Verma, van der Wal, and Fischer 2015, 657–58). Non-human charisma is the *distinctive properties* of a non-human being that determine whether humans perceive that being and the value they ascribe to it (Lorimer 2007, 915). In other words, charisma is a relational rather than an innate quality. To understand how environmental tracking platforms leverage charisma to create spectacular natures, we draw from Lorimer's (2007, 916–23) framework. Lorimer outlines three types of charismatic human–non-human relations: ecological, aesthetic, and corporeal.

Ecological charisma describes the "ecological affordances" or core behaviours and characteristics that non-human beings possess that intersect with humans. Human bodies have physiologies with specific traits, senses, and so on, and the specificities of bodies "filter" human perception such that some non-humans are more (or less) perceptible (charismatic) than others. Ecological charisma derives from colour, shape, size, sound, movement, and the nature and frequency of encounters between human and non-human bodies (e.g. seasonality and migration).

Aesthetic charisma is the visual and behavioural properties of non-humans that elicit emotional responses in humans (not necessarily positive responses). Examples of aesthetic properties include fierceness, cuddliness, cuteness, danger, tameness, independence, or other attributes that appeal to human morality and ethics, in addition to feelings of awe or fear. Corporeal charisma describes when emotions and attentions form through practical human–non-human interactions such as memories of being moved by a first encounter.

Corporeal charisma is particularly characteristic of conservation science-based encounters, such as the feelings one gets from identifying species in the field, doing species censuses, and making lists and notes about encounters (Lorimer 2007, 916–23).

In digitally mediated human-environment relations, charisma is co-constructed through technology. According to Kirksey et al. (2018, 604–5), environmental technologies and social media, in particular, open new spaces for relationships between human and non-human animals. As Kirksey et al. (2018) describe Australian cockatoos, these charismatic birds that respond well to humans in real life generated a *technological charisma* through their social media reach and

Facebook followings. In the case of Kirksey et al.'s (2018, 611–12) cockatoos, real-life in-person experiences formed the basis for digital encounters; however, technologies can also produce human–non-human encounters that might not otherwise ever occur in real life. For example, close-circuit television wildlife cameras seem to provide humans with an intimate look into the lives of "wild" animals, allowing humans to experience places and natures they might not otherwise (Adams 2019, 342–43; Verma, van der Wal, and Fischer 2015, 655–56).

However, for all their part in generating conviviality between humans and non-humans (Kirksey et al. 2018, 609) or "new networks of care" (Adams 2019, 343; Verma, van der Wal, and Fischer 2015, 655–56), others would argue that the spectacle of digital nature visualisations commodifies non-humans for human consumption and enjoyment (Adams 2019, 342–43; Altrudi 2021, 25). For example, trail cameras and drone footage underpin popular nature documentaries such as *Planet Earth III* (Adams 2019, 343; Rose 2017). In the context of conservation projects, nature commodified as a visual spectacle creates interest and support for environmental causes (Igoe 2010, 383–85). Organisations might leverage nature's charisma to garner financial donations, and the public can pay for the experience of engaging with nature as a spectacle (Verma, van der Wal, and Fischer 2015, 657). Indeed, by enabling users to "save" nature "through mouse-clicks and double-taps," conservation platforms are connecting "user affects to the political economy of conservation" (Büscher 2016, 727, 732). In summary, technology does more than emphasising non-human charisma; it mediates new forms of charisma and, in turn, emotional responses through the visual spectacles of maps, charts, and other imagery. Understanding the world-making potential of maps and other data visualisations used in conservation is essential, given their potential to unmake and remake nature's value and consumption (Campbell et al. 2021, 425–28).

eBird

As a citizen science endeavour launched in 2002, eBird bills itself as rooted in two goals: leveraging the "unique knowledge experience" of every birdwatcher and "developing tools that make birding more rewarding." In terms of the former, the focus of eBird is on the checklist submission process. They provide registered birders with an expert-tailored checklist of species known to occur in an area and then tasked with documenting the presence or absence of those species while visiting a location. Its web page declares that

> eBird began with a simple idea – that every birdwatcher has unique knowledge and experience. Our goal is to gather this information in the form of checklists of birds, archive it, and freely share it to power new data-driven approaches to science, conservation and education. At the same time, we develop tools that make birding more rewarding. From being able to manage lists, photos and audio recordings, to seeing real-time maps of species distribution, to alerts that let you know when species have been seen, we strive to provide the most current and useful information to the birding community.
>
> *(eBird 2021)*[5]

In terms of making birding "more rewarding," eBird enables birders to upload and collate photos and audio, digitally secure their bird lists, and learn from other birders about where a species can be found. eBird also synthesises the data it collects into abundance and range maps for dozens of species, making these available for public download and illustrating them in animated seasonal migration maps for those interested in bird patterns and processes. The focus of eBird is

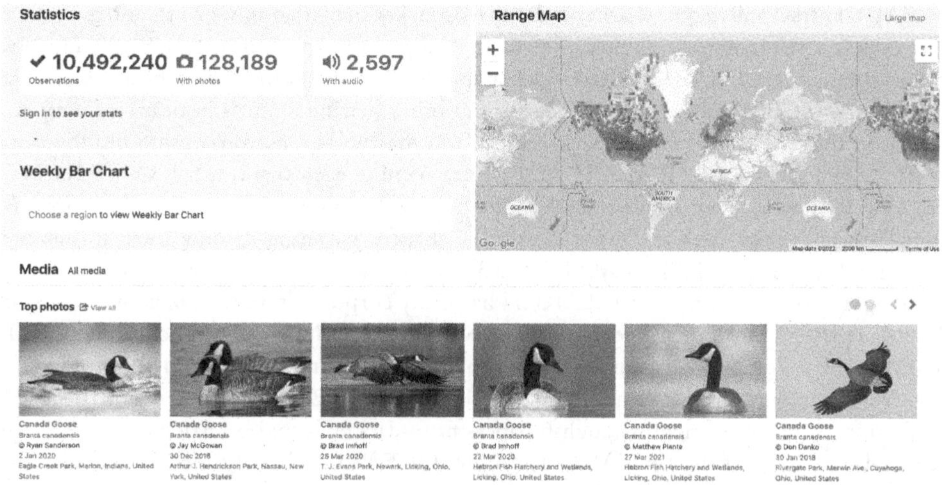

Figure 21.2 Image of the eBird dashboard for the Canada goose.

on the visual. Users log observations through a map-based interface. Accessing others' observations is also done through an interactive map. Most observations involve sightings of the species in question and may even include photos. eBird's home page shows the species distribution of the bird of prey black kite against a grey base map of political borders.

In contrast, the front page for eBird's science arm includes an image of the world lit up like those composite satellite images of nighttime lights – except, in this case, the bright spots are eBird data, not reflected light. Moreover, not everything about eBird is visual. For instance, users can make identifications based on birdsong and even upload audio to the eBird servers. However, nearly users have logged 100,000 photos of Canadian geese worldwide, but there are not even 2,000 audio samples (**Figure 21.2**).

OCEARCH

OCEARCH was founded in 2007 by Chris Fischer, who is also known for featuring in a few ocean-related reality television shows, including *Offshore Adventures* and *Shark Wranglers*.[6] OCEARCH undertakes several highly publicised expeditions per year, explicitly intended to locate, capture, sample, and fit sharks with satellite tags. The expeditions bring research scientists from various universities, mainly in the United States, onboard the *MV OCEARCH*, a 581-ton vessel custom fitted with the hydraulic lift and research platform. The platform takes a sample of sharks, and it features many of OCEARCH's YouTube videos and photos in the background. Its website states,

> OCEARCH is a data-centric organization built to help scientists collect previously unattainable data in the ocean. Our mission is to accelerate the ocean's return to balance and abundance through fearless innovations in scientific research, education, outreach, and policy, using unique collaborations of individuals and organizations in the US and abroad.
>
> (OCEARCH 2021)

OCEARCH tracks all tagged sharks on the shark-tracker map; that is, when their tags make satellite contacts, they ping on the map. The map is on the front page of the OCEARCH website and features in the OCEARCH shark-tracker app. A comment at the top of the app says, "Welcome to the OCEARCH app! Track sharks and other marine animals in near real time. Each animal on the Tracker is sending back critical data that will be used to ensure healthy oceans for future generations" (OCEARCH 2021). After naming each shark, it tags OCEARCH and creates a Twitter account for the shark. Often, these accounts tweet screenshot maps of an animal's recent pings, with text written as if the shark is narrating its movement in the ocean (e.g. "gulf life = pure bliss"). Sharks have also been known to tweet at human celebrities and give plugs to corporate brands. OCEARCH has many corporate sponsors, including SeaWorld, Costa Sunglasses, and even Cisco Brewers of Nantucket – a New England craft brewery. The OCEARCH website and app encourage visitors to donate and consider buying from various sponsors, including co-branded products like the Costa-OCEARCH Stoneham Trucker Hat. In addition, as research scientists publish papers from data collected on *MV OCEARCH*, they are listed on a page of the OCEARCH website. OCEARCH has also developed curriculum packages on various topics targeted to children from kindergarten through grade 8.[7]

Making Nature Known: From Engagement to Environmental Outcomes

In our case, one needs to look no further than the emotional reaction of commenters on the OCEARCH app, which swing wildly from "we love you shark" to "where is the shark? Is she dead? nooooo!" to begin to examine technologically mediated charisma (2021). Unlinked to encounters with sharks in real life, these emotional responses result from the technology – whether Miss Costa pings or not – and the visualisation – where is she now? There she is! (Phew.) In other words, because shark habitat and behaviour do not lend themselves to regular human encounters, they are only made visible to humans through technology that their ecological charisma manifests. Likewise, although social perception reduces sharks to aesthetic, charismatic qualities, such as fierceness or being threatening, playful tweets from Miss Costa and her finned friends elicit a broader spectrum of human emotional responses such as care and excitement.

Nevertheless, while the pendulum swings from animal absence to presence, concern to relief, anticipation to enthusiasm – there is little description or education about why the sharks are where they are, simply that they are there. Using the OCEARCH app, we do not learn anything about shark habitats, whether sharks are endangered species or not, what sharks like to eat, how they live, or how they relate to other animals, including other sharks or humans. We do not get any images of Miss Costa in her natural habitat, and we do not get to see the ocean from anything other than the bird's-eye-view map (Figure 21.1). One sentence describes the purpose of the sharks being tagged to send back data to humans, but we do not learn what that data is or how it is used for shark conservation. Ultimately it is almost impossible to figure out the point of the OCEARCH app as an audience member.

Given that the platform's mission includes education, outreach and the digital display of critical data about ocean health, we might assume the app's intended purpose is awareness-raising. What awareness is exactly being raised, though, is unclear. The way an audience member engages with nature is mediated in such a way as to show us an exact version of a shark's life while at the same time telling us nothing more about it.

In comparison, eBird enables a digital form of corporeal charisma. As a citizen science platform, eBird provides the technological infrastructure for contributors to make lists that can then be shared and compared with other users. Just as Facebook or other social media draw on contributions of individual users, "rewarding" or compensating them with tools to optimise their social networks, eBird compensates its users with enhanced abilities and insights around the birding they already love to do.

The home page of the Cornell Lab of Ornithology (2021), which hosts the eBird initiative, includes an animated abundance map under the caption "We reveal how nature works" (Figure 21.3). Indeed, by "playing" the animated map and watching the species, one is given the sense that the inner workings of nature are being illustrated with all its movements, mechanisms, and gears. Unfortunately, only generic months (e.g. January) are indicated in the animation rather than specific points in time (e.g. January 2021). Thus, the animation reflects predictions of a general pattern, not observed results for a specific year. What is not clear is what turns nature's gears. Why do birds go where they do? Users can speculate about drivers, such as timing and habitat. As the sub-caption states, such a spectacle of nature aims to encourage everyone to join in on conserving bird species.

The eBird animations aim to tell primarily a neutral story about species. What we see on the map is the abundance of birds and political borders, for reference. What is missing are the sorts of threats to these birds – such as wind turbines, light pollution, or cats – that may be challenging to put on a map. So rather than tell a harmful or threatening story about birds through its maps, with all the obstacles birds encounter in making their migrations, eBird aims at something positive and remarkable – a "planet Earth style" – here is the wonder of the world worth protecting.[8] Although eBird's map animations are not analogous to a nature documentary, they still create a "nature as spectacle" experience that generates public engagement with nature through the platform and maps.

In the case of OCEARCH, the app appears to be almost exclusively a form of entertainment. The only scientific details referenced for each shark – other than its name, species type, and age category (e.g. juvenile or adult) –was its length and weight when the shark was initially tagged. Audiences can view exactly where the sharks were at times and places of their taggings and then trace the patterns of locations created by their various migrations over time. OCEARCH also does not ask audiences to interpret any information concerning other sharks or marine animals or broader environmental issues. It seems as if the app treats its users as nonscientists who are not interested in learning more complex information about sharks in their environments. The mention that the sharks are sending back data to scientists implies that it is something that the app user does not need to concern themselves with. Rather, OCEARCH scientists are taking care of the fundamental research and work. The developers could have added additional features to the app, such as a link to OCEARCH's findings from all of their shark research. The app could include links to learn more about sharks and their habitats, or why sharks may be in danger, or why sharks are an important species in the ocean, but such links are absent. Likewise, the app could link to campaigns where people might perform individual actions that could directly or indirectly help sharks – for example, saying no to shark fin soup or reducing their use of plastics. However, none of these and other potential information and activist features are available to app users. Although on the OCEARCH platform, there are no calls to take environmental action, there are still several calls to action: donate, shop, and follow. In the OCEARCH app, there is a big blue DONATE button under the description of the project. A tab across the top for support has a heart icon with a dollar sign inside it. On that tab is another donate button and then a section called "shop2give" with another big blue button and a description of the OCEARCH co-branded collections with a button for each that takes you out of their partner's corporate website, Costa sunglasses, for example. These requests to shop and donate are essentially part of how you engage with the animals. Whether or not you donate or shop, the option is always there. It also includes buttons allowing you to follow OCEARCH on Twitter, Instagram, and

Facebook. Connecting through these platforms is about increasing the ideological and economic reach of OCEARCH rather than anything else.

Scales of Conservation Objects and Subjects

Digital technologies make nature and environmental phenomena more tangible through data. As an abstract rendering of the environment, data themselves must also translate into information that is recognisable and meaningful. Technological modes of representation can shift perceptions and experiences of the environment, particularly understandings of place and time, by their ability to bridge vastly different temporal and spatial scales (Jørgensen 2014, 97). Digital technologies are unique in that they allow for both immediacy and interactivity. The user can zoom in and out on a location or data point; they may offer a time slider that allows the user to explore five years of information in a matter of seconds. In short, the audience can see space and time in new ways.

Data visualisations are interfaces between people and otherwise spatially and temporally incomprehensible environmental phenomena. In the absence of numerical literacy or specialised scientific knowledge, it is difficult for public audiences to ascribe meaning to large datasets (Houser 2014, 319). Even then, tabular data only goes so far. Data visualisation addresses the "affective gap" between enumeration and human action (Houser 2016, 162). In particular, in conservation platforms, it does so by tacking back and forth scales and times, from individual animals to whole species and from one moment in place and time to vast movements over the years.

A stunning aspect of both the OCEARCH and eBird maps and platforms is the sheer number of animals that appear. With OCEARCH, the first screen is a map of the eastern United States, and the ocean around it is filled with so many blue dots that it is pretty spectacular and shocking (Figure 21.1). Part of this situation is the scale of the dots compared to the ocean. Another part is that the app has tracked and tagged many animals. Individual animals are "spectacularised" through tracking devices and the platform (Adams 2019, 343). The trackers enable humans to identify individual sharks and their movements. When a shark's tracker pings in real time, the app users are alerted to the shark's presence and location. This intimate awareness of the lively nature of shark geographies would be nearly impossible in the absence of digital technology. In addition, the platform provides a venue for the audience to develop a relationship with an individual shark. Through its digital lenses, the audience gets to "know" the shark through photos, tweets, and elaborate narratives on each shark's profile page.

While users can log any avian species with eBird, the focus is on one individual species at a time, enrolling users in a narrative about that particular bird in the aggregate, producing ecological charisma through the platform. eBird maps do not tell a story about all species in a place – just one species at a time.[9] The spectacle of viewing an entire species in a given place at a specific time is not one that humans would experience in real life and is only made possible through the affordances of the eBird platform and maps. Likewise, one of the most striking components of eBird is the animated maps of species abundance.[10] Unlike OCEARCH, eBird is a citizen science project, so it relies on active contributions from specific publics to work. eBirders' observations have been aggregated, run through Cornell's models, and then reflected back to eBirders as maps of expected or predicted relative abundance. Based on previous eBirder observations and environmental data, the maps show the relative number of birds that one should expect to see (Figure 21.3). Audiences can transcend time. They can see species sightings historically at different locations. Also, they can anticipate what will arrive in the future. In other words, part of the spectacle of eBird is the ecological charisma of "yet-to-be-realized natures" made real and encounterable through predictive data visualisations.

TheCornellLab of Ornithology

We reveal how nature works

We bring together scientists, students, and people from all walks of life in the quest to generate new knowledge and conserve our shared natural world. You can help.

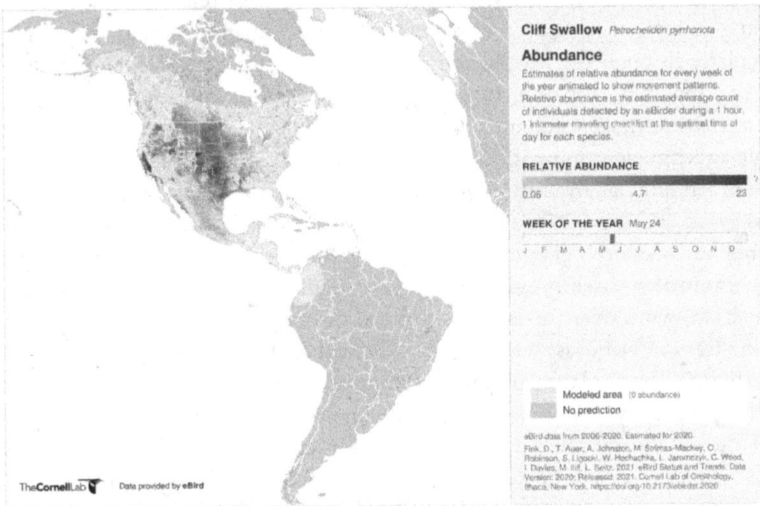

Figure 21.3 Still image of eBird's animated abundance map.

While the spectacle of sharks traversing the ocean is a compelling aspect of the OCEARCH app, equally interesting, from the perspective of data visualisation, is what the user cannot see. As an audience member, you see a map from a bird's eye view with all of these dots of sharks and then when you click on an individual dot, you see a photo of the shark. Many of the photos are of the sharks out of the water on the boat's platform and being tagged or swimming away from the boat's platform. In that sense, it is a close-up view of the shark, but it is not a realistic view because often, as in Miss Costa's photo (Figure 21.1), people are working on her. In the photo, she has a black towel over her eyes. Somebody is crouching down next to her with a measuring tape around her middle. These are particular views of sharks and the environment that an audience member gets.

App users can see the map where Miss Costa has travelled and a photo of what she looks like – at least the visible pieces visible in the photo – but users do not get any additional information

(Figure 21.1). Audiences do not learn why she has travelled where she has, for example, to find food or to mate or because of ocean temperatures. They also do not get any sense of whether or not Miss Costa's travels are unusual for a shark. The user-contributed comments below her photo suggest that she travels a lot. However, unless you click on every other shark, there is no sense of how her journey compares to other sharks or how it fits within broader understandings of shark distribution and behaviour. App users learn detailed information about where *exactly* Miss Costa is (in terms of location) but without any additional information to put that locational data in any context, scientific or otherwise. In short, there is no holistic overview that helps the audience to make sense of individual shark behaviours concerning the species as a whole or concerning ocean balance and abundance – which OCEARCH states are its focus.

Conclusion

We close this chapter by reflecting on the significance of conservation tracking platforms for broader human-environment relations. Maps and other visualisations are integral to how digital conservation platforms such as OCEARCH and eBird tell stories about nature. Part of their appeal is that they enable users to experience non-human species in ways not otherwise possible, particularly through the platforms' maps and other visualisations. The platforms foreground, or remake altogether, non-human charisma – the qualities of an animal that make it noticeable to humans and make encounters meaningful – engendering new emotional relations between people and the environment. Specifically, platform visualisations mediate spectacular visions of non-human animals by shifting the scales of an encounter between humans and non-humans across space and time. Not only can humans learn about the intimate geographies of animals, but they can see those geographies in aggregate. In other words, rather than an encounter with a single animal, a shark fin visible above the water line at the beach, a user can see the paths 20 sharks have swum over the last year. Instead of simply seeing a flock of birds flying overhead, a model shows in elaborate, animated colour where those birds and many others are going.

Although these platforms provide captivating visualisations of the beings and doings of non-humans, they also render non-human nature knowable in a narrowly prescriptive and stylised form already filtered through the affordances of the technology. A shiver of sharks and a flock of birds seem to be knowable entities and ephemeral or confusing to the general public. These platforms are mapping individual objects – an individual shark or an individual bird. As the audience, we are using the maps of the movement of those individuals to try and understand the conservation of a more significant entity – shark populations, bird populations, habitats for birds, habitats for sharks. This situation raises important questions about what scale means for understanding environments, the threats they face, and their conservation. Does tracking sharks in isolation tell audiences anything about the interconnected web of ocean ecosystems as a whole or just sharks' place in it? Can an emotional connection with an individual shark or bird be extrapolated to an entire species? Is the most meaningful conservation action that the public can take to support shark conservation buying products from the organisation's corporate sponsor?

What is more, the apps focus on their users' repeated engagement. This focus creates a digitally mediated form of contact charisma and potentially encourages a consumptive relationship between users and non-human nature. However, we also wonder if the ability to track a shark on your phone, get notifications about where sharks are, and see other people comment about them is, in a way, making nature more mundane. George Swenson, a radio engineer and wildlife tracking supporter, once stated, "You ecologists, you're stupid. You have this big topic you could address, but you're thinking too small." Swenson's point was that scientists needed to track all creatures simultaneously and across the planet rather than in small groups or discrete places

(Shah 2021). We also speculate on how a DEH framework might inform how we understand the world-making potential of these platforms and how these platforms are themselves a form of DEH practice. Conservation tracking platforms and visualisations are disrupting scientific practice in enabling new forms of monitoring and visualisation. However, a DEH framework troubles assumptions that knowledge about the environment can only emerge from the academy and views humans and non-humans alike as collaborators rather than just objects and subjects of conservation (Holm et al. 2015, 988–89). Therefore, we suggest a fruitful direction for future research is to explore these platforms' potential to remake their public as both passive audiences and active experts.

Notes

1 eBird (users can create an account to access the site: https://ebird.org/submit/map).
2 eBird Map (https://ebird.org/map).
3 eBird Featured Status and Trends Visualizations (https://ebird.org/science/status-and-trends/cangoo).
4 See the British Cartographic Society Design Group principles in Field 2015 (http://cartonerd.blogspot.com/2015/10/principles-of-cartographic-design.html).
5 eBird (https://ebird.org/about).
6 OCEARCH (www.ocearch.org/about).
7 OCEARCH (www.ocearch.org/education/#curriculum).
8 To be clear, eBird scientists do research these barriers. For instance, they have investigated the role of light pollution in migration. It is just not something visualised in the animated "We reveal how nature works" maps.
9 However, users can look in eBird at species observations in checklist format for a particular (e.g. the county Guelph is in; https://ebird.org/region/CA-ON-WL?yr=all&m=&rank=mrec).
10 eBird (https://ebird.org/science/status-and-trends/cangoo/abundance-map-weekly).

Sources

Adams, William M. 2019. "Geographies of Conservation II: Technology, Surveillance and Conservation by Algorithm." *Progress in Human Geography* 43 (2): 337–50.

Altrudi, Soledad. 2021. "Connecting to Nature Through Tech? The Case of the iNaturalist App." *Convergence* 27 (1): 124–41.

Bergthaller, Hannes, Rob Emmett, Adeline Johns-Putra, Agnes Kneitz, Susanna Lidström, Shane McCorristine, Isabel Pérez Ramos, Dana Phillips, Kate Rigby, and Libby Robin. 2014. "Mapping Common Ground: Ecocriticism, Environmental History, and the Environmental Humanities." *Environmental Humanities* 5 (1): 261–76.

Büscher, Bram. 2016. "Nature 2.0: Exploring and Theorizing the Links between New Media and Nature Conservation." *New Media & Society* 18 (5): 726–43.

Campbell, Lisa, Noella J. Gray, Sarah Bess Jones Zigler, Leslie Acton, and Rebecca Gruby. 2021. "World-Making Through Mapping: Large-Scale Marine Protected Areas and the Transformation of Global Oceans." In *The Routledge Handbook of Critical Resource Geography*, edited by Matthew Himley, Elizabeth Havice, and Gabriela Valdivia, 425–40. New York and London: Routledge.

eBird. 2021. *About eBird. The Cornell Lab of Ornithology*. Ithaca: Cornell University. https://ebird.org/about.

Field, Kenneth. 2015. "Principles of Cartographic Design." *Cartography*, October 12, 2015. http://cartonerd.blogspot.com/2015/10/principles-of-cartographic-design.html.

Holm, Poul, Joni Adamson, Hsinya Huang, Lars Kirdan, Sally Kitch, Iain McCalman, James Ogude et al. 2015. "Humanities for the Environment – A Manifesto for Research and Action." *Humanities* 4 (4): 977–92.

Houser, Heather. 2014. "The Aesthetics of Environmental Visualizations: More Than Information Ecstasy?" *Public Culture* 26 (2) (73): 319–37.

———. 2016. "Climate Visualizations as Cultural Objects." In *Teaching Climate Change in the Humanities*, edited by Stephen Siperstein, et al., 162–71. New York and London: Routledge.

———. 2017. "Climate Visualizations: Making Data Experiential." In *The Routledge Companion to the Environmental Humanities*, edited by Ursula K. Heise, Jon Christensen, and Michelle Niemann, 374–84. London and New York: Routledge.

Igoe, Jim. 2010. "The Spectacle of Nature in the Global Economy of Appearances: Anthropological Engagements with the Spectacular Mediations of Transnational Conservation." *Critique of Anthropology* 30 (4): 375–97.

Jørgensen, Finn Arne. 2014. "The Armchair Traveller's Guide to Digital Environmental Humanities." *Environmental Humanities* 4 (1): 95–112.

Kirksey, Eben, Paul Munro, Thom van Dooren, Dan Emery, Anne Maree Kreller, Jeffrey Kwok, Ken Lau et al. 2018. "Feeding the Flock: Wild Cockatoos and Their Facebook Friends." *Environment and Planning E: Nature and Space* 1 (4): 602–20.

Leszczynski, Agnieszka. 2019. "Platform Affects of Geolocation." *Geoforum* 107: 207–15.

Lorimer, Jamie. 2007. "Non-Human Charisma." *Environment and Planning D: Society and Space* 25 (5): 911–32.

OCEARCH. 2021. "Sharktracker." www.ocearch.org/about/.

Rose, Chris. 2017. "Planet Earth III? For Nature's Sake, no Thanks." *Ecos* 38 (1).

Shah, Sonia. 2021. "How Far Does Wildlife Roam? Ask the 'Internet of Animals.'" *The New York Times Magazine*, January 12, 2021. www.nytimes.com/interactive/2021/01/12/magazine/animal-tracking-icarus.html.

Travis, Charles, and Poul Holm. 2016. "The Digital Environmental Humanities – What Is It and Why Do We Need It? the NorFish Project and SmartCity Lifeworlds." In *The Digital Arts and Humanities*, 187–204. Cham: Springer.

Verma, Audrey, René van der Wal, and Anke Fischer. 2015. "Microscope and Spectacle: On the Complexities of Using New Visual Technologies to Communicate About Wildlife Conservation." *Ambio* 44 (4): 648–60.

22

IMAGES OF NATURE THROUGH PLATFORMS

Practices and Relationships as a Research Field and an Epistemic Vantage Point of DEH

Paolo Giardullo

Introduction

The present chapter addresses the opportunity to consider digital images of nature as research objects and from an epistemic vantage, as a point of debate in the DEH, to analyse relationships between environment and society. In our contemporary cultural context, often defined as a digital one, images can consist of the digital conversion of paintings, in addition to genuinely generated digital pictures of subjects and objects. In this chapter, I will concentrate on the latter, specifically on photographs. Besides considering such pictures as cultural products, I will illustrate how photographs, in general, offer an opportunity to focus on cultural practices. Pooles states that visual images are "part of a comprehensive organisation of people, ideas, and objects" (1997, 8), and this analytical point will be of pivotal relevance in developing my argument over the following pages. Images are a crucial part of broader sociocultural systems; this was true when photography was inaugurated, and contemporarily with amateur and personal photography, its social and cultural impacts have grown considerably (Gye 2007; Van Dijck 2008; Huhtamo 2011). If we take photographs as our units of analysis, it means keeping in mind at least three interconnected elements: first, the socio-technical history evolution of photography itself; second, the actors who take pictures; and third, the purposes for which the pictures are taken. Regarding the former, pictures of natural environments are as old as photography. Indeed, many pioneering photographers in the 19th century engaged in photography to portray landscapes (Seelig 2014). The second and third elements are even more interconnected: besides the aims of artistic and cultural spheres, even the scientific community encourages natural environment photography as evidence for scientific knowledge creation (Tucker 2005). In our current global environmental crisis, photographers can play a role beyond the pure artistic representation of natural environments. For instance, portraying wildlife can make people aware of endangered species and their habitats (McGarr 2016).

Indeed, we should keep in mind that photography as figurative art developed as a popular activity at the centre of a more comprehensive array of practices and usages. We no longer talk of professional photographers as unique or even as the main category of social actors able to

DOI: 10.4324/9781003082798-27

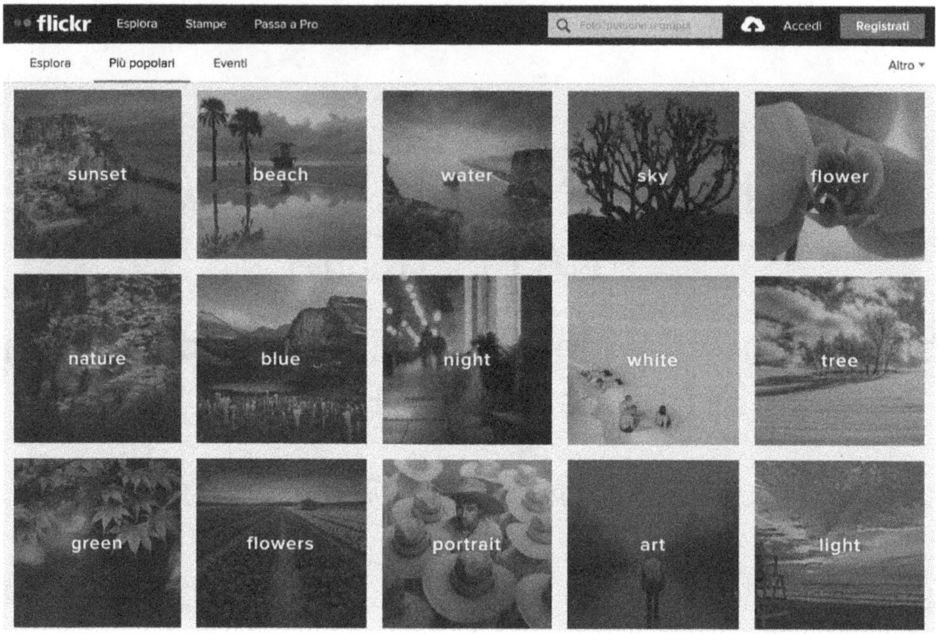

Figure 22.1 Most popular tags on Flickr.

snap pictures. Twenty-first-century digital technologies have fostered the ongoing 20th-century popularisation of photography, coalescing into the so-called *camera epidemic* – further reducing the skill and technical requirements of an individual to obtain a "good shot" (Huhtamo 2011). At first digital cameras, followed by cameraphones (now smartphones), further enabled the autonomy of controlling the editing and circulation of pictures (Gomez-Cruz and Meyer 2012). This digital turning point fostered the personal self-representation of people (the selfie) who snap pictures (Schwartz and Halegoua 2015; Van House 2009). But landscapes and pictures of natural environments contribute to the tremendous array of pictures snapped daily. Figure 22.1 presents the most popular tags on Flickr, arguably the leading social media platform dedicated to photography.

In addition to the tag "nature," other digital photo tags refer to natural environments: "tree," "flowers," and "green." The ubiquity of digitally produced and disseminated images of nature offer an opportunity for scholars in DEH to understand representations of environments as narrative proxies of individual relationships with nature. Parsed through the lens of science and technology studies (STS) offers intersecting avenues of study for DEH and other transdisciplinary focused researchers. This chapter will focus on practices shaped and enacted by web platform algorithms (Gillespie 2014) to address a key issue in DEH debates concerning the notion of "field" for online research of practices connected with images of nature. STS literature on digital technologies provides a framework for DEH studies on visual representations of nature or, to put it more simply, to research environments through pictures.

This chapter will outline a socio-technical historical review of the relationship between the production and usage of images about nature and environments. This review will discuss the changes that digitalisation (first) and datafication (afterwards) brought to society and the social sciences. Such changes affect the main narratives and practices connected with the production and dissemination of images of nature and the environment on digital platforms. This has facilitated a reshuffle of previous digital practices and new configurations of use – including a plethora of "citizen science" web platforms. In DEH debates, less attention has been given to such projects, where non-professionals contribute to scientific activities, often based on digital platforms that collect pictures and other data about "nature." This chapter's examination of such sites will illustrate issues such as the ubiquity of infrastructures and the reinvention and reconfiguration of already-known practices connected to the production and dissemination of images of nature and environments. The conclusion will briefly reprise the evolution of this new field of study for online research on practices connected with images of nature, further highlighting the epistemic value of research involving digital images and their connected practices in relationship to nature and environments.

Images and Pictures of Nature and Environments

Reviewing the socio-technical historiography about the production and use of images of nature and environments from the early development of photography in the mid-19th century entails exploring a threefold relationship. First, the photography of nature aimed to illuminate artistic concepts such as the *sublime* and the *picturesque* (Jakobs 2008). Second, photography represented a tool of colonial dominance by European empires. In contributing to the mapping, classifying, and recording of new territories and peoples, photography aided imperial physical and cultural appropriations of nature (Jakobs 2008). Third, photography as a tool was deployed to represent nature for explicit scientific purposes (Tucker 2005). It was not uncommon for early photographers, influenced by the perspectives of painters, to concentrate on taking photos of landscapes (Seelig 2014). Indeed, many pioneering photographers, often painters themselves, were inspired by *vedute* – paintings of cities and towns that were lucid and faithful enough so that their locations could easily be identified. In pursuing a continuity with pictorial theories, some photographers captured images of specific *vedute* locations to showcase the full potential of photography as an innovative visual representation technique (Jakobs 2008).

By doing so, photographers situated themselves as performers who provided the perfect means for interpreting the picturesque. This practice made the photography of landscapes and natural environments a classic and, at times, unavoidable topic. Through the picturesque, nature became meaningful in and of itself, deserving to be captured best through photography rather than painting (Jakobs 2008). In terms of the cultural influence of photography on wildlife and landscapes, some consider that it fostered the distinction between nature and culture by objectifying and spectacularising environments as a sublime otherness (Brower 2005). In this sense, photography took part in the construction of a dominant western paradigm framing the opposition between nature and culture – one that justified extractivism and the capitalist exploitation of environments – and if we examine this binary from a postcolonial perspective, it goes even further (Latour 1993; Catton and Dunlap 1978).

During the 19th century, cameras portrayed landscapes with detail and fidelity, providing colonisers with new and powerful technology for exploiting territories. As a promoter of the sublime and the picturesque, photography applied the same concept of "otherness" to their colonies. In this sense, photographers configured the camera as a tool of dominance by producing images of nature. As Nicholas Dirks affirms in his foreword to Bernard Cohn's book *Colonialism and Its Forms of Knowledge* (1996), photography and statistics became novel tools that contributed to the scientific knowledge of colonies. Photography, but more specifically landscape photography, in its quest for the sublime and the picturesque, also supported the practical and symbolic management of lands controlled in India and Africa by the British Empire. Colonisers, in general, took advantage of landscape photography in terms of cultural and scientific appropriation and dominance. Indeed, pictures of nature allowed colonisers to produce classifications and frame statistical perspectives of the colonised – often providing the justification for racial and imperialist policies (Price 2015). In regards to the use of photography for scientific purposes, we can intertwine this endeavour with its already mentioned aesthetic and colonial framings of the natural environment.

Peter Henry Emerson, a photographer and theorist active between 1886 and 1894, promoted photography as a scientifically expressive and symbolic practice. Emerson worked hard to elevate photography to the level of "visual art." He believed that a pure representation of nature was possible and could be better performed through photography. In his opinion, a photograph could provide a more scientifically accurate portrayal of nature by assuring a proper and intimate relationship with the portrayed subject itself rather than requiring the performance of a mimicked representation through painting (Stewart Howe 2008). Being considered truthful rather than imitative, the photography of natural environments and wildlife also provided the idea of the medium as a proper tool for scientific research. In reconstructing the socio-technical history of scientific photography in Britain during the Victorian Age, Tucker (2005) points out how images were part of the complex work of producing evidence about nature and corroborating scientific hypotheses. In this regard, controversy about Charles Darwin's theory of evolution, for instance, took nourishment from photographic evidence while, during the same period, appeals for the use of photography in comparative zoology were in evidence (Prodger 2009). Thus, since its infancy, photography has been part of the toolkit of scientific knowledge production.

This brief socio-technical historical review of the threefold relationship between photography, nature and the environment illustrates such tropes are still relevant. However, their relations have evolved across time. Portraying landscapes, for example developed into specific professions such as nature photography. Reports and photos provide wildlife documentation with tools to aid conservation movements and provide proof of environmental degradation (McGaurr 2016). More militant ways of interpreting the role of the photographer have reversed the table. Rather than offering a "spectacle of otherness" and aesthetic images of natural beauty – photography now offers a "pictorial voice" to activists and organisations seeking environmental protection and justice (Mittermaier 2005). Nonetheless, pictures of natural landscapes and wildlife are often appraised for their intrinsic beauty, thus retaining an explicit function of artistic value in environmental communication. In this regard, Anderson (1997) notes that the presence (and the quality) of pictures as visual endowments of news positively influences the "newsworthiness" of topics. Contemporarily, the global ecological crisis makes the relations of photography to the natural environment to emerging digital infrastructures even more intimate and timely. For example, digital images of nature streamed live allow the monitoring and tracking of wildlife and the contamination of natural environments, such as oil spills, reflecting photography's 19th-century development as a scientific tool (McCormick 2012; Gabrys 2016).

It can be stressed that the study of such images, belonging to "visual culture," can contribute to environmental humanities research. However, as Heise (2017) states, humanistic approaches should not be limited to analysing images as such. Indeed, the digital turn provides us with more options to explore photography's usages and availability in connection with image sharing infrastructures. These facets of the digital turn have also contributed to the reconfiguration of the threefold historical relationship between photography and nature. Therefore, it appears to be of critical importance to consider this reconfigured relationship, as the digital turn offers an epistemic vantage point to better frame aspects of our current ecological crisis and useful methodological options.

The World Has Changed: From Digitisation to Datafication

Digitisation consists of coding sounds, images, and texts into "digits" by compressing information into a quicker, more compact, and more agile format that offers the opportunity not only to store it easily but to transfer it to portable storage and the World Wide Web (Lister et al. 2009; Balbi and Magaudda 2018). The digital turn manifested when a sufficient number of users included digital technologies in their daily routines. As part of a socio-technical network, photography is not an exception to this, and its practices have co-evolved with its technologies (Minniti 2016). According to renowned media archaeologist Erkki Huhtamo (2011), the first *camera epidemic* – the rapid diffusion of the device as a successful commercial product – emerged with portable film cameras that were easier to use and more affordable than previous more professional versions. The Eastman Kodak Company of Rochester, New York, established in 1892, advertised photography as an activity for amateurs, regardless of gender or age. Later, point-and-shoot cameras, with auto-focus functions, further provided non-professionals with easy-to-use and affordable portable devices that transformed photography into a much more ordinary activity, especially compared to early photographic ventures. Aside from its technological evolution, photography developed in connection with social practices. It created the opportunity to visually represent essential family rites of passage (e.g. weddings, graduations, birthdays, funerals) and consumption habits (e.g. trips, music events) that shaped the visual memories of many families (Van House 2009). Personal photography depicts social status, as illustrated in Pierre Bourdieu's (1996) analysis of middle-class family portraits, which finds social etiquette reflected in the objects and poses (re)presented by such photographic images. Recently, photography has merged digital technologies providing opportunities for research unexplored in "analogical times." Gomez-Cruz and Meyer (2012) reconstructed the shift from cameras being precious family objects, to becoming almost limitless personal and pocketable technologies, compared to devices requiring laboratories to process photo images. Moreover, the convergence with information communication technologies further enhanced the capabilities of amateurs in photography, providing them with unprecedented digital control in audiovisual production (i.e. editing, post-production) and circulation.

Social media take advantage of these options and encourage opportunities to add visual effects (e.g. filters, tags) to images. The portability of smartphones allows users to take pictures flexibly and quickly and share them immediately. The immediacy brought by social media personal photography removes the need to set up a one-to-one dedicated moment for showcasing pictures. Amateur photographers share their experiences, almost in real time, with their thoughts and feelings, enjoying the support of visual elements. In many cases, such pictures capture snapshots of natural environments with plants, insects, birds, and other living beings in the environment becoming main characters in the images rather than merely background (Flaherty and Choi 2016). Recent tourism research reveals that people actively seek out nature for inner restoration, consequently portraying and sharing its images on social media (Hitchner et al. 2019). Reasons for this may vary – from providing simple updates for close contacts or friends, to reaching a broader audience of followers, to giving an account of a specific experience – with the aim to have a successful post on Instagram (Smith 2019). This state of affairs is relatively easy to conceive and offers opportunities for DEH scholars since many representations of natural environments are shared publicly and visibly. Images of nature work together in a continuous data sharing ecosystem operating across digital web platforms with content that can also shape social interactions. In addition, we should emphasise the political economy of platforms, as their power is rooted in data access, availability, and circulation. These elements qualify what I refer to as part of a *datafied* society.

Images of Nature and Environment in a Datafied Society

The background which shapes the scenario described in preceding paragraphs consists precisely of how people experience their lives. Digitalisation changed significantly the way people share their experiences. Wearable technologies (e.g. smartwatches) and smartphones with broadband connections have increased the variety and availability of such internet-based practices. Moreover, such mobile, pocketable technology allows numerous actions to be made on the move. As Barry Wellman (2011, 21) notes, "the Internet has become an important thing, but it is not a special thing. It has become the utility of the masses, rather than the plaything of computer scientists." Our daily life remains integrated and entangled with portable technologies. Van Dijck, Poell, and De Waal (2018) distinguish between infrastructural platforms and sectorial ones. The former are the rule-setters and are the best known, as defined by the acronym GAFAM (Google, Amazon, Facebook, Apple, and Microsoft). Sectorial platforms often base their services on GAFAM structures. For instance, it is possible to register a Spotify or Academia.edu account directly, to name two, by using a Facebook or Google account. The same applies to internet-based services for images sharing. Apart from the well-known Instagram (Facebook is its parent company), photo-sharing platforms such as ImageShack and 500px grant subscriptions by logging in with a Facebook or Apple account. Users who share pictures, tag objects within them, and upload content to groups online produce value for GAFAM and other sectorial platforms. Prominent, influential economic players now belong to a new evolution of capitalism based on data circulation, dominion, access, and the consequent opportunity to sell such data products for advertisement and user profiling (Fuchs 2021).

Regarding user experience, Van Dijck (2008) explored how personal photography using digital media became a "preferred idiom" for social media users to present themselves in public. Consequently, the sharing of pictures on social media platforms created new market opportunities for professional photographers and non-professional photographers relying on images for their businesses. Such users now actively rely on digital infrastructures for digitised data as it enables a popular and desirable way to connect with people through visual images.

The transferability of such content characterises the contemporary period, and we should consider our current society as a datafied one, a society in which data sharing is at the core of daily digital ecosystem practices (Van Dijck, Poell, and De Waal 2018). Subsequently, web platforms have become necessary passage points in our daily life, and as a consequence, to use a data analyst slogan, "big data is here to stay" because society now heavily relies on their services (Franks 2012). Also, web platforms have seen their relevance grow because several components of society tend to be translated, reinvented, or even created from scratch through such platforms. The use of images of nature is not exempt and are often relevant constituents of self-presentation in public. These practices enrich the array of alternatives for configurations of personal memories, in addition to domestic representation analysed by sociologists (Bourdieu 1996) and media and STS scholars (van Dijck 2008).

Nonetheless, a datafied society configures new practices and reshapes the conditions for producing photographs of natural environments, with new actors entering the stage – specifically "media influencers" who share experiences and spread particular messages. From January 2020 to June 2021, relevant Instagram influencers contributed photographs with the hashtag "nature" in 3,148 posts (CrowdTangle 2021).[1] The tagged posts generated more than 79 million reactions globally. A 2020 Leonardo di Caprio post about wildfires in Australia had more than 1.6 million likes, and one by model Gisele Bundchen, who celebrated World Environment Day on 20 June 2020, who posed by embracing a giant sequoia, collected 437,000 likes. Other personalities show themselves standing among wildlife or walking through a forest. Many posts covered issues discussed previously – advocacy for wildlife threatened by a calamity, an appeal for protecting nature and its beauty, and the picturesque beauty of nature as a critical topic. However, it is clear that datafied worlds reinvented features of nature photography and conceived of nature as an element to play within self-representations. Reinforcing the idea of nature as something external, creating a kind of "spectacle of nature." In our datafied society, such representations could have specific effects on behaviour, on the way we experience environments – a new way of exploiting nature.

The magnitude of such practices and impacts on the natural environment is detectable if we consider the notion of "Instagrammable places" or "Instaplaces" (Leaver, Highfield, and Abidin 2020). These are overexposed locations featured on social media, with intrinsic features of interest that are recognisable and easily portrayed. These practices configure boosts of a post and encourage emulation by other users. Currently, it does not strike one as odd to find dedicated apps for smartphones – such as Photomapper – that recommend visiting and snapping such spots (Figure 22.2).

These two screenshots capture two Alpine lakes in Italy, marked on Photomapper –Sorapis Lake is located in Veneto, and Braies Lake is in Trentino Alto Adige. They are two examples of how the practice of visually sharing may result in the overexposure to wilderness and nature, with the lakes serving as examples of wildlife under siege. Because of their beauty, the picturesque "lakescapes" offer opportunities to create a successful post on Instagram. Braies Lake is well known and is a suggested spot since 2015, with 366,661 posts on Instagram.[2] These areas in

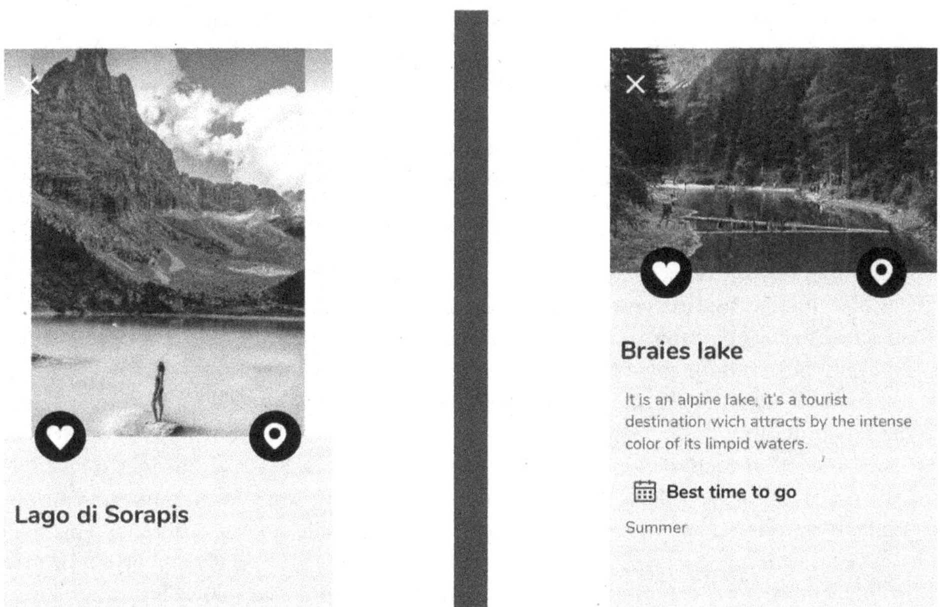

Figure 22.2 Screenshots of the App Photomapper on iOS recommending two Instaplaces in the Alps: Lake Sorapis (altitude 1,925 metres), left; Braies Lake (altitude 1,496 metres), right.

Figure 22.3 Collage of Images from Instagram account "Il mondo secondo Gipsy". On the left, the beautiful and picturesque Braies Lake as typically posted on Instagram; on the right, the parking area, tourists crowd along the lakeside and queuing for boat renting.

Source: Pictures courtesy of Beatrice Clerici – www.ilmondosecondogipsy.it

the Dolomites (a World Heritage site) became famous for a new kind of tourism. Rather than the destination of expert trekkers, both lakes became the perfect setting for memorable social media shots, at risk of cannibalising their local environments (Figure 22.3). Local newspapers denounced trends to favour tourism destinations that feature an Instagrammable view:

> In recent years, it [Lake of Sorapis] has become a star on social media, with thousands of photos posted by visitors. "Today it is very popular," admits Pais [owner of an Alpine Refuge in the area]. The result is that, in these weeks of high season, two thousand people a day take the paths that lead from Passo Tre Croci to Sorapis.
>
> *(Excerpt from Soave 2018)*

The hiking route consists of a round-trip just over 14 kilometres long with an altitude difference of about 800 metres. Tourists visit the site regularly, despite these challenges.

This state of affairs prompts us to better define a second reason for the relevance of images to the environmental components of a datafied society. It can be seen that there are specific rules of interaction set up by social media companies that are designed to take advantage of shared data and function of the values derived from it. Moreover, as many have repeatedly pointed out, algorithms and other technologies developed to improve services based on such data actively shape the practices of users (Beer 2017; Gillespie 2014). Algorithms need users' preferences as data inputs to improve content ranking, but these are "unstable objects, culturally enacted by the practices people use to engage with them" (Seaver 2017, 5). Specifically, on social media platforms based on visual content such as Instagram, research illustrates how algorithms are strategically deployed to increase content visibility. As an influencer observed: "It would be about creating cool and interesting content again, as opposed to the same 5 unoriginal images you routinely see now because we're all so afraid of no longer being relevant and doing something the algorithm doesn't like" (in Cotter 2019, 902). Though this prescribes a limit to creativity, it is a confirmation about the importance of algorithmic patterns and, therefore, how platforms influence and shapes the kind of content available on them.

Considering the role of images of nature, we cannot overlook the platforms' processes. As Helmond (2015) points out, platforms envisage the coexistence and flow of digital objects alongside other platforms. Flickr, for instance, sees the sharing of content among interest groups – in doing so, the platform contributes to developing a sense of community and a shared sense of aesthetics, further renovated in discursive practices among users through comment functions (Van Dijck 2011, 2013). To discipline this, Flickr requires users to tag pictures. Such a requirement is functional in the content searches of other users and in the platform's maintenance. I also outlined how it is possible to interpret social practices shaped by the mutual interactions of platforms and users. Platforms expect users to behave in a particular way, and users feed platforms with the data they share, adapting, more or less consciously, their choices. I concentrated mainly on social media and its actual effects on specific locations. To point out key features of the current production and sharing of images of nature in our contemporary, datafied context, we could affirm that amateur and professional photography of nature coexist and often use the same channels for the distribution of images. Conversely, we could ask ourselves – is social media the only kind of digital platform eager to receive images of nature? Indeed, its function in the current historical setting is ubiquitous and is embraced across different milieus, thus relaunching some of the original features of portrayals of natural environments.

Citizen Science and the Use of Images

I have mentioned the role of digital images in monitoring natural environments. Monitoring is conducted with fixed cameras, such as standing sensors and mobile technologies (Gabrys 2016). In this sense, citizen science projects are blooming worldwide (Vohland et al. 2021). Citizen science is defined in numerous ways (Haklay et al. 2021). The *Oxford Dictionary* describes it as the "collection and analysis of data relating to the natural world by members of the general public, typically part of a collaborative project with professional scientists" (Oxford English Dictionary n.d.). This participatory method of producing evidence for scientific purposes is made possible and facilitated by emerging information communication technologies. Both the availability of global connectivity and mobile app diffusion contribute to making the public part of such projects (Haklay 2015). Indeed, in most cases, data collection is the central activity individuals are asked to contribute, and many citizen science projects enable data collection through apps able to report georeferenced metadata for each observation (Hecker, Garbe, and Bonn 2018). Among them, possibly the most renowned is iNaturalist. Powered by National Geographic and the California Academy of Science, this app appears like a social media platform for those interested in sharing pictures of living organisms in the biosphere (Altrudi 2021). Moreover, iNaturalist presents itself as an opportunity as detailed on its website:

- Record your encounters with other organisms and maintain lifeform lists, all in the cloud.
- Create useful data: Help natural organisms and resource managers understand when and where organisms are.
- Share identifications: Connect with experts who can identify the life forms you observe.
- Become a Citizen Scientist: Find a project with a purpose that interests you, or start one yourself.
- Get to know Nature: Increase your knowledge by talking to naturalists and helping others.

(Excerpt from the iNaturalist landing page)

Each report recorded in iNaturalist consists of a photograph of a georeferenced specimen, with the data collected undergoing a validation process by the community. By taking and sharing pictures on the app, a user can be part of a community with more than four million registered members, all contributing to their knowledge and findings from more structured projects on biodiversity. Currently, iNaturalist has a collection of more than 69 million observations. However, I would like to stress a couple of points. First, it is worth underlining that also, in this case, we are talking about a sectorial platform – it is a dedicated community for naturalists, in a broader sense, and also relies on an Infrastructural platform since it offers the opportunity to sign up freely using Facebook or Google credentials. In this sense, iNaturalist operates as other sectorial platforms do.

As with many other platforms, it relies on data sharing with other platforms and other platforms to use photographic features of smartphones through an app. Such an element robustly seals the connection between the original use of images of nature as scientific proof and our current datafied society. A second element concerns the actual user experience within the platform. In addition to user profiles being required to maintain interest, expertise, and searchability, monthly and yearly rankings, according to the number of observations posted reported, are assigned to profiles. This practice, a gamification strategy, is oriented to encourage users to provide more observations in order to raise their position in the rankings (Haklay 2015). Users, by raising their rankings, contribute to the whole platform, enjoying the opportunity to see its number of records increase, for instance, during a BioBlitz. In such an event, during which people compete to find as many species as possible and thus observations, the platform exploits the competition among volunteers to enrich areas less covered by observations through gamification (Altrudi 2021).

For biodiversity scholars, checking iNaturalist is often the starting point for research articles or to read general ideas on the distribution and evolution of specific species (e.g. plants, animals, fungi).

Indeed, as with many other citizen science projects, iNaturalist enriches biodiversity data by filling gaps in many official datasets (Hurlbert and Liang 2012; Soteropoulos, De Bellis, and Witsell 2021). Thus, data for scientific research come from datafied practices and devices designed for personal photography. Who enjoys the output of these practices? Does the iNaturalist platform encourage a further configuration for a "spectacle of nature" that deepens the feeling of separation between nature and society? It may be a perverse effect of a technology that joins together different elements of our contemporary digitally mature society and a visual culture sharing images and experiences (Altrudi 2021). To answer such a provocative question would require further investigation that, starting from a DEH perspective, would fruitfully consider digital images of nature as a product of practices entangled with the technologies for communication.

Conclusion

I have illustrated how platforms in a datafied society enable and encourage specific practices connected to images by using algorithms developed to manage and create value from data. Many of these platforms directly affect the way people interact with natural environments. People are inclined to post pictures of what they like, and natural environments often encourage the quest for the beautiful and the picturesque. Such practice consists of reconfiguring images of nature, which can be traced back to the origin of photography in the early 19th century. Alternatively, portable digital technologies are both desirable and available to capture moments and create unforgettable views of a natural landscape. Such outcomes have ambivalent meanings. On the one hand, they could be opportunities to create resonances around environmental issues by media influencers and not only activists; on the other, they may provoke new forms of the exploitation of nature with the cannibalisation of so-called Instaplaces. In this sense, this echoes the second feature of the photography of nature, the one concerning the dominion and exploitation of natural environments. We are not talking of colonialism anymore; however, an extractivism based on the value of beauty assigned to nature is an evident effect, in a blurred sense.

It would be easy to point at GAFAM as the leading promoters and actors profiting from this phenomenon. Aside from environmental damage, the "spectacularisation" of nature has many critical scholars denouncing the injustice of user-generated content (e.g., pictures, selfies), which turns social media users into "unpaid workers" (Haraway 2008; Gidaris 2019; Fuchs 2021). We can observe that the same logic applies to citizen science projects which are broadly considered genuine opportunities to open up public participation in knowledge creation. In my description of the platform iNaturalist, I tracked how the same features that keep social media alive also pop up in the data production to monitor wildlife. A key difference (but not the only one) consists in the fact that images of nature (wildlife in this case) are openly required as data for scientific purposes. This practice comprises a revamp of the third original feature of photography and the natural environment – the production of scientific evidence. Citizen science, developed by relying on crowdsourced data through dedicated digital platforms, closes the circle of the socio-technical historical review outlined previously in this chapter. Informed by STS scholarship on media technologies, my contribution to DEH approaches considers images beyond the question of pure representation and the meaning they may impart. By outlining the evolution of practices connected with images, an association with socio-technical practices in different configurations of a datafied society can be made. This observes relational practices that embrace natural environments through a different form mediated by technology. Online activities offer several opportunities for researchers to exploit digital objects to obtain new kinds of data. Indeed, if the digital turn configures new user practices for capitalism and technology, researchers face new opportunities and challenges.

Compared with early studies of online images, the intensity of online practices, including but not limited to sharing images on the web, has increased. In parallel, the variety of data produced in interacting with platforms and users widens opportunities for researchers. Contributions by Nadav Hochman and Lev Manovich (2013) on the use of "urban rhythm" detected through shared images on Instagram in two cities offer a good example that emerged from media studies with an STS flavour. Specific contributions from the social sciences deserve attention, such as the Digital Methods Initiative (DMI) at the University of Amsterdam or MediaLab at Science Po in Paris. Both offer a wide array of freely available research tools for social research in parallel with valuable theoretical reflections on the methodological implications of using digital data. Developed in the early 2000s, DMI and MediaLab offer a solid basis for those dealing with social research on the web while seeking to avoid falling into the pitfalls of research on digital tools (Giardullo 2016). The problem of accessibility to data, in any event, is always behind the corner – since GAFAM owns most digital data, we should be aware that we can access only a limited amount until those who own the data guarantee access. Facebook has partially opened its archive to academic research through the project CrowdTangle.

Researchers with experience in digital methods have reflected the extent to which digital tools can effectively offer data about a specific phenomenon or a class of phenomena (Venturini et al. 2018). They warn, for instance, that a single data source such as a social media platform may be insufficient. Instead, researchers should ask themselves how much of the phenomenon under study takes place on a specific platform. This is certainly a crucial question to be addressed in order to produce fruitful research outcomes. Indeed, as other researchers recently stressed, digital phenomena are unlikely to be limited to a single platform – thus, as researchers interested in the DEH, we should be ready to follow cross-platform approaches (Pearce et al. 2020).

Environmental issues tend to be global or, at least, to transcend administrative borders, and the same applies to some social phenomena in a datafied society. As provided by digital research tools, transmedia research on digital practices may offer a specific vantage point for the DEH – which may involve considering images of nature as part of a mutual reinforcement process between practices made possible through technological mediation (platforms) and the actions of users. This configures socio-technical apparatuses that make the production and sharing of images possible in the current context. Aragona, Arvidsson, and Felaco (2020) recently promoted the ethnography of algorithms as a research approach to the current datafied context. Similarly, I propose the tracking of images through hashtags. A DEH approach to studying the images of nature should not be limited to analysing the content of a picture taken with a smartphone or an expensive mirrorless camera. Instead, it is crucial, from an epistemic point of view, to consider the practice of snapping as a proxy for understanding the role of natural environments in our daily lives. As discussed in this chapter, it also offers methodological options and enriches the tools for studying relationships between society and the environment.

Acknowledgement

This chapter was supported by the NEWSERA project funded by European Union's Horizon 2020 research and innovation programme, under Grant Agreement no. 873125. Furthermore, this chapter developed analytically some conversations about Instaplaces I had with Daniela Carazzai, a friend of mine and a travel blogger.

Notes

1 I obtained this evidence in an analysis carried out with CrowdTangle. The query I launched for the keyword "nature" included public accounts classified according to CrowdTangle lists of influencers as active in entertainment, sports, fashion, and lifestyle.

2 Last accessed on Instagram on 13 June 2021.

Sources

Altrudi, Soledad. 2021. "Connecting to Nature Through Tech? The Case of the iNaturalist App." *Convergence: The International Journal of Research into New Media Technologies*: 1–18. doi:10.1177/1354856520933064.

Anderson, Alison. 1997. *Media, Culture and the Environment*. London: UCL Press.

Aragona, Biagio, Adam Arvidsson, and Cristiano Felaco. 2020. "Introduction. Ethnography of Algorithms. The Cultural Analysis of a Socio-Technical Construct." *Etnografia e ricerca qualitativa* 13 (3): 335–49.

Balbi, Gabriele, and Paolo Magaudda. 2018. *A History of Digital Media: An Intermedia and Global Perspective*. London: Routledge.

Beer, David. 2017. "The Social Power of Algorithms." *Information Communication & Society* 20 (1): 1–13.

Bourdieu, Pierre. 1996. *Photography: A Middle-Brow Art*. Palo Alto: Stanford University Press.

Brower, Matthew. 2005. "'Take Only Photographs': Animal Photography's Construction of Nature Love." *Invisible Culture: An Electronic Journal for Visual Culture* 9. www.rochester.edu/in_visible_culture/Issue_9/issue9_brower.pdf.

Brunello, Lucia. 2020. "Dolomiti prese d'assalto, dai laghi alle ferrate. In coda sui sentieri (spesso senza mascherina) per una montagna sempre più modello Rimini." *Il Dolomiti*, August 15. www.ildolomiti.it/societa/2020/dolomiti-prese-dassalto-dai-laghi-alle-ferrate-in-coda-sui-sentieri-spesso-senza-mascherina-per-una-montagna-sempre-piu-modello-rimini.

Catton Jr. William R., and Riley E. Dunlap. 1978. "Environmental Sociology: A New Paradigm." *The American Sociologist* 13 (1): 41–49.

Cohn, B. S. 1996. *Colonialism and its Forms of Knowledge: The British in India*. Princeton, NJ: Princeton University Press.

Cotter, Kelley. 2019. "Playing the Visibility Game: How Digital Influencers and Algorithms Negotiate Influence on Instagram." *New Media & Society* 21 (4): 895–913.

CrowdTangle Team. 2021. "CrowdTangle." Facebook, Menlo Park, California, United States. [Platform: Instagram; Lists included: 557351,39108,124651,83020,493780,124652,267031,554870,1366161].

Dirks, Nicholas, foreword to Bernard Cohn. 1996. *Colonialism and its Forms of Knowledge: The British in India*. Princeton: Princeton University Press.

Flaherty, Gerard T., and Joonkoo Choi. 2016. "The 'Selfie' Phenomenon: Reducing the Risk of Harm While Using Smartphones During International Travel." *Journal of Travel Medicine* 23 (2): 1–3. https://doi.org/10.1093/jtm/tav026.

Franks, Bill. 2012. *Taming the Big Data Tidal Wave: Finding Opportunities in Huge Data Streams with Advanced Analytics*. Hoboken: John Wiley and Sons.

Fuchs, Christian. 2021. *Social Media: A Critical Introduction*. 3rd ed. London: Sage.

Gabrys, Jennifer. 2016. *Program Earth: Environmental Sensing Technology and the Making of a Computational Planet*. Minneapolis: University of Minnesota Press.

Giardullo, Paolo. 2016. "Does 'Bigger' Mean 'Better'? Pitfalls and Shortcuts Associated with Big Data for Social Research." *Quality & Quantity* 50 (2): 529–47.

Gidaris, Constatine. 2019. "Surveillance Capitalism, Datafication, and Unwaged Labour. The Rise of Wearable Fitness Devices and Interactive Life Insurance." *Surveillance & Society* 17 (1/2): 132–38.

Gillespie, Tarleton. 2014. "The Relevance of Algorithms." In *Media Technologies: Essays on Communication, Materiality, and Society*, edited by Gillespie Tarleton, Pablo J. Boczkowski, and Karen A. Foot, 167–93. Cambridge, MA: MIT Press.

Gómez Cruz, Edgar, and Eric T. Meyer. 2012. "Creation and Control in the Photographic Process: iPhones and the Emerging Fifth Moment of Photography." *Photographies* 5 (2): 203–21.

Gye, Lisa. 2007. "Picture This: The Impact of Mobile Camera Phones on Personal Photographic Practices." *Continuum: Journal of Media and Cultural Studies* 21 (2): 279–88.

Haklay, Muky. 2015. *Citizen Science and Policy: A European Perspective*. Woodrow Wilson International Center for Scholars. www.wilsoncenter.org/publication/citizen-science-and-policy-european-perspective.

Haklay, Mordechai Muki, Daniel Dörler, Florian Heigl, Marina Manzoni, Susanne Hecker, and Katrin Vohland. 2021. "What Is Citizen Science? The Challenges of Definition." In *The Science of Citizen Science*, edited by Katrin Vohland, Anne Land-Zandstra, Luigi Ceccaroni, Rob Lemmens, Josep Perelló, Marisa Ponti, Roeland Samson, and Katherin Wagenknecht, 1–12. Cham: Springer Nature. https://doi. Org/10.1007/978-3-030-58278-4.

Haraway, Donna. 2008. *When Species Meet*. Minneapolis: University of Minnesota Press.

Hecker, Susanne, Lisa Garbe, and Aletta Bonn. 2018. "The European Citizen Science Landscape – A Snapshot." In *Citizen Science: Innovation in Open Science, Society and Policy*, edited by Hecker Susanne, Muki Haklay, Anne Bowser, Zen Makuch, and Johannes Vogel, 190–200. London: UCL Press. www.jstor.org/stable/j.ctv550cf2.20.

Heise, Ulrike K. 2017. "Introduction: Planet, Species, Justice – and the Stories We Tell about Them." In *The Routledge Companion to the Environmental Humanities*, edited by Heise Ursula K, Jon Christensen, and Michelle Niemann. Oxon and New York: Taylor & Francis.

Helmond, Anne. 2015. "The Platformization of the Web: Making Web Data Platform Ready." *Social Media+ Society* 1 (2): 2056305115603080.

Hitchner, Sarah, John Schelhas, J. Peter Brosius, and Nathan P. Nibbelink. 2019. "Zen and the Art of the Selfie Stick: Blogging the John Muir Trail Thru-Hiking Experience." *Environmental Communication* 13 (3): 353–65.

Hochman, Nadav, and Lev Manovich. 2013. "Zooming into an Instagram City: Reading the Local Through Social Media." *First Monday* 18 (7). https://doi.org/10.5210/fm.v18i7.4711.

Huhtamo, Erkki. 2011. "Pockets of Plenty: An Archaeology of Mobile Media." In *The Mobile Audience*, edited by Martin Rieser, 23–38. Amsterdam and New York: Rodopi.

Hurlbert, Allen H., and Zhongfei Liang. 2012. "Spatiotemporal Variation in Avian Migration Phenology: Citizen Science Reveals Effects of Climate Change." *PloS One* 7 (2): e31662.

Jakobs, Steven. 2008. "Landscape." In *Encyclopedia of Nineteenth-Century Photography*, edited by John Hannavy, 818–24. New York: Routledge.

Latour, Bruno. 1993. *We Have Never Been Modern*. Cambridge, MA: Harvard University Press.

Leaver, Tama, Tim Highfield, and Crystal Abidin. 2020. *Instagram: Visual Social Media Cultures*. Cambridge, UK: Polity Press.

Lister, Martin, Jon Dovey, Seth Giddings, Iain Grant, and Kieran Kelly. 2009. *New Media: A Critical Introduction*. London: Taylor & Francis.

McCormick, Sabrina. 2012. "Transforming Oil Activism: From Legal Constraints to Evidenciary Opportunity." In *Disasters, Hazards and Law (Sociology of Crime, Law and Deviance*, edited by Mathieu Deflem, Vol. 17, 113–31. Bingley: Emerald Group Publishing Limited. https://doi.org/10.1108/S1521-6136(2012)0000017009.

McGaurr, Lyn. 2016. "The Photography of Debate and Desire: Images, the Environment and Public Sphere." *Ethical Space the International Journal of Communication Ethics* 13 (2/3): 16–34.

Minniti, Sergio. 2016. "Polaroid 2.0. Photo-Objects and Analogue Instant Photography in the Digital Age." *TECNOSCIENZA: Italian Journal of Science & Technology Studies* 7 (1): 17–44.

Mittermaier, Cristina. 2005. "Conservation Photography: Art, Ethics and Action." *International Journal of Wilderness* 11 (1): 8–13.

Oxford English Dictionary. n.d. "Citizen Science." Accessed June 12, 2021. www.lexico.com/definition/citizen_science.

Pauwels, Luc. 2005. "Websites as Visual and Multimodal Cultural Expressions: Opportunities and Issues of Online Hybrid Media Research." *Media, Culture & Society* 27 (4): 604–13.

Pearce, Warren, Suay M. Özkula, Amanda K. Greene, Lauren Teeling, Jennifer S. Bansard, Janna Joceli Omena, and Elaine Teixeira Rabello. 2020. "Visual Cross-Platform Analysis: Digital Methods to Research Social Media Images." *Information, Communication & Society* 23 (2): 161–80.

Poole, Deborah. 1997. *Vision, Race, and Modernity: A Visual Economy of the Andean Image World*. Princeton: Princeton University Press.

Price, Derrick. 2015. "Surveyors and Surveyed: Photography Out and about." In *Photography: A Critical Introduction*, edited by Liz Wells. 5th ed. Oxon, UK and New York: Routledge. 77–129.

Prodger, Phillip. 2009. *Darwin's Camera: Art and Photography in the Theory of Evolution*. Oxford: Oxford University Press.

Schwartz, Raz, and Germaine R. Halegoua. 2015. "The Spatial Self: Location-Based Identity Performance on Social Media." *New Media & Society* 17 (10): 1643–60.

Seaver, Nick. 2017. "Algorithms as Culture: Some Tactics for the Ethnography of Algorithmic Systems." *Big Data & Society* 4 (2): 2053951717738104.

Seelig, Michelle I. 2014. "Visual Exploration of Environmental Issues: Photographers as Environmental Advocates." *Media Watch* 5 (3): 306–20.

Smith, Sean. P. 2019. "Landscapes for Likes: Capitalising on Travel with Instagram." *Social Semiotics*. doi:10.1080/10350330.2019.1664579.

Soave, Franco. 2018. "Droni, frigo e ciabatte: così il turismo cafone invade il lago glaciale." *Il Gazzettino*, August 19. www.ilgazzettino.it/nordest/belluno/lago_sorapiss_turismo_cafone-3921321.html.

Soteropoulos, Diana L., Caitlin R. De Bellis, and Theo Witsell. 2021. "Citizen Science Contributions to Address Biodiversity Loss and Conservation Planning in a Rapidly Developing Region." *Diversity* 13 (6): 255. doi.org/10.3390/d13060255.

Stewart Howe, Kathleen. 2008. "Naturalistic Photography." In *Encyclopedia of Nineteenth-Century Photography*, edited by John Hannavy, 980–82. New York: Routledge.

Sturm, Ulrike, Sven Schade, Luigi Ceccaroni, Margaret Gold, Christopher C. M. Kyba, Bernat Claramunt, Muki Haklay, Dick Kasperowski, Alexandra Albert, Jaume Piera, Jonathan Brier, Christopher Kullenberg, and Soledad Luna. 2018. "Defining Principles for Mobile Apps and Platforms Development in Citizen Science." *Research Ideas and Outcomes* 4: e23394. https://doi.org/10.3897/rio.4.e23394.

Tucker, Jennifer. 2005. *Nature Exposed: Photography as Eyewitness in Victorian Science*. Baltimore: John Hopkins University Press.

Van Dijck, José. 2008. "Digital Photography: Communication, Identity, Memory." *Visual Communication* 7 (1): 57–76.

———. 2011. "Flickr and the Culture of Connectivity: Sharing Views, Experiences, Memories." *Memory Studies* 4 (4): 401–15.

———. 2013. *The Culture of Connectivity: A Critical History of Social Media*. New York: Oxford University Press.

Van Dijck, José, Thomas Poell, and Martijn De Waal. 2018. *The platform society: Public values in a connective world*. New York: Oxford University Press.

Van House, Nancy A. 2009. "Collocated Photo Sharing, Story-Telling, and the Performance of Self." *International Journal of Human-Computer Studies* 67 (12): 1073–86.

Venturini, Tommaso, Liliana Bounegru, Jonathan Gray, and Richard Rogers. 2018. "A Reality Check (List) for Digital Methods." *New Media & Society* 20 (11): 4195–217.

Vohland, Katrin, Anne Land-Zandstra, Luigi Ceccaroni, Rob Lemmens, Josep Perelló, Marisa Ponti, Roeland Samson, and Katherin Wagenknecht. 2021. "The Science of Citizen Science Evolves." In *The Science of Citizen Science*, edited by Vohland, Katrin, Anne Land-Zandstra, Luigi Ceccaroni, Rob Lemmens, Josep Perelló, Marisa Ponti, Roeland Samson, and Katherin Wagenknecht, 1–12. Cham, Switzerland: Springer Nature. https://doi. Org/10.1007/978-3-030-58278-4.

Wellman, Barry. 2011. "Studying the Internet through the Ages." In *The Handbook of Internet Studies*, edited by Mia Consalvo and Charles Ess, 17–23. Chichester: John Wiley & Sons.

23

A NOVEL METHOD SUGGESTION FOR THE ACHIEVEMENT OF ENVIRONMENTAL CITIZENSHIP BEHAVIOUR IN THE DIGITISING WORLD

Selin Süar Oral, Hasan Volkan Oral, Serhat Yilmaz, Hasan Saygin, and Gizem Naz Gezgin Direksiz

Introduction

The Brundtland Report, published in 1980, is widely recognised as the formal starting point for sustainable development (SD). In 2012, 30 years after the publication of this report, 17 Sustainable Development Goals (SDGs) were proclaimed, covering environmental, economic, and social approaches, respectively. After eight years later, in 2020, these goals are updated and renewed as follows: (1) end poverty in all its forms everywhere; (2) end hunger, achieve food security and improved nutrition and promote sustainable agriculture; (3) ensure healthy lives and promote well-being for all at all ages; (4) ensure inclusive and equitable quality education and promote life-long learning opportunities for all; (5) achieve gender equality and empower all women and girls; (6) ensure availability and sustainable management of water and sanitation for all; (7) ensure access to affordable, reliable, sustainable, and modern energy for all; (8) promote sustained, inclusive, and sustainable economic growth, full and productive employment, and decent work for all; (9) build resilient infrastructure, promote inclusive and sustainable industrialisation, and foster innovation; (10) reduce inequality within and among countries; (11) make cities and human settlements inclusive, safe, resilient, and sustainable; (12) ensure sustainable consumption and production patterns; (13) take urgent action to combat climate change and its impacts; (14) conserve and sustainably use the oceans, seas, and marine resources for sustainable development; (15) protect, restore, and promote sustainable use of terrestrial ecosystems, sustainably manage forests, combat desertification, and halt and reverse land degradation and halt biodiversity loss; (16) promote peaceful and inclusive societies for sustainable development, provide access to justice for all, and build effective, accountable, and inclusive institutions at all levels; and (17) strengthen the means of implementation and revitalise the global partnership for sustainable development (VNRSDG 2020).

Currently, the SD strategy provides more advantages in combating one of the severe environmental drawbacks, such as global climate change. Relevant to this strategy, the concept of

 DOI: 10.4324/9781003082798-28

environmental citizenship (EC) includes the most fundamental strategic approach to mitigating this environmental drawback. This concept can be defined as a set of behaviour that individuals must protect the environment. In a broad sense, the citizenship perspective in general and environmental responsibility imposes some responsibilities on individuals to pay more attention to the environment. Based on this responsibility, different political dimensions of the concept of EC are ongoing discussions in the literature (Hadjichambis and Reis 2020; Oral et al. 2020). By definition, EC requires the understanding that public resources, such as the environment, are sometimes not preserved or retained by self-interested actions. It stems from the implications of the view that environmental duties arise from environmental rights as a matter of natural justice (Dobson 2007). According to European Cooperation in Science and Technology (COST) project, a project known as European Network for Environmental Citizenship (ENEC) (2018) and Smerederevac-Lalic et al. (2020), EC could be regarded as a specific bundle of environmental rights, duties, responsibilities, knowledge, awareness, and willingness to engage for the protection of the common environmental good. This definition of EC as an essential and specific behaviour or set of behaviours within a specific context includes environmental and citizenship issues and suggests that individuals need both environmental knowledge and citizenship knowledge from these bodies to develop their own EC. While there is a philosophical difference between SD and sustainability, both concepts support understanding environmental, economic, and social aspects and transferring environmental capital to future generations. According to Dobson and Bell (2021), supporting EC as a means of achieving sustainability by encouraging people to act in the public's interest offers an alternative to the policies currently employed by most governments.

Education is, of course, an essential tool to disseminate the EC perception in a community. The acceleration of educational programme development efforts among disciplines and the intensity of the studies conducted within the scope of bringing EC awareness increase the need for studies in this field. The fact that curriculum development studies are based scientifically and that contemporary orientation is included in these studies constituted a fundamental reason for the emergence of such a study. While presenting this study, the idea of establishing a bridge between theory and practice has been set out. In this context, it is thought that this book section will serve as a resource for those who want to do both theoretical and applied work. One of the most effective ways to achieve the desired results in the education and applied science fields is to continuously improve education programmes in parallel with the changes and developments in science and technology (Stevenson 2007; Henderson and Tilbury 2004). Curriculum development can be defined by taking the dynamic relationships between the purpose, content, learning-teaching process, and evaluation elements of the education programme. According to another definition, programme development is a study that deals with the fundamentals, principles (theory), and activities (practice) utilised for the healthy and effective determination and realisation of the objectives covered by the programme (Varış 1988). The achievement of the targeted results at the end of the educational activities requires consistent and detailed planning and effective implementation. The efficiency of education depends on realistically determining the behaviours to be acquired by the individual, arranging the appropriate educational environment for these changes to occur, providing systematic guidance in performing behaviour change, and reliably controlling the extent of the designed behavioural changes (Levine 2002).

The primary goals and functions of environmental education differ according to the approaches adopted. In this context, approaches related to environmental education appear in the literature as environmental education, ecology pedagogy, ecological learning, nature experience, and education for sustainable development (Payne 2006). Undoubtedly, the methodology to be followed has a decisive role in fulfilling the aims and expected functions of environmental education. In addition to education and involvement, technology is an important tool that cannot be avoided. It depends on a new concept being discussed more frequently in the last ten years: digitisation. By definition, digitisation is the increased availability of digital data enabled by advances in creating, transferring, storing, and analysing digital data, which can structure, shape, and influence the contemporary world (Ritter and Pedersen 2019). Digitalisation is the process of converting something to a digital form (Merriam-Webster 2021), or it is "the adoption or increase in the use of digital or computer technology by an organisation, industry, country" (Schumacher, Sihn, and Erol 2016).

Ubiquity, affordability, reliability, speed, usability, and skill are the significant measurement units of digitalisation. Ubiquity is all about the extent to which consumers and enterprises have universal access to digital services and applications. Affordability is the extent to which digital services are priced within a range that makes them available to as many people as possible. Reliability is also known as the quality of available digital services; speed can be described as how digital services can are accessed in real time; usability concerns the ease of use of digital services and their ability of local ecosystems to boost adoption of these services, and skill is relevant to the ability of users to incorporate digital services into their lives and businesses (Sabbagh et al. 2012). Digitisation and digitalisation have separate meanings as concepts (Schumacher, Sihn, and Erol 2016). One of the essential benefits of digitisation is to access information more easily and establish communication with individuals more quickly over the internet (Solomon 2014). When it comes to disseminating these benefits to children, one of the first examples that come to mind is digital gaming. As a result of the advancement of life digitisation, digital games have invaded the world and provide interactive learning experiences, making them one of the first examples that come to mind when it comes to providing these benefits to people of all ages, especially children and adolescents (Süar Oral 2021). The convergence of the EC concept and the digitisation concept opens up many possibilities for helping to solve environmental problems such as climate change and global warming. In this era, when the rapidly developing internet technology makes the internet indispensable, what sort of connection exists between digitalisation and EC?

Touir (2020) explains this connection in a way related to social media tools offered by the internet as follows: "The widespread digitalisation of civilisation has led to many changes in the participation and involvement of social actors in civil society. Citizen environmental initiatives have often emerged on an individual basis through different digital photo and video sharing platforms for example, on Fotolia, Flickr, Dailymotion, and YouTube within blogs and digital social networks." Glas et al. (2019) report that "the conceptions and hopes of what citizen participation means have dramatically changed with the development of digital and mobile technologies. It seems that interactive, networked, and affordable technologies have significantly democratised the generation and understanding of literacy, information, and power structures in everyday life and that they have increased and have more potential to increase the degree of civic engagement."

According to McCallum et al. (2018), game mechanics or tactics may involve people in environmental issues. On the other hand, gamification turns activities into games to make them more fun or enjoyable (Cambridge Dictionary 2021). According to a literature survey conducted for this book chapter, relatively few studies are being conducted. As a result, to fill a gap in the literature, this book chapter introduces a novel approach and explores the methods for achieving EC action in the digital age. Using the concept of EC following digitalisation can provide strategic opportunities for different environmental issues such as climate change and global warming, which is relevant to this context. As a result, this chapter has been written to incorporate a novel model suggestion approach to developing an EC awareness educational programme in a digitalised world.

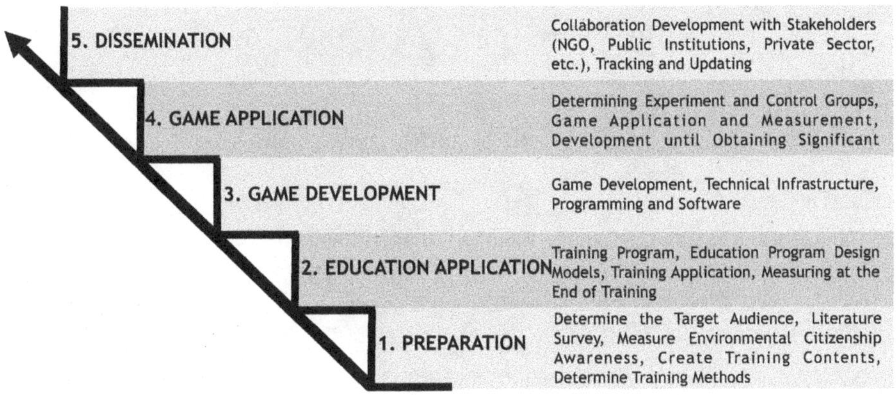

Figure 23.1 The organisational structure of the study.

The organisational structure of the study (Figure 23.1) is designed with the following sections as follows: Section 1 presents information about preparation, Section 2 is about education application, Section 3 provides the information about game development, Section 4 details the game application, Section 5 shows the dissemination ways, Section 6 reveals the challenges and opportunities, and Section 7 concludes the book chapter.

Section 1: Preparation

This section includes details on preparation steps and five other critical components of a novel method recommendation.

Determine the Target Audience: In any area that includes communication, the definition of the target audience is a critical criterion. The dynamic message must be communicated to the target audience using symbols and graphics, and the editing must meet the standards of the target audience. Digital games are platforms that enable users to immerse themselves in fantastic worlds where they can assume various identities, have unique experiences, and learn faster, thanks to their rich visual content. Today's digital games are characterised by long, challenging, and complex structures. They consist of the sum of different components. These include the platforms on which they are played, the interaction with other players, the type of the game, the mechanics, and the perspectives of Cheng and Cairns (2005), Harrison and Roberts (2011), and Bayraktar and Amca (2012). Digital games that create a hybrid platform between the game and the computer medium have a wide range of target audiences (Murray 2011). As a result, when deciding the target audience for digital games, it may be beneficial first to decide the type of digital game.

Serious games, which include the gamification of an educational subject or course or that aim for a financial result and are referred to as "serious games" in the literature, are an essential reference in terms of providing a high probability of input and making a substantial difference and/or tendency in behavioural changes (Michael and Chen 2005; Duin et al. 2011; Teichmann et al. 2020). As a result, serious games aim to gamify non-entertainment topics like training, education, and health care (Loh, Sheng, and Ifenthaler 2015, 3; Ratan and Ritterfeld 2009, 11). Braad, Zavcer, and Sandovar (2016, 96) imply that the audience targeted by a challenging game is an essential source of design requirements. However, the general purposes of serious games, target audiences addressed by serious games, and ways of embedding serious content into a serious game make it complicated to discuss the design of serious games in general. In almost all

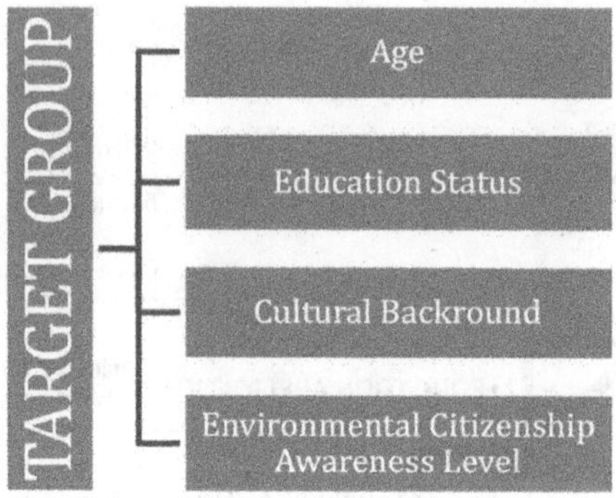

Figure 23.2 Target audience levels determining for the EC awareness.

cases, the specific area of application or the specific goals must be considered. The classification of learning outcomes distinguishes between cognitive, skill-based, and affective learning outcomes and provides a suitable framework to address the different goals we find in serious games (Swain 2007; Lee et al. 2017; Andrade et al. 2020).

According to Timur and Yılmaz (2013, 319), behavioural change is a complex process. It has been demonstrated that socio-economic status, demographic characteristics, mass media, attitude towards the environment, knowledge, education campaigns, values, environmental beliefs, environmental ethics, developer life experiences, verbal responsibility, age, and gender are all factors that influence environmental behaviour. As a result, determining the correct target audience is critical for developing positive behavioural changes and the most fundamental. Therefore, the target audience can be determined according to demographic, psychological, and sociological criteria. It is essential to know the EC level of the target audience to grow EC knowledge, ensure its sustainability, and build a model that can be distributed. Therefore, Figure 23.2 can be considered to determine the target audience:

Age, academic level, socio-economic status, and cultural context are not only excellent parameters in game production and should be known holistically. They also stand out as variables that directly impact EC understanding, according to the concepts of EC education, which should include the lifelong learning process.

***Literature Survey*:** It is desired to disclose the degree of understanding of the EC of the target audience determined through field research. Since it is a fact that the behaviours expected from individuals at the primary school level vary from those expected from adults, according to the target audience, the type of information to be given for EC awareness often varies. Therefore, these realities will be defended with theoretical approaches by literature analysis during the writing of this chapter in the model.

***Measure Environmental Citizenship Awareness*:** In terms of literature, assessing the degree to which the target audience follows the expected EC behaviours by age group should be clarified. It should be emphasised while writing this section that different scales can be used in the knowledge measurement study according to the age group, and some scale examples should be given according to age groups. Another criterion that will be emphasised when writing this section is to assess the degree of EC activity that should be found according to the age group according to the data in the literature report.

***Create Training Contents*:** This section explains the information to be transmitted in education so that the level of EC awareness measured in the literature study of the target audience can be met. That means that information limitations for the target audience to gain EC awareness will be explained in this section.

Determine Training Methods: In this section, it should be made clear that different training approaches may be preferred compared to allowing information transfer more efficiently. Following the techniques selected, it is essential to prepare content.

Section 2: Education Application

This section is prepared to present the information about the education application.

Training Program: The training programme includes activities such as aims to determine the objectives (goals) to create the learning of the target audience, to choose the content to be used to achieve these gains, to plan the learning-teaching activities where the content will be presented, to decide the methods and techniques to be used, to determine the necessary tools, and to determine the evaluation criteria and tools (Ceyhan 1995). The goal, also expressed as acquisition, is the qualities that can be acquired through education, which are deemed appropriate to be found in the person for whom education is to be applied. This goal reflects the behaviourist school and considers more outcomes. On the other hand, achievement reflects the cognitive school and focuses on the process and the result. Thus, a measurable output can be viewed, observed, and evaluated according to criteria (Harden 2002; Hartel and Foegeding 2004; Kennedy, Hyland, and Ryan 2006; Melton 2014).

Training programmes depend on having some basic features to be effective. First of all, education programmes should have national and local characteristics. Every educational programme should be socio-economic culture, traditions, customs, and values of the society it is in and should not contradict. Undoubtedly, while preparing future-oriented programmes, ensuring international competencies and technological developments into the programmes is critical. In other words, education programmes should be developed to consider the needs of future generations and reflect national and local characteristics and carry international competencies and skills.

Another critical point is that, while developing training programmes, it is necessary to analyse where to start accurately. With the need's analysis made, it is guided how the design of the training programme will be shaped. Therefore, before developing a training programme, the training programme must first be structured according to a specific design approach. Although design constitutes one of the three dimensions of programme development with its implementation and evaluation dimensions, it is the essential element in which the understanding and philosophy of the programme are revealed (Kennedy, Hyland, and Ryan 2006).

Education Programme Design Models: Programme designs consist of the essential elements that make up an education programme. Programme design aims to handle the organisation of education with meaningful integrity. The essential elements of a programme, as mentioned before, are goal/acquisition, content, learning-teaching processes, and evaluation. These four elements are in constant relationship with each other. Therefore, the items in question should be used in all designs.

Based on an interdisciplinary approach, according to Smith and Ragan (1999), learners' attitudes towards cooperation, tendencies towards cooperation or competition, peer relations, socio-economic status, moral development, and similar social characteristics are important factors in teaching. One of the most used designs in educational programming is the problem-centred design model (Demirel 2007). According to this model, the problems of the individual and society are at the centre of education. This design, which considers the culture and needs of the society, should be planned before training. Social problems and the interests, requirements, and abilities of the target audience are considered together. Thus, active participation of the target audience in the learning-teaching process is ensured. The most important skill this design wants to bring to the target audience is problem-solving. Problem-centred programme designs are divided into subheadings as life-contingent, core, social problems, and reconstructionist.

Regarding environmental education, the target audience needs to gain generalisation skills about the problems related to the real world, living conditions, and the environment. The target audience must be confronted with real problems in society, and studying these issues contributes to the development of society. This design focuses on real-life problems and provides solutions. The purpose of this design centres on making learning meaningful and ensuring it is adapted to life.

Training Application: When training programmes are viewed in terms of acquiring EC awareness, training contents will be prepared to achieve the optimal level of EC awareness after the target group's EC consciousness is determined as a priority. Content is a tool since goals/acquisitions are set first; then, the content for gaining these features is arranged. The content can be considered the arrangement of the subjects to gain goals/acquisitions. Some factors should also be considered while selecting and determining the educational content (Hartel and Foegeding 2004). These factors are listed as social benefit, individual benefit, learning and teaching, and the horizontal and vertical relations of the subjects to be learned and the activities to be done. However, the educational content should be organised according to the goals. While making this arrangement, the level of the target should be taken into account. Methods and techniques used in solving problems related to subject areas should be presented and appropriate to the target audience's readiness level.

The literature has determined that using measurement tools is more effective in determining in-service training needs (Wood and Leadbeater 1986). As a result of this literature study, the training content to be applied is created. After deciding on the subjects included in the training program's content and the methods to be used, unique measurement methods should be used for each of them by analysing them. Analyses based on the research in the literature should be made to reveal the knowledge, skills, and attitudes that are primarily present in the training programme to raise awareness of EC.

Measuring at the End of Training: Curriculum development and evaluation in education are intertwined, respectively. Evaluation is an important phase of a programme development activity and constitutes a continuous aspect. The results or feedback obtained in this process are used to develop the programme (Varış 1988) better. According to Tyler (1949), evaluation is the primary function of a programme study. The evaluation process determines precisely to what extent a program's goals and behaviours expected to change are achieved. In this context, programme evaluation can be defined as the process of collecting data about the effectiveness of the education programme with observation and various measurement tools, comparing and interpreting the obtained data with the criteria that are the indicators of the effectiveness of the programme, and making a decision about the effectiveness of the programme (Erden 1998). With the measurements taken at the end of the training, curriculum innovation, development, or execution of the training programme is supported. Thus, the continuity of the programme is tried to be maintained. Besides, programme evaluation serves different purposes, from providing insight into how a programme or practice can improve the programme implementation's efficiency and effectiveness (Klenowski 2010).

There are three types of evaluations generally made for education development processes and various decisions regarding the programme. These are reflective, formative, and summative evaluations. Reflective evaluation includes the evaluations made by taking the opinions of the relevant parts of the draft training programme before its implementation. This evaluation, which forms the basis of the training preparation phase, is made to know the education entry levels of the sample and to form a basis for evaluating their development. Formative evaluation is done to provide feedback on the implementation of existing programmes. It is done to identify and eliminate the students' learning deficiencies and difficulties and increase their learning while the education continues. Moreover, formative evaluation provides students with information and feedback on their learning. Besides, summative evaluation studies include both the learning at the end of the learning-teaching practices and the previous learning during the implementation of the programmes (Erden 1998). In short, an evaluation must be made in every training programme. This process is mandatory. Significantly, in terms of providing information on successful activities, the form of evaluation may vary depending on the purpose and nature of the programme. The evaluation study constitutes both the last stage of a completed activity and the first stage of the activity. Besides, the fact that the programme development activities are applied requires the evaluation to be continuous (Lavelle and Donaldson 2015).

In summary, according to Smith and Ragan (1999), the instructional design process starts with determining the outcome goals. The organisation of instructional strategies follows this. At the last stage, the evaluation process occurs (Akkoyunlu, Altun, and Yılmaz Soylu 2008). Reigeluth (1989) emphasised that there are four essential aspects of instructional design theory. As mentioned before, these are goal/acquisition, content, learning-teaching processes, and evaluation. Acquisition statements included in the programmes' objectives require exhibiting the behaviours learned at the end of the learning-teaching process. Therefore, it is essential to create a suitable learning environment for the target audience to show these behaviours. In this way, an effective learning environment can be created, and teaching processes by the programme objectives and content can be realised by considering the needs. The appeal of the learning-teaching processes to the target audience is one of the most important factors in informing an effective teaching method. A digital game method is also an approach that has been developing in recent years and appeals to a general target audience. In the next section, we explain game development steps.

Section 3: Game Development

Game Development: Game development is an integral part of game production which consists of multiple disciplines such as education, psychology, game script, graphic design, gaming, modelling and simulation, software engineering, and visual arts. Writing the game scenario to be designed based on statistical results, deciding the technical infrastructure, and programming and software processes to be designed based on the target audience selection defined in the introduction of the method proposed and the results exist at this stage. Without a doubt, converting abstract statistical data into a fictional text presents challenges. Motivational elements such as growth, competitiveness, escape, socialisation, privatisation, and exploration, which should be found in a game, must be fed into and encouraged by these data. Acceptability, challenge ability, consistency, efficacy, enjoyability, interactivity, localisability, and rewardability. These attributes should be found in educational games that target behaviour change (Aslan and Balcı 2015, 308).

Serious games listed in the target audience can be a roof type in and of themselves. Different types positioned within this genre and decided based on the target audience's characteristics can develop EC behaviour (Gal et al. 2002; Arsenault 2009). This situation may emerge as a significant benefit in selecting game materials appropriate for the target audience's characteristics. Furthermore, while designing the game, slight changes to the prototype for individuals within the target audience allowed for the development of improved game versions. Different preferences, desires, and demands exist among these audiences. There are several forms of serious games aimed at improving the enthusiasm of the target audience. Serious games strive to encourage learning by establishing an immersive way of teaching the topic desired to be taught.

Various researchers classify game styles based on age group, gender, number of players, game platforms, whether the game is played online or not, and/or the player's perspective. Simulation, strategy, action, and role-playing games are among the most common genres for serious games (Apperley 2006). Narayanasamy et al. (2006, 141) state that dividing simulation games into four define them as a mixture of a game of skill, chance, and strategy and results in the simulation of a complex structure.

The second phase in the game development process is to model a feasible scenario structure using game mechanics and materials, with the genre defined based on the target audience's characteristics. The storytelling technique (scenario), which can be expressed as game dynamics, is supported by mechanics and gamification: components, achievement, points, badges, level, user images (avatars), bosses, collections, contest, solving game content, gifting/sharing, leaderboard, tasks, social graphics, teams, and winning conditions; mechanics, a term that includes essential elements, such as competition, cooperation, feedback, sourcing, rewards, luck (random or unknown reward), transactions/swap, turn turns, and winning conditions; components, achievement, points, badges, level, and user images (avatars) (Bitirim-Okmeydan 2018, 15). However, it should not be forgotten that the mechanics are diversifying with the emergence of new platforms. Therefore, games that can be determined as a new genre can be designed through this diversification. For example, while the dynamics that require in-depth monitoring in mobile games have been reduced, today, it has been possible to design serious games that require physical activity with the increasing use of VR technology and motion sensor cameras.

Technical Infrastructure: Creating the game infrastructure, which includes the modelling processes of the game environment, is a step that requires engineering discipline. This process, which is different from traditional engineering, coincides with the visual production process. At this stage, the scenario is revealed, and conceptual drawings are made about the scenario. Oğuz Tunç (2019, 26–27) states that although the definitions of all production work in games are broadly kept in some exceptional cases, they are evaluated under alpha-beta stages and release version titles and that each element is modelled. Animated one by one following the predetermined conceptual content, it was drawn and solidified as functional in the game code. In three-dimensional games, the editor of the game engine used creates the map, world, and stage designs, which are then added to the in-game elements to make them navigable-made available in the alpha-beta phase, the game interface is designed and created, the game is made functional, and the game can be used roughly. The release version of the game, on the other hand, refers to a continuity period in which the visual design of the game, which is available and up-to-date, is not finalised. It is required to develop a new narrative and graphic production by developing other games that employ the same game's dynamics and materials when adding new and small improvements to the game. Maya, ZBrush, and Blender are modelling and drawing programmes that include the requisite material and content before entering the game (Braad, Zavcer, and Sandovar 2016; Şahin 2019). The contents are then moved to the game engine, and the game's final stage is launched using the game engine's supported programming language.

Programming and Software: The last process in the first step of game development, the design part, is deciding on the programming language. Programming languages include Assembly, C, C++, C#, Java, Modula 3, Dylan, Perl, Python, Ruby, and Smalltalk (Ouahbia et al. 2015; Parveen and Nazish 2016; Wertz 2016; Yassine et al. 2017). The most widely used programming language is C++ because of its fast speed and availability for all platforms. However, the third-generation Pascal, C, C ++, C #, and Java are categorised as procedural, functional, and object-oriented programming languages. They are frequently preferred in digital games as their programming goals become more and more complex (Xu 2018, 6). Game engines are used to create video games and simulations for computers, consoles, and mobile devices, and are widely used for the type of game, number of players, game mechanics, and character designs. Unreal Engine, CryEngine, Game Maker, 3D Game Studio, and Torque are examples of 3D game engines (Indraprastha and Shinozak 2009; Vasudevamurt and Uskov 2015; Alan 2017). As can be seen, game development takes place in the interdisciplinary line where design and engineering intersect after transferring the educational content to the scenario and determining the game type. After determining the target audience in game development, modelling depends on the educational content applied by considering the target audience's interests, and the game is brought to the final stage with programming processes. The following section reveals the steps of game application in detail.

Section 4: Game Application

Recent advances in communication technologies have driven a significant shift in contemporary society's lifestyle (Katz 2006, 127). Individuals have become open to a creation that will help the learning process in any sector due to this transition, which also affects education life, by choosing to use and communicate with the screen contents and images of the communication resources in their hands (Nygren et al. 2019). Owing to these opportunities provided by the interaction with screen content and images of individuals, mathematics education can be given to primary school students, and young people can receive foreign language education or contribute to the solution of the water problem, which is a social problem for adults (Raquel et al. 2007; Elaish et al. 2019; Anwar et al. 2020). There are other examples where such a learning process has been successfully used instead of the traditional book-based approach (Chang, Chang, and Shih 2016).

With this approach, however, it should be noted that a lack of motivation would harm the learning process (Elaish et al. 2017). As a result, educators and educational organisations fail to maintain and improve the target audience's motivation in the learning process (Prensky 2003, 7). Therefore, the concept of gamification emerges as a means of enhancing motivation in such training. Furthermore, it is viewed as an approach that can overcome the limitations mentioned because learners have a greater sense of ownership and internalisation of the learning process (Bozkurt and Genç-Kumtepe 2014). Although a digital-based educational approach based on gamification has the desired effect on the target audience, the contents must go through several stages. To achieve the goal, this phase of the approach proposed by this criterion requires first determining the experimental and control groups based on experimental studies, measuring the outcomes of the applications to be carried out for these groups, and developing the contents following the findings.

Determining Experiment and Control Groups: At this stage, as with all experimental research, a sample that will represent the universe determined for the target audience should be selected for digital-based game applications (Fraenkel and Wallen 2003, 19). This sample should be split into two identical groups, one for the experimental group and one for the control group. The control group should be regarded as the group that received no other intervention and was only used for data collection. In contrast, the experimental group should be regarded as the group that received a different application or intervention whose effect is being investigated. In this splitting process, it should be desired to see to what extent a specific intervention will effectively solve a specific problem in controlled conditions under a systematic method. A pre-test application should be carried out for the determined experimental and control groups to determine the initial levels of both groups before the experimental intervention. While the experimental group undergoes an experimental intervention, no particular intervention is made for the control group. A post-test is administered to both groups following the application to determine the experimental group's results level. As a result, after being exposed to the independent variable,

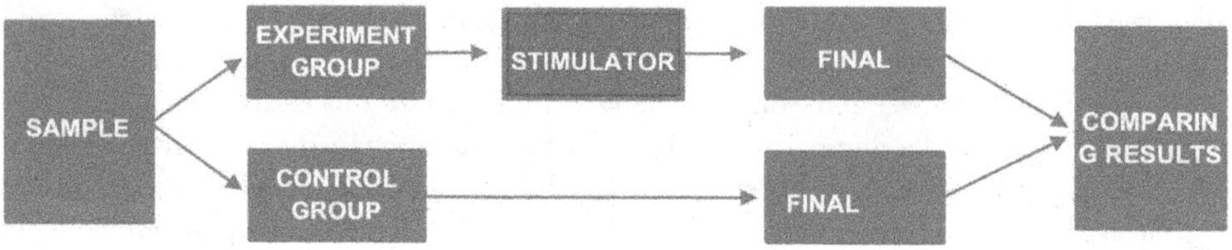

Figure 23.3 Experiment and control group design in game application.

it will be possible to remeasure the dependent variable and compare the results using statistical methods (Christensen, Johnson, and Turner 2014, 187; Metin 2014, 27; Fellows and Lui 2015, 159). As shown in Figure 23.3, this process has been systematised.

According to the literature review, studies using an experimental approach should be carried out systematically, passing through specific stages. Some issues, including the experimental and control groups' selection, the effect of exposure to the conceptual designs, and the measurement methods to be utilised, are crucial to the proposed system's functionality. In this context, first, the experimental and control groups should be as similar as possible in their selection. Otherwise, even if the applied design is flawless, the results obtained may be deceptive. In other words, if this similarity is ignored, the control group's response to the question "what would have been like if the stimulus had not been exposed" cannot be adequately represented. Another critical issue is the development of a valid and reliable measure to assess the dependent variable.

Consequently, when determining whether to create their scales or use one that is already usable, practitioners of this proposed method should consider the validity and reliability of this scale. The concept of neutrality should be upheld when assessing the groups in related studies using an experimental method. External variables must be kept under control, as well as at least one independent variable. Statistical comparisons are generally accepted to test the obtained findings (Bentler and Bonnet 1980; McCallum, Browne, and Sugawara 1996; Daşdemir 2016, 38; Bard et al. 2000).

Game Application and Measurement: The application and measurement stage of the game is the phase in which the product stream is tested and effectiveness investigated concerning the method proposed, following the preparation, training application, and training phases. At this point, the digital education strategy is used in the specified sample for the experimental group based on the idea of gamification developed within a particular system within the scope of previous steps. However, the method's successful operation due to this application process depends on the method practitioners' ability to compare many different datasets. As a result, method practitioners must meticulously collect the data they will obtain in the pre-tests and post-tests, the data they will obtain during the observation process during game implementation, and the interviews with the individuals included in the experimental group. As a result, some sensitivities must be observed in the studies for the experimental group.

First, a digital-based gamification approach for educational purposes is an application that, with its framework for conceptualising and evaluating a wide range of related player interactions, challenges a single approach (Hefner, Klimmt, and Vorderer 2007). Consequently, the most fundamental challenge that method practitioners will face is a lack of consistent and detailed tools for accurate, reliable, and valid measurement of the experience. However, studies in the literature show that this deficiency can be overcome with data obtained by simultaneously incorporating standards, such as self-report, behavioural, neural, and psychophysiology criteria, into the game set during the application process to individuals in the experimental group (Brown and Ryan

2003; Cowley et al. 2008; Yannakakis and Hallam 2009; Whitton 2011; Plass, Homer, and Kinzer 2015). Furthermore, to apply the standards recommended in these studies, the sensitivity, reliability, and validity criteria for each standard criterion must be met. These standards and criteria differentiate seven dimensions of the player's experience: sensory and imaginary immersion, tension, competence, flow, negative emotion, positive emotion, and difficulty.

Thus, valid and reliable data can be obtained from specific dimensions, such as open expressions and facial expressions of each individual in the experimental group, and hidden expressions, such as pressure applied to the interaction device, boredom, flow, and disappointment. Moreover, data on the relationship between the experiences of the individuals in the experimental group and the behaviours they will exhibit will be available (Demasi and Cruz 2003; Spronck et al. 2006; Poels, de Kort, and Ijsseltein 2007; Browne and Maire 2010; Hooshyar, Yousefi, and Lim 2018). If the target goal is statistically reached during the game implementation and measurement process, the method's final stage, the dissemination process, should be initiated. However, to account for the potential of not achieving a meaningful result, this strategy includes an interim step in which content flaws will be detected and developed, respectively.

***Development until Obtaining Significant Results*:** When evaluating the literature on gamification research and approaches in teaching experiences that rely on a digital basis, it is observed that there is a lack of a directive study if the desired level of consciousness or behaviour cannot be achieved through education. In this case, the aim is to partially eliminate this deficiency within the confines of the prescribed procedure. If the measurements made between the experimental group and the control group during the game implementation process do not differ significantly, or if the target result in the experimental group cannot be achieved, the gamification content development process should start once more. The data collected during the implementation of the game and the measurement process is decisive at this point. The standards and criteria used to interpret the correlation between each individual's experience and behaviour in the experimental group should be reviewed one by one. The development process should be shaped following the data obtained. Another requirement in this method is to research the contents prepared after the development process is completed on a new experimental and control group representing the target audience. If a meaningful difference or the targeted result in the experimental group cannot be achieved, as a result of the studies for the new experimental and control groups, the process of developing the gamification content should be resumed. Added to that, the process of content development should be continued until the desired difference is reached. If the statistical goal is met, the method's final stage, the dissemination, should be initiated. Therefore, the next section is about the dissemination.

Section 5: Dissemination

A dissemination strategy is required to deliver the application prepared by these proposed method steps to the identified target audience. The requirements outlined in the following paragraphs should be taken into account when preparing this dissemination strategy.

***Collaboration Development with Stakeholders*:** The development of a public opinion agenda on the subject is regarded as a critical success factor in social work initiatives, such as increasing environmental awareness. However, since there are such a wide variety of subjects competing for attention in social life, and people are instantly bombarded with hundreds of messages, it is difficult for a dedicated subject to get on the agenda. Therefore, it is essential to establish some cooperation with the subject's stakeholders as part of a strategy, to address this challenge. Furthermore, transparency should be acknowledged as the guiding principle in implementing these collaborations with public agencies, non-governmental organisations, and private businesses, and assistance from specialists in communication techniques should be sought.

***Tracking and Updating*:** Input from the application users should be ensured constantly during the delivery process to keep the existing application up-to-date and not lose the target audience's attention. In response to these suggestions, updates to the application should be made and made available again.

Section 6: Challenges and Opportunities

The most challenging part of performing digital research is maintaining sufficient technical infrastructure. This technology includes the internet, cable, mobile networks, communication satellites, data centres, end-user computers, and the internet of things (Designing Buildings Wiki 2021). Failure to supply these materials, or technical inadequacy, would directly affect the performance of the applied work. Another significant concern is the shortage of technical staffing to complete these applications. According to Yamoah (2013), capacity-building encompasses people's skills and attitudes related to the design, growth, management, and maintenance of locally applicable institutional and operational infrastructures and processes. Regarding EC, the following social issues can make it difficult for societies to internalise the concept: gender equality issues, civil rights and racial injustice, a lack of leadership, and a lack of academic knowledge. These barriers often hamper communities' ability to respond to environmental concerns. On the other hand, local government elements are often ineffective in raising community awareness of the EC approach. One well-known example is a lack of institutional resources (Oral and Saygın 2021).

Learning and presentation are aided by digitisation and the use of tools, which speed up solving tasks that additional students can complete simultaneously. In terms of opportunities, digitisation speeds up growth, advanced communication, and educational advancement, resulting in a mutually circular joint process between educators and students. It also makes it easier to observe the tasks, and videos of various phenomena and processes can be seen (European Commission 2021). Digital games for education offer opportunities to improve students' sense of balance, develop problem-solving skills, improve memory enhancement, and enhance multitasking skills (Advancement Courses 2014)

Conclusion

EC is needed for the development of environmentally conscious communities capable of finding solutions to environmental issues. The adoption of environmental education curricula in schools is the first step in forming this principle of citizenship. Recently, EC is now widely regarded as one of the most significant aspects of the sustainability concept. Besides, digitalisation is being used as a method to help society internalise EC more quickly and clearly. The development of digital-based games and their use for this purpose is the most specific example of this situation. Therefore, this chapter aims to present a novel model recommendation to create an educational programme for EC awareness in a digitalised world. The stages of this method are grouped under the five steps as follows: Preparation, education application, game creation, game application, and dissemination. In the most basic sense, incorporating these approaches introduces the idea of EC to young people in society. Consequently, digital games are the most effective way to reach these young people, also recognised as Generation Z by some sources.

The improvement of technical infrastructure and the incapability to find skilled and certified workers to use this infrastructure are challenges throughout this new method. In terms of EC, issues emerge primarily as a result of sociocultural factors and local governments. To address these challenges, experts should first conduct initiatives to raise society's awareness level. However, the most important thing is that society's decision-makers and administrators grasp the principles of digitalisation and EC and their significance. Therefore, awareness-raising about EC is essential, and it should be conducted to obtain significant results besides digitalisation. Examples of awareness-raising activities include publicising news releases, briefings, and commentaries and disseminating papers, studies, and publications. These examples can also be multiplied as writing or oral submissions to parliamentary committees and inquiries, collaborating with the media, organising public meetings and events, convening conferences and workshops, and producing and contributing to educational materials.

Acknowledgements

The authors acknowledge the Istanbul Aydın University Research Fund (project no. 2021/3, due to a decision taken on 19 March 2021). The authors also thank Dr Andreas Ch. Hadjichambis (chairman of the European Network for the Environmental Citizenship, COST Action CA16229), who inspired us to write this book chapter.

Sources

Advancement Courses. 2014. "Educational Benefits of Video Games." Accessed March 28, 2021. https://blog.advancementcourses.com/articles/educational-benefits-video-games/.

Akkoyunlu, Buket, Arif Altun, and Meryem Yılmaz Soylu. 2008. *Öğretim Tasarımı*. Ankara: Maya Akademi.

Alan, Davut. 2017. "Dijital oyun tabanlı yaklaşım ile yazılım geliştirme öğretimi." Master thesis, Selçuk University.

Andrade, Alexandro, Whyllerton Mayron da Cruz, Clara Knierim Correia, Ana Luiza Goya Santos, and Guilherme Guimarães Bevilacqua. 2020. "Effect of Practice Exergames on the Mood States and Self-Esteem of Elementary School Boys and Girls During Physical Education Classes: A Cluster-Randomised Controlled Natural Experiment." *PLoS One* 15 (6): e0232392. doi:10.1371/journal.pone.0232392.

Anwar, Nizirian, Dedy Prasetya Kristiadi, Faris Ahmad Novezar, Patrick Alexander Tanto, Kein Septha, Prahastiwi Ardhia, Khalid Evan, and Audrey Chrysler. 2020. "Learning Math through Mobile Game for Primary School Students." *SYLVAN* 164 (5): 346–52.

Apperley, Thomas H. 2006. "Genre and Game Studies: Toward a Critical Approach to Video Game Genres." *Simulation & Gaming* 37 (1): 6–23. https://doi.org/10.1177/1046878105282278.

Arsenault, Dominic. 2009. "Video Game Genre, Evolution and Innovation." *Eludamos Journal for Computer Game Culture* 3 (2): 149–76.

Aslan, Serdar, and Osman Balcı. 2015. "GAMED: Digital Educational Game Development Methodology." *Simulation: Transactions of the Society for Modeling and Simulation International* 91 (4): 307–19.

Bard, Christine C., Kathleen J. Bieschke, James T. Herbert, and Amy B. Eberz. 2000. "Predicting Research Interest Among Rehabilitation Counseling Students and Faculty." *Rehabilitation Counseling Bulletin*, 44 (1): 48–55. https://doi.org/10.1177/003435520004400107.

Bayraktar, Fatih, and Hasan Amca. 2012. "Interrelations between Virtual-World and Real-World Activities: Comparison of Genders, Age Groups, and Pathological and Nonpathological Internet Users." *Cyberpsychology, Behavior, and Social Networking* 15 (5): 263–69. https://doi.org/ 10.1089/cyber.2011.0337.

Bentler, Peter M., and Douglas G. Bonnet. 1980. "Significance Tests and Goodness of fit in the Analyses of Covariance Structures." *Psychological Bulletin* 88 (3): 588–606. https://doi.org/10.1037/0033-2909.88.3.588.

Bitirim-Okmeydan, Selin. 2018. "Pazarlama 'Oyun'a Geldi: Pazarlamada Oyunlaştırma Yaklaşımı ve Örnekleri." *Journal of Social and Humanities Sciences Research* 5 (31): 4750–768.

Bozkurt, Aras, and Evrim Genç-Kumtepe. 2014. "Oyunlaştırma, Oyun Felsefesi ve Eğitim: Gamification." *Akademik Bilişim 2014, 5–7 Şubat 2014, Mersin Üniversitesi, Mersin*: 147–56.

Braad, Eelco, Gregor Zavcer, and Alyea Sandovar. 2016. "Processes and Models for Serious Game Design and Development." In *Entertainment Computing and Serious Games*, edited by Ralf Dörner, Stefan Göbel, Michael Kickmeier-Rust, Maic Masuch, and Katharina Zweig, 92–118. Cham, Switzerland: Springer.

Brown, Kirk Warren, and Richard M. Ryan. 2003. "The Benefits of Being Present: Mindfulness and its Role in Psychological Well-Being." *Journal of Personality and Social Psychology* 84 (4): 822–48. https://doi.org/10.1037/0022-3514.84.4.822.

Browne, Cameron, and Frederic D. Maire. 2010. "Evolutionary Game Design." *IEEE Transactions On Computational Intelligence and AI Games* 2 (1): 1–16. https://doi.org/10.1109/TCIAIG.2010.2041928.

Cambridge Dictionary. 2021. "Gamification." Accessed February 1, 2021. https://dictionary.cambridge.org/dictionary/english/gamification.

Ceyhan, Erdal. 1995. *Eğitimde İzlence ve Yöntem Kuramı*. Gaziantep: Gaziantep Üniversitesi Fen Edebiyat Fakültesi Yayını.

Chang, Ching, Chih-Kai Chang, and Ju-Ling Shih. 2016. "Motivational Strategies in a Mobile Inquiry-Based Language Learning Setting." *System* 59: 100–15. https://doi.org/10.1016/j.system.2016.04.013.

Cheng, Kevin, and Paul A. Cairns. 2005. "Behaviour, Realism, and Immersion in Games." *CHI'05 Extended Abstracts on Human Factors in Computing Systems, New York, NY, USA, 2005*: 1272–275. https://doi.org/10.1145/1056808.1056894.

Christensen, Larry B., R. Burke Johnson, and Lisa A. Turner. 2014. *Research Methods, Design, and Analysis*. Upper Saddle River, NJ: Pearson Education, Inc.

Cowley, Ben, Darryl Charles, Michaela Black, and Ray Hickey. 2008. "Toward an Understanding of Flow in Video Games." *Computers in Entertainment* 6 (2): 1–27. https://doi.org/10.1145/1371216.1371223.

Daşdemir, İsmet. 2016. *Bilimsel Araştırma Yöntemleri*. Ankara: Nobel.

Demasi, Pedro, and Adriano J. De O. Cruz. 2003. "Online Coevolution for Action Games." *International Journal of Intelligent Games and Simulation* 2 (2): 80–88.

Demirel, Özcan. 2007. *Eğitimde program geliştirme*. Ankara: Pegem Akademi.

Designing Buildings Wiki. 2021. "Digital Infrastructure." Accessed March 27, 2021. www.designingbuildings.co.uk/wiki/Digital_infrastructure.

Dobson, Andrew. 2007. "Environmental Citizenship: Towards Sustainable Development." *Sustainable Development* 15: 276–85. https://doi.org/10.1002/sd.344.

Dobson, Andrew, and Derek Bell. 2021. *Environmental Citizenship*. Cambridge, MA: Massachusetts Institute of Technology Press.

Duin, Heiko, Jennicke Baalsrud Hauge, Felix Hunecker, Felix, and Klaus-Dieter Thoben. 2011. "Application of Serious Games in Industrial Contexts." In *Business, Technological, and Social Dimensions of Computer Games: Multidisciplinary Developments*, edited by Maria Manuela Cruz-Cunha, Vitor Hugo Varvalho, and Paula Tavares, 331–47. Hershey, PA: International General Insurance Co. Global.

Elaish, Monther M., Norjihan Abdul Ghani, Liyana Shuib, and Ahmed Al-Haiqi. 2019. "Development of a Mobile Game Application to Boost Students' Motivation in Learning English Vocabulary." *IEEE Access* 7: 13326–37. https://doi.org/10.1109/ACCESS.2019.2891504.

Elaish, Monther M., Liyana Shuib, Norjihan Abdul Ghani, Elaheh Yadegaridehkordi, and Musaab Alaa. 2017. "Mobile Learning for English Language Acquisition: Taxonomy, Challenges, and Recommendations." *IEEE Access* 5: 19033–47. https://doi.org/10.1109/ACCESS.2017.2749541.

ENEC. 2018. "COST Action CA16229." Accessed February 1, 2021. https://enec-cost.eu/.

Erden, Münire. 1998. *Eğitimde Program Değerlendirme*. Ankara: Anı Yayıncılık.

European Commission. 2021. "EPALE." Accessed March 28, 2021. https://epale.ec.europa.eu/en/blog/digitization-and-education.

Fellows, Richard F., and Anita M. M. Lui. 2015. *Resource Method for Construction*. West Sussex: John Wiley & Sons Ltd.

Fraenkel, Jack R., and Norman E. Wallen. 2003. *How to Design and Evaluate Research in Education*. New York: McGraw-Hill.

Gal, Viviane, Cécile Le Prado, Stéphane Natkin, Liliana Vega, and Cedric Cnam. 2002. "Writing for Video Games." *Proceedings Laval Virtual (IVRC), June 2002*: 245–52. Laval: France.

Glas, René, Sybille Lammes, Michiel de Lange, Joost Raessens, and Imar de Vries. 2019. "The Playful Citizen: An Introduction." In *The Playful Citizen: Civic Engagement in a Mediatized Culture,* edited by René Glas, Sybille Lammes, Michiel de Lange, Joost Raessens, and Imar de Vries, 9–30. Amsterdam: Amsterdam University Press.

Hadjichambis, Andreas Ch., and Pedro Reis. 2020. "Introduction to the Conceptualisation of Environmental Citizenship for Twenty-First-Century Education." In *Conceptualizing Environmental Citizenship for 21st Century Education*, edited by Andreas Ch. Hadjichambis, Pedro Reis, Demetra Paraskeva-Hadjichambi, Daphne Goldman, Jan Cincera, Jelle Boeve-de Pauw, Niklas Gericke, and Marie-Christine Knippels, 1–14. Switzerland: Springer.

Harden, Ronald M. 2002. "Learning Outcomes and Instructional Objectives: Is There a Difference?" *Medical Teacher* 24 (2): 151–55. https://doi.org/10.1080/0142159022020687.

Harrison, Brent, and David L. Roberts. 2011. "Using Sequential Observations to Model and Predict Player Behavior." *Proceedings of the 6th International Conference on Foundations of Digital Games, New York, NY, USA, June 2011*: 91–8. https://doi.org/10.1145/2159365.2159378.

Hartel, Richard W., and E. Allen Foegeding. 2004. "Learning: Objectives, Competencies, or Outcomes?" *Journal of Food Science Education* 3 (4): 69–70. https://doi.org/10.1111/j.1541-4329.2004.tb00047.x.

Hefner, Dorothée, Christoph Klimmt, and Peter Vorderer. 2007. "Identification with the Player Character as Determinant of Video Game Enjoyment." In *Entertainment Computing – ICEC 2007. ICEC 2007. Lecture Notes in Computer Science, vol 4740. Springer, Berlin, Heidelberg*, edited by Lizhuang Ma, G. W. Matthias Rauterberg, and R. Nakatsu, 39–48. https://doi.org/10.1007/978-3-540-74873-1_6.

Henderson, Kate, and Daniella Tilbury. 2004. *Whole-School Approaches to Sustainability: An International Review of Sustainable School Programs*. Sydney: Macquarie University.

Hooshyar, Danial, Moslem Yousefi, and Heuiseok Lim. 2018. "Data-Driven Approaches to Game Player Modeling: A Systematic Literature Review." *ACM Computing Surveys* 50 (6): 731–9. https://doi.org/10.1145/3145814.

Indraprastha, Aswin, and Michihiko Shinozaki. 2009. "The Investigation on Using Unity3D Game Engine in Urban Design Study." *ITB Journal of Information and Communication* 3 (1): 1–18. https://doi.org/10.5614/itbj.ict.2009.3.1.1.

Katz, James E. 2006. *Magic in the Air: Mobile Communication and the Transformation of Social Life*. Piscataway, NJ: Transaction Publishers.

Kennedy, Declan, Áine Hyland, and Norma Ryan. 2006. *Writing and Using Learning Outcomes: A Practical Guide*. Bologna: European Higher Education (EHEA).

Klenowski, Val. 2010. "Curriculum Evaluation: Approaches and Methodologies." In *International Encyclopedia of Education*, edited by Eva Baker, Penelope Peterson, and Barry McGaw, 335–41. 3rd ed. Amsterdam: Elsevier.

LaVelle, John M., and Stewart I. Donaldson. 2015. "The State of Preparing Evaluators." *New Directions for Evaluation* 145: 39–52. https://doi.org/10.1002/ev.20110.

Lee, Seungmin, Wonkyung Kim, Taiwoo Park, and Wei Peng. 2017. "The Psychological Effects of Playing Exergames: A Systematic Review." *Cyberpsychology, Behavior, and Social Networking* 20 (9): 513–32. http://doi.org/10.1089/cyber.2017.0183.

Levine, Tamar. 2002. "Stability and Change in Curriculum Evaluation." *Studies in Educational Evaluation* 28 (1): 1–33. https://doi.org/10.1016/S0191-491X(02)00010-X.

Loh, Christian Sebastian, Yanyan Sheng, and Dirk Ifenthaler. 2015. "Serious Games Analytics: Theoretical Framework." In *Serious Games Analytics: Methodologies for Performance Measurement, Assessment, and Improvement*, edited by Christian S. Loh, Yanyan Sheng, Dirk Ifenthaler, 3–30. Cham: Springer.

Loos, Eugene, and Annemiek Zonneveld. 2016. "Silver Gaming: Serious Fun for Seniors?" In *Human Aspects of IT for the Aged Population. Healthy and Active Aging, Second International Conference, ITAP 2016, Held as Part of HCI International 2016 Toronto, ON, Canada, July 17–22, 2016, Proceedings, Part II*, edited by Jia Zhou and Gavriel Salvendy, 330–41. Berlin: Springer.

McCallum, Ian, Linda See, Tobias Sturn, Carl Salk, Christoph Perger, Martina Duerauer, Mathias Karner, Inian Moorthy, Dahlia Domian, Dmitry Schepaschenko, and Steffen Fritz. 2018. "Engaging Citizens in Environmental Monitoring via Gaming." *International Journal of Spatial Data Infrastructures Research* 13: 15–23. https://doi.org/10.2902/1725-0463.2018.13.art3.

McCallum, Robert, Michael W. Browne, and Hazuki M. Sugawara. 1996. "Power Analysis and Determination of Sample Size for Covariance Structural Modeling." *Psychological Methods*, 1 (2): 130–49. https://doi.org/10.1037/1082-989X.1.2.130.

Melton, Reginald. 2014. *Objectives, Competencies and Learning Outcomes: Developing Instructional Materials in Open and Distance Learning*. New York and London: Routledge.

Merriam-Webster. 2021. "Digitalisation." Accessed January 23, 2021. www.merriam-webster.com/dictionary/digitalization.

Metin, Mustafa. 2014. *Kuramdan Uygulamaya Eğitimde Bilimsel Araştırma Yöntemleri*. Ankara: Pegem Akademi Yayıncılık.

Michael, David R., and Sandra L. Chen. 2005. *Serious Games: Games That Educate, Train, and Inform*. Muska & Lipman/Premier-Trade. https://dl.acm.org/doi/book/10.5555/1051239.

Murray, Janet H. 2011. "Are Games a Medium?" *Inventing the Medium*. Accessed March 15, 2021. https://inventingthemedium.com/2011/10/24/are-games-a-medium/.

Narayanasamy, Viknashvaran, Kok Wai Wong, Chun Che Fung, and Shri Rai. 2006. "Distinguishing Games and Simulation Games from Simulators." *Computer Entertainment* 4 (2): 141–44. https://doi.org/10.1145/1129006.1129021.

Nygren, Eeva, Seugnet Blignaut, Verona Leendertz, and Erkki Sutinen. 2019. "Quantitizing Affective Data as Project Evaluation on the Use of a Mathematics Mobile Game and Intelligent Tutoring System." *Informatics in Education* 18 (2): 375–402. https://doi.org/10.15388/infedu.2019.18.

Oral, Hasan Volkan. 2020. "Sustainable Development." In *The Palgrave Encyclopedia of Global Security Studies*, edited by Scott Romaniuk, Manish Tapa, and Péter Marton, 1–6. Cham, Switzerland: Palgrave Macmillan. https://doi.org/10.1007/978-3-319-74336-3_438-1.

Oral, Hasan Volkan, Özge Eren, Aliye S. Erses Yay, and Hasan Saygın. 2020. "Environmental Citizenship Perception and Behavior Among University Engineering Students in the Marmara Region of Turkey." *Environment, Development and Sustainability* 23: 3638–652. https://doi.org/10.1007/s10668-020-00736-8.

Oral, Hasan Volkan, and Hasan Saygın. 2021. "Presenting the Challenges and Offering New Strategies to Private and Public Organisations for Environmental Sustainability." In *Environmental Sustainability and Development in Organizations Challenges and New Strategies*, edited by Clara Ines Pardo Martinez, and Alexander Cotte Poveda, 89–102. London: Taylor & Francis.

Ouahbia, Ibrahim, Fatiha Kaddaria, Hassane Darhmaouib, Abdelrhani Elachqara, and Soufiane Lahmine. 2015. "Learning Basic Programming Concepts by Creating Games With Scratch Programming Environment." *Procedia – Social and Behavioral Sciences* 191 (2015): 1479–82. https://doi.org/10.1016/j.sbspro.2015.04.224.

Parveen, Zahida, and Fatima Nazish. 2016. "Performance Comparison of Most Common High-Level Programming Languages." *International Journal of Computing Sciences Research* 5 (5): 246–58.

Payne, Phillip G. 2006. "Environmental Education and Curriculum Theory." *The Journal of Environmental Education* 37 (2): 25–35. https://doi.org/10.3200/JOEE.37.2.25-35.

Plass, Jan L., Bruce D. Homer, and Charles K. Kinzer. 2015. "Foundations of Game-Based Learning." *Educational Psychologist* 50 (4): 258–83.

Poels, Karolien, Yvonne A. W. de Kort, and Wijnand A. Ijsseltein. 2007. *D3.3: Game Experience Questionnaire: Development of a Self-Report Measure to Assess the Psychological Impact of Digital Games*. FUGA Technical Report. Holland: Technical University Eindhoven.

Prensky, Marc. 2003. *Digital Game-Based Learning*. New York: McGraw Hill.

Raquel, Salazar, Szidarovszky Ferenc, Coppola Emery Jr, and Rojano Abraham. 2007. "Application of Game Theory for a Groundwater Conflict in Mexico." *Journal of Environmental Management* 84 (4): 560–71. https://doi.org/10.1016/j.jenvman.2006.07.011.

Ratan, Rabindra, and Ute Ritterfeld. 2009. "Classifying Serious Games." In *Serious Games: Mechanism and Effects*, edited by Ute Ritterfeld, Michael Cody, and Peter Vorderer, 10–24. New York: Routledge.

Reigeluth, Charles M. 1989. "Educational Technology at the Crossroads: New Mindsets and New Directions." *Educational Technology Research & Development* 37 (1): 67–80.

Ritter, Thomas, and Carsten Lund Pedersen. 2019. "Digitisation Capability and the Digitalisation of Business Models in Business-to-Business Firms: Past, Present, and Future." *Industrial Marketing Management* 86: 180–90. https://doi.org/10.1016/j.indmarman.2019.11.019.

Ryan, Richard M., C. Scott Rigby, and Andrew Przybylski. 2006. "The Motivational Pull of Video Games: A Self-Determination Theory Approach." *Motivation and Emotion* 30 (4): 344–60. https://doi.org/10.1007/s11031-006-9051-8.

Sabbagh, Karim, Roman Friedrich, Bahjat El-Darwiche, Milind Singh, Sandeep Ganediwalla, and Raul Katz. 2012. "Maximising the Impact of Digitization." In *The Global Information Technology Report 2012: Living in a Hyperconnected World*, edited by Soumitra Dutta and Beñat Bilbao-Osorio, 121–34. Geneva: World Economic Forum.

Şahin, Can. 2019. "3D Karakter Modellemesi ve Animasyonu Aşamaları." *Idil* 8 (55): 387–92. https://doi.org/10.7816/idil-08-55-12.

Schumacher, Andreas, Wilfried Sihn, and Selim Erol. 2016. "Automation, Digitisation, and Digitalisation and Their Implications for Manufacturing Processes. Innovation and Sustainability International Scientific Conference." *Sustainable Innovative Solutions* 2nd Edition. *28–29 October 2016, Bucharest, Romania:* 1–6.

Smederevac-Lalic M., et al. 2020. "Knowledge and Environmental Citizenship." In *Conceptualizing Environmental Citizenship for 21st Century Education. Environmental Discourses in Science Education*, edited by A. Hadjichambis et al., Vol 4. Cham: Springer. https://doi.org/10.1007/978-3-030-20249-1_5.

Smith, Patricia L., and Tillman J. Ragan. 1999. *Instructional Design*. New York: Macmillan Publishing Company.
Solomon, David. 2014. "The Impact of Digital Dissemination for Research and Scholarship." *E Cancer Medical Science* 8 (ed44): 1–3. https://doi.org/10.3332/ecancer.2014.ed44.
Spronck, Pieter, Marc Ponsen, Ida Sprinkhuizen-Kuyper, and Eric Postma. 2006. "Adaptive Game AIwith Dynamic Scripting." *Machine Learning* 63 (3): 217–48. https://doi.org/10.1007/s10994-006-6205-6.
Stevenson, Robert B. 2007. "Schooling and Environmental Education: Contradictions in Purpose and Practice." *Environmental Education Research* 13 (2): 139–53. https://doi.org/10.1080/13504620701295726.
Süar Oral, Selin. 2021. "Adapting Digital Games to Course Contents As An Interactive Education Model." In *Istanbul Aydın University Research Fund Project 2021/3*. Istanbul: Istanbul Aydın University.
Swain, Chris. 2007. "Designing Games to Effect Social Change." Situated Play, Proceedings of DiGRA 2007 Conference, Volume 4, The University of Tokyo, September 2007, 805–9.
Teichmann, Malte, Andre Ullrich, Dennis Knost, and Norbert Gronau. 2020. "Serious Games in Learning Factories: Perpetuating Knowledge in Learning Loops by Game-Based Learning." *Procedia Manufacturing* 45: 259–64. https://doi.org/10.1016/j.promfg.2020.04.104.
Timur, Serkan, and Mehmet Yılmaz. 2013. "Çevre Davranış Ölçeğinin Türkçe'ye Uyarlanması." *GEFAD/GUJGEF* 33 (2): 317–33.
Touir, Ghada. 2020. "Digitalization and Civic Engagement for the Environment: New Trends." In *Digitalization of Society and Socio-political Issues 2: Digital, Information, and Research*, edited by Éric George, 93–102. Wiley. https://doi.org/10.1002/9781119694885.ch8.
Tunç, Oğuz. 2019. "Sanat Tarihinin Yeniden Yorumlanması Yöntemiyle Gerçeküstü Bir Oyun Kavram Tasarımı." Thesis in Proficiency in Art. Hacettepe University.
Tyler, Ralph W. 1949. *Basic Principles of Curriculum and Instruction*. Chicago: University of Chicago Press.
Varış, Fatma. 1988. *Eğitimde program geliştirme*. Ankara: Ankara Üniversitesi Basımevi.
Vasudevamurt, Vinay Bhargav, and Alexander Uskov. 2015. "Serious Game Engines: Analysis and Applications." *Electro/Information Technology (EIT), 2015 IEEE International Conference, 9–12 October, City University (CityU) of Hong Kong* 2 (1): 440–45. https://doi.org/10.1109/EIT.2015.7293381.
Voluntary National Review Sustainable Development Goals (VNRSDG). 2020. Accessed August 24, 2021. https://sustainabledevelopment.un.org/content/documents/26290VNR_2020_Bulgaria_Report.pdf.
Wertz, Harald. 2016. *Object-oriented Programming with Smalltalk*. Amsterdam: Elsevier.
Whitton, Nicola. 2011. "Game Engagement Theory and Adult Learning." *Simulation & Gaming* 42 (5): 596–609. https://doi.org/10.1177/1046878110378587.
Wood, Sue, and Patricia Leadbeater. 1986. "Stages of Entry for Target Groups Participating in Gifted Program Inservice and Staff Development." *Gifted Child Quarterly* 30 (3): 127–30. https://doi.org/10.1177/001698628603000307.
Xu, Chong-Wei. 2018. *Learning Jawa with Games*. Switzerland: Springer.
Yamoah, Emmanuel E. 2013. "Capacity Building and Employee Performance." *Canadian Social Science* 9 (3): 42–5. https://doi.org/10.3968/j.css.1923669720130313.1160.
Yannakakis, Georgios N., and John Hallam. 2009. "Real-Time Game Adaptation for Optimizing Player Satisfaction." *IEEE Transactions on Computational Intelligence and AI Games* 1 (2): 121–33. https://doi.org/10.1109/TCIAIG.2009.2024533.
Yassine, Alaeeddine, Driss Chenouni, Mohammed Berrada, and Tahiri, Ahmed. 2017. "A Serious Game for Learning C Programming Language Concepts Using Solo Taxonomy." *International Journal of Emerging Technologies in Learning* 12 (3): 110–27. https://doi.org/10.3991/ijet.v12i03.6476.

PART V

Digital Chronicles of Environment, Literature, Cartography, and Time

24

ONLINE TRANSCRIPTION OF REGIONAL ICELANDIC MANUSCRIPTS INITIATIVE

Steven Hartman, Viðar Hreinsson, Guðrún Ingólfsdóttir, Astrid E.J. Ogilvie, and Ragnhildur Sigurðardóttir

Introduction

In recent years the urgent need to address the climate and biodiversity crises, among other global environmental challenges, has seen sustainability science and environmental studies occupying ever more central positions in the international agendas of science, education, policy, and governance. At the same time, environmental studies approaches rooted in the humanities and social sciences have discernibly expanded over the past decade. While humanities disciplines have long been underrepresented in research on environmental change, a number of academic networks have been rewriting this script in recent years. Larger-scale international research collaborations addressing North Atlantic environments and societies have made it increasingly clear over the past two decades that ecological resilience cannot be meaningfully addressed in isolation from social and cultural factors.[1] A recognition of the so-called human dimensions of natural systems inevitably yields an appreciation that all biospheric systems are to some degree socio-environmental systems, an insight that the global change research community acknowledged explicitly in 1990 with the International Social Science Council's establishment of the Human Dimensions Programme on Global Environmental Change (Jacobson and Price 1990), rebranded in 1996 as the International Human Dimensions Programme (IHDP).

In light of this understanding that nature and the environment are inextricably implicated in societal development and activities (and vice versa), fields and disciplines such as historical studies, archaeology, anthropology, geography, literary studies, the arts, and digital humanities have as great a role to play in illuminating environmental change – recast as *socio-environmental change* (Hackmann, Moser, and St. Clair 2014) – as the life sciences and geosciences were understood to play when the International Geosphere-Biosphere Program was founded a decade before the IHDP (IGBP Report 1 1986).

Research networks in the North Atlantic with robust anchoring in the humanities began to practice unprecedented levels of collaboration across scientific domains and scholarly communities of interest already in the earliest years of the 21st century. While they may have begun as distinct academic groups and research programmes organised along disciplinary or, more narrowly, multidisciplinary lines, many of these scholarly communities have begun to overlap and

DOI: 10.4324/9781003082798-30

merge significantly in the past decade. This development also represents a general trajectory from disciplinary and multidisciplinary scholarly communities of interest to integrated, interdisciplinary (even transdisciplinary) scholarly communities of purpose (Hartman and Opperman 2020). At present, a number of these researcher networks are expanding their integrated approaches to knowledge production and assessment from regional to global collaborations through such programmes as BRIDGES, launched in 2021 as the Sustainability Science Coalition of UNESCO's international science programme Management of Social Transformations (MOST).

Concerted efforts among North Atlantic researcher networks to investigate long-term human ecodynamics and changing human-environment interactions through time have shed new light on the resilience and sustainability of island communities at various temporal scales through comparative analysis of an expanded range of environmental and cultural data.[2] This development reflects growing recognition of the value of historical documents and literary texts in environmentally oriented research, as well as a growing confidence in the utility and relevance of these previously untapped heritage archives in relation to other kinds of evidence (e.g. archaeological and environmental proxy data). It also reflects the significant growth and maturation of fields such as environmental history, ecocriticism, environmental archaeology, historical climatology, and historical ecology in recent decades, including the striking proliferation within the past decade of interdisciplinary environmental humanities. Scholarly communities of practice in these fields have begun to make significant advances illuminating the long-term challenges, failures, and sometimes even the surprising successes of island communities in the circumpolar north at the margins of human habitation.

A case in point is Iceland, famous as the land of fire and ice for its highly active volcanism and its location at the edge of the arctic circle, and also well known for its rich literary and historical traditions. The most famous examples of Iceland's prose works are undoubtedly the *Sagas of Icelanders*, written down in the 13th and 14th centuries and disseminated in copies through a sophisticated medieval and early modern manuscript culture that was at least partly secular. Although less well-known, a host of valuable literary and historical works continued to be written in manuscript from the late 16th century onwards. This time period witnessed a change in Icelandic literary culture (and writing traditions more generally), ushered in by the establishment of the country's first printing press and the acceptance of the Lutheran Reformation. While printed works eventually became the norm in ecclesiastical and administrative contexts, the widespread production of manuscript materials in many different local contexts continued until the late 19th century, in part due to the Church's effective monopoly on this technology through most of the 18th century. As late as circa 1950, some form of manuscript culture, though obsolescent, continued to exist in Iceland in certain niche environments.

The Online Transcription of Regional Icelandic Manuscripts Initiative (OTRIMI) is an outcome of the project ICECHANGE (2017–2020).[3] The initiative involves a trial of an online platform for curated citizen science and open science, enabling collaborative transcription and digitisation of previously unpublished Icelandic literary production in manuscripts found in the Icelandic National Archives (Þjóðskjalasafn Íslands) and the National and University Library of Iceland (Landsbókasafn Íslands Háskólabókasafn), as well as various regional archives covering the period 1550–1950.

OTRIMI is an open science digitisation project focused on making unique cultural heritage resources containing a wealth of information on past environmental change available through an open-science project. The manuscripts will be shared through digital photographs published on a dedicated site with the ambition of crowd-sourcing transcriptions from voluntary communities of interest, to be curated and professionally edited by specialists, and made openly available for the benefit of society. The aim is to preserve cultural heritage, involve non-specialists in vital preservation efforts in which they can collaborate with the scientific community and make vital data and knowledge accessible for posterity.

In its limited first iteration, launching in 2022, OTRIMI is intended as a pilot initiative for an anticipated expanded platform, with further technical refinements, within the developing research programme ILLUMINAS (Illuminating Social-Ecological Change, Adaptation, and Resilience in North Atlantic Island Societies 1250–1950). As with a number of the precursor projects on which it builds (ICECHANGE, MYSEAC, etc.), ILLUMINAS will consider a wide range of data from archaeology, physical geography, palynology, geology, and climatology, as well as new textual data drawn from previously unpublished manuscripts in historical and literary archives, to reconstruct and analyse the interactions of Icelandic communities and their environments over 700 years. One ambition of this developing research programme is to open up previously underutilised sources of data drawn from literary and historical documents from the later medieval and early modern periods through the early 20th century. Recorded evidence of environmental observation, social-ecological interactions, and/or natural events in specific local settings are of particular interest. As a highly interdisciplinary project, ILLUMINAS will draw on theories, methodologies and analytical approaches in environmental history, archaeology, ecocriticism, and integrated environmental humanities (Hartman 2016; Hartman et al. 2017), including historical ecology and historical climatology (Bell and Ogilvie 1978; Ogilvie and Jónsson 2001; Jones 2008; Ogilvie 2010; Pfister et al. 2018), literary and cultural studies (Hreinsson 2016, 2018a), digital humanities, and manuscript studies (Ingólfsdóttir 2016, 2017, 2021b).

A key ambition of OTRIMI is to facilitate the identification and analysis of significant instances of environmental representation and memory accessible in largely unexamined historical and literary archives. These archives are of great potential interest in light of recent studies exploring the *longue durée* of human impacts on island landscapes of the North Atlantic; the impacts of climate and other environmental changes in a range of comparable landscapes and communities (e.g. in Greenland, the Faroe Islands, Shetland and Orkney); and the interaction of human societies and their environments at different spatial and temporal scales (Sigurðardóttir et al. 2019; Ogilvie 2020; Ogilvie et al. 2020).

Theoretical Dimensions: Ecocritical Literary History, Manuscript Culture Studies and Integrated Environmental Humanities

OTRIMI approaches heritage and environment as inextricably intertwined. With a focus on manuscript culture, the platform is intended to facilitate the analysis of significant examples of environmental knowledge inscribed in local traditions of literary production that predominantly circulated in manuscripts. This approach foregrounds a heritage perspective in which authorship and literary production are viewed in light of their strong social significance (Ezell 1999). In other words, a premium is placed on the value of recorded ideas, observed phenomena, local history, (auto)biographical narratives, everyday perspectives, attitudes and lore, and whether or not the texts containing these elements exhibit features of an exemplary literary culture according to 19th- and 20th-century paradigms of virtuosity, which effectively set the tone, critical fashions, and research agendas of professional literary studies through the recent past (Hreinsson 2014, 2019; Ingólfsdóttir 2016; Magnússon and Ólafsson 2017; Ólafsson 2012, 2013; Hufnagel 2013; Lansing 2014).

The production and dissemination of writings in manuscripts are profoundly different from products of mechanical print culture, where the printing press delivers finalised works to a public readership. Production of handwritten materials was autonomous and uncontrollable (like the internet). Texts of literary works often change between individual manuscripts Ólafsson

2012, 2013). In this sense manuscript, culture can be regarded as more organic, less settled, and stimulated by diverse socio-environmental impulses (Hreinsson 2018c, 2019; Zapf 2014). Under such circumstances, the unpredictable but often autonomously organised dissemination of knowledge, entertainment and lore (in the form of stories, poetry and biographical/place-focused writings) represented to some degree a form of cultural self-preservation, perhaps even a slow cultural insurgency, answering the urge for expression and the need for knowledge. In Spinozan terms, this could even be seen as a kind of cultural conatus (Spinoza 2002; Damasio 2003, 2018; Hreinsson 2016, 2019).

New ecocritical, literary, historical, and environmental historical scholarship in the context of the ILLUMINAS research programme will seek to re-evaluate human perceptions/conceptions of nature and environments as these have developed over time in specific places (Hreinsson 2016, 2018a, 2022, 2023). The ambition is not only to shed light on modern conceptions of nature and the environment as these have evolved but also on the shifting social-ecological relations characteristic of local communities in small island societies over many generations. Novel ecocritical readings of poetry and narratives, including documentary and oral folkloric descriptions of particular places in Iceland (i.e. specific communities *and their environments*), can also help to renew understanding of these very concepts (e.g. place, community, landscape, environment, and nature). Such reconsideration is helpful because a number of these concepts are still used interchangeably, and sometimes normatively, in ways that obscure important distinctions among these analytical categories as reconsidered in landscape studies, geography, and environmental history in recent decades, both in Iceland (Karlsdóttir 2010a, 2010b) and in the development of these fields of study internationally (Olwig 2019). Interrogations of the semantic fields of *nature* and *environment* and other concepts long considered cognate have a deep and rich history that goes back to early ecofeminist, ecocritical, and environmental philosophical scholarly discourses (Gaard and Gruen 1993; Buell 1995; Soper 1995) and in a modern sense, such investigations have an even deeper history in traditions of nature writing and literary Transcendentalism that extend back to 1854 with Thoreau's *Walden* (1995 [1854]) and Emerson (1836).

Investigations of place-centred traditions of inscribing and transmitting environmental memory, as they are being designed for the ILLUMINAS research programme, are now achievable in ways not generally seen before the widespread use of digital humanities tools or the kinds of broader interdisciplinary and transdisciplinary efforts foregrounded in an integrated environmental humanities approach. Such an approach builds upon not just the possibility but the expectation that disciplines such as environmental history, cultural anthropology, historical geography, archaeology, ecocritical literary studies, and folkloristics will bring expanded theoretical refinement and methodological innovation to collaborative team-based study (Hartman et al. 2017). Drawing on a manuscript cultural studies approach, which does not try to resolve variant versions of texts in a single presumed (if usually non-existing) authoritative text, participating researchers in the ILLUMINAS research programme regard the gradual (intergenerational and wider diachronic) evolution of place-based narratives in cultural/societal, biographical, and environmental imaginaries in the light of organic (iterative) processes of observation, imaginative engagement, poiesis, transmission, and adaptation over time. Inscriptions of environmental observation, lore, and imagination are understood to develop dynamically in different local contexts, as the collective knowledge of communities and environments accrues and takes shape in communal discourses and memorial archives (both tangible and intangible). These may, in turn, yield regionally specialised understandings of place that are continuously negotiated and adapted in familial or communal networks of literary culture, then passed on as environmental memory (Buell 2017; Hartman 2016; Hartman et al 2016, 2017).

Opening Archives of Local Writing to Wider Analysis by Interdisciplinary Teams of Scholars

OTRIMI will focus on a variety of literary sources not previously analysed in relation to nature and the environment. A number of early works for Iceland (prior to BCE 1800) were analysed as part of the ICECHANGE project. Although the new ILLUMINAS research programme will draw on this prior research, an emphasis will be placed in OTRIMI on unpublished literary texts in manuscripts from the years 1800 onwards that are central to the research ambitions of the ILLUMINAS programme. Some texts extending back to the late medieval/early modern period that were not part of the earlier ICECHANGE project are also to be integrated into the transcription project now being planned, though these materials will make up a smaller portion of the corpus. A key continuing objective of the larger research programme is to elucidate the ways in which locally produced literary works reflect natural, climatic, and social changes in the period 1300–1950 in order to cast light on sociocultural aspects of sustainability and social-ecological resilience. Results will include the analysis of previously little-studied local literary production of the study area of northeast Iceland. Dissemination of new analyses concerning nature and place-based literary reflections of this region can provide more complete knowledge than previously available of various developments in social-ecological and socio-economic spheres as reflected in a vibrant local manuscript culture. Much pioneer work has been conducted on important yet forgotten poetry by women in the manuscript archives, often revealing different perceptions and expressions of nature than is typical in more male-dominated canonical literature that became more widely available and more widely known during earlier periods (Ingólfsdóttir 2021a). The time has never been riper for similar recovery efforts regarding texts on the environment and nature. Virtually all of these materials demand study and historical revaluation from ecocritical, environmental humanities, and indeed, ecofeminist perspectives.

Undertaking such a research agenda requires systematically reviewing, cataloguing, and analysing large archives of unpublished and previously unstudied literary works in manuscript. The materials to be examined include many local tales, histories and collections of poetry by Jón Guðmundsson the Learned (1574–1658), Stefán Ólafsson (1619–1688), and Bjarni Gissurarson (1621–1712), as well as the works of a number of modern writers from different localities in the north of Iceland in particular. Approximately 11,000 manuscript pages preserved in the local archives of Húsavík in northeast Iceland have been photographed (but not yet analysed), and these materials contain texts (encompassing many genres and forms: diaries, letters, poetry, local tales in prose, and even handwritten newspapers) by various inhabitants from all walks of life in the Lake Mývatn area and adjacent communities. Some 2,700 of these manuscript pages were written by local historian and poet Helgi Jónsson (1890–1969), arguably one of the most remarkable undiscovered writers in Iceland, containing poetry, biographies, a historical novel, and a large number of local tales drawn from the entire region; nearly all of these writings are unpublished, with the exception of a short monograph on the 18th-century woman poet Látra-Björg Einarsdóttir (1714–1784), republished in 2020 (Jónsson 1949).

The majority of manuscript materials and half-forgotten records of local lore now set to be examined in the ILLUMINAS research programme focus on poetry and literary reflections from a number of outlying areas, including the highlands of Vopnafjardarheiði and Jökuldalsheiði, the Lake Mývatn area, and the coastal areas of the Langanes peninsula. Many of these materials from northeast Iceland and the Eastfjords relate to nature, environment, and natural resources. Alongside other written historical sources, such as annals, official documents, and printed local history, as well as lore, these manuscript materials can provide valuable information on the farming and fishing communities of the past, on seasonal and meteorological details that prevailed at certain times, or on topographical conditions endemic to these communities, expressing local environmental knowledge and lore, at times in fairly straightforward language or sometimes in more sophisticated literary forms rich in metaphor and complex in sound patterning. The following poem from the archival materials to be studied in the ILLUMINAS research programme, from the turn of the 19th century, is a good example of the latter:

Nokkrar veðurspárvísur í Mývatnssveit Stefán Stefánsson í Ytri-Neslöndum.

1
Þegar vötnin verjast ís
vel þó svelli og hrími
þá er ótíð alltaf vís
upphefst neyðar tími.

2
Þegar hyllir hólma og strönd –
hærra en vanalega,
Hhirtast mun með hríðar vönd
hauðrið svaðalega.

3
Þá Kleifarfossar kveða hátt –
kryddað undirspili –
nálæg mundi norðan átt
með nauma og slærri bóli (sic – i.e. byli).

4
Drangseyjar þá digri foss
dreifir hljóði um munnann
sveitin þiggur kærleiks koss
kemur hann að sunnan.

A number of Weather-Forecasting Verses by eftir Ste-Stefán Stefánsson of the Outer Headlands

1
When the waters brace against the ice
though crystals form a glistening skin
foul weather traps all in its vise
as perilous times then begin.

2
When islets and shoreline appear
higher than usual
the land's skin can expect
a merciless birching of white.

3
When the chants of Kleifarfossar (cleft falls) peal –
lively accompaniment –
this way a northerly will steal
in weak and sluggish squalls.

4
When the swollen falls at Drangsey
resound throughout the gorge
the district will accept
the south's loving kiss.[4]

This poem is, in fact, a tiny sample from a profound meshwork of poetry and lore deriving from one family lineage (descendants of farmer-poet Gamalíel Halldórsson (1776–1858) over a period of 200–400 years. Much of these writings are preserved in the manuscripts of Helgi Jónsson mentioned previously, and others from a few members of this family lineage.

Some Methodological Challenges of OTRIMI

The inclusion of literary texts of varying degrees of accomplishment or virtuosity poses challenges only when the transcriptions are to be translated into a widely accessible language (English in this case) for the wider benefit of the research community. Transcription of analogue manuscript sources from photographs assembled in the online platform does not pose great challenges beyond the risk of mistranscription, substitution, or interpolation of linguistic elements not in the original source manuscripts, which is always a risk of copying, transcription, or digitisation. For this purpose, the platform is to be curated and edited by qualified Icelandic scholars trained in documentary editing practices. Depending on the nature of the research in which these materials may be used as primary sources, the quality of the texts (from the point of view of literary aesthetics as well as traditional philology) may or may not be a factor of interest or relevance. Additional challenges owing to processes of transmission and representation of these texts may present themselves, however, when the transcribed and edited digital texts in Icelandic are then selected (on the basis of noteworthy content) for translation into the smaller database of materials to be made available in English for the benefit of wider research communities (linguistic, literary, historical, archaeological, cultural geographical, etc.). Different researchers may be interested in drawing upon some of these materials for data of interest that they may contain, or the texts may be approached as valuable objects of study in their own right, for example, in the case of scholarship concerned with the totality of the work as a literary study object (or as a valuable snapshot of literary history against the background of the organic flow of manuscript culture).

Beyond the inclusion of texts in the platform and eventual digital transcription by citizen scientists, any further steps taken to make selected texts available to researchers who are not Icelandic speakers will inevitably subject the source materials to the vagaries of translation as a practice of linguistic, cultural, historical, and aesthetic mediation. Potentially a large number of additional variables as well as potential risks can be introduced into the scholarly chain of custody of the materials as they undergo adaptation for wider dissemination outside the native Icelandic context. Generally, these additional risks would not come into play in the same way if the texts were to be examined in their native Icelandic in digital transcribed form. While source criticism and cultural and historical contexts will always come into play to one extent or another (and transcription errors are always a possibility), scholars can work from the texts in Icelandic as reasonable facsimiles of the original texts in manuscript without being overly concerned about potential distortions of the original that may occur, deliberately or unintentionally, as a result of the translator's priorities. If the translator is a literary translator concerned with formal compositional techniques as much as he/she may be with the literal content of the texts, then this kind of risk can increase significantly, particularly if the researchers drawing on the text for analysis are hardly concerned with literary expression but heavily invested in explicit content.

Many of the texts to be incorporated into the OTRIMI platform, because they are literary works, defy hopes or expectations of a simple one-for-one correspondence of literal sense-making in translating the text from one language to another (and one cultural context to another) because of the heavy element of metaphor and other figurative devices employed in the text, which can rarely if ever be taken at face value when seeking to understand what these works actually say. This is partly because one cannot understand what many literary texts say without appreciating simultaneously *how* they say what they say, *how they make their sense*, through conceits, kennings, allegory, satire, and other complex figurative means or generic conventions and expected features, and this says nothing of the musical or sound-patterning elements of verse, or the formal structure of poems, in particular.

Part of the challenge of translating literary texts into another language for use as source materials in research derives from the different interests and practices germane to different disciplines and research traditions/methodologies. An agricultural historian, for example, may be primarily interested in specific details that can provide valuable data points concerning farm management, the number of household members on smallholder farms, or the cost of livestock at a particular place and time, or he/she may be equally interested in further details from historical archives or biographical sources that may add helpful qualitative context to these data points. A geoscientist may also be concerned with context, though perhaps not in as fully qualified a way as the historian, because at the end of the day, he/she may need to translate textual data into a form and interface that also incorporates data from soil samples and the geoscientist's standard methodology may not easily admit the kinds of qualitative gradations or qualification that may be possible to ascertain through a careful source-critical evaluation of datasets or individual data points. For example, the semi-legendary poet Hallvarður Hallsson (1723–1799) composed a verse-letter to a friend, dated 6 September 1744, where he describes the rough sailing north along the coast

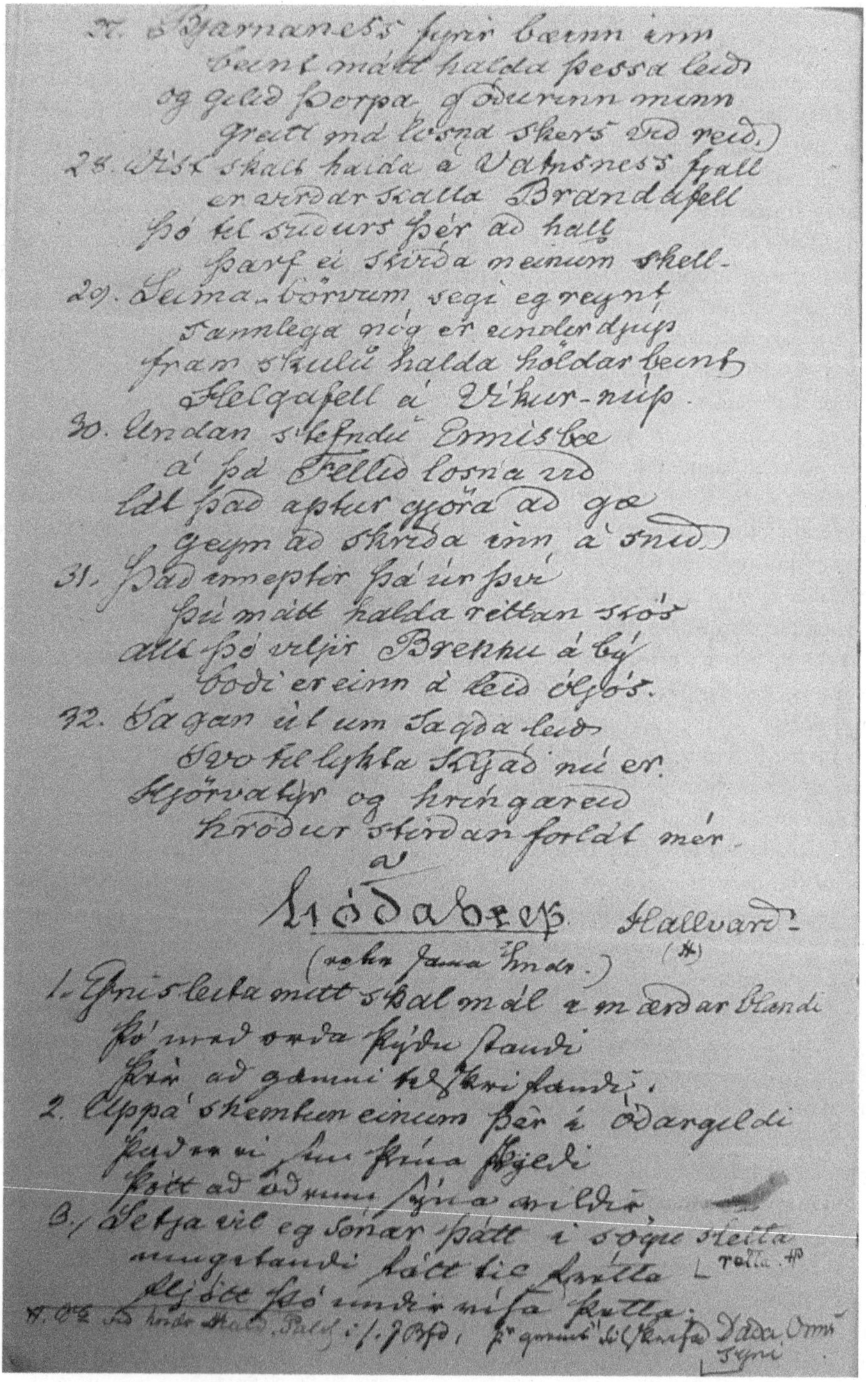

Figure 24.1 OTRIMI image 2: This manuscript is probably from the hand of Páll Pálsson in his second collection (see the next section). Hallvarður Hallsson's verse-letter from 1744 begins in the lower part of the page, a version slightly different from the one published online. The upper part of the page is the end of a poem incorrectly ascribed to Hallsson.

of Strandir and Hornstrandir regions (the eastern and northeastern shore of the Westfjords peninsula) in early June that same year. Among other things, he vividly describes some spectacular landslides on the magnificent slopes and cliffs of Hornstrandir. So far, these descriptions have not received much attention but are of considerable interest to geologists.

The value of this text may lie in its specific dating of the events whose effects the author reports observing, or it may lie in the particular descriptive details in the letter that provide significant qualitative (social, historical, and/or environmental) context. None of these aspects of the event may translate neatly into other modes of analysis (or evidence analysed) that geologists may more routinely consider central to their research methods. If nothing else, this example illustrates the importance of not thinking too narrowly concerning what may or may not be of interest in a manuscript text (or not thinking too stereotypically about what falls in the wheelhouse of a particular discipline) while also thinking beyond the traditional limits of one's own disciplinary perspective.

As suggested previously, by comparison with both the historian and the geoscientist, a literary scholar may seem overly concerned with the textuality of the text, with conventions and tropes employed as the fabric of the work studied, including the role of different stylistic elements within received literary traditions. Such details may suggest the need for even greater care in interpreting some texts as transmitters of reliable historical data without first qualifying (perhaps a great deal) any data we might hope to draw from narratives or lyrical descriptions of life in a particular place at a particular time. To put this concern into some useful perspective, it may be worth asking ourselves how comfortable we would feel with our descendants 300 or 400 years from now, drawing hard and fast conclusions about life in the Southern Confederacy during the American Civil War on the basis of Margaret Mitchell's *Gone With the Wind*, or about life in England during World War I based on the P.G. Wodehouse's stories of Jeeves and Wooster.

The OTRIMI platform must take into account a plurality of research disciplines that may wish to draw upon the texts it makes available for study, which in effect means acknowledging that a range of researchers addressing different questions may be interested in a range of different kinds of data. This is why the specific content of literary materials, when these are eventually translated into English, must take priority over stylistic concerns if a trade-off must occur. The *rímur* form of Icelandic poetry exemplified in the previous extract (prominent from the 16th through the 19th centuries) employs a specific set of formal features, including the use of alliteration and a great variety of stanzaic, metrical, and rhyming forms. In the first stanza of the previous poem, it was possible to maintain a reasonable reflection of the original content in the English translation while also retaining the rhyme scheme. In the third stanza, on the other hand, only the "A" rhymes (lines 1 and 3) could be retained while maintaining a reasonable fidelity to the specific content of the original quatrain in Icelandic. In the second and fourth stanzas, none of the rhyme schemes could be maintained, but the specific content details are reasonably preserved. Above and beyond attending to these formal and sound patterning elements, particular metaphors are approximated where possible (even if these invariably involve some degree of modification to work in the translation's target language), whereas alliteration was sacrificed in most of the stanzas included in the previous extract. In order to meet the needs of a potential plurality of researchers (including the different research methods involved in their disciplines and the range of different research questions they might be drawing on the text to address), all translation choices involve the principle of compensation, where retention of specific content from the original in the target language must invariably trump form and style, except where and when the latter can be achieved without sacrificing fidelity to content substance since aspects of form and style remain important considerations for literary researchers and need to be reflected wherever this is practicable without sacrificing substance.

The Variety of Manuscript Materials to Be Included in the OTRIMI Platform

A wide variety of hitherto largely unanalysed poetic texts covering many topics relating to nature and the environment are contained in manuscripts that were collected, repaired and bound at the National Library in Iceland by Páll Pálsson (1807–1877). These take the form of two collections of poetry from the 17th to 19th centuries that run to over 80 volumes in manuscripts. A large store of these have been surveyed and photographed in the context of the ICECHANGE project, but until recently, very few of these materials have been analysed in any detail (except in Viðar Hreinsson's paper, currently under peer review). The photographic archive available to the ILLUMINAS team includes 14,357 photos, including upwards of 3,000 poems by nearly 200 poets. Many of these relate to nature, with associated topics, such as farming, fishing, and travelling on land and sea. There is poetry on nature, landscape, water, weather, climate, sea ice, animals, birds, fishes, seafaring and mountain trails, preternatural beings, seasons, pagan lunar months, time reckoning, hardships, food, hunger, seal hunting, whales, walruses, diseases, and the Famine of the Mist after the Lakagígar volcanic eruption (1783–1784) (Gunnlaugsson et al. 1984; Ogilvie 1986), as well as poetry on places, geography, coal-making, the poor condition

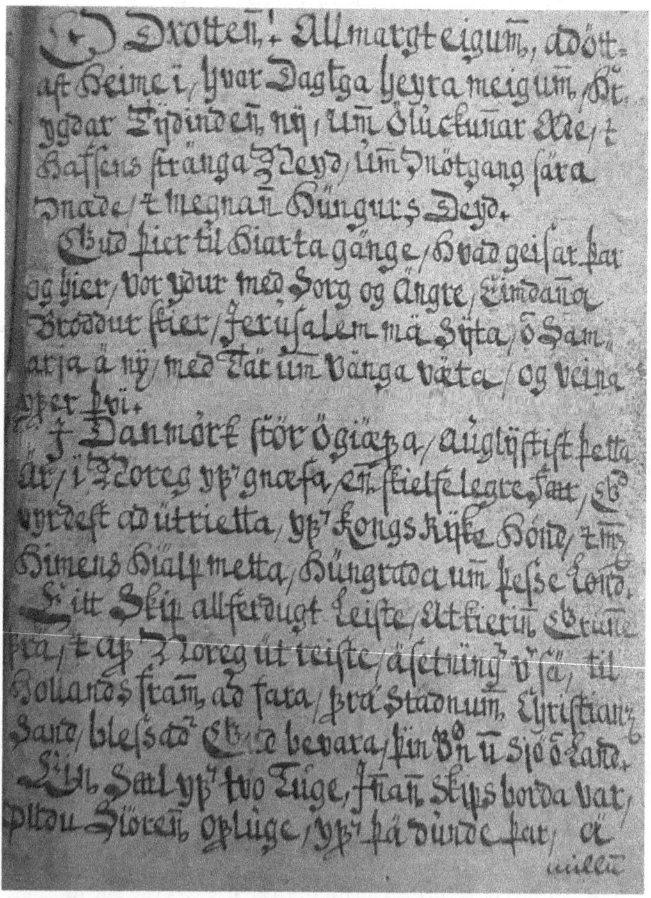

Figure 24.2 OTRIMI image 3: Manuscript in Páll Pálsson's collection concerning the terrible famine that struck Norway in 1696.

of the world, superstition, and Iceland's decline. This collection of nature/environment-related poems will serve as a basis for the curated open-science/citizen-science collaborative transcription project that is OTRIMI.

As an open science platform for curating citizen science-driven transcription and digitisation of previously unpublished Icelandic literary production in manuscript, the design and implementation of OTRIMI will involve surveying all the Icelandic National Library Manuscript catalogues, containing approximately 15,000 items, to help identify more nature-/environment-related material in literary manuscripts from 1550 to 1950 than is already known (from published works). The selected material will be photographed for further processing along with material from the local archives in Húsavík and Akureyri (already photographed and organised but not transcribed or analysed as part of two previous projects, ICECHANGE and MYCHANGE/MYSEAC).[5]

Manuscripts with environmentally significant contents that are identified during this survey are expected to provide a large store of materials for a planned open-access database (consisting of approximately 3,000 pages of materials) to be made publicly available in the form of a transparently organised open science collaborative platform (refined from the pilot model undertaken as an outcome of the ICECHANGE project). High-resolution photographs of the relevant manuscript pages will be organised on this platform and promoted in various communities of practice (the Icelandic studies community, saga-study hobbyists, cultural and scientific heritage groups, etc.) for collaborative open-science sourcing of citizen science transcriptions to be curated and edited to professional standards by ILLUMINAS team members. Curated transcriptions will then be made available to accompany the digital images of the manuscripts as digitised texts become available during the course of the project, with the aim of making the images and digital texts accessible in an online archive as a legacy of the project for the research community. Results will include (1) the transcription and digitisation of works in manuscripts that have never appeared in print through an open science platform and (2) the resulting availability of transcriptions as open-access texts to facilitate new research (both within the ILLUMINAS research programme and among the wider research community). One of the aims of the ILLUMINAS programme is to help reconstruct environmental conditions and changes over time, as reflected in local literary texts drawn from over three centuries of manuscript production. Henry David Thoreau, commenting in *Walden* on the then unfolding project to create an American transcontinental telegraph system, remarks,

> Our inventions are wont to be pretty toys, which distract our attention from serious things. They are but improved means to an unimproved end, an end which it was already but too easy to arrive at; as railroads lead to Boston or New York. We are in great haste to construct a magnetic telegraph from Maine to Texas; but Maine and Texas, it may be, have nothing important to communicate.
>
> *(Thoreau 1995, 33–34)*

When viewed against the social-ecological and wider sustainability challenges now facing the Earth's roughly 200 nation-states (and 431 mapped world ecosystems according to Sayre et al. 2020), the DEH we develop and apply in our research endeavours must ultimately be seen as improved tools and applications that cannot in themselves mitigate the considerable challenges we face as the pivotal middle decades of the 21st century draw ever nearer.[6] Tools are only as helpful as the limits of their users' vision, motivation and will. As Thoreau suggested in *Walden*, they can hardly guarantee the quality of our discourse or what may be achieved by it.

In the case of OTRIMI, the project will create the technical means to access and unlock archival resources in manuscripts for wider knowledge and use that can help us better understand how past societies living at the limits of human habitation responded to social-ecological changes, whether endogenous (e.g. volcanic activity), exogenous (e.g. globalisation of trade and economic systems), anthropogenic (e.g. deforestation, overgrazing), or naturally occurring (e.g. climate shocks).

OTRIMI is not a technically advanced project (nor does it need to be one). Its potential for success does not depend on groundbreaking applications in the vanguard of data science or IT. Rather, it will depend on the ability of the team constructing this platform to connect its archive of selected manuscripts with a network of motivated actors (e.g. the Icelandic studies community, heritage and scientific hobbyists, and armchair philologists, among others) whose efforts and interests in expanding knowledge and understanding of documentary sources will empower the citizen-science dimension of the project, thereby helping to create usable digital artefacts from these analogue sources for use by professional scholars and amateurs, including by eventually translating particularly rich or promising materials (in terms of content) into a language more widely accessible to scientific and scholarly users and non-professional communities of interest. The project aims to merge non-specialist efforts (transcription at a scale and a rate that would be very hard, maybe impossible, to achieve in a few years by a small team of scholars) and specialist efforts by scholars and educators involved in curating the manuscript materials, building the site and the interface, and then editing transcriptions according to professional documentary editing practices and standards. The digitised texts then submitted through the platform by volunteer citizen scientists are to be made available and viewable alongside the digital photographs of the original manuscripts for the benefit of each of these communities of interest and practice. In the process, the project can help to build a community of purpose, which is the very definition of transdisciplinary science and knowledge formation (Hartman and Oppermann 2020, 2, 16).

Conclusion

Ultimately the DEH are improved tools and applications that cannot in themselves mitigate the considerable social and ecological challenges we face approaching the pivotal decades of the 21st century in our efforts to achieve sustainable societies. Tools are only as helpful as the uses to which we put them. The OTRIMI project is an effort to make new uses of older analogue materials, recorded knowledge, and literary expression that can be of value in understanding how past societies coped with environmental change. In this sense, the platform and the uses to which our team hopes it may be put are also small but meaningful steps toward the preservation, reclamation and rejuvenation of priceless heritage – both *cultural heritage* and *scientific heritage* (in its own unassuming way). We hope that these resources and the collective wisdom they contain can see new lives and uses through partnerships among scholars, scientists, and citizen scientists, those who care for the history, language, literature, culture, nature, or identity of places (communities *and* environments) that are at risk of being lost forever in an urbanised, digital, present-focused world.

The project team will always keep in mind the words of the Icelandic bishop Brynjólfur Sveinsson (1605–1675) when he shipped off to Copenhagen a number of extremely valuable manuscripts in 1656. In a letter to the royal antiquarian, he wrote, "Að loka handritin hljóð inni í erlendum bókasöfnum þar sem enginn mun nokkurntíma skilja þau, . . . það er ekki að varðveita fornfræði, heldur týna þeim" (*To lock the manuscripts silently up in foreign libraries, where nobody will ever understand them, . . . that is not a preservation of ancient lore, but rather the loss of it*) (Helgason 1942, 72).

Acknowledgements

Steven Hartman, Viðar Hreinsson, and Astrid E.J. Ogilvie acknowledge support from the Swedish Foundation for Humanities and Social Sciences (Riksbankens Jubileumsfond) for the project Reflections of Change: The Natural World in Literary and Historical Sources from Iceland ca. AD 800 to 1800 (ICECHANGE), 2017–2020 (award number P16–0601:1). Astrid E.J. Ogilvie acknowledges support from the NordForsk-funded Nordic Centre of Excellence project (award 766654) Arctic Climate Predictions: Pathways to Resilient, Sustainable Societies (ARCPATH).

Notes

1 Some of the most prolific researcher networks active in the context of North Atlantic studies include the North Atlantic Biocultural Organization (NABO), the Nordic Network for Interdisciplinary Environmental Studies (NIES), the Circumpolar Networks of Future Earth's Integrated History and Future of People on Earth (IHOPE), the Oceans Past Initiative (OPI), and the Humanities for the Environment (HfE) Circumpolar Observatory and European Observatory groups.

2 Such projects have brought together interdisciplinary teams of archaeologists, literary scholars, historians, cultural anthropologists, and geographers. Examples include "Co-production of Knowledge and the building of local archaeological capacity in Greenland," supported by the United States National Science Foundation Arctic social sciences program (#181284), 2019–2022; "Reflections of Change: The Natural World in Literary and Historical Sources from Iceland ca. AD 800 to 1800 (ICECHANGE)," supported by the Swedish Foundation for Humanities and Social Sciences (P16–0601:1), 2017–2020; "The Mývatn District of Iceland: Sustainability, Environment and Change ca. AD 1700 to 1950 (MYSEAC)," supported by RANNÍS – The Icelandic Centre for Research (#163133–051), 2016–2019; "BCC Building Cyberinfrastructure for Transdisciplinary Research and Visualization of the Long-Term Human Ecodynamics of the North Atlantic," supported by the US National Science Foundation (NSF OPP ASSP #1439389), 2014–2016; and "Comparative Island Ecodynamics in the North Atlantic" (CIE) project (NSF OPP ASSP #1202692), supported by the US National Science Foundation, 2013–2017; and "RCN – SEES Global Long-term Human Ecodynamics Research Coordination Network: Assessing Sustainability on the Millennial Scale," supported by the US National Science Foundation (NSF SEES #1140106), 2011–2016.

3 Reflections of Change: The Natural World in Literary and Historical Sources from Iceland ca. AD 800 to 1800 (ICECHANGE). See www.rj.se/en/grants/2016/reflections-of-change-the-natural-world-in-literary-and-historical-sources-from-iceland-ca.-ad-800-to-1800-icechange.

4 Extract of a poem (in 16 quatrains) by Stefán Stefánsson (1855–1929), a capable poet of the Mývatn District, recorded by his niece Þura Árnadóttir (1891–1963), a renowned and accomplished versemaker in her own right. Translation by Steven Hartman and Viðar Hreinsson.

5 ICECHANGE (www.svs.is/en/projects/icechange) and MYCHANGE/MYSEAC (www.svs.is/en/projects/myseac).

6 An example is the European Climate Law, which codifies the goal set out in the European Green Deal for Europe's economy and society to become climate-neutral by 2030. The law also sets the intermediate target of reducing net greenhouse gas emissions by at least 55% by 2030, compared to 1990 levels. Approved by the European Parliament in 24 June 2021, this law reflects similar legislative and executive measures taking place in countries and territories around the world to meet the international and national targets of the Paris Climate Agreement and the Sustainable Development Goals as formalised in 2015 and subsequently updated.

Sources

Árnason, Þorvardur. 2005. "Views of Nature and Environmental Concern in Iceland." Doctoral thesis, Linköping University, Sweden.

Bell, W. T., and A. E. J. Ogilvie. 1978. "Weather Compilations as a Source of Data for the Reconstruction of European Climate During the Medieval Period." *Climatic Change* 1: 331–48.

Buell, Lawrence. 1995. *The Environmental Imagination: Thoreau, Nature Writing, and the Formation of American Culture*. Cambridge, MA: Belknap Press of Harvard University Press.

———. 2017. "Uses and Abuses of Environmental Memory." In *Contesting Environmental Imaginaries: Nature and Counternature in a Time of Global Change*, edited by Steven Hartman, 95–116. Leiden: Brill.

Damasio, Antonio. 2003. *Looking for Spinoza: Joy, Sorrow and the Feeling Brain*. London: Harcourt.

———. 2018. *The Strange Order of Things: Life, Feeling and the Making of Cultures*. New York: Random House.

Emerson, Ralph Waldo. 1836. *Nature*. Boston: James Munroe and Company.

Ezell, Margaret J. M. 1999. *Social Authorship and the Advent of Print*. Baltimore: John Hopkin University Press.

Gaard, Greta, and Lori Gruen. 1993. "Ecofeminism: Toward Global Justice and Planetary Health." *Society and Nature* 2 (1): 1–35.

Gunnlaugsson, G. Á., G. F. Guðbergsson, S. Þórarinsson, and Þ. Einarsson, eds. 1984. *Skaftáreldar 1783–1784. Ritgerðir og heimildir*. Reykjavík: Mál og Menning.

Hackmann, H., S. Moser, and A. St. Clair. 2014. "The Social Heart of Global Environmental Change." *Nature Climate Change* 4: 653–55. https://doi.org/10.1038/nclimate2320.

Haldon, J., L. Mordechai, T. P. Newfield, A. F. Chase, A. Izdebski, P. Guzowski, I. Labuhn, and N. Roberts. 2018. "History Meets Palaeoscience: Consilience and Collaboration in Studying Past Societal Responses to Environmental Change." *Proceedings of the National Academy of Sciences* 115: 3210–218.

Hallsson, Hallvarður. "Ljóðabréf Hallvarðs Hallssonar til Daða Ormssonar, in Bragi, óðfræðivefur." Accessed December 28, 2021. https://bragi.arnastofnun.is/ljod.php?ID=2794.

Hartman, Steven. 2016. "Revealing Environmental Memory: What the Study of Medieval Literature Can Tell us about Long-Term Environmental Change." *Biodiverse* 2. CBM Swedish Biodiversity Centre, SLU/Uppsala University, Sweden.

Hartman, Steven, A. E. J. Ogilvie, and R. Hennig. 2016. "Viking Ecologies: Icelandic Sagas, Local Knowledge, and Environmental Memory." In *A GlobalHistory of Literature and the Environment*, edited by J. Parham and L. Westling, 125–40. Cambridge: Cambridge University Press.

Hartman, Steven, A. E. J. Ogilvie, Jón Haukur Ingimundarson, A. J. Dugmore, George Hambrecht, and T. H. McGovern. 2017. "Medieval Iceland, Greenland, and the New Human Condition: A Case Study in Integrated Environmental Humanities." *Global and Planetary Change* 156. https://doi.org/10.1016/j.gloplacha.2017.04.007.

Hartman, S., and S. Oppermann. 2020. "Seeds of Transformative Change." *Ecocene: Cappadocia Journal of Environmental Humanities* 1 (1): 1–18. https://doi.org/10.46863/ecocene.29.

Helgason, Jón. 1942. *Úr bréfabókum Brynjólfs biskups Sveinssonar*. Copenhagen: Safn Fræðafélagsins um Ísland og Íslendinga.

Hreinsson, Viðar. 2014. "Cultural Amnesia – and Sustainable Development." *Култура/Culture* 7, Skopje: 27–36.

———. 2016. *Jón lærði og náttúrur náttúrunnar*. Reykjavík: Lesstofan.

Hreinsson, Viðar. 2018a. "A Matter of Context and Balance. Pre-industrial Conceptualizations of Sustainability." In *Cultural Sustainability and the Nature-Culture Interface: Livelihoods, Policies and Methodologies*, edited by I. Birkeland, R. J. F. Burton, C. Parra, and K. Siivonen, 79–92. Routledge.

———. 2018b. "Ghosts, Power, and the Natures of Nature: Reconstructing the World of Jón Guðmundsson the Learned." In *Framing the Environmental Humanities*, edited by H. Bergthaller and P. Mortensen, 67–85. Brill: Studies in Environmental Humanities 5.

———. 2018c. "Vicious Cycle of Violence: The Afterlife of Hervör." In *The Legendary Legacy: Transmission and reception of the Fornaldarsögur Norðurlanda*, edited by M. Driscoll, S. Hufnagel, P. Lavender, and B. Stegmann, Viking Collection 24, 71–90. Odense: University Press of Southern Denmark.

———. 2019. "Hannes tekur í nefið. Um vistfræði sagnalistar." *Skírnir* 193: 349–406.

———. 2022. "Rough Seas in Tattered Manuscripts." In *Paper Stories: Paper and Book History in Post-Medieval Europe*, edited by Silvia Hufnagel, Þórunn Sigurðardóttir and Davíð Ólafsson. De Gruyter (forthcoming, planned in 2022).

———. 2023. *Landsins meydómur* (working title) a forthcoming book, planned in 2023.

Hufnagel, Silvia. 2013. "The Farmer, Scribe and Lay Historian Gunnlaugur Jónsson from Skuggabjörg and His Scribal Network." In *Gripla* 24, 235–68.

IGBP Report 1. 1986. *The International Geosphere-Biosphere Programme: A Study of Global Change/Final Report of the Ad Hoc Planning Group*. Berne, Switzerland: ICSU 21st General Assembly, September 14–19, 1986.

Ingólfsdóttir, Guðrún. 2016. *Á hverju liggja ekki vorar göfugu kellíngar. Bókmenning íslenskra kvenna frá miðöldum fram á 18. öld*. Sýnisbók íslenskrar alþýðumenningar 20, Reykjavík: Háskólaútgáfan.

———. 2017. "Women's Manuscript Culture in Iceland 1600-1900." In *Mirrors of Virtue. Manuscripts and Printed Books in Post-Reformation Iceland*, edited by Margrét Eggertsdóttir and Matthew James Driscoll, 195-224. Copenhagen: Opuscula XV, Bibliotheca Arnamagnæana XLIX.

———. 2021a. *Skáldkona gengur laus. Erindi nítjándu aldar skáldkvenna við heiminn*. Reykjavík: Bjartur.

———. 2021b. "Just a homemaker? An eighteenth-century Icelandic housewife's manuscript miscellany." In *Hidden harmonies. Manuscript and print on the North Atlantic fringe, 1500–1900*, edited by Matthew James Driscoll and Nioclás Mac Cathmhaoil, 49-77. Copenhagen: Opuscula XIX, Bibliotheca Arnamagnæana LIV.

Jacobson, H. K., and M. Price. 1990. *A Framework for Research on the Human Dimensions of Global Environmental Change*. Paris: International Social Science Council, Human Dimensions of Global Environmental Change.

Jones, P. D. 2008. "Historical Climatology – A State of the Art Review." *Weather* 63 (7): 181–85.

Jónsson, Helgi. 1949. *Látra-Björg*. Reykjavík: Helgafell.

Karlsdóttir, Unnur Birna. 2010a. *Þar sem fossarnir falla: Náttúrusýn og nýting fallvatna á Íslandi 1900 – 2008*. Reykjavík: Hið íslenska bókmenntafélag.

———. 2010b. "Náttúrusýn og nýting fallvatna." Doctoral Thesis, University of Iceland.

Lansing, Tereza, 2014. "Manuscript Culture in Nineteenth Century Northern Iceland. The Case of Þorsteinn Þorsteinsson á Heiði." In *Vernacular Literacies – Past, Present and Future*, edited by Ann-Catrine Edlund, Lars-Erik Edlund, and Susanne Haugen, 193–211. Umeå: Northern Studies Monographs 3.

Magnússon, Sigurður Gylfi, and Davíð Ólafsson. 2017. *Minor Knowledge and Microhistory. Manuscript Culture in the Nineteenth Century*. London: Routledge.

Ólafsson, Davíð. 2012. "Vernacular Literacy Practices in Nineteenth-Century Icelandic Scribal Culture." In *Att läsa och att skriva Två vågor av vardagligt skriftbruk i Norden 1800–2000*, edited by Ann-Catrine Edlund, 65–85. Umeå: Umeå University.

———. 2013. "Scribal Communities in Iceland: The Case of Sighvatur Grímsson." *White Field, Black Seeds: Nordic Literacy Practices in the Long Nineteenth Century*, edited by Anna Kusimin and Matthew J. Driscoll. Helsinki: Finnish Literature Society.

Olwig, Kenneth R. 2019. *The Meanings of Landscape: Essays on Place, Space, Environment and Justice*. New York and London: Routledge.

Ogilvie, A. E. J. 1986. "The Climate of Iceland, 1701–1784." *Jökull* 36: 57–73.

———. 2010. "Historical Climatology, *Climatic Change*, and Implications for Climate Science in the 21st Century." *Climatic Change* 100: 33–47.

———. 2020. "Famines, Mortality, Livestock Deaths and Scholarship: Environmental Stress in Iceland ca. 1500–1700." In *The Dance of Death. Environmental Stress, Mortality and Social Response in Late Medieval and Renaissance Europe*, edited by Andrea Kiss and Katherine Prybil, 9–24. London: Routledge, Online 2019 https://doi.org/10.4324/9780429491085.

Ogilvie, A. E. J., Gao, Y., Einarsson, N., Keenlyside, N., and King, L. 2020. "The ARCPATH Project: Assessing Risky Environments and Rapid Change: Research on Climate, Adaptation and Coastal Communities in the North Atlantic Arctic." In *Nordic Perspectives on the Responsible Development of the Arctic: Pathways to Action*, edited by Douglas C. Nord, 137–56. Switzerland: Springer Nature. https://doi.org/10.1007/978-3-030-52324-4.

Ogilvie, A. E. J., and Trausti Jónsson, eds. 2001. *The Iceberg in the Mist: Northern Research in Pursuit of a "Little Ice Age"* (Reprinted from *Climatic Change* 48). Dordrecht: Kluwer Academic Publishers.

Pfister, C., R. Brázdil, J. Luterbacher, A. E. J. Ogilvie, and S. White. 2018. "Early Modern Europe." In *The Palgrave Handbook of Climate History*, edited by S. White, C. Pfister, and F. Mauelshagen, 265–95. London: Palgrave Macmillan. First Online July 18, 2018. https://doi.org/10.1057/978-1-137-43020-5_23. eBook ISBN 978-1-137-43020-5; Hardcover ISBN 978-1-137-43019-9.

Sayre, R., D. Karagulle, C. Frye, T. Boucher, N. H. Wolff, S. Breyer, D. Wright, M. Martin, K. Butler, K. Van Graafeiland, and J. Touval. 2020. "An Assessment of the Representation of Ecosystems in Global Protected Areas Using New Maps of World Climate Regions and World Ecosystems." *Global Ecology and Conservation* 21: e00860.

Sigurðardóttir, Ragnhildur, A. J. Newton, M. T. Hicks, A. J. Dugmore, Viðar Hreinsson, A. E. J. Ogilvie, Árni Daníel Júlíusson, Árni Einarsson, S. Hartman, I. A. Simpson, Orri Vésteinsson, and T. H. McGovern. 2019. "Trolls, Water, Time, and Community: Resource Management in the Mývatn District of Northeast Iceland." In *Global Perspectives on Long Term Community Resource Management, Studies in Human Ecology and Adaptation*, edited by L. R. Lozny and T. H. McGovern, 71–101, vol. 11. © Switzerland: Springer Nature 77. https://doi.org/10.1007/978-3-030-15800-2_5.

Soper, Kate. 1995. *What Is Nature? Culture, Politics and the Non-Human*. Oxford: Blackwell.
Spinoza, Baruch. 2002. *Spinoza. Complete Works*. Translated by Samuel Shirley, edited by Michael L. Morgan. Indianapolis: Hackett Publishing.
Thoreau, Henry David. 1995 [1854]. *Walden, or, Life in the Woods*. New York: Dover Publications.
Zapf, Hubert. 2014. "Creative Matter and Creative Mind: Cultural Ecology and Literary Creativity." In *Material Ecocriticism*, edited by Serenella Iovino and Serpil Opperman, 51–66. Bloomington, IN: Indiana University Press.

Manuscript Sources

Héraðsskjalasafn Þingeyinga (Archives of the Thingey County, Húsavík): HHus, E – 16/8.
The Icelandic National and University Library, Manuscript Archives: JS 479 8vo. Lbs 165 8vo.

25

"THICK MAPPING" FOR ENVIRONMENTAL JUSTICE

EJScreen, ArcGIS, and Contemporary Literature

Parker Krieg and Matthew N. Hannah

Introduction

As a form of cultural production, literature is inherently spatialised. Characters, and their readers, move through and interact with spaces and places just as they experience the narrative plot. Literary places often serve as metaphors for larger themes and concerns in the text, lending such spaces added mythological weight and a symbolic valence that often transcends the text itself. One thinks of ecotourists traipsing around Walden Pond, seeking a connection to Henry David Thoreau's book through the experience of place. Compared with film and visual art, the spatial dynamics of literature may be the most unrecognised in the popular imagination. Literary topography is vast and diverse because fiction navigates space as it builds worlds. From the fictionalisation of real-world locations to the creation of entirely new or abstract space, literature's relationship to space, place, and environment is complex. In some narratives, the environment is akin to a character; in others, it merely provides a stage for the action, but locality is inescapable. As Henri Lefebvre observes, "the problem is that any search for space in literary texts will find it everywhere and in every guise: enclosed, described, projected, dreamt of, speculated about" (1991 [1974], 15).

Many novels attempt to fictionalise the lived texture of real spaces, such as James Joyce's Dublin, Richard Wright's Chicago, or Willa Cather's Nebraska. Their works are so accurate, as Joyce once claimed, that reconstructions could be built from the text should the location itself disappear (Budgen 1960, 67–68). Some literary texts mythologise real places, such as Homer's Mediterranean islands or William Faulkner's Yoknapatawpha County, while others speculate places that defy attempts to locate them empirically, such as Jeff VanderMeer's Area X or Colson Whitehead's Zone One. Maps also offer the literary sociologist odd artefacts, such as the foldout maps of J.R.R. Tolkien's Middle Earth, featured on the back cover of the Houghton Mifflin edition. Literary plots are thus inextricable from the coordinates plotted therein and thus essential to the social experience of reading literature.

As our relationship to space and place has become increasingly significant in the age of climate change and ecological collapse, so do our imagined experiences of geography. Descriptors of space and place thus become essential components of narrative, serving what Roland Barthes might call the "reality effect" (1989). And it is accomplished through signifiers of

DOI: 10.4324/9781003082798-31

space, and layers of specific data points representing location as characters navigate both fictional and non-fictional worlds. The predominance of space and place, when combined with temporality, is "a formally constitutive category of literature" (Bakhtin 1981, 84). "We are thus confronted by an indefinite multitude of spaces, each one piled upon, or perhaps contained within, the next," claims Lefebvre about literary space (1991 [1974], 8). The recognised preponderance of locations in literature led to the "spatial turn," with the application of geographical analysis as a discrete set of concerns and methodologies. For Robert Tally, this orients the scholar "towards the world itself, towards an understanding of our lives as situated in a mobile array of social and spatial relations that, in one way or another, need to be mapped" (2013, 16). The link between narrative and location is thus an explicit aspect of literature as a medium where such social and environmental relations are enacted. "Narratives are, in a sense, mapping machines," Tally claims. "On the other hand, narratives – like maps, for that matter – never come before us in some pristine, original form" (2016, 3). Literary texts and maps are both embedded in sociopolitical discourses, what David Bodenhamer calls the "the dense coil of memory, artifact, and experience," and constructed through a complex layering of signifiers and symbols (2010, viii).

But turning toward space is also a geographical movement in itself, a recognition that our environment shapes how and why we experience the literary object – that space provides a rubric with which to interpret literature, both in relation to rootedness and environmental disruption. Tally points out that spatiality can also be understood negatively, dialectically: "Displacement, perhaps more than a homely rootedness in place, underscores the critical importance of spatial relations in our attempts to interpret, and change, the world" (2013, 13). Such dialectical understandings (e.g. country and city, displacement, gentrification, and anthropogenic disaster) are common if not fully acknowledged in environmental criticism. However, cartography is always bound up by questions of power and ideology. In his capacious study, *The New Nature of Maps* (2001), J.B. Harley illustrates the ideological nature of maps beyond their accuracy as texts: "Maps are never value-free images; except in the narrowest Euclidean sense they are not in themselves either true or false" (53). Maps are cartographic texts whose accuracy is linked to geopolitical and ideological dynamics. Heather Winlow describes the dynamics by which mapping contributed historically to "the social construction of race, which has been reinforced through cartographic power" (2009, 1). As colonial cartographers justified the spread of European power, such maps were created to support arguments for racial and ethnic superiority. Critiques of such mapping practices have generated a wealth of scholarship on colonialism and postcolonialism (Anthias 2019; Goldie 2010), Indigenous land rights (Sarkowsky 2020), and gendered landscapes (Kolodny 1975; Massey 2005).

As geographer Edward Soja argues, the spatial turn represents possible new horizons in social theory, turning from the modernist emphasis on time to the co-constitution of temporality by space. "Space still tends to be treated as fixed, dead, undialectical," he laments (Soja 1989, 11). Soja's synthesis stakes out a territory apart from the focus on historical *durée* and positions the spatial turn squarely within a Marxist project through which space itself becomes dialectical. Similarly, geographical accounts of gender, race, and finance illustrate how spaces are not empty but are rather immanently shaped by processes of cultural production (Harvey 1996; Massey 2005; Woods 1998). As the Italian school of post-Fordist critics recognise, the production and accumulation of value have moved "from the factory to the metropolis" and into the environment of daily life (Negri 2018). We situate our own project alongside the critiques that have been mobilised in this period. With a biopolitical account of culture as a proliferating constructive force, we understand that narrative texts can be interventions in the spaces they depict and produce. In a similar fashion, digital maps may also enable the juxtaposition of data points and layered information, generating visual supplements to multiple (even contradictory) ways of knowing, living, and transforming measured space.

This spatial turn exposes the explicitly political contours of shared material environments that environmental justice criticism has long taken as its starting point. As the environmental humanities focus on cultural narratives concerning issues such as climate change, land rights, water usage, toxicity, pollution, agriculture, farming, ecology, and other topics, the field provides a generative site for further convergences with the digital humanities through geospatial analysis. From the most general macro level to microclimates of injustice, such mapping may contribute to what David Naguib Pellow (2017) calls a "critical environmental justice." This critical mapping goes beyond a neoliberal conception of justice as representational proportionality across unequal conditions to explore the constitutive role of material environments in the production and reproduction of unequal (and disposable) life. Turning to the places where injustices and struggles occur likewise reveals histories of contemporaneous yet disjunctive spaces. As the editors of *Latinx Environmentalisms* argue, this spatialised vector creates possibilities for environmental interpretations that decentre the "material projects of capitalism, racism, and colonialism" with an "epistemological and material project" for knowing and making the world otherwise (Wald et al. 2019, 7).

If, as Doreen Massey observes, aspatial globalisation homogenises the world along Cartesian coordinates and a space for the development of capital accumulation, today we are confronted by the prospect of an aspatial Anthropocene in which periodisation masks the continued imperial management of discontinuous environmental effects (Massey 2005, 82; Sexton 2017, 15). We highlight these aspatial parallels to suggest that the expansive purpose of maps is to create disjunctures rather than to restore or reconfirm a romantic wholeness (a first nature, retroactively created by a second "nature"). By focusing on the US Environmental Protection Agency (EPA) data, we recognise that this information is shaped by the history of US regulatory bodies. As such, it is fraught and incomplete. Yet as a public resource, it is available for repurposing for critical and "commons"-oriented ends. Furthermore, we see such EPA data as one possible layer of information among many possible layers, and by theorising the layering functionality of digital maps, we reinforce our emphasis on spatial disjuncture and a dialectical rather than romantic, organic wholeness.

In this chapter, we explore the applications of digital mapping tools for expanding the topography of humanities research through a process of "thick mapping," which we situate at the intersection of the digital and the environmental humanities. This method provides a means to analyse literary data and environmental data. We follow Todd Presner, David Shepard, and Yoh Kawano's definition of thick mapping, which goes further than GIS layering to include "cultural analysis trained on the political, economic, linguistic, social, and other stratificatory and contextual realities in which human beings act and create" (2014, 18; see also Furlan 2019; Carvalhaes et al. 2021). Or we might follow William T. Vollmann, who describes his own writing process of "delineating" geographic entities: "Whenever I went to Imperial, my chief joy was to record through words and photographs the splendid colors, the fruits and stories of that world, to map it and as an act of worship to fix it in time" (2009, 112). Here, *thick* mapping differs from recent *deep* mapping, which places a greater emphasis on representing temporal change and contextualising human culture within environmental history (Travis et al. 2020). As authors craft narratives, they must necessarily describe places and spaces by adapting the inherited idioms that delineate such milieus, especially when working in a meta-fictional mode describing "real" environments. Layering literary geographies onto a data layer derived from environmental science practices allows us to generate a "thick map" to focus on environmental justice and contested cultural representations of space.

But such a method also produces a new form of reading, one situated at the nexus of "close" and "distant" readings: a layered mode of reading that engages both narrative form and environmental data through the mapping interface. Nevertheless, surprising images of the world emerge where they are least expected. For instance, Sarah M. Broom's National Book Award–winning

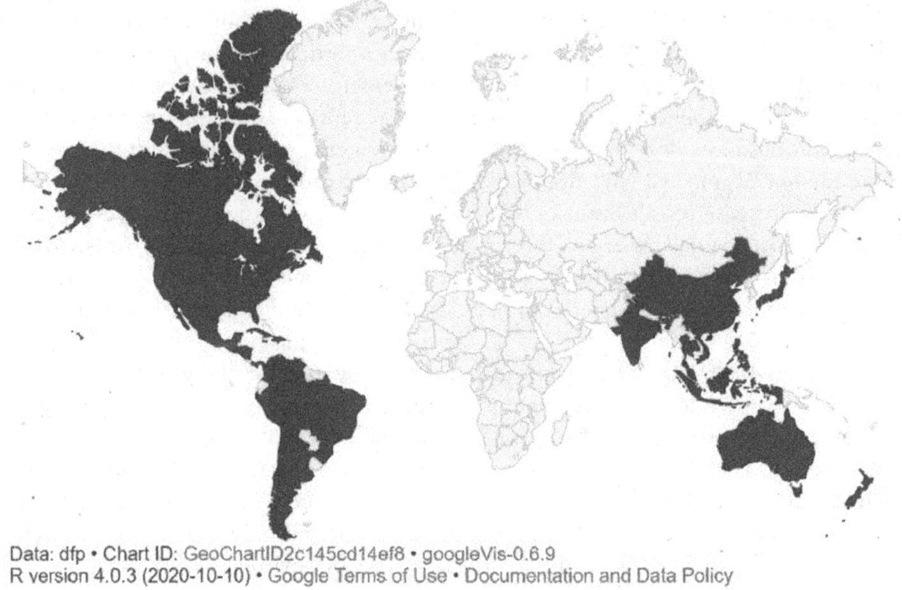

Figure 25.1a Countries named in *The Yellow House: A Memoir* (Broom 2019).

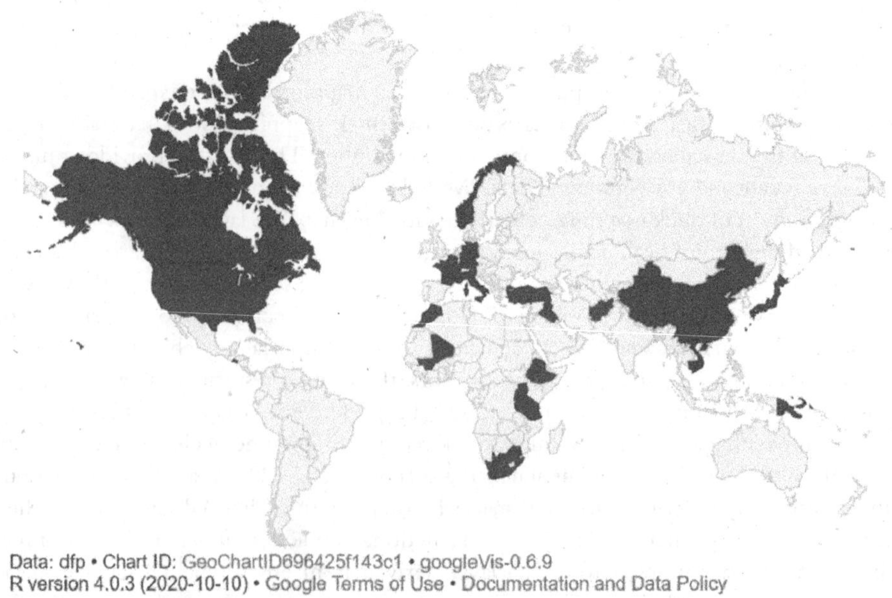

Figure 25.1b Countries named in *Tropic of Orange* (Yamashita 1997).

memoir, *The Yellow House* (2019), focuses on the impact of losing a family home in New Orleans during Hurricane Katrina, yet its range of geographic references places it in a much larger narrative world.

In the case of Karen Tei Yamashita's novel *Tropic of Orange* (1997), the characters enact the postmodern geography of Los Angeles, where the border between Global North and Global South shifts in the context of the North American Free Trade Agreement (NAFTA) policies, the agency of migrant labour, and moving commodities. However, the map that emerges from named countries in the text offers an image of a Pacific world. Indeed, given the "Pacific pivot" in US political and military postures, which has likewise been accompanied by a rise of Sinophobia and neo–Cold War rhetoric, it is possible that a map like this suggests the potential for critical readings against future frameworks that would seek to recast Anglophone literature on an east–west axis.

These are the global images of two of our chosen texts, yet they provide a starting point for rethinking the worlds represented in their narratives. Franco Moretti argues that mapping "is not the conclusion of geographical work; it's the beginning" (1998, 7). That is, spatial understanding of literature produces new ways to read the text itself, offering new interpretive permutations. Mapping literature opens up new vistas to consider how questions of form, plot, and style contribute to a sociology of literature. Furthermore, the increasing accessibility to such geospatial technology digital tools such as Google Maps and Esri's ArcGIS, contextualised within the emergence and spread of the digital humanities, has radically transformed the possibilities for cartographic analysis. The availability of such tools has sparked a revolution in spatial analysis in the humanities by focused applications and appropriations of digital mapping technology. Bodenhamer describes the implicit potentials for furthering humanistic research by enabling more complex analyses of environment and spatiality:

> This convergence of technologies has the potential to revolutionize the role of space and place in the humanities by allowing us to move far beyond the static map, to shift from two dimensions to multidimensional representations, to develop interactive systems, and to explore space and place dynamically – in effect, to create virtual worlds embodying what we know about space and place.
>
> *(2007, 101)*

The history and critique of such tools and methods have been detailed elsewhere (Bodenhamer, Corrigan, and Harris 2010; Gregory and Geddes 2014; Schindling and Harris 2018), but the impact of maps on digital humanities projects is undeniable. Projects such as Torn Apart/Separados, the Bdote Memory Map, Icelandic Saga Map, Mapping Inequality, Mapping Police Violence, and Queering the Map, among others, showcase the salience of digital mapping platforms in contributing to significant humanistic research on relations between geography and power.[1] In addition, such methods and tools indicate future and fruitful research integrations, especially with the environmental humanities, itself a multi- and interdisciplinary cluster of scholarly activity (Lethbridge and Hartman 2016). Kueffer et al. (2018) point out that "responses to environmental problems are primarily social and cultural issues," and cultural mapping provides one such critical site of analysis for our environmental humanities foci. We concur with Mary Kinniburgh that a spatial analysis of the environment with literature reveals "a complex web of meaning across categories of history, literature, and landscape" (2018, n.p.). Applications of GIS software to map this "complex web" reveal much about how locations in fiction are deployed as literary effects and, at the same time, relate to environmental justice frameworks, as deployed by the team at Environmental Justice

Atlas.[2] Their work models the kinds of interdisciplinary, intersectional projects we advocate, suggesting important future directions for projects that leverage existing tools to pose new scholarly questions.

Method

The search for locational data guarantees a preponderance of geospatial information even within a small corpus such as ours. Geospatial data ubiquity represents a significant challenge for researchers who want to apply spatial analyses to collections of literary texts. Analysing the geographic data in our corpus required the application of computational methods to map the contours of the selected texts. Because our data was unstructured, we needed a method to transform it into a dataset we could map with GIS tools. Literary texts are considered highly structured in terms of semantic density and complexity, often deploying narrative techniques of metaphor, irony, and ambiguity, which are notoriously difficult to parse computationally. In this regard, such data types do not conform to geospatial structural features and are difficult to analyse with GIS tools. Further, working with humanistic data is inherently fraught. Indeed, some scholars question the applicability of data as a concept to describe humanistic objects of study (Drucker 2011). When considering DEH approaches, we can look to Christoph Schöch's useful definition of humanistic data as "a digital, selectively constructed, machine-actionable abstraction representing some aspects of a given object of humanistic inquiry" (2013, n.p.). Jim Schindling and Trevor Harris note that working with unstructured data sourced from primary source documents presents unique and complex challenges: "These historical materials are usually text-based and spatially imprecise, and they stand in contrast to the tabulated structure of modern datasets which usually correspond to known boundary units" (2018, n.p.). Because we sought to apply GIS to a corpus of literary texts, we faced many of these challenges: extracting entities, followed by cleaning and structuring data so it can be effectively analysed and visualised by literary and cultural scholars.

To assist the geospatial analysis of the environment in our four selected texts, we turned to computational methods derived from natural language processing (NLP) methods. Applying a technique known as named-entity recognition (NER) produced a set of keywords associated with space, place, and locale. We applied NER to this data using the SpacyR package in R, which provides a Python wrapper to perform NLP and extract locational data (Benoit and Matsuo 2020). Although this method is necessarily imperfect as the computer algorithm will often make errors identifying location data that is obscure, obsolete, ambiguous, or pseudonymous, we managed to collect a robust list of key locations referenced in our four selected texts. We subsequently cleaned and structured the data, correcting errors and standardising entries where possible. For example, in our collection of locations from Vollmann's *Imperial*, we standardised "Salton Sea" and "the Salton Sea," which were scraped as separate entities, as "Salton Sea." Such standardisations were performed when appropriate, although, occasionally, the same locations were described using different languages (e.g. "Signal Mountain," "Centinela"), and we kept those entries separate to reflect the textual flavours of the original. An additional challenge with this method is the various informal references to places, such as nicknames or shorthands, that are best interpreted with local knowledge and read in the larger context of the text. As we argue, this thick mapping is intended to support, not replace, this living philology.

Having generated a set of location names from our four texts, we then created a digital map in ArcGIS. This platform allows us to create data layers that can be laid on top of one another, filtered, and manipulated. We can thus layer points on top of the raster image that serves as the base of our digital maps. Furthermore, our map of literary locations will produce an interactive digital map which can be accessed later and embedded on a project website. But unlike literary maps that layer locations on top of raster images, we advocate for "thickness" in our map. As we have argued, contemporary literary texts are themselves already layered documents, an intuition expressed in Yamashita's *Tropic of Orange*:

> There are maps and there are maps and there are maps. The uncanny thing was that he could see all of them at once, filter some, pick them out like transparent windows and place them even delicately and consecutively in a complex grid of pattern, spatial discernment, body politic.
>
> *(1997, 56)*

We argue for the geographical capacity to "filter" and "place" literary locations within "a complex grid of pattern" through which literary spaces are layered onto scientific data concerning environmental challenges. The added layering of scientific data sourced from publicly available data portals such as the EPA's provide vistas for possible future research avenues. These paths have yet to be fully explored by humanities scholars. However, Anastasia Lin's *Mapping Multi-ethnic Texts in the Literary Classroom* (2018), Kenton Ramsby's *Lost in the City* (2020), and Alejandra Ortega's *Calculating the Costs: Effects of Land Consumption in Margaret Atwood's MaddAddam Trilogy* (2020) suggest feasible mappings horizons for the DEH.

To create the maps discussed in this chapter, we sourced data from the EPA's Environmental Justice Screening and Mapping Tool (EJScreen).[3] This platform allowed us to add indexed data layers on climate, compromised water features, air quality, urban density, and industrial waste to our GIS map. When layered over important locations referenced in contemporary literature, these publicly available geospatial data layers provide an important context to integrate literary *and* environmental problems, one that showcases imagined literary spaces within an ecological frame. Thus, the environment is not simply constitutive of the text's "reality effect" but an essential core of the literary experience of space and place, even when the text may not be explicitly environmentalist. And while this chapter focuses on EJScreen and North American literature, we advocate a similar approach with appropriate and available datasets. Mapping ecological data onto literary maps provides a lens with which to consider the topography of literary spaces linked to environmental concerns outside the literary world but refracted through the text as light through a prism. Furthermore, each of the four authors of our selected texts explicitly engages space, place, and locatedness in different ways, and our mappings bring their textual relationships with the environment to the foreground.

The following examples illustrate the way this mapping can be generatively combined with autobiographical novels, memoirs, postmodern fiction, and metafictional journalism. We initially intended to include a work of speculative fiction, but the practical and theoretical implications would demand more explanation than this chapter allows. We nevertheless settled on what are basically two memoirs and two postmodern works: Sarah Broom's *The Yellow House: A Memoir*, Richard Wright's *Black Boy (American Hunger)*, Karen Tei Yamashita's *Tropic of Orange*, and William T. Vollmann's *Imperial*. Each illustrates possibilities for different interpretive uses for mapping. While by no means exhaustive, these examples provide a proof of concept accompanied by layered readings.

Sarah M. Broom in New Orleans

Sarah Broom's *The Yellow House* provides an example of how mapping can contribute to a process of memory building by authors and readers. The memoir positions the house as a carrier of intergenerational memory, which the narrator draws on to tell a history of race and environment

Figure 25.2a Map of percentage people of colour in East New Orleans.

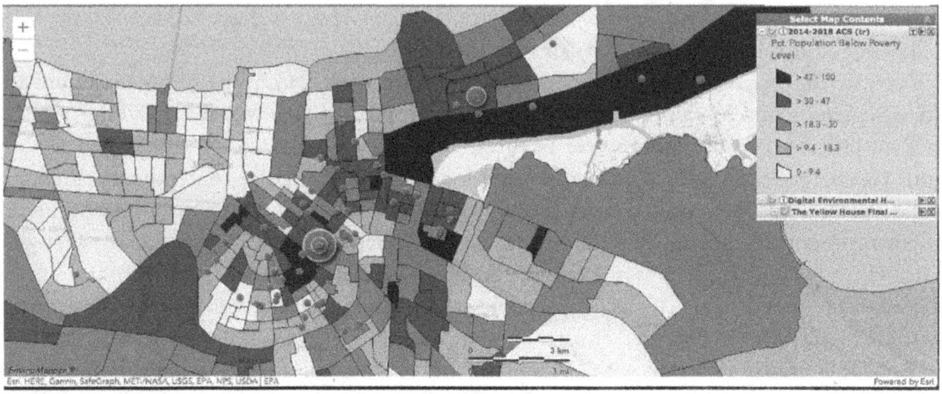

Figure 25.2b Map of populations below poverty level.

from the personal lives of those living in East New Orleans. "My beginning precedes me," she writes, evoking an immanent sense of writing as a trace in the wake of an external source of origin (2019, 9). A distinction is drawn early on between "the facts as they were recorded, [and] the story as the generations tell it" (2019, 13). The boundaries between lived experience, narrative or ideological framings, and the world of recorded facts (constructed out of observations, measurements, and valuations) are continuously challenged in Broom's narration. Supported by the data maps, we find locations within the city clustered in high concentrations of people of colour, which likewise correlate to a percentage of the population below poverty. The house "resides" on Wilson Avenue, the second-largest cluster, on the border of a region that has 95–100% non-white and between 47–100% below the poverty line.

As an "origin" that precedes the author, these maps fill out the narrative's history of the house within the historical development of East New Orleans. A residential garden since the 1800s, the East's middle-class and majority white population left during the oil bust of the 1980s, and the precarious "eastern frontier" became a new locus of subsidised housing as downtown real estate increased (2019, 143). *The Yellow House* likewise challenges media narratives that the district had fallen into disrepair and neglect by residents prior to Hurricane Katrina. Precisely *who*

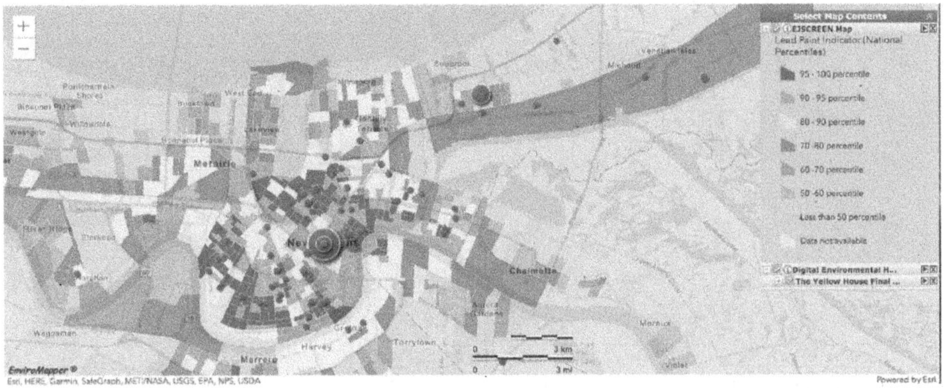

Figure 25.3 Map of lead paint indicators.

was neglecting this milieu is a question put to the city. This erasure is compounded further as parts of the East are now being rezoned as "light industrial" (2019, 334). The history of care and active construction (production) of the house by multiple generations of the Broom family is evidenced by the work of painting. As a form of upkeep, keeping up appearances, a metaphor, and a symbolic act, paint is referenced 52 times. The colours of painted houses are strictly regulated by different districts for heritage and tourism. However, there are no explicit references to lead paint, which is a significant environmental hazard and the subject of decades-long lawsuits against the Housing Authority of New Orleans.

A map of lead paint indicators is not as spectacular as flood data, which is well-documented. Nor is it as dramatic as the petrochemical refineries along River Road, the famous route that oil companies now share with plantations and the levees on which the severed heads of rebel slaves were mounted in the German Coast uprising of 1811 (2019, 14). Rather, a map of lead paint indicators reveals the *slow* violence (both physical and mental) by which the home itself becomes a material site for the devaluation of Black life as the city decides which properties are considered "historic" and deserving of remediation by the housing authority.

The map of lead paint indicators reveals that many of the locations referenced in *The Yellow House* correspond to such devalued areas. Writing on the lead poisoning of New Orleans' Black residents, journalist Vann R. Newkirk II argues that "for those in the poisoned generation [of the 1990s] and beyond, blackness is a tightrope, and lead poisoning is just one of the ways to fall" (2017). This toxicity undermines the fantasy of the American home as a refuge and the prospect of homeownership as a route to middle-class life. If the memoir frames memory as a trace of the built environment, these maps likewise reveal additional dimensions of this landscape that predate erasures by flood. The final image casts the locational data of the text in proximity to the "agriculture street landfill" superfund site, which stores decades of toxic waste. Black residents were encouraged to purchase homes on top of the site and now experience generational trauma of cancers and tumours.

Broom's memoir casts her house and city as a memory text, subject to refashioning and rewriting. An epigraph by Joan Didion declares that "a place belongs forever to whoever claims it hardest, remembers it most obsessively, wrenches it from itself, shapes it, renders it, loves it so radically that he remakes it" (2019, 286). However, Broom addresses how the mythology of New Orleans as "a progressive city open to whimsy and change" can also "suffocate the people who live and suffer under the place's burden, burying them within layers and layers of signifiers, making it impossible to truly get at what is dysfunctional about the city" (2019, 328). Citing

Figure 25.4 Map of proximity to superfund site.

writer-director David Simons and his television series *Treme*, which follows the lives of those living through post-Katrina "recovery," Broom suggests that it is precisely his love of New Orleans that keeps the series from exploring the systemic corruption that defined Simons' portrayal of Baltimore in *The Wire*. Indeed, the final chapters of *The Yellow House* are devoted to the author's own excavations of deeds and city planning. During Broom's investigation into the official documents by which a city makes, remakes, remembers, and investigates itself, she encounters a librarian who suggests that "we don't have the liberty of going around and examining things the way we think makes sense" (2019, 335). We suggest this mapping of environmental justice data can contribute to sense-making in similarly constrained investigations into environmental injustice, whether taken up by authors or critics.

Richard Wright in the Northern Migration

Turning to a text like Richard Wright's 1945 memoir, *Black Boy (American Hunger)*, raises the question of how mapping with contemporary data might illuminate historical narratives. For example, we considered the growing body of evidence that discriminatory *redlining* practices by banks in the 1930s have resulted in uneven urban heating today (Hoffman, Shandas, and Pendleton 2020; Ploomer and Popovich 2020). Given this and other historical effects of environmental inequalities, we believe that Wright's depictions of mid-century metropolis may reveal continuities with present data. He took a keen interest in sociological data and actively sought to incorporate this objectivity into his immanent explorations of Black social life (Wright 1962 [2015]). However, Wright's memoir contains few named local entities. Where they exist, they are often informal, even vague, references that require close interpretation to be placed at that time (e.g. coded areas, health institutions, public service buildings). Instead of an internal geography, we find names of cities and countries at larger scales.

This challenges the conventional reception of Wright that is framed solely through early works like *Uncle Tom's Children* (1938), *Native Son* (1940), and *Black Boy* (1945). Whether writing on the global "colour line" at Bandung or the decolonisation of Ghana at the invitation of Kwame Nkrumah, Wright's later literature is interested in scales of geography beyond that of the city. Rather, he thinks in terms of migration and the geopolitics of capitalist modernisation. Whereas our project hoped to link past and present environmental injustice in Wright's Chicago through contemporary data, the mapping process instead leads us to frame his memoir in the context of the author's global outlook and his work on the internal migration of African Americans northward from the Mississippi Delta region. To those familiar with his early work, this comes as no surprise. However, mapped onto his later work, *Black Boy*'s personal account of the Great Migration can be read in the context of global development and anti-colonialism. Thus, environmental justice takes on a scale concerned with global inequality and is typified in Wright's critical engagement with "Black Belt" theorists like Harry Haywood and the Chicago Left. The geography of Black poverty in the United States, for Wright, cannot be properly grasped at the city level but must be understood on a larger map.

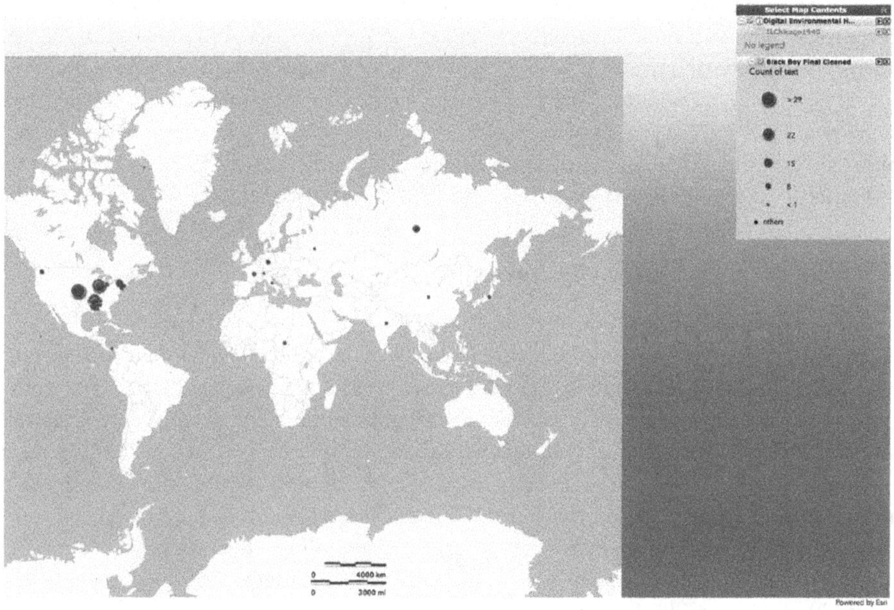

Figure 25.5a Global map of locations in Wright's *Black Boy*.

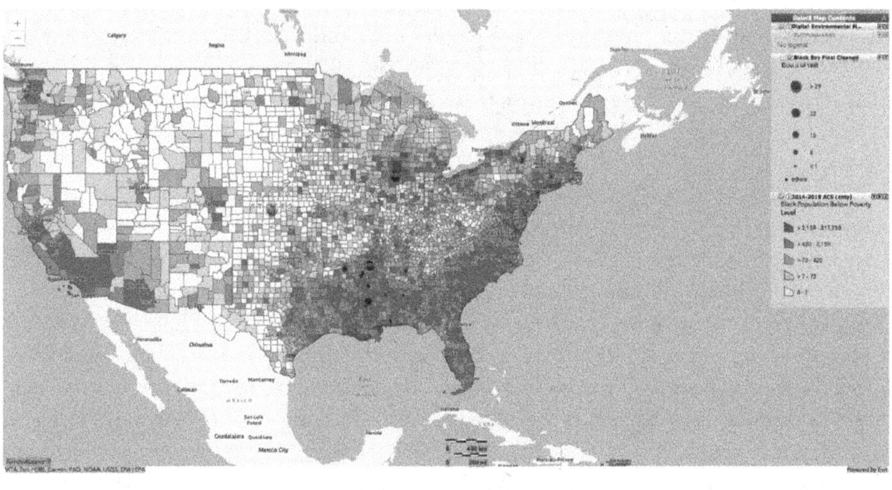

Figure 25.5b Map of locations in Wright's *Black Boy* on the Black population below poverty level.

Understanding his environment through the proper frame was a central concern of Wright's process of writing. On moving north, he realised, "I was persisting in reading my present environment in the light of my old one" (1945, 264). Getting by in Chicago is similarly framed as a challenge of spatial interpretation. Rather than asserting a deterministic naturalism, he differentiates separate spheres of environmental and human agency. By describing people and environment "with equal thoroughness," he differentiates himself from his environmental conditions that pose both constraint and opportunity (1945, 282). Wright's spatial orientation extends to the critique of his fellow Chicago communists. He attributes their disconnect between rhetoric and strategy to "the secret, underground tactics of the political movement . . . under the czars of Old Russia" and recognises that his "comrades were acting out a fantasy that had no relation whatever to the reality of their environment" (1945, 363). The space of narrative thus becomes a means to critique the narrative of space in the political imagination of those who would combat economic and racial oppression. Wright turns his literary investigations of the social environment following the 1927 Mississippi Flood, the debt peonage of sharecropping, and New Deal migration toward the spatial and existential terrain of the northern metropolis but does so in a global frame.

Karen Tei Yamashita in Los Angeles

The third example illustrates how thick mapping allows critics to valorise the multiplicity of postmodern texts. Yamashita's novel *Tropic of Orange* is often read in the context of environmental justice, globalisation, and multi-ethnic space. The narration specifically draws attention to mapping as a representational practice that is thoroughly embedded in cultural geography. Two commonly cited passages serve to focalise these themes: "*There are maps and there are maps and there are maps*" (1997, 56). Another character suggests, "If someone could put down all the layers of the real map, maybe he could get the real picture" (1997, 81). Yamashita's novel has been digitally mapped to explore its multi-ethnic urban space, while its challenge to conventional objectivity undermines the divisions between nature and culture that produced the Anthropocene (Lin 2018; Sexton 2017). However, as these passages suggest, the position of the novel is that the space of the city cannot be completely known or measured. Every attempt to represent the space is always undone by the movement and becoming of the subjects that compose and produce the city. For this reason, Blyn argues that the novel enacts the theoretical shift from Fredric Jameson's epistemic approach of "cognitive mapping" to the ontological approach of Michael Hardt and Antonio Negri's "network" (2016, 192). Blyn ultimately reads Yamashita against the latter's network, suggesting that the novel's magical realism places its faith outside (rather than immanent to) capitalist development, infrastructures, and subjectivities. We do not believe in magic.

The ontological turn not only predates the network metaphor made popular by neoliberal flexibility but is itself a product of the radical movements in the 1960s and 1970s as capital accumulation moved outside the factory and into the biopolitical sphere of daily life. In an essay on "midway terrains," Negri outlines possibilities of subjects that are neither wholly determined nor determining of the infrastructures of the social factory. "If the metropolitan hive is an ensemble of places and non-places," he writes, "the important, indeed fundamental thing is *to grasp this* ensemble *as a relationship between old and new, between the place of the factory and the non-place of metropolitan dissipation of the proletariat*" (Negri 2018, 20, emphasis in original). The space of the globalised metropolis is thus remade (along with subjectivity) at the points of production, distribution, and exchange. Understood this way, the noted freeway presence in *Tropic of Orange* is a metaphor not simply for the information superhighway but for the material infrastructure

Figure 25.6a Map of locations in Yamashita's *Tropic of Orange* on Traffic Proximity EJ Index.

Figure 25.6b Map of locations in Yamashita's *Tropic of Orange* on Traffic Proximity indicator.

that moves people, material, and value throughout the city as part of the logistics enterprise that makes NAFTA possible. The locations scraped from the novel reveal what might be considered a "midway terrain" when layered onto Traffic Proximity maps.

When the novel's locational data are layered onto the Traffic Proximity index and indicator maps of the greater Los Angeles region, an ambiguity becomes visible. The index (figure 4.1) automatically references traffic in relation to compiled demographic data on ethnic minority and low-income areas. It is not a perfect fit. In fact, there are a number of locations that appear outside of any hotspot for traffic-indexed environmental risk. However, when layered onto the Traffic Proximity indicator map (figure 4.2), the locations more closely follow the high traffic corridors. This might be taken as evidence that the narrative follows the networks of neoliberalism much more closely than anticipated, which lends credence to the critical discussion of the novel's vision of emancipatory politics. Of course, it is altogether possible that the locations mapped into GIS represent only those spaces that are legible by power and thus correspond only to the metropolis as it is constituted rather than the way it is lived by insurgent subjects who might desire to make it otherwise. This underscores the importance of reading with the text as it complicates and adds additional layers of meaning to social space.

William T. Vollmann on the Border

The final example of thick mapping offers a way of *continuing* the empirical work of the author in imagining or composing a landscape. Vollmann's 1,300-page book, *Imperial*, offers a metafictional historiography of the border region between California and Mexico. Originally intended as a nonfiction novel about border-crossing farmworkers, it expanded to encompass the region's centuries-long obsession with water and the seemingly countless economies of speculation, irrigation, and impairment that regulate the flow of produce and people across the hemisphere. Here, thick mapping contributes new layers to Vollmann's project of critical description. His reflexive narration continuously confronts readers with the metaphysics of textual representation of (and within) the material world:

> "People say it was miraculous that Christ walked across the water," he observes, "and yet they don't think twice when the same is performed by this entity [Imperial] invisible everywhere except in its representations, whose substance is comprised of equal parts imagination, measurement, memory, authority, and jurisdiction!"
>
> *(Vollmann 2009, 44)*

Distinguishing his "infinite" project of writing the space of *Imperial* from the historical projects of inscription, both by successive empires and fugitive subjects that evade colonial delineation, Vollmann includes his own effort within a fraught genealogy. The word "water" appears roughly 1,900 times in the novel, or almost one and half times per page. The material and discursive project of producing water as an object of investment, governance, control, and fertility is reflected in the history he compiles. A significant portion of *Imperial* follows Vollmann through the Salton Sea, the New River (Rio Nuevo), and the landscapes that would otherwise be arid if not for the diversions of the Colorado River. The agriculture of this region and the migrant farmworkers who cultivate it create roughly two billion dollars' worth of food per year and supply a sizable portion of domestic produce. However, the region's waterways are notorious for their toxicity resulting from a combination of agriculture and sewage run-off, salinity, and algae blooms. The postwar tourist boom at Salton Sea resorts has been replaced by seasonal fish die-offs as locals struggle on the margins of agriculture and the illicit economies produced by the border. The EPA's term for these aqueous bodies is "impaired," meaning that the water exceeds acceptable levels of pollution as specified by federal and state regulations. The Salton Sea itself is classified

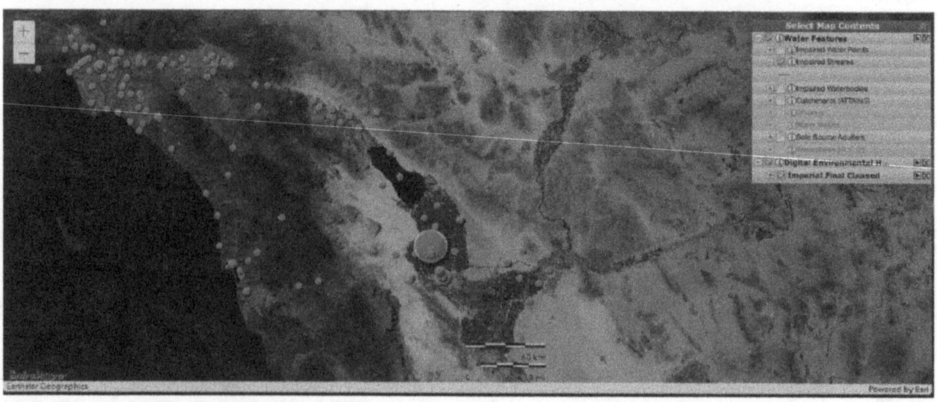

Figure 25.7 Map of locations in Vollmann's *Imperial* on impaired water streams.

as impaired; however, in the figure 5.1 map, the locations referenced in *Imperial* are plotted onto impaired streams.

The EJScreen map illustrates Vollmann's travel near these impaired streams, but this also provides greater context to his excursions. For instance, he takes multiple trips along the New River and the Salton Sea to gather water samples to send to a university researcher, all the while gathering his own anecdotal data, such as stinging sensations, smells, and carcasses floating in foam (2009, 78). In a literary sense, these river trips are an ironic play on the great river voyages of US literature, and Vollmann uses them to explore the contradictions between sense experience, knowledge, and belief. However, by EPA standards, the qualifications for "impairment" include both *numerical* and *narrative* data. As this EJScreen map likely contains narrative data, this means that Vollmann's own narrative descriptions may likewise serve as evidence in a case for regulatory intervention in the water systems of this region. The impairment data visibly stops at the US-Mexico border, which recapitulates Vollmann's critical observation about the imagination of the region as a constructed blankness.

While obsessing over the presence and absence of water in *Imperial*, Vollmann touches on the airborne toxic hazards and particulate matter released by evaporating bodies of water. These are carried by the wind into working-class and largely immigrant residential areas. One woman interviewed relayed that "kids have respiratory problems just from living here" (2009, 75). For the county's nearly 200,000 residents (85% "Hispanic or Latino" according to the census), these hazards have resulted in skyrocketing levels of asthma in children and adults, respiratory diseases, and cancers. Vollmann's investigation of the selenium stored in the evaporating lake bed contains exchanges with journalists and scientists who suggest that continued evaporation would release "over 400 square miles" of toxic selenium dust over Southern California, virtually ending agriculture and tourism, while "health problems would escalate to insurmountable proportions" (2009, 95). If concerns over a future "toxic cloud" are "overblown," he suggests, the realities of toxic dust and particulate matter are already being felt by local residents who have been raising the alarm for years over long-term issues created by the flow of water in the region alongside industrial *maquiladoras* south of the border (2009, 96).

These anecdotal accounts contained in Vollmann's metafictional historiography are supported by EJScreen data from the National Air Toxics Assessment (NATA) Respiratory Hazard Index, the Particulate Matter 2.5 (fine particles) percentiles, and the percentile of people of colour in the region. Compared with water (and its absence), air quality is a necessary component of an environmental justice reading of *Imperial*. These digital maps draw into relief passages that may

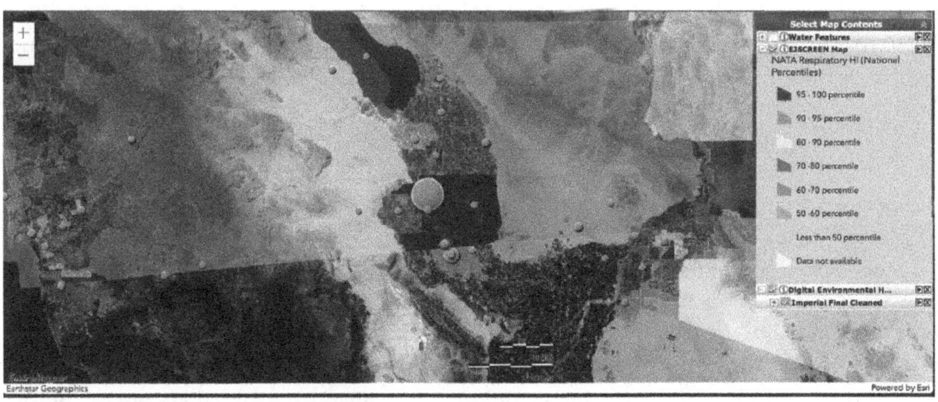

Figure 25.8a Map of Vollman's *Imperial* locations NATA Respiratory Hazard Index.

Figure 25.8b Map of Vollman's *Imperial* locations in relation to Particulate Matter 2.5.

Figure 25.8c Map of Vollman's *Imperial* locations in relation to percentile people of colour.

be overshadowed by Vollmann's accounts of neocolonial state violence against migrant workers, water pollution, and counter-pastoral landscapes of nostalgic ruin, all produced by successive fantasies of paradise. Combined with Vollmann's text, these maps illustrate how spatial analysis collates both numerical and narrative data. Moreover, they expose the disastrous project of border creation and management in the interests of transnational capital that Vollmann himself wishes to transform.

Conclusion

The examples from our project discussed in this chapter offer a starting point for developing "thick maps" that add layers of ecological and environmental information into the discourses of narrated space. At the same time, thick mapping places the discourse of historical narratives within the built environment. Predictably, the limitations to this approach exist at the named-entity recognition phase, which relies on automated, algorithmic processes to identify particular locations according to pre-existing categories. NLP can only approximate actual locations mentioned in the text due to the complexity of human language. If an author uses slang terms or local references to a place, the computer will be unable to scrape the entities, requiring a human reader to confirm and clean the output. Rather than a limitation, this necessity forcefully demonstrates the need for close readings and interpretations.

At the same time, computational methods, like maps themselves, only point to something more complex and nuanced, and we believe our maps offer a model for new forms of reading, operating between the dichotomy of "close" or "distant." Like space and place, experienced as both incredibly granular *and* stunningly vast at the same time, our method suggests possibilities for layered readings, attentive to the nuances of the text but also aware of the horizon, the data, and the information that ground the text within the geopolitical realities of environmental devastation and justice. Situated within the spatial turn of the humanities, our project occupies a third space between focused mapping projects closely attentive to one text (Lin 2018; Ramsby 2020) and massive data collection efforts that scrape locational entities from all English-language fiction published between 1701 and 2011 (Wilkens and Ruan). Our project combines both approaches by scraping geographical references from a small, thematically linked corpus and layering those locations with data from publicly available datasets in an effort to suggest new models for engaging literary spaces in the context of environmental data. With the development of new computational tools such as we apply here, we anticipate such projects will only become more capacious and significant.

Notes

1 Torn Apart / Separados (https://xpmethod.columbia.edu/torn-apart/volume/2)
Bdote Memory Map (https://bdotememorymap.org/mnisota
Icelandic Saga Map (http://sagamap.hi.is/is/#)
Mapping Inequality (https://dsl.richmond.edu/panorama/redlining/#loc=5/39.1/-94.58)
Mapping Police Violence (https://mappingpoliceviolence.org)
Queering the Map (www.queeringthemap.com)

2 Environmental Justice Atlas (https://ejatlas.org).

3 EJSCREEN: Environmental Justice Screening and Mapping Tool (www.epa.gov/ejscreen).

Sources

Ahmed, Manan, Maira E. Álvarez, Sylvia A. Fernández, Alex Gil, Merisa Martinez, Moacir P. de Sá Pereira, Linda Rodriguez, and Roopika Risam. n.d. "Torn Apart/Separados." https://xpmethod.columbia.edu/torn-apart/credits.html.

Anthias, Penelope. 2019. "Ambivalent Cartographies: Exploring the Legacies of Indigenous Land Titling through Participatory Mapping." *Critique of Anthropology* 39 (2): 222–42.

Bakhtin, Mikhail. 1981. *The Dialogic Imagination*. Austin: University of Texas Press.

Barthes, Roland. 1989. "The Reality Effect." In *The Rustle of Language*, translated by Richard Howard, 141–48. Berkeley: University of California.

Benoit, Ken, and Akitaka Matsuo. 2020. "Package 'spacyr.'" https://cran.r-project.org/package=spacyr.

Blyn, Robin. 2016. "Belonging to the Network: Neoliberalism and Postmodernism in *Tropic of Orange*." *MFS: Modern Fiction Studies* 62 (2): 191–216.

Bodenhamer, D. J. 2007. "Creating a Landscape of Memory: The Potential of Humanities GIS." *International Journal of Humanities and Arts Computing* 1 (2): 97–110.

Bodenhamer, David J., John Corrigan, and Trevor M. Harris. 2010. *The Spatial Humanities: GIS and the Future of Humanities Scholarship*. Bloomington: Indiana University Press.

Broom, Sarah M. 2019. *The Yellow House: A Memoir*. New York: Grove.

Budgen, Frank. 1960. *James Joyce and the Making of* Ulysses. Bloomington: Indiana University Press.

Carvalhaes, T., V. Rinaldi, Z. Goh, S. Azad, J. Uribe, A. Chester, and M. Ghandehari. 2021. "Integrating Spatial and Ethnographic Methods for Resilience Research: A Thick Mapping Approach for Hurricane Maria in Puerto Rico." Available at SSRN 3863657.

Drucker, Johanna. 2011. "Humanities Approaches to Graphical Display." *Digital Humanities Quarterly* 5 (1). https://ejatlas.org/.

Furlan, Cecilia, 2019. "Unfolding Wasteland: A Thick Mapping Approach to the Transformation of Charleroi's Industrial Landscape." In *Mapping Landscapes in Transformation*, edited by T. Coomans, B. Cattoor, and K. De Jonge, 131–48. Leuven: Leuven University Press.

Goldie, Matthew Boyd. 2010. *The Idea of the Antipodes: Place, People, and Voices*. Routledge Research in Postcolonial Literatures 26. New York: Routledge. http://search.ebscohost.com/login.aspx?direct=true&scope=site&db=nlebk&db=nlabk&AN=302929.

Gregory, Ian N., and Alistair Geddes. 2014. *Toward Spatial Humanities: Historical GIS and Spatial History*. Bloomington: Indiana University Press.

Harvey, David. 1996. *Justice, Nature, and the Geography of Difference*. Malden: Blackwell.

Harley, J. B. 2001. *The New Nature of Maps: Essays in the History of Cartography*. Baltimore: Johns Hopkins University Press.

Hoffman, Jeremy, Vivek Shandas, and Nicholas Pendleton. 2020. "The Effects of Historical Housing Policies on Resident Exposure to Intra-Urban Heat: A Study of 108 US Urban Areas." *Climate* 8 (1). https://doi.org/10.3390/cli8010012.

Kinniburgh, Mary Catherine. 2018. "Spatial Reading: Digital Literary Maps of the Icelandic Outlaw Sagas." *Digital Medievalist* 11 (1): 1. https://doi.org/10.16995/dm.66.

Kolodny, Annette. 1975. *The Lay of the Land: Metaphor as Experience and History in American Life and Letters*. Chapel Hill: University of North Carolina Press.

Kueffer, Christoph, Philippe Forêt, Marcus Hall, and Caroline Wiedmer. 2018. "Applying the Environmental Humanities." *Gaia (Heidelberg, Germany)* 27 (2): 254–56. https://doi.org/10.14512/gaia.27.2.16.

Lefebvre, Henri. 1991 [1974]. *The Production of Space*. Cambridge: Blackwell.

Lethbridge, Emily, and Steven Hartman. 2016. "Inscribing Environmental Memory in the Icelandic Sagas and the Icelandic Saga Map." *PMLA* 131 (2): 381–91.

Lethbridge, Emily, Hjördís Erna Sigurðardóttir, Gísli Pálsson, Zachary Melton, Trausti Dagsson, and Logi Ragnarsson. n.d. "Icelandic Saga Map." http://sagamap.hi.is/is/.

Lin, Anastasia. 2018. "Mapping Multi-ethnic Texts in the Literary Classroom: GIS and Karen Tei Yamashita's *Tropic of Orange*." In *Teaching Space, Place, and Literature*, edited by Robert T. Tally, Jr., 40–48. New York: Routledge.

Mapping Inequality. n.d. https://dsl.richmond.edu/panorama/redlining/#loc=5/39.1/-94.58.

Massey, Doreen. 2005. *For Space*. London: Sage.

Moretti, Franco. 1998. *Atlas of the European Novel*. London: Verso.

Negri, Antonio. 2018. *From the Factory to the Metropolis*. Translated by Ed Emery. Cambridge: Polity.

Newkirk II, Van R. 2017. "The Poisoned Generation." *The Atlantic*, May 21, 2017. www.theatlantic.com/politics/archive/2017/05/the-poisoned-generation/527229/.

Ortega, Alejandra. 2020. "Calculating the Costs: Effects of Land Consumption in Margaret Atwood's MaddAddam Trilogy." *ISLE*, October 14. doi.org/10.1093/isle/isaa154.

Pellow, David Naguib. 2017. *What is Critical Environmental Justice?* London: Polity.

Ploomer, Brad, and Nadja Popovich. 2020. "How Decades of Racist Housing Policy Left Neighborhoods Sweltering." *New York Times*, August 24, 2020. www.nytimes.com/interactive/2020/08/24/climate/racism-redlining-cities-global-warming.html.

Presner, Todd, David Shepherd, and Yoh Kawano. 2014. *Hypercities: Thick Mapping in the Digital Humanities*. Harvard University Press. https://escholarship.org/uc/item/3mh5t455.

Queering the Map. n.d. www.queeringthemap.com/.

Ramsby, Kenton. 2020. "Lost in the City." https://uta-arcgis.maps.arcgis.com/apps/View/index.html?appid=b24f6dbdefb54753927e502513141da6.

Sarkowsky, Katja. 2020. "Cartographies of the Self: Indigenous Territoriality and Literary Sovereignty in Contemporary Native American Life Writing." *Journal of Transnational American Studies* 11 (1): 103–25.

Schindling, Jim, and Trevor M. Harris. 2018. "Deepening Historical GIS: An Integrated Database Solution for Linking People, Place and Events through Unstructured Text." *International Journal of Humanities & Arts Computing: A Journal of Digital Humanities* 12 (2): 120–37. https://doi.org/10.3366/ijhac.2018.0218.

Schöch, Christof. 2013. "Big? Smart? Clean? Messy? Data in the Humanities." *Journal of Digital Humanities*. Accessed April 6, 2021. http://journalofdigitalhumanities.org/2-3/big-smart-clean-messy-data-in-the-humanities/.

Sexton, Melissa. 2017. "*Tropic of Orange*, Los Angeles, and the Anthropocene Imagination." *Concentric* 43 (1): 13–32. doi:10.6240/concentric.lit.2017.43.1.02.

Sinyangwe, Samuel, DeRay McKesson, and Johnetta Elzie. n.d. "Mapping Police Violence." https://mappingpoliceviolence.org/.

Smith, Mona. n.d. "Bdote Memory Map." https://bdotememorymap.org/.
Soja, Edward. 1989. *Postmodern Geographies.* London: Verso.
Tally, Robert T. 2013. *Spatiality*. New York: Routledge.
———. 2016. *Literary Cartographies: Spatiality, Representation, and Narrative*. Geocriticism and Spatial Literary Studies. New York: Palgrave Macmillan.
Travis, C., F. Ludlow, A. Matthews, K. Lougheed, K. Rankin, B. Allaire, R. Legg, P. Hayes, R. Breen, J. Nicholls, and L. Towns. 2020. "Inventing the Grand Banks: A Deep Chart." *Geo* 7 (1).
Vollmann, William T. 2009. *Imperial.* New York: Viking.
Wald, Sarah D., David J. Vazquez, Prescilla Solis Ybarra, and Sara Jaquette Ray, eds. 2019. *Latinx Environmentalisms: Place, Justice, and the Decolonial.* Philadelphia: Temple University Press.
Wilkens, Matthew, and Guangchen Ruan. "Geographic Locations in English-Language Literature, 1701–2011 (1.0) [Dataset]." HathiTrust Research Center. https://doi.org/10.13012/2K5C-RF13.
Winlow, Heather. 2009. *Mapping, Race and Ethnicity*. Elsevier Ltd. https://doi.org/10.1016/B978-008044910-4.00048-1.
Woods, 1998. *Development Arrested: The Blues and Plantation Power in the Mississippi Delta.* New York: Verso.
Wright, R. 1938. *Uncle Tom's Children*. New York: Harper & Brothers.
———. 1940. *Native Son*. New York: Harper and Brothers.
———. 1945. *Black Boy (American Hunger)*. New York: Perennial.
———. 1962 [2015]. "Introduction." In *Black Metropolis: A Study of Negro Life in a Northern City*, edited by St. Claire Drake and Horace R. Clayton. Chicago: University of Chicago.
Yamashita, Karen Tei. 1997. *Tropic of Orange*. Minneapolis: Coffee House Press.

26

ONE MAP CLOSER TO THE END OF THE WORLD (AS WE KNOW IT)

Thinking Digital Cartographic Humanities with the Anthropocene

Laura Lo Presti

Introduction

In a recent work concerning the "emergent ecologies" of the Anthropocene (Kirsley 2015), Bill McKibben (2010, 2) affirms, "The world hasn't ended, but the world as we know it has – even if we don't quite know it yet." With the end of the Holocene, the search for a new imaginary and grammar capable of explicating the unhomely transformations of the planet has become urgent among critical thinkers in several disciplines. For the title of his 2010 book, McKibben replaced the word *Earth* with *Eaarth*, suggesting we attuning ourselves to emergent and radical planetary changes with an overtly pessimistic, even alarmist, stance. For his book's cover image, the Earth is visually represented by the famous 1972 Apollo 17 photograph *22727* – popularly known as the *Blue Marble* or *Blue Planet*. But on the cover of *Eaarth*, the photo is cut in half to reveal an angry and red planet underneath, corroded by high temperatures and disasters.[1] Reflecting on the messianic and apocalyptic impulses of exhaustion, regeneration, finitude, and transformation induced by the first wave of scientific works on anthropogenic climate change, geoscientists and human geographers have also paid increasing attention to the challenge of deconstructing and reconstructing spatial allegories to describe this new climactic epoch. Neologisms have included *Anthropo-scene*, *Anthropobscene*, *Plantationocene*, *Capitalocene*, *Misanthropocene*, *Chthulucene*, *Plasticine*, *Necrocene*, and so on. More interestingly, as the geohumanities grow, original collaborations with artists, poets and writers are strengthening the field, with many geographers not missing the opportunities it allows to exhibit their own creative sides (Berry and Keane 2019; Engelmann 2020; Mateless 2016; Magrane 2020).

During the past 20 years, there has been explosive growth in humanistic and artistic research into environmental issues. Ecocritical perspectives offering a wide range of both dystopian and utopian scenarios have found an accommodating place in literary studies (e.g. Opperman and Iovino 2017). Commencing with the Land Art movement of the late 1960s, care for and attention to the environment have intensely manifested in contemporary art (e.g. Davis and Turpin

 DOI: 10.4324/9781003082798-32

2015). Toby Miller speaks about "the two humanities . . . literature, history, and philosophy on one side and communication and media studies on the other" (2012, 2). But despite the presence of hybrid socio-humanistic fields such as geohumanities, and more specifically, cartographic humanities, these perspectives are still far from being widely acknowledged in environmental humanities scholarship.

In contrast, the digital humanities have integrated the use of creative digital maps into text-oriented studies such as history and literature and subsequently cultivated a growing interest in spatial analysis and cartography as heuristic and investigative tools for these disciplines. Adopting a cultural cartography perspective and a humanist position, this chapter demonstrates other ways through which mapping and maps can assemble, elicit, and embody a plethora of discourses, actions, and feelings about the Anthropocene. It does so by exploring the wider dissemination of the cartographic imaginations of the Anthropocene across a variety of media to consider how broad intersections between the visuality, materiality, and movement of images give rise to different configurations of anthropocentric and post-anthropocentric maps.

Beyond the explicit reference to the humanities – maps, atlases, and globes are tools that have been widely employed to archive, convey, and produce ecological knowledge for public, scientific, mass media, and governmental communications. As the cover image of McKibben's *Eaarth* suggests, the globe serves as an image of both the Anthropocene and post-Anthropocene scenarios. It is an emotive rather than informational icon of the interconnected and potentially controllable planetary dimensions of environmental change (Edwards 2010). While the globe, due to its spherical dimension, can be grasped in halves by the human eye, the atlas, conceived through a progression of assembled thematic maps and pages, has been used to exhibit seductively ecological issues (Struck 2014). Images framed by globes and atlases both work to transform climate change into an epistemic object of research and a vehicle of imagination. In addition, individual charts, planispheres, and maps supplement textual information on issues of global warming, toxic landscapes, and climate change, as visualisations provided by the United Nations' Intergovernmental Panel on Climate Change (IPCC) periodically show.

These heterogeneous media ecologies and mapping and cartographic visuals have significantly impacted the creative practices of environmental thought. As such, the cartographic imagination has undertaken both tangible and metaphorical explorations and create pessimistic or hopeful narrations on the urgency for driving change to boost new ecological and sustainable futures. This chapter draws on the richness of such images and practices, to offer a repertoire of cartographic illustrations of the Anthropocene to discuss the role of the cartographic humanities within the horizons of environmental thought. By searching for emerging theoretical dispositions and projects that make sense of the Anthropocene's catastrophic and slow transformations through the experience of maps and map-like presences, this chapter revolves around the following questions:

- Can we speak of digital cartographic humanities?
- If so, what does it mean for (digital) cartographic humanities to address the concept of the Anthropocene?
- How do digital and nondigital maps convey different senses of ecological transformation?

To unravel these threads of analysis, this chapter is structured as follows. The next section discusses the legacy and development of the cartographic humanities and the great ambiguity through which the advent of the digital has been welcomed in the field. It then considers the visuality, materiality, and movement of images from three vantage points through which maps can be explored: "fast-moving," "slow," or through the "exhausted" imaginations of the Anthropocene.

Subsequent sections highlight these different characteristics of maps and, consequently, the wide spectrum of rhythms imbued in mapping (at) the end of the world as we know it.

(Digital) Cartographic Humanities: Visual, Material, Moving

Since the 1980s, the conception of cartography as a form of vertical power geometry and abstract machine of territorial control and order has dominated debates in political geography and digital geographies (Harley 2001; Crampton 2003; Wilson 2017). Such perspectives often run the risk of overlooking the creative and even progressive possibilities by which cartographic imaginings can be mobilised through humanistic lenses. Referring to cultural cartography as the imprint left by the cultural turn on the field of map studies, Denis Cosgrove fairly assigns a positive place for the map in the development of a cultural theory of space, one where "new concepts of cartography and new mapping practices are generating an active and intensely practical engagement with everyday cultural life" (2008, 26). Within the fabrics and encrustations of a more profane, modest, and everyday ecology, created by impromptu encounters with a variety of cartographic imaginings (embedded in smartphones, photographs, paintings, cinematic objects, panels, and logos), the map can no longer be read as the archetype of the Western episteme and its ordering principle of space (Farinelli 1998). Rather, it breaks down into a blinding plurality. In recent decades and in line with Cosgrove's expectations, the figure of the map, as Tania Rossetto recognises, "has increasingly travelled across the humanities" (2021, 1). These travels have been imbued with a sensitivity that combines the long-standing critique of maps as political, social, and cultural constructions with new perspectives gathered from non-representational and visually oriented investigations. In restoring the richness and plurality rather than the limitedness of cartographic ontology, maps have been rediscovered as "images among other images, visual objects among other visual objects and things among other things" (Rossetto 2019, 7). Cultural, humanistic, and social perspectives on cartography can be regarded as synonyms to the extent that

> [t]he cultural context of a map might be compared to a pattern of concentric circles surrounding the map. We can move from the inner circle of map making to the remote circles of economic, social, political, intellectual and artistic context.
>
> *(Jacob 1996, 193)*

In literary studies, visual anthropology, material culture, the history of science, art history, and visual culture, the cartographic object has rapidly begun serving heterogeneous subjects and is now studied through "concentric" readings. This offers humanist scholars and art practitioners generally unfamiliar with geographical knowledge the chance to experiment with synoptic information, spatial visions, material narratives, and counter-narratives. Through maps and mapping practices, artists have developed a geo-aesthetic filled with emotion, trauma, and delight (Harmon 2009); several animated and interactive geovisualisations have fertilised academic fields and activist organisations as a means to foster critical awareness of the political, social, and economic issues we are presently facing (e.g. Kollektiv Organgotango 2018). In the language of deep mapping, cartographic toolboxes have increasingly facilitated the enactment and narrative of places by encompassing alternative explorations of natural environments and disclosing new ways of storytelling that even include non-cartographic uses of maps. In environmental aesthetics, for instance, poetic and political explorations of space have been conducted by walking, thereby reconfiguring the map as more than a geometrical and abstract technology of calculation and spatialisation (Careri 2006; O' Rourke 2013).

Given the tensions within which both critical theory and the humanities have addressed the trope of the map, especially notable in the fractures between normative, conventional cartographies and alternative mappings, the arrival of the digital into the terrain of humanities has been greeted with great ambiguity. Like Janus, digital mapping has two faces, bringing both techno-optimistic and techno-pessimistic positions to the fore. On the one hand, environmental artists and humanist scholars have often perceived "natural" space as an uncanny, disorienting, and sensory ecology whose experience can be more authentically represented through a genuine, technologically unmediated, and multi-sensual encounter. In the search for an intimate connection with the natural landscape, teeming with non-human living presences, any technological means, like the map, can be thus impugned as a noise – an intrusive object that is an obstacle to the artist's claim for contingency and immediacy. In this sense, the mediation of a digital screen, the quintessence of artificiality, has been greeted by humanist scholars with some concern. On the other hand, as Finn Arne Jørgensen recognises "this idea of nature is becoming very hard to separate from the digital tools and media we use to observe, interpret, and manage it" (2014, 109). Recent advancements in visual and media studies have allowed art practitioners and critical scholars to appreciate the aesthetics, materiality, decay, waste – let's say the organicity – of these same digital artefacts. As Maxwell and Miller (2012, 165) evocatively put it, "media technologies generate meaning, but also detritus and disease. Their industrial life cycles extend far-flung injuries into natural and bio-physical environments."

The digital turn has heavily impacted and transformed the academic field of cartography, situating geovisualisation as an appealing tool for humanists, especially historians and literary scholars. According to its technicians, a GIS guarantees a much more effective spatial analysis than traditional cartography because a GIS is capable of generating as much information as was formerly required by reading several maps (Schuurman 2004). In this sense, the GIS database can be applied to include attribute information from a variety of different maps; it can also build multiple and contrasting representations of the same phenomena. Furthermore, there is no limit to the number and types of data that can be collated in a GIS once the data is assigned to its appropriate class. Many other techniques, as recently listed by Charles Travis, have led to renewed attention to cartographic tools in what he refers to as the Digital Anthropocene:

> Influenced by narrative, storytelling, cinematic, gaming, and network analysis techniques, these digital and environmental humanities practices represent the fluidity of human-environmental symbiosis captured by the concept of the Anthropocene, in contrast to the static snapshots of human-environmental binaries portrayed within the frame of the Holocene.
>
> *(Travis 2018, 173–74)*

While the digitalisation of the everyday is certainly occurring at a sustained pace, we have now entered a new phase in which the digital and analogue spheres of life cannot be so easily disentangled. Instead, they can be experienced through a hybrid approach that is alternatively dialectic and collaborative. From a phenomenological perspective, analogue and digital technologies are, in fact, equivalent: both influence our relationship with the environment. Each technology becomes a means of the production of reality and the attribution of its meaning. Digital media, visual theorist Hans Belting has further argued, "change our perception – as do all the other technical media before them – yet this perception still remains linked to the body" (2011, 35). Likewise, traditional and digital cartographies share embodied visions and coexist in many ambiences, giving rise to a particular coalescence of artefacts (maps) and digital objects (interfaces), even though they are produced with different materials. Jussi Parikka, an exponent of contemporary media archaeology, acknowledges that, although new forms of media have been slowly changing our habits, the "old" media has never left us. Continually repaired, it re-emerges unexpectedly to find new uses, contexts, and adaptations (Parikka 2012, 3).

In summation, whether digital or nondigital, "maps take a wide variety of material forms and thus fall within the remit of both the cultural history of representation and of things" (Cosgrove 2008, 9). Cosgrove's observation on map studies is fundamental, as it echoes the representational and non-representational shift that cultural geography has experienced in regards to its study of images. Rose and Tolia-Kelly (2012) made clear a decade ago that visuality and materiality are co-constitutive elements of both digital and nondigital images and require cognitive, semiotic, and multisensory modes of inquiry. The co-constitutive presence of the visual and the material, the act of seeing and sensing "images as things" and "things as images," can be intuitively rendered through what has been defined as the practice of "seensing" (Lo Presti 2018). This wordplay is useful for underlining the conceptual and experiential modes through which the perceptions of images such as maps occur. Through "seensing," the aesthetic experience of the Cartographic Anthropocene, can be experienced in all its intellectual, emotional, attentive, fleeting, symbolic, and material nuances.

Movement, along with the visual and the material, is conceived in terms of speed, change, and temporality, but also as processes of circulation and dissemination. Movement, therefore, is the last piece that can be added to the mosaic of the renewed humanistic sensitivity toward maps, or what we might now call the (digital) cartographic humanities. In fact, since the experience and navigation of natural environments have become suffused with digital devices and information, we must try to understand whether the advent of the digital has really made the movement that traditional maps tried to represent obsolete for the practice of environmental thought? In light of this question, we must consider that (1) a drawn or a printed map can be digitally converted or remediated with ease, (2) many physical experiences can be also lived digitally, and (3) the digital is a corrosive and corroded technology, polluting the planet as much as its analogue predecessor. In fact, in the examples of my forthcoming discussion, seeds of environmental rumination multiply over an intense web of cartographic materiality that often transcend the digital sphere or, at best, collaborates with it.

Such eco-graphic transformations certainly concern maps that represent change through innovative digital designs in animation and moving images but also involve maps that are physically changed by the environment that nurtures and hosts them. We might encounter maps made of, or modified by, organic matter like plants, insects, and bacteria or inorganic materials like plastic. Conceived as a geomorphic agent in the Anthropocene, the map can also embody the circadian rhythms of ecological change rather than merely "englobing" them over its surface. In this sense, through a processual approach that focuses on geological and geographical rhythms, mapping acts as a near or remote mutable sensor of environmental action and thought.

Considering, especially, the entanglement between the visuality, materiality, and movement of mapping in the context of the Digital Anthropocene, we might refer to "fast-moving mapping" as the attempt to visually solicit, through dynamic maps, ideas of irremediable change and, consequently, "an increasing sense of urgency to report 'facts' as fast as possible" (Mah 2017, 122). This category falls within the framework of what art historian Steven Shaviro (2015) calls "accelerationist aesthetics." In cartographic theory, Monmonier (2018) uses the label fast maps to mean online maps resulting from the ability to create and disseminate them infinitely more rapidly than static paper maps; however, the concern of the Anthropocene's dynamic visual storytelling maps is more intuitively to show, at a glance, the spatial distribution of a given phenomenon over time or changes that occurred in an area after the introduction of that phenomenon. On the other hand, maps produced in environmental art and humanities can be perceived as traces of meditating, deep-time, stratigraphic, and curious exploratory activities and should be considered as an alternative mode of mapping the Anthropocene. This slow mapping also denotes cartographic presences made of organic matter that grow slowly and follow the cadences of the earth. In this sense, such maps can be addressed through an object-oriented ontology that brings, through speculative thinking, the life of objects to the fore (Rossetto 2019).

This philosophical stance rethinks map realities from a decentralised perspective by recognising the presence of organic movements in unliving things that are even knowable in their autonomy from the subject. Slow maps engage alternatively with environmental issues that are represented by fast-moving mapping in alarmist tones, drawing our attention instead to degrowth practices and a vision of sustainable futures. Finally, as the most extreme outcome of the two, there are also "exhausted maps," which can invigorate, physically or representationally, ideas and imagination of decay, collapse, and the finitude of the world *as we know it*.

Mapping Closer to the End of the World

Anthropocène, a short video animation released in June 2018 by artist Martin Hardouin Duparc and geographer Philippe Rivière, depicts a strange atmosphere made up of everyday human and non-human presences that are ultimately revealed to serve an allegorical function.[2] Using the stop-motion technique, a pair of scissors representing physical science gives shape to a tetrahedral papercraft globe that turns around very rapidly until a cat grabs and eats it (Figure 26.1). As the final credits explain, the human fingers through which the globe is put in motion represent the *Cosmos*, a cohesive force capable of giving life to the earth, while the pet cat capturing the planet (a planet now bereft of any natural connotations as it is turned into the coherent, controllable, and manageable world through scientific, cartographic rendition) stands for the rapaciousness and avidity of the human race.

Riddled with deep irony, the animation nicely unfolds the textual meaning of the Anthropocene as "a geo-historical period, in which humans are said to have become the biggest threat to life on earth" (Zylinska 2014, 10). When attempting to make the public sphere aware of the dramatic changes that the planet faces – and blaming human beings for such degradation – scientists, artists, and writers are confronted with a problem of vision and imagination that

Figure 26.1 Video stills from *Anthropocène*, 2018, animation. Authors: Martin Hardouin Duparc, Philippe Rivière. Creative Commons License.

Source: https://visionscarto.net/anthropocene

mainly relates to the scale, intensity, and duration through which such phenomena occur. Geological temporalities do not coincide well with the human sense of time and, on a psychological level, only the pressure exerted by the escalation of dangerous events can create urgency for action among audiences (including governments). This asynchronicity between the "long dyings" (Nixon 2011, 2) and calls for immediate action results in – as novelist Kim Stanley Robinson (2017) describes – a "state of indecisive agitation." Charlotte, a fictional character in Robinson's novel *New York 2140*, calls the period between 2005 and 2060 as the Dithering – a condition of underlying procrastination that largely informs climate change policies. In *Slow Violence*, Nixon (2011, 2) makes a similar point, suggesting that climate change "and a host of other slowly unfolding environmental catastrophes present formidable representational obstacles that can hinder our efforts to mobilize and act decisively."

Many advancements in digital technologies, especially the possibility of experiencing mapping as a dynamic language that incorporates or is incorporated by other media like video, photographs, and audio have situated the cartographic imagination as a highly visible act of representation and anticipation of the conundrums of the Anthropocene. Animated maps, including small multiple maps, flow maps, long-form infographics, and dynamic slideshows, are often used as an intriguing opportunity to show the long-term spatial effects of climate change at an accelerated speed (Roth 2020). *Climate Time Machine*, a series of visualisations released by NASA's Global Climate Change website, is a compelling example (Figure 26.2). Divided into four topics (sea ice, sea level, carbon dioxide, global temperature), these animations provide a linear narrative of the main environmental changes and impacts, compressing long-term and

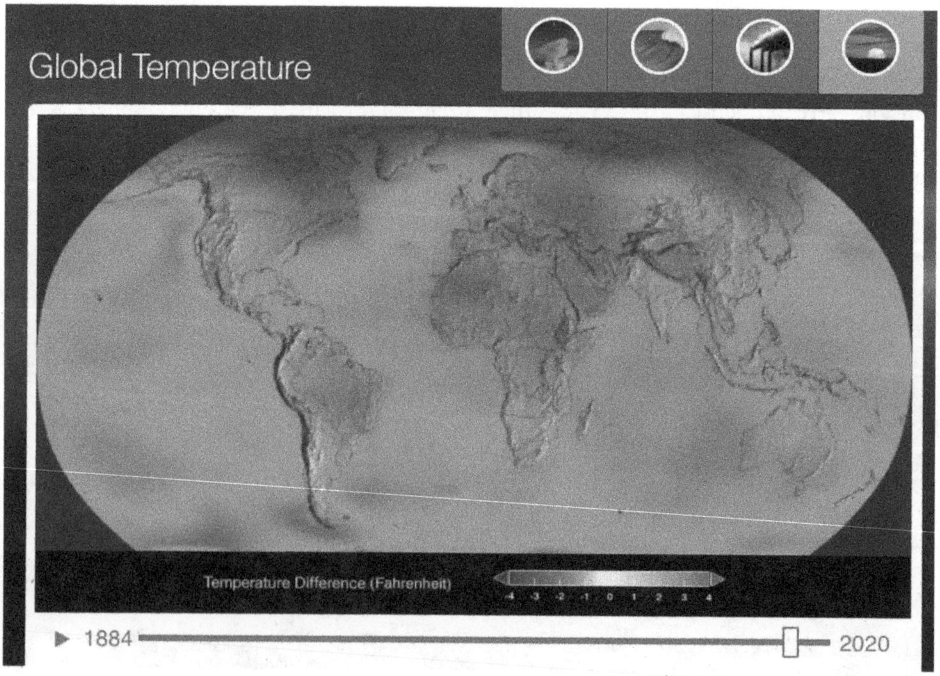

Figure 26.2 An animated map from the *Climate Time Machine* (https://climate.nasa.gov/interactives/climate-time-machine). As an example of fast-moving mapping, it shows changing global surface temperatures since 1884. Data source: NASA/GISS. Credit: NASA Scientific Visualization Studio. Image in public domain.

future activities into an accelerated cartography of anticipation. Many other examples are on offer; Shipmap, created by the data visualisation company Kiln based on a dataset provided by University College London's Energy Institute, was one of the first projects to gain attention for its 2012 animated and interactive visualisation of cargo shipping activities around the globe. Guided by a voiceover, users can digitally navigate a bathymetric map and gain a sense of the carbon dioxide emitted and maximum freight carried by vessels.[3]

While fast mapping might be seen as an easy strategy to signal both the drivers and effects of climate change and the increasing perturbation of natural rhythms caused by human-technological agencies, many scholars are aware that a different imagery should be cultivated to accommodate the perception of non-human movements and temporalities. In fact, Jørgensen (2014, 98) recognises that speed and slowness are relational: "[t]he 'slow' is attributed by us, accustomed to higher speeds." As a consequence, a set of aesthetic postures that oppose the time scale of the now digitally induced "great acceleration" (Steffen et al. 2015) has matured in the last decades. Walking often becomes the first step to grasping such natural changes, precisely because it suggests an action always in progress, slow and cultured in its making, of which the map may constitute a trace or an enduring mark.

For instance, in the case of the Ghost River project that set out on the trail of the "ghost" Saint-Pierre River in Montreal, Tricia Toso, Kassandra Spooner-Lockyer, and Kregg Hetherington (2020) initially relied on archival maps, the traces of an absent presence, to produce "unruly maps . . . that would change (and often tear, or simply blow away) as we walked" (2020, 1). As they nicely put it,

> [t]hrough the winter of 2017–18, we mapped the divergent lines drawn by a number of nineteenth and twentieth-century cartographers onto present-day street maps and began to speculate about where the river might have flowed, as well as to construct a chronology of its canalization and burial. Often, the river disappeared from maps, buried sometimes in the gap between renderings, but occasionally it reappeared or headed off in a different direction, even changing names.
>
> *(2020, 1)*

Figure 26.3 *A screenshot from the Ghost River project created by the Montreal Waterways research group at Concordia University's Ethnography Lab.* Image courtesy of Tricia Toso. As an example of slow mapping, including both digital and nondigital methodologies, the whole project can be followed at this link: https://ethnographylabconcordia.ca/ghostriver.

In the Ghost River project, mapping as a process of spatio-temporal discovery and the map as the ultimate tangible output of such exploration are intensely appreciated through geo-aesthetic ambulatory practices. Interestingly, walking-generated maps often address the legacy of the Anthropocene differently, "not just as a time of rumbling disaster but as a time littered with the disasters of the past" (Toso, Spooner-Lockyer, and Hetherington 2020, 2). Through slow movements and promenades, artists and academics attempt to craft alternative digital or paper (but digitally remediated) cartographies that are more sensitive to the fleeting and slippery experience of landscape mutation and adaptation (Figure 26.3). One way to challenge Euclidian conceptions of cartography has been especially inspired by the process of deep mapping. Drawing the concept from the famous book *PrairyErth: A Deep Map* by author William Least Heat-Moon (1991), Mike Pearson and Michael Shanks describe the deep map as an attempt to

> [r]ecord and represent the grain and patina of place through juxtapositions and interpenetrations of the historical and the contemporary, the political and the poetic, the discursive and the sensual; the conflation of oral testimony, anthology, memoir, biography, natural history and everything you might ever want to say about a place.
>
> *(2001, 64–65)*

The slow process of deep mapping should not be necessarily conceived in representational terms but grasped in its non-human and material performative nuances. Several maps created in artistic contexts are "made" slow because of the material used to create them. For instance, on the Beijing Expo, a green world map was co-created by visitors to the 2019 International Horticultural Exhibition. On that occasion, the continents, first represented by stones on barren ground, were gradually replaced by flowers and plants planted by tourists and visitors, which slowly gave life to the familiar shape of the planisphere. While the world map image was transformed into organic matter, the digital component of the UNESCO Garden's project ensured that the day-to-day mutation of the vegetal map was registered. Every day, a drone was sent to fly over the garden and take pictures of its changes. The process of repeat photography was used to reproduce a video animation of the growing green map.[4] In this example, it is interesting to notice how mapping is sensed through two different levels of speed: a natural map, artificially conceived by humans yet following the growth rhythms of plants, and a digital moving image of the natural map that accelerates the various phases through which the green map has been put into existence, thus making the whole experience perceptible and conceivable for a techno-human sensorium.

However, in critical understandings of the Anthropocene, the idea of growth, if considered from an economic point of view, is hardly associated with positive meaning or feelings. To challenge the ideology of economic growth, many scholars draw on the oppositional concept of degrowth, alluding to a subtractive idea of development and expansion. Degrowth posits a need for society's reorganisation through the possibility of living *with less* by reducing resources and decelerating energy consumption. In degrowth storytelling, the (digital) map still plays a crucial role, fostering new operations and imaginations of sustainable futures while denouncing the subtle processes of "slow violence." For instance, several degrowth organisations rely on interactive mapping as a network enabler because it favours connections and visualises the proliferation of such initiatives at both local and global scales. The map can also retain traces of the environmental violence inflicted on the territory. For instance, The Environmental Justice Atlas monitors the distribution of ecological conflicts in the world.[5] Finally, a map can represent a degrowth society of the future, like the one represented by Cedric Price Architects in the Duck-lands project (1993). It represents a proposal for the transformation of the Hamburg Docklands into wild wetlands through an imaginative application of economic degrowth principles. In this utopian vision, resilience and sufficiency become the guide for a frugal, non-capitalistic Anthropocene.[6] Overall, in slow mapping, the urgency of acceleration infused by fast-moving maps leaves spaces for more accommodating and modest tones, opening up practices of care and respect for nature, but perhaps sacrificing the urgent cry for action and the rapid search for timely solutions.

Mapping (at) the End of the World

Fast mapping implies that our planet is radically changing and elevates the entire human race to the role of destroyer of the Earth instead of distinguishing the different and varied impacts each human society has on the planet. In contrast, slow mapping adopts a much more optimistic tone and proposition by feeling, listening to, and taking care of the environment by attuning itself to the planet's extended geological rhythms and solicitations. In one way or another, growing fast or slow or making other things or ideas grow means, above all transformation, a change in status and, ultimately, *the end of the world as we know it.* From epistemological and ontological perspectives, Haraway is quite correct to suggest that the rationale of the Anthropocene is "the destruction of places and times of refuge for people and other critters" (2015a, 160). Economic growth cannot help but create its opposite – death. In turn, the mass extermination of human and non-human beings, ideas, and technologies charges Anthropocene discourses with "the threat of imminent doom" (Morton 2010, 123). This may result from catastrophic events that brings several forms of exhaustion to the fore (Figure 26.4); extinction can, however, follow much slower rhythms, sometimes even regenerative, to be observed in the processes of waste, decay and unbecoming (DeSilvey 2006; Crang 2010; Gandy 2013). On the one hand, the feared extinction of humans mirrors the finitude of humanism and its technologies. On the other, this doom illuminates the capacity of technologies to become part of the future ecological system – as residuals of an out-of-joint world: "products at the end of their lives, dumped, discarded, and being dismantled" (Crang 2010, 1086). Archaeologists, trained to be most sensitive to stories of doom, distinguish between the *artefact* (an object created out of human activity), the *ecofact* (a relic of a living organism), and the *manuport*, a non-human entity displaced from its original context (e.g. minerals, shells). How could artefacts, like maps, become ecofacts and manuports of the Anthropocene if not through the process of mouldering and degradation? In the absence of neat boundaries between the human and non-human, should an artefact be always accounted as an ecofact? Could an ecofact become an artefact? Such transformations, parsed in terms of "ecocritical materialism," stand

> behind the nodes of the ecological crisis – pollution, mass extinctions, poverty, enslavement of humans and animals, and many other forms of oppression – are tangles of natures and cultures that can be unraveled only by interpreting them as narratives about the way humans and their agentic partners intersect in the making of the world.
>
> *(Iovino and Oppermann 2014, 6)*

In the last section of this chapter, the visuality, materiality, and movement inherent in maps and cartographic objects are provided with agencies to frame narratives of exhaustion, decay, and extinction more vividly within the contexts of the Capitalocene and Plasticene debates. For example, in 2019, Cattle Decapitation, a death-grind music band from San Diego, California, released the album *Death Atlas*, which provocatively engages their audience with songs on global climate change issues and laments about wasted landscapes. Along with the album cover image featuring a kneeling Grim Reaper carrying a burning Earth on his back like the Atlas of Greek

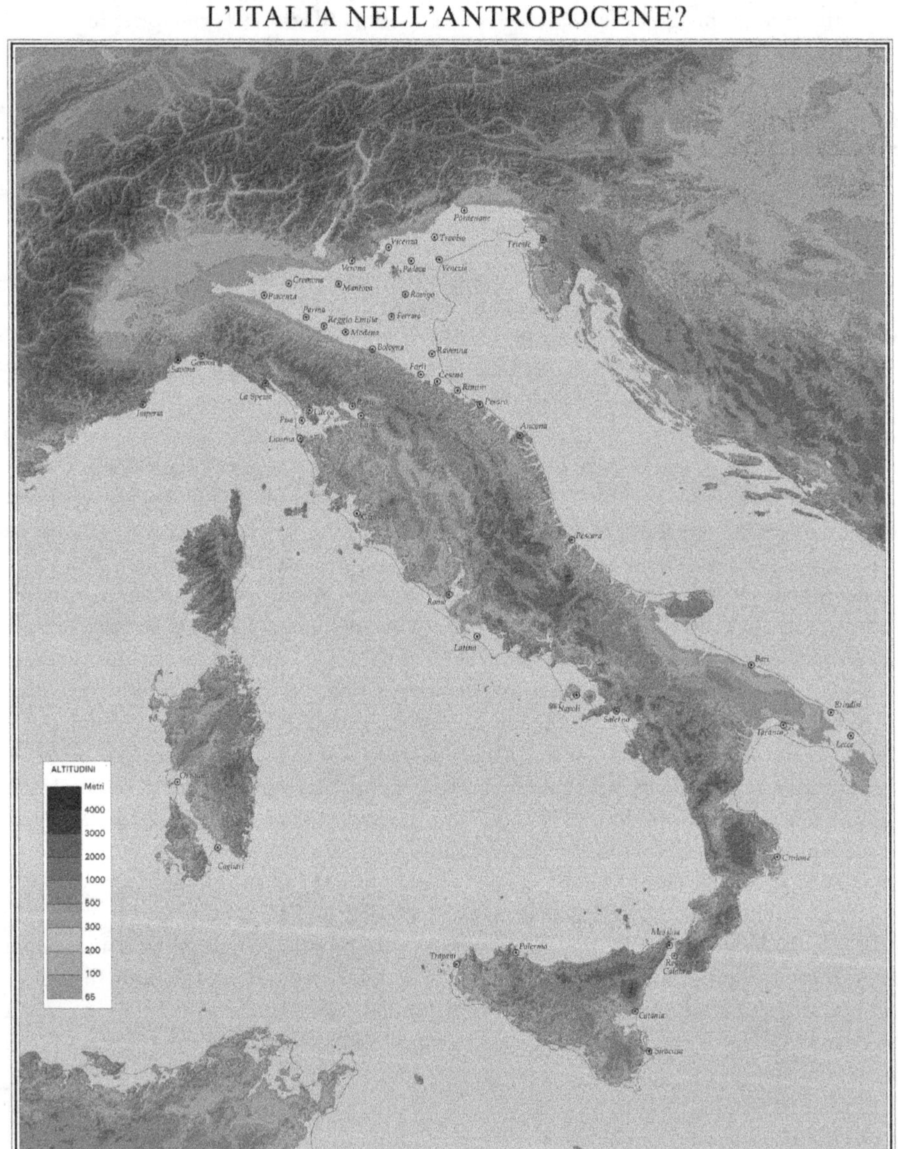

Figure 26.4 An example of exhaustion conveyed by a map predicting the effects of the Anthropocene in Italy is exhibited at the Museum of Geography, University of Padua. Credit: Museum of Geography. Data processing by Francesco Ferrarese. Image courtesy of the museum.

mythology, the band published the "Post-Anthropocene Map," a planisphere plotting the dystopic end of the world. Cattle Decapitation's map is an exhausted and failed imagination of the world; the sea covers the surface of many countries while masses of garbage float on ocean waves. The white polar polygon normally representing glaciers was replaced by an expanse of open ocean. This kind of dystopian imagination, as Squire (2012, 212) argues, "can have the effect of collapsing the political into the existential, enclosing humanity within 'thoughts' of inevitable doom, while rescinding our arrival in the present, thereby forestalling means to action." However, many critical thinkers often court the idea of collapse precisely for its underlying emancipatory politics. Referring to the impossibility of providing modern solutions to problems that can no longer be conceived through classic Western epistemology, new possibilities and clarifying spaces for action emerge by thinking of "the end of the world" (De la Cadena and Blaser 2018). Especially in the field of political aesthetics, there is a tendency to push thought to extreme ends to grasp the inherent contradiction of humanism and the Anthropocene itself: "In order to overcome globalized neoliberal capitalism, we need to drain it to the dregs, push it to its most extreme point, follow it into its furthest and strangest consequences" (Shaviro 2015, 2).

Cartography, conceived as the quintessence of modernity, would serve as an antagonist figure herein – an obstacle that must be overcome to envision a non-modern and non-Western imagery of the planet. However, the reconceptualisation of cartography in cultural geography and cognate disciplines is distanced from the map as a universalist trope of order and surveillance, shifting attention instead to mappings as processual and contingent space-making practices (Kitchin, Dodge, and Perkins 2009). The Westernism of maps can be challenged from different directions, not least by unearthing Indigenous mapping and non-Western traditions of cartography. For instance, Fujikane's *Mapping Abundance for a Planetary Future* (2021, 3–4) claims that "the vibrant cartographies of Indigenous and settler ally artists, scientists, writers, and activists" can transform "the exhausted cartographies of capital" and "restore more sustaining arrangements of life." Additionally, *Feral Atlas* (Tsing et al. 2020), an interactive online platform, allows users to drift across several "Detonator landscapes" – each a collage evoking four posthumous worlds created by "Invasion, Empire, Capital, and Acceleration," respectively. *Feral Atlas* constitutes one of the most compelling attempts to navigate the digital cartographies of the exhausted ecologies of the Anthropocene by processual and post-human approaches. The user is asked to choose a feral entity as an avatar before floating through the interlinked anthropogenic scenarios of toxic, colonialist, and vicious human activities. *Feral Atlas*' examples suggest that the discovery of post-anthropocentric scenarios passes through map contingencies and their vibrant materialities, corresponding with recent theories where "visuality as a becoming-with or being-with" is "opposed to surveying-from" (Haraway 2015b, 258). Escaping from a technological and calculative digital gaze, the Anthropocene "becoming-with" or "being-with" is especially notable in the process of decay, with the map as both a representational and an organic scheme. In everyday life as well as in art projects, maps – because of the material of which they are made – often emerge as residual and fragile connective tissues. Just like human skin, they are flexible and resistant but also vulnerable and perishable, marked by violence, holes, and wounds of different kinds. Symbolically, maps are finite representations of spatial phenomena; physically and temporally, their materiality suggests that they are destined to die. DeSilvey offers a description of a worn-out decaying US Forest Service map found in an abandoned house in the state of Montana:

> [T]he insects had intervened to assert the materiality of the map, and in doing so they offered their own oblique commentary on human intervention in regional ecologies. The forests in the physical territory depicted by the disfigured paper map suffered from decades of poor management and fire suppression, which made them vulnerable to the depredations of other organisms. Over the last few decades, an infestation of destructive bark beetles has killed many of the trees represented by the map's green patches. The destruction on the root cellar's map can be read as a metonym for the destruction of the surrounding forest.
>
> *(DeSilvey 2006, 329)*

In this example, the organic degradation of the map is activated by non-human actors (e.g. insects), and this materiality quickly takes on a symbolic meaning.[7] Acting as a surrogate of the territory, the disfigured US Forest Service map, re-sensed through a digital screen, becomes a palpable landscape on which to reflect on real ecological disasters. Jamie Lorimer, remembering an entomological survey to a graveyard in South London, embraced the narratological power associated with the decomposition of cartographic matter, stating that "we were there to count the beetles, to put decay on the map, and to help foment popular support for rot" (2016, 235). Finally, another interesting posthuman outcome of the post-Anthropocene's map emerges in the *naturecultures* of waste. As Haraway argues, "the effects of our species are literally written into the rocks," (2015b, 259) and proof of these artificial inscriptions are the many *plastiglomerates* found on Hawaii's shorelines. Proposed by geologist Patricia Corcoran, oceanographer Charles Moore, and artist Kelly Jazvac, this term indicates the presence of new stones made of molten plastic and organic materials, representing not only the most vivid effect of the Plasticene but also the future fossils of the post-Anthropocene. In this case, the proposed link between the plastiglomerate and the globe is an imaginative one. One of the plastiglomerates portrayed in the series evokes *apophenically* (the tendency to perceive meaningful connections between unrelated things) the melting and collapse of the globe, the best icon of the Anthropocene's legacy.[8] According to Bratton (2013), the most tangible effect of post-anthropocentric aesthetics is, in fact, the exercise of apophenia, the tendency to see familiar patterns in random natural images.

Conclusion

The spectre of a cartographic imagery of the Anthropocene, now further charmed by the potentials of digital cartographic projects, looks to have never ceased to haunt and fertilise academic and public opinion and imagination. Because "the issues of climatic change are too complex to be reduced to a single narrative" (Scranton 2015, 21), the growing salience of animated and multisensory mapping activities within the horizons of Anthropocene and post-Anthropocene imaginings is demonstrated in different lines of inquiry. All suggest one way or another that cartographic visuals, materials, and mobiles have the power to spur us to action, sending alternative messages of "impending catastrophe," resilience, or hope (Dobson 2007, 1). This speaks to the ability of cartography to convey the adaptable, mutable, and heterogeneous power of our spatial imaginations. In fact, when maps are mute, artists and geohumanist scholars attempt to fill them with different words and provide them with speech. When maps are perceived as abstract and inanimate, such scholars work to unearth their vibrant materiality and lives. And when maps refuse to move, motion is infused into them through digital injections of animation and interconnectivity. If the environmental humanities revolve around "the need to see how human stories emerge from and converge with the stories of the more-than-human beings around and within us" (Iovino, Cesaretti, and Past 2018, 3), the digital cartographic humanities deserve a special place in this new narratological effort. Being either human-centred representations or non-human objects, maps have a significant and hybrid capacity to heighten public environmental awareness. In the cacophony of presences and representations, maps may then appear differently, but they all work to build a collective imagery of the Anthropocene. In this respect, when Haraway (2015a, 160) makes a plea for endorsing the new tentacular and entangled vision of the Chthulucene, she admits that "[m]athematically, visually, and narratively, it matters which figures figure figures, which systems systematize systems." Likewise, mapping is a holistic language encompassing mathematical, visual, and narrative geo-graphs that can help us understand how societies collectively imagine the past, present, and alternative futures of the environments they inhabit. Cartographic imagination is, in fact, a beguiling entryway not just to understanding the past of the Anthropocene or to acting upon its present but also to fantasising about its future and inviting us to move beyond the limits of our current imagination. Such alternative cartographic imaginations, as Purdy (2015, 7) puts it, "also enables us to do things together politically: a new way of seeing the world can be a way of valuing it – a map of things worth saving, or of a future worth creating."

Notes

1 The book cover image of *Eaarth* can be viewed here: www.blackincbooks.com.au/books/eaarth.
2 *Anthropocene* (https://visionscarto.net/anthropocene).
3 Shipmap (www.shipmap.org).
4 UNESCO Garden Green World Map (https://news.cgtn.com/news/2019-09-25/UNESCO-Garden-at-Beijing-Expo-Creating-a-green-world-with-everyone-Khf64EL6DK/index.html).
5 Environmental Justice Atlas (https://ejatlas.org).
6 See Doucet, Isabelle. 2019. "Anticipating Fabulous Futures" (Overgrowth Series), *E-Flux* Journal (www.e-flux.com/architecture/overgrowth/284918/anticipating-fabulous-futures).
7 For an interpretation of this map, see Rossetto, Tania. 2019. *Object-Oriented Cartography: Maps as Things*. New York: Routledge.
8 The apophenic encounter with the plastigomerate globe can be appreciated here: www.kabk.nl/en/lectorates/design/plastiglomerate.

Sources

Belting, Hans. 2011. *An Anthropology of Images: Picture, Medium, Body*. Princeton: Princeton University Press.

Berry, Kaya, and Jondi Keane. 2019. *Creative Measures of the Anthropocene: Art, Mobilities, and Participatory Geographies*. Singapore: Palgrave Macmillan.

Bratton, Benjamin. 2013. "Some Race Effects on the Post-Anthropocene: On Accelerationist Geopolitical Aesthetics." *E-Flux Journal* 46.

Careri, Francesco. 2006. *Walkscapes: Camminare Come Pratica Estetica*. Turin: Einaudi.

Cosgrove, E. Denis. 2008. "Cultural Cartography: Maps and Mapping in Cultural Geography." *Annales de géographie* 660/661 (2): 159–78.

Crampton, W. Jeremy. 2003. *The Political Mapping of Cyberspace*. Chicago: University of Chicago Press.

Crang, Mike. 2010. "The Death of Great Ships: Photography, Politics, and Waste in the Global Imaginary." *Environment and Planning A* 42 (5): 1084–102.

Davis, Heather, and Etienne Turpin, eds. 2015. *Art in the Anthropocene*. London: Open Humanities Press.

De la Cadena, Marisol, and Mario Blaser, eds. 2018. *A World of Many Worlds*. Durham and London: Duke University Press.

DeSilvey, Caitlin. 2006. "Observed Decay: Telling Stories with Mutable Things." *Journal of Material Culture* 11 (3): 318–38.

Dobson, Andrew. 2007. *Green Political Thought*. New York: Routledge.

Doucet, Isabelle. 2019. "Anticipating Fabulous Futures" (Overgrowth Series), *E-Flux Journal*. www.e-flux.com/architecture/overgrowth/284918/anticipating-fabulous-futures/.

Edwards, Paul N. 2010. *A Vast Machine: Computer Models, Climate Data, and the Politics of Global Warming*. Cambridge, MA: The MIT Press.

Engelmann, Sasha. 2020. *Sensing Art in the Atmosphere: Elemental Lures and Aerosolar Practices*. 1st ed. London and New York: Routledge.

Farinelli, Franco. 1998. "Did Anaximander ever Say any Words? The Nature of Cartographical Reason." *Ethics, Place and Environment* 1 (2): 135–44.

Fujikane, Candace. 2021. *Mapping Abundance for a Planetary Future*. Durham, NC: Duke University Press.

Gandy, Mathew. 2013. "Marginalia: Aesthetics, Ecology, and Urban Wastelands." *Annals of the Association of American Geographers* 103 (6): 1301–16.

Haraway, Donna. 2015a. "Anthropocene, Capitalocene, Plantationocene, Chthulucene: Making Kin." *Environmental Humanities* 6: 159–65.

———. 2015b. "Anthropocene, Capitalocene, Chthulhocene. Donna Haraway in Conversation with Martha Kenney." In *Art in the Anthropocene*, edited by Heather Davis and Etienne Turpin, 255–69. London: Open Humanities Press.

Harley, J. Brian. 2001. *The New Nature of Maps: Essays in the History of Cartography*. Baltimore: The Johns Hopkins University Press.

Harmon, A. Kathrine. 2009. *The Map as Art: Contemporary Artists Explore Cartography*. Hudson, NY: Princeton Architectural Press.

Iovino, Serenella, Enrico Cesaretti, and Elena M. Past, eds. 2018. *Italy and the Environmental Humanities: Landscapes, Natures, Ecologies*. Charlottesville: The University of Virginia Press.

Iovino, Serenella, and Serpil Oppermann, eds. 2014. *Material Ecocriticism*. Bloomington, IN: Indiana University Press.

Jacob, Christian. 1996. "Towards a Cultural Theory of Cartography." *Imago Mundi: The International Journal for the History of Cartography* 48: 191–98.

Jørgensen, Finn Arne. 2014. "The Armchair Traveller's Guide to Digital Environmental Humanities." *Environmental Humanities* 4: 95–112.

Kirksey, Eben. 2015. *Emergent Ecologies*. Durham, NC: Duke University Press.

Kitchin, Rob, Martin Dodge, and Chris Perkins. 2009. *Rethinking Maps: New Frontiers in Cartographic Theory*. New York: Routledge.

Least Heat-Moon, William. 1991. *Prairyerth*. New York: Houghton.

Lo Presti, Laura. 2018. "Extroverting Cartography: 'Seensing' Maps and Data Through Art." *Journal of Research and Didactics in Geography (J-READING)* 7 (2): 119–34.

Lorimer, Jamie. 2016. "Rot." *Environmental Humanities* 8 (2): 235–39.

Magrane, Eric. 2020. "Climate Geopoetics (the Earth Is a Composted Poem)." *Dialogues in Human Geography* 11 (1): 8–22.

Mah, Alice. 2017. "Environmental Justice in the Age of Big Data: Challenging Toxic Blind Spots of Voice, Speed, and Expertise." *Environmental Sociology* 3 (2): 122–33.

Matless, David. 2016. "Climate Change Stories and the Anthro-poscenic." *Nature Climate Change* 6 (2): 118–19.

Maxwell, Richard, and Toby Miller. 2012. *Greening the Media*. Oxford: Oxford University Press.

McKibben, Bill. 2010. *Eaarth: Making Life on a Tough New Planet*. Melbourne: Penguin Books.

Miller, Toby. 2012. *Blow Up the Humanities*. Philadelphia: Temple University Press.

Monmonier, Mark. 2018. *How to Lie with Maps*. 3rd ed. Chicago, IL: University of Chicago Press.

Morton, Timothy. 2010. *The Ecological Thought*. Cambridge: Harvard University Press.

Nixon, Ron. 2011. *Slow Violence and the Environmentalism of the Poor*. Cambridge: Harvard University Press.

Orangotango Kollectiv, ed. 2018. *This is Not an Atlas: A Global Collection of Counter-Cartographies*. Bielefeld: Transcript Verlag.

O'Rourke, Karen. 2013. *Walking and Mapping: Artists as Cartographers*. Cambridge, MA: The MIT Press.

Opperman, Serpil, and Serenella Iovino. 2017. *Environmental Humanities: Voices from the Anthropocene*. Latham: Rowman & Littlefield.

Parikka, Jussi. 2012. *What Is Media Archaeology?* Cambridge, UK: Polity Press.

Pearson, Mike, and Michael Shanks. 2001. *Theatre/Archaeology*. New York: Routledge.

Price Architects, Charles. 1993. "Ducklands, Hamburg. Over havenfronten." *OASE* (35): 2–7. https://www.oasejournal.nl/en/Issues/35/DucklandsHamburg.

Purdy, Jedediah. 2015. *After Nature: A Politics for the Anthropocene*. Harvard: Harvard University Press.

Robinson, Kim Stanley. 2017. *New York 2140*. London: Orbit books.

Rose, Gillian, and Divya P. Tolia-Kelly, eds. 2012. *Visuality/Materiality: Images, Objects and Practices*. London: Ashgate.

Rossetto, Tania. 2019. *Object-Oriented Cartography: Maps as Things*. New York: Routledge.

———. 2021. "Not Just Navigation: Thinking About the Movements of Maps in the Mobility and Humanities Field." *The Cartographic Journal*. doi:10.1080/00087041.2020.1842144.

Roth Robert, E. 2020. "Cartographic Design as Visual Storytelling: Synthesis and Review of Map-Based Narratives, Genres, and Tropes." *The Cartographic Journal*. doi:10.1080/00087041.2019.1633103.

Schuurman, Nadine. 2004. *GIS: A Short Introduction*. Malden, MA: Blackwell Publishers.

Scranton, Roy. 2015. *Learning to Die in the Anthropocene*. San Francisco: City Light Books.

Shaviro, Steven. 2015. *No Speed Limit: Three Essays on Accelerationism*. Minneapolis, MN: University of Minnesota Press.

Squire, Louise. 2012. "Death and the Anthropocene." *The Oxford Literary Review* 34 (2): 211–28.

Steffen, Will, Wendy Broadgate, Lisa Deutsch, Owen Gaffney, and Cornelia Ludwig. 2015. "The Trajectory of the Anthropocene: The Great Acceleration." *The Anthropocene Review* 2 (1): 81–98.

Struck, Wolfgang. 2014. "Genesis, Retold: In Search of an Atlas of the Anthropocene." *Environmental Humanities* 5: 217–32.

Toso, Tricia, Kassandra Spooner-Lockyer, and Kregg Hetherington. 2020. "Walking with a Ghost River: Unsettling Place in the Anthropocene." *Anthropocenes – Human, Inhuman, Posthuman* 1 (1): 3. https://doi.org/10.16997/ahip.6.

Travis, Charles. 2018. "The Digital Anthropocene, Deep Mapping, and Environmental Humanities' Big Data." *Resilience: A Journal of the Environmental Humanities* 5 (2): 172–88.

Tsing, Anna L., Jennifer Deger, Alder Keleman Saxena, and Feifei Zhou. 2020. *Feral Atlas: The More-Than-Human Anthropocene*. Redwood City: Stanford University Press.

Wilson, W. Matthew. 2017. *New Lines: Critical GIS and the Trouble of the Map*. Minneapolis: University of Minnesota Press.

Zylinska, Joanna. 2014. *Minimal Ethics for the Anthropocene*. Ann Arbor: Open Humanities Press.

27

THE DEAFENING ROAR OF THE DIGITAL ENVIRONMENTAL HUMANITIES

Case Studies in New Scholarship

William Hansard and Kevin Moskowitz

Introduction

In their article "Mapping Common Ground: Ecocriticism, Environmental History, and the Environmental Humanities" (2014), Bergthaller et al. write that "more and more environmental historians and eco-critics are coming to see their work as part of a broadly interdisciplinary enterprise labeled 'the environmental humanities'" and that "close collaboration with the emerging digital humanities will be of crucial importance." Bergthaller et al. are concerned that scholars in various fields of environmental study do not communicate well with each other. Scientists, literary critics, and historians must "map common ground" to solve environmental problems, they argue. Of course, humanists often worry that scientific and digital methods will encroach upon the methodologies to which they are accustomed. But even prior to the 21st century, cutting-edge work using digital tools and methods was used to construct new environmental narratives. William Cronon, one of the foremost scholars in environmental history, contributed to a critical element of his groundbreaking work *Nature's Metropolis* (1991) by using advanced (for the time) computer processing to analyse the accounts of over 19,000 creditors, an unthinkable task just a few decades earlier. Bankruptcy records examined by Cronin through a computational lens illustrated regional representations of changes in an environmental reorganisation by Chicago creditors, who were able to reshape vast swaths of the American West's landscapes with the stroke of their fountain pens. It can be argued that environmental history has come of age alongside the rise of the digital humanities and has contributed to DEH discourses and methods that, rather than depart from traditional humanities approaches such as interpretation, critique, exploration, and communication, seek to apply such methods to creating critical perspectives on environmental change (Sinclair and Posthumus 2017).

Haitian scholar Michel-Rolph Trouillot's *Silencing the Past* (1995) suggests that the production of history generates silences – the selection of information and loss of details and narratives based on ideology – at four distinct points in the creation process: the making of sources, creation of archives, narration of historical events, and inclusion in the corpus (historiography). Today, the

DOI: 10.4324/9781003082798-33

digital resources available to historians and archivists suggest that this turn in the humanities could alleviate many of Trouillot's criticisms on the production of historical narratives. Environmental historians face the dual challenge of giving agency to the non-human and investigating how humanity has silenced elements of itself. For example, a recent study by Thomas Almeroth-Williams (2019), using obscure digital sources such as court proceedings from the *Old Baily Proceedings Online* and digital newspaper archives, unearthed the untold history of urban animals that fed, moved, and protected Londoners in the 19th century. As such work demonstrates, Trouillot's observations about elisions and omissions remain critical to praxis in environmental history concerning the silences of non-humans in many narratives.

In this chapter, we investigate the impact of the digital turn in the environmental humanities in exposing or creating silences in the archives and the historical narration process. We also suggest the existence of an additional form of silence inherently created by the digital turn in the humanities – one created during the intermediate steps of converting (often) quantitative data and information from archival sources into narration-friendly formats. We believe that supplemental forms of archival research and processing – such as entering spatial data into a GIS database – can help us to recover environmental narratives that have been silenced, intentionally or otherwise. However, we must also remain aware that DEH projects can and do contribute to silences in the corpus (historiography).

Theory and Method

Reflecting on the predominant historical narratives framing the journeys and "discoveries" of Christopher Columbus, Michel-Rolph Trouillot (1995) notes "[the] creation of that historical moment [Columbus' landfall in 1492] facilitates the narrativization of history, the transformation of what happened into that which is said to have happened" (113). The narrativisation of the environment leads us to place an emphasis on what the environment was perceived to be like, rather than as it actually was. What makes *Silencing the Past* an important critique for digital humanists is the work's emphasis on the process of historical production. "What matters most," Trouillot argues, "are the processes and conditions of production of such narratives" (25). When we manipulate quantitative historical materials through GIS, optical image recognition, digital imaging, or machine learning, we are inherently subjecting it to the accompanying cultural and technical values of the Information Age.

In this age, the need for information literacy and an understanding of how historical narratives are produced is paramount. Historians, for example, have often railed against the lack of interpretive ability by scholars who rely on quantitative data. In *Computing and the Historical Imagination* (2004), W.G. Thomas recounts decades of resistance by historians to the often impersonal and ahistorical works produced by statisticians and cliometricians, who perceived only numbers and not narratives. A particularly notorious example of such work, Thomas argues, is Robert Fogel and Stanley L. Engerman's *Time on the Cross: The Economics of American Negro Slavery* (1974), which reduced the abject horrors of that "peculiar institution" to statistics and did not accurately account for the experiences of enslaved persons. In the ensuing decades, humanities scholars have mapped common ground between quantitative and qualitative methodologies. For example, Charles Travis et al. (2020) have described how the literary and cartographic "invention" of the Grand Banks of Newfoundland initiated the North Atlantic Fish Revolution in the early modern period. The new human perception of a previously existing environment altered sociopolitical reality, which in turn had serious ramifications for the natural environment. This process of alteration, both physical and psychological, occurred over many centuries, but today, modern technology allows for more rapid and profuse dissemination of new environmental perceptions than ever before.

In addition to the Information Age, another term employed to describe the current period of technological development and informational landscape is the Digital Anthropocene, which describes a period in which the digital has replaced the analogue, and human perception is the primary driver of environmental transformation. Whereas the Information Age calls for informational literacy, the Digital Anthropocene calls for technological literacy. DEH scholars Charles Travis and Poul Holm (2016) have argued that in order to meet the challenges of the Digital Anthropocene, the next generation of students must be trained in terms of digital literacy as well as consider new ideas concerning the perception, construction and conceptualisation of "Nature" (202). Indeed, as scholars we must engage in several layers of metacognition in order to fully understand how we perceive the world around us. In this regard, we can be aided by engagements with Big Data, artificial intelligence, and other techno-tropes gathering under the umbrella of the DEH.

Travis and Holm are among a growing group of environmental scholars who emphasise the importance and impacts of digital projects and information in constructing environmental narratives. It is worth noting that such concepts have deep roots in environmental history scholarship. In his seminal work, *The Railway Journey: The Industrialization of Time and Space in the 19th Century* (2014), cultural studies scholar Wolfgang Schivelbusch describes the ways in which the advent of the railroad system not only altered the natural world but altered humanity's perceptions of nature as well. The so-called annihilation of space and time brought on by the industrialisation of the Western world, he argues, was a complex process that both contracted and expanded perceptions of space-time (33–35). Building on the work of Schivelbusch, environmental historian Finn Arne Jørgensen (2014) draws a parallel between the effects of railroad technology and the impacts of the DEH on humans' understanding of the environment. Jørgensen argues that the DEH is essentially a continuation of this process of new technologies mediating humanity's relationship with nature. More specifically, he sees DEH as the newest method of "armchair travel" and a new window through which both experts and laymen are developing their perceptions of the natural world.

Jørgensen further argues that, in terms of physical science, the very nature of "nature" means that humans cannot actually "know" the natural world directly and that all human perception of nature is in some way mediated (109). Taking these ideas in conjunction with the work of Trouillot, we can see that the silences produced by historical scholarship may, in some cases, be alleviated through the use of more advanced technological methods of analysis, but they can never be completely eliminated due to the idiosyncrasies of human experience and perception. In order to compose more comprehensive environmental narratives and to prevent the creation and amplification of additional silences, we must take care to consider the ways in which DEH methods and projects mediate, at foundational levels, our understanding of the subjects under study.

Of course, this set of arguments assumes a traditional and monolithic concept of human agency being exercised over the environment. But because human perception is not independent of the world in which it is developed, this approach is inadequate – especially if the goal is to give voice to environmental silences. In environmental history, the very concept of agency needs a reworking, argues Linda Nash in *The Agency of Nature or the Nature of Agency?* (2005). While taking care to avoid slipping into environmental determinism, Nash argues that "environmental history should not strive merely to put nature into history, but to put the human mind back into the world" (69). Nash, working along the same line of thought as Schivelbusch and Jørgensen, argues that human experience and actions, if not completely determined by the environment, are certainly mediated and shaped by structures provided by the environment. More directly, Nash builds on the work of anthropologist Tim Ingold (2002), who argues that human agency should be studied through the framework of "the developing organism-in-its-environment, as opposed to the self-contained individual confronting a world 'out there'" (4). Although Nash limits her arguments to structures of the natural world, these could easily be extended to the built environment as well.

In addition to theoretical concerns posed by rapid alterations in human cognition being shaped by the influence of the digital humanities, Big Data, and the environment itself, Travis and Holm also find themselves concerned with the practical matters of collaboration on DEH projects. This is made difficult, they argue, due to a "host of methodological, institutional, and funding issues," which find many (though not all) DEH projects "operating in a fragmented, patchwork landscape dotted with solipsistic disciplinary silos" (203). As with the analogue forms that preceded the DEH, difficulties hindering attempts at digital collaboration generate and amplify their own silences in the production of historical narratives. And if we cannot innovate new methods and practices to overcome such difficulties, we are missing opportunities to uncover the past and present silences in environmental history. To demonstrate the manner in which DEH methods can be used to uncover such silences, we present two case studies. The first discusses an understudied subject and concerns the environmental narratives of the American Railroad Circus. The second explores the implications of making public policy decisions about automobile manufacturing by uncovering historical silences in the face of vanishing archives.

The Circus

Research on the history of the American Railroad Circus in the late 19th and early 20th centuries lends itself especially well to the DEH. Given the remarkable mobility of circuses under canvas and their impact on the places they visited, circus history is an inherently environmental topic. From its unloading in the trainyard and parade of animals and performers to the show lot that attracted gathering crowds, the travelling circus made drastic changes to a town's geography on the day it came to visit. And despite being transitory, the circus also made some permanent changes to the environment, especially through the construction of winter quarters, many of which still stand today. One of the aspects that left the greatest impact on the environment was circus billing which promulgated "billing wars" between travelling and competing circuses. American studies scholar Janet Davis notes in *The Circus Age* (2002) that "circus billposters marked the landscape, claimed it, and transformed it months before the actual onslaught of crowds, tents, and animals" (45). We can learn much about the American environment of the Gilded Age (ca. 1870s–1900s) and Progressive Era (ca. 1900s–1930s) from these narrative sources left behind by circus advertisers. The men employed on circus advertising teams – known as advance men or opposition gangs – knew very well the importance of understanding the local environments due to be visited by the circus. Given the nature of their work, advance men were masters of mobility and geography on both large and small scales. As renowned circus historian Charles Philip "Chappie" Fox puts it, these men were "walking gazetteers" (1985, 71).

In their popular survey *The Circus in America* (1969), Fox and fellow circus historian Tom Parkinson drew up a laundry list of the different types of advance men and their specific areas of expertise: billposters knew "every shed and fence in the nation"; billers recognised "the principal streets of every city" and "the multitudes of little towns"; press agents identified the newspapers and their areas of circulation; contracting agents dealt with merchants, feed dealers, and show lots; general agents recognised alternative routes; and all advance men were experts in appreciating local hotels and restaurants (53–54). Circus route books, newspaper articles, and memoirs of press agents have the potential to tell us much about the American environment during the period from the perspectives of men who experienced its regional milieus more than most people.

With the growing number of large railroad circuses touring the United States and Canada at the turn of the 20th century, hyperbolic print advertising became more and more crucial, with competition to play larger and more desirable cities growing ever more intense. Circus advertisements were plastered over towns by the thousands on a daily basis – a larger show might place as many as 20,000 posters at a single stand (Hoh and Rough 1990)! Such practices led to a new form of competition between circus shows called billing wars. At times, these "wars" involved violence and weapons, but more commonly, these battles were fought with words, pictures, paste, and tacks. Billing wars often involved ruthless oppositional advertising methods. These include "rat bills" accusing rival shows of misdeeds, stealing or destroying a rivals' handbills, and plastering over previously placed advertisements. "Wait sheets," imploring customers to "wait for the big show," were a common tool – so common, in fact, that the Ringling Bros. Circus became known to some as the Wait Bros. show (Hoh and Rough 1990)! And of course, advance agents could also weaponise the local press, bribing reporters with free tickets to print favourable news and reviews.

Perhaps no billing war in circus history was more intense than the so-called Great Circus War of 1903. The Barnum and Bailey Circus had returned from a four-year grand tour of Europe to find that the Ringling Brothers (1903) had made significant gains in brand recognition and

Figure 27.1 Forepaugh circus poster. At the turn of the 20th century, extravagant posters such as this one for the Forepaugh-Sells Circus, printed by the Courier company of Buffalo, New York, blanketed North American towns for much of the year.

Source: Adam Forepaugh and Sells Brothers. America's shows consolidated. Representative riders of every class and country. United States, ca. 1900. Photograph retrieved from the Library of Congress, www.loc.gov/item/94507620/. Public domain.

territory, and this led to more serious competition between the two than had ever been known. All over the United States and Canada, citizens took note of how their towns were being overrun by circus advertising, and not just by those two shows. A journalist for the *Morning Star* in Rockford, Illinois, reported on 14 May 1903, "Yesterday the real work of the combat was commenced, though for several days past there have been side-line firings from both sides in the way of small stands of bills and banners," referring to advertising campaigns in the city by the Great Wallace and Forepaugh-Sells Circuses (*Rockford Morning Star* 1903a). D.F. Lynch, the head of the advance department for the Great Wallace Circus, informed the reporter that the circus benefited from this war, saying,

> It draws a larger crowd, though not in proportion to the additional expense. But the fact that a circus comes out ahead in the war is worth more in advertising than in the matter of dollars and cents for the fact is sent out broadcast and is worth much in the next stand as an advertisement.
>
> *(Rockford Morning Star 1903a)*

Lynch went on to note that smaller circuses such as his also benefited from the popularity of the spectacle between Barnum and Bailey and Ringling Bros. and the war both circus giants waged against each other. Many thousands of people were turned away when their behemoth shows reached capacity and so were eager to see the next circus that came to town. The war was not viewed as a merry one by all, however, due to its impact on the landscape. Another Rockford paper, the *Daily Republic*, featured an article complaining of "the bill board nuisance." "The bill posters have made Rockford look like a veritable bedlam," the author grumbled. "Two circuses are competing and there is a natural rivalry as to the greatest and ugliest display" (*Rockford Daily Republic* 1903). The reporter went on to note that the bill posters had missed the courthouse, Carnegie Library, and Veteran's Memorial Hall, which was to be dedicated by the president in June. This sarcastic journalist mockingly suggested that the bill posters ought to "get the stand built from which President Roosevelt is to speak to the multitudes June 3 and let the circus men decorate that with flaring posters and gay bunting, on which is printed truths about the greatest show on earth" (*Rockford Daily Republic* 1903). The temporary presences of the circuses in towns was only part of the problem. The detritus left behind was a different matter; after the "bill battles" were over, the warring circuses left town, leaving others responsible for tearing down the bills, scooping up the dung, and picking up the garbage. This example of environmental degradation during the Gilded and Progressive Eras is an aspect of American environmental history whose silence has yet to be fully examined.

The exaggerated nature and histories of the so-called Great Circus War surely must have caused aspects of their environmental dimensions to be ignored. GIS methods were employed to uncover the silences in the historical narrative and especially to explore just how intense territorial competition between circuses actually was during the 1903 season. Data and information from newspaper reports and circus route books were collated in GIS to create an animated time map of several circus routes. The aim was to expose some of the environmental truths obscured by the war of words between circuses, by newspaper reporters, and even by historians. Some circus employees claimed this war was largely a myth; journalists hyped it up far beyond what was necessary, and historians, for whatever reason, have largely ignored it. But the 1903 billing war proved a significant turning point in the history of the American circus industry and reflected changes in US culture and society at the dawn of the 20th century.

Tracing the routes of three circuses – Barnum and Bailey, Ringling Bros., and Pan-American Shows – in GIS contributed to creating a more nuanced and geographically contextual narrative

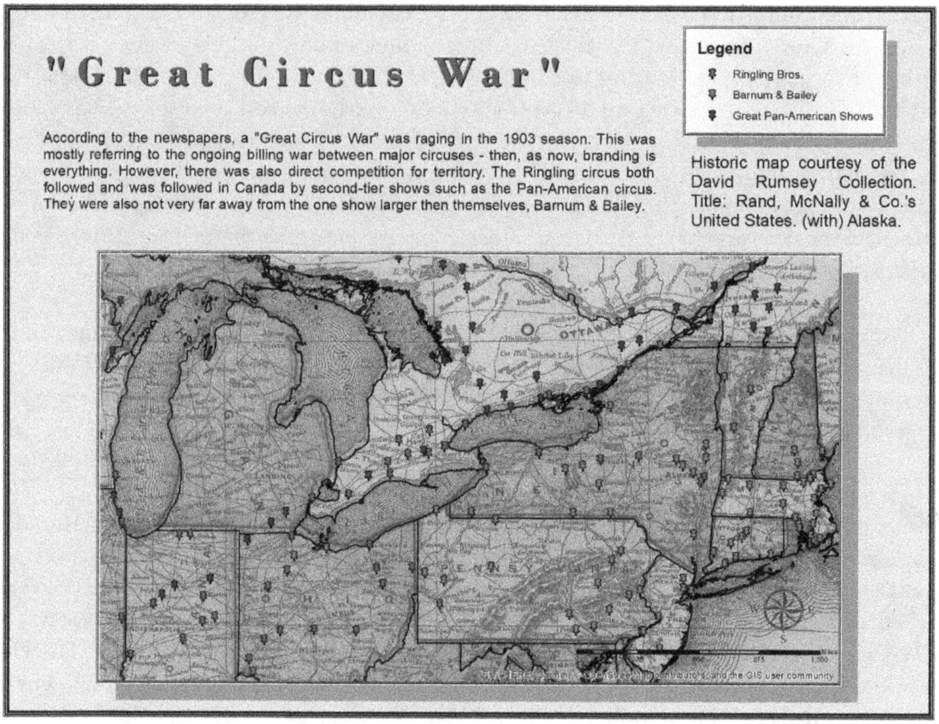

Figure 27.2 Circus route map. This map was produced by Mr Hansard for a GIS course in which he was enrolled. Original base map courtesy of the David Rumsey Map Collection, David Rumsey Map Center, Stanford Libraries United States, 1903. Rand McNally and Co.'s United States (with Alaska)

than provided by text sources alone. In 1903, despite bombastic press coverage, the two largest circuses, Ringling and Barnum, were ironically engaged in almost zero direct competition for territory; the Great Circus War was, for them, an issue of branding and billing above all else. The only town that both shows played was Youngstown, Ohio, and were dated far enough apart – more than three months – that it is unlikely to have been related to any direct attempt at dominance over that territory. However, this does not negate the fact that the branding war was still going strong. In fact, it may prove this notion, as neither show had gained dominance in brand loyalty enough to encroach on the other's territory to any meaningful degree

Mapping circus routes also revealed that the region of Upstate New York and Ontario seemed to be the greatest hotbed of territorial competition for most major shows. The Ringling and Pan-American circuses followed parallel paths north and south of Lakes Erie and Ontario. In the Ringling route book, this is briefly acknowledged by noting that their show was competing with several other second-tier circuses in Upstate New York (*The Circus Annual* 1903, 62). The Ringling and Barnum shows would come physically closest to each other during this leg of the tour but still not close enough for it to amount to significant territorial competition. The two major shows steered a wide berth of each other's traditional territories. The Barnum and Bailey show stayed largely clear of the Midwest, just as the Ringling show stayed largely clear of the Northeast, with the exception of Upstate New York. Further research could potentially uncover the reasons why regions in the Northeast were a particular hotbed of circus activity at the turn of the 20th century and how this influenced the circus industry in North America.

The Great Circus War was less a conflict between major competitors than it was one between major competitors and second-tier shows, such as the Pan-American and Great Wallace shows. And of course, these second-tier shows were in serious competition with each other, in part fighting over the scraps left behind in the wake of the Ringling and Barnum war. Although this conclusion had not been completely silenced – D.F. Lynch explained this very point to the reporter for the Rockford *Morning Star* – one that had been deeply buried beneath layers of narratives built by both circus management, employees and historians of the circus.

As a final aside, it is worth noting that circus history can help us to give voice to silences in other ways. Despite their flaws – especially unabashed biases that favour the circus companies – primary sources of circus history have the potential to be a goldmine for environmental historians and digital humanists. Route books are essentially a type of yearbook which include the dates and cities to which the circus travelled, rosters of employees, photographs and advertisements, and generally a narrative diary of events. These books are a wealth of information not just for historians of the circus but for environmental historians who seek to learn historical tidbits about towns and cities in North America. Circus employees often recorded their impressions of the town, its size, its people and their demeanour, its accommodations, its weather, and more. If a show visited a place multiple times, change over time and changing perspectives may also be present in the records. When seeking to eliminate silences in the corpus, those working in the DEH might do well to turn to the circus route books as a source.

The Automobile

By 2022, most of the world's largest automakers will have pledged to replace most or all of their consumer offerings with battery-powered, zero-emission vehicles by the end of the 2030s (Walton 2021). Carbon dioxide emissions, along with other noxious tailpipe gases, have become the metric for the ecological consequences of automobilism's contribution to global warming. As suggested by John Urry in his landmark article "The 'System' of Automobility" (2004), once the car industry is freed from burning hydrocarbons, it will become a ready partner in the fight against climate change, waste, and pollution. This narrative is not by any means a new one. Over the past half-century, politicians, activists, businesses, and academics have shaped the narrative of automobility and the environment as one of air pollution being a detrimental side effect of using vehicles. Indeed, the most visible story of the auto's relationship with the environment, both in public discourse and in academic literature, is that of emissions. By challenging this narrative using the techniques of the digital turn in the humanities, scholars can lead the charge against prevailing, unhelpful narratives of automobilism by offering more spatially and environmentally comprehensive alternatives.

In the United States, the pervasive environmental automotive emissions narrative commences in the manure-and-horse-carcass-strewn streets of the big city, where rising populations at the turn of the end of the 19th century created a sanitation nightmare. Motorised transportation saved urban spaces from the filth and squalor of biological transportation. Promising to be a cleaner and more democratic form of transport, the automobile offered an unprecedented expression of freedom to those who could afford it (McShane and Tarr 2007, 178–81). A three-way battle between electric-, steam-, and gasoline-powered vehicles resulted in victory for the latter, which offered greater range, easy refueling, and a mixture of pleasing noises and vibrations appealing to the young, adventurous purchasers of early automobiles (Mom 2014, 61–63). This gas-powered victory shaped the relationship between the automobile, society, and the environment for the next century.

In this emissions narrative, increasing demand for faster, more powerful vehicles in the 1920s resulted in the proliferation of gasoline additives, namely tetraethyllead, which reduced engine knock but pumped millions of tons of lead into the atmosphere.[1] While activists and doctors warned of the dangers caused by noxious additives, the lead industry, in lockstep with the petrochemical and automotive industries, downplayed these threats. Harder to ignore were the growing clouds of fumes over major cities, such as the terrible clouds of smog that periodically covered Los Angeles. By the early 1970s, particles such as hydrocarbons, carbon monoxide, and nitrogen oxide, threatened to label the automobile as a cancer-causing product (Neumaier 2014, 448). The formation of the Environmental Protection Agency (EPA) and the oil crisis forced automakers to address these flaws. Regulation and the introduction of the catalytic converter (which could only operate using unleaded gasoline) reduced smog and created a car with cleaner emissions. Since the 1970s, carbon dioxide and higher levels of greenhouse gasses contributing to global warming have continued to be the focus of public concern (McCarthy 176–77, 254). With the arrival of the 21st century, automakers have experimented with alternatives to gasoline-driven automobiles, first with hybrid electric vehicles and most recently with natural gas, hydrogen, and battery-electric options. Today, the latter is seen by automakers, politicians, and the public as a complete panacea to the lead-clogged, smoky past of automobilia and the start of a Jetson-esque future.

Ultimately this narrative is focused on consumer choice rather than the decisions of the manufacturers. If a better fuel existed, these narratives suggest, then automakers, pushed by consumers, would adapt to them. However, the rise of the sport utility vehicle (SUV) and proliferation of light-duty trucks as personal transportation in the last decade wiped away any greenhouse gas emissions declines from the previous decades. Automotive historian Tom McCarthy laments that "consumer decisions consistently served the personal desires of individuals that for most rarely, if ever, gave precedence to matters involving the wider social and environmental consequences of automobile use" (2007, 253). The electric SUV, then, serves as the promise of the future: satisfying the demands of consumers for large, heavy vehicles while emitting nothing from non-existent tailpipes.

In this narrative, the environmental legacy of the car is set by its fuel. The core principles driving the adoption of the automobile in the broader transatlantic world were democracy and modernity – a good idea that needed the maturation of appropriate technological systems to make the car "sustainable" (Mom 2014). Automobile manufacturers, politicians, and the public have latched on to this narrative for several reasons. One, it is reinforced by technological determinism or an assumption that technologies continue to improve over time as if by destiny. Automakers can point to the large and small innovations (such as the catalytic converter and hybrid electric powertrain) in ways that suggest that there will eventually be a "clean" car. Meanwhile, manufacturers continue to operate under the system of planned obsolescence; each generation of cleaner vehicles provides consumers with yet another reason to upgrade. Electric vehicles are now synonymous with "[bringing] the United States into the 21st century," according to politicians such as United States House Representative Tim Ryan of Ohio, a vocal proponent of vehicle electrification (Coller 2021). If the 19th century was an age of coal and the 20th an age of petroleum, then electricity symbolises the hopes of the 21st. Additionally, emissions have the appearance of being geographically agnostic. While air pollution affects some places more directly than others, the collective concern of climate change provides a useful call to arms for the public while not requiring a full assessment of the transportation systems that underpin motorisation.

I assert that rather than looking at the automobile's use, historians should refocus their interests on the complex network involved in the automobile's creation. By the 1920s, the automobile industry was the largest in the United States and continued to contain the most powerful and valuable corporations in the world for most of the 20th century, employing millions of people and swallowing up millions of tons of iron, coal, petroleum, aluminium, copper, lumber, and more every year. The emissions narrative is so pervasive because of the silences created at each step of the history-making process. Understanding the environmental consequences of manufacturing are incredibly challenging as it requires a diverse set of primary sources from a large geographic range. Historians who have investigated the manufacturing process have centred their attention on the assembly plant – the complex at which thousands of parts come together to form a finished vehicle.

In the first two decades of mass production, understanding the environmental consequences of the industry was comparatively easy as massive factories, such as Ford's Highland Park, produced almost every part from raw materials, which were often sourced from mines and forests owned by the manufacturers. However, the focus on the assembly plant is an outmoded means by which to gauge automobile manufacturing and obscures the larger environmental consequences of automobilia. While early mass-produced vehicles might have had most of their components produced at a single massive facility, by mid-century, increased complexity and consumer demand rendered such vertically integrated systems obsolete. By 1950, Buick assembly plant of General Motors (GM) at Flint, for example, pulled components from 1300 suppliers across 42 US states and Ontario. Sea and rail transportation carried some of the material, but motor trucks hauling parts ranging from alternators to suspension bushings across 600 square miles of the United States and Canada were increasingly important to the network as it grew (Henrickson 1951, 7–12). While scholars have explored the role of road construction in shaping automobile consumption and culture, the automakers themselves needed the construction of motorways just as much as consumers (Merriman 2009).

Thus, these narratives provide an incomplete and problematic understanding of the automobile's environmental consequences. There are practical reasons why analogue historians, such as David Nye, Brian McMahon, and Tom McCarthy, have selected the assembly line narrative without exploring the role of suppliers. Spatially, automotive historians who study manufacturing end up looking at very small geographic spaces or very large, generalised ones, obscuring the complex regional relationships required by industry at the scale of GM or Ford. While choices at each point in the historical narrative creation process create silences, perhaps none are as consequential to the state of automotive history as the condition of relevant automobility archives in the United States. The creation (or more aptly, destruction) of archives has severely impeded researchers' access to industrial records. While the non-profit Benson Research Center at the Henry Ford Museum is a notable exception, the condition of corporate and internal papers from the other major American automakers is shameful. In 2009, investment group Cerberus purchased Chrysler. Automotive journalist Bob Elton laments,

> With little notice and no planning, Cerberus literally abandoned the engineering library at the Chrysler Technical Center. The library was shuttered and the librarian laid off. And then the real crime: all the library's books and materials were offered to anyone who could carry them away. I repeat: the documents were free for the taking. Within a week, a collection spanning decades was scattered to the winds; the books and other materials will never again be available in any coherent, comprehensive form.
> *(2009)*

In the case of Chrysler's archival materials, there was no Hercules to subdue Cerberus, the mythical hound of Hades. GM corporate archives suffered a similar fate, with records from many of the corporations' divisions disappearing. The GM Heritage Center, home to the remaining archives, does not even publish a guide for searching its collection. Instead, and like many online automotive archives, the records most easily accessible are not necessarily the ones most useful for researchers in manufacturing or environmental fields. Rather, these records tend to be photographic: advertisements, racing paraphernalia, and walkarounds of the most valuable items in any automobile museum: the cars. In total, this means that if only a fraction of materials gets archived, and only a fraction of those records become digitally available, then we can understand why very little about the design, finance, and manufacturing of the automobile is available to the digital scholar.

Making matters more challenging is that as the automobile industry grew, suppliers located across a vast geographic space became much more important to the production of larger, more complicated vehicles assembled from an increasing variety of materials. The records of these suppliers are even harder to access, as it is not always clear where to look for them. Some suppliers were subsidiaries of the car companies, such as AC Delco and Fisher Body. The fate of these records is often tied to those of the main corporate archives, which do not bode well for their availability. Others, independent manufacturers of all shapes and sizes, may have records scattered across the continent and find themselves often relying on information from assembly plants managers and the financial departments of Ford, Chrysler, and GM. As a result, automotive emission and assembly plant narratives are easier to produce than the manufacturing-networks story. The DEH offer three ways in which to challenge the latter narrative: by improving access, interpreting data, and offering collaboration.

The opportunity to digitally "armchair travel" across North America provides significant opportunities to scholars looking to challenge or complicate existing automobile narratives. Just as the automobile and railroad before they were technologies that compressed time and space, surfing online archives allow historians to cover great distances at a lower cost and in less time. Scholars should be wary to not rely on corporate records and archives alone; the creation of these archives is also a means of silence, and as digital humanists, we should remember to consult other resources, such as newspaper archives and governmental records. In particular, the records at the Crittenden Library (now hosted by Archive.org) offer access to historical footage and documents regardless of one's academic affiliation.

Even curated digital sources about automobile manufacturing can provide historians with ways to develop new environmental narratives. While the narrative focus on lead pollution and the automobile centres around tailpipe emissions, digital close readings of promotional materials (one of the few online manufacturing documents readily available) can hint at other ways in which leaded substances were impactful. *Factory Facts from Ford* (1917), a brochure printed by the Ford Motor Company and provided to dealerships across the country, proudly proclaims that the Highland Park factory, a workplace of over 35,000 men, maintained a "department of about 27 men [that] does nothing but paint the walls and ceilings of the factory, keeping everything fresh and clean." When we examine the accompanying photographs, it becomes clear that most every surface in the factory was kept a shade of bright white, almost universally formulated during the period from lead pigment (12–13). It is not hard to imagine the health consequences for thousands of employees breathing in fresh lead paint on a daily basis. Even though the lead industry in the 1920s denied any danger of its product to a child's normal development, it was willing to admit that industrial exposure could be toxic (Markowitz and Rosner, 22–26). Scholars may have fewer options in digital archives than they would like, but with creative surfing and reading, there is still much to learn from these collections.

Utilising documents from online archives becomes a more powerful and revealing tool when engaged in concert with other digital tools. An illustration of the ability to address silences is the

Figure 27.3 Dodge auto factory. Lead was not the only hazardous chemical used in great quantities in early automotive manufacturing. The Dodge Brothers' Hamtramck factory used 1,000 pounds of cyanide a day in 1917 for the hardening of steel parts.

use of GIS to map suppliers for the Buick assembly plant at Flint, Michigan. Utilising digitised records from the Institute for Human Adjustment at the Rackham School of Graduate Studies, historians can begin to expand the narrative of automobile construction beyond the spaces of the assembly plant. Published in 1951 by George Rex Henrickson at the University of Michigan, *Trends in the Geographic Distribution of Suppliers of Some Basically Important Materials Used at the Buick Motor Division, Flint, Michigan* offers us a glimpse into the complexity of automobile manufacturing with incredible detail and scope. We are fortunate to have Henrickson's report, as much of the information it contains is virtually impossible to find anywhere else. Not only does the report inform us where many of the plant's parts and materials originate from, but it tells us how they arrived, giving the reader insight into transportation networks that extended the environmental transformations caused by automobile manufacturing beyond the plant at Flint. Although Henrickson's report is far from perfect, of the 1,300 suppliers Buick utilised at the Flint plant, he only identifies the locations of 245 of these, describing little more than what the suppliers produced and the names of the cities where they were located – its information is sufficient enough from which to glean adequate geospatial data in order to begin mapping out new ideas on the industrial impacts of motorisation. For example, this data informs scholars that they need to consider the role of the machinery manufacturing industry of New England in evaluating the impact of Flint's automobile industry. It also challenges scholars to answer questions about the ecological impact of similar industries on different places. For instance, how is the run-off from a rubber-moulding plant in rural Indiana perceived by locals in comparison to one by the denizens of Cleveland, Ohio?

In such a manner, the DEH offer us collaborative tools to transcend the traditional research boundaries of individual labour, time, and travel costs. The American automobile industry is a very large machine to study alone. Constructing a historical narrative to frame understandings that even a single assembly plant in a single year as part of a network that connected 1,300 other places, each with their own local and unique environmental histories, will require us stodgy

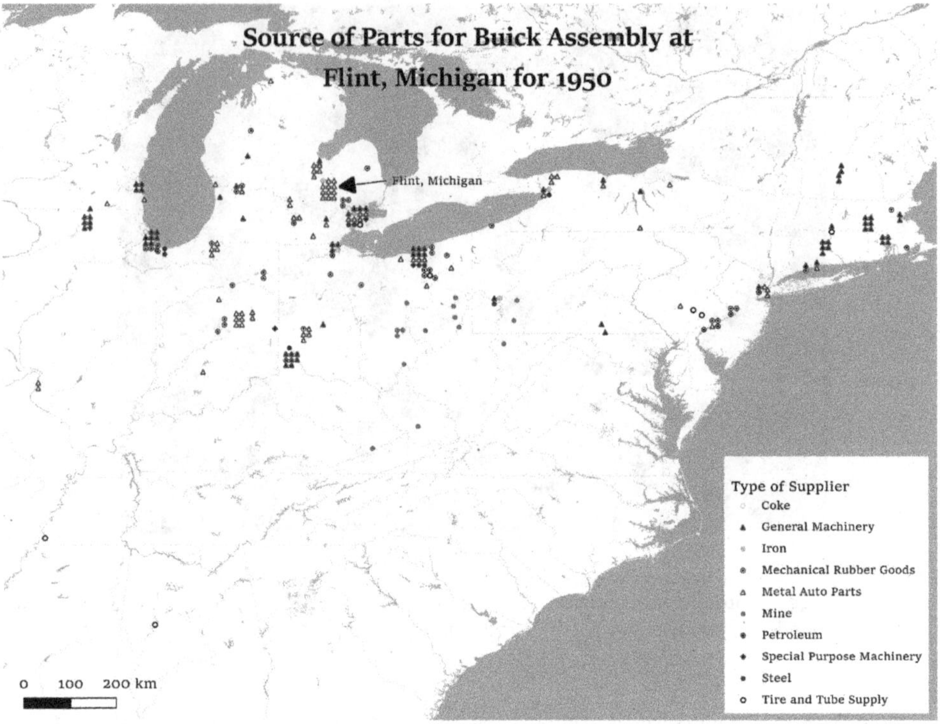

Figure 27.4 Auto parts map. By the 1950s, automobile manufacturing had matured into a complex technical system, with an ecological footprint stretching hundreds of kilometres in every direction (map created by Kevin Moskowitz using open-source base map from OpenStreetMap). © OpenStreetMap contributors.

scholars to get out of our cosy offices and quiet headspaces in order to interact with other scholars and the public. Just as classical and medieval scholars have created in Harvard University's collaborative Mapping Past Societies project (formerly the Digital Atlas of Roman and Medieval Civilization), automobility scholars need a digital platform to host and publish data on where and when auto manufacturing took place, and links to what additional archival resources are available. Additionally, the DEH offer a democratising opportunity to crowdsource information on suppliers. The internet has spawned hundreds of dedicated online communities teeming with automotive enthusiasts from diverse backgrounds. Historians should utilise their enthusiasm and nostalgia for the automobile in order to canvas global continents for mines, smelteries, factories, and assembly plants. By thinking beyond the scope of traditional print medium tools and engaging the public directly, scholars are offered the ability to reach out to more people and contribute more widely and effectively to public policy discussions.

Conclusion

Michel Rolph Trouillot concludes in *Silencing the Past* that "professional historians will have to position themselves more clearly within the present, lest politicians, magnates, or ethnic leaders alone write history for them" (152). Practitioners of the DEH are well situated to re-engage and re-established narratives with relevant environmental dialogues and to engage in critical cultural, economic, and political debates on local, national, and international scales. By analysing the ways in which perceptions of nature are mediated by technology and the experience of environment, we are able to better understand both the agency of nature and the nature of agency. This enhanced understanding, then, allows us to better engage with silences in historical narratives of the environment. To contribute new meaningful narratives to the corpus, DEH scholars must be cognisant of where and how silences in past narratives were generated and formed. By learning to reinterpret archival materials and searching out new, unconventional archives scholars can look past the most commonly used sources of historical information and learn to read such new sources for stories beyond the narratives intended by their creators. Lastly, by engaging the DEH, scholars should be prepared to present such information in new, unorthodox ways, utilising the democratic potential of digital tools to position their historical narratives as qualified alternatives to the hubris of the "politicians, magnates, or ethnic leaders" that so concerned Trouillot.

Note

1 Engine knock occurs when combustion of some of the air/gasoline mixture results not from from propagation of the flame front ignited by the spark plug but by other air/gasoline pockets in the cylinder.

Sources

Almeroth-Williams, Thomas. 2019. *City of Beasts: How Animals Shaped Georgian London*. Manchester: Manchester University Press.

Bergthaller, H., R. Emmett, A. Johns-Putra, A. Kneitz, S. Lidström, S. McCorristine, . . . L. Robin. 2014. "Mapping Common Ground: Ecocriticism, Environmental History, and the Environmental Humanities." *Environmental Humanities* 5 (1): 261–76. https://read.dukeupress.edu/environmental-humanities/article/5/1/261/8152.

"The Bill Board Nuisance." May 14, 1903a. *Rockford Morning Star*. Rockford, Illinois. 4.

"Circus War Is On In Rockford." May 14, 1903b. *Rockford Morning Star*. Rockford, Illinois. 3.

Coller, Patty. 2021. "Rep. Tim Ryan Introduces House Measure to Pull USPS Electrical Vehicle Contract." News. *WKBN.com* (blog), March 9, 2021. www.wkbn.com/news/local-news/rep-tim-ryan-introduces-house-measure-to-pull-usps-electrical-vehicle-contract/.

Cronon, William. 1991. *Nature's Metropolis: Chicago and the Great West*. New York: W. W. Norton.

Davis, Janet M. 2002. *The Circus Age: Culture and Society under the American Big Top*. Chapel Hill: The University of North Carolina Press.

Dodge Brothers Motors. 1917. *Dodge Motor Cars*. Documentary. http://archive.org/details/dodge-motor-cars-ca-1917.

Elton, Bob. 2009. "Editorial: Chrysler Destroys Its Historical Archives; GM to Follow?" *The Truth About Cars* (blog), July 26, 2009. www.thetruthaboutcars.com/2009/07/editorial-chrysler-destroys-its-historical-archives-gm-to-follow/.

Factory Facts from Ford. 1917. Detroit: Ford Motor Company.

Fogel, Robert William, and Stanley L. Engerman. 1974. *Time on the Cross: The Economics of American Negro Slavery*. Boston, MA: Little, Brown and Company.

Fox, Charles Philip. 1985. *Billers, Banners and Bombast: The Story of Circus Advertising*. 1st ed. Boulder, CO: Pruett Pub Co.

Fox, Charles Philip, and Tom Parkinson. 1969. *The Circus in America*. Waukesha, WI: Country Beautiful.

Henrickson, George Rex. 1951. *Trends in the Geographic Distribution of Suppliers of Some Basically Important Materials Used at the Buick Motor Division, Flint, Michigan*. Ann Arbor. http://hdl.handle.net/2027/mdp.39015007583266.

Hoh, LaVahn G., and William H. Rough. 1990. "Chapter Five: Back Yards And Getting There." In *Step Right Up! The Adventure of Circus In America*. White Hall, VA: Betterway Publications. http://xroads.virginia.edu/~MA02/amacker/circus/ch_5.txt.

Ingold, Tim. 2002. *The Perception of the Environment*. London: Routledge. https://doi.org/10.4324/9780203466025.

Jørgensen, Finn Arne. 2014. "The Armchair Traveller's Guide to Digital Environmental Humanities." *Environmental Humanities* 4 (1): 95–112. https://doi.org/10.1215/22011919-3614944.

Markowitz, Gerald, and David Rosner. 2002. *Deceit and Denial the Deadly Politics of Industrial Pollution*. Berkeley: University of California Press. https://uta.alma.exlibrisgroup.com.

McCarthy, Tom. 2007. *Auto Mania: Cars, Consumers, and the Environment*. New Haven: Yale University Press.

McShane, Clay, and Joel Tarr. 2007. *The Horse in the City: Living Machines in the Nineteenth Century*. Edited by Harriet Ritvo. Baltimore, MD: Johns Hopkins University Press.

Merriman, P. 2009. "Automobility and the Geographies of the Car." *Geography Compass* 3 (2): 586–99. https://onlinelibrary.wiley.com/doi/pdf/10.1111/j.1749-8198.2009.00219.x.

Mom, Gijs. 2014. *Atlantic Automobilism: Emergence and Persistence of the Car, 1895–1940*. New York: Berghahn Books.

Nash, Linda. 2005. "The Agency of Nature or the Nature of Agency?" *Environmental History* 10 (1): 67–69.

Neumaier, Christopher. 2014. "Eco-Friendly versus Cancer-Causing: Perceptions of Diesel Cars in West Germany and the United States, 1970–1990." *Technology and Culture* 55 (2): 429–60.

Pinkus, Karen. 2008. "On Climate, Cars, and Literary Theory." *Technology and Culture* 49 (4): 1002–9.

Ringling Brothers. 1903. *The Circus Annual: A Route Book of Ringling Brothers World's Greatest Shows, Season 1903*. Chicago, IL: Central Engraving and Printing.

Rockford Daily Republic. 1903. "Circus Men Overlook A Bet – Fail To Put Bills On Memorial Hall And Carnegie Building." May 14, Rockford, IL, 1.

Rockford Morning Star. 1903a "Circus War Is On In Rockford." May 14, Rockford, IL, 3.

Rockford Morning Star. 1903b "The Bill Board Nuisance." May 14, Rockford, IL, 4.

Schivelbusch, Wolfgang. 2014. *The Railway Journey: The Industrialization of Time and Space in the Nineteenth Century: With a New Preface*. Oakland: University of California Press.

Sinclair, S., and S. Posthumus. 2017. "Digital? Environmental: Humanities." In *The Routledge Companion to the Environmental Humanities*, edited by U. K. Heise, J. Christensen, and M. Niemann, 369–77. London, Routledge.

Thomas, W. G. 2004. "Computing and the Historical Imagination." In *A Companion to Digital Humanities*, edited by Susan Schreibman, Ray Siemens, and John Unsworth, 56–68. Oxford: Blackwell. http://www.digitalhumanities.org/companion/.

Travis, Charles, and Poul Holm. 2016. "The Digital Environmental Humanities – What Is It and Why Do We Need It? The NorFish Project and SmartCity Lifeworlds." In *The Digital Arts and Humanities*, edited by Charles Travis and Alexander von Lünen, 187–204. Springer Geography. Cham: Springer International Publishing. https://doi.org/10.1007/978-3-319-40953-5_11.

Travis, Charles, Francis Ludlow, Al Matthews, Kevin Lougheed, Kieran Rankin, Bernard Allaire, Robert Legg, et al. 2020. "Inventing the Grand Banks: A Deep Chart." *Geo: Geography and Environment* 7 (1). https://doi.org/10.1002/geo2.85.

Trouillot, Michel-Rolph. 1995. *Silencing the Past: Power and the Production of History*. Boston: Beacon Press.

Urry, J. 2004. "The 'System' of Automobility." *Theory, Culture & Society* 21 (4–5): 25–39. https://journals.sagepub.com/doi/pdf/10.1177/0263276404046059.

Walton, Robert. 2021. "Carmakers in US to Spend $250B on Electrification by 2023, Push for National Standard, Group Says." *News. Utility Dive*, February 10, 2021. www.utilitydive.com/news/carmakers-in-us-to-spend-250b-on-electrification-by-2023-push-for-nationa/594833/.

28

THE COVID-19 TESTIMONIES MAP

Representing Italian "Pandemic Space" Perceptions with Neogeography Technologies

Francesco De Pascale and Charles Travis

Introduction

Accessing the sense of place of a location or environment via digital media and geospatial technology is problematic. Affective and subjective dimensions of place, mediated by technology of 1s and 0s and by Cartesian and Euclidean spatial discourses, can appear static and devoid of the vagaries and idiosyncrasies of the human condition. However, Torsten Hägerstrand's *Time-Geography* and Anne Buttimer's *Lifeworld* studies revealed that an individual's internal mental experiences were often in symbiosis with surrounding environmental phenomena. Their studies underscored that simply plotting human behaviour in isometric space and on time grids only scratches the surface of the human condition in space and time but can open the door to exploring subjective experiences of place and time. Deep joy, anger, and grief as emotions colour individuals' perception and experience of place. Geospatial technology approaches to such phenomena, to paraphrase John Corrigan, must "chase the butterfly, rather than pin it" (Corrigan 2010; Travis 2017, 2014).

This chapter discusses research conducted in Italy during the 2020 COVID-19 pandemic that engaged digital communication and geospatial platforms to map and collate discursive, visual, and oral testimonies, stories and narratives of individuals experiencing lockdown conditions. The purpose of the research was to explore physical distancing, resistances, and practices that occurred in the daily spaces of homes and local communities. The research identified which types of social and spatial activities were considered most significant for individuals and in what ways these interactions occurred, when individuals defined their living places as "pandemic spaces." Entitled *Il Mio Spazio Vissuto* (*My Lived Space*), our research explores a concept developed by the French geographer Armand Frémont (1933–2019) *l'espace vécu* (lived space.)[1] Lived space is a collage of the paths, perceptions, representations, signs, drives, and passions of an individual during their everyday life (Frémont 2007). Testimonies received were processed, along the following three thematic indices:

DOI: 10.4324/9781003082798-34

Figure 28.1 A Testimony: "Little Pots of Hope" (Charles Travis and Francesco de Pascale).

1 What were the activities deemed most significant, carried out by the witnesses within their lived space?
2 What types of interactions occurred with other individuals who live in the same house or in the same building (partner, friends, roommates, etc.)? How did the witness define his/her/their own lived space? Would it be a space in which some perceptions prevail over others (visual, sound)?
3 How did these interactions take place (through the balcony of the house; on the phone; via e-mail, internet, social networks, etc.)?

Testimonies collated on the geospatial platform Google Maps were useful in studying the geographical diffusion of the witness population. Such a perspective can direct the interventions of local policymakers, stakeholders, and the national government on (1) possible cultural gaps, (2) enhancement of risk communication, and (3) implementation of adaptive behaviours and strategies of emergency pedagogy and psychology useful for reducing the impact of any future pandemics and other extreme events.

Methodologies and Theories

We employed a qualitative survey methodology and assembled a collection of documents relating to testimonies and private documents. We define documents as "any material that can be used for study purposes, generally in the form of text or video, images, audio" (Lucidi et al. 2008, 67). According to Corbetta (2003), the strength of this technique consists in the use of completely natural data, which, therefore, are generally not affected by the possible distortions generated by researchers. The survey aimed to collect brief reflections and thoughts of subjects who revealed, through stories or narratives, the experiences of living through the pandemic and in the spaces of their homes. The collection of different testimonies, thoughts, and imaginaries was useful in identifying spatial practices that constitute the "geography of the house." Three hundred testimonies were sourced via e-mail from all regions of Italy during March and April of 2020 – the period of a nationwide lockdown. The collection of testimonies also continued during the partial lockdowns of May and early June 2020. Testimonies were published on an on-rolling basis in *Il Sileno Edizioni*, a free open-access website.[2] Locations can be accessed via *Il Mio Spazio Vissuto* or *Mappa delle Testimonianze* (*Evidence Map*) – an interactive map with videos and images sent by witnesses and produced from their own personal data.[3] Such "neogeography" platforms are increasingly employed to collect, compare, analyse, and map data and involve people who use and create their own maps, combining elements of an existing set of tools. The term, apocryphally coined in 2006 by Di-Ann Eisnor, is defined as "a set of techniques and tools that fall outside the realm of traditional GIS" (Jackson 2006; Turner 2006, 3). Consequently, such practices constitute a radical new potential for knowledge and information gathering, particularly for real-time disaster management (Goodchild and Glennon 2010; Callaghan 2016). As an umbrella term for a series of practices that embrace the proliferation of playful and everyday uses of geospatial technologies, neogeography, according to Michael Goodchild,

> implies a reinvention of geography, in which the traditional roles of expert producer of geographic information and amateur user are been interrupted, with the amateur becoming both producer and user, or what some have called a prosumer.
>
> *(Wilson and Graham 2013, 10; Wilson 2017)*

Goodchild (2007) places user-generated cloud-computing phenomena and contents within volunteered geographic information (VGI) and contrasts them with more conventionally produced and mediated forms of GIS to emphasise their role in increasing our knowledge of the geographic world by the efforts of volunteers and "amateurs" (Elwood, Goodchild, and Sui

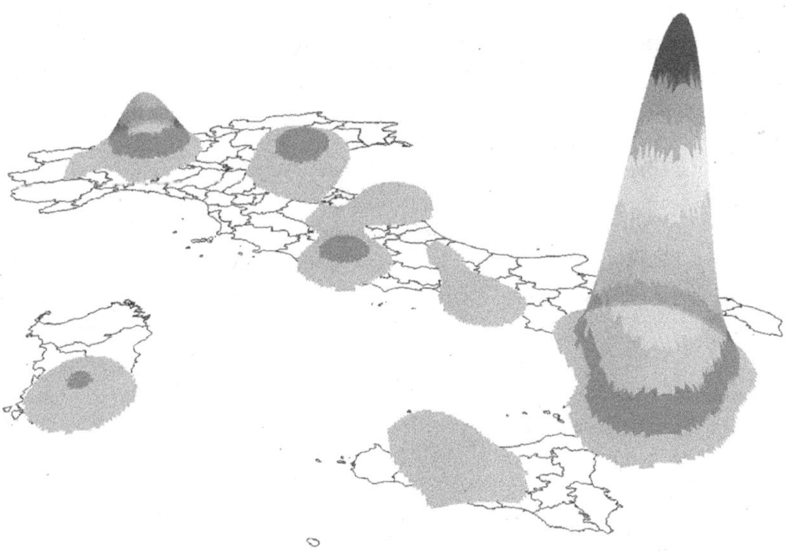

Figure 28.2 The spatial gestalt of the testimony mapping project *Il Mio Spazio Vissuto* (Charles Travis).

2012). Neo-geography offers new opportunities, as well as challenges in disaster risk reduction arising from the intersection between citizen science and VGI (Connors, Lei, and Kelly 2012). With the advent of cloud-computing and crowdsourcing technologies, citizens have the ability to customise spatial content, generate mashups of maps and combine information with multiple sources such as social media, e-mails and mobile phones (Kankanamge et al. 2019). On a global scale, social media and digital platforms have become the official channel for communications concerning COVID-19 pandemic information, from civil and corporate service messaging to logistical details of where to undergo tests, get vaccinations and seek help from health and social services. The evidence collected in this chapter was processed by performing thematic analysis (Braun and Clarke 2006). Following the three indices previously listed, themes were identified through an in-depth reading of the testimonies to form a *spatial gestalt* of the collective experience, positions, perceptions and knowledge of the participants (Aronson 1995; Braun and Clarke 2006; Forino, Von Meding, and Brewer 2018).

Testimonies

From its inception, the testimony mapping project *Il Mio Spazio Vissuto* was appreciated by solicited witnesses "for the operation of memory and hope, between anthropology and literature, a duty, ethical, therapeutic, which also offers psychological support in emergencies" (Vito, 70, Italy). Testimonies revealed multifaceted situations in which, paradoxically, often the joy of finding the closeness of the loved ones, but also oneself, prevails over the discomfort, the boredom, and having to adapt to the difficult context of "permanent disaster." In particular, many people rediscovered new dimensions of their intimate spheres that their pre-pandemic daily lives were jeopardising. Periods of confinement, and the physical isolation of people in the spaces of their homes, revealed, particularly amongst younger witnesses an "open mind" (Martina, 22, Italy).

Removed from the duties of work, study, other responsibilities, and anxieties, thoughts that had not been given space or time emerged, such as the taken-for-granted aspects of life prior to confinement. Having a family, loved ones, a roof under which to feel protected, and particularly among students, the privilege of being able to attend university "whose lessons, we students, we all remember with melancholy, in whose corridors we walked snorting and which we promise, instead, to retrace with a smile, when all this is over" (Martina, 22), were viewed with a new type of appreciation. Nostalgia for the past is a recurring component in quarantine testimonies, but also there were various attempts to imagine an uncertain future:

> And I find myself inventing dystopian futures, a generation of the sixties with one foot in the past and one in the future. Generation that lives in eternal balance between the memory of a world that no longer exists and updating itself to continuous change to survive the future that will come and is already consumed within us. And in the meantime I live the present of a future imagined only in my invented stories.
>
> *(Danila, 56, Varese, Italy)*

Another frequent theme that emerged concerned travel and the inability to visit and discover new places due to confinement. However, this also presented an opportunity for witnesses to participate and learn more about the natural and cultural heritage of their own community:

> This situation made me understand the true meaning of the word freedom. I, who have always carried the sense of travel inside me, I who felt free only when I was traveling, I only needed to change the city for two days . . . that I felt part of it immediately, I who

> have never given so much weight to everything what surrounded me. I who, after all, have never felt like an Italian citizen, but a citizen of the world. Here, I have rediscovered the meaning of the word freedom, connected in all this to the word homeland. Freedom now for me means leaving the gate of my house, running in the woods or taking a walk by the lake. I will undertake to give more importance to my land, to my homeland, to what I really belong to. I will visit and discover my country, before all the others.
>
> *(Serena, 21, Com, Italy)*

As places, balconies represented for many a point of contact with the outside world, with one witness declaring that "it is a great privilege to be able to use it even just to take a breath of fresh air, which, in these spring days, is equivalent to a dream" (Luca, 29). Conversely, Emma had never taken into consideration the value of having a balcony, through which she realised the changes in the urban landscape of the neighbourhood where she lives in Varese. From its vantage point, she grasps the conditions of emptiness, desolation, and an instantaneous image of the nation struck by the pandemic:

> From the balcony, which I now conceive as a trait d'union between my lived space and the outside, I observed the changes in the urban landscape which, if in the first photo (December 2019) was crowded, noisy, polluted and alive, now, as in the second photo (April 2020), it is empty, silent, peaceful and bleak as well as the whole nation during this unprecedented health emergency.
>
> *(Emma, 20, Varese, Italy).*

Witnesses who had the opportunity to experience gardens, often in the company of pets, found that such spaces and encounters played key roles in alleviating loneliness: "I'm lucky because I have a fairly large piece of garden, which is the place of residence of my six cats (yes, I know maybe they are a bit too many) who always combine one!" (Giada, 21, Monza, Italy). Another aspect that emerges from testimonies is the love for nature. Visual and aural perceptions allowed human beings in "recluse" to contemplate on a daily basis "being in the world":

> In my lived space, sound perceptions prevail, but also visual ones because I often go to the terrace to observe how nature has flourished, as if it were free to continue its life cycle, since the "recluses" are us human beings, but not her.
>
> *(Giulia, Como, Italy)*

Not all witnesses, however, had the privilege of being able to contemplate nature by looking out the window of their homes. Rather, they observe and experience the natural and cultural landscapes of nearby places and their local communities by creating metaphorical games:

> Sometimes I felt a strong need to breathe deeply, to feel the sun warm my skin and watch the clouds dance. The windows were the only door to the world, but the view they offer is claustrophobic: a narrow street and many neighboring houses. The only element that stands out is the bell tower that rises against the sky, marking the passage of time with the tolling of its bells.
>
> *(Giulia, 20, Como, Italy)*

Soundscapes also played fundamental roles in the bottom-up construction of solidarity and closeness between citizens – creating messages of resistance and resilience:

> From the terraces of our houses, the eerie silence of the city is was broken by the various flashmobs, voices and sounds that suddenly opened a dialogue between the houses. We need to make people feel that there is someone out there who resists like us, wants to talk, to win. We are getting used to a different, more supportive city and a more sonorous landscape. I am sure that when all this ends, we will look at our "collective home" with greater respect and care.
>
> *(Kristian, 21, Olgiate Comasco, Italy)*

Video calls via mobile phone or computer with family and friends were the most used tools to communicate at a distance. All witnesses agreed, however, that although they were useful for feeling closer in physical distances, "the natural coldness of a telephone contact" was only ameliorated if "it was transformed into an affectionate desire to meet again as soon as possible" (Giada, 21, Italy). Evidence reveals that the most awaited moment of the day was precisely the one in which some video call took place since it allowed the space inside one's home to be disowned. Subsequently, the creation of new spaces emerged from the interactions of calls originating and received from different locations:

> This has pushed me to try to be able to maintain contacts as real as possible through the means of communication, so much so that my favorite moment of the day has become that of video calls. I think this means that, perhaps, in this moment of quarantine and social distancing, I am not in my space, despite being within the walls of my home.
>
> *(Sara, 21, Busnago, Italy)*

Although one's home is considered the first place to take refuge and be welcomed, according to some witnesses, perceptions and feelings associated with this place changed for some witnesses during their confinements:

> Home is the place of refuge, always ready to welcome, a place where one feels protected. But when it becomes the only dimension of life, the perception changes. It is the alternation between external life and internal life that enhances both, the inside-outside dialectic that gives meaning to everything. . . . I feel, then, that I am living a suspended time in which I am unable to go forward or backward, a sort of dimension parallel that takes away from life, stealing something precious that cannot be recovered in any way. And, then, the only prospect to keep me alive is that of a return to proximity, closeness, human contact, to a moment in which the other is not viewed with suspicion. It's a long way, but I need to think that all this will come back.
>
> *(Alessandra, 26, Vibo Valentia, Italy)*

Yi-Fu Tuan's (1977, 186) observation that "sense of time affects sense of place" underscores the changes in the perception of space and time, often cited by witnesses that stress an indissoluble association between the two categories of *chorology* and *chronology*. Pandemic dimensions of space-time reveal the liminality of *terrae incognitae* which "lie in the minds and hearts of men" (Wright 1947, 15; Lowenthal 1961, 241). According to Fabio Lando (2012, 264), J.K. Wright's *geosophical* perspective invites us to explore those unknown and difficult to penetrate sectors that constitute the sphere of individual subjectivity as they intersect with various social groups. One witness testified,

> It is in the newfound conviction of the usefulness of social distancing that I find the reason to activate defense mechanisms, invest energy to find the right personal balance between space and time, with the awareness that they are, despite the undisputed mathematical rationality, variables in perception; the same space can be sufficient and protective or a cage that, despite its size, makes us prisoners of ourselves; thus time can appear slow and infinite in anticipation of an uncertain future or run fast chasing tomorrow.
>
> *(M. Francesca, 61, Terranova di Pollino, Italy)*

Interesting anthropological elements also emerge, such as the various and significant metaphors through which SARS-Cov-2 is defined: monster, dragon, invisible or dark enemy, and alien. Such appelations recall the popular and collective memory of other types of past disasters and extreme natural events:

> My life smelled of happiness. It was a sweet, intense perfume, it flooded all the rooms of the world around me, I lived in a perfect world. I have always felt, more than a princess, a warrior, the modern Mulan. But I had never really come to terms with some terrible dragon to defeat. Never, until this time . . . I found myself catapulted into a new world, disoriented, terrified. The dragon is so real and frightening, and the perfume that flooded my life has disappeared, it has left room for a feeling of weight that oppresses my chest every day.
>
> *(Giusy, 26, Cosenza)*

By mapping the landscape of testimonies during the Italian COVID-19 lockdown, a complex, variegated, psychological portrait of pandemic spaces and the places from which they were experienced fades into view. Collectively, these testimonies speak to the fragility and vulnerability of the human condition but also bear witness to its dimensions of resilience and resistance.

Conclusion

The 18th-century Italian political philosopher Giambattisto Vico (2010 [1710]), 11) critiqued René Descartes' Cartesian methods for studying "civic life" by stating that "to import the geometric method into practical life" was like "going mad by means of reason . . . as though desire, temerity, occasion, fortune did not rule in human affairs." Buttimer's (1976, 287) phenomenological approach to mapping recognises the inner contingencies of human agency and observes that our "behavior in space and time [is like] the surface movements of icebergs, whose depths we can sense only vaguely."

This chapter's testimony mapping illustrates that plumbing such depths of emotion and human subjectivity during the Italian COVID-19 lockdown seems to have had beneficial psychological effects, despite a qualitative use of Descartes' Cartesian methods. One witness reflected that it provided "a moment to carve out a space for reflection, or not to think only in distressing terms about what was happening." The cases presented in this chapter illustrate applied methods for assessing an individual's senses of place and social vulnerability during a pandemic or any other civic or natural crisis to plan mitigation measures in the fields of emergency psychology and disaster risk management. The geospatial mapping employed in this chapter blended techniques in historical, anthropological, geographical, psychological, pedagogical, and literary fields. Such a multidisciplinary approach is necessary in order to develop commensurate training models for teachers and students to map out relations between the locations of epidemiological and environmental disasters and the human experiences (daily lives, emotions, spatial interactions, mental maps, etc.) of various actors, stakeholders, citizens, students, and socio-health workers, affected by such events.

In conclusion, though this chapter discussed the practical and theoretical dimensions of capturing the slices of lives of witnesses at numerous locations in Italy during the pandemic via geospatial technology, it has not been able to map out the voices and human souls lost to COVID-19. However, Hagerstrand's *Time-Geography* diagrams portray a "sensitivity to the micro-topographies of everyday life," and by tracking phenomena that can "easily escape linear language" and plotting "the mass of the departed," Hägerstrand created a precedent for practices of a "post-mortem" type of geography (Gregory 1991, 32). The shadowed absences of missing testimonies lost to the pandemic throw our life-filled senses of place, though tinged with grief, into the colourful bas-relief of grateful survivors.

Dedication

To my mother, Kathleen Brigid Travis, and the invaluable others who died as a result of the global COVID-19 pandemic.

Acknowledgements

This research was promoted and conceived by the authors, together with Giovanni Gugg (University of Nice, France), Stefano Montes, and Gaetano Sabato (University of Palermo) in the context of the scientific-cultural association and publisher Il Sileno. The research was cited in the May 2020 newsletter of the American Association of Geographers: https://news.aag.org/2020/05/aag-newsletter-may-2020.

Notes

1 Also explored by Henri Lefebvre in *La production de l'espace* (1974) and Edward Soja in *Thirdspace: Journeys to Los Angeles and Other Real-and-Imagined Places* (1996).

2 Il Sileno Edizioni, Testimony page: https://www.ilsileno.it/rivistailsileno/ilmiospaziovissuto/testimonianze/.

3 *Il Mio Spazio Vissuto / Mappa delle Testimonianze*: www.ilsileno.it/rivistailsileno/ilmiospaziovissuto/ilmiospaziovissuto_mappa.

Sources

Aronson, J. 1995. "A Pragmatic View of Thematic Analysis." *The Qualitative Report* 2 (1): 1–3.

Braun, V., and V. Clarke. 2006. "Using Thematic Analysis in Psychology." *Qualitative Research in Psychology* 3 (2): 77–101.

Buttimer, A. 1976. "Grasping the Dynamism of Lifeworld." *Annals of the Association of American Geographers* 66 (2): 287.

Callaghan, C. W. 2016. "Disaster Management, Crowdsourced R&D and Probabilistic Innovation Theory: Toward Real Time Disaster Response Capability." *International Journal of Disaster Risk Reduction* 17: 238–50.

Casti, E. 2013. *Cartografia critica. Dal topos alla chora.* Milano: Guerini e Associati.

Connors, J. P., S. Lei, and M. Kelly. 2012. "Citizen Science in the Age of Neogeography: Utilizing Volunteered Geographic Information for Environmental Monitoring." *Annals of the American Association of Geographers* 102 (6): 1267–289.

Corbetta, P. 2003. *La ricerca sociale: metodologia e tecniche.* Bologna: Il Mulino.

Corrigan, J. 2010. "Qualitative GIS and Emergent Semantics." In *The Spatial Humanities: GIS and the Future of Humanities Scholarship*, edited by David Bodenhamer, John D. Corrigan, and Trevor Harris, 76–88. Bloomington: Indiana University Press.

De Pascale, F. 2021. "Paesaggi nei mondi virtuali e neogeografia. 'Il mio spazio vissuto": una mappatura delle testimonianze di quarantena durante il lockdown in Italia." In *Configurazioni e trasfigurazioni. Discorsi sul paesaggio mediato*, edited by G. Messina and L. D'Agostino, 145–58. Torino: Nuova Trauben.
Elwood, S., M. F. Goodchild, and D. Z. Sui. 2012. "Researching Volunteered Geographic Information: Spatial Data, Geographic Research, and New Social Practice." *Annals of the Association of American Geographers* 102 (10): 1–20.
Forino, G., J. Von Meding, and G. J. Brewer. 2018. "Challenges and Opportunities for Australian Local Governments in Governing Climate Change Adaptation and Disaster Risk Reduction Integration." *International Journal of Disaster Resilience in the Built Environment* 9 (3): 258–72, doi:10.1108/IJDRBE-05-2017-0038.
Frémont, A. 2007. *Vi piace la geografia?* Translated by D. Gavinelli. Roma: Carocci.
Goodchild, M. F. 2007. "Citizens as Sensors: The World of Volunteered Geography." *GeoJournal* 69 (4): 211–21.
Goodchild, M. F., and J. A. Glennon. 2010. "Crowdsourcing Geographic Information for Disaster Response: A Research Frontier." *International Journal of Digital Earth* 3 (3): 231–41.
Gregory, D. 1991. "Interventions in the Historical Geography of Modernity: Social Theory, Spatiality and the Politics of Representation." *Geografiska Annaler: Series B, Human Geography* 73 (1): 17–44.
Howe, J. 2006. "Crowdsourcing: A Definition." Accessed November 10, 2020. http://crowdsourcing.typepad.com/cs/2006/06/crowdsourcing_a.html.
Jackson, J. 2006. "'Neogeography' Blends Blogs with Online Maps." *National Geographic News*, April 25, 2006.
Kankanamge, N., T. Yigitcanlar, A. Goonetilleke, and M. D. Kamruzzaman. 2019. "Can Volunteer Crowdsourcing Reduce Disaster Risk? A Systematic Review of the Literature." *International Journal of Disaster Risk Reduction* 35 (101097): 1–12.
Lando, F. 2012. "La geografia umanista: un'interpretazione." *Rivista Geografica Italiana* 119: 259–89.
Lowenthal, D. 1961. "Geography, Experience and Imagination: Towards a Geographical Epistemology." *Annals of the Association of American Geographers* 51 (3): 241–60.
Lucidi, F., F. Aliverninni, and A. Pedon. 2008. *Metodologia della ricerca qualitativa*. Bologna: Il Mulino.
Soja, E. W. 1989. *Postmodern Geographies: The Reassertion of Space in Critical Social Theory*. London: Verso.
———. 1996. *Thirdspace: Journeys to Los Angeles and Other Real-and-Imagined Places*. Malden, MA: Blackwell.
Travis, C. 2014. "Transcending the Cube: Translating GIScience Time and Space Perspectives in a Humanities GIS." *International Journal of Geographical Information Science* 28 (5): 1149–164.
———. 2017. "Geohumanities, GIScience and Smart City Lifeworld Approaches to Geography and the New Human Condition." *Global and Planetary Change* 156: 147–54.
Tuan, Y. F. 1977. *Space and Place: The Perspective of Experience*. London: Arnol.
Turner, A. 2006. *Introduction to Neogeography*. Sebastopol, CA: O'Reilly Media.
Turri, E. 1998. *Il paesaggio come teatro. Dal territorio vissuto al territorio rappresentato*. Venezia: Marsilio.
Vico, G. 2010 [1710]. *De Antiquissima Italorum Sapientia* (*On the Most Ancient Wisdom of the Italians*). Translated by J. Taylor. New Haven and London: Yale University Press, 11.
Wilson, M. W. 2017. "Neogeography." In *Oxford Bibliographies*. Accessed November 20, 2020. www.oxfordbibliographies.com/view/document/obo-9780199874002/obo-9780199874002-0152.xml.
Wilson, M. W., and M. Graham. 2013. "Neogeography and Volunteered Geographic Information: A Conversation with Michael Goodchild and Andrew Turner." *Environment and Planning A* 45: 10–18.
Wright, J. K. 1947. "Terrae Incognitae: The Place of Imagination in Geography." *Annals of the Association of American Geographers* 37 (1): 1–15.

PART VI

Algorithmic Landscaping

29

DIGITAL OIL AND THE PLANETARY OILFIELD

John Kendall

Introduction

In August 2019, leading oilfield services company Schlumberger announced that it would be donating the codebase for its DELFI data ecosystem to the cloud-native data platform being developed by the Open Subsurface Data Universe (OSDU) Forum (Schlumberger 2019). Composed of a global network of field operators, cloud vendors, application developers, and academic researchers, the OSDU Forum has become a fulcrum for the entire oil and gas (O&G) industry, helping to break down historical O&G data silos, migrate server maintenance and computational processing onto cloud architecture, and provide a ubiquitous and universally accessible data platform for the upstream sector.

While standards-driven initiatives existed before OSDU, such as the Professional Petroleum Data Management Association, the forum has in recent years become *the* premier effort to reformat O&G for a rapidly digitising world. And as their representatives never fail to repeat, Schlumberger's contribution amounts to the open-sourcing of "well over 200 person years" of an otherwise lucrative and proprietary codebase. The donation's announcement thus ostensibly marks a serious sacrifice of short-term gains in the philanthropic effort to help advance wholesale the digital transformation of the O&G industry (Open Group 2021). To be sure, Schlumberger's move is quite significant for an industry where operations are so notoriously veiled behind, as Sara Wylie has aptly put it, "regimes of imperceptibility" (2018; cf. Murphy 2004). But the donation is, of course, also a carefully calculated business decision insofar as it affords the oilfield services an ideal spot to capitalise on the industry-wide shift to a new kind of interoperability as technical as it is political and cultural in scope. That is, what this codebase donation announces is not just a new compatibility with cloud vendors but an alliance with the purportedly more socially conscientious and green-minded information and communication technologies (ICT) industry, against which O&G appears increasingly antagonistic in an era of unabated climate change. This recent move is, in fact, but one of the latest in a series of actions taken by Schlumberger to appear less like an *oilfield services* company and more like a *digital technology* company. To grapple with waning numbers of college graduates interested in joining the O&G industry, for instance, the firm hosts hackathons and design sprints at its Software Technology and Innovation Center to recruit fresh young talent in Silicon Valley (Slav 2020). Schlumberger has also worked hard in recent years to leverage its expertise in extractive sectors beyond oil and gas, such as

DOI: 10.4324/9781003082798-36

geothermal (2020a) and lithium mining (2021). Digitisation thus signals no minor adjustment to O&G operations but a significant transformation in governance, operations, and ethos, such that the industry at large might learn how to disassociate itself from the dirty image of fossil fuel extraction to which it, all the while, remains committed (cf. Amy-Vogt 2020).

What is thus clear is that, far from being left behind by the "greening" of the global political economy, oil – right alongside solar, wind, and other renewable sources of energy – is becoming further de-territorialised and recoded into the latest, greatest, most highly technologised configurations of capital flourishing today. Now, it perhaps comes as no surprise that an industry today facing so many existential uncertainties – from the increasingly sensitive oil price volatility to heightened public and regulatory scrutiny – is scrambling to seek refuge in high tech, which for decades has fancied itself the guarantor of the future.

What is interesting to me, however, how this new mode of interoperability is changing the oilfield. Much like Martín Arboleda's "planetary mine" (2020), the oilfield can no longer be regarded as a "discrete sociotechnical object," cleanly demarcated by geological surveys, property regimes, and national strategic interests. Today, the oilfield extends well beyond the conventional territoriality of extraction as it becomes integrated within the network technologies ostensibly supposed to supersede it. As a result, extraction gets shaped more by the technical demands of standards compliance, machine learning algorithms, and interoperable functionality than by the political wants of state legislatures, national jurisdictions, or climate activists. Oil is indeed taking on an entirely new mode of existence – it is becoming a digital object: a dynamically scalable, recombinatory, and relational database. And as it leaks into cloud computing stacks, digital oil operates at a significantly higher order of abstraction than the forms of oil intelligible to the public or those which are subject, however insufficiently, to regulatory controls. Digitisation, in turn, makes oil even more integral to the "impersonal form of social domination" of capital (Postone 1993, 30).

In this chapter, I argue that the emergence of "digital oil" demands a fundamental rethinking of what extraction *is* in its various modes of existence. To be sure, extant research in political ecology on the fossil fuel industry is crucial as it tracks the precarity of money, labour, and life flowing into and out of oil booms (Caraher and Conway 2016), the carcinogen-laced fracking fluids unleashing unthinkable and unaccountable harm on humans, non-humans, and environments and the efforts of Indigenous water protectors to save ancestral lands (Whyte 2017; Wylie 2018). But I want to suggest that the digitisation of oil poses new problems for extraction scholarship, simultaneously conceptual and practical in scope. Contesting oil requires grasping it in all its various and dynamic modes of existence. Accordingly, we can no longer focus solely on its materiality or sociality but must confront its emergent digitality.

This chapter is an exploratory inquiry into these newfound interfaces of oil and ICT. First, I ask, what is this thing, digital oil? What kinds of relations does it presuppose, and what new kinds of relations does it bring about? Finally, what role does the digital transformation of oil play in the ever-evolving technopolitics of extraction? My aim is not to definitively answer any of these questions but rather introduce them into the ongoing scholarly conversation on oil.

Approaching the Digital Object: From Heidegger and Simondon to Hui

To demonstrate the role digitisation is playing in the technopolitics of extraction, it is necessary to dwell further on the notion of a digital object – a far more complex concept than it first appears. In this paper, I build my understanding of the digital object off the philosophical investigations of Yuk Hui, whose initial description can help orient this chapter. Digital objects, he writes, are

> objects on the Web, such as YouTube videos, Facebook profiles, Flickr images, and so forth, that are composed of data and formalized by schemes or ontologies that one can generalize as metadata.
>
> *(Hui 2012, 380)*

The main goals of this chapter are, first, as to elaborate on the operations through which oil is being added to this list, and second, to explain how digital objects ground new relations between extraction and capitalist society. For his part, Hui (2016) draws on a wide range of thinkers to help him inquire into digital objects, ranging from formal ontology to the tradition of phenomenology extending from David Hume to Edmund Husserl to the philosophies of technology of Martin Heidegger, Gilbert Simondon, and Bernard Stiegler. It is impossible to give a full account of his complex approach in the space provided here, so I will focus only on a few aspects pertinent to my own investigation. The first thing to say, however, is that Hui insists we cannot arrive at a concept of the digital object by merely comparing it to other objects and abstracting from these comparisons a list of attributes specific to the former. For one, a digital object appears to challenge the very notion of an object insofar as objects are said to occupy space. Digital objects do not physically extend beyond the screens which project them, yet they still seem to occupy a sense of space with which we interact – what has been called cyberspace (Hui 2016, 110). The existence of digital objects thus forces us to reconsider what, in essence, an object is.

This reconsideration compels Hui to reject hylomorphism. This manner of grasping objects goes back to Aristotle – even if the Greek philosopher does not employ the concept "object" but only the *hypokeimenon*, or the underlying substratum which remains the same in a thing as it changes. What is important to retrieve for this discussion is the idea that, while an individual thing for Aristotle "comes into being" as a composition of matter (*hyle*) and form (*morphe*), the true essence of a thing resides solely in its form (1994, 1029a26–32, 32b1–2). Hylomorphism is indeed a common engineering principle today, where matter (or in my case, data) is treated as *a priori* passive and accidental, becoming necessary and useful only through its determination by forms. It has heavily influenced the OSDU data platform, just as it has informed the kinds of technological developments (XML, web ontologies, etc.) Hui studies. We can see its legacy, for example, in the typification of resource instances on the OSDU platform through a standardised data schema stringified in JavaScript Object Notation, or JSON (Figure 29.1).

While this is certainly one way to grasp digital objects, it presents a limited view of what the digital object is in its varied modes of existence. As I will explore in this section, the main issue is that hylomorphism detaches the thing being contemplated from the worldly relations which constitute it – or as Hui writes, it detaches the thing from the "totality of its production" (2016, 62, 102–5). In defence of this claim, I follow Hui's synthesis of Heidegger and Simondon, who both find hylomorphism an insufficient way to comprehend objects and especially *technical* objects, given their essential artificiality and historicity. Now, to be sure, the two philosophers find very different motivations for this refusal. Heidegger critiques hylomorphism as a "conceptual schema," which does not regard things as they exist in their functionalities ("ready-to-hand") but as objects rendered for consciousness ("present-at-hand") (1993, 163). He characterises the issue as such: the philosopher can sit and think about the essence of objects all he wants, but when he actually gets to using the

```
{
    "data": {
        ...
    },
    "kind": "opendes:osdu:well-master:0.2.1",
    "namespace": "opendes:osdu",
    "legal": {
        "legaltags": [ "opendes-public-usa-dataset-1" ],
        "otherRelevantDataCountries": [ "US" ],
        "status": "compliant"
    },
    "id": "opendes:doc:2a77f17aa61e4ac1958cf4628e320247",
    "acl": {
        "viewers": [ "data.default.viewer@opendes.contoso.com" ],
        "owners": [ "data.default.owner@opendes.contoso.com" ]
    },
    "type": "well-master",
    "version": 1585760889387388
}
```


Figure 29.1 An example of a JSON document on the OSDU data platform. Applications retrieve the right-hand data by querying the left-hand tags (i.e. forms) (Open Group 2020a, 13–14).[1]

hammer, his attention is not turned toward the idea of a hammer (its properties, its nature, and so on) but toward what is being built. To treat the hammer as an object for consciousness, as "present-at-hand," is therefore to formalise it, to take it out of its everyday use and obscure its "being-in-the-world." Heidegger's entire corpus could be described as an attempt to think beings differently so as to more closely "reveal Being." To be sure, Heidegger is not alone among philosophers in attempting to think things in their unthematised worldliness, but he stands out insofar as this compels him to inquire further specifically into the nature of *technical* objects.

For his part, Simondon criticises hylomorphism on the basis that it occludes an account of the ontogenesis of forms. In the hylomorphic account, that is, forms are always already individuated elements – *their* individuation is externalised from the process of individuation and treated arbitrarily as a "principle of individuation" (2020a, 3). In rejecting this proposition, Simondon's aim is to provide a more adequate theory of individuation, one which does not depend on external causes it cannot itself explain. It follows that, for Simondon, no individuated being can serve as a "model" for the process of individuation, as the existence of any individual presupposes the operations of a "pre-individual reality," and it is precisely this pre-individual reality which must be grasped in thinking individuation. But this is also to say that thought cannot grasp the process of individuation in the same way it grasps individuated beings. Rather, thought grasps the individuation of beings analogically – that is, by *itself* individuating: "the relation between thought and the real becomes a relation between two organized reals that can be analogically linked by their internal structure" (ibid., 170). There is thus no "knowledge of individuation" in the "ordinary sense of the term," only the "individuation of knowledge" (ibid., 17).

In summary, the hylomorphic schema does not account for either a thing's being-in-the-world or the process of individuation necessary for its ontogenesis. Rather, in hylomorphism the process of individuation is substituted with the "finished," "separate," and abstract terms of matter and form (Simondon 2020a, 5). Cognition accordingly becomes detached from the thing as it is encountered ready-to-hand and, in turn, thought does not grasp the operations which bring both the things it thinks and thinking itself into being.

If we are not to conceive technical objects as compositions of matter and form, then how are we to conceive them? Hui's answer is this: "A technical object, if we can understand it ontologically, is a unity of relations" (2016, 14). In developing this thesis, I first move to Simondon, who avoids detaching beings from their worldiness by thinking beings not through the form-matter coupling but through the operational relations which constitute them (2017, 248–49). The French philosopher sees an individual brick of clay, for example, not as what results from the form of the mould after it is applied to the matter of clay but as the convergence of two "half-chains of transformation" toward a common operation (2020a, 24). The clay, in other words, is not some inert, undifferentiated mass when it encounters the mould; it is already the result of, among other things, its removal from the marsh and its drying, shaping, and kneading, all of which is necessary to prepare the clay to "embrace the contours of the mold" (ibid., 23). And likewise, the mould is not "just any form" but already contains a "certain schematism" that had directed its own construction (ibid., 23–24). The brick of clay is, in turn, only the latest result of an ongoing and dynamic "communication," composed of operations which converge "two realities of heterogeneous domains" (2020a, 22). And like every object for Simondon, the individuated brick is nothing but a temporary resolution of the tension between different orders of magnitude – a unity of relations in an "evolving energetic system" (Combes 2013, 6).

While central for Simondon, a theory of relation is more marginal in Heidegger, as Hui notes (2016, 115–17). This is because, early on in *Being and Time*, Heidegger denounces the concept of relation as too formalistic to authentically address Being (1962, 107–8). Despite himself, however, Heidegger provides the possibility of developing a fruitful theory of relation which, when put in conversation with Simondon, can help to understand better what technical objects are, whether we are referring to clay bricks or well log data. First, we must understand the distinction Heidegger makes between relation (*Beziehung*) and reference (*Verweisung*). Whereas relations are, for the German philosopher, improper to Being, references are grounded in the "Being-structure of equipment" (ibid., 109). Despite the awkwardness of this phrasing (especially in English translation), it is important to note the deliberate emphasis Heidegger places on the essential technicity of referentiality. It is precisely *because* equipment is essentially technical that it is also referential, and this is therefore why referentiality addresses Being, whereas relationality, as an idealisation, conceals Being. As Heidegger goes on to write, equipment is always a "being-for," such as the hammer insofar as it "references" the nail. Moreover, such "beings-for" never simply correspond with a single reference. The being-for of the hammer also references the being-for of the table one is constructing, and the work-bench, and the cottage, ultimately the "totality of equipment" through which the "worldly character of the ready-to-hand announces itself" (ibid., 110). It is thus *in and through technics* that ontological knowledge concerns itself with the totality of references which, as Heidegger says, signifies being-in-the-world.

With this in mind, Heidegger can be put back into conversation with Simondon. The latter was also concerned with a sense of "interobjectivity," as Hui terms it, insofar as thinking about technical objects means for him thinking about the relations to exteriority they develop. Simondon uses the concept of the "associated milieu" to describe this process. When a technical object "individualizes," he writes, it establishes a "recurrence of causality within a milieu that the technical object creates around itself and that conditions it, just as it is conditioned by it" (ibid., 59). "Recurrence of causality," or "recurrent causality" (see Simondon 2020a, 2020b), is one way Simondon translates the cybernetic notion of "feedback" (Wiener 1961; see Hui 2019, 190). It is meant to describe a kind of causality which, as opposed to a mechanistic causality which moves linearly from cause to effect, refers to a cause which realises its effect in itself. The key example Simondon gives is the Guimbal turbine, which improves upon the design of the turbine by using oil to both lubricate the engine and isolate the crankcase from water (2017, 57). This creates for the turbine a new "techno-geographical milieu," which draws the river into its own operations to act as a cooling agent. The associated milieu is thus not simply external to the technical object but acts as a kind of folding of exteriority into the functionalities of the technical object. Importantly, however, the associated milieu does not simply collapse into an identity with the object qua "technical individual" but continues to play the "role of information," particularly in the development of machines Simondon describes as "open" insofar as they allow for a certain "margin of indeterminacy" (2017, 17–18, 61). This distinction between object and milieu is crucial because only through information are forms capable of participating in ground and, through this participation, transforming into something else:

> Gestalt psychology, while recognizing the function of totalities, attributed force to form; a deeper analysis of the inventive process would no doubt show that what is determinant and plays an energetic role are not forms but that which carries the forms, which is to say their ground; the ground, while perpetually marginal with respect to attention, is what harbors the dynamisms; it is through which the system of forms exists; forms do not participate in forms, but in the ground, which is the system of all forms or rather the common reservoir of the formes' [sic] tendencies, well before they exist separately and constitute themselves as an explicit system. The relation of participation that links forms to ground is a relation that bestrides the present and diffuses an influence of the future onto the present, of the virtual onto the actual. For the ground is the system of virtualities, of potentials, forces that carve out their path, whereas forms are the system of actuality.
>
> *(Simondon 2017, 60–61)*

Simondon thus defines two kinds of relations – relations between forms and relations between form and ground – analogous to what Heidegger drew our attention to previously. Hui calls the former kind of relations "discursive relations" – that is, "discursive" in the sense that they are relations which emerge from the utterable and are thus premised on the "analyticity of language" (Hui 2016, 133). These relations are similar to the ones Heidegger denigrates as formalistic, and Simondon describes as the "schemes of the creative imagination" concretised in technical objects (2017, 60). Hui refers to the latter relations as "existential relations," or "sedimentations of experience and nonexperience that constitute the 'already-there' and the *Umgang* with the world" (Hui 2016, 133). Existential relations cannot be fully represented because they include some differential margin or absence, which "escapes description and quantification" (ibid.). They are like the relations Heidegger locates in the "gatherings" insofar as they reveal Being, as well as the relations which allow for the kind of convergence of form and ground which Simondon calls individuation. Now, for Hui, the importance of distinguishing discursive relations and existential relations is not to abandon one in favour of the other but to regard them as concerning two different "orders of magnitude" which correspond with different "modes of existence of things" (2016, 29). This, again, is where Hui finds a shared concern in Heidegger and Simondon, as he reads both as diagnosing the problem of alienation within industrial modernity as symptomatic of the disjuncture between two orders of magnitude: for Heidegger, between thought and Being; for Simondon, between culture and technics. Despite their many differences, both philosophers strive to affirm a "higher degree of convergence," which is "more profound than efficient connections and reticulations" comprising discursive relations alone (ibid., 186).

Two final distinctions must be made before closing in on Hui's concept of the digital object. First, Heidegger's own diagnosis of alienation limits his understanding of the "*dynamics* of ontological difference" in the evolution of technical objects (ibid., 117). Hui criticises Heidegger for being unable to think the structure of Dasein as in itself evolving in its correspondence with the technical evolution of interobjective relations. This, for one, informs Heidegger's prescription to abscond modern technology and reinvigorate poetic, non-mediated ways of being with the "hammer" and the "jug." Insofar as the digital milieu provisions contexts drawn from a totality of references quite unlike those which concern hammers and jugs, we must inquire further into the dynamics of ontological difference than Heidegger allows (ibid., 148). Second, while Simondon affords us a way of thinking individuation alongside the technical objects, he did not anticipate a milieu which associates not just machines but entire networks – that is, a properly *digital* milieu. Instead, Simondon treats networks as beyond the purview of what the technical individual can affect and thus beyond the politics of individuation (2017, 229).

It is against both Heidegger's shortcomings with respect to the problematic of givenness, and Simondon's inability to conceive of the possibility of grasping networks as manipulable, technical objects, that Hui raises the provocative concept of the digital object and its associated milieu. Together, they provision not merely new contexts for technical individuals but also, and more critically, transformations in existential relations (Hui 2016, 165). Thus, in my case, digital oil, as a specific instance of the digital object, operates in (at least) three modes of existence. Firstly, it materialises discursive relations (e.g. in new political and cultural compatibilities between oil and ICT); secondly, it provisions new programmable contexts (e.g. new selections of significations premised not on intersubjective experiences of [and with] physical oil but on predictive models generated from machine learning algorithms trained on representative data from other wells, seismic surveys, etc.); and thirdly, it involves a transformation in existential relations – a new form of spatio-temporality integral to what will be defined in the next section as the planetary oilfield.

Interobjectivity and the Planetary Oilfield

I want to put what I have said so far in conversation with critical scholarship on extraction, but a rigorous convergence would take much more space than what is provided here. So while acknowledging the numerous frictions between the phenomenological-existential approach to digital oil I have thus far undertaken and the methodological approaches more familiar to the empirical social sciences, I would like to focus on elaborating what I find to be a few fruitful compatibilities. The first thing to say is that I am, of course, not alone in arguing that the dynamics internal to technical operations shift not just our "discursive" understandings of spatio-temporality but spatio-temporality itself. In the context of challenging the dominant narratives of the global capitalism, such inquiries have been pivotal for the rapidly growing fields of "critical infrastructure" (e.g. Easterling 2014; Bratton 2015; Starosielski 2015) and "critical logistics" (e.g. Cowen 2014; Khalili 2020; Mezzadra and Neilson 2019). I also owe a great debt to work in the social sciences which has for some time now unearthed the "frictions" (Tsing 2005) of globalisation, identifying in them routes toward "alter-globalization" (Bakker 2007), "cosmopolitanism" (Appiah 2006), and other "transnational" modes of being in common (Sassen 1996; Smith and Guarnizo 1998). All of this work rethinks the expansion of capitalist modernity from the perspective of those who had never received it passively as some monolithic form imposed by the so-called industrial core. Rather, capitalist modernity is treated in these accounts as a differentiating process continuously being resisted, repaired, and remade through concrete and contingent participation in its production and reproduction.

Combining these two strains of literature – critical studies of technological modernisation and critical studies of globalisation – has been crucial in displacing what Arboleda (2020) calls methodological nationalism. This bias arises when the conventional, Westphalian political geography of nation-states becomes the exclusive terrain for the critique of political economy. In so doing, methodological nationalism ignores, for one, how global supply chains have integrated directly with urban systems in "the sociometabolic production and reproduction of the mine" (ibid., 5). Moreover, insofar as it pits resource-rich countries against those at the manufacturing centre, it impedes emancipatory political consciousness by obfuscating how, despite national variations, the international working class lives in increasingly convergent and common conditions of existence. Against this trend, Arboleda shows how the geography of advanced industrialisation destabilises former geometries of power which had been structured around the more familiar Global North/Global South binary. This can be witnessed, for instance, in the political and economic rise of China to the global stage, which has forged major new flows of resources, labour, and capital – and accordingly, new chains of dependency – between countries once considered "peripheral" and "semiperipheral." But it can also be seen in the ways technical operations from formerly distinct economic realms (e.g. manufacturing, circulation, and extraction) converge toward an infrastructural-logistical system dispersed at the planetary scale, transcending traditional state jurisdictions while still remaining ruthlessly committed to the exploitation of workers in the expanded production of relative surplus value.

To be clear, there is no doubt that the political sovereignty of the nation-state and the hegemony of the Global North still play a heavy hand in the mediation of international flows of resources, labour, and capital. The point, however, is that from a Marxist perspective, the "polarizing tendencies of uneven geographical development" cannot be confined to the spatial relations between nation-states. Through the convergence of the technical operations which support capital accumulation at a planetary scale, such tendencies have "become immanent to the production of space under capitalist society" (ibid., 22). Mazen Labban (2014) provides the useful example of bacteria which have been genetically modified to conduct metabolic processes capable of extracting minerals not just from ores *in situ* but also in the recycling of e-waste. Biomining, as such procedures have been termed, blurs together manufacturing and extraction processes, allowing the logic of capital to transcend "geological space-time" and extend the territoriality of extraction into the waste dumps of the metropoles (ibid., 572). At least today, the geography of extraction therefore cannot be regarded as a linear, one-way supply line of resources taken from the periphery and dumped onto the industrial core but as itself something "intimately bound up with and constitutive of processes of capitalist urbanization" (ibid., 564). As Labban has aptly put it, capitalist urbanisation is not the result of but "secretes" the planetary mine, such that "periphery needs to be understood as a ubiquitous sociospatial condition" (Arboleda 2020, 16).

Accordingly, we can see that the development of technical operations for extraction not only resolves tensions between extraction and other economic realms but also restructures the very spatio-temporality within which capitalism operates – via, as Simondon would say, the evolution of a new "techno-geographical milieu." What I further appreciate about both Labban and Arboleda, in contrast to other accounts of newer geographies of extraction, is that they remain committed to treating capital as a systematising process while being careful to avoid the pitfalls of structuralist readings of Marx in doing so. Arboleda makes this distinction quite explicit. Even as they frequently evade legislative and institutional mediation, he argues, spaces produced *by* capital do not exist on a "separate plane of reality" than social or political mediations *of* capital (2020, 22). Indeed, analysis of capital must start from the "*modes* or *forms of existence*" whence it emerges:

> To decipher the real social relations behind the reified forms of appearance of the state, then, one must first interrogate the evolving modalities in which the process of socio-ecological metabolism is mediated, produced, and organized.
>
> *(ibid., 121–23)*

Such an immanent critique helps explain how and why heterogeneous experiences of labour are compelled to reproduce homologous relations of production, even and especially as those heterogeneous experiences remain mutually unrecognised. And with this in mind I argue that the "planetary oilfield" operates in an analogous way to, and in conjunction with, the planetary mine. It describes the process through which technical activities used in oil production are converging with not only other forms of extraction but, more broadly, the planetarised associated milieu of advanced industrialisation. The planetary oilfield is evinced, for instance, in Chevron's adoption of cutting-edge technologies of drones and robotics to perform remote maintenance across its vast infrastructure of rigs, refineries, and pipelines (Lee 2019). It is also apparent in the capacity of Schlumberger, as previously mentioned, to leverage its expertise in drilling and surveillance technologies in lithium mining. Indeed, given that the rapid expansion of lithium extraction is driven by the ballooning production of electric vehicles, this also exemplifies how the planetary oilfield frustrates efforts to excise oil from the very technologies supposed to supersede it. The advent of digital oil is central to this obfuscation, as it allows oil to bleed into the "fourth industrial revolution" in new and thus far unchallenged ways.

Now, where does all of this leave my existential inquiry into technics and digital oil? Despite their differences, I do see some productive resonances between Arboleda's "form-analysis Marxism" and the kind of phenomenology of the digital object I presented through the preceding discussion of Hui. For one, they both are very much concerned with understanding objects in terms of relations, and both reflect deeply on the ontogenesis and contingencies of social reality. They also commonly strive toward a resolution of the problem of alienation. Indeed, in a gesture of which Hui would no doubt approve, Arboleda concedes that the "abolition of capital does not necessarily imply that the rift between algorithmic and folk knowledge will be overcome" (2020, 258). The democratisation of the relations of production is a transformation in "discursive relations," which will be no less alienating if it does not also result in "dereification: restoring sensuous objectivity via the liberation of things, and people, from circuits of abstraction" (ibid., 259).

But there are (at least) two crucial incompatibilities which must be addressed. The first is the apparent absence in Hui's text of the question of class and, by extension, the question of value. Labour is not at all an operative concept in Hui's diagnosis of the problem of alienation. Now, one reason for this is that Hui's focus on interobjectivity necessarily displaces his attention from intersubjectivity (hence class struggle). Even still, when he does finally return to this question, he does not do so through Marx but through Husserl and Stiegler and only then to reassert the primacy of interobjectivity as that which conditions intersubjectivity (Hui 2016, 219). Now, I do not think this is a flippant move but a deliberate methodological decision concerning his object of inquiry – for Hui, even the "critique of capital is fundamentally a critique of technology" (2019, 218). One reason for this move, then, is to make room for the consideration of the concretisation of the technical object as something distinct from, and indeed circumscribing, the dialectic of labour and capital. Hui sees the technical object as concretising through resolutions of tension which develop not dialectically but through what Simondon calls transduction. The brick of clay is not what results from the dialectic between form and matter but from transduction wherein operations converge through the communication of technical elements across different domains. Transduction is thus driven not by negation but the "transformation of forms and structures" in the convergence of heterogeneous realities (Hui 2015, see also 2016, 192, MacKenzie 2002) or the "individuation of the real itself" (Barthélémy 2012, 230).

In the spirit of Hui, I think we can say that the dialectical account of social transformation is not "wrong" but that it concerns itself with orders of magnitude which, at best, only partially overlap those which concern interobjective relations. Dialectical relations unfold in the self-transformation of substance as subject; however, precisely because this self-transformation turns *on* the subject, it omits or at the very least does not exhaust the transduction of technical elements which arises during the process of technical individuation. This is perhaps why, as Hui laments, "there is no place for technical objects" within the dialects of substance and subject – a remarkable failure of thought when considering the contemporaneity of Hegel with the onset of the Industrial Revolution (2012, 384). And while, to be sure, Marx had much to say about the technicity of labour (that is, in particular, insofar as an increase in the organic composition of capital corresponds with the intensification of the application of technoscience to capitalist production), this dialectic still turns for him on the self-transformation of substance as subject. This can be seen, for instance, in Marx's notion of the "general intellect," where social knowledge concretises through technics into a productive force without the ontological dynamism of interobjectivity having any apparent effect. By supposing that interobjective relations pertain to a different order of magnitude, Hui thus provides crucial insight into the concretisation of the technical object which otherwise remains hidden.

The second important difference between the existential analysis I am proposing and Arboleda's analysis concerns the role of digitality itself. Arboleda would probably say that if there are such things as digital objects, they are products of the externalisation of labour. The concept of the digital object is thus, at best, an effect and, at worst, a mystification of social relations; in either case, it does not in itself condition transformations in existential relations. This aligns with the aforementioned scholarship on infrastructure and logistics, which tends to privilege the materiality of social relations in the capitalist production of space while having far less to say about the digitality which accompanied its dramatic expansion over the past several decades (in oil scholarship specifically, see Mitchell 2011; Huber 2013; Appel, Mason, and Watts 2015 for such a materialist bias). But as I want to insist, digital objects *do* ground a mode of interobjectivity, which contains its own unique existential relations. Accordingly, the existence of the "planetary oilfield" concerns not only its materiality (cloud-computing stacks, physical buildout of transmission lines, undersea cables) and its sociality (divisions of labour, the value form) but also its emergent digitality (metadata schemes, cloud architecture, Big Data analytics). The latter cannot be reduced to the former but must be integrated into a general critique of the political economy of oil.

Now, to be clear, none of this is meant to give credence to the "techno-paradigm" of digitalism, defined by Matteo Pasquinelli as the

> cult of the *code* against the materiality of *energy* . . . a basic designation for the widespread belief that Internet-based communication can be free from any form of exploitation and will naturally evolve towards a society of equal peers.
>
> *(2008, 63)*

As I will return to later, digitality does not at all liberate digitised subjects from uneven relations of production. Rather, it expands and recomposes these relations into a new digital terrain, conditioning them according to their own dynamics, contours, and logic. But what I nevertheless want to suggest is that there is a wholly different and irreducible set of relations partially constituting the planetary oilfield unaddressable at the level of its social or material relations alone. There is another mode of existence of oil, digital oil, which concerns the resolution of tensions between oil and the "digital milieu," as Hui says, or in the echo of Labban and Arboleda, we might say between oil and the digital dimension of the planetarised technosphere.

The Open Subsurface Data Universe: Making Oil (More) Relational

The Open Subsurface Data Universe (OSDU) began as the Subsurface Data Universe (SDU), a proprietary data platform developed by Shell in 2017. The project was motivated by the strenuous labour expended by the Shell Exploration and Production (E&P) team in simply tracking down and reformatting relevant subsurface data across a myriad of non-standardised and non-interfaceable data silos. This is a problem widely felt across the industry: as Feblowitz (2013) puts it, oil E&P has for a long time been plagued not with *a lack of* but *too much* data. The issue is that this data is often very noisy and application-specific and has little metadata attached to it. This makes it difficult to locate, query, analyse, and more broadly, integrate the technical operations of the petroleum industry into recent cutting-edge innovations in ICT, such as machine learning, automation, and cloud computing.

Recognising that segregated data evinced an industry-wide lack of digital interobjectivity, the SDU team quickly realised that the problem of aggregating, managing, and querying subsurface data needed to be an industry-wide solution. So in March 2018, Shell's SDU team formally convened a meeting with five other oil majors (BP, Chevron, Devon, Equinor, ExxonMobil) and two cloud vendors (Amazon and Microsoft) to discuss a new and much broader project to standardise and centralise oil data at a planetary scale. Given the massive size and complexity of both the physical networks of sensors used in E&P and the data these networks collect, the implementation of a cloud-based digital architecture proved favourable. This is because, first, it promotes industry-wide interoperability and thus facilitates the breaking down of historical data silos. Second, it helps reduce overhead costs of ICT by offloading certain "non-competitive" industry operations, such as data storage and processing, onto cloud vendors.

This initial meeting was followed shortly after by another in June, when the expanded project officially announced its partnership with the Open Group, a global consortium of over 800 organisations dedicated to the promotion of "open, vendor-neutral technology standards and certifications" (Open Group 2021). Consequently, the project also committed to open-sourcing its cloud platform architecture and technology standards. By March of next year, 35 companies, including field operators, oilfield service providers, cloud vendors, and IT firms signed on for the launch of the R0 (demo) release of the OSDU in 2019. As of September 2021, the open-source data platform is now in its deployment-ready R3 commercial release phase and supports a burgeoning number of third-party software applications and services. Perhaps most significantly, as mentioned in this chapter's introduction, this includes Schlumberger's entire DELFI cognitive E&P environment.

Since its inception at Shell, the OSDU project has thus grown from the data platform of a single large firm to a massively distributed, open-source, and cloud-native platform-as-a-service (PaaS). Accordingly, its purpose has shifted significantly beyond the better management of proprietary Shell data toward the development of open-standard data schemas and a set of unified public application programme interfaces (APIs) through which O&G data across the industry can be "collected, described, and served" (Open Group 2020a, 9). In Simondonian terms, we could say that what is witnessed in these changes is the "concretisation" of digital oil as it technically progresses toward a greater and greater degree of coherency, both internally and in relation to its associated digital milieu. Internally, digital oil evinces a technical progression, that is, from stranded, incompatible data silos, to a centralised database for faster and more automated querying, to a consolidated, open-sourced, API-based data platform upon which not only legacy operators and service providers but also new independent software vendors are integrated into the operations of the oil industry. And thus, with respect to its associated digital milieu, the OSDU data platform facilitates the integration of the upstream petroleum industry with the "fourth industrial revolution," an adaptation for which it notoriously trails behind nearly every other sector (Johnson 2019). In Hui's terms, we might generalise this process as the "objectification of data," through which digital objects become more precise yet more flexible precisely because the data they incorporate becomes more relational (2016, 66).

A few concrete examples will prove illustrative of the degree of optimisation and expanded capacity afforded by the concretisation of digital oil. The first is in the improvement of the productivity and reliability of electronic submersible pumps (ESPs), which are used to create artificial lift when bottom-hole pressure is low such that the flow rate is less than desired or oil is otherwise incapable of rising to the surface on its own. This usually occurs after enough petroleum is already recovered to begin to diminish the higher pressure of the oilfield relative to the surface. As Sarapulov and Khabibullin (2017) demonstrate, advanced data analytics drawing on historical production data were successfully used at an oil firm to better predict down-well emergency events such as jamming and overheating, which would cause the ESP to shut down (see also Gupta, Saputelli, and Nikolaou 2016a). Automating this process helps minimise well downtime and reduces the costs of in-field maintenance. Another major benefit of Big Data analytics for the petroleum industry is that it allows much better prediction of well productivity prior to drilling. This is especially useful in plays where dry wells are catastrophically costly, such as deep-water drilling (Gupta et al. 2016b). This advantage results from the fact that well-defined data-driven methods of reservoir modelling have proven better at predicting subsurface rock matrices and fluid distribution than older models premised on geophysics principles and theoretical equations alone (Brulé 2015).

It is important to note that such an instance is precisely what I mean by the provision of new contexts within the digital milieu. The decisions of oil firms, that is, are being drawn from contexts derived neither through directly surveying the reservoir nor the expertise of petroleum engineers but through automated data analyses trained on historical datasets. Such new contexts are associated, then, with a spatio-temporality which is thoroughly digital. One significant result of this is that they can lead to the discovery of insights which would otherwise remain imperceptible to humans, such as Southwestern Energy's AI-driven discovery that a different proppant loading and spacing between fracturing stages would yield higher overall productivity (Betz 2015). It is insufficient to describe such a discovery as the result of an augmentation to already existing human faculties. Digital oil is not simply a prosthetic extension, which allows a better sense of the "natural" objects beneath the subsurface. What must be accounted for is the *nonexperience* of interobjective relations, constituted through programmable algorithmic computation, which participates concretely in the petroleum engineer's imagination of what the oilfield is (Hui 2016, 222–23).

Now, recalling Simondon's critique of hylomorphism in the individual brick of clay, it is important to note the other "half-chain of transformation" which allows for the emergence of digital oil. Improvements to the "objectification of data," that is, often correspond with improvements to what Hui calls the "dataification of the object," i.e. processes through which individuated objects are rendered more addressable to the digital milieu (2016, 50). Thus, as Mehdi Mohammadpoor and Farshid Torabi (2020) have shown, the digitisation of oil production is not just the result of applying algorithms to readymade oilfields but also requires significant renovation of the networks of sensors already embedded therein. Moreover, given the latency issues associated with cloud computing, oftentimes these new devices must be equipped with edge or fog computing capabilities to automatically clean up and analyse the data *in situ* before being served to human-user-facing software applications. Considering simultaneously the physical renovations made to sensing networks and the development of Big Data analytics also helps us better understand the previously mentioned concept of transduction. The creation of new interfaces with oil and ICT initiated by new digital elements requires reconfigurations of the petroleum industry at multiple orders of magnitude. For one, a recurrence of causality must be established between the physical oilfield and digital oil through the implementation of a thick network of smart sensors. At the same time, the physical oil underground is made more amenable to Big Data analytics through the concretisation of well-defined data and metadata schemas compliant with cloud architecture. The emergent interobjectivity of digital oil thus contains both material and digital dimensions. Digital oil, considered as a unity of such relations, provisions a new mode of existence of oil, which is ultimately more variable and versatile precisely because it is more relational.

I want to spend the rest of this section discussing the specific role of the cloud, as I think it best exemplifies the explicit digitality of the planetary oilfield. It is first important to distinguish this digitality from earlier interfaces between ICT and oil. In truth, despite its "stodgy" reputation, the petroleum industry had been an early and eager adopter of ICT, with the implementation of real-time online computing in process facilities beginning in the late 1960s (Cortada 2003, 168). Indeed, ICT played an indispensable role in helping the industry survive the infamous 1980s oil market glut (Cortada 2002, 18). However, as I have been arguing, the transduction of new digital element, such as machine learning algorithms, themselves only recently rendered compatible with oil through the restructuration of massive datasets and augmentation of in-field sensing networks, has initiated an entirely new mode of interobjectivity in the planetary oilfield.

Adapting current business practices in the petroleum industry to cloud architecture begins with cloud migration, a process which requires highly specialised labour practices. It is important to note that "cloud migration" is an umbrella term for a number of pathways composed of even more numerous operations firms need to perform in order to make their legacy applications and databases compliant with cloud architecture. Cloud migration is often a tedious and very labour-intensive process, involving significant fixes or enhancements to codebases, the reformatting and recompiling of legacy databases, and rounds of testing and debugging. Moreover, cloud migration demands a dramatic technical recomposition of the labour operating within oil firms, as workers must possess a host of new skills not provided by their previous education in petroleum engineering, geology, and so on. And while 92% of O&G executives recently surveyed by Ernst and Young (2020) recognised the need to quickly reskill their workforces to survive the industry's rapid digital transformation, around half reported not having a robust plan to do so due to the lack of existing technological competency within their firms. Accordingly, recent industry hiring efforts skew heavily toward data scientists and other related professions with expertise in robotics, automation, cloud computing, and machine learning (Rigzone 2014). These changes in intersubjective relations, themselves introduced by the evolving interobjectivity of digital oil, are not merely technical in nature but also "cultural," as some industry figures describe it. The following interview with an academic researcher and petroleum engineer, published in the *Journal of Petroleum Technology*, illustrates this point:

> AI is a completely different way of solving problems from the complex-mathematics and first-principles-physics approach petroleum engineers have used for the past 30 years to understand and optimize oil- and gas-producing reservoirs, says Shahab Mohaghegh, professor of petroleum and natural gas engineering at West Virginia University. The math behind AI is simpler than that for complex engineering, but AI

involves neuroscience, philosophy, and other disciplines outside the engineering scope, explains Mohaghegh, and the lack of understanding around it can breed resentment, uncertainty, and fear.

(Feder 2020, 28)

Indeed, the "cultural" barriers are quite profound: 86% of executives surveyed from the previously mentioned Ernst and Young report identified "resistance to change among front-line employees" as a significant challenge to the adoption of new technologies (2020, 7). In the digital transformation of the oil industry, the "specter of 'Big Brother' is very real," as employees are forced to confront not just the new technical operations of automation and artificial intelligence but the different sets of values implied within them (Saputelli et al. 2013, 12). From the perspective of intersubjective relations, this is perhaps an even more significant disjuncture than that of technical reskilling, as it implies not only an impediment to prerequisite technical knowledge but also to affectivity.

Indeed, I would like to suggest that this feeling of anxiety among petroleum engineers is symptomatic of the kind of alienation with which I have been concerned throughout this paper. As one of the greatest thinkers of the relation between alienation and technology, Simondon is again helpful on this point. In the context of psychic and collective individuation, he describes the experience of alienation as a kind of anxiety in which the subject "feels as if it exists as a problem posed to itself, and it feels its division into pre-individual nature and individuated being" (2020a, 282). But in the attempt to resolve this tension, the subject "deserts itself," shedding its individuality in becoming "object and witnesses its own expansion according to dimensions it cannot assume" (ibid., 283–84). Importantly, then, anxiety concerns not only a feeling of being controlled by Big Brother but, more fundamentally, a failure to individuate (i.e. to discover a convergence between oneself and one's "pre-individual nature").

It is in this way Simondon opposes anxiety to affectivity, which he situates at the very heart of the possibility of individuation. As in anxiety, affectivity moves the individual outside itself, but it does so in an entirely different way. Unlike anxiety, affectivity does not absolutise exteriority; it does not relate absolutely to the outside but to the "preindividual share" which accompanies the individual. As Combes suggests,

[a]ffectivity includes a relation between the individuated being and a share of not-yet-individuated preindividual reality that any individual carries with it: affective life, as "relation to self," is thus a relation to what, *in the self*, is not of the order of the individual. Affective life thus shows us that we are not only individuals, that our being is not reducible to our individuated being.

(2013, 31)

Now, it is true that anxiety also expresses a relation to the "preindividual share," but it can do so only crudely. Anxiety merely casts the individual into solitude without escape (Simondon 2020a, 283–84). By contrast, affectivity recognises and affirms, as necessary for the individuation of oneself, the existence of others who are also accompanied by "preindividual shares." Against anxiety, affectivity thus demands that the resolution of the tension between the individual and pre-individual can only occur through the collective. In this way, affectivity "relates to a subjective transductive reality" (ibid., 288). Could we understand the anxiety felt by petroleum engineers as symptomatic of a similar rupture in the collective through a new form of interobjectivity they can no longer modulate? If this is the case, I want to suggest that it is precisely because of a disjuncture in not only the "discursive relations" amenable to new technical knowledge but with respect to the very spatio-temporality of digital oil. I end this section by elaborating further on this disjuncture.

First, I must stress that there are always multiple modalities of existential relations at play. We can speak, for instance, of clock time as an empty time through which modern technologies discipline and synchronise space, such as the standardised trading hours of the New York Mercantile Exchange (NYMEX), which (ostensibly) help regulate the paper oil trade. We can also understand oil through an entirely different temporality, what Hui calls topological time. Technical systems give presence to this temporality when they render "obsolete some interobjective relations in favor of others" (Hui 2016, 175). Consider, as Heidegger does, the experience of time which arises when one encounters an ancient piece of equipment in a museum (1962, 431–32). What sense of temporality is being experienced here? It is not the same temporality which I experience when I remember, for example, what I did yesterday, nor is it the same temporality which I experience when I look at the clock and realise I am late for work. Instead, temporality is encountered as interobjective relations detached from the contemporaneous habits and knowledge of Dasein. Unlike clock time, which is also in a way spatialising, topological time is thus not homogeneous. As a process of separation, it brings to presence the multiplicity of time. Considered as a planetary technical system, the cloud indeed depends on this multiplicity of topological time to buttress the planetary oilfield, among the many other things now included in the digital milieu. As an experience of decoupling, topological time can thus lead one either to profoundly inhibiting anxiety or to new forms of individuation (Hui 2016, 180).

The topological temporality of the digital milieu must be understood in terms of the evolution of both the intersubjective and interobjective relations which have constituted it. We can experience this topological temporality, for instance, in the coming to pass – or "percolation," as Serres says (1995) – of other kinds of interobjective relations, such as the data silos laboriously navigated by an older generation of petroleum engineers. These interobjective relations are both digital (objectification of data) and material (smart sensors) in scope. Just as importantly, new intersubjective relations also have to be established at the level of labour, of affectivity, and as we shall see in the next section, of property and governance. Again, I stress, all of this points to a different mode of existence of oil with its own dynamics and logic.

Limits to Contest: Digitalism, Information, and Capital

Now, it is all well and good to diagnose the anxieties of petroleum engineers, but the reader might be wondering: where does this leave the rest of us? Of course, in the epoch of climate change, the planetary oilfield concerns not just disaffected oil workers but every individuated being on the planet. Insofar as digital oil allows the petroleum industry to remain operating under increasing political scrutiny and economic insecurity, the planetary oilfield will no doubt merely ramp up the "slow violence" (Nixon 2011) already skewed toward the most vulnerable peoples and ecosystems. If I had privileged those subjects closest to the centre of the digitisation of oil and thus relatively less exposed to the violence of the periphery, it was not just to offer sympathy but to insist that, through an investigation of their encounters with the planetary oilfield, we might see that this is not the *only* thing going on. Its advent cannot be reduced to the augmentation and exacerbation of already-existing extractive processes but rather concerns a new mode of interobjectivity.

Alienation in the digital milieu, of course, extends far beyond the petroleum industry. Simondon regards alienation as a failure of collective individuation – or the "genesis and resolution of tensions to arrive at a metastable equilibrium" (Hui 2016, 15) – which rests at the heart of industrial modernity. Accordingly, I think the two prescriptions suggested by Simondon to reconstitute individuation will prove useful here. The first route, he says, is to restore the encyclopedism of the Enlightenment through the founding of a "mechanology" with which humans can relearn how to work with technical objects and resituate themselves as technical individuals. Against the stratified arrangements of industrial modernity, within which humans are either placed below technical objects as their labourers or above them as their masters, Simondon argues individuation can only occur when humans understand themselves alongside and amidst technical objects, attending to their ontogenesis in the reinvention of themselves (2017, 255).

Now, we might be tempted to think of a project like Wikipedia as such an effort to renew processes of individuation. But the issue is that, to resolve alienation, encyclopedism must work in concert with the second route: the deployment of philosophical thinking as a means of re-establishing the "reticulation of key-points, which is the direct mediation between man and the world" (2017, 194). "Key-point" is a very difficult concept in the philosophy of Simondon, as it points him rather contentiously back to a primordial magical unity wherein the split between figure and ground has not yet occurred. As he speculates, at some point, there must have been a rupture which bifurcated this magical unity into technology, which objectifies figures, and religion, which subjectifies ground. In contrast, magical thinking did not divide figure against ground but distinguished key-points which remain immanent to what surrounds them but nevertheless allow for singular focalisations (ibid., 178–79). The summit of a mountain is one of his more illuminating examples: it "governs a land" through its naturally privileged position with respect to other places. Moreover, it is explored not

> in order to dominate or possess it, but in order to exchange a relationship of friendship with it. . . . The magical universe is made of a network of access points to each domain of reality: thresholds, summits, limits, and crossing points, attached to one another through their singularity and their exceptional character.
>
> *(ibid., 179–80)*

Now, what does it mean to introduce such key-points into the digital milieu? To be sure, Simondon does not contend one can (or should) "go back" to this magical unity but rather identifies the task of philosophical thinking with the facilitation of new convergences of figure and ground in the associated milieu within which one finds oneself. Accordingly, to bridge these two paths toward dis-alienation – encyclopedism and the reticulation of key-points – I think it is crucial to recall how Simondon differentiates between form and information. Recall, first, that the associated milieu "plays the role of information" for technical individuals and, second, that forms serve a regulative function between the technical individual and the associated milieu in the establishment of a recurrent causality. Forms are what allow for the metastability necessary to, in the first place, receive information qua "variability of forms, the influx of variation with respect to form" (ibid., 150). *Pace* Norbert Wiener (1961), information is not the measure of organisation of a system: a perfect automaton conveys no information. On the other hand, as Simondon explains, information is never "pure chance" but can only be rendered significant "with respect to already existing forms" (2020a, 150). Finally, then, technology is what mediates form and information: it is the historico-practical activity through which the *a posteriori* (information) becomes the *a priori* (form).

By Hui's account, however, the digital object presents an immense challenge to the ability of humans to use technical knowledge to not only operate alongside the networks of information which shape them but to distinguish key-points within these networks. Now more than ever, the forms programmed into machines maintain such high margins of indeterminacy as to be frequently and thoroughly confused with information. So many metaphors which name techniques in predictive data analytics – artificial general intelligence, machine learning, neural networking – are testament to this confusion about the operations of machines which exchange forms and the operations of a mind which forms itself by adapting itself to new information. Moreover, through the advent of digital oil and its associated milieu, I think we can say that the planetary oilfield comes closer to approximating this existential indeterminacy. Thus, it likewise poses the same difficulty of distinguishing information from form. In its claim to transcend this division, the techno-paradigm of digitalism cultivates everywhere a profound distancelessness and immediately accessible openness. Indeed, perhaps the greatest irony of the whole digital transformation of the oilfield is that the technical operations of the petroleum industry are now more open to investigation than ever, yet this interoperability has not at all made the economy of oil any more democratic.

Recalling Pasquinelli's definition of digitalism as the "cult of the *code* against the materiality of *energy*," we can say that what most often occurs in the digital milieu is the disembodiment of politics away from the uneven terrain of material struggle and toward an entirely ephemeral and inconsequential "code fetishism" (2008, 72–73). We had been exposed to this ideological operation at the very beginning, through the OSDU Forum's claim to be open-source and open-standard, thus ostensibly more integrated into the liberal political paradigm of a "horizontal democracy of nodes that produce and exchange on an equal basis" (ibid., 66). It is also evident in recent claims made by oil majors to be on a path toward net-zero emissions by 2050 amidst shareholder-driven "rebellions" waged in the name of proactive disclosure of environmental and social governance, public accountability, and financialised climate risk (Ambrose 2021; Shell 2021). Of course, such disclosures often do little more than afford fossil fuel companies a way to reframe climate change as a "risk" linked to consumer demands and not their own business practices (Supran and Oreskes 2021). My point, however, is that they also, and indeed as consequence, advance the communicability of oil within the digital milieu.

Now, beyond a recomposition of labour, this process of digital transformation also necessitates a new transnational mode of governance between capitals at the planetary scale. As Schlumberger employee Trygve Randen states, the cloud architecture of the OSDU platform demands that "the way we organize, handle, and access our data as an industry would not be an area of competitive focus" (Schlumberger 2020b, 4). This long-held digitalist mantra, that "information is non-rival" (Benkler 2006), thus requires the mediation of a new disjuncture which partially, indeed very awkwardly and unevenly, brackets off the "discursive" regime of property rights from the "existential" relations of production. We see this conflict between communicative capital and industrial capital bear out in the rapidly increasing concerns about the risk of new digital contagions, such as cyberattacks and data breaches, which may result from the expanded interoperability and communicability of oil in the digital milieu (Yuan and Mahdavi 2011; Onyeji, Bazilian, and Bronk 2014; Lamba 2018). And as we saw with the ransomware attack on Colonial Pipeline in April 2021, such fears are certainly not without warrant (Turton and Mehrotra 2021).

After all, the OSDU data platform *is* open-source and open-standard and thus, in some way, collaborative, intersubjective, and non-proprietary. Accordingly, as Figure 30.2 shows, a bifurcation in the regime of property between areas of competitive and non-competitive operations must be made, precisely insofar as a commons of sorts is established through the OSDU platform. Of course, this still involves the oligopolistic propertisation of the physical infrastructure (servers, data centres, fibre optic networks, and so on) by the three planetary ICT behemoths: Google, Amazon, and Microsoft. But the point is that, at least at the order of magnitude which pertains to technical operations in oil E&P, this regime of property is mutating. We should appreciate just how sharp of a reversal this is for the petroleum industry. Bowker's studies of

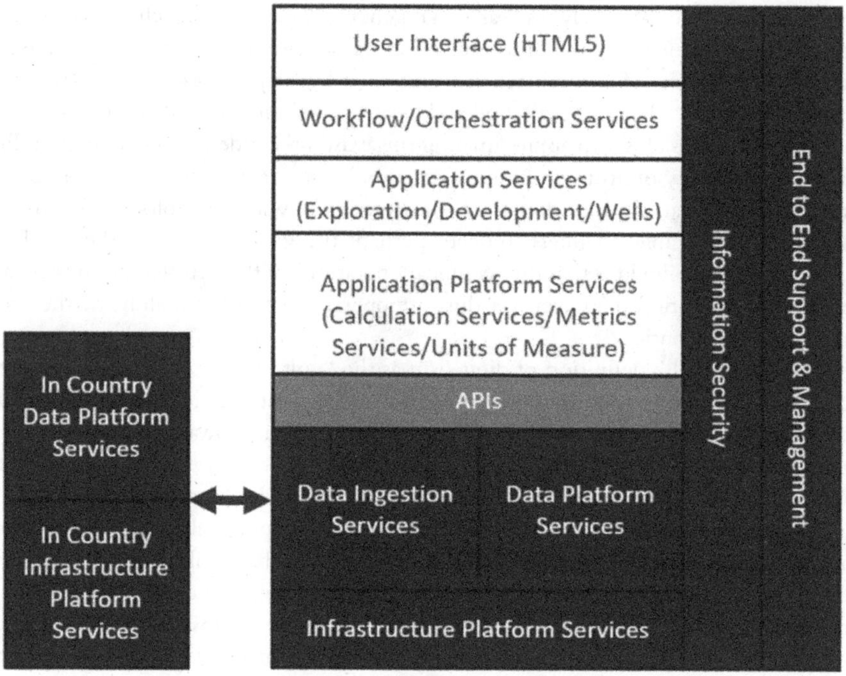

Figure 29.2 Diagram of the OSDU architecture. In blue are the non-competitive aspects of the platform and in white are the competitive aspects, with API hooks (orange) linking these two dimensions (Open Group 2020b, 9).[2]

Schlumberger (1987, 1994) are particularly illuminating: in its early days, the oilfield services company deliberately made its technologies more complex than necessary so as to be difficult to copy, and it was always in the process of inventing new ways to clandestinely survey the subsurface so as to avoid the detection of nearby competitors. Likewise, the Seven Sisters of the oil industry colluded in infrastructural sabotage so as to underdevelop the capacities of global oil production and maintain price control in the postwar years (Mitchell 2011). Indeed, oil firms have spent extensive resources for decades on the concealment of their technical operations (Wylie 2018) and have routinely relied on configurations of fixed capital which render the industry *less* interoperable so as to secure "costly investments" and protect exorbitant profits (Watts 2005).

The openness of the architecture of the cloud mutates the old regime of property into a new mode of governance, at least at certain orders of magnitude. To put it in Marxist terms, the digital milieu adapts to and absorbs some degree of the socialisation of technical knowledge without either abolishing the regime of property or emancipating the "social individual" qua living embodiment of the "general intellect" (Marx 1973, 706). Or to put it in Simondon's terms, digital oil evinces an "encyclopediazation" of intellectual property without establishing key-points and hence reigniting processes of individuation. This is symptomatic of a failure to distinguish technical objects as figures and instead regard technology as a totalising ground. What's left are "superficial engagements" between humans and machines impeding more inventive uses of technical objects in the discovery of information – or "significations," as Hui also describes them – which might serve as new key-points to help converge figure and ground at a higher degree (2016, 205). Hui has recently taken to describing such therapeutic practices as "cosmotechnics" (2019), through which digital technology would be resituated in heterogeneous cosmic realities and hence a genuine "technodiversity" reintroduced into otherwise totalising cybernetic systems.

But such philosophical thinking, I contend, requires further synthesis of the question concerning technology and the critique of political economy. Short of this, climate struggles which venture onto digital terrain will continue to fall under the spell of digitalism, falsely presuming that all that is needed to overcome the abuses of what Pasquinelli (2017) fittingly calls "cyberfossil capital" is to make it more communicable (e.g. Donaghy, Henderson, and Jardim 2020). This does little more than contribute to the same flat encyclopedism informing the rapid digital transformation of the O&G industry. In truth, anti-capitalist climate activism will have limited impact if it cannot address both the discursive and existential relations of digital oil. To put it another way: if it is true, as Arboleda says, that technology "plays a definitive role in the process whereby capital metamorphoses into conscious revolutionary action," an adequate understanding of such a metamorphosis today must include a critique of the digital object (2020, 233).

Conclusion

This chapter has sought to conceptualise digital oil as a specific mode of existence of oil which has emerged at the interface of the technical operations of oil production and the so-called fourth industrial revolution. Following Hui, I insisted that digital oil cannot be adequately understood from a hylomorphic perspective but comprises a new mode of interobjectivity occurring at multiple orders of magnitude. Further, I argued that digital oil is amenable to ICT not just because of the imposition of new conceptual schemas borrowed from the tech industry but because of its convergence toward the existential relations which subtend the digital milieu. This digital milieu, in turn, led me to conceptualise the planetary oilfield as not only containing material and social folds but also one which is irreducibly digital.

Such existential inquiries into the digital object and its associated techno-geographical milieu must be made part of our understanding of the capitalist infrastructures of advanced industrialisation, as the latter are neither only social nor material but also thoroughly digital undertakings. Digitality, as I argued in the final section, opens the planetary oilfield for excavation on entirely new terrain, compelling entirely new technical practices. To be sure, this terrain contains its own ideological traps, such as digitalism, but also, just as importantly, new engagements and opportunities for political action. I followed Simondon in identifying alienation as rooted in the rupture between ground and form, which, as it manifests in the digital milieu, has made it increasingly difficult for humans to distinguish information qua variability of form in the establishment of key-points which could help reconstitute modes of individuation. In lieu of a more robust account of digital oil, we will continue to fail to differentiate form from information and, what amounts to the same, the automaton of capital from the autonomy of social life.

Acknowledgements

In conducting research for this chapter, the author acknowledges the financial support provided by the William F. Stout Fellowship of the Graduate School at the University of Minnesota. The author also acknowledges the Open Group for permission to include figures derived from its copyrighted OSDU Application Development Guide. OSDU is a trademark of the Open Group.

Notes

1 ©2021 The Open Group. OSDU is a trademark of the Open Group in the United States and other countries.
2 ©2021 The Open Group. OSDU is a trademark of the Open Group in the United States and other countries.

Sources

Ambrose, Jilian. 2021. "ExxonMobil and Chevron Suffer Shareholder Rebellions over Climate." *The Guardian*. Accessed September 3, 2021. www.theguardian.com/business/2021/may/26/exxonmobil-and-chevron-braced-for-showdown-over-climate.

Amy-Vogt, Betsy. 2020. "Oil and Gas Industry Embraces Open-Source Collaboration, Encourages Greener Energy Solutions." *SiliconANGLE.com*. Accessed April 27, 2021. https://siliconangle.com/2020/12/01/oil-and-gas-industry-embraces-open-source-collaboration-encourages-greener-energy-solutions-reinvent/.

Appel, Hannah, Arthur Mason, and Michael Watts, eds. 2015. *Subterranean Estates: Life Worlds of Oil and Gas*. Ithaca: Cornell University Press.

Appiah, Kwame Anthony. 2006. *Cosmopolitanism: Ethics in a World of Strangers*. New York and London: W.W. Norton & Company.

Arboleda, Martín. 2020. *Planetary Mine: Territories of Extraction Under Late Capitalism*. London and New York: Verso.

Aristotle. 1994. *Metaphysics: Book Z and H*. Translated by David Bostock. Oxford: Clarendon Press.

Bakker, Karen. 2007. "The 'Commons' Versus the 'Commodity': Alter-globalization, Anti-privatization and the Human Right to Water in the Global South." *Antipode* 39: 430–55. https://doi.org/10.1111/j.1467-8330.2007.00534.x.

Barthélémy, Jean. 2012. "Fifty Key Terms in the Works of Gilbert Simondon." In *Gilbert Simondon: Being and Technology*, 203–31, edited by Arne de Boever, Alex Murray, Jon Roffe, and Ashley Woodward. Edinburgh: Edinburgh University Press.

Benkler, Yochai. 2006. *The Wealth of Networks: How Social Production Transforms Markets and Freedom*. New Haven: Yale University Press.

Betz, Jack. 2015. "Low Oil Prices Increase Value of Big Data in Fracturing." *Journal of Petroleum Technology* 67 (4): 60–61. https://doi.org/10.2118/0415-0060-JPT.

Bowker, Geoffrey C. 1987. "A Well Ordered Reality: Aspects of the Development of *Schlumberger*, 1920–39." *Social Studies of Science* 17: 611–55. https://doi.org/10.1177/030631287017004003.

———. 1994. *Science on the Run: Information Management and Industrial Geophysics at Schlumberger, 1920–1994*. Cambridge: MIT Press.

Bratton, Benjamin H. 2015. *The Stack: On Software and Sovereignty*. Cambridge and London: MIT Press.

Bridge, Gavin. 2009. "The Hole World: Scales and Spaces of Extraction." *New Geographies* 2:43–48.

Brulé, M. R. R. 2015. "The Data Reservoir: How Big Data Technologies Advance Data Management and Analytics in E&P." Presented at SPE Digital Energy Conference and Exhibition, The Woodlands, Texas, USA, March 2015. https://doi.org/SPE-173445-MS.

Caraher, William, and Kyle Conway, eds. 2016. *The Bakken Goes Boom*. Grand Forks: The Digital Press @ The University of North Dakota.

Combes, Muriel. 2013. *Gilbert Simondon and the Philosophy of the Transindividual*. Translated by Thomas LaMarre. Cambridge and London: MIT Press.

Cortada, James W. 2002. "Studying the Increased Use of Software Applications: Insights from the Case of the American Petroleum Industry, 1950–2000." *Iterations: An Interdisciplinary Journal of Software History* 1: 1–26.

———. 2003. *The Digital Hand: How Computers Changed the Work of American Manufacturing, Transportation, and Retail Industries*. Oxford and New York: Oxford University Press.

Cowen, Deborah. 2014. *The Deadly Life of Logistics: Mapping Violence in Global Trade*. Minneapolis and London: University of Minnesota Press.

Donaghy, Tim, Caroline Henderson, and Elizabeth Jardim. 2020. "Oil in the Cloud: How Tech Companies Are Helping Big Oil Profit from Climate Destruction." *Greenpeace Reports*. Accessed April 26, 2021. www.greenpeace.org/usa/reports/oil-in-the-cloud/.

Easterling, Keller. 2014. *Extrastatecraft: The Power of Infrastructure Space*. New York and London: Verso.

Ernst & Young. 2020. *How Do You Reshape when Today's Future May Not Be Tomorrow's Reality?* Oil and Gas Digital Transformation and the Workforce Survey 2020. Accessed April 28, 2021. https://assets.ey.com/content/dam/ey-sites/ey-com/en_gl/topics/oil-and-gas/ey-oil-and-gas-digital-transformation-and-the-workforce-survey-2020.pdf.

Feblowitz, Jill. 2013. "Analytics in Oil and Gas: The Big Deal about Big Data." Presented at SPE Digital Energy Conference and Exhibition, The Woodlands, Texas, USA, 5–7 March 2013. https://doi.org/10.2118/163717-MS.

Feder, Judy. 2020. "Upstream Digitalization Is Proving Itself in the Real World." *Journal of Petroleum Technology* 72 (4): 26–28. https://doi.org/10.2118/0420-0026-JPT.

Gupta, Supriya, Luigi Saputelli, and Michael Nikolaou. 2016a. "Big Data Analytics Workflow to Safeguard ESP Operations in Real-Time." Presented at SPE North American Artificial Lift Conference and Exhibition, The Woodlands, Texas, USA, October 2016. https://doi.org/10.2118/181224-MS.

Gupta, Supriya, Luigi Saputelli, Alexander Verde, Jose A. Vivas and G. M. Narahara. 2016b. "Application of an Advanced Data Analytics Methodology to Predict Hydrocarbon Recovery Factor Variance Between Early Phases of Appraisal and Post-Sanction in Gulf of Mexico Deep Shore Assets." Offshore Technology Conference, Houston, Texas, May 2016. https://doi.org/10.4043/27127-MS.

Heidegger, Martin. 1962. *Being and Time*. Translated by John Macquarrie and Edward Robinson. Oxford: Basil Blackwell.

———. 1966. *Discourse on Thinking*. Translated by John M. Anderson and E. Hans Freund. New York: Harper & Row.

———. 1993. "The Origin of the Work of Art." In *Basic Writings*, edited by David Farrell Krell, 139–212. New York: HarperCollins Publishers.

Hoberg, George. 2013. "The Battle over Oil Sands Access to Tidewater: A Political Risk Analysis of Pipeline Alternatives." *Canadian Public Policy* 39 (3) (September): 371–91. https://doi.org/10.3138/CPP.39.3.371.

Huber, Matthew T. 2013. *Lifeblood: Oil, Freedom, and the Forces of Capital*. Minneapolis and London: University of Minnesota Press.

Hui, Yuk. 2012. "What Is a Digital Object?" *Metaphilosophy* 44 (4) (July): 380–95. https://doi.org/10.1111/j.1467-9973.2012.01761.x.

———. 2015. "Induction, Deduction and Transduction: On the Aesthetics and Logic of Digital Objects." *Networking Knowledge* 8 (3): 1–19. https://doi.org/10.31165/nk.2015.83.376.

———. 2016. *On the Existence of Digital Objects*. Minneapolis and London: University of Minnesota Press.

———. 2019. *Recursivity and Contingency*. London and New York: Rowman & Littlefield.

Johnson, Bill. 2019. "DCP Midstream – Enabling Business Transformation with the PI System: The DCP 2.0 Journey." Keynote presentation at PI World, San Francisco, April 2019. Accessed April 28, 2021. https://resources.osisoft.com/presentations/dcp-midstream – enabling-business-transformation-with-the-pi-system – the-dcp-2–0-journey-1x/.

Khalili, Laleh. 2020. *Sinews of War and Trade: Shipping and Capitalism in the Arabian Peninsula*. New York and London: Verso.

Krebbers, Johan, and Stephen Whitley. 2020. "The OSDU™ Data Platform: Why We Built It." Filmed June 18, 2020 online for World Oil Webcast, 59:38. www.youtube.com/watch?v=KvxsE8J1J8o.

Labban, Mazen. 2012. "Deterritorializing Extraction: Bioaccumulation and the Planetary Mine." *Annals of the Association of American Geographers* 104 (3): 560–76. http://doi.org/10.1080/00045608.2014.892360.

Lamba, Anil. 2018. "Protecting 'Cybersecurity & Resiliency' of Nation's Critical Infrastructure – Energy, Oil & Gas." *International Journal of Current Research* 10 (12): 76865–6876. https://doi.org/10.24941/ijcr.35045.12.2018.

Lee, Mike. 2019. "Robots in the Permian? Climate Concerns Drive Innovation." *E&E News*. Accessed April 28, 2021. www.eenews.net/stories/1060201281.

MacKenzie, Adrian. 2002. *Transductions: Bodies and Machines at Speed*. London and New York: Continuum.

Marx, Karl. 1973. *Grundrisse: Foundations of the Critique of Political Economy*. Translated by Martin Nicolaus. London: Penguin.

Mezzardra, Sandro, and Brett Neilson. 2019. *The Politics of Operations: Excavating Contemporary Capitalism*. Durham and London: Duke University Press.

Mitchell, Timothy. 2011. *Carbon Democracy: Political Power in the Age of Oil*. London and New York: Verso.

Mohammadpoor, Mehdi, and Farshid Torabi. 2020. "Big Data Analytics in Oil and Gas Industry: An Emerging Trend." *Petroleum* 6: 321–28.

Murphy, Michelle. 2004. "Uncertain Exposures and the Privilege of Imperception: Activist Scientists and Race at the U.S. Environmental Protection Agency." *Osiris* 2 (19): 266–82. www.jstor.org/stable/3655244.

Nixon, Rob. 2011. *Slow Violence and the Environmentalism of the Poor.* Cambridge and London: Harvard University Press.

Onyeji, Ijeoma, Morgan Bazilian, and Chris Bronk. 2014. "Cyber Security and Critical Energy Infrastructure." *The Electricity Journal* 27 (2): 52–60. http://dx.doi.org/10.1016/j.tej.2014.01.011.

Open Group, The. 2020a. *The Open Group Guide: OSDU™ Application Development Guide.* Berkshire, UK: The Open Group.

———. 2020b. *The Open Group Guide: OSDU Geomatics Conceptual Solution Architecture: Geodetic Principles and Policies.* The Open Group: Berkshire, UK.

———. 2021. *The Open Group: Leading the Development of Open, Vendor-Neutral Technology Standards and Certifications.* The Open Group. Accessed April 26, 2021. www.opengroup.org/about-us.

Pasquinelli, Matteo. 2008. *Animal Spirits: A Bestiary of the Commons.* Rotterdam: NAi Publishers.

———. 2017. "The Automaton of the Anthropocene: On Carbosilicon Machines and Cyberfossil Capital." *The South Atlantic Quarterly* 116 (2): 311–26. https://doi.org/10.1215/00382876-3829423.

Postone, Moishe. 1993. *Time, Labor, and Social Domination: A Reinterpretation of Marx's Critical Theory.* Cambridge: Cambridge University Press.

Rigzone. 2014. "Data Scientists in Demand in Oil, Gas to Address Big Data Challenge." *Rigzone.com.* Accessed April 28, 2021. www.rigzone.com/news/oil_gas/a/132874/Data_Scientists_in_Demand_in_Oil_Gas_to_Address_Big_Data_Challenge/?all=HG2.

Saputelli, Luigi, Cesar Bravo, Michael Nikolaou, Carlos Lopez, Ron Cramer, Toshi Mochizuki, and Giuseppe Moricca. 2013. "Best Practices and Lessons Learned after 10 Years of Digital Oilfield (DOF) Implementations." SPE Paper 167269, SPE Kuwait Oil and Gas Show and Conference, 2013. http://doi.org/10.2118/167269-MS.

Sarapulov, Nikolay, and Rinat Khabibullin. 2016. "Application of Big Data Tools for Unstructured Data Analysis to Improve ESP Operation Efficiency." Presented at SPE Russian Petroleum Technology Conference, Moscow, Russia, October 2017. https://doi.org/10.2118/187738-MS.

Sassen, Sakia. 1996. *Losing Control? Sovereignty in the Age of Globalization.* New York: Columbia University Press.

Schlumberger. 2019. "Schlumberger Open Sources Data Ecosystem and Contributes to The Open Group Open Subsurface Data Universe Forum." *SLB.com.* Accessed April 26, 2021. www.slb.com/newsroom/press-release/2019/pr-2019-0822-osdu-data-ecosystem.

———. 2020a. "Schlumberger New Energy and Thermal Energy Partners Enter into Agreement to Create GeoFrame Energy, a Geothermal Project Development Company." *SLB.com.* Accessed April 26, 2021. www.slb.com/newsroom/press-release/2020/pr-2020-0827-geoframe-energy.

———. 2020b. "Understanding the OSDU Opportunity: A Schlumberger Guide to OSDU Data Platform." *SLB.com.* www.software.slb.com/-/media/software-media-items/software/documents/external/product-brochures/a-schlumberger-guide-to-the-osdu-data-platform.pdf.

———. 2021. "Schlumberger New Energy Venture to Launch a Lithium Extraction Pilot Plant in Nevada." *SLB.com.* Accessed April 26, 2021. www.slb.com/newsroom/press-release/2021/pr-2021-0318-sne-lithium-extraction-plant-nevada.

Serres, `Michel, and Bruno Latour. 1995. *Conversations on Science, Culture, and Time.* Ann Arbor: University of Michigan Press.

Shell. 2021. "Shell Accelerates Drive for Net-Zero Emissions with Customer-First Strategy." *Shell.com.* Accessed April 26, 2021. www.shell.com/media/news-and-media-releases/2021/shell-accelerates-drive-for-net-zero-emissions-with-customer-first-strategy.html.

Simondon, Gilbert. 2017. *On the Mode of Existence of Technical Objects.* Translated by Cécile Malaspina and John Rogove. Minneapolis: Univocal Publishing.

———. 2020a. *Individuation in Light of Notions of Form and Information, Volume I.* Translated by Taylor Adkins. Minneapolis and London: University of Minnesota Press.

———. 2020b. *Individuation in Light of Notions of Form and Information, Volume II: Supplemental Texts.* Translated by Taylor Adkins. Minneapolis and London: University of Minnesota Press.

Slav, Irina. 2020. "Can Digital Tech Solve Oil's Talent Crisis?" *OilPrice.com.* Accessed April 27, 2021. https://oilprice.com/Energy/Energy-General/Can-Digital-Tech-Solve-Oils-Talent-Crisis.html.

Smith, Michael Peter, and Luis Eduardo Guarnizo, eds. 1998. *Transnationalism from Below.* New Brunswick: Transaction Publishers.

Starosielski, Nicole. 2015. *The Undersea Network*. Durham and London: Duke University Press.

Stiegler, Bernard. 1998. *Technics and Time, 1: The Fault of Epimetheus*. Translated by Richard Beardsworth and George Collins. Stanford: Stanford University Press.

Supran, Geoffrey, and Naomi Oreskes. 2021. "Rhetoric and Frame Analysis of ExxonMobil's Climate Change Communications." *One Earth* 4: 696–719.

Tsing, Anna. 2005. *Friction: An Ethnographic of Global Connection*. Princeton and Oxford: Princeton University Press.

Turton, William, and Kartikay Mehrotra. 2021. "Hackers Breached Colonial Pipeline Using Compromised Password." *Bloomberg*. Accessed September 5, 2021. www.bloomberg.com/news/articles/2021-06-04/hackers-breached-colonial-pipeline-using-compromised-password.

Watts, Michael. 2005. "Righteous Oil? Human Rights, the Oil Complex, and Corporate Social Responsibility." *Annual Review of Environment and Resources* 30: 373–407. https://doi.org/10.1146/annurev.energy.30.050504.144456.

Whyte, Kyle Powys. 2017. "The Dakota Access Pipeline, Environmental Injustice, and U.S. Colonialism." *RED INK: An International Journal of Indigenous Literature, Arts, & Humanities* 19 (1): 154–69.

Wiener, Norbert. 1961. *Cybernetics, or Control and Communication in the Animal and the Machine*. Cambridge: MIT Press.

Wylie, Sara Ann. 2018. *Fractivism: Corporate Bodies and Chemical Bonds*. Durham and London: Duke University Press.

Yuan, Herb, Mehrzad Mahdavi, and Donald Paul. 2011. "Security: Digital Oil Field or Digital Nightmare?" *Journal of Petroleum Technology* 63 (8) (August): 16–18. https://doi.org/10.2118/0811-0016-JPT.

30
BETWEEN DIGITAL AND TERRITORIAL TURNS
A Forking Path

Chiara Cavalieri and Elena Cogato Lanza

Introduction: The Territorial and Digital Era

Nowadays, the concept of *digital urbanism* refers to the planning and governance of urban phenomena based on computational tools (Kitchin 2014). This involves the collection of a big quantity of data. *Intelligent*, *smart*, and *programmable cities* are among the formulas that designate both the object of such urbanism and its planning objectives (Stonor 2018). If the adjective "digital" evokes a turning point, and the shift between "pre" and "post," such a junction, is not unique in its methods and implications. Suffice it to say that *digital urbanism* activates a set of contradictory imaginaries, linked, on the one hand, to top-down control, and on the other, to social empowerment. This raises a fundamental question about the relationship between computational approaches and the specificity of places. This chapter intends to explore the complex relationship between digitisation and urbanism.

Our hypothesis is that *digital urbanism* can be properly outlined as an incremental parallel and dialectic process with territorial urbanism. The latter identifies an arborescence of theoretical positions and projects that have developed throughout the 20th century to the present day. As the problem of urban agglomeration emerged, new approaches to city design advocated for territorial contextualisation as the relevant scale to consider the dynamics of material and cultural urbanity and the appropriate frame for any planning deliberations. Observing this process through both nominal and technological representations of territory, our discussion discloses the interdependencies between the *territorial* turn and the *digital* turn, in which *digital urbanism* emerges as only one of the most recent developments.

In particular, we focus on *transformative cartographies*, which, over centuries and with all cartographical techniques employed by architects and urbanists, have revealed, enhanced, and generated territorial transformations. Conceived as the function of a specific project or formalised by an analytical descriptive logic but also aiming to have operational impacts, the transformative cartographies discussed in this chapter are situated at the intersection of the digital and the territorial turns (Ash, Kitchin, and Leszczynski 2018; Carpo 2017; Cavalieri Cogato 2020).

This chapter follows a chronological perspective oscillating from one development to another to highlight the specific contexts of exchanging trends and traditions. We employ shifts from the point of view of urbanism to the techniques and technologies of (its) representation. Within

 DOI: 10.4324/9781003082798-37

these rhythmic shifts, we firstly expand the notion of territory, dedicating a part of our discussion to excavation of the "archaeology" of scholars, projects, and experiences that initiated the territorial turn. Secondly, we define transformative cartographies and read this expansive scale of investigation as an advance towards the digital (aerial photography and GIS technologies) in urbanism. We describe these advances by defining André Corboz's (1983) concept of subject-territory, whereby territory is viewed as an entity endowed with its own specificities, which is impossible to simply reduce to a model. Then we discuss the appropriation of technology by architects, marking a summit beyond which a "descent" towards a position in opposition to Corboz's perspective emerges to reveal that the "territory" itself is at stake.[1]

Emergence of Territory as "Context": A New Look at Urbanisation

The need to understand the urban phenomenon within the scale of territory, well beyond the boundaries of the traditional city, is posited – both in theory and practice – in opposition to the conventional practices of town planning, framed by municipal administrative limits. At the start of the 20th century, Scottish naturalist, geographer, reformer, and city planner Patrick Geddes (1854–1932) coined the term "city-region" (Geddes 1915). Indicating the emergence of British con-urbation, the phrase described urban transformation resulting from the Industrial Revolution, from a landscape that had been previously "a province covered with houses." The city-region was envisioned by Geddes not as an expanding pattern of urbanity, absorbing the resources of its natural environment, but rather as a process of a continuous urban evolution (Geddes 1925, 288–90; 322–25; Ferraro 1998, 46; Cavalieri 2021).

Geddes' spatial analysis was characterised by two original innovations – the Outlook Tower and the Valley Section (Geddes 1915). These types of analysis and representation aimed not only to "overcome the bi-dimensionality of paper," but also to shape new, organic visualisations within the scale and concept of the city-region. Installed on the top of a small hill in the heart of Edinburgh, Scotland, the Outlook Tower was a place from which to observe the surrounding territory – a diversely inhabited space located beyond the boundaries of the built city. The Valley Section was a *typical portrait* of the territory, topographically representing the evolution of civilisation from the perspective of a "general slope" reaching "from the mountains to the sea, which is found everywhere in the world" (Geddes 1925, 288–89).[2] This type of spatial analysis operated as a lens to reveal the fundamental principles of territorialisation, replacing a paradigm that positioned the political and cultural power of the city over that of the countryside. Geddes' two tools of representation allowed him to disclose the city-region as a territory ultimately defined by both environmental and civilisational boundaries. Geddes' work became a primary influence on American ecological planning and was crucial to the development of the Regional Plan Association of America (RPAA).[3] The association's objective was to reform and repair the industrialised, overcrowded, and polluted metropolises of the United States by offering Geddes' city-region model as an urban alternative.

One of the most emblematic projects of this reformist approach is illustrated by the creation of the Appalachian Trail (MacKaye 1921), conceived some years before the establishment of the RPAA. As a hiking trail in a wild, mountainous region, the project had the objective not only of offering accessible landscape and recreational spaces but also to create employment and dwelling opportunities for local communities. As with Geddes' Valley Section, Benton MacKaye (1879–1975) largely used regional topography as a tool to environmentally represent territorial spatial, temporal and metabolic relations. As a project conceived from a geographical feature, the Appalachian Trail is fundamentally a linear infrastructure shaped by the regions' natural hydrology and

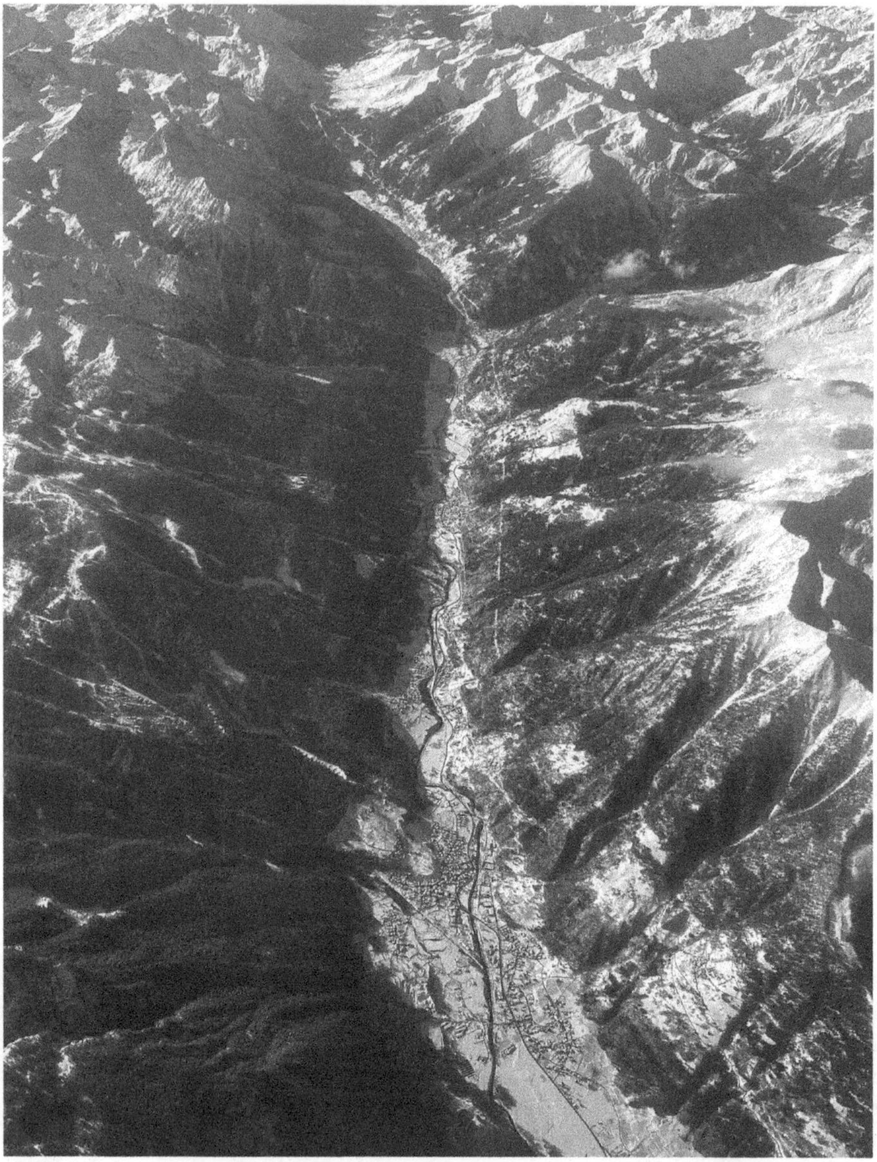

Figure 30.1 The scale of territory: Alps, as viewed from a plane. Picture by authors.

appropriately belongs to the tradition of the *park system* (Skjonsberg 2018). Commonly considered an expression of the discipline of landscape architecture and especially its father, Frederic Law Olmsted (1822–1903), the park system is a comprehensive territorial design scheme. The park system (as exemplified in Boston and Chicago) is an open structure with a double organising function that articulates urbanisation within a regional watershed and delineates land usage – mainly creating distinctions between built and green spaces, roads, and agricultural production. Considering regionalism as the relevant scale and approach for ecological and economic planning, it is not by accident that one of the more accomplished experiments in territorial design was initiated by Adriano Olivetti (1901–1960). An Italian engineer, politician, and intellectual, he was an industrialist who established and ran the northern Italian Olivetti Factories in Ivrea and was a promoter of the Italian National Institute of Urbanism (INU). Olivetti, during his travels, absorbed ideas from the sociological and economic cultures of America and England. On his return to Italy, he disseminated these ideas through his publishing house Comunità, in addition to reorganising methods of industrial production in his factories which manufactured typewriters, calculators, and later on, computers.

Olivetti can be considered both a digital and territorial pioneer. His company created the first computer in Italy, the Elea 9003, in 1959, after initiating a territorial plan for the Valle d'Aosta, which shares a border with France and Switzerland in Northern Italy. Co-authored in 1930 by a multidisciplinary team led by architects, the plan dealt with the geomorphological and social dimensions of the territory. It operated on two major scales – a regional scale, featuring a series of thematic plates and brilliant photomontages of Valle d'Aosta, and on an architectural scale, detailing various projects outlined for the city of Aosta. From the perspectives of representation and urban practice, the plan's de-emphasis on the urban core as the scale for planning illustrated a departure from the bi-dimensional approaches that dominated traditional planning practices. The Valle d'Aosta Plan also exhibited a retreat from the international Congrès Internationaux d'Architecture Moderne (CIAM) doctrine and confirmed the inner character of a three-dimensional regional approach that would come to frame urban issues in relation to both territory and built structures (Ciucci 2001). About ten years later, on the other side of the Alps, the Swiss Association for the National Development Plan (ASPAN, created in 1945) oriented urbanisation planning towards the principle of decentralisation. Theorised during the 1930s by Armin Meili, president of ASPAN, the decentralised metropolis aimed to curb the growth of large urban concentrations (Cogato Lanza 1998; Hildebrand 2006). Erroneously judged as conservative, the philosophy of the ASPAN revealed, on the contrary, a search for a renewed concept of the city as an alternative to hierarchical and non-symmetrical city-countryside relationships. The shift in considering territory simply from the scale of urbanisation to an alternate asymmetrical conception of city and countryside in balance intensified after the Second World War.

In particular, Ludwig Hilberseimer (1885–1967), employed by the Illinois Institute of Technology after leaving Germany, where he had been associated with the Bauhaus School, broke with the paradigm of dense, concentrated metropolises in the seminal text *The New Regional Patterns* (1948). Hilberseimer's concept of a network of linear cities situated within the scale of the United States placed emphasis on the ability to control the conditions of economic territorialisation. By planning routes for transit and access to resources and raw materials, *The New Regional Patterns* highlights the flexibility of investment and employment between primary and secondary sectors of a territorial economy. Hilberseimer's perspective stood in contrast to Jean Gottmann's *Megalopolis: the urbanized northeastern seaboard of the United States* (1961), which places emphasis on the city as the centre of a heterogeneous territory (Viganò 2014).

Hilberseimer's regionalism and Gottmann's metropolitanism represent two interpretations of the role of the territorial scale in relation to the urban realm. The former insists on a balanced homogeneity, the latter accentuates the centrality of the urban core. Faced with these two contrasting hypotheses, Paola Viganò seeks a third way, that of urban fragmentation and isotropy, closer to the reading of the *Zwischenstadt* proposed by Thomas Sieverts in his reading of German urbanisation (Sieverts 1997). The *Horizontal Metropolis* brings theoretical and procedural maturity to the emergence of the territory in assemblage and in scale with the urban, from which the city-region leads to the *city-territory*, and in turn, to the emergence of *territorialism* (Viganò 2013, 2014; Viganò, Cavalieri, and Barcelloni 2018; Cavalieri and Viganò 2019).

A second theoretical line, for which the Valle d'Aosta Plan serves as a precedent, considers territory as the field and scale of the expansion of "architectural rationality," particularly in the tradition of urban morphology studies. In 1966 Vittorio Gregotti's seminal essay, "La Forma del Territorio" (The Shape of Landscape), called for a renewed relationship between acts of architectural design and the specificities of places. Gregotti echoed the ideas of Manfredo Tafuri, Giorgio Piccinato, and Vieri Quilici:

> To place the problem of territorial settlement in a wider and different dimension should therefore lead, as a consequence, to the introduction of a working hypothesis that does not translate into a model, but is organized and structured in a configuration that ensures flexibility not only on the scale of the single urban sector, but also and principally on the scale of the overall organism.
>
> *(1962, 22)*

Following this train of thought, it is worth noting that Aldo Rossi's (1962, 6) research on the design of monuments in "a wider metropolitan territory" contributed to nullifying distinctions between centre and periphery. Rossi stressed the validity of the "primary structure" as a fundamental architectural category, relevant to both the periphery and the historic urban fabric, regardless of the size of the city (Lampariello 2020). To summarise our overview, territory emerges as both a specific place and context according to the *ecological principle* (an understanding of the systemic relationships between individual, social, material, and cultural processes), the *reconceptualisation of the city* (its scales, themes, and design procedures), and the *morphological* approach (territory as the form). Collectively, these three dimensions share a recognition of the specificity of each territory within the framework of its own historical evolutionary process. Such ideas resonated through 20th-century debates on the concept of "territory" with an *incessant crescendo* until the 1980s, when they crystalised into the territorial turn and met the irruptions of digital mapping. This led cartographic discourse to a breakthrough in theory and practice that had been bourgeoning since the 19th century.

The Emergence of Transformative Cartographies

The emergence of the territorial turn was accompanied by a parallel evolution in cartography and the use of digital technologies to embrace the wider scales of territorial studies and shape a new gaze over large surfaces of the earth. This new gaze observes, traces, maps, and reads the existent to envision its own transformation. It is a gaze that adopts a transformative eye – an urbanist's eye in distinction to a cartographic or geographic one (Chapel 2018). We now turn to a discussion on the notion of transformative cartographies, where the term transformative refers to images produced by architects and urbanists to support, produce, enhance, and reveal territorial transformations. In this perspective, the evolution of transformative cartographies is intimately intertwined with applications of the digital in cartographical practices. Indeed, much has been discussed about the influence of digital technology on the field of cartography and geography and about the role of the digital in design thinking – but few have considered cartographies as *prior* yet necessary to design processes (Wood 2003; Lynn 2004; Crampton 2009; Picon 2010; Lévy 2015; M'Closkey and Vandersys 2016; Wallis 2018; Carpo 2020).

It is from the specific perspective of mapping as a tool for transformation that one could trace a specific chronology of the "digital" (Corner 1999) This chronology deals with the evolution of the capacity of map images in capturing, representing, and transforming large earth surfaces in support of territorial transformations. In this sense, territory itself and its representation become closely intertwined. Emerging as an object of both study and design, such a "carto-territory" triggers a new method of representation, creating images able to describe large and complex regions. This reconceptualisation needs new technologies able to embrace, collect, and process the enormous amount of data produced by the territorial gaze.

Prior to the 20th century, the bird's-eye-view image of the "world from above" was not a common one – territory was mainly represented in topographical and cadastral maps and large national surveys. Aerial photography and GIS technology had yet to be developed. The evolution of aerial pictures and of GIS cartographies in the mid and late 20th century can be observed as attempts to grasp and conceptualise extensions of the territorial gaze that questioned the canonical binary of city and countryside, by observing territorial dynamics from a wider scale. This new scale incorporated observation, design, and physiography in representing the surfaces of three-dimensional features. Arguably, it was not by chance that the first aerial pictures, taken by Gaspard-Félix Tournachon, better known as Nadar, recorded the city of Paris transformed by the seminal Plan Haussmann (1853–1870). Photographed for the Universal Exhibition of 1868, these images mark an undeniable articulation between the urban project and the need for both recording and representing it on the wider scale of the territory (Waldheim 1999).

As for aerial pictures, their intimate relationship with transformation processes was already embedded in Le Corbusier's work, who in the 1930s collaborated with the London publishing house, the Studio Ltd., on a series of books titled *The New Vision* (Boyer 2003).[4] After the Second World War, the strong development of aerial photography, empowered by national states, became a metaphor for surveillance, control, and protection of military powers while at the same time providing enormous support for territorial studies and analysis (Waldheim 2012).[5] The development of GIS technology followed a parallel path. Besides the capacity to process ever-increasing amounts of data that could represent large portions of the Earth's surface, the premise of GIS was to link quantitative data to space, thus spatialising figures and territorialising statistics.

In early-19th-century precedents for contemporary GIS applications, epidemiological information was linked to physical space in a "map of the cholera outbreak across 48 districts of Paris" plotted by Charles Piquet in 1832. This was followed in London by John Snow's 1855 map "Showing the Deaths from Cholera in Broad Street, Golden Square, and the Neighbourhood," which not only spatially localised cholera but also linked deaths and the probable source of infection to a public water pump in Broad Street (Akerman and Karrow 2007; Water 2017). In these instances, cartography became transformative. Maps became the ultimate panels on which to visualise spatial connections that had otherwise been difficult to represent. In addition, in 1869, French engineer Charles Joseph Minard gained worldwide recognition for his seminal cartographic representation of Napoleon's 1812 failed winter campaign against Russia that merges flows and time within the bi-dimensional space of a paper map (Rendgen 2020; Kraak 2021).

This emerging capacity of representation, that of embedding different kinds of information overlaid onto a common ground of a map would later become crucial in city planning, which from Geddes onward, would use *layers* as a way for deconstructing territory, long before the same term would distinguish GIS computer techniques. Even the official creation of GIS in 1962 (Canada GIS, Roger Tomlinson) is somehow the result of a larger territorial operation – a survey that sought to collect, classify and monitor the natural resource of Canadian forests. Indeed, from its very first applications, GIS seemed closely intertwined with the development of the territorial gaze – one that required a wider scale of investigation, more information to be processed, and more powerful computing and storage capacities.

During the so-called *pioneer period* of GIS technology – Harvard's Laboratory for Computer Graphics (1964), the software Symap (1964), and the United Kingdom's Experimental Cartography Unit (1967) – geospatial technologies, territorial gazes, and multiple scales nourished and reinforced each other (Coppock and Rhind 1991). Ian McHarg, designated the father of ecological planning at the University of Pennsylvania (UPenn), is undoubtedly one of the authors of the geospatial technology territorial gaze. McHarg's seminal text *Design with Nature* (1969) and its emphasis on environmental layering – an influence shaping the development of GIS was published the same year that the Environmental System Research Institute (Esri) was established. Originating as a land-use consulting firm, Esri is now a worldwide supplier of ArcGIS software and services. However, *Design with Nature* did not provide any methods for computerising the overlay process, nor was it based on the use of GIS technology. Rather it illustrated the aggregation of quantities and planning on a territorial scope by overlaying and observing its multiple features: geology, pedology, climatology, ecology, hydrology, agronomy, and forestry. However, McHarg, in *The History of Geographic Information Systems: Perspectives from the Pioneers* (1998, ix), declared that his methods

> based in a comprehensive chronologically layer approach, have popularized and advanced the application of multiple "cake layers" for incorporating the environment and the social constraints into the myopic developer's dream for paving the planet.

In spite of this, McHarg claimed that his team at UPenn originated computerised ecology prior to 1962 and supported the hypothesis that cartography and planning were mutually influenced (1998, x). With the influence of pioneering GIS methods technology on the field of transformative cartographies, the 1960s closed with critiques of the technology and its limitation. Indeed, McHarg's retrospective clarification on the publication of *Design with Nature* and the creation of GIS illustrates the relation and co-evolution of digital cartography techniques and territorial thinking. A relationship worth addressing in terms of actual practices but also in potentialities and respective projections. The 1960s proved to be decisive from this perspective. For instance, the English word *layer*, reiterated in Gregotti's essays and in reference to the archaeological study of historical processes, bypasses the Italian archaeological metaphor *strata* and establishes a direct relation with fundamental principles of organising information in digital cartography. A second example of a fertile resonance between digital and territorial fields is illustrated by the 1968 documentary *Powers of Ten* produced by Charles and Ray Eames – architects, scenographers, and specialists in scientific communication (Morrison 1982). Re-released in 1977 and commissioned by International Business Machines (IBM) Corporation for the exhibition *A Computer Perspective*, the film chronicles the development of the computer from 1890 to 1950. The Eameses aimed to provide a glimpse of the potential of computers for scientific investigation as tools for investigation and simultaneous visualisations. The view of the Earth taken by NASA in 1968 is at the centre of a montage displaying different forms of representation that suggest the potential of digital technology to visualise physical "reality" at all scales – from the sub-microscopic quark to beyond our galaxy.

Powers of Ten is a dream – its representations of a magnitude and cognitive efficiency that in 1968 was only at promising stages. Although we speak of films, the illusion of cinematic continuity actually springs from images produced for the most part by analogue techniques (photography, painting, photomontage, etc.). Reviews of the film reflect its ambiguous nature: "The unknown has surrounded us. The world of the everyday seems now like an illusion," wrote one critic (Lightman 2005, 123). Actually, *Powers of Ten*'s extremely rigorous structure, based on the highest precision of algorithmic measurements, postulates indirectly an agenda for a research programme, where de-discretisation of digital power meets the overwhelming complexity of human life and the unpredictable relations and non-linear interdependence between various environmental scales (Cogato Lanza 2015). Conceived by two architects, familiar with mechanical planning systems, *Powers of Ten* illuminates the great expectations promised by the territorial turn, which had been addressing problematic interdependencies between phenomena of distinct natures, dimensions and temporalities from the mid-20th century.

The Territorial Turn: From Context to Subject

In 1983 the essay "Le Territoire Comme Palimpseste," published by the Swiss historian of architecture and urbanism André Corboz, established a benchmark for the territorial turn (Cavalieri Cogato 2020). Corboz begins by chronicling an increasing enthusiasm for territorial themes across a breadth of disciplines, including political science, geology, topography, planning, zoology, and cultural history. This, he asserts, was the culmination of a process that paralleled the broadening territorial scope of public policies. In addition, Corboz commented on the incredible success of exhibitions such as *Cartes et Figures de la Terre*, held in Paris, at the Centre Pompidou in 1980. No less popular than a retrospective of Impressionist paintings, *Cartes et Figures de la Terre* revealed how maps could be understood as cultural artefacts with their representations of land as a topic of broad social interest, worthy of debates in public spaces. The renewed multidisciplinary focus in the early 1980s on the notion of territory, which went well beyond classical urban science to embrace the commercialisation of images, imaginaries, maps, and cartographies, allowed Corboz to declare that a new collective *horizon of reference* had emerged, fulfilling the paradigm shift and parable of the territorial turn (1983, 15).

The essay's title, "Le Territoire Comme Palimpseste," announced Corboz's theoretical proposal and is itself inscribed within the new horizon of reference, summarising his conceptual aspirations in cultural and operational terms deployed in planning and the study of urbanism. On a broader cultural level, Corboz theorises that each territory is "the result of a very lengthy and very slow stratification which should be understood before acting" with a unique form, irreducible to pre-established models, generic planning, or a policy based on abstract principles. Corboz claims the failure of the modern *tabula rasa*, which postulates space as "a quasi-abstract field of operation," was inevitable – territory instead manifests as palimpsest[6] rather than an empty vessel (1983, 227). The metaphor of the palimpsest has tremendous potential for cartography – an original prototype is illustrated by the *Atlas du Territoire Genevois* (1993), published by the Canton of Geneva. The *Atlas* comprises a corpus of mappings that juxtapose Napoleonic and federal cadastres across three historical thresholds that are about 170 years apart (Léveillé et al. 1993).

Based on the layer-cake technique, the *Atlas* is completely analogue and, like McHarg's method, employs an extremely simple set of observations. The *Atlas*' legend lists parcels, buildings, roads, vegetation, hydrography, and topography. Sequential map images facilitate a comparative analysis of the same territory across three historical thresholds, providing the means to identify different types of territorial transformations over time. The *Atlas* also reveals what has remained unchanged (permanence), what has been transformed (persistence), and what has been erased (disappearance). The shift from the complexity of the metaphor of the territory as a palimpsest to an elementary, descriptive mapping strategy must be read within the idea of disclosing a new image for the city of Geneva. One that reveals a hidden dimension, that of history, one that typifies territorial modifications, and ultimately one that empowers future transformations – in other words, a transformative cartography.

Considering the territory as a palimpsest implies reading a history of its modifications over a *longue durée*. It involves reading carefully the form of what has been added beyond the perspectives of governance and looking for traces of what has been demolished or deeply transformed. In this manner, territory can be recognised not only as an object but as a personality "who has a name," a body, a voice. Corboz evokes the mythological or ancient anthropomorphic personifications of territories as a *process* and also a *projection* of its culture. In this regard, the specificity of a territory is inseparable from the effects of its cultural representations and the material traces of its production.

According to Corboz, in such a manner, it becomes a subject: "being a project, the territory is semanticized. It can be parsed. It bears a name. Projections of all kinds are attached to it, transforming it into a subject." The subject-territory, however, is represented in a map, a photograph,

Figure 30.2 Transformative cartographies: Polder landscape in the Veneto region. Map by Cavalieri (2012).

or a poem as a construction, with its "value attributed to its configuration" (1983, 225). This postulate lies at the very heart of the map exhibition held at the Centre Pompidou, where the perception of the territory as a subject became a collective consciousness. Similar perceptions emerged in the 1980s with the acknowledgement of the Earth as a fragile subject which in turn grew global resistances to the "accelerated anthropisation process" (*processus d'antropisation accelerêré*) and worries for its future (Meadows et al. 1972; WCED 1987). As Paola Viganò (2020) notes, the recognition of the territory as a subject implies a need to recognise its legal right to survive.

The Digital Turn through Transformative Cartographies

While territory was drifting from context to subject, in the early 1980s digital technology was going through a commercialisation period, when applications engaged by specialists or pioneer users become more widely employed in other disciplines, not least the fields of urbanism and emerging territorial design (Coppock and Rhind 1991). In parallel the study of cartography, in the 1980s like academic perspectives on space, time and text experienced a paradigm shift. J.B. Harley's seminal paper *Deconstructing the Map* (1989) defined an important distinction between the *external* and *internal* power of maps. The latter situates power as exerted from the centres of political powers *through* cartographies; the former designates the *intrinsic* power of cartographic processes – by revealing, unfolding, and ultimately shaping perceptions of reality (Harley 1989).

In 1992, the Cooper-Hewitt National Museum of Design in New York launched an exhibition entitled *The Power of Maps*, the result of a study by the Institutional Studies Office in Washington, DC. Through the use of panels and text labels, the exhibition sought to demonstrate that "all maps – whether rare or familiar, new or old, Western or non-Western – are more than simply guides to 'help you find your way'" (Doering et al. 1993, iii); they also provide individual power, in line with Harley's perspective. In this context, Denis Wood, Professor of Landscape Architecture at North Carolina State University and co-curator of the exhibition, not only contributed a critical review of map analysis but published a text titled *The Power of Maps* (1993), discussing the democratisation of cartography. The exhibition and publication promoted cartography and its technologies to a larger public, allowing map-making to become a weapon not only for every *writer* but also for every *reader*. As Corboz (2001) later noted, in describing a territory, the reader inevitably transforms the object into a subject and thus a reading into a rewriting.

With the commodification of digital technologies and democratisation of cartography in the 1980s, transformative cartographies found themselves following two parallel pathways.

One track sharpened the gaze of the reader through technology; the other tackled the complexity of the world with computational capacity, which as Charles Waldheim (2012) points out is at the risk of being placed in an epistemological *cul-de-sac*. However, transformative cartographies embraced the digital turn by generating two main foci. The first was to engage technology to empower the capacity to record, shape, and describe the subject-territory, thus visualising metrics, strata, and remotely sensed features. Landscape architect James Corner and photographer/pilot Alex Mc Lean's *Taking Measures Across the American Landscape* (1996) stands as a pioneering work that established a major benchmark for transformative cartographies.

Their text, the result of many years of flying, surveying, and picturing American landscapes, was infused with cartographical techniques that reinterpreted territorial context by manipulating United States Geological Survey (USGS) maps and their "neutral" descriptions of the United States' physiography. Corner's maps and McLean's images have the rare privilege of revealing, synthesising, and reinterpreting landscapes viewed from above by integrating their cultural dimensions within USGS topographical maps. Although Corner (1999) described the maps as possible rhizomes or game boards, *Taking Measures Across the American Landscape* manifests more as an exquisite exercise in representation than a means to empower cartographical transformations.

The second focus generated by this field is how digital technology itself became an agent of transformation by allowing the creation of computational images to represent large-scale hypotheses. Computer capacities in image processing (beyond GIS) are creating better and more realistic simulations of territories leading to completely different horizons of transformative mapping and thought. One example is the *Metacity/Datatown* visual installation exhibited in 1998 at the Stroom Center for the Visual Arts in The Hague, produced by Dutch architectural and urbanism firm MVRDV (1999). The work explores the possibility of exploring large-scale territories and cities from the perspective of data rather than just geographical context:

> Datatown is based only upon data. It is a city that wants to be described by information; a city that knows no given topography, no prescribed ideology, no representation, no context. Only huge, pure data. What are the implications of this city? What assumptions can be identified? What agenda would result from this numerical approach?
>
> *(MVRDV 1999, 58–59)*

Within this second focus, digital technology simply takes over context and seeks to overcome the topographies of the territory as being the key to its transformation. Subsequent to MVRDV's exhibition, James Corner was invited to contribute to a volume titled *Mappings* (1999), curated by British geographer Denis Cosgrove. His chapter "The Agency of Mapping" defined and described how cartography supported, revealed, and empowered territorial transformation (Corner 1999). Meanwhile, McHargh, Corner's mentor at UPenn, was sketching a balance between his protégé's concept of *the agency of mapping* and emerging geospatial technologies, in which he foresaw a future radicalisation of ongoing digital capabilities:

> [W]hile problems increase in complexity, it is gratifying to observe that our ability to understand and manage has been enormously expanded by the new prostheses: environmental science, sensors, satellite, and, not least, computers. The one advertised benison of computation is its capability of integrating data and perceptions from the full range of environmental science. This might well be its most significant contribution. We are buried into data. We desperately need integration. Computers can assist triumphantly in this quest.
>
> *(McHargh 1998, x)*

McHargh's observation sounded like a burdensome bequest for the next generation of geospatial technology scholars, one he imagined being overwhelmed by a coming deluge of digitally sourced environmental data. Indeed, the dawn of the 21st century was greeted by the creation of Keyhole EarthViewer 1.0 (launched in 2001), the predecessor of Google Earth and Google Maps, launched in 2005 (Brotton 2013). With the launch of these "global aerial navigators," anybody could navigate across the surface of the earth, as these geospatial technology platforms achieved the logarithmic ability depicted in the *Powers of Ten* to zoom up and down scales from one power of ten to another, without employing any visual cinematic tricks.

The process and dream of building a unique fictional map on "the scale of a mile to the mile" of the Earth evoke the Victorian and Fairyland worlds depicted in Lewis Carroll's *Sylvie and Bruno Concluded*, where a character asserts "we now use the country itself, as its own map, and I assure you it does nearly as well" (Carroll 1893, 169). In contrast, in Jorge Luis Borges' *On Exactitude in Science* (1946), a similar "map of such Magnitude" is seen as "cumbersome" and in "the western Deserts, tattered Fragments of the Map are still to be found, Sheltering an occasional Beast or beggar" (Borges 1975).

In their distinct literary styles, both Carroll and Borges present mapping as mainly a top-down construction of world imagery. Conversely, digitalisation has shifted the focus on mapping to one of one rooting – and shaping. Such processes employ the more bottom-up processes of counter or participatory cartographies that share "global" open databases like OpenStreetMap that, from 2008, have been freely downloadable. Following its launch, digital cartography was given the appellations Neo-Geography and Web 2.0 to describe platforms capable of accessing massively distributed and hyperlinked datasets, mash-ups, and customisable open-source geo-spatial tools. Neo-Geography/Web 2.0 methods are profoundly different from their precursors because they allow collaboratively linked mappings. In other words, cartography's latest "technological transition" is not only a technical question but a bricolage of open-source collaborative tools, mobile phone mapping applications, and geospatial web platforms that democratically rebalanced the collective and traditional powers of cartography.

A Forking Path: From Hypercontext to Hyperterritory

Again following a train of thought that interleaves *territory/territories* and *its/their* representations, one can observe how digitally empowered transformative cartographies emerged as a key for envisioning 21st-century metropolitan futures as a form of governance trying to enlarge its boundaries. Over the last decade, many European metropolises have assigned multidisciplinary teams of architects and urbanists to conceive "territorial vision" projects proposing shifts of scale – both in terms of space and time – that ultimately bypass policies and physical borders to promote long-term imaginaries of the future (Cavalieri 2020).[7] The increase in the computing capacities of the tools of digital cartography is one of the facilitators of studies and projects drawing on the concept of the subject-territory, where its physical dimensions come to the fore (Desimini and Waldheim 2016).

Likewise, many metropolises (e.g. Sao Paulo and London) have invested in massive data collection devices and real-time dashboards to support emerging forms of digital urbanism. In such systems of urbanism, data collection and computing protocols become planning tools, often without the benefits of design operations or transformative cartographies. In the 1990s, such urban planning transitions involving digital data led to a forking path in which territorial thinking diverged from its representations. The paradigm of territory has been amplified by a digital data *hypercontext* as technological practices increasingly record the context, shape, sound, light, and features of a territory. This focus on representational metrics, involving point-cloud and 4D scanner experimentations, urban sensing, monitoring, and other emerging digital technologies, emphasise data collection over territorial transformations. Such paths ultimately deploy the finest digital technology to shape and reshape models of territory, but nevertheless, the territory remains a subject (Urech 2020; Kaplan and Di Lenardo 2020; Llaguno-Munitxa and Bou-Zeid 2020).

Conversely, and in another respect, territory mutates into a *hyperterritory* – a cyberspace of data points, an extreme example of the no-context paradigm featured in MVRDV's exhibit (Dodge and Kitchin 2001). This hyperterritory is a non-physical space where technology takes over material space, where data shapes territory rather than the opposite. This path embodies current tendencies in digital urbanism, where data and their representations substitute territory, up to the point of replacing the context with its digital twin. Hyperterritory signifies the tendency toward planning rather than an urbanism of transformation (Ratti 2004; Greenfield 2013; Kitchin 2014; Lock 2019).

The forking path where territory and representation diverge is proposed as a lens through which to read a short – and necessarily incomplete – history of the territory as a subject related to the technology of digital representation. This history explores how the former informed the latter and vice versa. As for the field of architecture, for which the second digital revolution accentuation of "design beyond intelligence" has been advocated, our objective was to trace the steps of how the digital turn shaped territorial approaches via transformative cartographies (Carpo 2017). Our understanding of the evolution of the territorial turn requires its parallelisation with the digital turn to reveal how the latter is multivocal in its forms and implications. In the field of urbanism, this ranges from the ultimate goal of hypercontexting to that of denying the material support in the hyperterritory and ultimately pluralising rather than unifying a notion of a digital urbanism.

Notes

1 The sections "The Territorial and Digital Era" and "A Forking Path: From Hypercontext to Hyperterritory" are written by the two authors together; the sections "The Emergence of Territory as 'Context': A New Look at Urbanisation" and "The Territorial Turn: From Context to Subject" are written by Elena Cogato Lanza; the sections "The Emergence of Transformative Cartographies" and "The Digital Turn through Transformative Cartographies" are written by Chiara Cavalieri.

2 The Section Valley establish a bi-univocal relationship between the natural environment and man's occupations – from upstream to downstream, miners and woodmen inhabit the mountains; shepherds, hunters, and small farmers, the hilly belt; the rich farmer and the fisherman, the main plain. What emerges from this graphic categorisation is a reconstruction of man's original relationship with his natural environment, where physical conditions and human activities become the basis for a more complex social organisation. An organisation that marks the shift from what Geddes defines a palaeotechnic civilisation (that of the section) to a neotechnic one (an industrial one).

3 Formalised in 1923 by the architect and planner Clarence Stein, gathered people such as Lewis Mumford and Benton MacKaye.

4 With Le Corbusier images in mind, in 1936 the pilot-ethnographer Chombart de Lauwe, called *la vision aerienne du monde* (the vision of modernity) (Coste Roncayolo 1980).

5 While in 1968 the first picture of the Earth's surface – taken from the moon – was broadcasted; during the '70s aerial pictures guided the studies of the French Centre de Recherche d'Urbanisme (Pinchemel 1971), where the aerial picture was becoming the privileged background image for performing multiple urban analysis and comparison.

6 The fortunate metaphor of the palimpsest was used one year before Corboz by Gerard Genette that used the palimpsest as a metaphor for the thickness of literature texts (Genette 1982).

7 See, for example, the experiences of AIGP (Atelier International Gran Paris), 2008; Great Moscow, 2011; Brussels 2040, 2012; Montpellier 2030, 2012; Grand Geneve, 2018; Great Berlin, 2019; Luxembourg in Transition, 2020; and Liege 2050, 2020.

Sources

Akerman, James R., and Robert W. Jr Karrow, eds. 2007. *Maps: Finding Our Place in the World*. Chicago and London: The University of Chicago Press.

Ash, James, Rob Kitchin, and Agnieszka Leszczynski. 2018. "Digital Turn, Digital Geographies?" *Progress in Human Geography* 42 (1) (February 2018): 25–43. https://doi.org/10.1177/0309132516664800.

Borges, Jorge Luis. 1946. "On Exactitude in Science." *Los Anales de Buenos Aires* 1 (3).

———. 1975. *A Universal History of Infamy*. Translated by Norman Thomas de Giovanni. London: Penguin Books.

Boyer, M. Christine. 2003. "Le Corbusier's Spatial Transformations in the 1930s and 1940s. 'Diacritics.'" *New Coordinates: Spatial Mappings, National Trajectories* 33 (¾) (Autumn–Winter 2003): 93–116.

Brotton, Jerry. 2013. *A History of the World in Twelve Maps*. London: Penguin Books.

Caniggia, Gianfranco. 1976. *Le strutture dello spazio antropico*. Florence: Uniedit.

Carpo, Mario. 2017. *The Second Digital Turn: Design beyond Intelligence. Writing Architecture*. Cambridge, MA: The MIT Press.

———. 2020. "Storia brevissima, ma si spera veridica, della svolta numerica in architettura." *Casabella* 914 (10): 28–35.

Carroll, Lewis. 1893. *Sylvia and Bruno Concluded*. London: Palgrave Macmillan.

Cavalieri, Chiara. 2012. "Città Sommerse. Geografie d'acqua nel territorio costiero veneto." PhD diss., Iuav University of Venice.

———. 2020. "Beyond Limits. Multiple Rather Than Fragmented." In *Boundary Landscapes*, edited by Dalzero Silvia, Andrea Iorio, Olivia Longo et al., 299–304. Roma: Tab Edizioni.

———. 2021. "The City-Region. Patrick Geddes." In *The Horizontal Metropolis: The Anthology*, edited by Martina Barcelloni Corte and Paola Viganò. Cham: Springer.

Cavalieri, Chiara, and Elena Cogato Lanza. 2020. "Territories in Time: Mapping Palimpsest Horizons." *Urban Planning* 5 (2) (June 30, 2020): 94–98. https://doi.org/10.17645/up.v5i2.3385.

Cavalieri, Chiara, Michael Stas, and Marcelo Rovira Torres. 2020. "The 'Analogue City': Mapping and Acting in Antwerp's Digital Geographies." *Urban Planning* 5 (4) (December 15, 2020): 289–300. https://doi.org/10.17645/up.v5i4.3426.

Cavalieri, Chiara, and Paola Viganò, eds. 2019. *The Horizontal Metropolis: A Radical Project*. Zurich: Parkbook.

Chapel, Enrico. 2018. "The Urbanist's Eye." In *Mapping the Urban Question*, edited by Sabina Favaro, Cecilia Furlan, Alvise Pagnacco, 13–22. Rome: Officina.

Ciucci, Giorgio. 2001. "Le premesse del Piano regolatore della Valle d'Aosta." In *Costruire la città dell'uomo. Adriano Olivetti e l'urbanistica*, edited by Carlo Olmo, 55–82. Torino: Edizioni di Comunità.

Crampton, Jeremy W. 2009. *Mapping: A Critical Introduction to Cartography and GIS*. 1st ed. New York: Wiley-Blackwell.

Cogato Lanza, Elena. 1998. "Alla scoperta del territorio. Congressi e associazioni di urbanistica in Svizzera negli anni quaranta." In *Tra guerra e pace. Società, cultura e architettura nel secondo dopoguerra*, edited by Patrizia Bonifazio, Sergio Pace, Paolo Scrivano, Michela Rosso, 77–86. Milan: FrancoAngeli.

———. 2015. "The Legacy of Cadre de Vie." in *Territories in Crisis*, edited by Cristina Bianchetti, Elena Cogato Lanza, Angelo Sampieri, 286–95. Berlin: Jovis.

Coppock, John T., David W. Rhind. 1991. "The History of GIS." *Geographical Information Systems*, edited by David J. Maguire, Michael F. Goodchild, and David W. Rhind, 21–43. London: Longman.

Corboz, André. 1983. "Le Territoire Comme Palimpsteste." *Le Territoire Comme Palimpsteste* 121, Diogene.

———. 2001 [1995]. "La Description Entre Lecture et Écriture." In *Le Territoire Comme Palimpseste et Autres Essais*, edited by Sébastien Marot. Collection Tranches de Villes. Besançon: Editions de l'Imprimeur.

Corner, James. 1999. "The Agency of Mapping: Speculation, Critique and Invention." In *Mappings*, edited by Denis E. Cosgrove, 213–52. London: Reaktion Books.

Corner, James, and Alex McLean. 1996. *Taking Measures Across the American Landscape*. New York: Yale University Press.

Coste, Michael, and Roncayolo, Marcel. 1980. "La photo-interprétation des formes urbaines: remarques d'usage." '*L'Espace géographique* 9 (1) (Janvier–Mars 1980): 57–69.

Desimini, Jil, and Charles Waldheim. 2016. *Cartographic Grounds: Projecting the Landscape Imaginary*. New York: Princeton Architectural Press.

Dodge, Martin, and Rob Kitchin. 2001. *Atlas of Cyberspace*. Harlow: Addison-Wesley.

Dodge, Martin, Rob Kitchin, and Chris Perkins, eds. 2011. *The Map Reader*. Chichester, UK: John Wiley & Sons, Ltd.

Doering, Zahava D., Adam Bickford, Audrey Kindlon et al. 1999. "The Power of Maps: A Study of an Exhibition at Cooper-Hewitt, National Museum of Design." 1993. Report further published as: Zahava D. Doering, Adam Bickford, Audrey Kindlon et al. Communication and persuasion in a didactic exhibition: *The Power of Maps* study. *Curator: TheMuseum Journal* 42 (2): 88–107.

Ferraro, Giovanni. 1998. *Rieducazione alla Speranza: Patrick Geddes planner in India, 1914–1924*. Milano: Jakabook.

Geddes, Patrick. 1915. *Cities in Evolution*. London: Williams & Norgate.

———. 1925. "The Valley Plan of Civilization." *The Survey* 54: 288–90, 322–25.

Genette, Gérard. 1982. *Palimpsestes. La littérature au second degré*. Paris: Edition di Seui.

Girot, Christophe, Anette Freytag, and Albert Kirchengast, eds. 2013. *Topology: Topical Thoughts on the Contemporary Landscape*. Landscript 3. Berlin: Jovis.

Gottmann, J. 1961. *Megalopolis: The Urbanized Northeastern Seaboard of the United States*. Cambridge, MA: MIT Press.

Greenfield, Adam. 2013. *Against the Smart City: A Pamphlet. This Is Part I of "The City Is Here to Use."* New York City: Do projects.

Gregotti, Vittorio. 1966. "The Shape of Landscape [Italian: la forma del territorio]." *Edilizia Moderna*, 87–88: 1–13.

Harley, John B. 1989. "Deconstructing the Map." *Cartographica* 26 (2): 1–20.

Hilberseimer, Ludwig. 1948. *The New Regional Pattern*. Chicago: Paul Theobald.

Hildebrand, Sonia. 2006. "Urbane Schweiz. Urbanistische Konzepte für die Schweiz von 1930 bis heute." In *Das Ende der Urbanisierung? Wandelnde Perspektiven auf die Stadt, ihre Geschichte und Erforschung*, edited by Karsten Borgmann, Matthias Bruhn, Sven Kuhrau, and Marc Schalenberg. Berlin: Historisches Forum; 8.

Kaplan, Frederic, and Isabella Di Lenardo. 2020. "The Advent of the 4D Mirror World." *Urban Planning* 5 (2) (June 30, 2020): 307–10. https://doi.org/10.17645/up.v5i2.3133.

Kitchin, Rob. 2014. "Big Data, New Epistemologies and Paradigm Shifts." *Big Data & Society* 1: 311.

Kitchin, Rob, and Martin Dodge. 2007. "Rethinking Maps." *Progress in Human Geography* 31 (3) (June 2007): 331–44. https://doi.org/10.1177/0309132507077082.

Kraak, Menno-Jan. "The Best Map Ever?" *International Journal of Cartography* 7 (2) (May 4, 2021): 205–10. https://doi.org/10.1080/23729333.2021.1909404.

Lampariello, Beatrice. "Aldo Rossi pour une théorie du territoire et de ses éléments premiers." Conference "Entre héritage des Ciam et invention du territoire: revisiter le débat architectural italien, 1952–1966," Ecole d'architecture de la ville & des territoires Paris-Est, 13.1.2020.

Léveillé, Alain, Yves Cassani, Marie-Paule Mayor, and André Corboz. 1993. *Atlas du Territoire Genevois. Permanences et modifications cadastrales aux xix et xx siècles* [Atlas of the Geneva territory: Permanences and cadastral changes in the 19th and 20th centuries] (4–7). Geneva: Département des travaux publics du canton de Genève, Service des monuments et des sites, Centre de recherche sur la rénovation urbaine.

Le Corbusier. 1930. *Précisions sur un état présent de l'architecture et de l'urbanisme*. Paris: Éditions Crès, Collection de "L'Esprit Nouveau."

Lévy, Jacques, ed. 2015. *A Cartographic Turn*. Lausanne: EPFL Press.

Lightman, Alan. 2005. "A Sense of the Mysterious." In *The Work of Charles and Ray Eames: A Legacy of Invention*, edited by D. Albrecht et al. New York: Harry N. Abrams.

Llaguno-Munitxa, Maider, and Elie Bou-Zeid. 2020. "Sensing the Environmental Neighborhoods. Mobile Urban Sensing Technologies (MUST) for High Spatio-Temporal Resolution Urban Environmental Mapping." In *Digital Futures World 2020, Robotic Vision*. Cham: Springer.

Lock, Oliver, Tomasz Bednarz, and Christopher Pettit. 2019. "HoloCity – Exploring the Use of Augmented Reality Cityscapes for Collaborative Understanding of High-Volume Urban Sensor Data." In *The 17th International Conference on Virtual-Reality Continuum and Its Applications in Industry*, 1–2. Brisbane, QLD: ACM. https://doi.org/10.1145/3359997.3365734.

Lynn, Greg, ed. 2004. *Folding in Architecture*. Rev. ed. Architectural Design. Chichester, West Sussex and Hoboken, NJ: Wiley-Academy.

MacKaye, Benton. 1921. "An Appalachian Trail: A Project." *Regional Planning Journal of the American Institute of Architects* 9: 325–30.

M'Closkey, Karen, Keith Vandersys, Editorial. 2016. "Simulation." *LA+, Interdisciplinary Journal of Landscape Architecture* (4).

McHarg, Ian. 1969. *Design with Nature*. New York: American Museum of Natural History.

———. 1998. *The History of Geographic Information Systems: Perspectives from the Pioneers*. Edited by Foresman Timothy ix–x. Upper Saddle River, NJ: Prentice Hall.

Meadows Donatella, H., Dennis L. Meadows, Jorgen Randers, William W. Behrens. 1972. *The Limits to Growth: A Report for the Club of Rome's Project on the Predicament of Mankind*. New York: Universe Books.

Morrison, P., P. Morrison, and The Office of Charles & Ray Eames. 1982. *Powers of Ten. About the Relative Size of Things in the Universe*. New York: Scientific America Library.

Muratori, Saverio. 1960. *Studi per un'operante storia urbana di Venezia*. Rome: La Libreria dello Stato.

MVRDV. 1999. *Metacity/Datatown*. Rotterdam: 010 Publishers.

Picon, Antoine. 2010. *Digital Culture in Architecture: An Introduction for the Design Professions*. Basel: Birkhäuser.

Pinchemel, Philippe. 1971. "Photographie aérienne et urbanisme, édité par le Centre de Recherche d'Urbanisme, préface Jean Canaux, 463–464." *Annales de Géographie*, t. 80, n°440.

Presner, Todd Samuel, David Shepard, and Yoh Kawano. 2014. *HyperCities: Thick Mapping in the Digital Humanities*. MetaLABprojects. Cambridge, MA: Harvard University Press.

Ratti, Carlo. 2004. "Space Syntax: Some Inconsistencies." *Environment and Planning B: Planning and Design* 31 (4) (August 2004): 487–99. https://doi.org/10.1068/b3019.

Ravagnati, Carlo. 2012. *L'invenzione del territorio: l'atlante inedito di Saverio Muratori*. Milano: Franco Angeli.

Rendgen, Sandra. 2020. *Le système Minard: anthologie des représentations statistiques de Charles-Joseph Minard*. Paris: B42 Eds.

Rossi, Aldo. 1962. "Nuovi problemi." *Casabella continuità*, [s.vol.], giugno 264: 2–7.

Secchi, Bernardo. 1992. "Urbanistica descrittiva." *Casabella* 588: 22–23.

Sieverts, Thomas. 1997. *Zwischenstadt. Zwischen Ort und Welt, Raum und Zeit, Stadt und Land*. Berlin: Birkhauser.

Skjonsberg, Matthew. 2018. "A New Look on Civic Design: Park Systems in America." PhD Dissertation, EPFL Lausanne, p. 512, 10.5075/epfl-thesis-8095.

Steinitz, Carl, Paul Parker, and Lawrie Jordan. 1976. "Hand-drawn Overlays: Their History and Prospective Uses." *Landscape Architecture* 66 (5): 444–55.

Stonor, Tim. 2018. "Intense Relationships: Measuring Urban Intensity." *The Architectural Review*, April 30, 2018.

Tafuri, M., G. Piccinato, and V. Quilici. 1962. "La città territorio: verso una nuova dimensione." *Casabella continuità* 270: 16–25.

Urech, Philipp R. W. 2020. "Editing Cumulated Landscapes: Point Cloud Modeling as a Method of Analysis in Landscape Design." *Urban Planning* 5 (2) (June 30, 2020): 296–306. https://doi.org/10.17645/up.v5i2.2885.

Viganò, Paola 2013. "The Horizontal Metropolis and Gloeden's Diagrams. Two Parallel Stories." *OASE* 89.

———, ed. 2014. *Territorialism*. Cambridge: Harvard University Press.

———. 2020. "Territorio-Soggetto." In *Territori post rurali. Genealogie e prrospettive*, edited by De Marchi Marta and Hessam Khorasani Zadeh, 219–s29. Rome: Officina Edizioni.

Viganò, Paola, Chiara Cavalieri, and Martina Barcelloni Corte, eds. 2018. *The Horizontal Metropolis Between Urbanism and Urbanization*. Cham: Springer International Publishing.

Waldheim, Charles. 1999. "Aerial Representation and the Recovery of Landscape." In *Recovery Landscape. Essays in Contemporary Landscape Architecture*, edited by Corner James, 121–40. New York: Princeton Architectural Press.

———. 2012. "Provisional Notes on Landscape Representation and Digital Media." In *Landscript 1: Landscape Vision Motion. Visual Thinking in Landscape Culture*, edited by C. Girot and F. Truniger. Berlin: Jovis.

Walliss, Jillian. 2018. "Landscape Architecture and the Digital Turn: Towards a Productive Critique." *Journal of Landscape Architecture* 13 (3) (September 2, 2018): 12–15. https://doi.org/10.1080/18626033.2018.1589119.

Waters, Nigel. 2017. "GIS: History." In *International Encyclopedia of Geography: People, the Earth, Environment and Technology*, edited by Douglas Richardson, Noel Castree, Michael F. Goodchild, Audrey Kobayashi, Weidong Liu, and Richard A. Marston, 1–12. Oxford: John Wiley & Sons, Ltd. https://doi.org/10.1002/9781118786352.wbieg0841.

WCED (World Commission for Environment and Development). 1987. *Our Common Future*. Oxford University Press.

Wood, Denis. 2003. "Cartography Is Dead (Thank God!)." *Cartographic Perspectives* 45 (June 1, 2003): 4–7. https://doi.org/10.14714/CP45.497.

31

LANDSCAPES IN MOTION

Cartographies of Connectivity and the Place of Physical Geography in the Environmental and Spatial Humanities

Ryan Horne and Ruth Mostern

Introduction

The environmental humanities are a transdisciplinary field that draws from the humanities, social sciences, environmental sciences, geography, and ecology while advocating for viewing environmental challenges and change within a conceptual framework that encompass the social and cultural critique offered by the humanities (Adamson 2016, 347; Travis 2018, 172–73; Schmidt, Soentgen, and Zapf 2020). The digital humanities and spatial humanities likewise incorporate methods and approaches from social sciences, information sciences, and physical sciences within a humanities lens (Lin 2012, 295–98; Murrieta-Flores and Martins 2019; Giordano, Shaw, and Sinton 2020). Environmental, spatial, and digital approaches in the humanities all centre on the work of documenting and analysing connections rather than describing and understanding phenomena in isolation. These fields have in common an aim to identify links among people and between people and places throughout complex and emergent ecological systems. These approaches use methods that range from the interpretive work of "close reading" to investigations of events and systems covering large geographical extents, long time spans, and vast corpora of data. Such methods, some of which emerged outside the humanities, are used for the discovery and visualisation of complex, dynamic, and multi-scalar systems. In these ways, such fields are akin to one another and distinctive from many other humanistic approaches. They surface entanglements between human and non-human worlds, between data and experience, and between qualitative and quantitative methods in order to explore the place of humanity within global, environmental, and information ecosystems.

It is difficult to model, describe, and visualise social, environmental, and knowledge systems in their complexity and as they interact and evolve over time. This is even truer because environmental, spatial, and digital humanities projects may seek to synthesise data from a variety of scales, both temporal and spatial, themselves constituted by the activities that occur in them. Moreover, they do so with information that derives from any number of different source traditions and approaches. Such projects need to integrate and model quantitative data – from maps, historical documents, dendrochronology datasets, sensors, and other sources – while managing

DOI: 10.4324/9781003082798-38

uncertainty intervals, metadata standards, and specialised knowledge associated with that data and retaining the humanistic recognition that texts are complex and situated, that interpretation of them is a crucial element of the methodological toolkit, and that the concept of information is not universal. Indeed, uncertainty is not only a computational problem. From another angle, it is the favoured epistemological stance for all humanistic inquiry rather than a problem to be managed.

To help abstract such complexity, it is conceptually feasible to describe evolving and intricate networks as social-ecological systems (SES; Kluger et al. 2020, 1101). However, it is very challenging to identify and create data – to deploy methods characteristic of digital and spatial humanities – to surface connectivity within these complex co-constitutive systems while remaining anchored to human experience, meaning, and understanding. Often, visualisations, primarily maps, are used to communicate spatial and environmental phenomena. Alternative approaches include interactive timelines and network analysis in online publications, and these may also incorporate scientific data from other academic fields. However, while these are effective at communicating broad trends, they do not readily capture multivalent and temporally dynamic linkages. In this paper, we argue for leveraging geospatial and environmental data and systems at the intersection of spatial, digital, and environmental approaches, with the goal of creating an open, accessible digital ecosystem that enables the discovery, use, and publication of digital environmental history (DEH) data. We survey current innovations from the long-term and large-scale history of China, the ancient Mediterranean, and the globe, which collectively point toward a vision for a networked and cloud-based graph of historical environmental data.

At the core of this proposed methodology, we explain the merits and feasibility of creating a vast and collectively authored index of assertions about past ecology and past landscapes, each one of which is supported by complex interlinked metadata on place and chronology, using linked open data (LOD) practices to focus on connections between the human, environmental, spatial, and digital worlds and knowledge systems. The goal is to create cartographies of connectivity and a new digital ecosystem that expands upon the growing graph of digital gazetteers and spatial humanities by emphasising entanglements between diverse entities, disciplines, and the environment. The key advantage will be to move beyond the current situation in which ecology is often rendered as a static base layer to society's superstructure, and instead to ensure that historical projects in the environmental-spatial humanities can incorporate their analysis and data with information about the river courses, shorelines, terrain, and climate that existed during any given time period (Rankin 2020).

Space, Place, and the Environment

The most exciting contemporary work in the spatial humanities – scholarship that facilitates conceptual and analytical understanding of how complex systems vary and evolve throughout space and over time in ways that are simultaneous and mutually constitutive – focuses on models rather than maps. It is work that focuses on place rather than on Newtonian absolute space with its clear distinction between objects (relational and emergent) and their precise coordinates and the commercial GIS that instantiate that approach. People speak, write, and reason about geography with reference to distinctive named locations. We routinely say "my house" and refer to it by its address rather than according to its latitude-longitude coordinates. Names are the referents around which people formalise spatial inclusion and exclusion, through which they make meaning, and within which people are positioned in social hierarchies. Uluru and Ayers Rock, Jerusalem and Al-Quds, Istanbul and Constantinople – these pairs of names refer to approximately the same location and material setting on the earth's surface, but their appellations evoke entirely different histories and relationships.

Place is a multivalent concept in the spatial humanities. Within the indexical tradition of GIS, places are characterised by the fact that they have coordinates on the earth's surface. Geographers like David Harvey and Waldo Tobler have long recognised that coordinate systems are themselves social and historical.[1] The scale of coordinates may vary, and the locations of places (ships, encampments, sprawling cities, or locales impacted by rising seas or desertification) may not be fixed in perpetuity. Places are also material settings for social relations. Geographers refer to this by the term locale. Finally, places create attachment – a "sense of place." Location, locale, and sense of place are the core characteristics of places (Agnew 2011). In addition, places may have attributes associated with them that describe them and connect them semantically to one another. A set of places may have in common the fact that they were all inundated by the same flood. Finally, places come into being at particular times. They are human creations, and they exist because of human activity that makes them meaningful. They may cease to exist when they are no longer sites of meaning. Within the spatial humanities, practitioners tend to turn to the concept of place to affirm the inherent historicity of geographical arrangements rather than grappling with insights from a generation of critical geography, even though that direction of inquiry would be valuable as well.

In the spatial humanities, place is often juxtaposed with space. Space, in the tradition of commercial GIS rather than critical geography, is defined as abstract and undifferentiated expanses of terrain that occupy some portion of the earth's surface in which individual sites are described by latitude and longitude coordinates rather than by names and which are not endowed with social value. Places have space between them.[2] As the geographer Tim Cresswell (2013, 18) puts it, "When we look at the world as a world of places, we see different things. We see attachments and connections between people and places. We see worlds of meaning and experience." The reason why we advocate place as a critical concept for the environmental humanities is that it is an abstraction that makes it possible to link human and non-human worlds and to associate history with geography. Named places are the pivot points for the cartographies of connectivity that we propounded in the introduction to this paper. Data models constructed around the idea of place are conceptually legible, although they may be painstaking to build in practice. In a recent paper, Ross Purves, Stephan Winter, and Werner Kuhn (2019) approach the formalisation and modelling of place from the perspective of information science. They explain that places (1) are unique geographic objects, (2) have locations, and (3) emerge from some form of human consensus, even if the perception of the properties of a place may be contentious or impermanent. Seen as objects, places can become nodes or edges in networks. If need be, they can be located qualitatively through discourse and network topology without recourse to coordinates. Places can participate in events. For example, a historian may assert that a certain place experienced a drought in a particular year. All of this can be managed in data models, as Purves, Winter, and Kuhn demonstrate.

Databases organised around named places are called gazetteers. Historical gazetteers are ones in which all of the attributes of places (their multiple names, their locations, their characteristics, their networks of relationships) can be associated with dates and date ranges and with information about the sources for the assertions about them. Historians and humanists are beginning to realise that gazetteers, though less visually arresting than maps, are often better suited than univariate thematic maps to gather and model information about the complexity and heterogeneity of places, the ways that places change over time, and the attributes associated with them, such as their temperatures at given times, their elevations, the biomes in which they are situated, the amount of carbon dioxide that they emit at certain times,

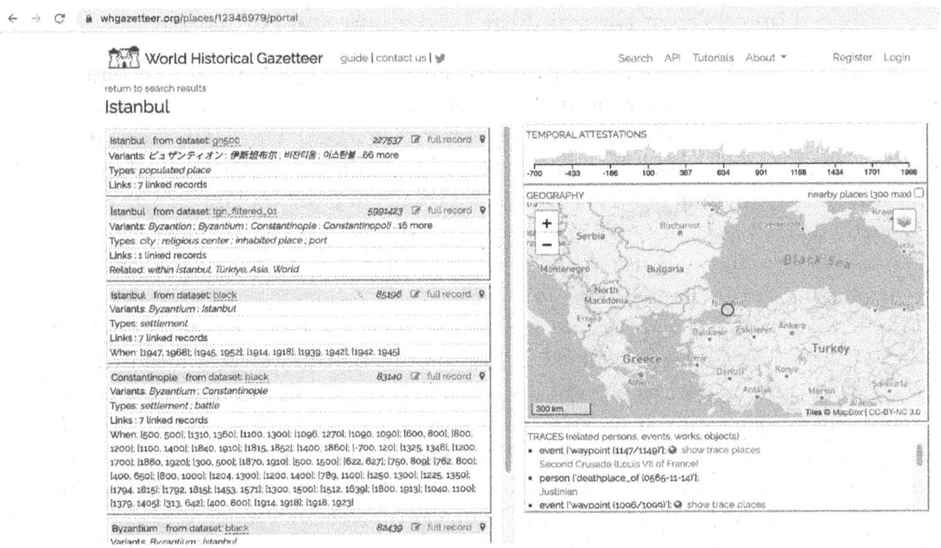

Figure 31.1 The World Historical Gazetteer (whgazetteer.org) is an initiative to create a common index for multiple linked attestations about places. This screenshot depicts how the WHG index collects multiple names for a single place that are drawn from numerous sources, as well as links to web-accessible third-party sources in the LOD ecosystem like Geonames, VIAF, Wikidata, and the Library of Congress. This record also includes references to the existence of the place for over 2,000 years and information about events associated with the place. Ruth Mostern is the project director of the WHG, and Ryan Horne is a member of the advisory board.

the occasions when they have been flooded, and the times when they have been protected by levees (Berman, Mostern, and Southall 2016). Because of the historical specificity of place, creating historical gazetteers requires a substantial amount of specialised knowledge and research.

Gazetteers, like the World Historical Gazetteer (WHG) in Figure 31.1, model place rather than absolute Cartesian space, and they scale up from individual instances about attestations of existence and naming into potentially vast and multiply authored datasets of information about individual places that change over time, form relationships with one another, and reflect histories of contestation. Histories of places occur in concert with environmental change. Cities name new streets as they fill in bays and wetlands. New settlements appear as glaciers recede, or they disappear as deserts expand. Places maintain names that reflect ghostly presences of past land use. The namesake for the Kappabashi neighbourhood in Tokyo, like many other places in that sprawling metropolis, is a long-gone bridge (*bashi*) that once spanned a body of water that has been drained or culverted for decades. Near the banks of the Yellow River in China, Lingzhou ("the miraculous prefecture") derived its name from its extraordinary propensity to avoid floods when the river ran high. Now abandoned, it is more than ten kilometres away from the current river course (Mostern 2021). As these examples suggest, places and their names, especially in combination with one another, often mark relationships between people and the non-human world much more effectively than maps do.

Linked Open Data and the Environmental Humanities

We advocate for linked open data (LOD) approaches to the digital spatial humanities because such a methodology is necessary for linking gazetteers with one another as well as linking gazetteers with other information about the places that they index. The WHG (see **Figure 31.1**) is a project that is creating tools, infrastructure and core content to facilitate this for the spatial humanities. LOD is a group of methodologies for connecting web-published datasets that are of an explicitly defined type, machine readable, and that reference one another. These references do not have to share the same data types or even be from the same study domains; for instance, demographic and climate information can be linked to data about places if some correspondence is made between unique identifiers, such as place-name IDs. LOD is, additionally, published with an open license agreement, and its format must be non-proprietary, like a CSV file, and open standards must be used to identify it (Berners-Lee 2007). In practice, most LOD systems use stable and unique uniform resource identifiers (URIs) to identify and disambiguate data (Bizer and Berners-Lee 2009, 1–2). URIs are familiar to anyone who has used a browser; a web address, otherwise known as a uniform resource locator (URL), is a URI and forms a hierarchical naming scheme that uniquely identifies resources on the web (Berners-Lee, Masinter, and McCahill 1994).

These URIs are often linked through the use of the Resource Description Framework (RDF), a metadata standard that is used to describe data with properties and values (Latif et al. 2009, 76–78). In practice this is done with a triple, or a declaration formatted as "<subject> <predicate> <object>." In this format, there is a relationship expressed between the subject of a statement and an object using a predicate, all of which are URIs in their own right. For example, one could employ URIs to say that the place known as Carthage (subject) also has the name or title (predicate) of Carthago (object).

A very simplified version using the Pleiades Gazetteer and Dublin Core Metadata Initiative (DMCI) metadata terms could look something like <https://pleiades.stoa.org/places/314921> <http://purl.org/dc/terms/title> <https://pleiades.stoa.org/places/314921/carthago>. Although the use of URIs in this way is nearly incomprehensible to most human users, this type of structured information is ideal for use in digital systems. Computers can quickly link, search, and harvest information about any entity in the growing and interconnected ecosystem of information that LOD practitioners refer to as a graph and potentially store in a graph database. In the digital humanities and adjacent fields, libraries, museums, and archives have been early adopters of LOD methods because they provide a powerful means to connect data on artworks, artists, media, and genres both within and outside their institutional setting. In the wider humanities communities, LOD practitioners are increasingly gathering around the Linked Pasts consortium, which "brings together scholars, heritage professionals and other practitioners with an interest in Linked Open Data as applied to the study of the ancient and historical worlds" (Linked Pasts 6 2020).[3] LOD is ideally suited for use by digital gazetteers, as it provides a framework and methodology for identifying, disambiguating, and representing unique entities whose precise definition and conceptual parameters may vary greatly between datasets and disciplines. For example, the Simple Knowledge Organization System (SKOS) is a series of specifications and standards which are used to express the relationships between different knowledge systems (thesauri, classification schemes, etc.) on the web.[4] When we use SKOS and other standards, it is possible to express relationships between entities, from exact correspondence to contested definitions using a standard vocabulary. Due to the complicated nature of place, relationships between places and names are complex and often contested. LOD methods and specifications like SKOS permit contradicting interpretations of place to coexist in linked datasets; they do not merely permit more knowledge to accrue. In the WHG, contributors themselves determine whether or not to designate any one of their records as a close match with one in the WHG index. As places are linked to one another through political, cultural, geographic, or other conceptual means, information from any individual gazetteer is likely to be small and/or sparse when viewed against the entire corpus of information on a given place. Digital gazetteers can, and should, incorporate or link to information in other gazetteers or projects that have overlapping spatial footprints. Given that structured data and unique identifiers are essential elements of both gazetteers and LOD, it is a relatively straightforward process to mint stable URIs to represent each record in a traditional gazetteer and to reconcile those records with other digital projects without requiring that distinct or contradictory attestations must be merged into a single record. A digital knowledge ecosystem is formed when more projects use these URIs to describe their data, which can lead to the development of new knowledge systems and scholarly approaches. Given the centrality of multiple readings and situated knowledge to humanistic epistemologies, such divergences and differences are not seen as a problem that needs to be rectified, as they might be in some other kinds of information systems.

This is the foundational principle of the Pelagios Commons[5] which began as an effort to build a graph of disparate information that was connected by common references to place URIs from the Pleiades Gazetteer of the ancient world.[6] These URIs uniquely identify different ancient places and form the *bodies* of annotations from other datasets that have different *targets* which are URIs to data in their respective projects. An inscription, text, or any other entity that has some spatial information can be related to a specified Pleiades ID for that place, which is then discoverable through the Pelagios graph of links. The result is a system that is capable of

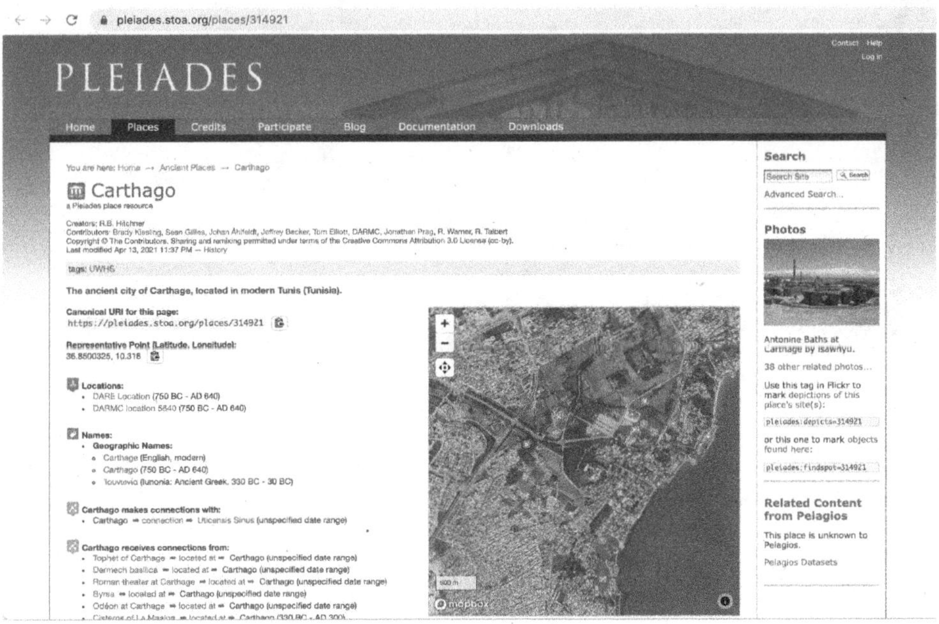

Figure 31.2 A The entry for Carthage in Pleiades (2A), the WHG (2B), and Recogito (2C). Although Pleiades and the WHG offer information about Carthage, they have their own URIs, which can be linked together using LOD. The resulting graph can then be queried in a platform like Recogito.

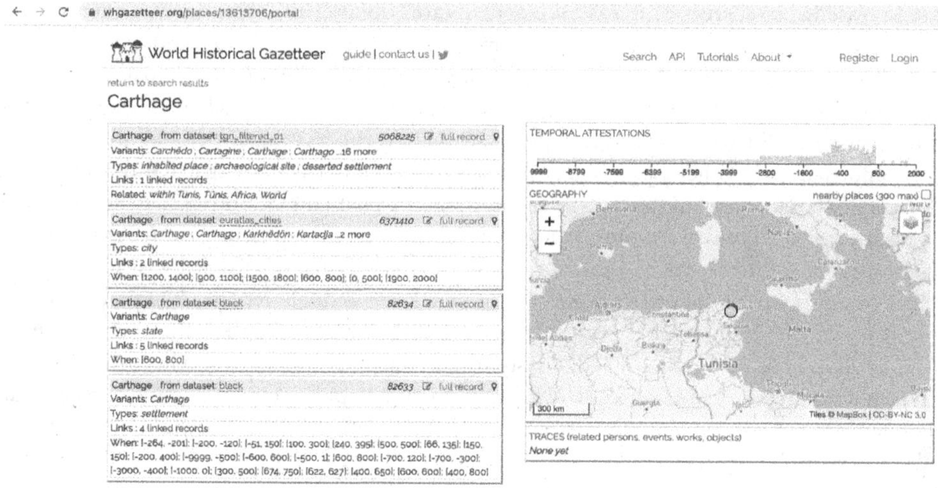

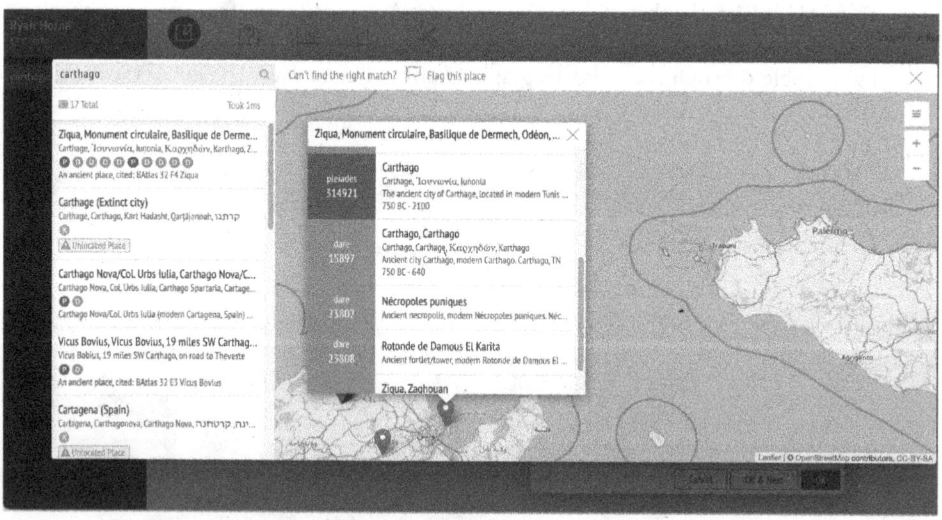

Figures 31.2 B (top) C (bottom)

expressing relationships between geography, material culture, text, and historical sources, which has now expanded to incorporate digital gazetteers and projects from a variety of temporal and spatial contexts, as shown in **Figure 31.3** (Isaksen et al. 2014, 198).

Developed in collaboration with Pelagios, the WHG exemplifies current best practices in the deployment and modelling of LOD in spatial humanities. The WHG indexes place data drawn from historical sources, contributed by research projects and individuals studying the past from many disciplinary perspectives. Version 1.2, launched in June 2021, includes 60,000 temporally scoped place records along with 1.8 million modern records. The WHG records include name variants, coordinates, and chronological information, all identified through individual URIs.

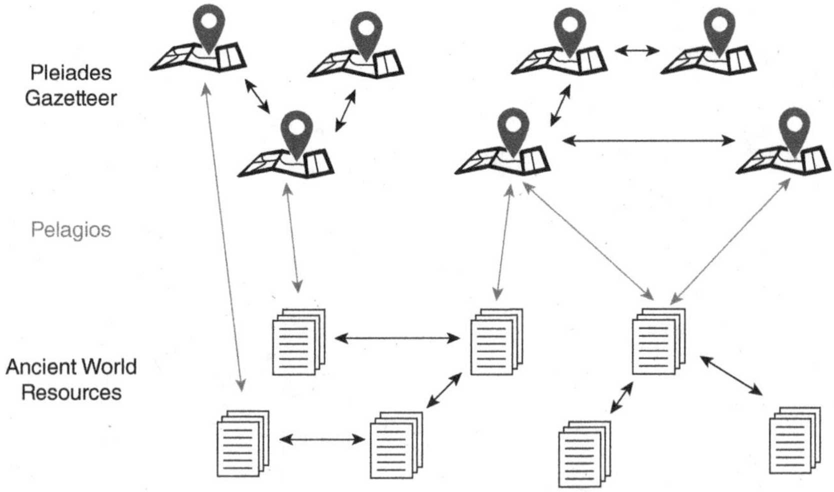

Figure 31.3 An abstraction of Pelagios Commons. Note the direct links between *Ancient World Resources* and gazetteers – this represents projects that have aligned their spatial data with one or more digital gazetteers. Different projects that reference the same gazetteers can be indexed and placed on the Pelagios graph; efforts are currently underway to link the gazetteers themselves, which would expand the graph even further (Barker, Simon, and Isaksen 2014).

Within a larger linked data ecosystem, partner projects can link their gazetteers to places in the index.[7] To be sure, human verification is still a critical part of the process. A core feature of the WHG is its reconciliation services, which permit contributors to upload place records and find authority matches for them. The scripts that the WHG has developed to suggest potential matches make use of all name variants, modern country or study area bounds, place type, and any provided coordinates. Contributors themselves determine whether or not to accept any potential match based on their own expert knowledge and interpretive framework and use the SKOS specifications to classify their assertions. Nevertheless, even though it is computationally assisted, the review of potential matches is a painstaking expert process. Contributors to the WHG review proposed matches before asserting that they are viable links to their records. Likewise, the Recogito programme, a semantic annotation tool for historical texts that is part of the Pelagios Network, can suggest matches for named places found in the gazetteers linked via an interface, but only an expert human can determine whether those matches are accurate (Simon et al. 2017). This process of reconciliation between different records and the creation of a LOD graph is a complex product of intense scholarship that necessarily proceeds at the pace of humanistic research directed by people with deep domain expertise. The promise of linkage through LOD is a promise of digital infrastructure that enables the connection of disparate disciplinary domains through convergences in common interests. Fully understanding the data and the implications of linkages facilitated by LOD still requires significant research effort and the application of conceptual and interpretive frameworks.

There are a growing number of data ontologies, vocabularies, and URI authorities in digital and spatial humanities as well environmental sciences, with specialisations including cultural heritage, ecological research, and other areas (Horne 2021a, 4–12).[8] In information science, an ontology is a formal declaration of categories and their properties. For humanists, the term refers to philosophical claims about the nature of existence. It is a powerful concept in the digital

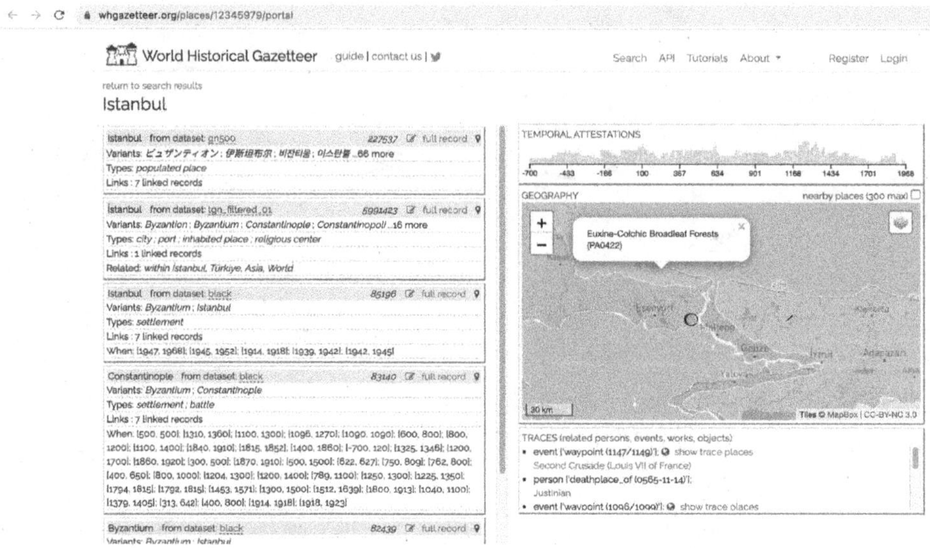

Figure 31.4 Istanbul-Constantinople-Byzantium in the WHG with rivers, watershed, and ecoregion layers enabled. An environmentally minded historian may find it meaningful to realise that this extraordinary world city lies at the intersection of several different forest ecologies. Even better than simply including these layers in a map visualisation would be to include this information in a database associated with the place record itself.

humanities – and the spatial environmental humanities in particular – precisely because it invites people to pivot between two meanings – that of data modelling and that of interpretive critique. In data modelling, the environment may be a collection of objects, while simultaneously, in the humanities, it is a domain of cultural construction and discursive practice. With a sufficiently supple data ontology and a sufficiently multivocal linked data system, it is nearly possible to bridge the gulf between these approaches. However, despite remarkable advances and increasing use of LOD in these areas, nobody has yet created a single usable LOD digital ecosystem. There are few efforts to collect and publish LOD linkages between human and environmental data from quantitative and qualitative approaches, and almost no projects that have provided stable URIs or generated communities of best practices in how to combine these study domains. The WHG includes a limited amount of environmental content that is formatted according to the principles of linked data. This means that WHG users can discover connections between any named place and its contemporary ecological setting. While this is a proof of concept and a down payment for linking spatial and ecological information, there is much more that can be done to make the ecology of the spatial humanities as temporally changing, interlinked, and richly attested as the rest of the field, and this requires interdisciplinary collaboration, not just technology

Beyond Base Layers

The first key concept for a historical and linked spatial environmental humanities is the notion of place, with an index of connected gazetteers using LOD methodology as its core infrastructure. The related second concept is to challenge the framework of the base map, with its assumptions of a single, static, hegemonic, and inert environmental world of a historical absolute space upon which human activity transpires in the foreground. The notion of the base map emerged as part of the visual vocabulary of thematic mapping in the 19th century, and it was woven into the development of certain kinds of cartographic software in the late 20th century. Now, a conceptual and technological domain is starting to open up for new kinds of approaches.

Here we are following a lead from a recent article by William Rankin (2020). As Rankin argues, contemporary spatial history is founded on the potential for maps and other visualisations to show the historical "constructedness" of space, but the visual argument of the base map undercuts that mission since the notion of foreground and background reifies the natural environment, makes it appear to be outside of spatial subjectivity and the historicity of space, and falsely separates human and non-human worlds from one another. Rankin reminds us that the visual makes an argument, just as text and data do, and that images shape our understanding of the world. He points readers toward Fernand Braudel and the Annales School. Braudel and his cartographer Jacques Bertin readily acknowledged that the geographic scale of the *longue durée* (the scale of erosion and climate change) is dynamic and integrated with the political and economic *moyenne durée* (the scale of environmental policy) and likewise with the *courte durée* of individuals and events (including environmental events like hurricanes and volcanic eruptions).

It is not that any part of the world is static or separate from the other parts: it is just that the scale of change tends to be distinctive in various domains. To reflect this, Braudel's text and Bertin's maps, created decades prior to the digital turn, invited analysis and reading that moved among these three scales and acknowledged the relationships among them. Rankin introduces his Remapping the Desert initiative as an alternative, depicting the Phoenix metropolitan area as a "triple interaction of topographic disposition, human activity, and human activities, each in historical interaction with the others" (Rankin 2020, 339). He has produced a static map, but its layers are numerous, inter-referential, and non-hierarchical. Rankin describes the objective he has sought to achieve for his map of land management status and race and ethnicity around Phoenix, Arizona: "Rather than heap more attention on the conspicuous boundary between city and desert – with the city portrayed as a metastasizing blob expanding into a featureless *tabula rasa* – these maps focus on the internal boundaries within both city and desert. The result shows the desert as already quite full in a legal sense, and the city as a complex field of different kinds of segregation" (Rankin 2009).

Despite the existence of such experiments, both within the LOD domain and elsewhere in the field, most spatial humanities projects generally use modern base maps, over which they may provide a geo-referenced historical map or some other visualisation. The current use of historical geographic information systems (HGIS) is largely based on a base map/layer approach. Appropriate data, often taking the form of satellite imagery or a digital elevation model (DEM), is selected as a base map, over which different layers of information (such as human settlement locations, roads, meteorological phenomena, biomes, etc.) are placed. Base maps may also take the form of digitised images of historical maps, which are often themselves georeferenced with respect to satellite or DEM data (Gregory and Ell 2007, 28–33, 48–49). In practice, almost all base maps are raster images where each individual pixel represents a discrete value. This is extremely useful for abstracting large geographic areas, but the data format does not have a mechanism for readily identifying or providing data on features like rivers, lakes, and roads. The only way to create features that can be assigned attributes and incorporated into spatial analysis is to painstakingly hand-trace them from georeferenced raster maps in order to create new vector layers. This is what it means to refer to these raster maps as base maps. They can orient readers spatially, but they cannot be used to visualise or analyse continuous or ongoing changes to coastlines, rivers, and other geographic features on a single base map. Moreover, georeferencing a flat map onto the spherical earth inevitably introduces error, and distortions in the original map, such as imprecise modelling of dynamic features like rivers and coastlines, also limit the utility of projecting historical data onto modern maps.

To overcome these limitations, most GIS systems and approaches turn to the concept of layers to express detailed data on discrete entities such as settlements, mountains, rivers, and biomes. These layers are largely composed of vector data rather than raster data and contain detailed spatial information about the bounds of a point, line, or polygon, along with attribute data that describes the entity.[9] This attribute data can be of any type, often listing names, chronological data, and some form of classification. Each entity within a layer has a unique ID, which can be used with an API to create a URI for use in LOD applications. For example, one can download a file from OpenStreetMap (OSM) data that contains information on places in China, and the ID associated with Shanghai, 244081648, is also in the URI for accessing Shanghai directly from the OSM site (www.openstreetmap.org/node/244081648). If a project has data that relates to Shanghai, it can use the OSM URI to indicate that its data is related to the conceptual and geographic entity of Shanghai.

The distinction between raster base maps and vector layers in GIS originates from the evolution of cartography prior to the digital era. For centuries, only states and other large entities were well positioned to produce print maps that purported to offer an accurate visualisation of the Earth's surface. These served as base maps, and they reflected the self-representation of individual states to promote their own borders and present themselves as geographic facts internationally (Rankin 2016, 26–27). As part of their utility to powerful state and economic interests, national and colonial mapping projects often obscured or ignored local spatial realities and perceptions in favour of an imposed centralised conception of neatly classified and bordered geographic space (Anderson 2006, 170–78; Winichakul 1994, 53–61, 120–21). The pre-eminence of these powerful interests continued with the development of GIS, which was first created by government agencies in Canada and the United States for land management, including the Canada Land Inventory, the US Fish and Wildlife Services, and the US Army Corps of Engineers (Neteler et al. 2012, 205; Presner and Shepard 2016, 203).[10] Still, the distinction between the base map and thematic layers is never complete, and among cartographers

Figure 31.5 The record for Shanghai in OSM. Notice that the ID forms part of the URI.

and academic geographers, the ideal of accuracy relative to the metrics of absolute space has always been in tension with fidelity to complex social and natural processes. It is the centrality of state and corporate power in the history of cartography that tends to obscure some of these nuances.[11] Today, modern technology and new political actors, in many cases massive international corporations like Alphabet/Google and Microsoft, are the creators and proponents of base maps that are products of their own economic, political, and social agendas. Although MapBox and other open-source tools, and even ESRI developer tools, permit cartographers to create their own base maps and merge them with thematic maps, the default visualisations of the underlying topography and map states are still products that are crafted through a corporate decision-making process.[12] While the use of DEM data to represent spatial "reality" of the present and deviations from it, including environmental changes, have greatly improved, a broad-based historical visualisation and conceptualisation of the dynamic past are still lacking. The new Google Earth Timelapse feature offers guided tours that permit anyone to "watch time unfold and witness nearly four decades of planetary change" based on a database of 24 million satellite photos from the past 37 years. This is fantastic data, but it is rendered and defined in a way that replicates the base map fallacy. The rhetoric on the Google blog post announcing the Timelapse feature envisions its users as spectators "marveling at changing coastlines, following the growth of megacities, or tracking deforestation" rather than as scholars or activists engaging in historical and environmental spatial analysis, dynamically modelling spatial change at multiple time scales, or seeking to change the world (Moore 2021).

Simply creating more raster base maps combined with distinct and separate vector layers is not a goal that aligns with a humanities approach to spatial history that propounds the co-creation of social and ecological realities. The issue remains that most modern manifestations of digital mapping projects use the base/layer paradigm. This implicitly produces a visual logic and an analytical imperative in which a static and "scientific" base is the stage upon which human activity transpires, one which its users and readers have no choice but to view as "'basic' and universal" even if they may know that ecology changes over time (Rankin 2016, 26). When spatial humanities projects of necessity rely upon these types of base maps, they obscure or ignore changing linkages between places, people, and natural phenomena, especially those that are difficult to visualise or for which vector data and database information are not easily available. At issue here is not just a quest to depict the past more accurately but to propound a version of the spatial, environmental, and digital humanities which construes place, human activity, the environment, and geography as entangled in an intricate web of dynamically changing interactions that cannot be reduced to elements in different layers that are simply stacked on one another.

Critical geographers have propounded this approach for decades. It is ironic to realise that it has been slow to find traction in the spatial humanities, a field that has often been seen as coterminous with historical GIS and with the cartographic assumptions that implies. To be sure, spatial and environmental historians are well aware of these multifaceted relationships, but at present, they can generally describe them only in prose text. This means that they are not open to queries, computationally actionable, or publishable as data. For these reasons, there is a critical practical and philosophical need in the research community for a system that can provide environmental data and visualisations for multiple historical periods and locations, and that can incorporate humanistic epistemologies and insights from critical geography. Such a system should also provide a means to connect that data with historical sources, scientific literature, and environmental information. And in contrast to the "base map/layer" paradigm that abstracts geography to a static background for human activity, the system we propose must model physical geography itself as a changing part of a dynamic, interconnected network of human activity, ecology, and time. Our proposal to accomplish this is by associating attestations about physical geography, from historical sources and from environmental science investigations, with stable URIs from existing and emerging historical spatial linked data ecosystems like Pleiades and the WHG. We anticipate that this will create a complex and decolonial archive that includes a growing depth of information about given places, as well as traces of the richly heterogeneous and sometimes conflicting names and histories that so often accrue around named places. Given the significant contributions to scholarship from the Linked Pasts community, the increasing use and release of open-access environmental and ecological data, significant work on infrastructure to connect earth science data with gazetteers, and our own initial steps into historical environmental humanities linked data, we believe that the technology, data, and digital methodologies are now in place to fulfil this need.

Cartographies of Connectivity and Spatially Entangled Ecosystems

We envision a system that builds upon the work of digital gazetteers and reconciliation software to annotate humanities data sources with historical and contemporary environmental and geospatial data. Such a system would be built upon a foundation of LOD principles and would link human and environmental data through stable URIs. This system would need to emphasise movement and connections and be capable of modelling events with complex temporospatial footprints, scales, and contested meanings by constructing a graph of complex relationships and using linked data approaches for indexing multiple interpretations. A focus on these entanglements coupled with representative geographic data (which may itself be a kind of entanglement as well) would be capable of producing striking visualisations and insights which would otherwise be highly distorted or even obscured by the common base map/layer paradigm using modern data (Horne 2021b). The goal of this system would be to model connections between different entities, be they conceptual, physical, or digital. We wish to expand the highly successful use of gazetteers and LOD in the digital and spatial humanities to link space, place, and environmental data with materials from the humanities, social sciences, and environmental sciences.

The key methodology of this approach would be for contributors to use a controlled vocabulary that best reflects their favoured interpretation of complex discourse and social reality. Multiple vocabularies would be, wherever possible, "crosswalked" with each other to form an ontology and graph of interrelated environmental and spatial humanities concepts that preserves multiple definitions and meanings. A user would be able to select elements from their own data to reconcile with this graph in much the same manner as current geospatial gazetteers. For example, a user would be able to select a word ("drought") or extended text ("a harsher winter than normal") and associate those statements with a URI for the concept.[13] If there is a connection in the data between a place and some kind of environmental attestation, like a flood that impacted a region or a tornado that devastated a number of towns, this place data could then also be linked to URIs from spatial gazetteers such as the WHG, Pelagios, and Pleiades. These attestations would also be temporally scoped; the user will be able to either enter their own chronological data or select an appropriate periodisation from the PeriodO gazetteer of historical, art-historical, and archaeological periods.[14]

Data from the environmental sciences, earth science, climatology, and geography could be entered into the graph in the same manner. Studies as a whole, along with their individual records, can be associated with URIs representing different conceptual, geospatial, and chronological information. For example, research on soil composition, erosion, or changing climate can be associated with any number of URIs. A drought, as revealed through dendrochronology and soil composition, would be associated with the same conceptual URIs used by a text that mentions the impact of drought in a specific historical period, along with URIs that are associated with any specific places mentioned or inferred in the study. In our proposed system, these URIs representing elements of social-ecological systems are expressed as nodes in a network graph, and interlinkages between them are edges. This mirrors some recent work deploying network analysis to model relationships between humans and the environment, although this work is often disconnected due to differing foci, vocabularies, and scales of analysis. In addition, the emphasis of such scholarship is almost exclusively modern. While there is significant work to model and predict future changes in the geographic and ecological landscape, such investigations rarely address long-term historical forces or analysis (Kluger et al. 2020, 1101–2; 1110).

Interest in viewing complex systems through a lens of network analysis has largely developed in concert with the extraordinary growth in the World Wide Web, proliferation of social network platforms, and the rise of new security states and technologies since the dawn of the 21st century. Originally the domain of computer scientists and largely quantitative inquiry, this "network turn" is being embraced by a growing group of humanities scholars and represents a new confluence of quantitative studies, natural and computer sciences, humanities, and graphic design (Ahnert et al. 2021, 1–4). Network analysis is increasingly used in environmental sciences to model complex systems, although different terminologies, methodologies, and domain knowledge has so far limited interoperability between different datasets (Kluger et al. 2020, 1110). Some preliminary steps have been taken to create ontologies to bridge study domains in the sciences, but these have largely remained disconnected from the growing graph of environmental, spatial, and digital humanities data (Fallahi et al. 2008, 341–44; Buttigieg et al. 2016, 1–3 and 9–10). For our proposed system to have success, it is not enough to provide annotations and expand the LOD graph to contain environmental humanities data. It is also necessary to provide tools that situate and visualise data in its proper geospatial and temporal context. A study on the changing courses of the Yellow River should have some spatial data on the courses themselves; in our proposed system, each record of a course change would be associated with a URI for the Yellow River, along with chronology from PeriodO, while retaining its own individual URI for reference and disambiguation. This URI could itself be annotated with different potential paths and attribute information from additional research. We envision the OpenStreetMap and OpenHistoricalMap datasets as a starting point for such work; the set would be expanded with more extensive attributes and spatial data that models the dynamic nature of features, such as rivers, over different time periods.

Some preliminary steps have been taken to create the data and infrastructure for such a system. The Ancient World Mapping Center (AWMC) at UNC-Chapel Hill released a base map that reflects the geography of the Roman Empire at 1:1,000,000 scale through MapBox for use in web-based projects and GIS systems.[15] Derived from the *Barrington Atlas*, the spatial and chronological data underlying the map, such as river courses, inland water, and coastline changes, is available through the centre's GitHub page and a custom API that has linkages to Pleiades. This data extends through the coverage of the *Barrington Atlas* and contains high-level changes in coastlines and inland water from the archaic period to late antiquity (before 550 BCE to 640 CE).[16] However, the base map itself is still static, in the sense that the selection of different features and coastlines is pre-selected by the AWMC and is only reflective of a specific, limited time at the height of the Roman Empire. Although the data underlying the map can be downloaded, queried, and used in GIS systems, the base map itself is a raster that is primarily intended to give a visual approximation of historical geography.[17]

Ruth Mostern's new book *The Yellow River: A Natural and Unnatural History* (2021), with cartography and data management by Ryan Horne, documents the ways that the river and the

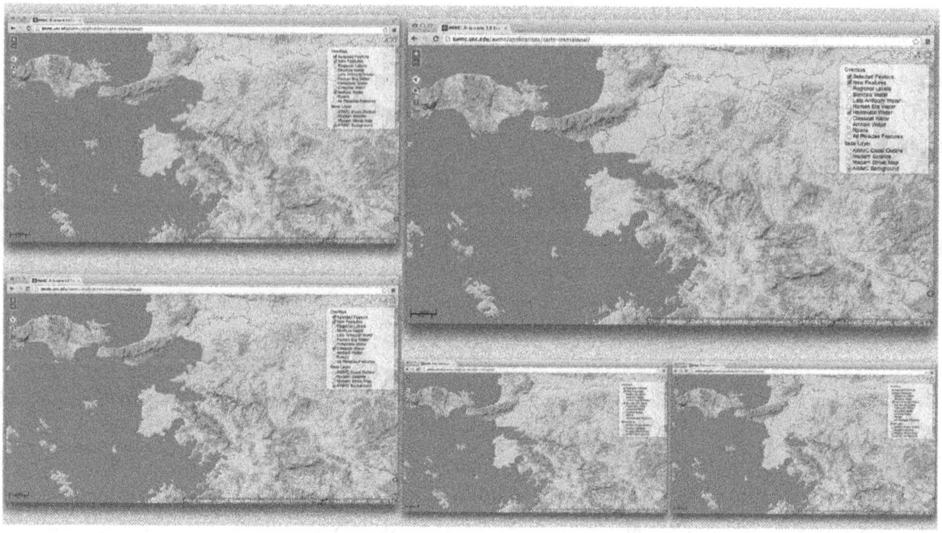

Figure 31.6 Detail of the AWMC tile set showing sea-level change around ancient Miletus. The base map itself is static; the changes in sea level are stored in a separate vector file that has temporal attributes tied to distinct water polygons in order to model coastal change. Although describing the same general geographic area, these datasets do not treat the terrain itself as a node within a larger LOD digital ecosystem.

human societies that coexisted with it evolved through their interactions with one another over thousands of years of history and throughout the whole watershed. River histories and historical documents about rivers most often focus on alluvial plains, which may be sites of intensive agriculture, dense populations, large cities, and close state scrutiny. By contrast, *The Yellow River* pays equal attention to the Huáng Hé (Yellow River) floodplain and to the Ordos Plateau, a semi-arid region in the middle reaches of the river's watershed that is dominated by loess soil, a form of sediment that erodes catastrophically when it is exposed to wind and water as a result of deforestation and other land-cover disturbance. The prevalence of floods and course changes on the historical Yellow River and the staggering investments of Chinese imperial regimes in dams and levees that were intended to forestall these processes varied in direct proportion to the rate of erosion on the Ordos Plateau. The interlinked dynamics of settler colonialism and erosion upstream and flooding and engineering interventions downstream, all pivoted together. They did so around three inflection points. The first one happened in the first century before the common era, the second transpired during the tenth and eleventh centuries of the common era, and the final one spanned the 16th through 18th centuries. The book disproves the notion that the Yellow River is inherently prone to unpredictable and devastating disaster. That stereotype emerged only in the 19th century, a time when the river, engorged with silt from the Ordos Plateau, could no longer be maintained according to the ingenious engineering interventions, discourses, and fiscal policies that constituted its previous logic. The dynamics that the book describes are seldom visible at the scale of years and decades. It relies on close readings of historical texts but also the creation and analysis of spatial databases and interpretations of environmental science data. The landscape changes frequently, and it does so at various rates at different times and places. Any one map of the river landscape is simply a snapshot of a given time and place, and it does not depict dynamic interrelationships of climate, settlements, erosion, water, and people in motion. For that purpose, an information system is a necessity.

The information system created for this project, the Tracks of Yu Digital Atlas (TYDA), is the result of over a decade of research and development. Built from a meticulous review of literature on the Yellow River, the TYDA links records on natural disasters, environmental management, ecological change, historical events, and source research. The TYDA is a relational database that is built on interrelated tables. There is an events table for 3,752 events which lists specific ecological or management events with their own unique ID and chronological information. The events table has a one-to-many relationship to a table that describes the event type (flood, construction, etc.) drawn from a mini-ontology created for the project. The TYDA also functions as a mini-gazetteer, with place information for 3,657 places located in its own table. This table combines data from upstream and downstream places, which were derived from different source traditions and, as such, had different data formats. The place table contains attributes for the establishment and disestablishment of individual settlements and the position of that place within the administrative hierarchy of imperial China. The places and events tables are connected on a many-to-many relationship, as any place can experience multiple events and any event could impact more than one place. The TYDA also contains information on Yellow River course changes, biomes, soil erosion, and a moisture index; however, this data is not directly linked with individual place entries (Mostern and Horne 2021, 247–56).

The structure of the TYDA is a preliminary and limited step towards the implementation of our proposed networked approach to environmental and spatial humanities. Places, sources, and events are directly linked in the TYDA and as such form a graph of human and environmental interaction. Although the other ecological data in the system is not explicitly connected to this graph, the spatial information that it contains can be used to create complex queries that combine any number of the data tables. Facilitated by the use of Jupyter Notebook, these queries are capable of visualising conjunctions in moisture variation, natural disasters, human management, and settlement patterns that are related to the graph (**Figure 31.7**).

Although capable of generating striking visualisations and offering new insights into human-environmental systems, the TYDA is only the first step into a new project to connect

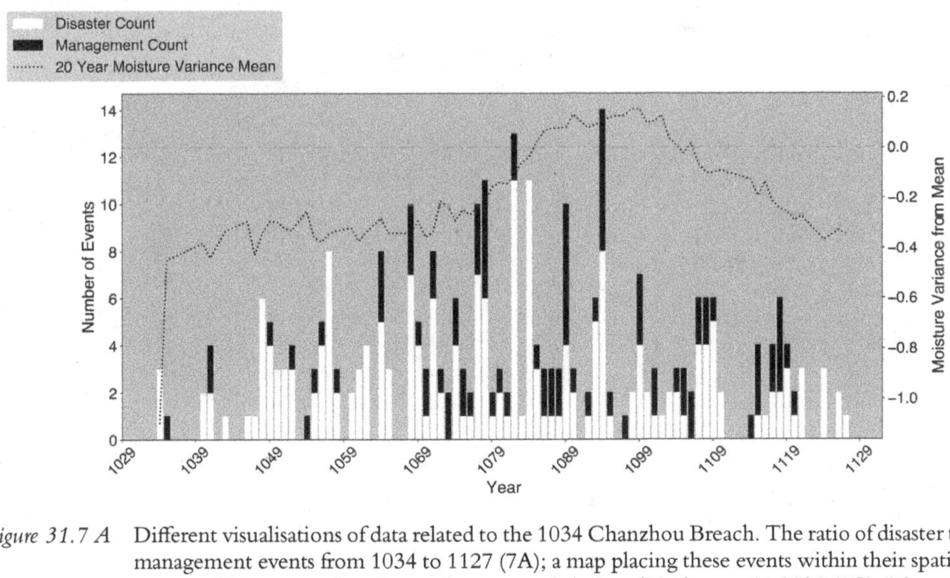

Figure 31.7 A Different visualisations of data related to the 1034 Chanzhou Breach. The ratio of disaster to management events from 1034 to 1127 (7A); a map placing these events within their spatial context (7B); a map showing settlements and their political status in 1034 (7C) (Mostern 2021, 165–67).

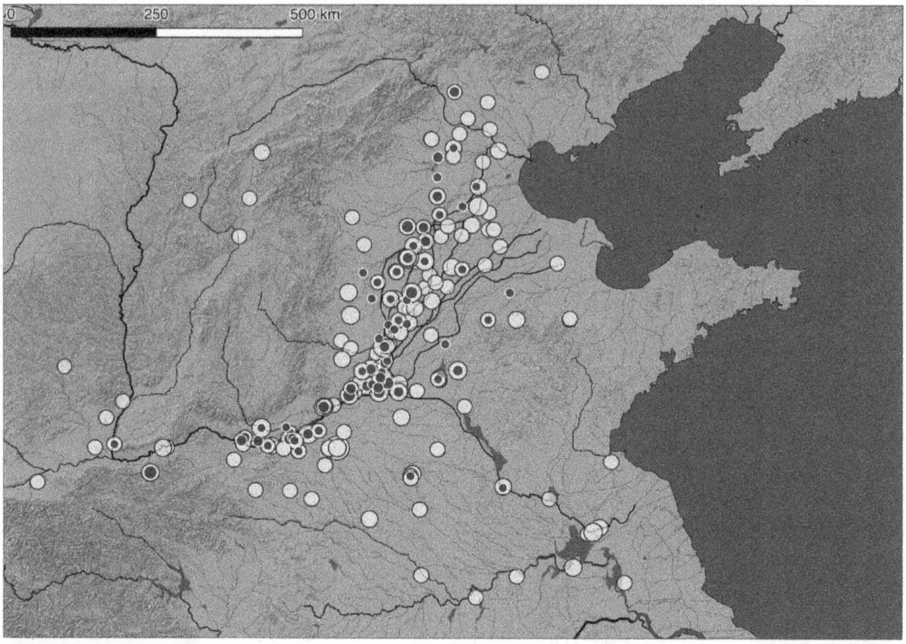

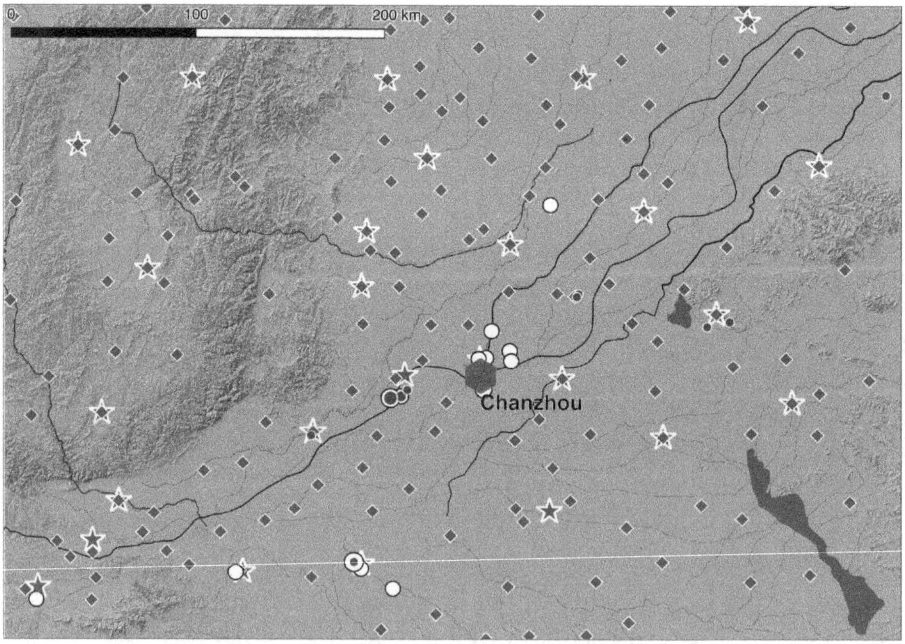

Figures 31.7 B (top) C (bottom)

environmental and spatial humanities. The authors are beginning preliminary steps to reconcile TYDA data with external resources like the WHG and are exploring new ways of associating place, source, and environmental data together into an open-access graph of associated environmental, spatial, and historical concepts.

Conclusion

The fields of environmental humanities and spatial history are entangled conceptually and practically, sharing datasets, digital tools, and methodologies. For that reason, digital approaches to the environmental humanities – at least insofar as practitioners in this domain seek to inquire about how people and the non-human world have coexisted and shaped one another on the face of the earth over time – should not start by privileging cartography of a particular type and place. Most maps are poorly suited to uncovering dynamic connections between people, place, and the environment. That is even more the case when projects seek to incorporate multivocal and contested information derived from people with many different areas of expertise and commitment and many types of data.

In spite of the origins of GIS in environmental management, spatial history, thus far practiced as an outgrowth of historical GIS, rarely makes use of environmental data that can reveal dynamic changes in the relationship between people and the planet. Indeed, the field of spatial history as a whole has not extensively theorised or modelled interactions between people and the non-human world. In this article, we are advocating for approaches to thinking about visualisation, spatial primitives, and spatial data that do not start with the imperatives of GIS and its limited notions of space. We favour methods that better model complex and humanistic engagement with the world. We therefore believe that it is imperative to embrace a methodology that is based on networks and relationships, one in which instances of entanglements between human and non-human worlds, along with the different academic domains that study them, are connected theoretically and practically.

Acknowledgements

Thank you to Luke Bergmann for a careful reading of this article from the perspective of critical geography, which much improved our thinking on various matters, and to Karl Grossner for a careful reading of the paper, excellent suggestions, and many conversations that have helped to shape this work.

Notes

1 Luke Bergmann, personal communication.
2 For an introduction to many versions of the distinction between space and place, see Hubbard and Kitchin (2011).
3 See https://ics.sas.ac.uk/events/linked-pasts-6.
4 www.w3.org/2009/08/skos-reference/skos.html.
5 https://pelagios.org.
6 https://pleiades.stoa.org. Ryan Horne is an editor for the Pleiades Gazetteer.
7 http://whgazetteer.org/tutorials/guide.
8 For an example vocabulary, see the Long-Term Ecological Research (LTER) site: https://vocab.lternet.edu/vocab/vocab.
9 Raster data can be used as layers as well; however, such layers have all of the same limitations as a traditional base map.
10 For other versions of this history, see Chrisman (2006) and Wilson (2017). Thank you to Luke Bergmann for recommending both of these titles.
11 Luke Bergmann, personal communication.
12 There are many open-source mapping tools that enable the construction of custom base layers, overlays, and other components of thematic mapping; in addition to the ones listed previously, see https://mapnik.org and https://github.com/tilemill-project/tilemill. However, most custom base maps based on modern elevation data use DEMs that are derived from NASA's Shuttle Radar Topography Mission

(SRTM), the Digital Elevation Model over Europe from the GMES RDA project (EU-DEM), and/or commercial satellite data.

13 Open Annotation is a model for such efforts; see www.w3.org/TR/annotation-model/#bodies-and-targets.

14 https://perio.do/en.

15 http://awmc.unc.edu/wordpress/tiles/. Ryan Horne is a former director of the AWMC and was the creator of these maptiles.

16 https://github.com/AWMC/geodata; http://awmc.unc.edu/api.

17 Unfortunately, changing technologies coupled with increased hosting costs due to the success of the AWMC tiles has now temporarily prevented their hosting through the commercial MapBox service provider. There are efforts underway to leverage new technologies like MapBox GL to create vector tiles based on the same underlying data; for now, the data used to build the original rasters is available at https://github.com/AWMC/geodata.

Sources

Adams, Benjamin. 2017. "Wāhi, a Discrete Global Grid Gazetteer Built Using Linked Open Data." *International Journal of Digital Earth* 10 (5): 490–503. https://doi.org/10.1080/17538947.2016.1229819.

Adamson, Joni. 2016. "Networking Networks and Constellating New Practices in the Environmental Humanities." *PMLA/Publications of the Modern Language Association of America* 131 (2): 347–55. https://doi.org/10.1632/pmla.2016.131.2.347.

Agnew, John. 2011. "Space and Place." In *The Sage Handbook of Geographical Knowledge*, edited by John Agnew and David Livingstone, 316–30. Thousand Oaks, CA: Sage Publications.

Ahnert, Ruth, Sebastian E. Ahnert, Catherine Nicole Coleman, and Scott B. Weingart. 2021. *The Network Turn: Changing Perspectives in the Humanities*. Elements in Publishing and Book Culture. Cambridge: Cambridge University Press. https://doi.org/10.1017/9781108866804.

Anderson, Benedict. 2006. *Imagined Communities: Reflections on the Origin and Spread of Nationalism*. Revised ed. London: Verso.

Barker, Elton, Rainer Simon, and Leif Isaksen. 2014. "Pelagios 3: Towards a Graph of Ancient World Data & an Ecosystem of Gazetteers." *DH2014 Workshop*. Lausanne, Switzerland. July 8, 2014. www.slideshare.net/aboutgeo/pelagios.

Berman, Merrick Lex, Ruth Mostern, and Humphrey Southall. 2016. *Placing Names: Enriching and Integrating Gazetteers*. Bloomington, IN: Indiana University Press.

Berners-Lee, Tim. 2007. "Linked Data." W3 Design Issues. www.w3.org/DesignIssues/LinkedData.html.

Berners-Lee, Tim, Larry Masinter, and Mark McCahill. 1994. "'Uniform Resource Locators (URL),' RFC 1738." https://doi.org/10.17487/RFC1738.

Bizer, Christian, Tom Heath, and Tim Berners-Lee. 2009. "Linked Data – The Story So Far." *International Journal on Semantic Web and Information Systems* 5 (3): 1–22.

Buttigieg, Pier Luigi, Evangelos Pafilis, Suzanna E. Lewis, Mark P. Schildhauer, Ramona L. Walls, and Christopher J. Mungall. 2016. "The Environment Ontology in 2016: Bridging Domains with Increased Scope, Semantic Density, and Interoperation." *Journal of Biomedical Semantics* 7 (1) (September 23, 2016): 57. https://doi.org/10.1186/s13326-016-0097-6.

Chrisman, Nicholas. 2006. *How Computer Mapping at Harvard Became GIS*. Redlands: ESRI Press.

Cresswell, Tim. 2013. *Place: A Short Introduction*. Malden, MA: Blackwell Publishing.

Fallahi, Gholam Reza, Andrew U. Frank, Mohammad Saadi Mesgari, and Abbas Rajabifard. 2008. "An Ontological Structure for Semantic Interoperability of GIS and Environmental Modeling." *International Journal of Applied Earth Observation and Geoinformation* 10 (3) (September 1, 2008): 342–57. https://doi.org/10.1016/j.jag.2008.01.001.

Giordano, Alberto, Shih-Lung Shaw, and Diana Sinton. 2020. "The Geospatial Humanities: Transdisciplinary Opportunities." *International Journal of Humanities and Arts Computing* 14 (1–2): 1–5.

Gregory, Ian, and Paul S. Ell. 2007. *Historical GIS: Technologies, Methodologies, and Scholarship*. Cambridge and New York: Cambridge University Press.

Horne, Ryan. 2021a. "Digital Approaches to the 'Big Ancient Mediterranean.'" In *Access and Control in Digital Humanities*, edited by Shane Hawkins, 78–95.

———. 2021b. "Digital Tools and Ancient Empires: Using Network Analysis and Geographic Information Systems to Study Imperial Networks in Hellenistic Anatolia." *Journal of World History* 32 (2).

Hubbard, Phil, and Rob Kitchin. 2011. *Key Thinkers on Space and Place*. London: Sage Publications.

Isaksen, Leif, Rainer Simon, Elton T. E. Barker, and Pau de Soto Cañamares. 2014. "Pelagios and the Emerging Graph of Ancient World Data." In *Proceedings of the 2014 ACM Conference on Web Science*. Bloomington, IN: Association for Computing Machinery. https://doi.org/10.1145/2615569.2615693.

Kluger, Lotta C., Philipp Gorris, Sophia Kochalski, Miriam S. Mueller, and Giovanni Romagnoni. 2020. "Studying Human – Nature Relationships Through a Network Lens: A Systematic Review." *People and Nature* 2 (4) (December 1, 2020): 1100–16. https://doi.org/10.1002/pan3.10136.

Latif, Atif, Muhammad Tanvir Afzal, Patrick Hoefler, Anwar Us Saeed, and Klaus Tochtermann. 2009. "Turning Keywords into URIs: Simplified User Interfaces for Exploring Linked Data." In *Proceedings of the 2nd International Conference on Interaction Sciences: Information Technology, Culture and Human*, 76–81.

Lin, Yu-wei. 2012. "Transdisciplinarity and Digital Humanities: Lessons Learned from Developing Text-Mining Tools for Textual Analysis." In *Understanding Digital Humanities*, edited by David M. Berry, 295–314. London: Palgrave Macmillan UK. https://doi.org/10.1057/9780230371934_16.

Linked Pasts 6. 2020. "University of London and British Library, December 2–16." ICS. https://ics.sas.ac.uk/ics-digital/linked-pasts-6.

Moore, Rebecca. 2021. "Time Flies in Google Earth's Biggest Update in Years." Google Earth Blog, April 15, 2021. Accessed November 18, 2021. https://blog.google/products/earth/timelapse-in-google-earth/.

Mostern, Ruth. 2021. *Yellow River: A Natural and Unnatural History*. New Haven: Yale University Press.

Mostern, Ruth, and Ryan Horne. 2021. "Tracking Yu: Developing a Data System for Yellow River History." In *Yellow River: A Natural and Unnatural History*, edited by Ruth Mostern, 247–66. New Haven: Yale University Press.

Murrieta-Flores, Patricia, and Bruno Martins. 2019. "The Geospatial Humanities: Past, Present and Future." *International Journal of Geographical Information Science* 33 (12) (December 2, 2019): 2424–429. https://doi.org/10.1080/13658816.2019.1645336.

Neteler, Markus, M. Hamish Bowman, Martin Landa, and Markus Metz. 2012. "GRASS GIS: A Multi-Purpose Open Source GIS." *Environmental Modelling & Software* 31 (May 1): 124–30. https://doi.org/10.1016/j.envsoft.2011.11.014.

Presner, Todd, and David Shepard. 2016. "Mapping the Geospatial Turn." In *A New Companion to Digital Humanities*, edited by Susan Schreibman, Ray Siemens, and John Unsworth, 201–12. Malden: Wiley Blackwell.

Purves, Ross S., Stephan Winter, and Werner Kuhn. 2019. "Places in Information Science." *Journal of the Association for Information Science and Technology* 70 (11): 1173–82. https://doi.org/10.1002/asi.24194.

Rankin, William. 2009. "Radical Cartography: Phoenix." Accessed November 18, 2021. www.radicalcartography.net/index.html?phoenix.

———. 2016. *After the Map: Cartography, Navigation, and the Transformation of Territory in the Twentieth Century*. Chicago: University of Chicago Press.

———. 2020. "How the Visual Is Spatial: Contemporary Spatial History, Neo-marxism, and the Ghost of Braudel." *History and Theory* 59 (3): 311–42.

Schmidt, Matthias, Jens Soentgen, and Hubert Zapf. 2020. "Environmental Humanities: An Emerging Field of Transdisciplinary Research." *GAIA – Ecological Perspectives for Science and Society* 29 (4) (December 16, 2020): 225–29. https://doi.org/10.14512/gaia.29.4.6.

Simon, Rainer, Elton Barker, Leif Isaksen, and Pau De Soto Cañamares. 2017. "Linked Data Annotation Without the Pointy Brackets: Introducing Recogito 2." *Journal of Map & Geography Libraries* 13 (1) (January 2, 2017): 111–32. https://doi.org/10.1080/15420353.2017.1307303.

Travis, Charles. 2018. "The Digital Anthropocene, Deep Mapping, and Environmental Humanities' Big Data." *Resilience: A Journal of the Environmental Humanities* 5 (2): 172–88.

Wilson, Matthew. 2017. *New Lines: Critical GIS and the Trouble of the Map*. Minneapolis: University of Minnesota Press.

Winichakul, Thongchai. 1994. *Siam Mapped: A History of the Geo-Body of a Nation*. Honolulu: University of Hawaii Press.

32

(RE)IMAGINING THE IBIS

Multispecies Future(s), Smart Urban Governance, and the Digital Environmental Humanities

Hira Sheikh, Marcus Foth, and Peta Mitchell

Introduction

Environmental sensing and monitoring technologies are increasingly being deployed to gather data on climate and biodiversity (Gabrys 2016; Bratton 2019). Since the advent of digital technologies like GPS, off-the-shelf sensors, and citizen science applications (Verma, van der Wal, and Fischer 2015; Gabrys 2019), environmental monitoring has become more readily available, accessible, and applicable, leading to critiques that natural ecosystems and the many species that inhabit them are "increasingly registered and documented as digital data" (Whitelaw and Smaill 2021, 80). As environmental historian Finn Arne Jørgensen (2014) has pointed out,

> [t]he idea of nature is becoming very hard to separate from the digital tools and media we use to observe, interpret, and manage it. Our ideas, our standards, for what is natural are distributed and maintained in digital tools and media like databases, computer models, geographical information systems, and so on.
>
> *(109)*

Amongst the plethora of digital tools (some detailed previously by Jørgensen) being used to understand nature, we will focus on biodiversity databases. Media theorist Lev Manovich (2002) describes the digital database as a distinct genre: "a new symbolic form of the computer age . . . a new way to structure our experience of ourselves and . . . the world" (219). Ursula Heise stretches Manovich's conception of databases to biodiversity databases as a new way of structuring human experience of non-human life (Heise 2016). Rafi Youatt (2008) extends Michel Foucault's concept of biopower – classifying humans into distinct data repositories that try to shape citizens – to biodiversity databases, arguing they exercise a similar categorisation of non-human

DOI: 10.4324/9781003082798-39

life. Biodiversity databases are one genre of environmental monitoring whereby "the scale, diversity, and complexity of the living world come[s] to us through [a] chain of technological mediation" (Whitelaw and Smaill 2021, 80). Most digital biodiversity databases comprise maps, spatial data, and statistics on species supplemented by photographs, videos, and hyperlinks (Heise 2016). To what extent each database integrates the mentioned components differs depending on what information it is designed to represent (Heise 2016). Biodiversity databases, amongst other digital tools, are increasingly being used to inform environmental governance (Edwards 2010; B. P. Braun 2014; Bakker and Ritts 2018; Gabrys 2020). Karen Bakker and Max Ritts (2018) claim the utility of such digital tools within environmental governance is apparent – they offer accessibility and new understandings of nature or species (in case of biodiversity databases).

In this chapter, we explore the application of biodiversity databases in the context of smart urban governance. We understand smart urban governance as the transformative impact of digital tools on urban governance practices. First, we consolidate critiques arising from DEH (while also engaging plural epistemologies and ontologies) on smart urban governance's approach to biodiversity conservation. Second, we offer a sketch of a more-than-human turn in DEH. This more-than-human turn integrates sensorial engagement with species, a framework that considers non-humans as thinking beings where humans learn both *from* and *with* them. The chapter explores this empirically through an analysis of how the Australian white ibis – a native bird species that has, over recent decades, migrated from its traditional wetland habitat into the highly urbanised environments of Australia's capital cities – is represented in and governed through digital biodiversity databases. Today, humans know the Australian white ibis through encounters and stories but also through biodiversity databases. When white ibises are visualised, classified, and governed with biodiversity databases, their records are captured – to some extent – from within the human cultural experience of the species. "What does it mean to govern white ibis through biodiversity databases?" is a question that partly frames this chapter's scope but is also one of critical significance to the broader multispecies justice movement (Celermajer et al. 2020). To respond to this question, we explore two biodiversity databases featuring our protagonist, the Australian white ibis – namely, the Atlas of Living Australia (ALA) and Big City Birds. The concluding discussion poses and responds to a second question, namely, "Can biodiversity databases be created to encapsulate the non-human experience rather than the human experience of non-human life?"

Environmental Governance and the Digital Environmental Humanities

As a named disciplinary formation, the DEH emerged at a similar time to the previously mentioned critiques of technology-driven environmental governance. In their meta-review of what they collectively call "Smart Earth" technologies, environmental geographers Karen Bakker and Max Ritts (2018) mention DEH as one recent disciplinary emergence of relevance to understanding the implications of these technologies (like GISs or data visualisations) for environmental governance. Yet apart from this passing mention by Bakker and Ritts, there has been no research that has directly explored the connections between and among environmental monitoring technologies, environmental governance, and the DEH. In this chapter, we are interested in approaching the question of technology-driven environmental governance – and particularly smart urban governance – through the lens of DEH, which itself represents the disciplinary conjoining of the digital and the environmental humanities (Posthumus and Sinclair 2014).

What then does DEH offer to, an understanding of environmental governance and vice versa? DEH draws on an ecocritical approach that underpins the environmental humanities. Environmental humanities scholars like Ursula Heise, Valerie Plumwood, Deborah Bird Rose, Thom van Dooren, Donna Haraway, and Anna Tsing have contributed to the exploration of human-environment relations from an ecocritical approach. Greg Garrard (2011) describes ecocriticism as the literary and cultural examination of environmental problems. In support of such investigations, he writes, "[E]nvironmental problems require analysis in cultural as well as scientific terms" (14). Ursula Heise (2006) and Lawrence Buell (2011) have illustrated the journey of ecocriticism, which was initially focused on nature writing but has travelled to different disciplines engaging with environmental justice, for example, bioregionalism, urban ecologies, more-than-human geographies, and now environmental digital humanities. A growing number of disciplines (including DEH) and diverse voices emerging from them are exploring the interconnected and interdependent relations with the living world. Ecocriticism, Ursula Heise (2006) narrates, differed from other postmodern constructs as it sought to redefine humans' relation with the non-human lifeforms instead of other humans. Evidently, ecocritical thinking is not new to DEH; rather, the emerging field offers an opportunity to consolidate prior research from social sciences (Heise 2016; Bakker and Ritts 2018), digital humanities (Parikka 2011; Gabrys 2016), and feminist disciplines (Hayles 2007). Additionally, to avoid the risk of diminishing the centrality of subaltern voices, it is critical to acknowledge that ecocritical approaches often stem from outside Western discourse. That is, they are often inspired by prior knowledge from diverse communities, including Indigenous and First Nations knowledge (Graham 1999; Watts 2013; Todd 2015) that may challenge entrenched anthropocentric and neoliberal epistemologies (ways of knowing) and ontologies (ways of being). Although ecocritical thinking primarily addresses human-environment relations, it also acknowledges the relationship between environmental issues and social exclusion (Martínez-Alier 1997; Bennett and Teague 1999). In this sense, DEH is an endeavour to merge plural knowledge to understand how the digital turn has and will transform the investigation of the natural world, providing a valuable perspective on the future of environmental governance.

Recent scholars whose work can be considered a critical contribution to DEH have scrutinised the digital turn in nature conservation by following a neoliberal mode of control that regards nature as an economic resource (Nost 2015), operating from human perception (Gabrys 2016), exercising spatial control on non-human species (Adams 2019), and reducing non-human species to numerical data that inform policies (Youatt 2008). William Adams (2019) maintains that neoliberal control in environmental conservation often stems from "science-based modes of understanding nature" (339). The scientific approach to environmental governance, Machen and Nost (2021) argue, hides the "political nature (via claims to objectivity), establish[es] an appearance of totality (universality), and assert[s] an inevitable, natural order of things (necessity)" (6), and facilitates what Adams (2019) terms "conservation by algorithm" (337). Elaborating further, Adams (2019) states that environmental conservation practice is an "exercise of power over . . . nature (keeping species and ecosystems within specific bounds in terms of state and location)" (338). In the digital era, the display of power or dominance over nature is often interconnected with the data that is gathered, analysed, and used for policymaking (Adams 2019). Consequently, the proliferation of digital tools in environmental conservation has often been known to legitimise unequal powers (Machen and Nost 2021) and perpetuate technological solutionism (Morozov 2014).

Despite the criticism, digital tools are increasingly claiming their space in urban governance, including biodiversity conservation. Within the Australian context, biodiversity databases like ALA,[1] iNaturalist,[2] Birdata[3] (offered by BirdLife Australia), and Big City Birds[4] are gaining increased traction with governments and citizens. Ursula Heise (2016) likens such biodiversity databases to what Franco Moretti (1996) dubbed a *modern epic*, stating they are designed "to inventory the totality of biological life" (62). These spatially oriented (using maps) biodiversity databases are used to represent both quantitative (numerical) and qualitative (narrative) data. Nevertheless, in recent history, databases and narratives have been posed as "enemies" (Manovich 2002, 225). Where the social science discourse has been preoccupied with quantitative data, humanities scholars have challenged this approach in favour of narrative forms of representations. For example, Johanna Drucker (2011) notes that the perception of data as an objective, unbiased representation of reality (species) requires adjustment in humanistic (and more-than-human) circumstances. Despite the difference in the two approaches, it is critical to note that quantitative data is not an objective representation of reality (or species), and qualitative accounts (narrative) are not natural or unmediated (by humans) representations of realities (or species). Consequently, scholars across disciplines have worked to deconstruct quantitative-qualitative dichotomies within databases. Ursula Heise (2017) describes the integration of quantitative and qualitative approaches, stating that

> the challenge for the environmental humanities in [the digital] context is not just the study of digital [visualisations], but the integration of digital tools and methods with older humanistic procedures: the combination of close reading with computational criticism, for example, of thick description with newly accessible statistics about ecological processes and cultural practices, of storytelling with database creation, or of photography with zoomable maps.
>
> *(7)*

Additionally, Katherine Hayles (2007) writes, "[D]atabase[s] can construct relational juxtapositions," but they require a "narrative to make [their] results meaningful" (1603). Lev Manovich (2002), elaborating on his initial positioning of databases and narratives as "enemies," argued narratives emerge when data is strung together in specific ways. Adding to the argument, Mitchell Whitelaw and Belinda Smaill (2021) write, "[G]iven that data and its representations are never immediate, we must come to grips with the mediated translation between data and the visual" (82). The authors (2021) further draw on Manovich, Hayles, and Heise's thoughts on databases to derive: narrative is a valuable tool for understanding biodiversity databases because it is a critical tool within database discourse and multispecies studies.

Similar quantitative-qualitative dichotomies have been witnessed for how humans have understood the function of maps over the years. Denis Wood (1987) deconstructed the false dichotomies that conceptualise maps as tools representing factual realities and narratives as a technique for imagining worlds. Maps, like databases, no matter their claims to objectivity, Wood writes, "[C]reate a discourse, a mediation, . . . [and] tell a story" (29). Similarly, John Pickles (2012) has discarded the notion that maps are objective tools of a producer/observer (humans) epistemology that positions the producer/observer as controllers of the worlds (species) they represent. Drawing on Pickles' observation on maps, we suggest, though biodiversity databases will always be entangled with the narrative assigned by the producer or the narrative deciphered by the observer, they do not have to bestow the producer/observer a hierarchical status over the species they represent.

As humans continue to understand and govern other species through biodiversity databases, there is an urgent need to understand their implications for other species and how they are managed. We take up this investigation in the smart city context, where governments often fail to adopt an ecocritical standpoint when informing decisions regarding non-human life based on what the biodiversity databases reveal. The smart city premise is significant because, with the increased urbanisation of the world's population, cities will have to play a leadership role in achieving global environmental objectives (Bongaarts 2019). Scholars have established that environmental governance in smart cities does not adequately account for the non- and more-than-human (Luusua, Ylipulli, and Rönkkö 2017; Clarke et al. 2019). Further, it reinforces hierarchies between humans and other species through the exercise of power – that is, control over non-human species and their data (Fish 2020). Human epistemologies and ontologies primarily inform databases. Under these circumstances, a critical question introducing axiological concerns may be what if non-human epistemologies and ontologies are used to inform databases depicting them.

More-than-Human Digital Environmental Humanities

The smart city discourse prioritises digital tools to improve the environmental performance of the built environment (Loh et al. 2020), with little explicit concern for making cities nurturing habitats for multiple species. Nevertheless, smart urban governance's human-centred inclinations are being challenged as a more comprehensive understanding of human–non-human interconnectedness is being translated into urban (Braun 2005; Whatmore 2006; Houston et al. 2018), digital (Vallee 2021; Wakefield, Chandler, and Grove 2021), and political (Celermajer et al. 2020) discourses. In recent decades, a resurgence of concepts exploring the human–non-human interconnectedness has been witnessed as the more-than-human turn. More-than-human turn outlines the significance of human–non-human interconnectedness (Abram 1997) across a body of literature in Indigenous ontologies (Graham 1999; Donald 2009; Watts 2013; Graham 2014; Todd 2015), posthumanism (Barad 2003; Braidotti 2013; Haraway 2016; Forlano 2017), and multispecies ethnography (Kirksey and Helmreich 2010; Van Dooren, Kirksey, and Münster 2016).

More-than-human ontologies are reshaping human–non-human associations in diverse disciplines, including urban political ecology (Gabriel 2014; Connolly 2019; Tzaninis et al. 2020), urban planning (Metzger 2016; Houston et al. 2018), and digital geographies (McLean 2020). Correspondingly, the DEH as a field combining prior and plural knowledge also emerged from research foregrounding more-than-human perspectives (Posthumus and Sinclair 2014; Heise, Christensen, and Niemann 2017) to study the digital turn in relation to the exploration of the natural environment. Many scholars in DEH have engaged with a more-than-human standpoint through review of data-driven environmental governance (Gabrys 2016), tracking of non-human species in biodiversity conservation (Adams 2019), biodiversity databases (Bowker 2000; Youatt 2008; Heise 2016), and biodiversity data visualisation (Whitelaw and Smaill 2021). Having explored the present discourse, we note the role of biodiversity data and how it can and will affect smart urban governance remains understudied in DEH, especially the political implications of how digital tools are used to control and silence urban species.

From the wider discussions on more-than-human turn, we focus on acknowledging the agentic and communicative abilities of non-human lifeforms. The erasure of non-human voices can be credited to the presumption that only humans speak and tell stories (Ghosh 2021). Many disciplines have contributed to non-human muteness, even in their commitment towards a more-than-human turn. For instance, in law, the *rights of nature* discourse (Stone 1975; Donaldson and Kymlicka 2011) – which gives non-human beings rights within human systems – has been criticised for continuing non-human beings' muteness by sustaining the narrative of humans giving a voice/speaking for them instead of listening to them as communicative beings (Anker 2017; Fitz-Henry 2021). Nonetheless, the voicelessness of non-human life is a minority view – not a concept many communities around the world have contributed to or abide by today

(Ghosh 2021). Despite differences in their teachings, many Indigenous communities worldwide have long acknowledged the agentic and communicative capacities of non-human lifeforms. For example, Haudenosaunee and Anishinaabe scholar Vanessa Watts maintain that "land is alive and thinking, and that humans and non-humans derive agency through the extensions of these thoughts" (Watts 2013, 21). Robin Wall Kimmerer (2013) has termed non-human life's ability to exhibit and understand signs as "grammar of animacy" (55). Eduardo Abrantes (2021) writes that each species has its own unique "acoustic niche" (Krause 1993), where the species live an entire lifecycle – engaging in mating, territorial battles, and various other communications. Western philosophical tradition appears to be the prevailing thought that has not supported the agency and wisdom of multiple species. After an extended erasure of the non-human voice in recent years, Western philosophy has also recognised that different species and lifeforms have agency and can communicate. In the 1930s, Jakob von Uexküll confirmed that non-human beings understand and interact with their environment through signs. Eduardo Kohn (2013) affirms that all non-human beings use semiotics to communicate by expressing, interpreting, translating, and responding to signs. Many scholars have strengthened these claims by demonstrating how non-human lifeforms communicate by performing signs through bodily movement, sounds, odours, and other ways (Wohlleben 2016; Westerlaken 2020).

Today, following Western philosophical thought, the majority of disciplines have adopted the notion of non-human muteness, including biodiversity conservation and its application through tools like biodiversity databases. Biodiversity databases are entirely bound to human forms of language that are often used to objectify species through classifications and human cultural framings. Shannon Mattern (2021) describes databases as "frame[s] of human agency" (27). As a result, the databases fail to account for the complexity of other species. To analyse biodiversity databases, we understand non-human life as agentic beings by adopting more-than-human perspectives emerging from plural communities. The knowledge of how non-human species communicate through signs has rarely been applied to modify databases and governance structures used to inform decisions regarding their life. A few scholars whose work is closely related to the field of DEH have called for the integration of non-human agentic and communicative abilities into biodiversity monitoring and governance practices (Vallee 2021; Wakefield, Chandler, and Grove 2021)

Listening to Other Species

David Abram (2017) contends that humans cannot perceive the non-human lifeworlds entirely but that those lifeworlds are "purveyors of secrets, carriers of intelligence" that "can inform us" (14). Similarly, Tim Ingold (2002) states humans can never step outside their framing, but they can attune to the worlds of other creatures. Abram (2017) maintains that being attuned to non-human communication is a way to exist with the local ecosystem. In today's cities, the voice of non-human nature is suffocated by continuous human noise. However, as Abram (2017) points out, we dwell in an "animate landscape" (80) teeming with natural life that is anything but silent. Non-human species are in constant communication with other species and their environment. It is we who do not know how to listen. Deep listening is one more-than-human approach that can help humans attune to the natural world. Deep listening, often affiliated with Indigenous cultures, comprises observing nature with the entire body to stimulate sensory awareness (Berry 2018). Geoff Berry (2018) states that deep listening is about "decolonising consciousness and opening the individual self to the more-than-human communications going on all around (and within) us all the time" (28). It requires submitting to relational ontologies to confront the "grand narratives of colonial conquest" (Country et al. 2021, 5). Deep listening offers what Anna Tsing (2015) refers to as "the arts of noticing" (37) to cultivate attentiveness towards multispecies worlds. To listen attentively to non-human species and experience our entanglements with nature, we need to understand multispecies' realities. Deep listening reframes the narrative of humans exercising control and acknowledges that non-human species can assert their preferences. Giving non-human species the ability to respond allows humans to regard them as subjects.

In many Indigenous cultures, deep listening is also connected to the practice of oral storytelling (Abram 1997; Kane 1998). Storytelling is increasingly being linked to creating empathy towards more-than-human lifeworlds, which is considered essential in enacting moral agency (Gruen 2009). Thom Van Dooren (2014) connects the role of non-human species as subjects with their abilities to produce storied relationships with their environment and other species. Thom van Dooren (2014), reflecting on a study about penguins, reasons that the birds are attached to places through storying. He pens, "[E]xperiencing beings like penguins 'represent' the world to themselves, too: they do not just take in sensory data as unfiltered and meaningless phenomena, but weave meaning out of experiences, so that they, like humans, 'inhabit an endlessly storied world" (78). Adding to the discourse, Michelle Westerlaken (2021) describes deep listening as a possible way to minimise the risk of telling on behalf of other species. The responsibility of learning with the voices of non-human beings necessitates embracing the fact that telling is not limited to human language. Deep listening focuses on the tells arising from non-human life. If humans listened carefully, they would support other species by understanding their ontologies through signs, thereby reducing the prospect of narrating the *Other*. Likewise, Astrida Neimanis (2017) and Emilia Terracciano (2021) maintain that nature is rendered mute not because it does not speak but because humans fail to listen. Deep listening offers humans a space to attune to the storied places of multiple species that account for how non-human beings inhabit physical space and time scales (Van Dooren, Rose, and Others 2012).

A close attunement to non-human lifeworlds may be one way biodiversity databases that objectify, mute, and reduce non-human species to mere numbers can engage with species' descriptions connected to their realities and experiences. Mitchell Whitelaw and Belinda Smaill (2021) note how different species "are posed within a graphical display" (83) can affect how decision-makers "experience multispecies worlds in digital form" (81). The authors (2021) further explain that "biodiversity data . . . provides specific affordances: allowing, encouraging or discouraging certain insights and possibilities that condition our knowledge of and engagement with living things" (80). To increase more-than-human governance actions, Whitelaw and Smaill (2021) encourage moving "beyond generic quantitative forms of graphical representation to ask how biodiversity data might be conveyed in ways that are specific to the materiality of species" (92). We suggest attunement through deep listening as a way to disrupt "anthropocentric borders" (Castricano 2008, 5) and to "rupture the politics of exclusion" (10), which still dominates the species' representations in biodiversity databases. To offer our contribution to how data can better encapsulate multispecies worlds through deep listening, we first offer a critique on the kinds of governance actions afforded by two biodiversity databases, ALA and Big City Birds, featuring the bird Australian white ibis. Second, we question: how biodiversity databases might convey a fuller set of (more-than-human) sign practices?

The Australian White Ibis

Urban landscapes are composed, as Raymond Pierotti (2010) has put it, of "many non-human persons – the fourleggeds, winged ones, plants, and even landforms" (30). Across many Australian cities, a notable non-human person of the winged variety that has begun to predominate in urban spaces is the Australian white ibis. This wading bird is recognised by its mostly white body plumage and featherless black head and neck (Australian Museum 2020) (Figure 31.1).

The white ibis thrives near water bodies and has traditionally lived in wetlands. In recent decades, like many other wild animals displaced because of habitat loss, the Australian white ibis populations have migrated from primary wetland habitats to urban environments and are increasing across all major Australian coastal cities (Smith 2009). Today the urban white ibis is commonly found in parks (Figure 2), in landfills, and near urban water and food sources (Figure 3) (Ross 2004).

Figure 32.1 Australian white ibis, illustration by Hira Sheikh.

Figure 32.2 Australian white ibis walking in the park, illustration by Hira Sheikh.

Figure 32.3 Australian white ibis eating leftover food at restaurants, illustration by Hira Sheikh.

Since the migration of the white ibis into cities, there are two predominant narratives around ibis in urban spaces: namely, ibis-as-pest and ibis-as-victim (McKiernan and Instone 2016). The ibis-as-pest narrative positions the ibis as unworthy of cohabiting urban space because, as McKiernan and Instone (2016) have argued, the "ibis presence in the city disrupts human positions of control" as the ibis challenges how both city governments and citizens perceive the "domesticated urban wilds" and "desirable nature" (476–77). Most citizens and city governments across Australia consider the white ibis as a pest as they can spread diseases (Epstein et al. 2007), cause air traffic hazards (Corben 2003), and adversely impact biodiversity (Kentish 1994). Therefore, the ibis is seen as a "bio-invasive species, a feral pest, a fly in, fly out opportunist and scavenger, an unwelcome space invader – now aligned with the abject geographies of human waste" (Figure 32.4) (Allatson and Connor 2020, 372).

For these reasons, urban ibis populations often "face steady eviction from spaces that are increasingly privatised, ghettoised, [and] developed" (Narayanan 2017, 476). On the other hand, the ibis-as-victim narrative emphasises how the ibis migrated to urban locations because of human-inflicted damage to their original habitats (McKiernan and Instone 2016). In this narrative, white ibises are considered "refugees from drought" (Allatson and Connor 2020, 372), "cult-hero[es]," or "Aussie battler[s]" (Stevens 2018). Following the two dominant narratives, in urban management plans, white ibises appear mainly as a target of intervention and never as fellow urban residents and coinhabitants (Foth 2017; Smith, Bardzell, and Bardzell 2017; Liu 2019).

In the context of environmental governance, drawing on Jamie Lorimer (2007), Paul Allatson and Andrea Conner (2020) regard the Australian white ibis as a charismatic species that is "able to elicit affective investments that are then mobilised within political assemblages" (374). Their charismatic presence is also why white ibises have "become particularly despised urban trespassers, partly because they, in all their animality, are so public" (Jerolmack 2013, 73). Further, William Adams (2019) states, "[C]onservation organisations actively select charismatic species as flagships for technological projects" because of their inherent ease of traceability (341). White ibises embody "such a highly visible urban presence" (Allatson and Connor 2020, 373) and are increasingly being studied through digital technologies. Presently, environmental decision-makers consider datasets on the bird's population, age, and distribution essential to effective conservation (Davis et al. 2017). Some scholars maintain "no organism lends itself more readily

Figure 32.4 Australian white ibis digging in the garbage, illustration by Hira Sheikh.

to the concept of citizen participation in data gathering than birds" (Sullivan et al. 2009, 2282). This is visible in the way that digital technologies have altered how the white ibises are governed by offering unparalleled knowledge of their population, movement, anatomy, foraging patterns, and migration routes (Martin et al. 2011). This knowledge is gathered through radio tracking, geotags (Figure 32.5), and sensors (Martin and Major 2010; Martin et al. 2011).

In what follows, we investigate what role digital tools play in mainly promoting the ibis-as-a-pest narrative. To explore this, we focus on two biodiversity databases: (1) the ALA – Australia's national biodiversity database that gathers information from different universities, museums, herbaria, and government agencies – and (2) Big City Birds – a community database driven by citizens. We use both to investigate how data represents the Australian white ibis. Our exploration mainly focuses on how data visualisation methods illustrating population records aid the ibis-as-pest narrative, which in turn invites city governments to create management plans around their eradication.

White Ibises as Objects in Biodiversity Databases

City governments across Australia have different white ibis management plans[5] to actively manage the species, including regulating the population of the urban bird. These management plans recommend the monitoring of the species to control their population in cities. Here we ask: how do biodiversity databases end up objectifying and legitimising control over the white ibis? Objectification and control are a direct outcome of the design decisions that demonstrate the

Figure 32.5 Australian white ibis geotagged, illustration by Hira Sheikh.

documentation of the white ibis and their sightings. The ibis's objectification guides how the observers (city governments, citizens, and environmental agencies) act upon the information to make governance decisions. Following Ursula Heise (2016), who maintains "structural inclusions and exclusions" of what data is represented "shape[s] the available information and cultural memory" (67), in the next section, we explore how relational ethics are restricted through solely quantified data representations. Of course, what quantified data means depends on *how* it is woven together and *what* stories it is telling (Heise 2016).

White Ibises in the Atlas of Living Australia

The Atlas of Living Australia (ALA) is a digital open-access biodiversity database that reports white ibis occurrence records – documenting the time and location of white ibis sightings (Figure 32.6). The platform attempts to "create a more detailed picture of Australia's biodiversity for scientists, policymakers, environmental planners and land managers, industry and the general public" (ALA 2020). The ALA has played and continues to play an important and admirable role in opening science to the public and engaging citizen science. Yet its driving focus is on presenting and mapping biodiversity data – and biodiversity *as* data – rather than articulating or visualising more-than-human entanglements of biodiversity and data.

The ALA interface offers a scientific reading of different species, including the Australian white ibis. The ALA classifies species data within spatial data to represent species distribution. Moreover, the white ibis occurrences on the ALA interface are marked as data points on the map that prompt "neat cartographic representations" over the messiness of on-ground reality (Billé 2021, 13). To add to the neatness, the images associated with the respective data points are not visible on the map by design. The interface design, therefore, restricts any association with the species or its stories through data visualisation. This homogeneous representation of the white ibis reduces the species to an object or a point on the map (Figure 32.7).

Further, the descriptions of sightings use scientific names (*Threskiornis molucca*) (Figure 32.8) and quantify the white ibis as numerical data. Geoffrey Bowker (2000) has criticised scientific databases

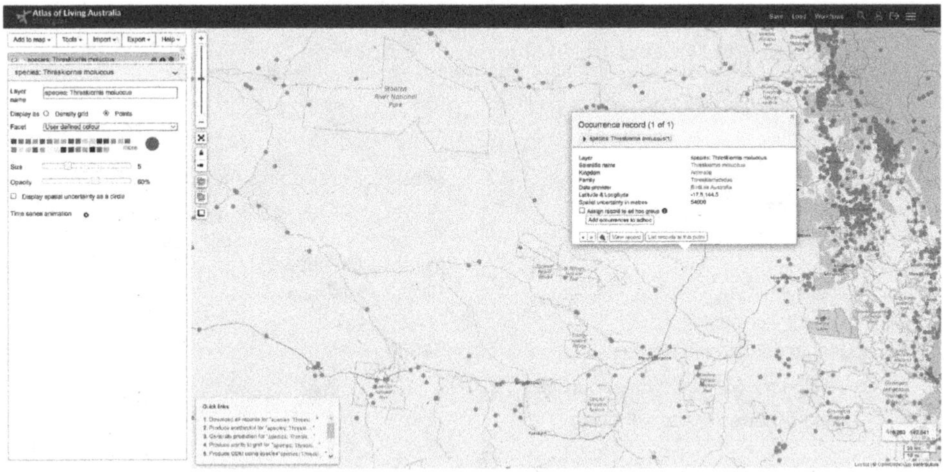

Figure 32.6 *Australian white ibis, Atlas of Living Australia | Spatial Portal*, https://spatial.ala.org.au, © OpenStreetMap contributors, www.openstreetmap.org (data visualisation). Screen capture by authors.

Figure 32.7 Australian white ibis as a data point, illustration by Hira Sheikh.

like ALA for rendering specific data (for example, classification or occurrences of species) visible while, on the other hand, rendering invisible other data (for example, Indigenous knowledge on the natural world, uncharismatic species, or sign communication of non-human lifeforms).

Jason Moore (2014) associates such representations of nature with capitalism. He writes, "[E]arly capitalism's world-praxis, fusing symbolic coding and material inscription, moved forward an audacious fetishization of nature. This was expressed dramatically in the era's cartographic, scientific, and quantifying revolutions" (Moore 2014, 288). The ALA interface showcases how the white ibis inhabits physical space and time scales as abstract points rather than any meaningful stories describing their connection to place and other species. Therefore, it can alienate observers from the white ibis communities rather than build relationships with them. Moreover, such representations exacerbate the disconnect between human decision-makers and non-human species they make decisions about. The abstraction of non-human life as data points, for instance, may make it easier

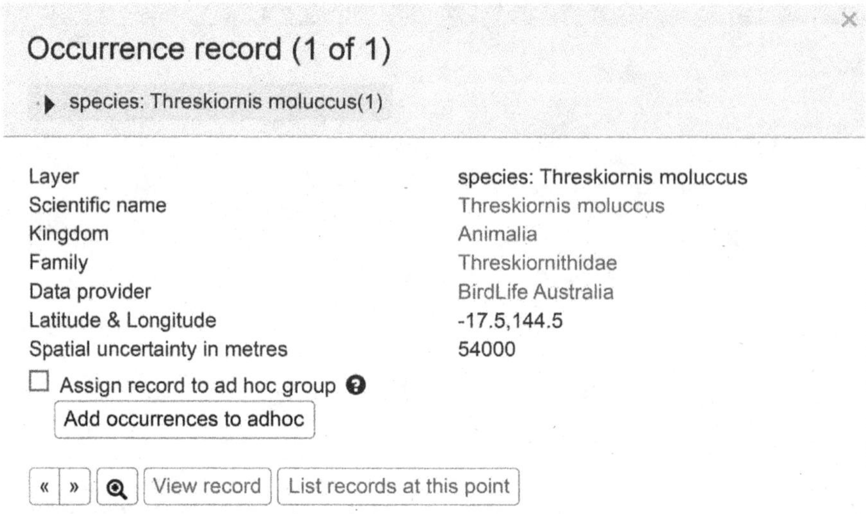

Figure 32.8 *Australian white ibis, Atlas of Living Australia | Spatial Portal*, https://spatial.ala.org.au (data visualisation). Screen capture by authors.

or more politically acceptable for policymakers to implement eradication plans when species are showcased as mere data points rather than living beings. Therefore, the dot point representation of species can encourage governance at the threshold of species abstraction and disembodiment. In other words, representations of species distribution on the ALA fail to capture the white ibis as an "alive" being. As a GIS, the ALA is embedded in Western colonial-cartographic and positivist traditions (Pickles 1995) that continue to silence non-human species. Reflecting on data practices that are neat and disconnected from realities, Orit Halpern (2015) writes,

> How did knowledge come to be about data analysis, perhaps even in real time, not discovery? How did data become "beautiful"? How did sustainability and environment come to replace structure, class, and politics in the discourses of urban planning, corporate marketing, and governmental policy?
>
> *(5)*

Orit Halpern (2015) suggests aesthetically *beautiful* scientific data, like the one offered by ALA, has played a vital role in endorsing and validating data that is disconnected from environmental reality. She associates the shift to increasing knowledge grounded on diagrammatic and schematic visuals across many disciplines (we add biodiversity databases to the mix). Aesthetically pleasing data, in biodiversity databases like ALA, is often used to mobilise the narrative of control and management to justify the neoliberal logic of conservation. Similar to criticisms about databases on human life, such databases on non-human life are scrutinised for legitimising algorithmic governmentality and control (Adams 2019).

Following Halpern's inquiry, we question this neat rhetoric of biodiversity databases as a smart solution to governance in nature conservation. Since the recognition of the Anthropocene, the interest in visualisation of unknown characteristics of biodiversity has snowballed. The increased use of *beautiful* biodiversity data visualisations in policy arenas is a testimony to their alluring success as decision-making tools. Following Halpern, we question the consequences of aesthetic legitimation of biodiversity data and oppose the temptation of neat data representations instilled into our biodiversity governance structures. Through neat representations, ALA erases the storied presence of the urban white ibis. Further, it illustrates how the white ibis represented through neat data can impact how they become objects of governance. As Heise noted about biodiversity databases elsewhere, such data reductions further enable the white ibis into categorical labels emerging from cultural memory – "an invasive pest" (Allatson and Connor 2020, 373), a "scientific object," and an "object of local government containment" (374). These labels reflect multiple human understandings of the ibis. However, they do not "regard ibis as active city-making agents" (Allatson and Connor 2020, 374), which reveals the Western ideologies of the societies using the tool. Ultimately, in cultural memory and databases, such anti-ibis rhetoric in datasets promotes urban policies that legitimise control over the species.

White Ibises as Subjects in Biodiversity Databases

To move beyond the objectification of the white ibis, we look at an alternative mode of data visualisation that encourages a less control-based urban management of the ibis. This section guides a deliberation on how more meaningful white ibis ontologies can be represented through data. Like humans, the white ibises are hard to capture through only quantitative data. Combining qualitative and quantitative data might unravel different ways humans experience interactions with the Australian white ibis. White ibises are not static but living "data" that manifest across time. The ibis as living data across time resonates with Thom Van Dooren's concept of *flight ways* (van Dooren 2014) – a means to discuss how birds are not just individuals but "vast evolutionary lineages stretched across millions of years" (van Dooren 2014, 22). Urban ibises carry histories that intersect with humans since their increased migration to Australian cities in the 1970s. Scientific data platforms like ALA fail to visualise the embodied histories of the white ibis and their narratives in cities. At this juncture, scholars and practitioners need to question: how can the addition of qualitative data visualisations might support thick engagement with white ibis ontologies and regard them as subjects that respond, interact with and co-inhabit the urban fabric?

White Ibises in Big City Birds

Smartphone applications like Big City Birds (Figure 32.9) are part of the big-data paradigm shift in biodiversity governance that attempts to engage with thick-er descriptions. The app invites citizens to track five species of big city birds, including the Australian white ibis. Big City Birds users share white ibis data by describing sightings, sharing photographs, and tagging the encounter's location

The various citizens upload data through the smartphone application. In this sense, the creators of Big City Birds favour bottom-up data gathering through community engagement instead of expert-based methods. The researchers behind the application intend to aid scientific data collection through citizen science (Paulos et al. 2008; Oliver et al. 2020), including movement, diet, and breeding – concerning Australia's most common native birds. The application "allows users to note any tagging or marking on the bird, update nest movements, and even note foods the birds are eating or scavenging" (Rachwani 2020). Although the app design's intentions are grounded in scientific motivations, the outcome is primarily guided by the end users' sensibilities that invite engagement with qualitative accounts and photographs of the white ibis.

The integration of qualitative narratives in biodiversity databases, like Big City Birds, highlights the epistemological differences that are often advanced through citizen participation. Unlike ALA, Big City Birds is less concerned with species distribution and more focused on (pleasant or unpleasant) cultural entanglements between humans and white ibises. This shift is

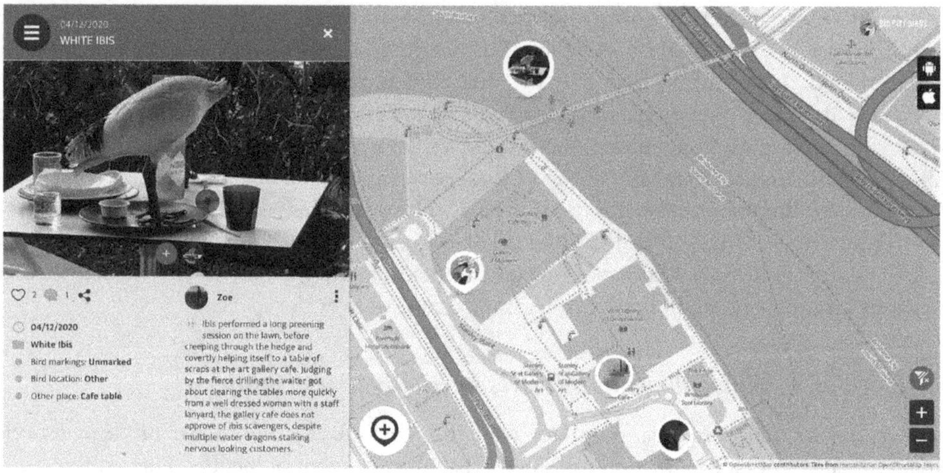

Figure 32.9 *Australian white ibis, BigCityBirds, App: SPOTTERON Citizen Science Platform*, www.spotteron.net (data visualisation). Screen capture by authors.

Figure 32.10 Australian white ibis as an image in a location pin, illustration by Hira Sheikh.

dependent on the flexibility allowed by the visual interface but, more critically, the broadening of what Heise terms the *cultural memory* through the union of the non-expert user and their entanglement with the white ibis. The resulting ibis representations on Big City Birds are shaped by human attention rather than scientific studies tracking ibis movement. Therefore, Big City Birds invite cultural narratives from citizens not present within scientific databases like Atlas of Living of Australia, where experts decide what categories of information are offered by the interface. In the Big City Birds app, the integration of cultural narratives arising from the community is made easier with the use of colloquial language over scientific terminologies and numbers. Moreover, instead of representing ibises as dot points, each entry on the pinned location is marked by the image of the individual ibis (Figure 32.10).

Such data representation steps away from reducing the subject into a data point, which strips ibises of having an identity beyond the representation of a dot denoting its existence. Much like critiques offered by critical data studies (Dalton and Thatcher 2014) on how Big Data erases the social aspects of human life, we conclude a comparable understanding of ibis as dot points in databases. Such representations do not consider the ontologies and epistemologies that might capture ibises beyond their mere presence.

Big City Birds' interface creates space for creative expression that helps sketch descriptive human-ibis encounters. Qualitative narratives in humanities are often connected to thick descriptions. However, the descriptions often render the human experience of species rather than offering "thick accounts of the distinctive experiential worlds, modes of being, and biocultural attachments of other species" (Van Dooren, Kirksey, and Münster 2016, 6). For example, one entry (marked by the pin location) on the app (Figure 32.11) illustrates how an ibis was treated at the Queensland Art Gallery in Brisbane:

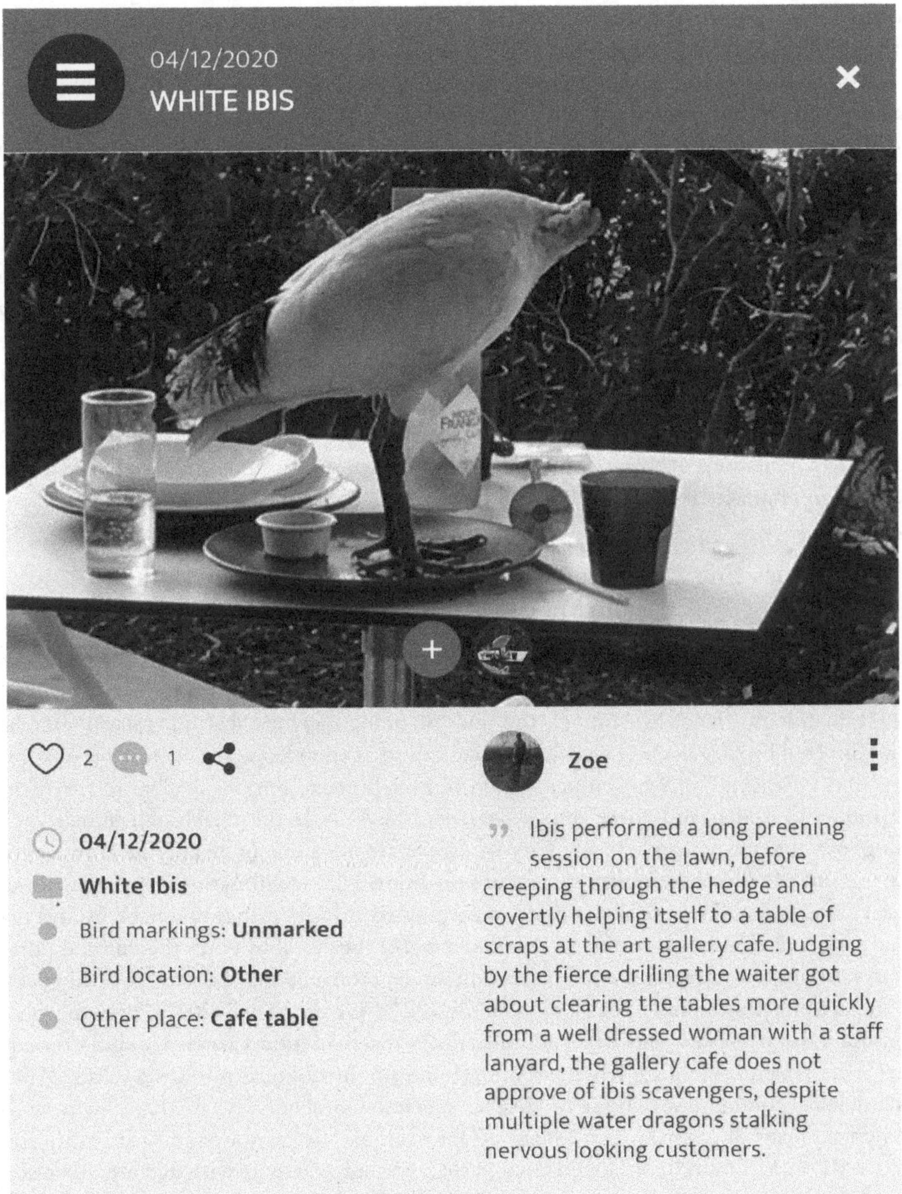

Figure 32.11 *Australian white ibis, BigCityBirds, App: SPOTTERON Citizen Science Platform,* www.spotteron.net (data visualisation). Screen capture by authors.

> The ibis performed a long preening session on the lawn before creeping through the hedge and covertly helping itself to a table of scraps at the art gallery cafe. Judging by the fierce drilling the waiter got about clearing the tables more quickly from a well-dressed woman with a staff lanyard, the gallery cafe does not approve of ibis scavengers, despite multiple water dragons stalking nervous-looking customers.

Evident from the interface design, compared to the ALA, the app attempts to regard the white ibis as a subject deserving of attention for its own sake. The motivations behind the application encourage a richer understanding of how ibises are adopting human-made landscapes. By allowing attentiveness towards the place-based white ibises narratives, Big City Birds demonstrates how urban space can be inclusive to marginalised non-human species. However, in staying limited to accounts of the human experience with the ibis, rather than exploring the experiential world of the ibis, the application fails to create deeper attunement to their wisdom and modes of being. Ursula Heise (2016) highlights how our engagement with species is culturally assembled. She explains that the widespread study of charismatic species (like white ibis) in databases reveals what future(s) citizens care about or do not. The described encounters represent human attention towards the charismatic species through amazement or repulsion. They do not seem to reveal an interest in meaningful future cohabitation with the white ibis, rather in exploring its awkward Otherness. Consequently, the centrality of human experience mostly limits the data to reflect a spectrum of ibis-as-pest and ibis-as-victim narratives. For example, while the cited example treats the ibis as a subject, the narrative regards it as "chaotic, untamed nature in spaces designated for humans" (Jerolmack 2013, 73). The review of the ibis's portrayal in Big City Birds unravels "the potential and limitations of anthropomorphic projection in understanding, . . . representing, [and governing] nonhuman existence" (Chao and Enari 2021, 37) from biased human cultural memory.

Translating More-than-Human Turn to Biodiversity Databases and Smart Urban Governance

Biodiversity databases use both quantitative and qualitative dimensions to represent the white ibis: cultural memories unfold through qualitative narrative and scientific inquiries are published through quantitative records. And yet, the understanding of white ibis is primarily established on and directed by the Western worldview that fails to acknowledge the agency of non-human beings (the *Othered*). The Western perception of non-human beings is evident in the management model to understand white ibis as witnessed in ALA or the established human cultural framings of white ibis as visible in Big City Birds. We are not alone in making such observations. Paddy Bresnihan observes a similar control of non-human life – within the Irish fishing industry, where coastal boundaries are demarcated according to human management of fishing quotas instead of fish mobilities (or realities) (Bresnihan 2016). Leah Gibbs notes the cultural portrayal of sharks as dangerous creatures encourages human decision-making that consequently has negative governance implications for sharks (Gibbs 2021). Ursula Heise (2017), drawing on Kari Norgaard, Dale Jamieson, and Mike Hulme, notes that scientific knowledge and consequent governance remain inadequate when disconnected from the political and social values of diverse (human) local communities about biodiverse species. Consequently, we have witnessed the detrimental effects of ignoring knowledge of, for example, Indigenous and First Nations communities who have always considered non-human species as beings with agency. Accordingly, the present databases exploring quantitative or qualitative dimensions of white ibis accounts leave no room for the experience of white ibis as beings with agency. To surpass this limitation, biodiversity databases need to engage with a more-than-human *design* approach to collecting and representing data on depicted and governed species. Such an approach translates environmental humanities' scholarship into design research through more-than-human thinking (Foth 2017; Smith, Bardzell, and Bardzell 2017; Clarke et al. 2019; Liu 2019). Our chapter suggests the need for a two-way dialogue between design and DEH. This conversation then begs the question of what creative practices can be used to embody "more-than-human agencies [that are] silenced through documentation processes" (Country et al. 2021, 7). As Ursula Heise (2016) argues, biodiversity databases "may be one of the most useful tools we have" in the attempt to articulate stories about the more-than-human world (86). Having quoted Heise, we note that white ibises have stories that are not data (represented in databases) but are lived. The bird exhibits ontologies that are plural: beyond what the human language and datafication can capture. Keeping this in mind, we suggest databases be expanded by epistemologies of listening to focus on other species (and their ontologies) as tellers. In other words, learning to create a database where humans do not create a narrative about species through their lens of control and cultural underpinnings but by regarding non-human signs as data. We elaborated earlier how the more-than-human turn is grounded in acknowledging non-human species as agentic and communicative beings and tellers of their own stories. Consequently, if biodiversity databases are to adopt a more-than-human *design* approach, they need to regard the white ibises (and all other species) as agentic and communicative beings (5.1) and tellers of their own stories (5.2).

White Ibises as Agentic and Communicative Beings

White ibises, as *flight ways*, have cultures, much like humans – they have their forms of expression and communication (van Dooren 2014). David Haskell, in his essay *The Voices of Birds and the Language of Belonging*, declares attentive listening to birdsongs can reveal an embodied knowledge of a place (Haskell 2019a). He maintains every bird species has its own unique "sonic signature" that expresses different meanings (Haskell 2019a). They have specific purposes and reveal individual bird personalities. Birds can communicate with one another – they warn their kin of predators, call to mates through courtship rituals, have territorial boundaries, and speak about their hunger. These are only the essential aspects of bird communications that science has been able to identify. With a myriad of unidentified birdsongs, birds probably engage in far more complex conversation than humans have been able to interpret. In the *Planet Earth* documentary, David Attenborough narrates that white ibises' birdsongs (sounds like nasal honks)[6] (Figure 32.12) have evolved to help them communicate with their kin through traffic noise in cities (Johns 2017).

Listening carefully to birdsongs can be a "powerful connector" between humans and their "avian cousins" (Haskell 2019a). Haskell maintains that in "attending to the sounds of bird species, our senses learn the language of belonging" (Haskell 2019a). Haskell further narrates that scientific studies prove bird sounds have grammatical rules. Birds are capable of learning as they

> hear and remember nuances of sound, connecting abstract acoustic patterns to the physicality of their ecological and social worlds. They listen to the voices of other species and understand what is meant. Social interaction with kin and neighbours moulds the shape of individual sounds and the organisation of these parts into a whole.
>
> *(Haskell 2019a)*

In this sense, scientific studies (often quantitative) help sketch (a qualitative) understanding of bird sounds. Understanding bird language can be a creative "leap across species boundaries" – which aids humans in learning their "stories of continuity, of extinction, of blossoming" and, at

Figure 32.12 Australian white ibis's birdsong, illustration by Hira Sheikh.

the same time, weave human-bird relations into a "communicative whole" (Haskell 2019a). The intention is to use scientific (quantitative) knowledge to reveal thick descriptions (as described by Van Dooren) of the bird species and their experiential worlds rather than objectifying them. Furthermore, how do we translate this more embodied scientific knowledge on non-human sign practices to biodiversity databases, so bird sounds and their different meanings might help policymakers, for example, better understand the experiential world of the ibis. Can our future biodiversity databases be designed to represent white ibises through sign practices that humbly focus on the bird as the teller?

The COVID-19 pandemic, in many ways, brought urban noise pollution to a halt and offered citizens a space to reconnect with ancestral birdsongs (Lovatt 2021). The pandemic brought a renewed awareness to deep listening practices, where human urban dwellers more than started attuning to the *grammar of animacy* through birdsongs. Deep attunement to ibises as tellers and agents may raise ethical tensions between humans and the white ibises in cities, especially when species preferences collide. Such political conflicts might expose opportunities to view the white ibis as a species beyond the human-focused framings. Any meaningful way to explore how the ibis inhabits the city would recognise them as power negotiators, constantly forging new associations with the urban landscape. Acknowledging their agency helps humans understand what is at stake for the ibis in cities. In turn, it helps humans adopt policies that negotiate their claim to urban spaces.

White Ibises as a Species with Their Own Stories

Amitav Ghosh (2021) asks, "[W]hat if the idea that Earth teems with other beings who act, communicate, tell stories, and make meaning is taken seriously?" Following Ghosh's proposition, we suggest that although we cannot directly approach the white ibis as humans, reading signs emerging from them might help humans regard them as the tellers of their stories. Thom Van Dooren contends, "[T]elling stories has consequences: one of which is that we will inevitably be drawn into new connections and with them new accountabilities and obligations" (van Dooren

2014, 10). Following Van Dooren, in the context of the discussed examples of biodiversity databases, we suggest how the stories rendered through data representations of the white ibis impact how their needs are conceptualised and governed upon. Planetary survival depends on stories that invite "attentiveness to the speech of other species" as "without their voices to guide us, we act in ignorance" (Haskell 2019b). Therefore, to act in awareness of the multispecies worlds and their stories – it is critical for smart urban governance and biodiversity databases to move beyond human language and legitimise sign communications of other species. Thom van Dooren and Deborah Rose (2012) describe multispecies storytelling as "willingness to recognise storied-experience in non-human places – to accept non-humans as "narrative subjects" with their abilities to trade in "signs and wonders" (4).

Edward Wilson (2017) explains that humans have limited sensory abilities to perceive non-human species, guiding constraints for stories that orient more-than-human life. Lizbeth Lipari (2014) maintains that listening encourages "a recognition of an unknown other" (176), even if the sensory capacities of others exceed humans. Similarly, Manulani Aluli-Meyer (2001) regards listening as a way of attuning to the more-than-human world. Willis Jenkins (2021) proposes technologies as one way to expand humans' sensory experience for attunement with other species. David Dunn (1997) proposes listening as a critical practice for healing the living world in visually oriented cultures, where the environmental study is increasingly represented through eye-pleasing data (Jenkins 2021). There is no defined path to decentralise the human language and minimise our reliance on human interpretations of the white ibis in databases. We suggest a reorientation of data representation towards how non-human beings use signs to reveal their stories can expand biodiversity databases from being tools premised only on human experience. For example, designers can experiment with biodiversity databases that use birdsongs to explore their storied places (Van Dooren, Rose, and Others 2012): (1) What do the birds (like the Australian white ibis) communicate to each other? (2) Where (physical space) and when (time scales) do these communications take place? (3) Are their communications being disrupted by urban noise? (4) How are the species and their communications being impacted by the climate crisis? And (5) what kinds of alternative urban environments would facilitate their communications to strengthen their communities?

Conclusion

The chapter unravelled the reductive representations of the Australian white ibis in biodiversity databases and legitimisation of control-based governance actions through them. Over the past few years, theorists from different disciplines who adopt an ecocritical approach have dismantled the Cartesian dichotomies (e.g. quantitative/qualitative, feral/domestic, native/non-native) that lead to a particular treatment of species (Head and Muir 2004; Whatmore 2006; Hinchliffe 2007; Donaldson and Kymlicka 2011) and, in turn, are challenging the biodiversity databases and governance structures that divide species into categories of desirable/undesirable nature (Srinivasan 2017; Crowley, Hinchliffe, and McDonald 2018). Unfortunately, the dichotomies continue to prevail in fields engaging with the protection of biodiversity. Describing the "current tyrannised status of animals" in biodiversity governance, Sue Donaldson states, "[T]hey are governed without consideration, representation, or political voice" (Donaldson, Vink, and Gagnon 2021, 78). Pushing past this status of non-human species, smart urban governance needs to regard non-human species as beings with agency.

DEH brings together plural knowledge to open space for recognition of non-human agency within the biodiversity (or environmental) monitoring and governmentality discourse. In uniting dialogues arising from more-than-human studies and Indigenous and First Nations knowledge to reflect on the digital study of the natural world, DEH has stretched the multispecies justice movement to the digital realm. Due to this union, there is increased recognition of the call to reorient digital tools (like biodiversity databases) that impact decisions regarding non-human life (environmental governance) to capture their experience by attuning to the signs they emit into the world. It is time we (re)imagine our tools to facilitate non-human beings and "consideration of their intrinsic interests in political deliberation, policy, and law" (Donaldson, Vink, and Gagnon 2021, 76). We cannot find examples that integrate non-human signs within biodiversity databases. Therefore, we have great scope for experimentation on how quantitative and qualitative data can help us realise databases and consequent governance processes that are in tune *with* the depicted and governed species. Since we don't have answers, we leave the readers to ponder two questions: (1) What would a biodiversity database look like if it focused on non-human beings as tellers (by listening to signs emitted by them)? And (2) how will the biodiversity databases focused on non-human experience affect environmental governance to encourage multispecies urban future(s)?

Notes

1 www.ala.org.au.
2 www.inaturalist.org.
3 https://birdata.birdlife.org.au.
4 www.spotteron.com/bigcitybirds.
5 Two examples of these white ibis management plans are from Camden and Canterbury-Bankstown Councils in New South Wales.
   (1) www.camden.nsw.gov.au/assets/Uploads/Adopted-Australian-White-Ibis-Management-Plan-Website.pdf
   (2) https://s3.ap-southeast-2.amazonaws.com/hdp.au.prod.app.cbnks-haveyoursay.files/6915/7533/9458/Ibis_Final_Management_Plan_June_2018.pdf
6 Listen to Australian white ibises' birdsongs at https://dibird.com/species/australian-white-ibis.

Sources

Abram, David. 1997. *The Spell of the Sensuous: Perception More Than Human*. New York: Vintage Books.
———. 2017. "The Spell of the Sensuous." *CSPA Quarterly* (17): 22–24.
Abrantes, Eduardo. 2021. "Wild Arrangements: Sonic and Performative Strategies for Interspecies Encounters." September. https://forskning.ruc.dk/en/publications/wild-arrangements-sonic-and-performative-strategies-for-interspec.
Adams, William. 2019. "Geographies of Conservation II: Technology, Surveillance and Conservation by Algorithm." *Progress in Human Geography* 43 (2): 337–50.
ALA. 2020. "About Us." 2020. www.ala.org.au/about-ala/.
Allatson, Paul, and Andrea Connor. 2020. "Ibis and the City: Bogan Kitsch and the Avian Revisualization of Sydney." *Visual Communication* 19 (3): 369–90.
Anker, Kirsten. 2017. "Law as Forest: Eco-Logic, Stories and Spirits in Indigenous Jurisprudence." *Law Text Culture* 21: 191.
Australian Museum. 2020. "Australian White Ibis." 2020. https://australian.museum/learn/animals/birds/australian-white-ibis/.
Bakker, Karen, and Max Ritts. 2018. "Smart Earth: A Meta-Review and Implications for Environmental Governance." *Global Environmental Change: Human and Policy Dimensions* 52 (September): 201–11.
Barad, Karen. 2003. "Posthumanist Performativity: Toward an Understanding of How Matter Comes to Matter." *Signs: Journal of Women in Culture and Society* 28 (3): 801–31.
Bennett, Michael, and David Warfield Teague. 1999. *The Nature of Cities: Ecocriticism and Urban Environments*. Tucson: University of Arizona Press.
Berry, Geoff. 2018. "Speaking English with Country: Can the Animate World Hear Us? Can We Hear It?" *PAN: Philosophy Activism Nature* (14): 24–29.

Billé, Franck. 2021. "Auratic Geographies: Buffers, Backyards, Entanglements." *Geopolitics*, April: 1–23.
Bongaarts, John. 2019. "IPBES, 2019. Summary for Policymakers of the Global Assessment Report on Biodiversity and Ecosystem Services of the Intergovernmental Science-Policy Platform on Biodiversity and Ecosystem Services." *Population and Development Review*. https://doi.org/10.1111/padr.12283.
Bowker, Geoffrey C. 2000. "Biodiversity Datadiversity." *Social Studies of Science* 30 (5): 643–83.
Braidotti, Rosi. 2013. "Posthuman Humanities." *European Educational Research Journal* 12 (1): 1–19.
Bratton, Benjamin H. 2019. *The Terraforming*. Moscow: Strelka Press.
Braun, Bruce P. 2005. "Environmental Issues: Writing a More-than-Human Urban Geography." *Progress in Human Geography* 29 (5): 635–50.
———. 2014. "A New Urban Dispositif? Governing Life in an Age of Climate Change." *Environment and Planning. D, Society & Space* 32 (1): 49–64.
Bresnihan, Patrick. 2016. *Transforming the Fisheries: Neoliberalism, Nature, and the Commons*. Lincoln: University of Nebraska Press.
Castricano, Jodey. 2008. *Animal Subjects: An Ethical Reader in a Posthuman World*. Waterloo: Wilfrid Laurier University Press.
Celermajer, Danielle, David Schlosberg, Lauren Rickards, Makere Stewart-Harawira, Mathias Thaler, Petra Tschakert, Blanche Verlie, and Christine Winter. 2020. "Multispecies Justice: Theories, Challenges, and a Research Agenda for Environmental Politics." *Environmental Politics*. https://doi.org/10.1080/09644016.2020.1827608.
Chao, Sophie, and Dion Enari. 2021. "Decolonising Climate Change: A Call for Beyond-Human Imaginaries and Knowledge Generation." *eTropic: Electronic Journal of Studies in the Tropics* 20 (2): 32–54.
Clarke, Rachel, Sara Heitlinger, Ann Light, Laura Forlano, Marcus Foth, and Carl DiSalvo. 2019. "More-Than-Human Participation: Design for Sustainable Smart City Futures." *Interactions* 26 (3): 60–63.
Connolly, Creighton. 2019. "Urban Political Ecology Beyond Methodological Cityism." *International Journal of Urban and Regional Research* 43 (1): 63–75.
Corben, D. 2003. "Population Composition, Abundances, and Movements of the Australian White Ibis (Threskiornis molucca) (Threskiornithidae), in an Urban Environment." B. Sc. (Hons) Thesis, University of Technology.
Country, Ngalakgan, Margaret Duncan, Rhonda Duncan, and Lillian Tait. 2021. "Traiyimbat Olkainbala Wei Ov Dum Tings | Trying Out All Kinds of Ways of Doing Things: Co-Creative Multisensory Methods in Collaborative Research." *Social & Cultural Geography*. https://doi.org/10.1080/14649365.2021.1896027.
Crowley, Sarah L., Steve Hinchliffe, and Robbie A. McDonald. 2018. "Killing Squirrels: Exploring Motivations and Practices of Lethal Wildlife Management." *Environment and Planning E: Nature and Space* 1 (1–2): 120–43.
Dalton, Craig, and Jim Thatcher. 2014. "What Does a Critical Data Studies Look Like, and Why Do We Care? Seven Points for a Critical Approach to 'Big Data.'" *Society and Space* 29.
Davis, Adrian, Richard E. Major, Charlotte E. Taylor, and John M. Martin. 2017. "Novel Tracking and Reporting Methods for Studying Large Birds in Urban Landscapes." *Wildlife Biology* 2017 (4). https://doi.org/10.2981/wlb.00307.
Donald, Dwayne. 2009. "Forts, Curriculum, and Indigenous Métissage: Imagining Decolonization of Aboriginal-Canadian Relations in Educational Contexts." *First Nations Perspectives* 2 (1): 1–24.
Donaldson, Sue, and Will Kymlicka. 2011. *Zoopolis: A Political Theory of Animal Rights*. Oxford: Oxford University Press.
Donaldson, Sue, Janneke Vink, and Jean-Paul Gagnon. 2021. "Realizing Interspecies Democracy: The Preconditions for an Egalitarian, Multispecies, World." *Democratic Theory* 8 (1): 71–95.
Dooren, Thom van. 2014. *Flight Ways: Life and Loss at the Edge of Extinction*. New York: Columbia University Press.
Drucker, Johanna. 2011. "Humanities Approaches to Graphical Display." *Digital Humanities Quarterly* 5 (1): 1–21.
Dunn, David. 1997. "Nature, Sound Art, and the Sacred." *The Book of Music and Nature*: 95–107.
Edwards, P. N. 2010. *A Vast Machine: Computer Models, Climate Data and the Politics of Global Warming MIT Press*. Cambridge, MA: MIT Press.
Epstein, Jonathan H., Jeffrey McKee, Phil Shaw, Vicki Hicks, Gino Micalizzi, Peter Daszak, A. Marm Kilpatrick, and Gretchen Kaufman. 2007. "The Australian White Ibis (Threskiornis Molucca) as a Reservoir of Zoonotic and Livestock Pathogens." *EcoHealth*. https://doi.org/10.1007/s10393-006-0064-2.

Fish, A. 2020. "Seadrones: Sensing Oceancultures." *Journal of Environmental Media*. www.ingentaconnect.com/content/intellect/jem/2020/00000001/00000002/art00003.
Fitz-Henry, Erin. 2021. "Multi-Species Justice: A View from the Rights of Nature Movement." *Environmental Politics*. https://doi.org/10.1080/09644016.2021.1957615.
Forlano, Laura. 2017. "Posthumanism and Design." *She Ji: The Journal of Design, Economics, and Innovation* 3 (1): 16–29.
Foth, Marcus. 2017. "The Next Urban Paradigm: Cohabitation in the Smart City." *It – Information Technology* 59 (6). https://doi.org/10.1515/itit-2017-0034.
Gabriel, Nate. 2014. "Urban Political Ecology: Environmental Imaginary, Governance, and the Non-Human: UPE: Imaginary, Governance, and the Non-Human." *Geography Compass* 8 (1): 38–48.
Gabrys, Jennifer. 2016. *Program Earth: Environmental Sensing Technology and the Making of a Computational Planet*. Minneapolis, MN: University of Minnesota Press.
———. 2019. "Sensors and Sensing Practices: Reworking Experience across Entities, Environments, and Technologies." *Science, Technology & Human Values* 44 (5): 723–36.
———. 2020. "Smart Forests and Data Practices: From the Internet of Trees to Planetary Governance." *Big Data & Society* 7 (1): 2053951720904871.
Garrard, Gred. 2011. *Ecocriticism, New Critical Idiom*. Hoboken: Taylor & Francis.
Ghosh, Amitav. 2021. "Orion Magazine – Brutes." September 1, 2021. https://orionmagazine.org/article/brutes/?mc_cid=870d0a7573&mc_eid=b8fa3a2b2d.
Gibbs, Leah. 2021. "Agency in Human – Shark Encounter." *Environment and Planning E: Nature and Space* 4 (2): 645–66.
Graham, Mary. 1999. "Some Thoughts About the Philosophical Underpinnings of Aboriginal Worldviews." *Worldviews: Global Religions, Culture, and Ecology* 3 (2): 105–18.
———. 2014. "Aboriginal Notions of Relationality and Positionalism: A Reply to Weber." *Global Discourse* 4 (1): 17–22.
Gruen, Lori. 2009. "Attending to Nature: Empathetic Engagement with the More Than Human World." *Ethics and the Environment* 14 (2): 23–38.
Halpern, Orit. 2015. *Beautiful Data: A History of Vision and Reason since 1945*. Durham, NC: Duke University Press.
Haraway, Donna. 2016. *Staying with the Trouble: Making Kin in the Chthulucene. Edition*. Durham, NC: Duke University Press.
Haskell, David G. 2019a. "The Voices of Birds and the Language of Belonging." May 26, 2019. https://emergencemagazine.org/essay/the-voices-of-birds-and-the-language-of-belonging/.
———. 2019b. "Listening to the Language of Birds." June 24, 2019. https://emergencemagazine.org/practice/listening-to-the-language-of-birds/?fbclid=IwAR2Slbpwa8tIjlp79wZ0Wz_rk4NSjUaG-Nz6wZFIVOPUAoHsy6zdCMo7dd2I.
Hayles, N. Kathrrine. 2007. "Narrative and Database: Natural Symbionts." *PMLA/Publications of the Modern Language Association of America* 122 (5): 1603–8.
Head, Lesley, and Pat Muir. 2004. "Nativeness, Invasiveness, and Nation in Australian Plants." *Geography Review* 94 (2): 199–217.
Heise, Ursula K. 2006. "The Emergence of Ecocriticism." *The Hitchhiker's Guide to Ecocriticism*: 503–16.
———. 2016. *Imagining Extinction: The Cultural Meanings of Endangered Species*. Chicago, IL: University of Chicago Press.
———. 2017. "Introduction: Planet, Species, Justice – and the Stories We Tell about Them." In *The Routledge Companion to the Environmental Humanities*, 17–26. New York and London: Routledge.
Heise, Ursula K., Jon Christensen, and Michelle Niemann. 2017. *The Routledge Companion to the Environmental Humanities*. New York and London: Routledge.
Hinchliffe, Steve. 2007. *Geographies of Nature: Societies, Environments, Ecologies*. SAGE.
Houston, Donna, Jean Hillier, Diana MacCallum, Wendy Steele, and Jason Byrne. 2018. "Make Kin, not Cities! Multispecies Entanglements and 'Becoming-World' in Planning Theory." *Planning Theory* 17 (2): 190–212.
Ingold, Tim. 2002. *The Perception of the Environment: Essays on Livelihood, Dwelling and Skill*. Routledge.
Jenkins, Willis. 2021. "Coastal Futures Conservatory: Listening as a Model for Integrating Arts and Humanities into Environmental Change Research." *Environmental Humanities* 13 (1): 201–23.
Jerolmack, Colin. 2013. *The Global Pigeon*. Chicago, IL: University of Chicago Press.
Johns, David. 2017. "Planet Earth: Bin Chicken (4K)." *Youtube*. March 29, 2017. www.youtube.com/watch?v=w4dYWhkSbTU.

Jørgensen, Finn Arne. 2014. "The Armchair Traveller's Guide to Digital Environmental Humanities." *Environmental Humanities* 4 (1): 95–112.

Kane, S. 1998. "Wisdom of the Mythtellers." https://books.google.com/books?hl=en&lr=&id=-Yz-meNDmrFsC&oi=fnd&pg=PA23&dq=Kane+Sean+1994+Wisdom+of+the+Mythtellers+Broad-view+Press&ots=Tl0Sw5PDKg&sig=guOHH5SnLHsRv-o0POxWwolkgpo.

Kentish, Barry. 1994. "The Effect of Revegetation on Silver Gull and Sacred Ibis Populations at Winter Swamp, Ballarat." *Corella* 18 (3): 71–76.

Kimmerer, Robin Wall. 2013. *Braiding Sweetgrass: Indigenous Wisdom, Scientific Knowledge and the Teachings of Plants*. Minneapolis, MN: Milkweed Editions.

Kirksey, S. Eben, and Stefan Helmreich. 2010. "The Emergence of Multispecies Ethnography." *Cultural Anthropology: Journal of the Society for Cultural Anthropology* 25 (4): 545–76.

Kohn, Eduardo. 2013. *How Forests Think: Toward an Anthropology Beyond the Human*. Berkeley, CA: University of California Press.

Krause, Bernard L. 1993. "The Niche Hypothesis: A Virtual Symphony of Animal Sounds, the Origins of Musical Expression and the Health of Habitats." *The Soundscape Newsletter* 6: 6–10.

Lawrence Buell. 2011. "Ecocriticism: Some Emerging Trends." *Qui Parle* 19 (2): 87–115.

Lipari, Lisbeth. 2014. *Listening, Thinking, Being: Toward an Ethics of Attunement*. University Park, PA: Penn State Press.

Liu, Szu-Yu (cyn). 2019. "Designing for Multispecies Collaboration and Cohabitation." In *Conference Companion Publication of the 2019 on Computer Supported Cooperative Work and Social Computing – CSCW'19*, 72–75. New York: ACM Press.

Loh, Susan, Marcus Foth, Glenda Amayo Caldwell, Veronica Garcia-Hansen, and Mark Thomson. 2020. "A More-Than-Human Perspective on Understanding the Performance of the Built Environment." *Architectural Science Review*. https://doi.org/10.1080/00038628.2019.1708258.

Lorimer, Jamie. 2007. "Nonhuman Charisma." *Environment and Planning. D, Society & Space* 25 (5): 911–32.

Lovatt, Steven. 2021. "'The Earth Could Hear Itself Think': How Birdsong Became the Sound of Lockdown." *The Guardian*, February 28, 2021. www.theguardian.com/books/2021/feb/28/birdsong-in-a-time-of-silence-steven-lovatt-lockdown-coronavirus.

Luusua, Anna, Johanna Ylipulli, and Emilia Rönkkö. 2017. "Nonanthropocentric Design and Smart Cities in the Anthropocene." *It – Information Technology* 59 (6). https://doi.org/10.1515/itit-2017-0007.

Machen, Ruth, and Eric Nost. 2021. "Thinking Algorithmically: The Making of Hegemonic Knowledge in Climate Governance." *Transactions*, trans. 12441 (March). https://doi.org/10.1111/tran.12441.

Manovich, Lev. 2002. *The Language of New Media*. Cambridge, MA: MIT Press.

Martínez-Alier, Juan. 1997. "Environmental Justice (Local and Global)." *Capitalism Nature Socialism* 8 (1): 91–107.

Martin, John M., Kris French, Geoffrey A. Ross, and Richard E. Major. 2011. "Foraging Distances and Habitat Preferences of a Recent Urban Coloniser: The Australian White Ibis." *Landscape and Urban Planning* 102 (2): 65–72.

Martin, John M., and Richard E. Major. 2010. "The Use of Cattle Ear-Tags as Patagial Markers for Large Birds – a Field Assessment on Adult and Nestling Australian White Ibis." *Waterbirds* 33 (2): 264–68.

Mattern, Shannon. 2021. *A City Is Not a Computer: Other Urban Intelligences*. Princeton, NJ: Princeton University Press.

McKiernan, Shaun, and Lesley Instone. 2016. "From Pest to Partner: Rethinking the Australian White Ibis in the More-Than-Human City." *Cultural Geographies* 23 (3): 475–94.

McLean, Jessica. 2020. "Delivering Green Digital Geographies? More-Than-Real Corporate Sustainability and Digital Technologies." In *Changing Digital Geographies: Technologies, Environments and People*, edited by Jessica McLean, 139–58. Cham: Springer International Publishing.

Metzger, Jonathan. 2016. "Cultivating Torment: The Cosmopolitics of More-Than-Human Urban Planning." *Cityscape* 20 (4): 581–601.

Meyer, Manulani Aluli. 2001. "Our Own Liberation: Reflections on Hawaiian Epistemology." *The Contemporary Pacific* 13 (1): 124–48.

Moore, Jason W. 2014. "The End of Cheap Nature, or, How I Learned to Stop Worrying About the Environment and Love the Crisis of Capitalism." *Structures of the World Political Economy and the Future of Global Conflict and Cooperation*: 285–314.

Moretti, Franco. 1996. *Modern Epic: The World-System from Goethe to García Márquez*. New York: Verso.

Morozov, Evgeny. 2014. *To Save Everything, Click Here: The Folly of Technological Solutionism*. Reprint ed. New York: PublicAffairs.

Narayanan, Yamini. 2017. "Street Dogs at the Intersection of Colonialism and Informality: 'Subaltern Animism' as a Posthuman Critique of Indian Cities." *Environment and Planning D: Society and Space*. https://doi.org/10.1177/0263775816672860.

Neimanis, Astrida. 2017. "Nature Represents Itself: Bibliophilia in a Changing Climate." *What If Culture Was Nature All Along*, 179–98.

Nost, Eric. 2015. "Performing Nature's Value: Software and the Making of Oregon's Ecosystem Services Markets." *Environment & Planning A* 47 (12): 2573–90.

Oliver, Jessica L., Margot Brereton, Selen Turkay, David M. Watson, and Paul Roe. 2020. "Exploration of Aural & Visual Media About Birds Informs Lessons for Citizen Science Design." In *Proceedings of the 2020 ACM Designing Interactive Systems Conference*, 1687–700. DIS'20. New York: Association for Computing Machinery.

Parikka, Jussi. 2011. "Insect Media." https://doi.org/10.5749/minnesota/9780816667390.001.0001.

Paulos, Eric, Marcus Foth, Christine Satchell, Younghui Kim, Paul Dourish, and Hee-Jeong Choi. 2008. "Ubiquitous Sustainability: Citizen Science and Activism." https://eprints.qut.edu.au/14130/.

Pickles, John. 1995. "Representations in an Electronic Age: Geography, GIS, and Democracy." In *Ground Truth: The Social Implications of Geographic Information Systems*, edited by John Pickles, 1–30. New York: Guilford.

———. 2012. *A History of Spaces: Cartographic Reason, Mapping and the Geo-Coded World*. New York: Routledge.

Pierotti, Raymond. 2010. *Indigenous Knowledge, Ecology, and Evolutionary Biology*. Routledge.

Posthumus, Stephanie, and Stéfan Sinclair. 2014. "Reading Environment(s): Digital Humanities Meets Ecocriticism." *Green Letters* 18 (3): 254–73.

Rachwani, Mostafa. 2020. "App Allows City-Dwellers to Turn Citizen Scientists and Track Australia's Urban Birds." *The Guardian*, November 11, 2020. www.theguardian.com/environment/2020/nov/12/app-allows-city-dwellers-to-turn-citizen-scientists-and-track-australias-urban-birds.

Ross, Geoffrey A. 2004. "Ibis in Urban Sydney: A Gift from Ra or a Pharaoh's Curse." In *Urban Wildlife: More Than Meets the Eye,'* edited by D. Lunney and S. Burgin, 148–52.

Smith, Andrew Charles Michael. 2009. "Population Ecology of the Australian White Ibis, Threskiornis Molucca, in the Urban Environment." https://opus.lib.uts.edu.au/handle/2100/1340.

Smith, Nancy, Shaowen Bardzell, and Jeffrey Bardzell. 2017. "Designing for Cohabitation: Naturecultures, Hybrids, and Decentering the Human in Design." In *Proceedings of the 2017 CHI Conference on Human Factors in Computing Systems*, 1714–25. ACM.

Srinivasan, Krithika. 2017. "Conservation Biopolitics and the Sustainability Episteme." *Environment & Planning A* 49 (7): 1458–76.

Stevens, Rick. 2018. "Bin Chickens: The Grotesque Glory of the Urban Ibis – in Pictures." *The Guardian*, April 9, 2018. www.theguardian.com/cities/gallery/2018/apr/09/bin-chickens-grotesque-glory-urban-ibis-in-pictures.

Stone, Christopher D. 1975. *Should Trees Have Standing?* Toward Legal Rights for Natural Objects.

Sullivan, Brian L., Christopher L. Wood, Marshall J. Iliff, Rick E. Bonney, Daniel Fink, and Steve Kelling. 2009. "eBird: A Citizen-Based Bird Observation Network in the Biological Sciences." *Biological Conservation* 142 (10): 2282–92.

Terracciano, Emilia. 2021. "Sounds of Silence: Conducting Technology and Nature." *Oxford Art Journal* 43 (2): 261–79.

Todd, Zoe. 2015. "Indigenizing the Anthropocene." *Art in the Anthropocene: Encounters Among Aesthetics, Politics, Environments and Epistemologies*: 241–54.

Tsing, Anna Lowenhaupt. 2015. *The Mushroom at the End of the World: On the Possibility of Life in Capitalist Ruins*. Princeton, NJ: Princeton University Press.

Tzaninis, Yannis, Tait Mandler, Maria Kaika, and Roger Keil. 2020. "Moving Urban Political Ecology Beyond the 'Urbanization of Nature.'" *Progress in Human Geography*. https://doi.org/10.1177/0309132520903350.

Vallee, Mickey. 2021. "Animal, Body, Data: Starling Murmurations and the Dynamic of Becoming In-Formation." *Body & Society* (May): 1357034X21992846.

Van Dooren, Thom, Eben Kirksey, and Ursula Münster. 2016. "Multispecies StudiesCultivating Arts of Attentiveness." *Environmental Humanities* 8 (1): 1–23.

Van Dooren, Thom, Deborah Bird Rose, and Others. 2012. "Storied-Places in a Multispecies City." *Humanimalia* 3 (2): 1–27.

Verma, Audrey, René van der Wal, and Anke Fischer. 2015. "Microscope and Spectacle: On the Complexities of Using New Visual Technologies to Communicate about Wildlife Conservation." *Ambio* 44 (Suppl 4) (November): 648–60.

Wakefield, Stephanie, David Chandler, and Kevin Grove. 2021. "The Asymmetrical Anthropocene: Resilience and the Limits of Posthumanism." *Cultural Geographies*. https://doi.org/10.1177/14744740211029278.

Watts, Vanessa. 2013. "Indigenous Place-Thought and Agency Amongst Humans and Non Humans (First Woman and Sky Woman Go On a European World Tour!)." *Decolonization: Indigeneity, Education & Society* 2 (1). https://jps.library.utoronto.ca/index.php/des/article/view/19145.

Westerlaken, Michelle. 2020. *Imagining Multispecies Worlds*. Malmö: Malmö University.

———. 2021. "The Telltale Worlds of the Octopus." 2021. www.e-flux.com/architecture/survivance/379308/the-telltale-worlds-of-the-octopus/.

Whatmore, Sarah. 2006. "Materialist Returns: Practising Cultural Geography in and for a More-Than-Human World." *Cultural Geographies* 13 (4): 600–9.

Whitelaw, Mitchell, and Belinda Smaill. 2021. "Biodiversity Data as Public Environmental Media: Citizen Science Projects, National Databases and Data Visualizations." *Journal of Environmental Media* 2 (1): 79–99.

Wilson, Edward O. 2017. *The Origins of Creativity*. New York: Liveright Publishing.

Wohlleben, Peter. 2016. *The Hidden Life of Trees: What They Feel, How They Communicate – Discoveries from a Secret World*. Vancouver, BC: Greystone Books.

Wood, Denis. 1987. "Pleasure in the Idea/the Atlas as Narrative Form." *Cartographica: The International Journal for Geographic Information and Geovisualization* 24 (1): 24–46.

Youatt, R. 2008. "Counting Species: Biopower and the Global Biodiversity Census." *Environmental Values* 17 (3): 393–417.

33

ELEMENTAL COMPUTATION

From Non-human Media to More-than-Digital Information Systems

Bronislaw Szerszynski and Nigel Clark

Introduction

Pervasive, high-powered digital information gathering and processing has played a significant role in constituting the "whole Earth" as an object of thought and practice. Coming shortly after the launch of the first satellite, the International Geophysical Year (IGY) of 1957–1958 – a collaborative endeavour involving scientists from 67 nations – is often taken as a turning point in the technologically mediated sensing of our planet (Gabrys 2016, 1–3). Not only did the Soviet Union's Sputnik satellite and subsequent space voyages initiate an "overview" perspective on the Earth, but a whole raft of projects utilising new technologies from spectroscopes and cosmic ray recorders through to mainframe computers commenced producing vast amounts of information about the Earth and cosmic processes (Lövbrand, Stripple, and Wiman 2009).

Along with new insights into ice, earthquakes, volcanic activity, geomagnetism, and solar flares, research under the IGY umbrella gave rise to the observations expressed in the Keeling Curve, a graph showing a steadily increasing atmospheric CO_2 concentration that became an icon of anthropogenic climate change (Howe 2014, 20–11; Everts 2016). In a more general sense, political scientist Eva Lövbrand and her colleagues argue that IGY-generated geophysical and biogeochemical data opened a way to both viewing the Earth as a single integrated system and to conceiving of cumulative human activity as having become a significant part of this planetary system (2009). There is, however, a twist to this story. In coming to an understanding of the oneness and unity of the Earth, researchers came to recognise the planet's multiplicity and dividedness – including its capacity to reorganise its component parts, from time to time, into a radically different operating state (Clark and Szerszynski 2021, 23–27).

Without this inherent non-self-sameness of the Earth, it would not be possible for certain kinds of human activity to push global climate and other physical systems into a new state or regime. But the planet's self-differentiating tendencies are much more than a threat. Like other forms of life, humans become who they are by responding to the challenges raised by this changeability and by taking advantage of the opportunities opened up by processes of self-ordering that occur at every spatial and temporal scale in the planetary body (ibid., 9, 93–99).

In this chapter, we ask what digital mediation looks like when we conceive of it as an expression of the multiplicity and diversity that inherently exists on Earth. In other words, rather than simply asking how digital communication and data processing shape the way we apprehend and

DOI: 10.4324/9781003082798-40

relate to our dynamic planet, we are interested in what advanced technological mediation looks like when we conceive of it as a variation on the theme of the Earth's own capacity for self-organisation and self-transformation.

This raises fundamental questions about the relationship between information and materiality, text and flesh, signs and substance. The fantasy that a new generation of machines "are all light and clean because they are nothing but signal" was already disputed by Donna Haraway in her renowned *Cyborg Manifesto* (1991, 153), originally published in 1985. Subsequent researchers have detailed the environmental costs of the manufacture, operation, and disposal of digital hardware (Parikka 2015; Cubitt 2017). But in the process, this research has also opened up deeper issues about the relationship of human technological mediation to the operations of the Earth itself – and it is these questions that interest us. If Earth systems are sensitive to human impacts, we ask, what does this say about the Earth's own capacity for self-sensing or self-understanding? To put it another way, how might human efforts to develop and deploy information systems in response to planetary change draw upon and extend the material-semiotic capacities of the Earth itself?

We begin with a conceptual framing of the relationship between information and materiality that addresses some of the ways that theorists in different disciplines have opened up the issue of sensing, communicative, and cognitive capabilities that extend far beyond human subjects. From there, we turn to the deep history or "archaeology" of human modes of processing information and examine how these developments elaborate upon operations that are part of the dynamism and multiplicity of the Earth itself. This leads us to a consideration of certain "minority" strands of computation or communicative technology that offer ways of negotiating the material-semiotic properties of Earth systems which differ from those prevalent in today's pervasive digitised infrastructures. Extrapolating from these achievements, and with an eye to earlier lineages that might be revisited and developed in new directions, we speculate about the potential for alternative information technics and practices that might be better suited to the challenges of grappling with a planet undergoing major systemic transformation.

Materiality, Information, and Meaning

At the core of contemporary globalised informatics is the binary signal – a macroscopic state of a component of a digital information system, such as the amount of charge on a capacitor, the alignment of magnetic particles on tape, or the modulations of a beam of light that indicates yes/no, on/off, positive/negative, and nothing more (Negroponte 1995, 14; Piccinini and Scarantino 2011, 7–8). As a sociotechnical system embedded within human societies with their projects and imaginaries, computation involves not just the manipulation of information and binary signals but also meaning and purpose (Brier 2008). But it is the basic architecture of binary code, massively reproduced and coordinated, that enables different media to converge and exchange contents (Clark 1998). Already by the early 19th century, telegraphy based on binary or digital electromagnetic signals had instituted a regime in which data flows vastly outpaced analogue technological media in which information coding remained wedded to various kinds of material substrate – though the latter retained the advantage of much higher informational density or broader bandwidth (Wark 1992). By the 1930s, Alan Turing had postulated that a single, programmable "universal computing device" could conceivably simulate the workings of any other computing device – in this way, anticipating the capacity of digital architectures to merge the capabilities of previously distinct number-, text-, image-, and sound-processing devices into integrated "hypermedia" (DeLanda 1991, 129–30; Clark 1998).

Digital computing machines using transistors to do the basic work of switching and amplifying electronic signals were first developed for the US military in the early 1950s and became more widely available at the end of the decade (Riordan and Hoddeson 1997, 204, 273–74). An important impetus toward developing a convergent medium of information storage, processing, and transmission was the massive amounts of data recorded in incommensurate analogue media over the course of the 1957–1958 IGY programme – and the subsequent sense of "information overload" (Everts 2016). But if making sense of the complexity and dynamism of the Earth was part of the push towards a shared informational architecture, in other ways the digital revolution of the latter 20th century increasingly engendered the experience of matter and information pulling in different directions.

While some cyberculture enthusiasts gushed about abandoning flesh and substance to enter realities of purely digital fabrication, many other cultural commentators – including environmentalists – voiced concern about the growing detachment of digitally mediated life from material and embodied existence. As one critic noted of a computerised educational programme that enabled children to "virtually" generate flocks of birds – there are "no smells or tastes, no winds or bird song, no connection with soil, water, sunlight, warmth, no real ecology" (John Davy, cited by Rifkin 1989, 33–34). However, the duality between hefty, resistant matter and weightless, disembodied digitised information – what Massachusetts Institute of Technology (MIT) Media Lab founder Nicholas Negroponte described as "the fundamental difference between atoms and bits" (1995, 4) – has been troubled and unsettled in numerous ways (Clark 1998). The rest of this section sketches out some of these deconstructive steps concerning distinctions amongst matter, information and meaning – though, as we later suggest, there are good reasons not to entirely dispense with distinctions between digitised information and other forms of mediation.

One frequent rebuff to the atom – bit dualism (one is tempted to say binary) is to note the increasing implantation of digital processing capabilities in a range of objects and sites – the rendering "smart" of everything from appliances to clothing, cities to ecosystems (Luke 1997; Gabrys 2016). A related counterargument tracks the multiple ways – from nanotechnology to 3D printing – that researchers have sought to extend the power of universal computing to the assembling and manipulating of matter (Clark 1998; Birtchnell and Urry 2016). What we want to focus on, however, is a set of approaches that move beyond the realm of human technics to make a case for informational, hermeneutic, and cognitive capacities inhering in the wider physical world. Social scientists and humanities scholars have grounds to be cautious or downright sceptical when the computer is used as a metaphor for understanding other things, such as the human brain or, in *pancomputationalism*, the cosmos at large (e.g. Wolfram 2002; Lloyd 2006). Western history has seen many other ground metaphors for nature, not least nature as a kingdom, as an organism, and as a machine. However, with care, it is possible to use ideas of computation to understand more-than-human processes. We will explore the idea that computation on human devices can be seen as a riffing on planetary processes – processes that planetary matter engages in under the right conditions.

Computation and Cognition

To clarify what we might mean by talking about computation in non-human nature, we first need to sort out some terms. Literary scholar Katherine Hayles (2014) makes some distinctions along a rough spectrum. At one end are *material processes* that she describes as having no "intention towards" in themselves – in terms of Aristotle's (1956, V[2]) four causes, these processes involve only his *material* and *efficient* causation. At the other end, Hayles places *consciousness*, which she defines as involving an internal modelling of the self and of the intentional objects of thought, out of which representational practices emerge semiotic "meaning," and Aristotle's *final* causation oriented to purpose.

Roughly in the middle of this spectrum, Hayles uses *nonconscious cognition* to refer to a broad set of processes of modelling, anticipation and other "informational tasks" that supervene on material processes and are, in turn, sometimes supervened upon by conscious thought. In Hayles' schema, such processes are not in themselves conscious and do not involve meaning in the semiotic sense – however, they still involve the "intention towards" of final causation. For Hayles, most instances of cognition are of this nonconscious type and typically occur not in individuals but in systems (2014, 201). She assumes that this "nonconscious cognition" is confined to humans, other animals and technical systems – but we will ascribe nonconscious cognition to a wider range of forms of matter.

Computation is an ordered mapping of inputs to outputs. One can meaningfully say that an entity computes in this sense:

(i) if it is possible to identify phenomena that can serve as the entity's inputs and outputs,
(ii) if the entity behaves in a way that produces an ordered mapping or set of relations between the two, and
(iii) if this ordered mapping performs a function for some other entities, assemblages or systems.

It is because of this last criterion that, just as Claude Shannon's (1948) quantitative definition of "information" as a measure of the unlikeliness of a signal was criticised for neglecting the dimension of meaning (MacKay 1969; Bateson 1972), so too computation can be said to involve not just the storing, manipulation, and transmission of information (for example, in the form of digital bits) but also meaning and purpose. In the case of human-made computers, meaning and purpose are most obviously manifest in the human-computer interaction (HCI) that occurs around input and output peripherals, where we might imagine that meaning is added to an essentially meaningless (re)arrangement of 1s and 0s occurring within the devices by the presence of living and sentient human minds (Brier 2008). However, we will suggest that in the case of computation in more-than-human systems, a kind of non-representational meaning is involved, where the "nonconscious cognitive" powers of matter play a role in wider geophysical processes.

One notable feature of the recent development of human computational technologies is that it has overwhelmingly favoured *digital* computation, which involves the manipulation of discrete elements selected from a finite alphabet. Classical digital computation, as inaugurated by Alan Turing, is a version of this that takes a particular string or ordered set of digital elements and follows an algorithm or set of rules to produce another string as output. Neural networks also manipulate digital elements, but without necessarily having a clearly definable algorithm that they follow to do so (Piccinini and Scarantino 2011, 7–9). Computation in more-than-human systems also lacks sharply defined algorithms but is also typically analogue, involving continuously variable quantities, such as mass, velocity, position, or magnetic field strength. Indeed, it is out of this world of more-than-human computation involving analogue and continuous physical variables, such as electrical charge, that designers and fabricators of computers have to fashion and defend the fiction of a digital world of discrete elements – one that is constantly in danger of collapsing into analogue instability.

Nature as Computer

Computer scientist Gary Flake's (1998) *Computational Beauty of Nature* is more than a guide to how to use computation to model the complexity of non-human nature; it also makes the case that non-human matter *itself* computes by following simple recurrent rules in a massively parallel way. Such ideas had been explored earlier by the cybernetician Stafford Beer when he rhetorically asked which computer would be the best choice to calculate and simulate the movement of water and in what form its "output" would be best expressed. He answered both questions with the same two words: "[w]ater itself" (Beer, in Blohm, Beer, and Suzuki 1986, 51).

In his own exploration of the computational powers of matter, Flake looks at fractals (including the deterministic ones typically generated by digital computers, but focusing on the stochastic ones created by non-human systems, such as coastlines and mountain ranges), chaos (which is deterministic but unpredictable, sensitive to initial conditions), and complex adaptive systems (which learn and become more complex). He identifies three key features that allow us to see these non-linear phenomena as forms of computation (and thus in Hayles' sense a form of nonconscious cognition). The first feature is *spatial* – large numbers of entities acting in parallel and interacting with each other (see Szerszynski 2021); the second is *temporal* – like Hayles, Flake emphasised iteration, repetition, and recursion; finally, the third feature adds *directionality* in time – adaptation and learning, through the operation of filters and some kind of memory.

However, to understand the complexity and unpredictability of the more-than-human world, we need not just ideas of computation but also incomputability. Non-linear natural processes with continuous variables, parallelism, and feedback are inherently "incomputable" – not necessarily in the mathematical sense as defined by Turing, Kurt Gödel, Alonzo Church, and others in the 1930s, but in the broader sense that they cannot be completely modelled or predicted by a digital computer (Flake 1998, 57). However, here Flake invokes another spectrum – not Hayles' spectrum between material processes and conscious thought but one between computability and incomputability. As Flake puts it, "nature's most amazing and beautifully complex creations must exist at the juncture between computability and incomputability" (1998, 427).

Flake is here conducting a computational version of the observation made by many authors that self-organisation can only take place in a border zone between rigid order and complete chaos (von Foerster 1960; Atlan 1979; Kauffman 1995; Bak 1996). On this spectrum, one end might be described as hypermnesic: exhibiting an excess of memory, which locks systems into all-too-predictable and maybe even static, changeless order – like a crystal. The other end of the spectrum is hypomnesic: it has a lack of memory so that all that can occur is chaos (Szerszynski 2019). In the middle is a zone of constant change but an underlying structure of function in which new forms can arise, adapt, and even learn (Flake: 199, 426, 429). Natural systems in this middle zone can be seen as storing and transforming *information* and thereby computing their own dynamic evolution (Shalizi and Crutchfield 2001). But they can also be seen as involving a more-than-human *meaning* and *purpose*, to the extent that the calculative and self-organising powers of material assemblages and systems enable them to play a role in wider planetary processes of self-organisation.

Flake summarises thus: "[n]ature, then, appears to be a hierarchy of computational systems that are forever on the edge between computability and incomputability," in which at each level there is "structural and functional self-similarity, multiplicity and parallelism, recursion, feedback and self-reference" – and sometimes learning (1998, 429).

Planetary Computation and the Humanities

Although our exploration of ideas of "elemental computation" includes both biotic and abiotic matter, a major tributary to humanities thinking about the computational power of planetary matter involved changing ideas about the nature of life. In particular, thinkers across multiple disciplines from the 1950s onwards displayed an increasing willingness – informed by post-war biology's deciphering of the genetic code – to conceive of biological life as an informatic, semiotic or communication system (Johnson 1993; Clark 2011, 16–19). As philosopher Georges Canguilhem expressed it, "[l]ife has always done – without writing, long before writing even existed – what humans have sought to do with engraving, writing and printing, namely, to transmit messages" (1994, 317). A crucial dimension of this generalised thinking in terms of signs or "marked elements" was a move away from thinking of information systems primarily in terms of homeostasis and equilibrium towards an appreciation of the way that noise, interference, and imperfect translation allowed for the emergence of novelty (Johnson 1993,142–87; Hayles 1999, 131–59). Later feminist theorists would extend and deepen this deconstruction of the matter–meaning dualism, Haraway generally speaking of the living body as a "material-semiotic actor" (1988, 595), and Vicki Kirby insisting that "information informs the very matter of [a] body's material constitution" (1997, 3).

But Kirby goes further still, moving beyond the informed flesh of the biological body to "consider the very real possibility that the body of the world is articulate and uncannily thoughtful" (ibid., 5). Other thinkers too, travelling along different tangents, have also considered the possibility of forms of calculation or cognition that are neither confined to human intelligence nor to the broader category of organic life. Philosopher Manuel DeLanda muses on observations made by fluvial geomorphologists about the way that rivers sort the pebbles they transport into various sizes. Based on ongoing feedback between the properties of the mobile rocky matter and the dynamic properties of flowing water, DeLanda explains that these "hydraulic computers" perform the work of differentiation to generate distinct geological strata (1997, 59–60). Science fiction writer and speculative thinker Stanislaw Lem suggests that such processes could be harnessed for human purposes. He proposes that a kind of sieving mechanism inserted into a fast-flowing stream carrying variously sized rocks could serve as a selective device, in this way performing computational functions (2013, 260). Lem goes as far as to say that exploiting the computational power of planetary matter in such ways could automate the process of scientific knowledge production: "We are to invent a device," he writes, "that will gather information, generalize it in the same way the scientist does, and present the results of this inquiry to experts" (ibid., 242).

This brings us back to the idea, roughly contemporaneous with the rise of digitality, that the Earth has a propensity for self-organisation and generating its own otherness – raising the question of whether we might conceive of planetary multiplicity not simply as an unfolding of physical forces but as a play of information or even as a kind of self-intelligibility. As well as speculating whether humans might be bringing the Earth to self-awareness for the first time, chemist and Gaia theorist James Lovelock spoke of the much more ancient "intelligence network" of the living Earth (1987, 46, 148). His Gaia-theory collaborator, evolutionary biologist Lynn Margulis, was still more emphatic, insisting that "Gaia, the physiologically regulated Earth, enjoyed proprioceptive global communication long before people evolved" (1998, 142; see Clark 2017). Literary theorist Bruce Clarke makes a Gaia-inspired case for planet-scaled sensing and knowing:

> Some three or so billion years ago, when a critical mass of biotic, biogenic, and abiotic elements fell into a closed loop locking in an emergent level of metabiotic autopoiesis, life and its environment coupled together to produce a primal regime of planetary cognition.
>
> *(2020, 17)*

Unsurprisingly, Gaian notions of a sensate or auto-communicative Earth put the emphasis on the planet's coupled living and non-living components. It is worth noting, however, that other approaches to similar questions have been less centred on life. In more recent work, Kirby posits an Earth that explores its own possibilities, an astronomical body that "represents itself to itself" (2011, 41). When she asks "Is this not a geology, an earthly science?" the implication is that our planet is literally self-investigative – that there is an originary complication of matter and inquiry that is the condition of possibility for the human study of "geology" (ibid., 40). Kirby's stance may appear to be an extreme expression of the deconstructive impulse, but in important regards it echoes geologist Victor Baker's earlier championing of a notion of geosemiosis: "a semiotic that is continuous from the natural world to the thought processes of geological investigators" (1999, 633). Citing pragmatist philosopher C.S. Pierce's assertion that the universe "is perfused with signs" and making connections with continental philosophy, Baker, too, suggests that human geological inquiry is embedded in a broader planetary and cosmic semiosis – rather than simply imposing understanding on a lumpen, incognisant materiality (ibid., 637). John Durham Peters (2015) similarly extends the idea of media to include sea, earth, fire, and sky – all are media, both in the sense of carrying information and messages and as providing conditions for existence.

In both conceptual and scalar terms, we have journeyed some way from Negroponte's sharp atom–bit divide. Our takeaway point from this breakneck survey is that an Earth infused with multiplicity and self-differentiating potential can also be seen as a planet with its own mediative, computational, cognitive capacities. This, in turn, for us, opens up a way of understanding human cognition and its technical supplements less as a split from natural wholeness and more as a kind of tapping into and elaborating upon modes of intelligibility that are bound up in the dynamic materiality of the Earth. In the following section, we look at ways in which a range of information-rich human practices and technics can be construed in relation to the planetary affordances they build upon.

Archaeologies of Elemental Computation

Until relatively recently, weaving was assumed to be a Neolithic technology, a craft invented by sedentary people who had domesticated plants and animals. Then, in the 1990s, archaeologists working at the Dolni Věstonice and Pavlov sites in today's Czech Republic excavated fragments of fired clay that bore impressions of cloth so tightly knit that it could only have been produced on a loom – a discovery that pushed weaving back into the domain of semi-nomadic peoples living in the midst of a late-Pleistocene glacial epoch some 26,000–30,000 years ago (Vandiver et al. 1989).

Like the cordage, knot-tying, sewing, and basketry that preceded them, spinning and weaving take advantage of a structure-forming process found throughout the organic world – the dynamic equilibrium that arises out of two or more spirals with contrary forces coming together (Ingold 2013, 121). Weaving textiles – a systematic operation in which fibres are transversally threaded over and under each other on a frame – takes the structural logic of twisting and tangling to a new level. Like basket-making, weaving requires detailed premeditation. In this regard, for cultural theorist Sadie Plant, weaving on the loom is the predecessor of all subsequent automated machinery: "[t]he program, the image, the process, and the product: these are all the softwares of the loom" (1997, 189, see also 60–69). Just as pixelated images will reiterate much of the logic of images patterned into textile, so too for Plant, in a more general sense, is this incipient "programming" the precursor of the textile manufacturing machines that were central to the industrial revolution – flying shuttles, spinning jennies, water frames, spinning mules, and power looms (ibid., 63–5).

Though distinguished by the pronounced feminist slant she brings to the field, Plant is far from alone in her excavation of modern media. Alongside and sometimes in conversation with earlier historical accounts of numeracy and literacy (McLuhan 1964; Ong 1982), there is a well-established body of work exploring the idea that ostensibly "new" media or informational technologies actually have deeply layered histories. While Friedrich Kittler (1999) blazed unfamiliar trails between the gramophone and early computing, fellow media archaeologist Siegfried Zielinski (2006) tracked still more obscure philosophically, aesthetically, and even mystically infused precursors of contemporary audiovisual media as far back as the ancient world. Explicitly engaging with the Anthropocene and other framings of global environmental crisis, Jussi Parikka (2015) provides media archaeology with a much more literal focus by showing not just how different media leave physical traces within the geological Earth, but also the manners in which different elements and materials lend their affordances to the development of informatic technologies.

In a similar vein to Parikka, this section of our chapter probes "different ways of mobilizing the earth into and as media" (ibid., 26). From the fabric arts of the late Pleistocene that may well have gifted us with precursive programming, we turn now to the origins of literacy and numeracy in the burgeoning agrarian civilisations of the mid-Holocene. Much has been said about the invention of writing and numerical calculation in relation to the logistical demands of increasingly complex, hierarchical grain-fed social formations. What especially interests us are approaches that focus on the intimate relationship between materials involved in early notational practices and the gradual abstraction of alphanumeric systems. In the context of the Fertile Crescent, archaeologist Denise Schmandt-Besserat (2014, 2010) draws attention to the formative role of record-keeping tokens deposited inside and later impressed upon small clay envelopes. Around 5,000 years ago, she observes, the impressions themselves were doing the representational work. Schmandt-Besserat proposes that it was the tangibility of the objects in question, together with the definitive plasticity of clay, that made it possible to visualise and "grasp" signs and enable them to seem malleable or manipulable (2014, 762–64, 2010; see also Clark 2020).

It is also worth remembering that *calculus* is the Latin word for "pebble" and that *abacus* is thought to derive from *abq*, a Semitic word for "sand." The earliest known human calculating devices involved tracing symbols in a tray of dust or fine sand or placing pebbles in an arrangement of lines or grooves (Heffelfinger and Flom 2004; see also Ifrah 2001). In a more general sense, we should consider just how crucial working with clay, mud, water and variously sized rocks was in the construction and provisioning of the riverine urban centres. We also need to keep in mind the vital connections between technics of timekeeping, geometry, and mathematics and the demands of sediment-dependent social life (Wittfogel 1957, 29–30; Clark 2021). If, as material culture theorist Lambros Malafouris (2010, 40) sums up, "the intelligent use of clay" was critical for the embodied and cognitive shift to literacy and numeracy, we might also say that the intelligent collaboration with sedimentary computational processes – thereby allowing the channelling, collection, apportioning, and setting to work of sediment – was the condition of possibility for ancient floodplain civilisations.

While the twists and tangles of the organic world that inspired fabric arts can be viewed as a natural self-ordering process, in the case of river-borne sediment, this ordering is arguably of another level. As discussed previously, fluvial geomorphologists and their more speculative commentators have posited that the selective transportation of variously sized particulate matter by flowing water functions as a selective or even basic computational mechanism. So in this sense, we might consider how the intelligent social manipulation of water, sediment, stones, and clay – the underpinning of sedimentary civilisations – can be seen as elaborations upon some of the planet's own sorting, probing, calculating, and self-organising capacities (Clark 2020, 2021).

Building on the work of Plant, Parikka, Zielinski, and fellow informatic "archaeologists," it might be possible to reconstruct the late-20th-century binary-coded "universal computing device" out of all its constituent mobilisations of natural and human ordering processes. Along with making use of the self-referential signifying systems that emerged from the play of clay and inscriptive devices, this would include the repurposing of recursive shuttling and switching mechanisms of generations of weaving machines, the use of wheels and cogs ultimately derived from ancient fibre-twisting spindles, the utilisation of silicate-rich semiconductive compounds that elaborate upon both naturally occurring glass and the 5,000- to 6,000-year tradition of artisanal glassmaking, and lastly, the processes of copper patterning on microchips inherited from Bronze Age metalwork techniques of inlaying silver and gold (see Clark 2018; Plant 1997, 60–69; Templeton 2015).

Conclusion

What general conclusions can we draw from this brief investigation of the idea that digital computation is merely an instance of a far wider planetary phenomenon? Firstly, rather than understanding computation and mediation solely as a human-centred, technological, intentional process – one that has become central in the contemporary understanding of Earth-system processes – we also need to be attentive to the self-ordering, computational, cognitive, communicative, and investigative powers of matter itself. Human negotiation with non-human materiality is fraught, challenging, and perpetually open to misrecognition in this regard, precisely because the wider world is itself sensing, probing, and calculating. Secondly, far from computation necessarily involving a progressive disembedding of human calculating, signifying, and communicative capacities from any material substrate, what comes into relief is the profound importance of collective engagement with the stuff of the world in the shaping of informatic media. In this regard, Schmandt-Besserat and Malafouris' elegant paradox that sensorially rich, hands-on engagement with clay paved the way to the abstraction of number and text is anticipated in pioneering media theorist Marshall McLuhan's point that "number is an extension and separation of our most intimate and interrelating activity, our sense of touch" (1964, 105). Lem's ideas of using matter's self-organising powers to automate the production, testing, and dissemination of scientific hypotheses with cybernetic "information farming" practices may have been a proposal largely designed to provoke. Nevertheless, such speculations and provocations serve to remind us that digitised infrastructures, for all their unquestionable power and speed, are not the only option for dealing with the informational complexities of planetary matter – just as fossil-fuelled heat engines are not the only way of moving and shaping physical mass.

As media archaeology helps us to see, the development of modern information technologies has taken particular pathways, but in the process, other possibilities have been bypassed, marginalised, or extinguished. When most of us are so immersed in and reliant upon global digital networks, it can be difficult to imagine what course these other options might have taken and what forms they might yet take. One small step in this direction, we have been suggesting, is not only to acknowledge that our socio-material practices are also informational engagements, but also to recognise that many of these negotiations are familiar, widespread, and mundane. It is here, in the often rather ordinary sites where our own intermittently conscious cognition tangles with the non-conscious cognition of the wider world, that we might look for traces of a more gritty, textured, and colourful supplement to the information systems to which we have become accustomed. Although it would likely involve some relinquishing of the speed and raw processing power of the dominant digital regime, we speculate that more-than-digital informatic architectures could play a part in helping us to respond – skilfully, generously, and receptively – to a planet that is in the throes of rapid systemic change.

Acknowledgements

The authors would like to thank Luke Bergmann, Sergio Rubin, and Leandro Soriano Marcolino for very helpful comments on an earlier draft, and to Maxigas for conversations that informed our early thinking on these matters. However, we take full responsibility for the final chapter.

References

Aristotle. 1956. *Metaphysics*. Translated by John Warrington. London: Dent.

Atlan, Henri. 1979. *Entre le Cristal et la Fumée: Essai sur l'Organisation du Vivant*. Paris: Éditions du Seuil.

Bak, Per. 1996. *How Nature Works: The Science of Self-Organized Criticality*. New York: Copernicus.

Baker, Victor R. 1999. "Geosemiosis." *Geological Society of America Bulletin* 111 (5): 633–45. https://doi.org/10.1130/0016-7606(1999)111%3c0633:G%3e2.3.CO;2.

Bateson, Gregory. 1972. *Steps to an Ecology of Mind: Collected Essays in Anthropology, Psychiatry, Evolution, and Epistemology*. New York: Ballantine.

Birtchnell, Thomas, and John Urry. 2016. *A New Industrial Future? 3D Printing and the Reconfiguring of Production, Distribution, and Consumption*. London: Routledge.

Blohm, Hans, Stafford Beer, and David Suzuki. 1986. *Pebbles to Computers: The Thread*. Toronto: Oxford University Press.

Brier, Søren. 2008. *Cybersemiotics: Why Information Is Not Enough!* Toronto: University of Toronto Press.

Canguilhem, Georges. 1994. *A Vital Rationalist: Selected Writings from Georges Canguilhem*. Translated by Arthur Goldhammer. New York: Zone Books.

Clark, Nigel. 1998. "Materializing Informatics: From Data Processing to Molecular Engineering." *Information, Communication & Society* 1 (1): 70–90. https://doi.org/10.1080/13691189809358954.

———. 2011. *Inhuman Nature: Sociable Life on a Dynamic Planet*. London: Sage.

———. 2017. "PyroGaia: Planetary Fire as Force and Signification." *Ctrl-Z: New Media Philosophy* 7. www.ctrl-z.net.au/articles/issue-7/clark-pyrogaia/.

———. 2018. "Bare Life on Molten Rock." *SubStance* 47 (2): 8–22. https:/muse.jhu.edu/article/701283.

———. 2020. "(Un)Earthing Civilization: Holocene Climate Crisis, City-State Origins and the Birth of Writing." *Humanities* 9 (1). https://doi.org/10.3390/h9010001.

———. 2021. "Planetary Cities: Fluid Rock Foundations of Civilization." *Theory, Culture & Society*. https://doi.org/10.1177/02632764211030986.

Clark, Nigel, and Bronislaw Szerszynski. 2021. *Planetary Social Thought: The Anthropocene Challenge to the Social Sciences*. Cambridge: Polity Press.

Clarke, Bruce. 2020. *Gaian Systems: Lynn Margulis, Neocybernetics, and the End of the Anthropocene*. Minneapolis: University of Minnesota Press.

Cubitt, Sean. 2017. *Finite Media: Environmental Implications of Digital Technologies*. Durham: Duke University Press.

DeLanda, Manuel. 1991. *War in the Age of Intelligent Machines*. New York: Zone Books.

———. 1997. *A Thousand Years of Nonlinear History*. New York: Zone Books.

Everts, Sarah. 2016. "Information Overload." *Distillations*. Accessed August 31, 2021. https://www.sciencehistory.org/distillations/information-overload.

Flake, Gary William. 1998. *The Computational Beauty of Nature: Computer Explorations of Fractals, Chaos, Complex Systems, and Adaptation*. Cambridge, MA: MIT Press.

Gabrys, Jennifer. 2016. *Program Earth: Environmental Sensing Technology and the Making of a Computational Planet*. Minneapolis: University of Minnesota Press.

Haraway, Donna. 1988. "Situated Knowledges: The Science Question in Feminism and the Privilege of Partial Perspective." *Feminist Studies* 14 (3): 575–99. https://doi.org/10.2307/3178066.

———. 1991. "A Cyborg Manifesto." In *Simians, Cyborgs and Women: The Reinvention of Nature*, 149–81. London: Routledge.

Hayles, N. Katherine. 1999. *How We Became Posthuman: Virtual Bodies in Cybernetics, Literature, and Informatics*. Chicago: University of Chicago Press.

———. 2014. "Cognition Everywhere: The Rise of the Cognitive Nonconscious and the Costs of Consciousness." *New Literary History* 45 (2): 199–220. https://www.jstor.org/stable/24542553.

Heffelfinger, Totton, and Gary Flom. 2004. "The Bead Unbaffled." *Abacus: Mystery of the Bead*. Accessed August 31, 2021. http://totton.idirect.com/abacus/pages.htm.

Howe, Joshua P. 2014. *Behind the Curve: Science and the Politics of Global Warming*. Seattle: University of Washington Press.

Ifrah, Georges. 2001. *The Universal History of Computing: From the Abacus to the Quantum Computer*. Translated by E. F. Harding. New York: John Wiley.

Ingold, Tim. 2013. *Making: Anthropology, Archaeology, Art and Architecture*. London: Routledge.

Johnson, Christopher. 1993. *System and Writing in the Philosophy of Jacques Derrida*. Cambridge: Cambridge University Press.

Kauffman, Stuart A. 1995. *At Home in the Universe: The Search for Laws of Self-Organization and Complexity*. New York: Oxford University Press.

Kirby, Vicki. 1997. *Telling Flesh: The Substance of the Corporeal*. London: Routledge.

———. 2011. *Quantum Anthropologies: Life at Large*. Durham, NC: Duke University Press.

Kittler, Friedrich A. 1999. *Gramophone, Film, Typewriter*. Stanford, CA: Stanford University Press.

Lem, Stanisław. 2013. *Summa Technologiae*. Translated by Joanna Zylinska. Minneapolis, MN: University of Minnesota Press.

Lloyd, Seth. 2006. *Programming the Universe: A Quantum Computer Scientist Takes on the Cosmos*. New York: Knopf.

Lövbrand, Eva, Johannes Stripple, and Bo Wiman. 2009. "Earth System Governmentality: Reflections on Science in the Anthropocene." *Global Environmental Change* 19 (1): 7–13. https://doi.org/10.1016/j.gloenvcha.2008.10.002.

Lovelock, James E. 1987. *Gaia: A New Look at Life on Earth*. Oxford: Oxford University Press.

Luke, Timothy W. 1997. "Digital Beings & Virtual Times: The Politics of Cybersubjectivity." *Theory & Event* 1 (1). https://doi.org/10.1353/tae.1991.0011.

MacKay, Donald M. 1969. *Information, Mechanism and Meaning*. Cambridge, MA: MIT Press.

Malafouris, Lambros. 2010. "Grasping the Concept of Number: How Did the Sapient Mind Move Beyond Approximation?" In *The Archaeology of Measurement: Comprehending Heaven, Earth and Time in Ancient Societies*, edited by Iain Morley and Colin Renfrew, 35–42. Cambridge: Cambridge University Press.

Margulis, Lynn. 1998. *The Symbiotic Planet: A New Look at Evolution*. London: Weidenfeld & Nicolson.

McLuhan, Marshall. 1964. *Understanding Media: The Extensions of Man*. New York: McGraw-Hill.

Negroponte, Nicholas. 1995. *Being Digital*. New York: Knopf.

Ong, Walter J. 1982. *Orality and Literacy: The Technologizing of the World*. London: Methuen.

Parikka, Jussi. 2015. *A Geology of Media*. Minneapolis: University of Minnesota Press.

Peters, John Durham. 2015. *The Marvelous Clouds: Toward a Philosophy of Elemental Media*. Chicago: The University of Chicago Press.

Piccinini, Gualtiero, and Andrea Scarantino. 2011. "Information Processing, Computation, and Cognition." *Journal of Biological Physics* 37 (1): 1–38. https://doi.org/10.1007%2Fs10867-010-9195-3.

Plant, Sadie. 1997 *Zeroes + Ones: Digital Women + the New Technoculture*. New York: Doubleday.

Rifkin, Jeremy. 1989. *Time Wars: The Primary Conflict in Human History*. 1st Touchstone ed. New York: Simon & Schuster.

Riordan, Michael, and Lillian Hoddeson. 1997. *Crystal Fire: The Birth of the Information Age*. New York: Norton.

Schmandt-Besserat, Denise. 2010. "The Token System of the Ancient Near East: Its Role in Counting, Writing, the Economy and Cognition." In *The Archaeology of Measurement: Comprehending Heaven, Earth and Time in Ancient Societies*, edited by Iain Morley and Colin Renfrew, 27–34. Cambridge: Cambridge University Press.

———. 2014. "Writing, Evolution of." In *International Encyclopedia of the Social & Behavioral Sciences*, edited by James D. Wright, 2nd ed., 761–66. Oxford: Elsevier. https://doi.org/10.1016/B978-0-08-097086-8.81062-4.

Shalizi, Cosma Rohilla, and James P. Crutchfield. 2001. "Computational Mechanics: Pattern and Prediction, Structure and Simplicity." *Journal of Statistical Physics* 104 (3): 817–79. https://doi.org/10.1023/A:1010388907793.

Shannon, Claude E. 1948. "A Mathematical Theory of Communication." *Bell System Technical Journal* 27: 379–423 & 623–56. https://doi.org/10.1002/j.1538-7305.1948.tb00917.x.

Szerszynski, Bronislaw. 2019. "How the Earth Remembers and Forgets." In *Political Geology: Active Stratigraphies and the Making of Life*, edited by Adam Bobbette and Amy Donovan, 219–36. London: Palgrave Macmillan.

———. 2021. "Colloidal Social Theory: Thinking About Material Animacy and Sociality Beyond Solids and Fluids." *Theory, Culture & Society*. https://doi.org/10.1177/02632764211030989.

Templeton, Graham. 2015. "What Is Silicon, and Why Are Computer Chips Made From It?" *Extreme Tech*. Accessed August 31, 2021. www.extremetech.com/extreme/208501-what-is-silicon-and-why-are-computer-chips-made-from-it.

Vandiver, Pamela B., Olga Soffer, Bohuslav Klima, and Jiři Svoboda. 1989. "The Origins of Ceramic Technology at Dolni Věstonice, Czechoslovakia." *Science* 246 (4933): 1002–8. http://dx.doi.org/10.1126/science.246.4933.1002.

von Foerster, Heinz. 1960. "On Self-Organizing Systems and Their Environments." In *Self-Organizing Systems*, edited by M. C. Yovits and Scott Cameron, pp. ix, 322. New York: Pergamon Press.

Wark, McKenzie. 1992. "Autonomy and Antipodality in the Global Village." In *Cultural Diversity in the Global Village: The Third international Symposium on Electronic Art*, edited by Alessio Cavallaro, Ross Harley, Linda Wallace, and McKenzie Wark, 99–104. Adelaide: Australian Network for Art and Technology.

Wittfogel, Karl A. 1957. *Oriental Despotism; A Comparative Study of Total Power*. New Haven: Yale University Press.

Wolfram, Stephen. 2002. *A New Kind of Science*. Champaign, IL: Wolfram Media.

Zielinski, Siegfried. 2006. *Deep Time of the Media: Toward an Archaeology of Hearing and Seeing by Technical Means*. Cambridge, MA: MIT Press.

INDEX

Note: page numbers in *italics* indicate a figure and page numbers in **bold** indicate a table.